The Business and Professional Man's Lawyer

"... AND A COPY OF 'THE BUSINESS AND PROFESSIONAL MAN'S LAWYER', PLEASE ..."

EWAN MITCHELL

The Business and
Professional Man's Lawyer

Third Edition

Illustrations by Tobi

BUSINESS BOOKS
COMMUNICA-EUROPA

First published 1971
Second edition 1973
Third edition 1976

ISBN 0 220 66291 6

This book has been set 10 on 12 point Times.
Printed and bound in England by
W & J Mackay Limited, Chatham by photo-litho
for the publishers, Business Books Limited,
24 Highbury Crescent, London, N5

STOP PRESS—JANUARY 1977

All the Employment Protection Act provisions will be in effect by the beginning of 1977, except as follows:

1 FEBRUARY 1977 (1) Part-timers—unfair dismissal and redundancy protection and written particulars of contracts of employment—extended to those who 'normally work' 16 hours weekly (or 8 hours after 5 years);

(2) Guarantee payments effective.

6 APRIL 1977 (1) Maternity payments commence;

(2) Itemised pay statements required.

IN PIPELINE: ACAS Codes of Practice on disclosure; time off for trade union activities; disciplinary procedures; and collective bargaining.

EXPECTED by about spring 1977:

(1) Required disclosure of information to independent trade unions;

(2) Remaining (trade union) time off rules in force.

ALSO: Safety Committees and Representatives—implementation of Regulations, Code and Guidance (Health and Safety at Work Act).

EXPECTED, 1977: Worker participation legislation.

NOT YET IMPLEMENTED: Transfer of all contracts of employment disputes to industrial tribunals.

BEWARE: Appeal courts have held that employees who 'ordinarily work' partly within and partly outside UK are not normally protected against unfair dismissal.

WATCH OUT FOR: Implementation of Race Relations Act, 1976—administrative structures similar to those under Sex Discrimination Act.

For
MYRA
— always, and with
every edition

Contents

vii

Introduction

THIS BOOK describes and explains the everyday law which the independent business or professional man needs to know. It is designed for the man who runs his own company, for the salaried director or company secretary of a larger concern, for the partner in any firm, and for the self-supporting, professional man or woman. There are basic, worrying legal problems which afflict them all. To know the answers is not only to reduce the number and complexity of the problems themselves but also to appreciate how to use the law to increase profits.

For instance, every successful business or professional man must know the rules which apply to contracts of service, even if the only employee happens to be his wife, his son or his secretary. But many small companies and large firms have extremely substantial payrolls. And professional people are plagued by staff problems, which could be reduced considerably by some basic knowledge of employment law.

Equally, if you run a company and work for it, you are employed by it. It has a separate legal existence from yourself, even if you and your wife own 100 per cent of its shares. So you, too, are an employee.

Take restraint clauses. Can you compete with your own company when you leave it? How can you prevent your partner from destroying your goodwill by taking your clientele or customers or staff with him when he leaves? Conversely, are you entitled to poach staff from your competitors?

Again, whatever your business or profession, how can you best deal with theft? Must you report those whom you catch stealing from you? Are you entitled to take the law into your own hands? And anyway, when has the suspected thief (or any other employee, for that matter) made himself liable to summary dismissal?

Then there are times of financial hardship, for the reader and his debtor. So what are the legal rules on credit . . . on dealing with banks . . . on coping with creditors . . .? When is it worth suing? If the worst comes to the economic worst, how do you cope with bankruptcies and liquidations—actual or potential, on the part of those who owe you money or (alas) of your own company, firm, business or professional undertaking?

Again, this book looks at the legal duties and responsibilities of commercial and industrial executives, and of professional people, and at how they can keep within the law. Misrepresentations, mistakes and meetings . . . trade descriptions, the protection of depositors . . . even problems of legal costs and of conduct in courts— all come within our sphere.

From the tax angle, consideration is given to the problems of small, family companies, of the directors of close companies as well as those of the one-man band, who operates with the aid of limited liability. We cover the perils of partnership and of the individual, self-employed person (who comes under Schedule D of the Income Tax Acts).

All these worries are common to all business and professional people at one time or another. We do not deal with the individual, esoteric problems of the particular industry, trade or profession, but with the practical legal questions that affect and afflict them all.

Whether the reader is concerned with staff or premises, tax or transport, buying or selling, starting a new business or reviving an old one . . . whatever his field or speciality . . . this book is designed to make the law his ally, and his guide to profits and success. And when he retires, voluntarily or otherwise, there are some chapters designed to show him how to do so to his own best advantage.

I hope, then, that this book will not become redundant. It replaces *The Businessman's Lawyer and Legal Lexicon,* to which I bid a fond farewell. After two editions, numerous impressions and changes in the law beyond number, it has gone out of print for ever.

The Businessman's Legal Lexicon has already appeared separately —altered and up-dated as necessary. Now this book replaces *The Businessman's Lawyer.* The vast majority of this work is entirely new. And instead of being directed (as was the old book) towards the interests of the business community as a whole, this book is specifically intended in the main for those with actual or potential practical powers over their own destinies.

My thanks, as always, to those who have helped make this work possible. In particular, I am deeply grateful to Messrs Brian Clapham, Duncan Gee, Richard Slotover and Simeon Hopkins, and to my wife.

The Temple,   EWAN MITCHELL
London EC4
October, 1970

Introduction to Third Edition

HOWEVER GRIM the prospect, the businessman who wishes to keep out of trouble with the law must keep up with its changes. This edition is the result of massive legal change, mainly in statutes affecting employment.

The Health and Safety at Work Act–with up to two years' imprisonment and unlimited fines for 'directors, managers and secretaries' with whose 'consent or connivance' or as a result of whose 'neglect' an offence is committed; the Employment Protection Act, strengthening and altering the rules on unfair dismissal and introducing guaranteed payments, maternity benefits and a range of change affecting insolvency, redundancy and the rest; the Equal Pay Act–now buttressed and amended by the Sex Discrimination Act, providing (together with the Employment Protection Act) such power to the feminist arm that those in executive posts run new risks; and the Rehabilitation of Offenders Act, wiping clean many sad slates–these are only a few of Parliament's recent fingers in the business pie.

Add the Supply of Goods (Implied Terms) Act– with its new protection against misleading exclusion clauses (in business as well as in 'consumer' contracts); mix in the Fair Trading Act, giving tremendous new powers to the Director General of fair trading; salt with the wit and wisdom of judges; pepper with a glimpse of the future (but recently announced plans for employee participation await confirmation in years—and editions—to come)—and we must ring out the old edition and (with over 25 new chapters) ring in the new.

My special thanks to Mr Christopher Ashby, LLB, who has combed through every word of the old edition, to help bring it up to accurate date; to Mr Desmond Sturman and to my wife for their help.

GREVILLE JANNER

(Ewan Mitchell)

September, 1976

"IS SHE UNDER 'SUNDRY ASSETS' OR 'LIVESTOCK'?"

Part one

Laws and Businesses

Chapter 1

Confidential Information

THE SON of a well known company director is said to have emerged from college with a degree in business administration. His father asked him to replace a light bulb in the hall chandelier. The son duly climbed up a ladder and was about to change the bulb when his father gave the ladder a shove and the son fell to the ground.

'Why in heaven's name did you do that?' the son protested, rubbing his bruises.

'So that you will learn that in business you must trust no one—not even your own father!' he replied. 'Business studies are excellent in their own way. But the practical realities are rough.'

Still, you have to trust—your colleagues, your subordinates and, on occasion, complete strangers. But what help does the law give you, if that trust is betrayed?

An employee owes a duty to give faithful service and he may be sacked on the spot if he hands over secrets. If he is paid for the betrayal, then he may be prosecuted under the Prevention of Corruption Acts—corruption is a crime for both briber and bribed (see Chapter 105). Industrial espionage as such is no offence—but if the confidential information is given by stolen document, the taker is a thief.

If an employee leaves the service of your company, then (in the absence of a reasonable, valid, binding restraint clause — see Chapter 42) he may earn his living as, where and when he sees fit. He may make use of the skills, knowledge, know-how and contacts obtained in the service of your outfit, either for his own benefit or for that of his new employers. Theoretically, he must not use information given to him in confidence, but it is very difficult to prove that a confidence was abused. And anyway, what information is 'confidential', and what knowledge is run-of-the-mill?

One type of knowledge is peculiarly secret. It involves new inventions, ready for sale. If you create an idea in the course of your employment or one which comes within the scope of your employer's business, then that invention or idea belongs to your employer. But if you have a bright idea which belongs to you, you may decide to sell it—quite properly.

A Mr Seager invented a hidden carpet grip which he called the 'Invisgrip'. He took this to an executive of Copydex Limited and tried to sell him the idea—obviously in complete confidence.

At the time, Copydex were not interested but later they themselves applied for a patent in respect of a carpet grip very similar to that dreamed up by Mr Seager. They maintained that the grip was their own idea, but Mr Seager sued for damages 'for breach of confidence'. The case reached the Court of Appeal.

Lord Denning referred to 'the broad principle of equity that he who has received information in confidence shall not take unfair advantage of it. He must not make use of it to the prejudice of him who gave it, without obtaining his consent.'

Mr Seager had told Copydex 'a lot about the making of a satisfactory carpet grip which was not in the public domain. They would not have got going so quickly except for what they had learned in their discussions with him. . . .' True, Copydex 'were quite innocent of any intention to take advantage of him. They thought that so long as they did not infringe his patent, they were exempt. In this, they were in error. They were not aware of the law as to confidential information.'

Ignorance of the law is no excuse say the Judges. And innocence of any wicked intent is no answer, in a case like this. All the judges agreed that the employees of Copydex acted honestly. But the fact that they could not be convicted of any offence in a criminal court did not free their company from an obligation to pay damages.

Later, the Court of Appeal had to consider the basis upon which damages in a case like this should be assessed. They held that Mr Seager was entitled to 'reasonable compensation for the use of the confidential information, assessed on the market value of that information as between a willing buyer and a willing seller'.

Happily for Copydex, the judges said that once the damages were both assessed and paid, the company acquired ownership in the confidential information which became 'vested' in them and they had right to make use of it. Naturally, had they been dishonest and stolen the information, they would have acquired no right whatsoever. A thief can never acquire 'property' in that which he has purloined.

In *Fraser* v. *Evans and Others*, the Court of Appeal (again presided over by Lord Denning) considered another branch of the law on confidential information. The plaintiff was a public relations consultant, employed by the Government of Greece to make reports to them. He specifically undertook 'never to reveal to any person or organisation any information related to the work in the areas where it was operating, or information which comes to his knowledge during the course of the contract'. This sort of term often finds its way into contracts of service of industrial managers and other executives.

A translation of one of the reports was 'obtained surreptitiously' and came into the hands of a journalist employed by the defendants, the proprietors of *The Times* newspaper. Mr Fraser attempted to get an injunction, to prevent publication of the confidential information. He maintained that it was defamatory—and this the defendants admitted, although they alleged that in so far as it contained statements of fact, it was true and in so far as it represented opinions, these were 'fair comment on a matter of public interest'.

The Court held that the plaintiff had no right to prevent publication as there was no breach of confidence as against him. The people entitled to the information were the Greek Government and they were the only ones who could prevent the publication.

If you work for a company, then any information you obtain on behalf of the company belongs to your employers and not to you, and if anyone can take action to prevent its publication, it is your employers.

More interesting: 'There is no confidence as to the disclosure of iniquity. . . . It is an instance of just cause or excuse for breaking confidence. There are some things which may be required to be disclosed in the public interest, in which event no confidence can be prayed in aid to keep them secret . . .'.

If you find out that a crime or some other 'iniquity' has been committed, even though the disclosure would be defamatory, you will not be forced by law to keep the evil news to yourself.

Even if the statement is defamatory, you will be allowed to publish it provided that you intend to plead 'justification' or 'fair comment'. And although in Fraser's case the Court doubted whether there was such 'iniquity' as to justify publication, *The Times* was entitled to proceed because any defamation action would be defended.

'The right of free speech is one which it is for the public interest that individuals should possess and, indeed, they should exercise without impediment, so long as no wrongful act is done.'

It is a wrongful act to give away your company's secrets or those which have been imparted to the company in confidence. It is both right, proper and necessary that citizens should speak freely, when no wrong would be done.

In *Hubbard* v. *Vosper*, the founder of the Church of Scientology attempted to obtain an injunction, to prevent the publication by the defendants of a book highly critical of Scientology and containing many extracts from the books and other writings of Mr Hubbard. The application was made before trial (at a so-called 'interlocutory stage')—and was refused.

Lord Denning said this: 'I think there is ground for thinking that Mr Vosper may have used information knowing that Mr Hubbard claimed it to be confidential. Nevertheless, he may have a good answer . . . the Court will, in a proper case, intervene to restrain a defendant from revealing information or other material obtained in confidence, such as trade secrets, and the like. This depends upon the broad principle of equity that he who has received information in confidence shall not take unfair advantage of it . . .

'But information must be such that it is a proper subject for protection . . . there are some things which may be required to be disclosed in the public interest, in which event no confidence can be prayed in aid to keep them secret . . .'.

Pointing out that the Court could not decide on the facts at that stage, the Judge added: 'I think that, even on what we have heard so far, there is good ground for thinking that these courses contain such dangerous material that it is in the public interest that it should be made known'.

Lord Justice Megaw added: 'Counsel for the defendants is more than abundantly justified in his proposition that there is here evidence that the plaintiffs are or have been protecting their secrets by deplorable means . . . and, that being so, they do not come with clean hands to this Court in asking the Court to protect those secrets by the equitable remedy of an injunction'.

Suppose that your company had been engaged in a tax or customs fiddle. You come across the information and decide to reveal it—to the authorities, perhaps, or to the press. However confidential the information, the court will not force you to keep it to yourself. There is no confidence in an iniquity—and if the company wishes the court to exercise its discretion and to grant an injunction—a so-called 'equitable' remedy, available to ensure that justice is done—then it must come 'with clean hands'.

A worker's hands may be physically dirty through contact with your machinery or equipment. A company's hands may be metaphorically dirtied, through contact with 'iniquity'. It then loses its right to have its confidences kept secret.

Chapter 2

What Can You Bank On?

THE NEXT time you are on your knees before your bank manager, bolster yourself with the remarkable thought that his employers make their living through granting loans, not refusing them. But it would be more tactful to keep this thought to yourself. Naturally, you are in need. A client seldom makes an appointment with his manager to announce that he is paying off his overdraft. You have either come for more money today or to postpone payments until tomorrow. Either way, you must manage your manager. To do so, you must appreciate the nasty legal niceties of your situation.

When you are granted 'facilities' by the bank, it is making you a loan. And like most other loans, in the absence of some agreement to the contrary the money lent is repayable on demand. The moment the creditor requires the return of his cash, he may ask for it. You are then bound to pay up. Refuse to do so and you are in breach of the contract of loan—with all the miserable legal consequences to which contractual breaches may give birth.

If, then, you require facilities for a specified period, you should say so when you make the initial arrangements. 'All right,' says the manager. 'I'll mark a £500 limit on your overdraft.' Fine. But as the facility was not for any specified period of time, the bank may terminate it at any moment. 'Regretfully, we must ask you to clear your overdraft within the next seven days . . .' Alas.

Alternatively: 'We'll let this run for an initial six months and then the situation will have to be reassessed.' The loan cannot be called in for six months. Any attempt to force you to reduce the amount of the borrowing before the period has expired would be a breach of contract on the part of the bank. But once the half-year has gone, so has your right to refuse payment.

Incidentally, just in case you are thinking of trying to convince the bank that their oral agreement was for a longer term than they say, remember that every manager is required to note every lending limit and the period for which it is to run either before payment or up to review. If ever you have to do battle with your bank, these records will be powerful evidence—probably against you.

Suppose, now, that you are required to reduce or to liquidate your overdraft—and the money is simply not available. What can the bank do about it?

First, like any other creditor, the bank may sue for its money. Presumably you would have no defence to the claim: judgment would be given against you—and swiftly, at that: and the bank (now a 'judgment creditor') would be entitled to 'levy execution' on your goods and chattels . . . to take out a judgment summons, to show cause why you had not complied with the order of the court to pay the money . . . or to tip you into bankruptcy or your firm into dissolution. In a word, failure to comply with your manager's 'request' may spell ruin.

Next (or alternatively) the bank is entitled to 'realise' the securities which you have lodged as collateral. That, after all, was the object of requiring security. If circumstances have arisen under which the bank is entitled to sell your shares . . . cash in your life insurance . . . sell your house—then you must rely upon the benevolence of the bank not to exercise those rights.

A much earlier disaster tends to arise, of course, when the bank 'bounces' your cheque. A cheque is no more than an order to the bank to pay money from your account and if the cupboard is bare and there is no agreement under which the bank has agreed to restock it from its own resources, it is fully entitled to decline to accept your instructions. On the other hand, mistakes are sometimes made. Cheques are occasionally dishonoured in error. If this happens to you, you may well have a good claim against your bank, which is in effect saying to the person to whom the cheque is addressed: 'We regret that our client's credit will not come up to the sum specified.' And that is a highly defamatory statement.

Of course, if you 'stop' your cheque—countermand your instructions to pay—the battle will probably be joined between the payee and yourself. In that case, the bank simply stands in the sidelines. It has carried out its instructions and that is all that you can demand of it.

In practice, millions of satisfied customers have their cheques honoured when the bank is under no obligation whatsoever to do so. And we may all be grateful that the powers of the mighty are so seldom used. We sleep comfortably in our beds, confident that before our securities are sold, we will be given plenty of notice . . . that when the manager says that he will 'speak to Head Office', he will succeed in putting our case to them better than we have to him . . . that he will not drive us into ruin by keeping to his word regarding the reduction of our loans—even if we have been unable to keep to ours. The law provides the manager with powerful muscles. He flexes them from time to time—if only to prevent us from becoming spendthrifts. That he so rarely strikes against the borrower should be a source of gratitude to us all. We may provide his bread and butter—but without him, many of us could afford no jam.

Chapter 3

When Your Name's the Same

SENTIMENT APART, you may be as attached to your name as your name is to you. It represents your goodwill and that means money. An invented or adopted business or professional pseudonym, or firm or company name, may symbolise your life's work. It may even be your most valuable, capital asset. So consider how far it is yours to use as you please. If you use it unlawfully, then you may be restrained from doing so. You must not use your name in such a way as to 'pass off' your goods or business as those of someone else.

It is an 'actionable wrong' for anyone 'so to conduct his business as to lead to the belief that his goods or business are the goods or business of another'. This may be done not only by copying the name.

You have no absolute right to use your own name for the purposes of your trade, business or profession or as part of your business name. If confusion or deception would be likely to arise, then you may be banned from using your name. Still, 'the sole right to restrain a person using any name he pleases in his trade or business', as one judge put it, 'is when the name adopted, whether fictitious or real, is calculated to do injury to any other person by representing that such business is the business of that other person.'

On the face of it, the use of your own name will not be taken as 'evidence of intention to misrepresent your goods'. But if, in addition to using your own name, you 'do other things which show that you intend to represent, and are in point of fact making your goods represent, the goods of another person', then the courts may step in and protect the good name and goodwill of the other. 'The court will not restrain a man for trading in his own name except where he uses his name in such a way as to pass off his goods as the goods of another.' But the converse applies.

Suppose that you have built up an excellent business. You have done so under your own name, William Jones. Another William Jones opens up in the same line of country (and possibly in the same immediate neighbourhood), proudly displaying his name (and hence yours) on his notepaper, publicity or fascia. What are your chances of restraining him from using that name?

You must try to show that besides using his own name, he is doing 'other things which show that he is intending to represent, and is in point of fact making his business represent' the business you carry on. Alternatively, you may be able to establish fraud. In one old case, Mr Burgess Snr had for many years sold 'Burgess's Essence of Anchovies'. He fell out with his son, who sold a similar article under the same name. No fraud was proved and the court refused to restrain the son from cashing in on the family name.

But in a more recent case, Messrs Wright, Layman & Umney Limited succeeded in obtaining injunctions, restraining a Mr Wright from 'causing his goods to be passed off as theirs'. The plaintiffs 'had a wide reputation' under the name 'Wright's' in certain goods. Mr Wright called his similar goods 'Wright's'. Although he was found guilty of no dishonesty whatsoever, two injunctions were granted against him; he was restrained from trading under a name containing 'Wright' or 'Wright's' and further from using the name 'Wright' or 'Wright's' on his goods without sufficiently distinguishing them from the plaintiffs.

The Law Reports record battles between Vallantine and Ballantyne, Steiner Products and Willy Steiner. Valentine Meat Juice Company and Valentine Extract Company, Rodgers (Joseph) and Joseph Rodgers. Then there was the Mr Sidney Lyons, who changed his name to Joseph Lyons and had notepaper printed, headed: 'J. Lyons, Food Specialists'. The Court held that he 'intended to deceive and had deceived the public into buying his goods as and for those of the famous J. Lyons & Company'. He was restrained from so doing in the future.

While you may trade in your own name or use it as part of your business name, provided that you do so honestly, if your use of the name 'is calculated to deceive the public unless precautions are taken', you will be given the choice: either take precautions or else cease using the name. For instance, just as you may 'pass off' your goods by marketing them in the same wrapping or 'get-up' as those of some more famous competitor, so you may be able to distinguish them by using a contrasting 'get-up'. If your competitor cannot establish that he is carrying on a business with which others 'will be led to associate' your activities, then all will be well.

So while in most cases you are fully entitled to make use of your name for whatever business purposes you see fit, if your real intention is to cash in on the goodwill of your namesake, you may find yourself in trouble with the law. Where the name's the same, very often the first to use it gets the right to keep it.

Chapter 4

Laws of Copyright

FOR THE professional architect, surveyor, draughtsman, writer, artist, photographer . . . or any other professional man who puts his talents on to paper . . . there is no branch of the law more important than that concerned with copyright. And every businessman who creates ideas in any artistic form—or who would like to purloin the ideas of others—should study this branch of the law with equal care. Here are the main rules, as found in *The Copyright Act, 1956.*

*   *   *

Copyright (you will be pleased to hear) is a right to copy—or, to be more precise, the ownership of that right. It can subsist in 'an original literary, dramatic or musical work' or in an 'artistic work'. 'Artistic work' includes 'works of architecture, being either buildings or models for buildings' (Section 3). 'Drawings' are regarded as 'artistic', and by Section 48 these now include 'diagrams, charts, plans and maps'. So the plans of a projected factory are the subject of copyright. But who owns that copyright?

In general, 'the author of the work' is entitled to any copyrights subsisting in it. The man who makes the drawings, produces the designs, prepares the plans—he has the right to say who may or who may not copy his work. He may 'license' the use of his ideas . . . grant permission to reproduce them . . . or refuse that permission, if he sees fit.

'But when I commission someone to do the drawings for me, do I not get copyright?'

If you commission someone to take a photograph, to make a painting or engraving or to draw a portrait, you become entitled to the copyright in the work. Section 4(3) of the Act says so. But commissions not coming within Section 4(3) leave the copyright with the author. What you are acquiring is the right to make use of the commissioned work for the specified purpose. When you employ an independent architect, surveyor or designer to prepare plans or drawings for you, you in general acquire the right to use them only for the specified purpose.

Of course, all this is subject to agreement to the contrary. If your architect is prepared to allow you to use his design for all purposes, for ever and ever—that is a matter for him. If you want that privilege, negotiate for it. You may have to pay more heavily—but it may be worth it. Otherwise, to use the 'work' for some purpose other than that contemplated may involve you in paying for the right all over again. Alternatively, you may find yourself restrained by an injunction of the Court from continuing to make use of the other man's 'artistic efforts'.

'Does this apply if the architect or designer is on my staff?'

No. If the work is made 'in the course of the author's employment by another person under a contract of service or apprenticeship, that other person shall be entitled to any copyrights subsisting in the work'. If your employee in the course of his employment by you produces the masterpiece in question, you may use it as you see fit.

But note: where the work is done in your employee's own time and not in the course of his employment, the copyright vests in him. He may perhaps be prevented from using his spare time working for his own purposes or those of others. But nonetheless, the copyright is his. If you want to make use of the material produced in his spare time, you may have to pay him extra for it. But assuming that the work was done 'in the course of his employment', you are entitled to make use of it in the course of your business.

There is one interesting corollary to all this. While you cannot use the drawings for a second building without the architect's consent (which you should have been able to obtain fairly cheaply, because he would not have had to redo the work), he himself would be entitled to use those drawings again. Assuming that he was not acting in breach of some express or implied term in his contract with another client, he could reproduce the drawings for that other client. Just as your wife gets no exclusive right to wear the copy of the Paris model, so you cannot prevent the owner of the copyright in the design of the premises you have built from exploiting his ownership for his own benefit and that of others.

Naturally, these rules are capable of alteration by consent. For instance, suppose that you are an illustrator. Publishers offer you payment on an all-in basis, full copyright to go to them. Then make sure that the price is sufficiently lucrative before you accept.

Authors are often prepared to accept a fee for full copyright instead of selling book rights only. That is a matter for them.

Journalists (particularly of the freelance variety) seldom specify what rights they are selling. In the absence of any agreement to the contrary, the answer is: 'First British serial rights'—the publisher acquires the right to reproduce the work once only, in a British journal or newspaper. So what do you do if you receive a receipt or a cheque which purports to acknowledge that you have sold all copyright? Refuse to sign. Literally dozens of publishers have had the gay temerity to try that dodge upon 'Ewan Mitchell', in spite of his being a lawyer. Each in turn has apologised and said that it was 'only a standard form'—a very poor excuse indeed.

Artists, too, should take care to retain their copyright. If the man who commissions the portrait wants to do as he will with it, reproducing it where and when he sees fit, then he must pay for that privilege.

Or take the architect. He prepares a plan for one building and may be scandalised if it is used for 300 identical copies on other estates. This branch of copyright law is complicated. You should make your deal as clear as possible from the start and there will be no expensive misunderstandings at the end.

So copyright law spills over into the law of contract. If you have a deal to be done which involves the right to copy or reproduce, by all means know the basic copyright laws. But the more money that the arrangement involves, the more important it is for you to let a lawyer draw up your contractual documents. Whether you are a buyer or a seller of copyright material—or both—you are venturing into a field so narrow and so complicated that even amongst the gentlemen of the Bar there are only half a dozen who are acknowledged experts in the field.

One final, happy thought. 'Reproducing the work of one man,' it is said, 'may be a breach of copyright. Reproducing the works of many, in a suitable amalgam, is research!' Which suggests, does it not, the most common way to avoid copyright troubles? You then create an 'original work' out of the ideas of others—and the law (kindly creature that it is) bestows the copyright in your new, mongrel creation upon you.

Chapter 5

Registration of Trade Marks

THERE IS nothing like an inventive mind to propel a professional man into success or an employed executive into starting his own business. First, you will probably want an invention—the rules on ownership are in Chapter 4. Then you will need your own trade mark. *The Trade Marks Act, 1938,* lays down the rules on registration. Here is what it says.

For a mark to be registerable, it must contain or consist of at least one of the following essential features:

1 The name of a firm, individual or company, represented in a particular or special manner
2 The signature of the applicant for registration, of some predecessor in his business
3 An invented word or words
4 A word or words having no direct reference to the character or quality of the goods, and not being according to its ordinary signification a geographical name or a surname.
5 Any other distinctive mark.

If you want to register a mark which contains one of these features, then you must still come within Section 11 of the Act—and, in particular, you must ensure that the mark would not be 'calculated to deceive'. It must not be too near some other mark, or you will not get it registered.

'Suppose that I cannot have a mark registered. If I use it anyway, what extra risks do I run?'

That all depends on the reason for non-registration. There are many brand names which are not registered, but which are jealously preserved. Non-registration will prevent you from taking proceedings for an infringement of a trade mark, but will not rule out 'passing off actions' if you consider that some other product is being marketed under a name so similar to your own as to suggest that your competitors are trading on your goodwill and trying to 'pass off' their goods as yours.

Finally, some examples from industry, of registration allowed and disallowed. The following have been held registerable—'Solie' for photographic printing paper; 'Savonol' for soap—but not 'Absorbine' for an absorbent product or 'Lactobacilline' for a lactic ferment.

The former words were held to be 'invented'—but the latter were not. Which shows that the borderline between invention and actuality is a narrow one indeed.

Next, once you have registered your mark, what are your rights?

Everyone knows that it is an infringement of someone else's trade mark to use it to describe one's own product. If you were to market goods under the name of 'Q Brand', then Q Limited could doubtless obtain an injunction, to restrain you from doing so, plus damages, to compensate it (as registered proprietor of the brand name) for any damage suffered. But what is not obvious (and what few people realise) is that it is also an infringement of a trade mark simply to quote it when making comparisons with one's own product. There was a case in the Court of Appeal not so long ago in which a manufacturer of a famous chemical successfully restrained a competitor from publishing a circular which named that chemical under its brand name and pointed out that its quality in no way justified its price. The mere use of the other man's registered trade name was itself a breach of the proprietor's rights.

'But I thought that the object of giving the proprietor of a trade mark his rights was to prevent anyone else from passing off other goods as those of the registered proprietor. . . .'

That may be. But on the proper interpretation of the relevant section of the law, it has been decisively established that even if there is no question of passing off, there can still be an infringement of the registered proprietor's rights.

The let-out? There seems to be no reason why a manufacturer should not make a true and favourable comparison between his product and that of another producer, simply by saying, 'Our product is better and cheaper than the equivalent line manufactured by Q Limited.' Do not mention the other man's registered trade name and all will be well.

For the rules on the protection of your own marks, apply the above—in reverse.

Chapter 6

Travel Costs and the Tax Man

IF YOU travel for fun, you cannot expect the tax man to foot the bill. But if you are dragged out of bed to attend to the needs of a patient or client or customer, what then? In the past, you would probably have been in the same unhappy position as the famous recorder of Portsmouth, whose claim for expenses incurred in travelling from home to court was disallowed. Work began in Portsmouth. That was his place of employment. And just as his secretary could not claim the cost of her season ticket nor his clerk the running expenses of his car, incurred on the way to trial, so the learned judge had to pay his travel costs out of his taxed income.

But now? The case of *Owen* v. *Book* (Inspector of Taxes) has reached the House of Lords. By a majority of three to two, Dr David Owen—who held part time appointments as obstretician and anaesthetist at a hospital—was held entitled to deduct the expenses incurred by him in travelling from his home. At home, he carried on practice as a general practitioner. In hospital, he dealt with emergency cases. He had two places of work—and just as the barrister may charge for travelling from court to court . . . the businessman from shop to factory or from supplier to customer . . . so the doctor won the day.

Dr Owen was on stand-by duty at home at certain specified times. He had to be accessible by telephone. When a telephone call came through, he gave instructions to the hospital staff, and either waited for a further report or set out immediately. 'His responsibility for the patient began as soon as he received the telephone call.' The committee in fact paid his travelling expenses at a fixed rate a mile between home and hospital, up to a single journey of ten miles. The remaining five miles were paid out of the doctor's own pocket. He sought to deduct the whole cost of travelling—between two and three pounds a week—from his taxable income.

Now, where you are employed by a hospital (or anyone else), you are taxed under Schedule E. For expenses to be deductible, it must be shown that they were incurred wholly, exclusively and necessarily in the performance of your duties. But where you operate as a one-man band, you are taxed under Schedule D. You must then show that the expenses were 'wholly and exclusively' incurred in the course of your work. But, whatever the schedule, you must prove that you travelled in the course of your work, and not simply in order to get to the place of work.

The basis of Dr Owen's case was that he had two places of work. There was his home consulting room, where he dealt with his general practice and also received emergency calls. Then there was the hospital. The Court of Appeal held (as Lord Donovan later put it), 'that Dr Owen had one place of employment . . . the hospital . . . When he answered the telephone and gave any necessary preliminary instructions, of course, he was performing the duties of his office. But when he got into his car and drove to the hospital, he was not performing such duties. He incurred the expense of so travelling because he chose to live in one town when the hospital was in another.'

But happily for the doctor (and for all like him—probably including the other professional people who work both at home and elsewhere) a majority of the House of Lords thought otherwise.

Lord Guest: 'Dr Owen's duties commenced at the moment he was first contacted by the hospital authorities. . . . His responsibility for a patient began as soon as he received the telephone call. . . . He sometimes advised treatment by telephone. There were therefore two places where his duty was performed, the hospital and his telephone in the consulting room. If he was performing his duties in both places, then it was difficult to see why, on the journey between the two, he was not equally performing his duties. But the travelling expenses were necessarily incurred in the performance of the duties of his office.'

Lord Wilberforce: 'Dr Owen had two places of work. The expenses were incurred in travelling from one to the other in the performance of his duties.' So the expenses were deductible.

The name of Dr Owen, then, has become beloved of those who must travel in the course of their work. But there are still limits to the new and merciful doctrine. Your accountant will doubtless still have to haggle with the tax man over the percentage of your expenses which should be allowable . . . or whether you attended that congress in Hawaii, Hong Kong or Hungary 'in the performance of your duty'—a question which may not be so easy to answer, if your wife came with you. And anyway, what of her travel expenses? Can you prove as a matter of fact that she actually worked with you?

You are only entitled to deduct those business expenses which were incurred wholly and exclusively (if you are an employed person) in the actual performance of your duties. So travel between office and site, site and factory, factory and supplier and so on is all properly deductible. Travel from home to work is not. Like the cost of obtaining a post, it is incurred prior to and not in the course of your duties.

A bricklayer and labour-only sub-contractor named Horton has now made a benevolent dent in this rule—which is well worth knowing, if you happen to be a peripatetic person—and particularly if you, like Mr Horton, are self-employed.

Mr Horton supplied the labour of a three-man team, which he was the leader. His team worked exclusively for one employer, travelling according to that employer's requirements for labour, from one site to another through the South of England.

Mr Horton lived in Eastbourne and used his car to take his men to the sites and back again. He was assessed for income tax as a self-employed man, under Schedule D. Question: Was he entitled to set off his travel costs against his earnings?

The Revenue maintained that while expenses in travelling from site to site were allowable, those between home and site were not. They relied on the famous case of *Newson* v. *Robertson*, in which it was said that the place of business of a London barrister was his Temple chambers, so that his travelling expenses between home and chambers could not be allowed.

Mr Horton maintained that he carried on 'business activities' at home. His employer used to come round to negotiate labour-only sub-contracts and his house contained his tools and his business books. Still, the home business was described by Lord Justice Stamp as 'very small . . . involving exiguous office equipment and no doubt only a very few tools'.

Still, Mr Horton was allowed to set off a proportion of his household expenses against tax and as he received the part-time secretarial services of his wife, he paid her a modest salary and she got her own allowances.

The case eventually reached the Court of Appeal which unanimously held that Mr Horton's home was 'the locus' (or place) of his trade, 'from which it radiated as a centre'. It followed that his travel from home was indeed tax deductible.

So Mr Horton won an important victory. And it should operate as a shining light to the self-employed business or professional man or woman. If you can show that your business or profession 'radiates' from your home as a central point, then travel to and from your home will be tax deductible. So when the next unhappy accounting season arrives, remind your advisers accordingly.

Unfortunately, it is very unlikely that the kindly rules will help you, if you are employed by a company—even if you and your wife happen to own all the shares. You will be taxed under Schedule E, and your expenses will be 'perused' with far greater care by the tax men. Unless your company operates from your own home, you would hardly be able to show that the company's business 'radiates' from your study. Even if you have a home office, it is the company's HQ, that forms the centre of its undertaking.

Of course, the company may if it wishes pay you all your travelling expenses. But the sum you get will be lumped together with your taxable income, in the same way as any benefit in kind, including the appropriate proportion of the use of the company car, if you take that back and forth to your home.

One day, I suppose that the unfair advantage gained by 'independent contractors', self-employed and travelling tax free—will be nullified. Meanwhile, just as home buyers are much better off from the tax angle than home renters, the independent, self-employed person should be grateful for a mercy which may be small if he works in many places, or near home, but which will be proportionately much larger if his efforts take him far afield.

The law, then, has been clarified and made more merciful. But the facts upon which a court would base its decision would still have to be considered with care. If in doubt about the tax chargeable on your travel, you should see your accountant, who should certainly have studied the rise to victory of Dr David Owen of Fishguard.

Chapter 7

Starting in Business

THINKING OF branching out on your own? Then before you do so, consider the legal angles.

*   *   *

First, should you operate as an individual or in partnership, or through a limited liability company? The major beauty of a company is that the liability of its shareholders is limited to any money unpaid on their shares (which is usually nil). A partner or an individual on the other hand, may be forced to pay business debts out of his own pocket. His own entire fortune (if that is not an overstatement) is available for the benefit of the business creditors.

On the other hand, individual businessmen and partners generally pay less tax. There is no corporation tax to worry about, for a start. Legitimate expenses are normally easier to come by. So those who spurn limited liability are generally able to keep more profits for themselves. It is when the day of loss arrives that the businessman regrets his short-term tax savings.

Again, company accounts must now be filed and are available for the inspection of actual or potential creditors in particular, as well as the world in large in general. Personal and partnership accounts may be kept secret. However, if there is capital to be raised or shares to be doled out, company organisation is simpler.

You may set up a private business without legal formalities. Partnerships may be created without even the benefit of a partnership deed or formal writing. Formalities are desirable, but neither essential nor particularly expensive. If you want a company, though, you must buy one off-the-peg for anywhere between about £60 and £200 or have one made-to measure to your requirements, probably by your solicitor or accountant, which may cost you £200 or so. Either way, no memorandum and articles of association and no proper registration means no company.

Next, you must consider your capital. The main reason for the earlier failure of most businesses is lack of the money needed—not only to acquire and equip the premises and lay in stock or supplies but also to keep you in food while the business builds up, in those lean and early days. So you must consider the legal implications of fund-raising—problems of hire purchase; the rights of banks to call in money lent; and if you do run into serious debt, then how long your lawyer will be able to fend off your various debtors. Discuss this with him, and with your accountant, before you launch your venture.

Next, you will need some sort of premises. If you acquire a freehold, you pay more initially but have no landlord and pay no rent. Remember, too, that you may sell your freehold (perhaps to an insurance company) and take back a lease—thus releasing the capital you need.

If you take a lease, remember that the length is not as important as you might think. You will be protected by *The Landlord and Tenant Act, 1954* as amended by *The Law of Property Act, 1969*—details in Chapter 8. So if you can buy up a 'fag end' cheaply, it may be well worth doing. Discuss the proposition with your solicitor. Ask him to advise you in particular about the repairing covenants. These may not mean what they appear to say. For instance, if you covenant to 'maintain' the premises in good repair, you may have to put them into good condition first.

If the lease contains an absolute prohibition against assignment, then you will only be able to sell the business with your landlord's consent. This he will probably not give except at a considerable price. But if you may not assign 'without the landlord's consent', the law says that such consent shall not be 'unreasonably withheld'.

Finally, if you are the first tenant under a new lease, even if you do assign you will retain your responsibility to your landlord. So make quite certain that you really want the term offered—and be especially careful before you personally agree to be a party to the lease and hence to guarantee the performance by the business of its obligations.

Then, you must chose a name for your business. If you use your own, the chances are that all will be well. But business names must not be misleading and your solicitor or accountant will discover whether the name you have in mind will be permitted (see Chapter 3).

Firms or individuals not trading under the names of the partners or individual concerned must register under *The Registration of Business Names Act, 1916* (set out in full as Appendix 6). The fee is £1 and full particulars are obtainable from the Registry of Business Names, Department of Trade, Pembroke House, 40–56 City Road, London EC1Y 2ON.

However you trade, you must keep proper accounts. There are stringent regulations for companies (only an accountant can sort them out)—and even the smallest, one-man (or woman) shop must account to the tax man. Cash 'fiddles' may pay in the short run, but quite apart from the possibilities of criminal prosecution, the day of reckoning arrives when you want to sell the business and the prospective buyer inspects the books. He will go by what they show.

Conversely, before you take over a business (of whatever size) make certain that the books are inspected by your accountant. Never take the seller's word for his turnover, receipts, profits. If he has any hesitation in letting you inspect his accounts once your deposit is paid, be on your guard. If in doubt, take your custom elsewhere. If some misrepresentation is made to you before your purchase, you will be protected by *The Misrepresentation Act, 1967*. If you can prove fraud, you will have a good claim in law. But by the time your case comes to court, you will wish that you had taken no risks. There is no substitute for the guidance of your accountant.

The Misrepresentation Act does not apply to Scotland but under the common law of Scotland if you are induced by an innocent misrepresentation to purchase the business which you would not have done otherwise you are entitled to rescind the contract.

When acquiring your premises, you should employ a competent surveyor to warn you of wet rot, dry rot, subsidence and other defects in the structure of the premises which you yourself might miss. Obtain a written survey—and an estimate of the cost of putting the premises into proper order.

As for deposits, beware of 'the usual 10 per cent'—there is no such thing. As a token of goodwill, a small initial deposit is quite enough. Put it up to 10 per cent when contracts are exchanged—meanwhile do not tie up your own (or borrowed) money. And always ensure that deposits are paid 'subject to contract'—so that they are without doubt recoverable if the deal goes off, even through your own fault. And unless the vendor's estate agents are well known to you, pay your deposit to his solicitors as stakeholders not as agents.

What legislation is most likely to affect you? *The Health and Safety at Work etc. Act, 1974*, is now in full force and aiming at much higher standards of health and safety (see Part 6). Existing legislation (*The Offices, Shops and Railway Premises Act, 1963*, and *The Factories Act, 1961*, for instance) remains effective, but over the years new provisions and regulations will drastically amend their effect.

Do not forget that if you are likely to have a turnover in excess of £5000 per annum then you will need to register for VAT purposes. Discuss your worries with your accountant.

Unless you plan to operate the business entirely on your own, you must plan to meet staff problems—in advance. These (once more) include tax provisions. Your accountant will help you to deal with PAYE, National Insurance and so on.

Thanks to *The Contracts of Employment Act, 1972*, your staff are either entitled to written contracts of employment or to written particulars (which need not be in any special form) setting out the main terms of their employment.

If you want to provide a home for your staff, get your solicitor to draw up the appropriate licence—making it clear that the employee is 'required to occupy the premises for the better performance of his duties'. Terms such as 'rent' and 'landlord' must be avoided—if you confer a tenancy—as opposed to a 'service occupancy' or licence—

your employee will acquire the protection of the Rent Acts. You will then only get possession with grave difficulty, even when the employment ends. If you reasonably require possession for the occupation of a replacement employee whom you have actually engaged or who is ready to move in—and the County Court Judge thinks it 'reasonable' in all the circumstances to grant possession—all may be well, in due course. But if you may want a speedier eviction, plan for it in advance.

If you take over a business, you are not bound to buy stock, materials, plant or supplies at valuation or at all. If you agree to do so, make sure that you have a full and checked schedule, so that disputes do not afterwards arise. And if you are to buy 'at valuation', agree on who is to do the valuing.

If you are buying in new stock, be very careful not to overstock in an excess of initial enthusiasm. Remember that—unless you buy on sale or return—you will not be entitled to return the goods, ordered in a rash moment. And even on sale or return, it is up to you to reject or to 'give notice of rejection' within the agreed time—or, if no time has been agreed, then within a reasonable time.

You will need cover against burglary, flood, fire, liability to staff, public liability, loss of cash—and probably against many other forms of disaster. Find an experienced and reputable insurance broker and let him see what terms he can get for you. Remember that he normally gets his commission from the insurers with whom he eventually places your custom, so obtain a number of quotes. You should shop around for insurance in the same way as your customers do so for the goods or service you provide.

When filling in your insurance proposal form, be careful to be absolutely accurate. Failure to make proper disclosure . . . misleading or false statements in the proposal form . . . these may give your insurers the right to repudiate liability on the happening of the very matters which you are paying your premium to cover. If your policy is to protect you, honesty is your only wise policy when taking on insurance.

To find out what cover you are offered, read the policy. It is a contractual document. It sets out what you are to receive in return for your premium. Beware of phrases like 'comprehensive'—a policy comprehends' the cover stated, that and nothing more, and if you run into insurance difficulties, take the policy to an expert to interpret.

Finally, make certain that any terms of the policy are complied with. For instance, if you are required to install a burglar alarm or to link one up with the police, make absolutely certain that this is done. Failure to comply with a condition may lead to entirely justifiable repudiation of the contract by the insurers.

Before you acquire transport make certain (*a*) that you will get adequate insurance cover at a price you can afford; (*b*) that the proposed driver is properly licensed for the class of vehicle concerned; and (*c*) that you will have somewhere to park. You have no greater right to station your vehicles on the highway outside your own premises than has any other member of the public. If in doubt, check with your local police.

It remains to wish you the best of good guidance from your advisers, and the most excellent luck available.

Chapter 8

At Your Lease's End

No BUSINESS or professional man can operate without premises—and most premises are on lease. So consider the protection given to the tenant by *The Landlord and Tenant Act, 1954* which has been heavily amended by *The Law of Property Act, 1969*.

*   *   *

The 1954 Act applies 'to any tenancy where the property comprised in the tenancy is or includes premises which are occupied by the tenant, and are so occupied for the purposes of a business carried on by him or for those and other purposes'. Provided that you yourself occupy and carry on a business in the premises, then, even if you live there as well, the Act is designed for you. But if you are a property owner and rent out flats, you do not normally 'occupy' them, so your tenancy will not be protected.

A business tenancy no longer comes to an end, unless either the landlord or the tenant takes some step which determines it. The landlord can do so by serving notice on the tenant not less than six, nor more than twelve months, before the date when the tenancy would otherwise determine, specifying the date at which it is now to come to an end.

This notice must require the tenant, within two months of its being received, to tell the landlord in writing whether he will be willing to give up possession. It must also state whether or not the landlord would oppose an application to the court on the part of the tenant for a new tenancy, and if so, on which of the specified grounds.

If you are a tenant and the landlord has not served such a notice on you and you wish to remain in the property, then say nothing and do nothing. Of course, you won't have any absolute certainty of security. If you want that, then you yourself must give notice to the landlords, requesting a new tenancy. Within two months of your request, he is entitled to give notice to you that he would oppose an application to the Court for the grant of a new tenancy, and, once again, this notice must state which of the grounds specified by the Act he intends to rely upon.

Consider these grounds. If the landlord can satisfy the Court of any one of them, no new lease can be granted. They are seven:

1 That the tenant has not kept the property in good repair.
2 That the tenant has been persistently late in paying his rent.
3 That there have been 'other substantial breaches' by the tenant 'of his obligations under the current tenancy'.
4 That the landlord is willing to provide alternative accommodation.
5 That the landlord wishes to let off the property as a whole, and the tenant's current tenancy was created by sub-letting only part of it.
6 That on the termination of the current tenancy, the landlord intends to demolish or reconstruct the premises. Note that a landlord cannot now resist a tenant's application for a new business tenancy on this ground if the tenant is prepared to accept a new tenancy of all or part of the premises, and the

landlord can do the work 'without interfering to a substantial extent or for a substantial time' with the tenant's business. The tenant must agree to the new tenancy containing a term which would give the landlord reasonable 'access and other facilities for carrying out the work intended'.

7 That the landlord, not having acquired his interest in the property less than five years ago, intends to occupy the premises himself.

Now note Section 6 of the 1969 Act: 'Where the landlord has a controlling interest' in that company, then 'any business to be carried on by the company shall be treated . . . as a business to be carried on by him'. If he has power over a majority of the directorships or holds (in his own right) over one half of the share capital, then he will be able to control not only the company but its business premises.

Suppose the landlord fails to prove his contention and a new lease has to be granted. The next questions are what will be its terms, what rent will the tenant have to pay and how long will it be for?

In most cases, landlord and tenant indulge in some hard bargaining, either in person or through their solicitors, and the terms of the new tenancy are hammered out between them. But if no agreement can be reached, the Act provides that the Court shall decide all these points.

The tenancy shall be such as is 'reasonable in all the circumstances' but not for more than fourteen years. The rent generally speaking is 'that at which . . . the holding might reasonably be expected to be let in the open market by a willing lessor'.

In practice, the parties arrive in court, backed by expert estate agents or valuers. The landlord's agent will say, perhaps, that the rent should be £2,000 a year. He will justify this by giving examples of recent lettings of similar property in the neighbourhood.

The tenant's valuer, using the same criterion, will possibly suggest that £1,500 per annum would be a rent reasonably obtainable in the open market.

And the judge, who must decide between them, like as not will chop the difference in half and award £1750. However, there's no guarantee of this—in some cases judges accept in its entirety the evidence of one or other of the experts.

Next, how long a term will the tenant get? Obviously, in most cases he will wish for the longest possible term and will try for the fourteen years maximum. He will tell the Court how long he has been there, how he has built the place up, how his need is a great one whereas the landlord will lose little by the grant of a long term—and so on. The judge must consider all the circumstances and decide what is reasonable.

As for the other terms in the tenancy—such as the covenants as to repair of the property—normally no alteration is made. Judges do not like having to settle the terms of new leases any more than they can help and it is rare, in the absence of agreement between the parties, that terms other than rent and duration are altered.

Section 2 of the 1969 Act: 'Where the rent is determined by the Court the Court may, if it thinks fit, further determine that the terms of the tenancy shall include such provision for varying the rent as may be specified in the determination.' So the Judge may order that a rent revision clause be included in the new tenancy—whether or not there was one in the tenancy which has expired.

Section 8 of the 1969 Act extends the power of the Court when fixing the terms of a new tenancy. The fact that the tenant had certain rights in the past does not mean that a judge is now bound to grant him the same privileges under a new lease.

As for the landlord—assuming that his tenant has served the appropriate counter-notice within the time limit laid down by the Act—he will only be successful in opposing the grant of a new lease if he can bring himself within one of the statutory exceptions. If he can prove to the Court that he really does intend to demolish or reconstruct the place, for instance, then he will get possession. If he really does want to use the premises for his own business, or even as his home, then again he will be entitled to possession. But the onus of proof lies on him. So it is important to him to prove, for instance, that his Minute book shows that the company really is resolved to take the proposed steps.

Suppose now that the tenant can get no new lease and has to leave the premises, what compensation will he be entitled to for his loss of goodwill? In the old days, tenants like him got compensation for lost goodwill, under *The Landlord and Tenant Act, 1927*. Unfortunately for businessmen—in this respect, at least—this was superseded by the 1954 Act. In its place comes a provision which provides compensation on a much lower scale.

First, the tenant must prove that the only reason that he has not got a new tenancy is because the Court is precluded from granting him one through the landlord bringing himself within one of the last three exceptions. In other words, if he cannot get a new lease and this is entirely in order to suit the landlord's convenience and not through any default on his own part, then he is entitled to compensation.

The extent of the compensation depends on how long the tenant has been in business in the premises. Roughly speaking, if he or some predecessor in his business has been in occupation for fourteen years or more, then he will be entitled to twice the rateable value of the premises. If he has been there for less than this time, the compensation is the rateable value of the holding.

Section 1 of the 1969 Act provides that business tenants are not to be penalised for improving their property. If an improvement was carried out by the tenant, he cannot afterwards be forced to pay a higher rent because he has seen fit to spend money on his premises. Exception? If the work was done to comply with a covenant in the lease.

The 1969 Act recognises that the delays of the law may prejudice landlords. They may not only be forced to keep their business tenants, but also to allow them to pay rent at the old (and often highly uneconomic) rate, until the Court fixes a new rental. No longer. Now the landlord may apply to the Court to fix a reasonable rent during the interim between the date specified in the landlord's notice, or the tenant's request, or the date of the application to the Court (whichever is the later), and the commencement of the new tenancy (and rental).

Section 4 sews up one possible landlord's loophole in the 1954 Act. Tenants were sometimes required to hand their landlords their notice to quit before their tenancies began. Such a notice is now invalid if given or executed before the tenant has been in occupation for one month. But landlord and tenant may now make joint application to the Court, asking that the 1954 Act protection be excluded from a particular tenancy. There are times when both parties agree that it would be fair for the tenant to remain unprotected. If they can induce the Judge to agree with them, then the tenant may 'contract out' of his rights.

Still, the surest and the most popular way to lose your rights is to delay when you receive notice under the 1954 Act.

If you have missed your chance, you will never get it back. There is no prospect of getting leave from the Court to serve your notice late. If you are late, you are finished. But if you have the good sense to put the matter in the hands of your lawyer in good time, the Act can bring you enormous benefits. The end of your lease need not bring disaster after all.

Chapter 9

Problems of Partnerships

As ANY accountant or tax consultant will tell you, there is a good deal to be said for the partnership. Quite apart from professionals, whose disciplinary or ethical rules forbid them to practise with the benefits of limited liability, modern legislation has put a premium on partnerships—or, for that matter, on trading as an individual. The main considerations bear repetition.

First, the tax burden lies heavier on the company than on the firm. Corporation tax aside, the Revenue smiles far more upon the man who has to meet his debts and his expenses out of his own pocket than upon the company which can shrug itself into liquidation, if disaster strikes.

On the other hand, of course, where your entire personal fortune rests upon the success of your business, you take added risks. But as partnerships are on the increase—and partnership ventures are even engaged in by companies—let us spare an informed thought, for the firm. Whether you are an actual or only a potential partner, it is well worth considering the laws on partnerships—most of which are contained in *The Partnership Act, 1890*, the full text of which is reproduced in Appendix 7. That is the law; here is the commentary upon it.

*   *   *

Unlike a company, which has no life without a formal memorandum and Articles of Association and due registration, no formalities are required for a partnership. 'Partnership is the relation which subsists between persons carrying on a business in common with a view to a profit', says Section 1 of the Act, whether those persons know it or not. If you decide to embark on a partnership business or venture, you would be wise to set down the details in writing. The law will not insist that you do so.

In practice, it is sometimes difficult to know whether a partnership in fact exists. And those dealing with the firm have no right to examine its accounts—unlike, of course, the company, bound by the *Companies Act, 1948* and *1967*, to lay its corporate cards upon *The* Registrar's table. On the one hand, then, partners have the benefits of secrecy; on the other, those who deal with the firm have the security provided by the individual liability of each of its members.

Every partner is an agent for the firm and of his other partners 'for the purpose of the business of the partnership'. Each may bind the firm and all his partners, unless he has no actual authority to do so and the person with whom he is dealing knows that fact.

Equally, 'every partner in a firm is liable jointly with the other partners . . . for all the debts and obligations of the firm incurred while he is a partner'. His liability is not confined to debts which he himself has incurred on the firm's behalf. If the partnership goes into debt, its creditors may enforce their rights against the property of any individual partner. Even a 'sleeping partner' may have a rude and expensive awakening.

Naturally, the partners are free to regulate their own rights and liabilities, as between themselves. And a person who is admitted as a partner into an existing firm does not become liable to the creditors of the firm for anything done before he became a partner, unless he expressly agrees to assume that burden. But the converse does not apply. A retiring partner remains liable for partnership debts incurred before his retirement. His fellow partners may agree to discharge him from existing liabilities, but the creditors may still look to him.

It follows that while one partner may obtain an indemnity against another or make whatever arrangements he chooses with his fellow members of the firm, those who deal with the partnership and do not know of those special arrangements and are not party to them may still look to each individual partner for money due. 'The mutual rights and duties of partners, whether ascertained by agreement or defined by this Act,' says Section 19, 'may be varied by the consent of all the partners, and such consent may be either express or inferred from a course of dealing.' Equally, the normal rules regulating the relationship between a firm and its individuals and third parties may be altered by agreement between them.

In the absence of some special duty, Section 24 of the Act says that 'all the partners are entitled to share equally in the capital and profits of the business, and must contribute equally towards the losses, whether of capital or otherwise, sustained by the firm'. For its own part, the firm must indemnify every partner in respect of payments made and personal liabilities incurred by him 'in the ordinary and proper conduct of the business of the firm' or 'in or about anything necessarily done for the preservation of the business or property of the firm'. There is no right to an indemnity if a partner acts improperly, still less in respect of any outlay unconnected with the partnership business. As one judge put it: 'You could say that a member of a firm acts as a partner during his working day, but he does not take his partnership to bed with him at night.' The law, happily, makes a distinction between commercial and marital unions.

Unless some alternative agreement is made, the following important rules apply:

1 Where a partner makes any payment or advance 'beyond the amount of capital which he has agreed to subscribe', and he does so for the purpose of the partnership, then he is entitled to interest at the rate of 5 per cent (only), from the date of the payment or advance.
2 Before the ascertainment of profits, a partner is not entitled to any interest on the capital subscribed by him.
3 Every partner may take part in the management of the partnership business.
4 No partner shall be entitled to remuneration for acting in the partnership business.
5 No person may be introduced as a partner without the consent of all existing partners.

It follows that any partner who wishes to be paid for his efforts or to have the right to introduce his son into the business or to exclude another of the partners from the day-to-day management of that business or to claim interest on capital he subscribes (before profits are ascertained), must so provide in his partnership agreement (which, I repeat, *may* be made orally but *should* be set down in writing).

What of partnership disputes? 'Any difference arising as to ordinary matters connected with the partnership business may be decided by a majority of the partners, but no change may be made in the nature of the partnership business without the consent of all existing partners.'

Section 25: 'No majority of the partners can expel any partner unless the power to do so has been conferred by express agreement between the partners.'

So what happens if there is a dispute? Then we must see how the partnership can be dissolved.

First, the partnership may be for a fixed term or a specified object. If the term expires or the object is achieved, the partnership is automatically dissolved.

Next, where no fixed term has been agreed for the duration of the partnership, 'any partner may determine the partnership at any time on giving notice of his intention to do so to all the other partners'. Only where the partnership was originally 'constituted by deed', is a notice in writing essential. In all other cases, notice to dissolve may be given orally and may take effect forthwith. So if you do not want any partner to be entitled to put an end to the firm at any moment, you should make some agreement to the contrary.

Conversely, if you enter into a partnership for a fixed term and it continues after that term has expired and without any express new agreement, 'the rights and duties of the partners remain the same as they were at the expiration of the term, so far as it is consistent with the incidents of a partnership at will'. In other words, any partner may put an end to the partnership at any time, if he so wishes.

Meanwhile, the previous partnership arrangements will generally continue. As before, no partner may compete with the firm—and if he does so without the consent of the other partners and 'carries on any business of the same nature as and competing with that of the firm', then he may be forced to 'account for and pay over to the firm all profits made by him in that business'. He is bound to render true accounts and give full information 'of all things affecting the partnership', and is himself entitled to inspect and to copy the partnership books and accounts, as and when he sees fit.

Unfortunately, many partnerships break up in dispute and contention. If the partners cannot agree on the distribution of partnership property or upon the proper interpretation of the partnership agreement, or if there is a deadlock in the management of the business, what happens? As like as not, one partner will apply to the court to dissolve the business and to order that the proper accounts be taken and enquiries made, so that the rights of the parties can be ascertained.

Apart from cases where a partner is found to be of unsound mind or 'in any other way permanently incapable of performing his part of the partnership contract', the court may dissolve the partnership in four other circumstances. Here they are, as set out in Section 35.1:

(*i*)   'When a partner, other than the partner suing (for dissolution) has been guilty of such conduct as, in the opinion of the court, is calculated to prejudicially affect the carrying on of the business, regard being had to the nature of that business.

(*ii*)   'When a partner, other than the partner suing, wilfully or persistently commits a breach of the partnership agreement, or otherwise so conducts himself in matters relating to the partnership business that it is not reasonably practicable for the other partner or partners to carry on the partnership, in partnership with him;

(*iii*)   'When the business of the partnership can only be carried on at a loss;

(*iv*)   'Whenever in any case circumstances have arisen which, in the opinion of the court, render it just and equitable that the partnership be dissolved.'

So if the partners cannot agree, the court may intervene. The law appears clear enough. But if doubts arise, you should consult your solicitor.

The Act lays down the rules for the distribution of assets on the final settlement of the accounts . . . the rights of partners if there is fraud or misrepresentation . . . the rights of outgoing partners to share profits made after dissolution . . . and various other inevitable essentials. Where the parties have not made the rules for themselves, Parliament does so for them. 'What a pity we did not work out our own arrangements,' say the partners. But the time to have thought of that was when the partnership was first created.

Chapter 10

The End of a Business

SOLVENCY IS an art—and so is insolvency. You must know how to put a business on its feet but it is sometimes useful to understand how best to lay it to rest. It's not clever to leave it to others to cremate your hopes, in their own time and in their own way. If business is bad, then you may have to understand the best ways of putting it to a decent end. And even if business is good, it is pleasant to analyse the way in which your competitors come to a sticky termination—if only so as to appreciate when not to give them credit. So here they are—the basic rules on insolvency, corporate and incorporate, personal and impersonal.

Many a businessman with creditors howling hungrily around his door has considered bankruptcy as a possible solution. And many have rejected it because of the effects of the Bankruptcy Acts, carefully designed to make it unpleasant for the man who too readily attempts to rid himself of his liabilities. Quite apart from the stigma attached to a bankruptcy, an undischarged bankrupt is forbidden to obtain credit for £10 or more without revealing that he is an undischarged bankrupt—so there goes his hope of sloughing off one hungry heap of creditors so as to start right in accumulating another. It isn't so easy to get rid of your bankruptcy, either. You will have to apply to the Court for an order of discharge, but there is no saying that you'll get one. And if you do, it may be made conditional—and the Court has an absolute discretion.

Of course, while you can voluntarily throw in the bankruptcy towel, others may count you out whether you like it or not. If you fraudulently convey your property, conceal yourself or abscond to avoid paying your debts, fail to satisfy the judgment of the Court—in fact, commit any 'act of bankruptcy'—then you may have a bankruptcy petition served on you. A receiving order will be made and an official receiver placed in control of your property—all of it. You may treasure secrets from your wife, your mistress or your private secretary—but the Official Receiver will know all.

The job of the Official Receiver is to get in as much as possible for your creditors. As for your debts, they are paid according to strict and settled priorities.

Top of the list come funeral and testamentary expenses. This may prove troublesome to your widow, but is unlikely to make you turn over in your grave any faster than your stock managed to during your lifetime.

Next come a series of so-called 'preferred debts', which 'rank equally'—if there is money enough to pay them all, then well and good—if there is not then they share in the proceeds in the same proportion. These have now been altered by the Employment Protection Act. For details, see Part 5.

If and when all the preferential creditors are paid off, the rest of the world's lenders can queue up for the crumbs.

'Aha!' you exclaim. 'But how naïve can one get? The law may choose the preferred creditors—but I will get there first. And then it is woe betide the mean and nasty people who have trodden me down—and the best of luck to the kindly folk who have picked me up. The latter will get paid before I go down the drain—and the others can gurgle for their money.'

'We've thought of all that,' replied the law. 'If you attempt to favour one creditor at the expense of the others and go bankrupt within six months of any such preferential payment, the payment will be void as being "a fraudulent preference" and your effort will have been entirely in vain.'

'But suppose that one creditor threatens to sue me if I don't pay up, while the others don't bother me—will it be a fraudulent preference if I pay the one applying pressure?'

'No, it won't. You are not then voluntarily preferring anyone—you are submitting to pressure which you cannot be expected to resist.'

All of which goes to show that kindness to prospective bankrupts just doesn't pay.

So much, then, for the downfall of individual, business brilliance. What now of two penniless genii in concert? How can one terminate an unhappy or an unsuccessful partnership? The rules are in Chapter 10.

When the firm is dissolved, its assets are used first for the paying of partnership debts, on similar lines to those governing payment of creditors in a bankruptcy. If the assets exceed the liabilities, then well and good—the debts are paid off and the partners share the balance. But if the liabilities exceed the assets, then it's heaven help the partners—they have to share the losses in the same proportion as they share the profits and each one of them is liable for the partnership debts to the full extent of all his worldly possessions—if any.

Which leaves companies. Assuming that they are not extinguished by being struck off the register, they can be wound up in any one of three ways. First, there may be a voluntary winding up, secondly, there may be a winding up under the supervision of the Court—and third, the Court may order a compulsory winding up.

If the shareholders decide by special resolution to dissolve the corporation, then they voluntarily put an end to their own association. If the directors deliver to the Registrar of Companies, not more than five weeks before the passing of the resolution, a statutory declaration confirming that the company will pay all its debtors in full within twelve months of the start of the winding up, then it is described as 'a members' voluntary winding up'. The advantage of this is that the liquidator will be appointed and controlled by the shareholders who will, in effect, control the passing of their own, corporate legal entity.

If the directors cannot make the statutory declarations, the winding up is described as 'a creditors' winding up'. The day following the resolution, a creditors' meeting is called and a liquidator appointed— but if the shareholders and creditors disagree, it is the creditors' man that will do the job.

Mind you, even where there is a voluntary winding up, the Court is entitled to step in. It may order that the winding up proceed under its supervision. And it will then appoint an additional liquidator to keep his eye on the proceedings.

A compulsory winding up is much more unpleasant. A Court can wind up the company for any of nine reasons. They are these:

1 If the company has by special resolution resolved that it be wound up by the Court.
2 If default is made in delivering the statutory report to the Registrar or in holding the statutory meeting.
3 If the company does not commence its business within a year from its incorporation, or suspends its business for a whole year.
4 If the number of members is reduced, in the case of a private company below two, or in the case of any other company below seven.
5 If the company is unable to pay its debts.
6 If the Court is of opinion that it is just and equitable that the company should be wound up.
7 If on a petition by the Official Receiver or by any other person authorised to present a winding up petition, the Court is satisfied that an existing voluntary winding up, or a winding up subject to supervision, cannot be continued with due regard to the interests of creditors or contributors.
8 If it appears to the Department of Trade and Industry from any

inspectors' report or from any information or documents obtained under *The Companies Act, 1967*, Part 111, or under certain provisions of *The Protection of Depositors Act, 1963*, that it is in the public interest that the company should be wound up and the Court thinks it just and equitable for it to be wound up.

9 If one of the conditions specified in *The Protection of Depositors Act, 1963*, is satisfied on the petition of the Department of Trade and Industry.

The most interesting of these grounds is 'inability to pay debts'. This again is divided by the Companies Act, and comes under four heads. Here they are:

1 If a creditor who is owed more than £50 has demanded payment —but has gone three weeks without being satisfied.

2 If, in England or Northern Ireland, execution is levied, to attempt to realise money owing under a judgment—and that execution is returned unsatisfied, in whole or in part.

3 If, in Scotland, certain specified debts (such as 'the induciae of a charge for payment of an extract decree' . . . or certain other matters, equally mysterious to a Sassenach) have gone unpaid. (NB—Don't trouble to consult the Lexicon, it won't help you.)

4 If it is proved to the satisfaction of the Court that the company is unable to pay its debts; and, 'in determining whether a company is unable to pay its debts, the Court is to take into account the contingent and prospective liabilities of the company'.

It is not really as complicated as it sounds. If it looks to the Court as if there is a good chance of the company getting back on its feet, it won't be wound up. But if it seems that extra time would only lead to further and deeper wallowing in the mire, the company will have to go.

A company's creditors are paid off on much the same basis as those of a bankrupt—but the shareholders will only be liable for debts to the extent of any unpaid portion of their share capital. And—unless they are shareholders, or have committed some fraud or other—the directors will not be liable at all. Which is certainly a great advantage. Their wives can rest easy in their beds—no one will spring a surprise and remove the sagging springs from under them. The reason? An individual is a legal entity. The partners in a firm are separate legal entities—but the firm is not. But a company, while it has life, exists in law—and has an existence entirely separate from those of its shareholders. And that is why limited liability is the greatest boon to business ever invented by fertile, legal minds.

Finally, note that in a recent High Court appeal, the Judges all agreed that one partner could be found guilty of stealing the partnership assets or property. It was held that: 'In relation to partnership property, the provisions of *The Theft Act, 1968*, have the effect that . . . one partner can steal the partnership property, just as a stranger could commit the theft of the property of another.'

There are three provisos. First, there must be 'the basic ingredient of dishonesty'. If there was no 'dishonest intent', the partner would be acquitted.

Next, there must be 'no question of there being a claim of right made in good faith'. If your partner honestly believes that he is entitled to help himself as he has done, then he is not a thief.

Third, there must be 'an intention permanently to deprive'. If, for instance, the partner was 'only borrowing', he might get away with it.

Chapter 11

Retirement – Voluntary and Otherwise

WHETHER OR not the economists call the particular commercial era one of 'depression' or 'recession' is almost irrelevant. Every day in every year brings top level unemployment. Maybe the cause is bad business, bringing economies at the whim of imported management consultants or home grown economists, seeking economies in the salary list. The reason may even lie in business boom, accompanied by merger, take-over, boardroom battle—and the shifting of the mighty from the corridors of commercial power. Whatever the season or the reason, someone is hurt.

Thanks to the law, those who depart in peace and those who leave after battle are both accompanied, in the main, by financial hand-outs. Severance pay, redundancy pay, pay in lieu of notice . . . call it what you will. Those who leave for any reason other than provable misconduct are likely to take company money with them. This Chapter attempts to make sure that its readers make the best of this sort of bad situation—at least by consulting top-notch laywers, before they accept less money than they might properly claim.

The corporate goose generally lays a golden egg which is taken away by the dismissed industrial executive. How, then, can he breed other geese, to produce equally satisfactory results? There are other boardrooms to be staffed, to be sure—and other jobs to fill. But there are always too many top hats for the racks available. And the older the wearer the longer and more desperate the search is likely to be. Every industrial executive who values his future should provide some sort of home produced alternative to his current work, to be available in time of emergency. Consider some typical cases.

Mr X resigned from his Board after a take-over. He did so upon the (later fulfilled) promise of a handsome golden handshake. He immediately set himself up as an industrial consultant in the field in which he was an acknowledged expert. He used the available capital for advertising—and to live off while he acquired his clientele.

Legal problems? Practically none. No staff; no licence; no planning permission required, He had no need to consult his lawyer—only his accountant, so as to set up a proper system of bookkeeping. And by keeping adequate records, he would have some accumulated losses in his early days which could probably be set off against his profits as time marched on.

Mr Y decided to invest his redundancy money and accumulated savings in a South Coast lodging house. He had always intended to retire to that district. His wife was a former nursery school teacher and she would open a school on weekday mornings in the living room and conservatory.

First problem? Planning consent. They were changing the use of an ordinary residential dwelling to that of a boarding house and school. Then there were bye-laws and fire regulations to be considered. These problems were sorted out at the town hall.

Next, the property was leasehold. Like many leases, that of Mr Y contained a clause restricting the use of the property to the residence of one family only. The landlord was prepared to waive this clause, in return for a modest increase in rent—such waiver being restricted to

Mr Y, and not intended for his successors in title. In order to allow successors to have the benefit of the change—and hence to ensure that the business (as opposed to the remainder of the lease) would be saleable in due course, the rent went up still further.

Still, if Mr Y had simply charged ahead and opened his business without knowing the legal snags, he might well have seen his entire investment go down the legal drain. As we said, the time to consider the legal implications is before you leave one living for the next.

Incidentally, quite apart from the law, Mr Y learned that he mis-judged his district and his site, as much as his market. He discovered that in the summer months there was a shortage of staff but plenty of money. In the winter, there were plenty of men and women, looking for work—but very little money to pay them with. You do not leave business complexities behind you when you depart from the company and strike out on your own.

Mr Z was happy to retire to his converted, country cottage. He signed a lease just a month before he moved out of the board-room.

Unfortunately, Mr Z tried to save money on his purchase. He begrudged solicitors' fees—and did not know enough to make the necessary searches. So he did not discover that there were plans for driving a motorway through the countryside just a few hundred yards from his peaceful retreat.

Worse, Mr Z had learned to trust the evidence of his own eyes, and he did not employ a surveyor to check the property on his behalf. To his horror, he discovered after exchange of contracts that the place was riddled with wet rot and dry rot and suffered from a substantial subsidence. There was nothing he could do except to pay to have the place put right and made habitable.

Mr A had his eye on a small, antique shop. He was not altogether sorry to leave the Board. He collected his tax-free severance pay; he sold his house; and he bought the shop, with living accommodation up above.

Unfortunately, the vendor refused to complete the sale on the agreed date. Mr A was therefore forced to delay completion of the sale of his own home. The proposed purchaser started raising the legal roof. 'Notices to complete' flew in all directions. Legal costs increased. Eventually, everything was sorted out—but after more time, delay and expense than Mr A had reckoned on.

Then the unfortunate executive found that trade was not all that he had expected. The stock took a long time to move. And, anyway, although he and his wife were knowledgeable people, they found that retail trade is just as cut-throat in its own way as any industrial business—and requires just as much knowledge, experience and good fortune, before much money is made.

So Mr A was guilty of the most common error of all—he was heavily under-capitalised. He had not allowed enough money in his reckoning for his own and his wife's living expenses, during the lean years, nor had he made sufficient allowance for legal and other expenses, which cropped up so unexpectedly. His new business crashed. He staved off bankruptcy but was left living on his retirement pension—if 'living' was the right word.

Mr A also learned that it is not only a big business which should have the benefits of limited liability. In these days of corporation tax and careful perusal of directors' expenses, there is much to be said for operating as an individual or a partnership. But the individual trader or the partner may be made liable for the debts of the business, almost up to the last penny that he personally owns in the world. The shareholder of a company will only be liable for the corporate debts up to any amount which he has left unpaid on his shares—and that is normally nil.

Mr A could have bought a ready-made company. He could have created his own, tailor-made corporation (with the help of his solicitor or his accountant). His failure to do either cost him (almost literally) his shirt.

The trouble is that far too many executives leave their business acumen behind them when they retire (willingly or otherwise) from their industrial companies. To operate on your own account is an intelligent and potentially worthwhile move. But there are legal and financial angles which require careful study and preparation. And whether you are planning to spend your (voluntary or enforced) retirement running an hotel or restaurant, a sweet shop or car hire concern, a business or property or investment consultancy—or any other sort of commercial enterprise—look with a legal, eagle eye before you leap, or you may land in a mire of disaster from which you are too old to emerge unscathed.

Mr B was determined to retire into an independent future. He decided to take on a franchise for a particular business. In return for an investment of £X,000, he was assured—assuming that he worked hard—of an annual income of at least £Y,000. He noticed, in passing, that the sales literature was carefully worded to indicate that there was no absolute guarantee of success. Still, he said to himself, you cannot go far wrong with the sort of guidance, experience and success of the main company behind you.

Unfortunately, he forgot that the people who were anxious to obtain his capital were concerned primarily with their own living. They helped him to select a site and to acquire the necessary equip-ment. They even trained him in the necessary techiques. But when it turned out that he had chosen an unsatisfactory site and that trade fell way below expectations, they shrugged, said how sorry they were —and he lost his precious nest egg.

The shoemaker, we are told, should stick to his last. There are some great captains of industry who make the world of commerce their stage and can step with ease and an apparent Midas foot from one industrial enterprise to the next. But these men are rare. Far more common is the self-confident executive who knows one business or trade well and thoroughly and fancies that he can step merrily into another. He may be right. But if he is wrong, the law can do nothing to assist him.

The unfortunate Mr B soon found that he could obtain no damages from the sellers of the franchise. They had been guilty of no fraud and no misrepresentation. Neither was there any breach of contract. His own eagerness and enthusiasm combined with his inexperience in the field in which he ventured cost him his savings. And no lawyer in the land could help him. He had learned the hard way that successful and lucrative retirement requires quite as much acumen, knowledge and caution as any other commercial venture. So when you retire, mind how you go.

"FOR ONCE IN YOUR LIFE, MISS THOMSON, CAN'T YOU FORGET PROFESSIONAL ETIQUETTE?"

Part two

Problems of Professions

Chapter 12

The Professional Man – and the Legal Profession

THE PROFESSIONAL man approaches the law from three main directions. First, it may help provide him with his livelihood. Second, he may require it in order to bring his customers into line and his bank account into credit. Third, he may be at the receiving end of legal proceedings, civil or criminal. In either case, he will be thrown into contact with the legal profession. If he knows how to handle the lawyers—including those who have been elevated to benches on high —his contact with the law itself is likely to be comparatively pleasant, often lucrative and in any event a good deal less harrowing than otherwise.

'Young man,' a wise old lawyer once said, 'what matters is not so much to know the law but to know your judges and your fellow lawyers.' If you understand how to handle barristers, solicitors and judges, then there is every reason to hope that your contacts with the law will be satisfactory. Otherwise, beware!

So now let us take a long, cool look at the legal profession, from the viewpoint of the professional man.

The Lawyer—and You

In general, witnesses may only be interviewed by solicitors. If the engineer or accountant, doctor or surveyor or other professional person wants legal advice, unless he can swing along the old boy net to some friend at the bar, he must go to a solicitor. So must everyone else who wants to sue clients, acquire new premises, make a will, effectively fight a summons . . . or deal with any of the other legal necessities and miseries of modern life.

The solicitor, despite his name (and the sense in which Americans use it) is not entitled to chase ambulances, employ fire watchers or otherwise tout for custom. But he does hunt for witnesses, for the sake of his clients.

If litigation is important, then it will almost certainly be taken by a solicitor to 'counsel'. The solicitor is fully entitled to deal with all aspects of Magistrates' and County Court work. At the moment, the limit of County Court jurisdiction is, in general, cases in which the amount in issue does not exceed £1,000. But this may go up again. A solicitor may appear in these lower courts, prepare the 'pleadings' (or documents, setting out the case), decide upon the evidence, interview witnesses, examine them in the witness box . . . and do all other necessary work.

But even in the County Court, if the case is substantial (either because the facts or the law are complicated), counsel is likely to be involved. He will advise, 'settle' (or draft) the necessary documents and appear at the hearing.

In the High Court, only barristers have a right of audience. In most cases, the 'pleadings' are drafted by him. Assuming that the solicitor does his job, counsel will 'advise on evidence' and, in many cases, he will (at some stage before the hearing) interview his clients. But he will not see witnesses other than experts before he actually calls them to appear in the witness box.

Professional men are different. Like all 'experts', they may be interviewed by counsel as well as by solicitors. As a result, many warm, personal friendships grow up between professional people and barristers; and whilst solicitors often decide upon the professional man most suited in their view to advise in the particular case, the barrister is often consulted, even on that point.

A typical case? A difficult matter of architecture or engineering is in dispute. The papers are sent to counsel with instructions to advise. These include something like this: 'Instructing Solicitors consider that it would be of great assistance to the client if the opinion of an expert could be obtained, before the pleadings are settled. Counsel will please advise.' Alternatively: 'Does counsel consider that it would be of advantage to obtain the expert evidence of an architect and/or engineer on our client's behalf?'

If counsel does advise that a professional expert be called, as like as not the solicitor will say to him (in conference or by telephone), 'Whom shall we have?' Upon the answer to that question may depend your livelihood, if you are an expert in that particular field, and prepared to give evidence accordingly. Indeed, if lawyers have a sufficient regard for your ability. you may join the selected band of engineers, doctors, surveyors, architects and others whose appearances in court are fairly regular and whose evidence is valued by judges and lawyers alike.

Once the expert has been consulted, he will generally be asked to make an initial report in writing. Lawyers abhor reports scrawled on scruffy paper . . . replete with terms which only men in that particular profession can understand and which send the reader scurrying for his dictionary . . . or which are incomplete. Reports should be typed neatly, preferably on foolscap paper, and leaving adequate margins for legal comment. An extra copy is always appreciated, even in these days of the photostat machine.

All professions have their own jargon. This is a tremendously useful form of shorthand, which swiftly and efficiently conveys meanings to others in the same profession. While the lawyer is forced to become at least moderately conversant with anything from the calibre of a gun to the construction of bridges, at a few hours' notice, he does not necessarily find this easy. But when professional experts do not do him the courtesy of defining their terms in layman's language, then the lawyer is put to considerable inconvenience and aggravation.

Anyway, when the lawyer 'opens his case' to the judge—or addresses the court at any stage of the proceedings—he will have to explain the case to the judge (himself a former legal practitioner) who will decide upon the fate of his client's allegations. If the report is not only crisp, clear and concise but also contains the minimum of professional jargon and the maximum of pithy explanation of such jargon as is necessary (complete with plans or diagrams, as required), then the popularity of its writers will soar.

'We don't like to teach grandma lawyer to suck eggs,' you answer. Never mind. Provided that you do not talk down to or patronise the lawyers, they will be only too delighted to learn from you. After all, that is the object of the exercise.

So the wise expert, preparing a really useful report, will not suppose that its reader is particularly knowledgeable in that particular matter. He will also make his report very full—the lawyers can always extract what they want and reject the rest, but if essentials are left out, the odds are that a 'further report' or 'supplementary report' will be required.

In any event, when a report arrives, it will probably be shunted off to the barrister, with the request that he 'advise thereon'. If he raises further questions, the 'expert' who wrote the report should not be offended. Nor does it help to write back the sort of 'shirty' note that harassed men sometimes send to solicitors: 'Surely counsel appreciates . . .'; or 'I would refer to paragraph 3—which, I would have thought, makes the matter clear . . .'. This kind of discourteous comment—which points out to the lawyers those inadequacies in their education of which they are doubtless already painfully aware—will not usually prevent the man being employed in the particular case. After all, it would probably take too long and cost too much of the client's money to get someone else in the particular case. But the kiss of death will have been placed on any further employment.

The chances are that the expert will be asked to confer with counsel. Certainly the barrister will wish to pick his expert brain, either in conference or outside the door of the court. Indeed, he will probably expect the man to sit behind him when the case comes to court. More of this later.

As we saw when we started, witnesses are normally interviewed only by solicitors. The etiquette of the bar forbids counsel from holding conferences with lay witnesses who are not parties to the dispute. It is apparently believed that counsel may plant words upon the tongues of such witnesses and so place pitfalls along the paths of truth.

Conferences with experts are immensely appreciated by lawyers, They can far better assess the prospects of a case, as well as the manner in which it may best be fought, if they can 'kick it around' in conference, with the expert upon whose evidence the court will (it is hoped) rely.

Litigation is uncertain. Lawyers will seldom guarantee the outcome of a case. The uncertainty is increased by the relative nature of the word 'expert'. In fact, however extraordinary the proposition, the chances are that you can find some expert to support it. With luck, he will even be able to produce a text-book to back him up. Indeed, he himself may even have written it.

'I would respectfully draw your Lordship's attention,' says Counsel, 'to this definitive work . . . this now standard text-book . . . written by the learned engineer (doctor, surveyor or architect) whom it will be my privilege to call before your Lordship . . .'

Naturally, an expert on the other side will doubtless be called to say that the matter is highly disputed within the profession—and that it represents a minority opinion. Professional courtesy may restrain him from pointing out that the book has in any event only sold 280 copies, and these were probably bought by the author himself—but, anyway, the battle is joined.

Happily (except for professional witnesses and advocates), the vast majority of cases settle long before they reach court. But as the professional man is almost certain to be a witness at some time in his life, either in his own cause or (preferably) on behalf of others, we now turn to the subtle arts of witness-boxing.

In the Witness Box

Whether you are in the witness box in support of your client's case or your own, it is absolutely essential that you should at least give the impression of honesty, accuracy and expertise. I do not suggest for a moment that you would be dishonest, inaccurate or inexpert. But it is remarkable how easily you may be made to look all three, if you do not know and follow the basic rules of witness-box behaviour.

First, whether you take the oath on the Old Testament or the New —whether you affirm or (if you happen to be a Chinese of a particular persuasion) if you smash a saucer, do indicate that you mean what you say. Those who gabble oaths make bad impressions.

Nor should you rely upon your memory. The usher will hand you a card. Read from it. It is really incredible how many intelligent people misread the oath. Whether this is due to nervousness or over-confidence—or a state of partial shock induced by the usher's loud roar of 'Silence', just as you are about to intone the formula—the resultant bad impression is the same.

Next, oblige your counsel by letting him hear your answers—and by addressing them to the judge. Roses may blush unseen and still have their place on earth. Unheard words should not be pronounced in courts of law.

Next, do not expect your own counsel to 'lead' you too far. He will normally not ask you questions which presuppose an answer of 'Yes' or 'No'. Listen to his questions. If they are not clear, ask for them to be repeated. Then reply, calmly and carefully.

When under cross-examination, do not allow opposing counsel to make you lose your temper. This is probably what he wants. He will rarely be permitted to take unfair advantage or you—if he tries to do that, then your own counsel will leap to his feet, objecting vigorously. But by then, if counsel really has been unfair, the chances are that the judge will already have choked him off.

Address counsel as 'Sir' or 'Madam'. If in the High Court, call the judge, 'My Lord' or 'My Lady'; in the County Court, 'Your Honour' in a Magistrates' Court, 'Sir' or 'Madam'.

All judges like witnesses to stand still in the witness box and not (for example) to rattle coins, tap upon the box or engage in other nervous antics. They also appreciate straight answers to straight questions. But if you consider that a question does not have a real answer, say so. If you rely on your recollection and you are uncertain, then admit it. Do not allow yourself to be pushed into firm statements on unsure foundations.

Another good rule? Do not make jokes. Leave that to counsel and to the judge. If the court or counsel do laugh about matters which you consider terribly serious, forgive them. If they were to become emotionally involved in the troubles that surround their lives, they would be sad folk indeed.

Treat both judge and counsel with tact. A witness once referred to a man as 'very old and decrepit'. It turned out that he was sixty and the judge more than ten years older.

Anyway, cases are seldom better than the witnesses who put them forward—nor witnesses than the cases which they must support. You can only do your best. If you do that and someone else's case is lost, then you will not be blamed. And if you lose your own battle, at least you will not blame yourself.

Finally, what of the time before and after you actually give evidence? Do not disappear down the corridors, to inhale nicotine, attend to other cases or otherwise to show that you are not really interested in the case in issue.

Your lawyers (or those of your clients) may need your help at any moment. A surprise attack may be launched and without your presence they will not know how to react.

The chances are that if you are an expert you will be invited to sit behind your counsel and that he will turn to you, from time to time, for advice, guidance and suggestions. If you wish to draw a suggestion to his attention, please do not tug at his gown. Even though he appears to be stupid and deviating from the correct paths, you should consider the possibility that the deviation is intentional. To catch the monkey in the witness box, you must not only tread softly on occasion but sometimes by very devious routes.

So pass the man a note. Write it in large letters, so that he can take in its import at a glance. Better still, hand it to the solicitor, who should be sitting beside you. He can then decide when and whether to pass it along to the barrister.

It may be, of course, that 'leading counsel' has been employed. Queen's Counsel (or 'leaders' or—by reason of the silken gowns that they wear on State occasions—'silks') are barristers of at least ten years standing. They 'apply for silk'. The method by which 'silks' are chosen is not generally known, but apparently the Lord Chancellor takes the decisions, upon the appropriate advice. Many 'junior counsel' are both senior in experience and knowledge—and earning a great deal more money—than many 'silks'. 'Juniors' (so called) do the paperwork. 'Leaders' advise on especially heavy cases and always appear in court, with 'juniors' behind them. At enquiries (such as at planning appeals) they may appear with 'juniors'.

So the professional witness will in general deal with the solicitor; who will deal with junior counsel; who, on occasion, will pass your note, information or views inside the bar of the court to his 'leader'.

Courts and Fees

If you are consulted as a professional expert, the chances are that your fee will be fixed by and with a solicitor. Only experience (coupled, on occasion, with the advice and help of colleagues) can really tell you how much to charge. Remember that lawyers' generosity is often limited by clients' purses. The lawyer seeks to do his best by his client and to obtain the finest evidence at the most moderate fee. When you buy, you will shop around for the best bargain. The lawyer purchases your services.

Still, it is even more common for the professional man to require the help of the law in order to get in the fees that he himself is owed. However expert you may be in your own field, the chances are that you will need to leave its answer to your lawyer. He will look at your case with the eyes of the eventual judge. You will tell him the facts . . . you will assess the financial strength or stability of your client or customer . . . you will tell your solicitor and/or counsel whether you think that the other side are bluffing—and how they will react to a writ or a summons . . . and whether, if you obtain judgment, you are likely to get your money or to be faced with a company that rushes into liquidation, rather than payment. (See also Chapter 110, on when to sue.)

Your lawyers will then assess for you your prospects of success in the litigation—plus the likely costs. When all the facts, information, estimates and ideas are pooled, you then decide whether or not to proceed.

How, then, do you get the best out of your lawyer? First, you must pick the right man. Generally, you have the choice. You take a small firm (or a one man band) where you will get individual attention and general expertise. But just as no engineer can be an expert in every field of engineering endeavour, so no lawyer can know the lot (or even where to find it). So if you want expert advice in a particular field at an early stage, you may prefer a large firm, highly departmentalised.

Naturally, size is not necessarily a guide to efficiency. There are marvellously efficient and chronically inefficient firms, at every level.

When it comes to choosing counsel, you may ask your solicitor to instruct a particular man who has especially impressed you, when you have met him in the course of your professional career. You are fully entitled to insist on the barrister of your choice.

Usually, though, you will rely upon the advice of your solicitor. He may choose a particular expert in a specialist field. He may prefer a general 'common lawyer'—an advocate in all-seasons, with a broad knowledge of most fields of the law. Equally, just as there are general surgeons, who will wield the knife as directed and whose scope is the entire body of the patient, so there are many barristers whose field is the entire body of the law. You work out the possibilities; you pay your money and you take your choice.

Next, you should provide your lawyers with as much information as possible, complete with statements, plans and all relevant documents, letters and the like—preferably presented in typewritten form and chronological order. The greater the information you provide, the easier it is for the lawyers to read and assimilate; the less effort and aggravation you require of them—the lower will be your costs.

Then discuss the matter with them; pick their brains; by all means harry them and make sure that they do their jobs swiftly. Then, when they give their advice, listen. After all, they are experts in their own field. There is no point in getting advice and then ignoring it. Let them get on with their jobs To keep a dog and to do your own barking is a futile exercise.

If you lose confidence in your lawyers, then there is nothing what-soever to prevent you from changing. Your solicitor may have a 'lien' on your papers, pending payment of his proper fees—in exactly the same way as the man who repairs your vehicle is entitled to keep it until he has been paid his charges. When the lawyers are paid, the papers will be transferred. Often, liens are not exercised.

Counsel, too, may be changed. It is often stupid to change legal horses in mid-stream. But it is far better to do that than to retain lawyers in whom you have no confidence.

So whether you work with lawyers as part of a professional team or they work for you so as to achieve your ends in litigation in which you are personally involved, or even in non-litigious matters which are your own, if you can establish and maintain a friendly personal relationship founded on a mutual confidence and under-standing, the odds are that your battle will be won, your job done with efficiency and to the mutual satisfaction of all.

The Professional Man in Trouble

Unfortunately, no one is perfect. Professionals may find themselves (justly or otherwise) at the receiving end of summonses, writs or even warrants for your arrest. If you come into this unhappy category at any time, you should consult your solicitors forthwith.

How many times have you said to a client: 'If only you had come to me before . . .'? The lawyer's vocabulary is replete with 'if only's'. The sooner you take your troubles (civil or criminal, professional or matrimonial, it matters not) to your lawyer, the more likely they are to be able to help you. The later you wait, the less the prospect of satisfactory results in the long run. The more you save in costs at the outset, the more the proceedings are likely to cost you in the long run.

That said, all the suggestions I have made about the handling of lawyers and courts when you are dealing with the affairs of others apply just as much when you are coping with legal miseries of your own. Professionals who ignore or underestimate the pitfalls of the law are asking for trouble. And however easy you may find it to assist clients in coping with their troubles, personal and emotional involve-ment in legal disasters of your own provide special problems.

When your contacts with the law are professional, you should attempt to stand back and to avoid emotional involvement, wherever possible. When the legal battle involves your own personal pocket, reputation or good name, then you must still attempt to achieve detachment. 'Much easier said than done,' you say. Agreed. But if done, you are far more likely to succeed in your litigation; you will make your lawyer's task much easier; and your contact with the law is far more likely to be satisfactory than if your limited nervous energy is dissipated in worry and aggravation.

Finally, whatever the reason for your contact with lawyers, remember the old saying: 'The man who is his own lawyer has a fool for a client.' So try to pick the right lawyer for your purpose; give him the ammunition; and let him get on with his job. In other words, treat him in his profession as you would wish that he would treat you in yours. And if you would like some more reasons for not representing yourself, turn to Chapter 111.

Chapter 13

Employing Professionals

THE MODERN business world seems to be infested with professionals, semi-professionals and would-be professionals. And they all have to be paid. There are lawyers, architects, surveyors, estate agents, accountants, stockbrokers—and each one seems to have a finger in the till.

What is the answer? Do it yourself? Let us see.

*   *   *

First, take the lawyers. Bearing in mind that a company can only appear in court if represented by solicitor or counsel, how necessary is it to employ a lawyer? The answer, is—usually, very. And the trouble with most businessmen is that they consult when the time for consultation is past.

The most common example of lawyers' fees begrudged is on the transfer of property. 'What do they do? They sit behind a desk, write a few letters, fill in half a dozen forms, ask the right questions, and it costs you hundreds of pounds.'

That is what it looks like—but it is far from the truth. Proof? Some time, take a look at the National Conditions of Sale or The Law Society's Conditions of Sale. These standard conditions have been prepared to save Lawyers the necessity of drawing up separate contracts—bound to be identical in most particulars—every time they convey land for a client.

'What did we tell you?' you say. 'All they have to do is take the printed conditions. . . .' Yes—and vary them. The 'General Conditions' may be printed, but those you don't want—those that have no reference to your particular case or the inclusion of which could do you harm—must be amended or struck out. And items not covered—which you would never know about—that is, the 'Special Conditions of Sale'—must be filled in.

If you doubt the worth of a solicitor on the assignment of property, read the Conditions of Sale. The chances are that you will scarcely understand a word. You certainly will not know what items ought to be excluded or amended for your protection or what extra clauses you need.

Unfortunately, the law is not easy. When it comes to dealing with land, there are no short cuts to understanding the rules. But for all you know there may be short cuts across your property. Do the job yourself and you may discover, too late, that others have rights of way across your land which prevent you from using it in the way you wish. You may find restrictive covenants, whose existence you never discovered because you never asked the right questions. Worse, there may be a road widening scheme affecting your property, so that part of it is hacked away. The front of your factory, office or shop or the back of your garden may be taken from you. And all because you begrudged a solicitor's fee

If you go to an intelligent, experienced and reputable solicitor, he will soon tell you what you can do on your own and when you would be better off not to spend money on lawyer's fees. He will be too busy to waste his time with non-essentials. And he will realise that it is more important for him, in the long run, to retain your goodwill than to overcharge you.

If you are contemplating any major building, any important alteration to your property, any work of any consequences involving British Architects lays down the conditions of employment for its members and the scale of fees properly chargeable by them. By all means enquire from your architect what the charge is likely to be—or better still, ask him to give you a copy of the Conditions of Employment and Scale of Fees, and to direct your attention to the relevant parts. If you are contemplating any major building, any important alteration to your property, any work of any consequences involving architectural planning, then do not begrudge an architect's fee. Your builder may be prepared to do it without an architect at his side, but for you to let him is sheer stupidity.

Equally, to buy a property without having it surveyed by a qualified surveyor is idiotic. You know your business and realise that no person inexperienced in your line could possibly do your work for you. So do not expect to do a surveyor's job yourself.

Or consider the accountant. His job is not to show you tax fiddles or to teach you how to evade taxes which you should properly pay. You employ him to show you how to arrange your affairs so that they attract the least possible tax and so that they comply, in all respects, with the law. Once again, the law does not force you to employ an accountant—other, of course, than a man to audit the Company accounts. But to wade through the tax forms on your own is simply ridiculous. You may manage it. You may satisfy the tax inspector. But the chances are that you will pay a great deal more in tax than you would have done had you saved yourself the worry and aggravation of doing the job on your own.

Professional fees should pay for themselves.

Chapter 14

Business Transfer and Estate Agents – and the Law

EVERY BUSINESSMAN involved in the sale or purchase of premises—or of a business itself—is likely to become entangled with agents. The Law Reports tell of the clashes between estate agents seeking commission and men of commerce denying their liability to pay. The law has defined 'sole agencies' and 'sole selling rights'—but do you know their meaning, and when you should grant them? When is an estate agent entitled to his money—and from whom? What should the businessman know of the everyday laws of estate agency?

* * *

You are under no legal duty whatsoever to employ an estate agent* at any time for any purpose. Indeed, if you can sell your property without an agent's help, you will save a great deal of money and incur no additional legal hazards. Do your own conveyancing or surveying and (unless you are an expert), you are riding for a swift fall. But if you can find your own buyer, then you and he pass the matter over to solicitors and money may be saved all round.

On the other hand, are you in a position to judge what your property or your business would fetch on the market? Do you know the sort of prices achieved in recent, similar sales? Are you in a position to value your property? And even if you have a very good idea about prices, can you reach the sellers you want? Often, the services of the business transfer specialist or estate agent are invaluable—or at least worth a good deal more than their cost.

If you do employ an agent, then unless you grant him 'sole selling rights' (which you should never do), you are still free to sell your property or your business through your own efforts. If the agent achieves the introduction which results in the eventual sale, then he has earned his commission and you (the vendor) must pay it. But if you pull off the deal on your own, then you need pay no commission to anyone. If you sign away 'sole selling rights', then whoever achieves the sale the agent will get his money. But my advice is: Never grant such rights and if any agent asks for them, take your custom elsewhere.

Sole agencies are a little different. An agent may legitimately say: 'If you want me to spend money on advertising your property or business and I really do put myself out to dispose of it, then I want to be sure that you will employ no other agents.' If you are really satisfied that the agent will earn his sole keep, then give him his sole money—but, I suggest, for a limited period only. When that period

* It is worth noting that in Scotland the work of estate agents in the negotiations for the buying and selling of property is commonly carried out by solicitors.

has expired, you should be free to put the property into the hands of any other agents.

Incidentally, even if there is no fixed time for the termination of a sole agency, this does not mean that the agent is entitled to your undivided custom for ever. You may still give reasonable notice to terminate that agency—how long that notice will be will depend on all the circumstances.

Normally, the agent is entitled to his commission from the vendor. In certain circumstances (such as where the agent is prepared to scour the country for property), a purchaser may grant the agent a retainer at a commission on the purchase. But usually the vendor can reckon to pay commission on the scale laid down by the appropriate estate agents' professional body, if someone introduced by that agent buys. If the agent belongs to no professional body (and there is no law which says that he must do so), you are in general unwise to retain him. In any event, read carefully any document you are invited to sign. You should have to pay commission only if someone eventually buys your property as a result of an introduction effected by the agent. Do not (for instance) agree to pay anything merely because the agent takes a deposit on your behalf.

If the agents are established and reputable, there is no reason why you should not let them take deposits on your behalf. If in doubt, then insist that deposits are paid direct to your solicitors.

When dealing with agents, take care. If you agree (for instance) to pay an especially high rate of commission to business transfer specialists, then that is a matter for you. If you do not understand the agreement you are invited to sign, then refuse to do so—at least until your lawyers have checked it for you. Remember that estate agents are experts at their job and are usually well aware of their rights. If the businessman wants to deal with them on their own level, he should check any doubts with his solicitor. Most estate agents are thoroughly reputable businessmen, who earn their living. But precisely because anyone may start in estate agency at any time without any qualifications, the oceans of agency contain their fair share of sharks. Watch out for them and follow the rules I have given and they will not feed off you.

Chapter 15

Laws and Ethics

ALL PROFESSIONAL men and women must conform to two separate codes of conduct. First, they are citizens of (or at least resident in) a country. They must therefore obey the laws of the land. Failure to do so brings them into conflict with the courts.

Second, every profession has its own rules of etiquette, laid down by its professional body and enforced where necessary by some sort of internal disciplinary procedure. The two codes should be complementary but in practice at times conflict—with varying results.

It is the law of the land, for instance, which prescribes who may be a doctor or dentist—and that non-qualified people shall not hold themselves out as such. Once qualified and registered, the practitioner acquires duties to his patients, some prescribed by law and regulation and others by virtue of his Hippocratic oath.

A doctor is required to answer a subpoena—that is, an order, requiring him to appear in Court—in the same way as anyone else. If ordered to appear in court he must do so. If he receives a 'subpoena duces tecum', then he must appear, bringing with him the documents specified in the subpoena. He must then enter the witness box and answer such questions as the judge may consider proper.

'I decline to answer that question,' says the doctor, unwilling to divulge his patient's most confidential secrets. Declining, he is acting strictly in accordance with his professional code. But if the judge insists upon an answer and the doctor refuses to give it, he is breaking the law and liable to be imprisoned. Hence the modern doctor's dilemma: To tell or not to tell?

Until recently, it was a crime to keep knowledge of a felony to yourself. You could have been convicted of 'misprision of felony'. But now the doctor who knows that his patient traffics in drugs—or even that he has recently committed a murder—may keep the information to himself (see Chapter 108). But should he?

Everyone is entitled to be represented in court—even the biggest crook. So barristers have a duty to represent clients whom they may despise. They must do their best to put their client's case forward in the most favourable light.

On the other hand, they owe a duty to the court. They must not deceive the judge. A brilliant, kindly and highly respected Queen's Counsel deliberately neglected to inform the court that his policeman client had been demoted. The barrister himself was deprived of his right of audience for twelve long months.

Disciplinary procedures are generally controlled by bodies that meet in private. Except for the lawyers' own disciplinary committees, professional bodies which hold the livelihoods of their members in their hands are usually made up of fellow professionals with experience neither in the law nor in its application, still less in the sifting of legal evidence.

The law, for its part, retains some sort of theoretical control over private courts. If 'the rules of natural justice' are flouted, then the court may come to the rescue. But in general, courts prefer to leave discipline to the professionals concerned. Even the Privy Council, to which doctors and dentists have a statutory right of appeal, seldom intervenes.

What, then, should you do if you find a conflict between your ethics and the law? Probably, consult your professional body. Once a doctor has been advised by his medical overlords not to give evidence, then it will take a brave judge to commit a doctor to prison for contempt of court. In the annals of the law, this grim step has never been taken.

Are we advising you to break the law, if necessary . . . to refuse to obey the orders of the judge. . . ? Are we counselling a contempt of court? Heaven forbid. Perhaps you should take the advice of your lawyer. He will doubtless tell you to obey the word of the judge along with the letter of the law. After all, he has his own ethical worries to consider. At least he can be grateful that his communications with you (as his client) are completely privileged and can never be revealed without your consent. And that is a privilege—absolutely vital for the fair administration of justice—for which both lawyer and client often have cause for the deepest gratitude. At least this sort of conflict between ethics and the law remains closed from public view.

Chapter 16

Professions on Trial

THE HOUSE OF LORDS decision in *Pharmaceutical Society of Great Britain and Another* v. *Dickson* (which, in effect, enabled Boots and others to continue to sell merchandise which is 'non-traditional' for chemists' shops) has some fascinating angles. For the first time in legal history, the House of Lords had to consider in depth the limits on the powers of a professional body to impose restraints on the freedom of their members.

First, it was accepted that pharmacy (with its study, training, 'wide-ranging examinations' and required skills) is a profession. Therefore the Pharmaceutical Society was fully entitled (and indeed bound) to seek to impose high standards on its members.

'In every profession,' said Lord Reid, 'there is a code of conduct, written or unwritten, which makes it improper for members to engage in certain activities in which ordinary members of the public are entitled to engage. Normally, that is regarded as a domestic matter within the profession. But if a member could show that a particular restriction on his activities goes beyond anything that could reasonably be related to the maintenance of professional honour or standards, the court must be able to intervene.'

So that is rule one. The professional body of a profession is entitled to impose restraints on its members' freedom to engage in trade. The extent of the restriction is normally a matter for the profession and the courts will not interfere provided that the restriction is 'related to the maintenance or improvement of the status of the profession. . . .'

If doctors, for example, wish to restrict their members from operating private fertility clinics . . . or advertising the services they have to offer . . . that is a matter for them. If those modern, medical miracle men who transplant the heart are to be permitted personal publicity, that again is a matter for the profession. The law will not interfere.

On the other hand, the common law 'dislikes all restraints, voluntary or involuntary . . . and there is no exception from the general rule in favour of a profession'. But in the case of any profession, there is a special circumstance: 'A profession is a vocation of the highest standing: it calls on its members to serve (no doubt for reward) the public by offering to them highly technical and always confidential advice and services which require a different standard of conduct from that of the tradesman. . . .

'The professional code must be different by the nature of its calling and the reliance placed upon it by the public. Those seeking the advice of a professional man are entitled to expect of him the highest standards of ethical conduct. That means that he must submit to some restraints of trade, such as a prohibition against advertising, and a refusal, by undercutting or otherwise, to snatch the work from another practitioner (but of course there is no harm in letting the work come to one). Such restraints, necessary to establish, sustain and promote the ethical standards of a profession, are justifiable in law.'

So there we have the justification for the refusal of lawyers, doctors, accountants and architects to allow their members to advertise . . . the justification for scales of fees . . . the basis of the powers of professional bodies, including that of the medical profession.

In fact, the House of Lords unanimously agreed that the restraint which the Pharmaceutical Society sought to put on its members went beyond the powers of the organisation. 'The restraint of trade which it would impose could not be justified as reasonable either in the public interest or in the private interest of the parties', as one Judge put it.

Again: 'The proposed restraints could not reasonably be related to the Society's objects . . . the suggestion that the adoption of the motion would make the profession more attractive to new entrants . . . was not supported by the evidence, which indicated that entrants tend to go where there is trading as well as professional work, because prospects are better. . . .' The restraint was invalid.

Chapter 17

Laws – Ancient and Modern

THE MODERN pharmacist follows an ancient profession. The ancient herbalist, apothecary and maker of ointments appears in the history of most nations. And his work is taken by one ancient writer to illustrate the laws moral and spiritual as well as laws temporal to which they usually gave birth. Consider the cynical Book of Ecclesiastes and the afterbirth of some of its sayings.

'Did flies cause the ointment of the apothecary to send forth a stinking flavour,' says the unknown author, putting his words into the mouth of Solomon, the son of David. 'So doth a little folly him that is in reputation for wisdom and honour. A wise man's heart is at his right hand: but a fool's heart at his left.'

Nowadays, the apothecary must not only make up his ointment with care but ensure that, once made, it is kept away from the carriers of germs. Let your stock stand too long so that it harms the eventual user and you will be an easy prey for an action in negligence. It is not enough to have your heart on the right side—your hand must be used with care.

'A man to whom God hath given riches, wealth and honour, so that he wanteth nothing for his soul of all that he desireth, yet God giveth him not the power to eat thereof, but a stranger eateth it; this is vanity, and it is an evil disease.' How many comfortable citizens buy aids to slimming . . . cures for ulcers . . . tranquillisers . . . pharmaceuticals to deal with the digestion? Even the physical allures have changed little.

As for your good name, this is protected by the laws of defamation. The man who speaks ill of you, so as to 'lower you in the eyes of right thinking people', is asking for trouble. The ancient Chinese demonstrated the solution in their carved statues of grinning lions; each lion holds its jaws apart, its lips back, its teeth clenched—and behind the teeth the craftsman has carved a loose, rolling, rattling, stone ball. The gossip is never let loose.

'The words of a wise man's mouth are gracious; but the lips of a fool will swallow up himself. The beginning of the words of his mouth is foolishness: and the end of his talk is mischievous madness. A fool also is full of words; a man cannot tell what shall be; and what shall be after him, who can tell him?'

The person defamed will be 'after him'—and the Courts of Justice at his side. By all means think whatever you like; discuss it with your wife—in English law, for this purpose at least, you are regarded as one person. Tell someone else to his face what you think of him and there is no defamation—you are unlikely to lower a person in his own estimation and to publish the words to him direct is no offence.* But tell his wife and you are a slanderer (or guilty of a libel, if the words are written or in some other permanent form).

'Curse not the king, no not in thy thought; and curse not the rich in thy bed chamber; for a bird of the air shall carry the voice, and that which hath wings shall tell the matter.'

From a legal viewpoint, you may curse anyone you like in your thoughts. In practice, no one is prosecuted for speaking their mind about the monarchy. It is treason to 'encompass the death' of the sovereign—but the monarchy as an institution is freely attacked. Nevertheless, many is the slander action which has reached court because some 'bird of the air' has spread the nasty rumour.

Again, 'be not rash with thy mouth . . . let thy words be few . . . a dream cometh with a multitude of business; and a fool's voice with a multitude of words.' This is excellent advice for anyone interviewed by the police in connection with a possible prosecution. The majority of offenders are convicted out of their own mouths. The man who exercises his right to stay silent, most often escapes. And this applies to the honest man, as much as to the crook.

Not long ago, the author saw a man killed by a car. The driver—who was in no way at fault—told the police that the deceased had appeared from her nearside and walked across the front of her vehicle. Had she been right, she could have avoided striking him because he collided with her offside front wing. But (as several witnesses were able to testify at the inquest) she was wrong. He had come from the far side of the road and walked straight into her. She could not have avoided the collision. The greater the shock, the more important it is to keep silent until you have been able to gather your thoughts.

* In Scotland there may be defamation of a person even although you tell no one else because in Scotland the damages are recoverable for injured feelings.

'When thou vowest a vow unto God, defer not to pay it; for He hath no pleasure in fools; pay that which thou hast vowed. Better it is that thou shouldest not vow, than that thou shouldest vow and not pay.'

The author was not referring to promises made between man and man, but the same truth applies. Not that the law enforces every promise. There must be an 'intention to create legal relations'. A father once promised £100 to a man who intended marrying his daughter; the marriage took place—but the father refused to pay. The son-in-law sued. But he did not get his money; the words of the promise were simply 'general words spoken to excite suitors'.

'Mere social engagements,' we are told, 'are also not based upon the intention necessary to create a valid contract.' As one Judge put it: 'The ordinary example is where two parties agree to take a walk together, or where there is an offer and acceptance of hospitality. Nobody would suggest in ordinary circumstances that those agreements result in what we know as a contract.

But once there is an intention to create a contract, the law will usually enforce it. If one person changes his position to his detriment as a result of a promise made by another, it is rare that the other will not be held to his side of the bargain. If he had not wanted to 'pay' then he should not have made his 'vow'.

Of course, much of English law (particularly those parts of it which affect marital relations) have grown out of the laws of the Church. And there is no more fascinating pursuit for a lawyer than to delve into the laws of ancient people, to see the distant origins of those which concern him from day to day. And often, as he does so, he runs into facts and illustrations taken from a profession as ancient as his own—that of the apothecary and maker of ointments. Or, for that matter, the profession of the priest, the parson, the scribe, the rabbi, the man of the cloth.

Chapter 18

Professional 'Duties of Care'*

IF THE priest who attempts to save your soul bungles the job, you have no legal remedy against him. The heat he engenders for you is no fit subject for terrestrial courts of law. But what of the doctor who fails to cure your body . . . the psychiatrist who leaves your mind a wreck . . . the builder who wrecks your home . . . the dentist who dislocates your jaw . . . the hairdresser who turns your wife's head into an itching, orange mess? What standard of care does the law demand from those professionals who act for you in your business—the surveyor, solicitor, architect, engineer. . . .? Some of the answers, at least, appeared in the recent Privy Council decision in the sad case of *Madame Chin Keow* v. *The Government of Malaysia.*

The plaintiff's daughter worked in the Kuala Lumpur Social Hygiene Clinic. Amongst his other activities on behalf of the socially unhygienic, the doctor in charge gave some hundred injections a day. He jabbed happily away, never pausing to enquire whether the patient was allergic to the drugs injected—and without, it seems, any mishaps. Then, one grim morning, his nurse fell ill. The doctor decided that her ailment called for procaine penicillin. He unsheathed his trusty needle—and killed his patient. She was hyper-sensitive to penicillin. He did not know that she had previously suffered adverse reactions from the drug but her out-patient card was marked 'allergic to penicillin'. And everyone agreed that in such circumstances, the fatal injection should never have been given.

But was the doctor negligent? Should he have enquired into the history of the patient before administering the drug? Her mother, Madame Chin Keow, said Yes—and sued for damages. The trial judge upheld her claim. The Federal Court of Malaysia overruled him. And the case came before the Privy Council.

Was the doctor, then, in breach of his duty to his patient?

'Where you get a situation which involves the use of some special

* For more on Negligence, see Part 8.

skill or competence,' a Judge had said in a previous case, 'the test is the standard of the ordinary skilled man exercising and professing to have that special skill. A man need not possess the highest expert skill; it is well established law that it is sufficient if he exercises the ordinary skill of an ordinary competent man exercising that particular art.'

Applying that test to the case, the Privy Council found that 'the evidence was all one way'. It was plain that the doctor 'failed in his duty to make appropriate enquiry before causing the penicillin injection to be given'. The case was proved.

When you fall ill, your doctor does not promise to cure you. If he makes a faulty diagnosis or prescribes the wrong treatment this will not of itself give you any claim against him. To win your case you must show that the mistake was due to negligence—caused by his failure to exercise that degree of professional skill that you are entitled to expect of the ordinary, average doctor. We would all like our professional advisers to be men of genius. Some are. But the law only demands of any of them that they exercise reasonable competence.

Suppose you travel by taxi and there is an accident. An outstanding driver might have avoided the smash-up. But that does not mean that you have a good claim for damages against your cabbie. If he were the world's greatest driver, the odds are that he would not be working a ten hour, fume-filled, ulcerated day. As it is, all you are entitled to expect of him is as much care and competence as you would get from the average, sensible man on that job.

The business world is full of error. But not every mistake is negligent. It is possible and (alas) often probable that when the (imperfect) mind is applied to a problem it comes up with the wrong answer without any lack of due care on the part of its owner. So if you are let down by your architect, surveyor, draughtsman, expert adviser or (which heaven forbid) your solicitor, do not rush too readily for your writ. You will have to prove not just that the gentleman concerned was wrong but that the error of his ways was caused by lack of due competence . . . that he failed to exercise the ordinary skill to be expected of a practitioner of his art.

As usual, the converse also applies. If you or your company earn a living by working for others . . . take heart. To err while earning is both human and expected. Only if the cause of the mistake is a failure to live up to the ordinary standards of reasonable people doing the same job will those who suffer by the error be entitled to make their suffering your own. Otherwise, the law will forgive, even if they will not. Divinity and the law are sometimes akin.

That professional Homers frequently nod is of course, one reason why premiums on professional negligence policies are so expensive. And the misadventure in the VD clinic will produce side effects far beyond the realms of social hygiene and the Malaysian Federation. The tragic memory of the needled nurse lies embalmed in our Law Reports.

Chapter 19

Surgeons – and Explosive Gas

A PATIENT, tactfully known to the law reports only as 'Gabriel G——' suffered from haemorrhoids. He went to a doctor who advised treatment by internal cauterisation of the bleeding veins. In due course poor Gabriel arrived on the operating table. All of a sudden, it seems, there was a dreadful explosion. His natural intestinal gases came into contact with electrical apparatus used during the operation and—bang!

Now, this story may have its funny side for those of us who are not directly involved. But Gabriel was not amused. He enlisted the help of his lawyers, to see whether he could not obtain compensation. And who can blame him? As a result of his explosion, he endured a whole series of serious operations—and was rendered permanently incapacitated.

The question which the Court had to decide was whether or not precautions should have been taken by the surgeon concerned against the disastrous event complained of. On the one hand, experts marched through the witness box to say that when one sets great heat alongside gas, an explosion is the expected result. On the other side, experts—who, of course, were sufficiently expert to differ—maintained that natural gases are not normally explosive and that there was no reason to suppose that the patient would suffer in the way complained of, if the operation was carried out in the normal manner.

The Court found in favour of the doctor. The explosion, said Monsieur le Juge (for the trial occurred in Lyons) was 'fortuitous'. Therefore, the doctor was not responsible. And all the explosive hot air of all the lawyers in France could not change that legal decision.

There was a question of fact. Are natural gases in the body normally explosive? If the answer is affirmative, the doctor cannot win his case. If it is negative, he cannot lose it. And provided that there is evidence upon which the court can come to its decision, appeal is likely to be a waste of time. This is not law but fact. This is not opinion but scientific finding. Natural gases should not explode. But that will be cold comfort for the pauvre Gabriel G——.

Chapter 20

A Lawyer's Duties

ONE OF the men convicted in connection with the infamous Dulwich Art Gallery robbery had pleaded guilty. He later maintained that he did so against his wishes and, in effect, that 'he had been the subject of almost a plot "fixed" by his own and prosecution counsel and by the court'. The Court of Appeal decided that 'the proper course was to deal with the case as an appeal, in open court, in the full glare of publicity. There must be no suggestion that anybody was covering up for anybody else.' The man was given legal aid, with Queen's Counsel to represent him.

Evidence was then given before the Court of Appeal by the Counsel who had defended him, by the solicitor's managing clerk who had represented him, and by both prosecuting counsel who were against him. The prisoner himself testified that his counsel 'had used threatening language, intimidating him, and told him that he would certainly, if he pleaded not guilty, be found guilty on the more serious charge . . .' and would have got a higher sentence. The 'deal' whereby he had pleaded guilty to a less serious charge was not, he said, to his benefit. He was 'told categorically that if he pleaded not guilty, he would be found guilty of the more serious charge'. He had, in effect, been bludgeoned into admitting guilt.

The court 'unhesitatingly accepted' the evidence of the prisoner's counsel, in preference to that of the prisoner—which was not altogether surprising, as the barrister in question was a highly respected and (of course) had a blameless past—whereas the same could not be said for the prisoner who was 'not inexperienced in criminal proceedings'. 'What the court was looking to see,' said the Lord Chief Justice, 'was whether the prisoner had a free choice. The election must be his; the responsibility his; his to plead Guilty or Not Guilty.

'At the same time, it is the clear duty of any counsel representing a client to assist the client to make up his mind by putting forward the pros and cons, if need be strongly and to impress on the client what would be the likely results of certain courses of conduct.'

The prisoner's counsel had done his duty 'in strong language', and perfectly properly. The appeal was dismissed.

Now consider the moral. If you go to lawyers, you are entitled to expect to be advised. There is every reason why you should be helped to make up your mind. 'The pros and cons' may be impressed upon you. Provided that the decision you take is your own, your lawyers have done their job.

Suppose, now, that a doctor is faced with a similar situation in his consulting room. Does he advise his patient to submit to an operation? What treatment should he receive? The advice is the doctor's but, in general, it is up to the patient to decide whether or not he takes it. Naturally, if the doctor's advice is ignored, there is nothing to prevent him from saying: 'I'm afraid that I cannot accept responsibility for what will happen if you do not follow my guidance.' Exactly the same principles apply to a man of law.

But there are limits. From the lawyer's viewpoint, he must never put words into his client's mouth.

A well known counsel tells of the crook he represented at the Old Bailey, on legal aid—his services cost his client nothing. 'So what do I say if they ask me that question?' queried the client. 'I can't tell you that, my man,' answered counsel. 'You must tell the truth.'

'Why can't you tell me?' retorted the client. 'What am I *not* paying you for?'

But there is one misery that lawyers are normally saved. The doctor knows just how dangerous his patient's illness may be. The client is blissfully unaware of the truth. To tell, or not to tell, that is the doctor's dilemma.

It is rare that the wise lawyer hides the seriousness of the position from his client, whether the cause is civil or criminal. Place the facts before the client . . . by all means 'set forth the dangers' . . . but let him make up his own mind. Subject to the proprieties of professional etiquette, the job of a barrister is to give counsel, not orders.

Chapter 21

Fair Comment*

WHEN PROFESSIONAL men start slinging mud at each other, their clients and patients look on with mingled delight and apprehension. There is a certain feeling that the Gods ought not to descend into the arena. But the law recognises that controversy and argument are not only healthy but essential in a free society. The laws of defamation are only designed to prevent the bath from getting too bloody. But the question in any particular case will often be: Have the attackers overstepped the mark?

Whenever you speak ill of another, you defame him . . . you 'make a statement which tends to lower him in the eyes of right thinking people' . . . you hold him up to hatred, ridicule or contempt. But amongst the defences which the law provides to the defamer is that of 'fair comment'—which is absolutely essential for the freedom of the press—whether expressing its own views or reporting those of others. 'To whatever lengths the ordinary citizen may go, so also may the journalist . . . his privilege is no other and no higher. . . . The range of his assertions, his criticisms or his comments, is as wide as, and no wider than, that of every other subject. . . .' The profess-ional man's privilege to speak his mind is no different from that of the writer.

It is a defence to an action for defamation 'that the words com-plained of are fair comment on a matter of public interest'. But what precisely does this mean?

First, the allegation must be recognisable as comment, not fact.

* See also Chapter 47, for the law on defamation.

The speaker or writer is expressing his opinion, not putting forward what he alleges to be a fact. State facts and if they are true, you have the defence of 'justification' available to you. Comment upon them and your defence is different.

Nor is the defence intended to cover 'mis-statements of fact'. If the words complained of include allegations of fact, the defendant must show that the facts are correct—it is not enough to say that you honestly believed them to be true.

What, then, of the comment itself? In order to be 'fair', 'it must not contain imputations of corrupt or dishonourable motives on the person whose conduct or word is criticised, save insofar as such imputations are warranted by the facts'. And it must be the honest expression of the writer's or speaker's real opinion.

Your honesty, in expressing your opinion is highly important. 'Both in cases in which the defence of privilege and in those in which the defence of fair comment is set up,' said a judge, 'the state of mind of the defendant when he published the alleged libel is a matter directly in issue.' It follows that the defence will fail if the jury are satisfied 'that the libel is malicious . . . that the defendant was actuated by a malicious motive . . . that is to say, by some motive other than that of a pure expression of a critic's real opinion.'

Take the man who has a grudge against a fellow professional. He lashes out at the other man's work, hoping thereby to destroy the man, rather than the method. He will not be allowed to succeed in the defence of fair comment because he was actuated by malice . . . he was not simply expressing his honest opinion . . . he was venting his ill-will on his colleague, under the cloak of an attack on the man's working methods.

A judge summed up the scope of 'fair comment' like this: 'Every latitude must be given to opinion and to prejudice, and then an ordinary set of men with ordinary judgment must say whether any fair man would have made such a comment. . . . Mere exaggeration, or even gross exaggeration, would not make the comment unfair. However wrong the opinion expressed may be in point of truth, or however prejudiced the writer, it may still be within the prescribed limit. . . . The jury must consider—would any fair man, however prejudiced he may be, however exaggerated or obstinate his views, have said that which this criticism has said?'

People are entitled to 'entertain very, very strong opinions, and if they use strong language, every allowance should be made in their favour'. Provided they 'believe what they say, then if they are within anything like reasonable bounds, they come within the meaning of fair comment'.

Here, then, is the law's shield for the satirist . . . the protection provided for the politician (amateur or professional), speaking his mind outside Parliament . . . the writer who feels bound to speak out. . . . Only if the words stated are alleged fact and not comment . . . or the statement is made maliciously . . . are the vultures of the law likely to swoop down and pick at the remains of the reputation of the person making the defamatory statement.

Chapter 22

Protecting Reputations

THE *British Medical Journal* published a scientific paper which was critical of a technique for dental anaesthesia introduced, recommended and used by a named dental surgeon. He maintained that the article was 'unjustifiably critical of the way he carried on his practice' and that his professional reputation was 'thereby damaged'. He sued for damages for libel.

The British Medical Association attempted to have the action dismissed long before it was due to reach trial. It attempted to strike out the Statement of Claim on the basis that 'the words complained of were not reasonably capable of being understood as defamatory of the plaintiff personally'. The application reached the Court of Appeal whose majority decision will be of great importance in the world of libel—and of considerable interest to every professional man.

The first judgment was given by the Master of the Rolls, Lord Denning. He held that 'the scientific paper in question was no libel. A group of scientists had done a valuable piece of research. It is surely in the public interest, said the Judge, that they should make known their findings to the profession and that the scientific journal should be entitled to publish them without the fear of a libel action.

'It might be that in criticising the plaintiff's technique,' said the Judge, 'they cast reflection on him. That could not be helped. The scientists had no way descended to an attack on the plaintiff personally.'

So Lord Denning held that 'the defendants had not gone beyond the bounds of lawful criticism, but only exercised the right to such criticism. It would be a sorry day,' he added, 'if scientists were to be deterred from publishing their findings for fear of libel actions. So long as they refrained from personal attacks, they should be free to criticise the systems and techniques of others. It is in the interest of truth itself. Were it otherwise, no scientific journal would be safe.' Lord Denning was in favour of striking out the action.

Lord Pearson came next. He pointed out first that 'the power to strike out a Statement of Claim should be used in plain and obvious cases'. The parties to litigation are entitled to have their cases heard by a court, unless it is 'plain and obvious' that they cannot succeed—in which case, the party who obviously cannot lose should not be forced into the worry, aggravation and expense of litigation. But could it be said that the dentist's 'alleged cause of action had no chance of success?'. Were the words capable of bearing any meaning defamatory of the plaintiff?

The plaintiff, said Lord Pearson, 'was likely to have no great difficulty in satisfying the jury, or the Judge acting as a jury, that his name, practice and reputation had been and were closely associated with the technique in question. It would be open for twelve reasonably minded jurymen to conclude that the severe attack which the article made on the technique involved an attack on the plaintiff's reputation as a dentist.'

Lord Pearson carefully expressed no opinion on whether or not the attack was justifiable, or whether or not it was fair comment on a matter of public interest. The sole question at that stage was whether 'it was capable of bearing a meaning defamatory of the plaintiff'. The Judge made a distinction between a trader's goods and a professional man's technique; the former are impersonal and transient; the latter is 'at least relatively permanent, and it belongs to him (that is, to the professional man himself)'.

Words might be defamatory of a business or professional man even though they do not 'impute any moral fault or defect of personal character'. But it could be suggested, said the Judge, that the article 'impliedly imputed to the plaintiff lack of judgment and efficiency in that he had adopted, practised and recommended a method of anaesthetising patients which (as the article said) was dangerous to the patients and might impede good dentistry. That suggestion is really to be considered by the jury (or judge) and should not be withdrawn from them.' So Lord Pearson would not agree to the striking out—and the decision lay with Sir Gordon Willmer, who held the balance.

Sir Gordon said that he did not accept that there was any danger that to hold the words capable of bearing a defamatory meaning would be detrimental to the advancement of scientific knowledge because no scientific journal would in future feel safe in publishing an article critical of the views of an opposing school of thought. It is 'perfectly possible,' he went on, 'for scientists to criticise each other's views and theories without saying anything capable of being construed as defamatory, even though they might be, in Gilbert's words, "Maintaining with no little heat their various opinions".'

The Judge held that the essential feature of the present case was that the plaintiff, a practising dental surgeon, felt that the article was unjustifiably critical of the way he carried on his practice and that his professional reputation had been damaged. His case should not be struck out.

I do not know whether or not the dentist succeeded in his action—nor whether it was compromised. But leave to appeal to the House of Lords was refused to the BMA. And what matters from the legal point of view is that by a majority of two to one, the Court of Appeal has held that the scientific paper concerned which was critical of the technique 'introduced, used and recommended' by the named dental surgeon could be defamatory of him and therefore could give rise to a good claim for damages.

It follows that if you see fit to criticise the techniques or methods of other professional men, you must exercise very great care. You may be lowering the colleague 'in the eyes of right thinking people'. Whether or not you actually do so will depend upon the words used, the circumstances and nature of their use and all the facts of the particular case. But the colleague who feels that his professional reputation has been adversely affected by your statement will, it seems, at least be allowed to place his allegations before a judge and jury. He will not be 'driven forth from the seat of justice' without at least having had the opportunity to stake a legal claim to damages.

As usual, of course, there are two angles to this legal problem. On the one hand, if you wish to criticise or to attack the views, methods or techniques of others, you must recognise the risks. It may be arguable that you are attacking the man's reputation and that he may defend himself in a court of law. Conversely, if you find that you are attacked in a similar way, then you may welcome opportunity to call upon the law to remedy your wrongs.

Chapter 23

Miseries of the Misfit

CERTAINTY IN life and in law provides a rare blessing. Patients and cases alike fit ill into categories. And it is the misfits who get the most misery from both law and medicine.

Sensational examples abound. Consider the sad saga of the man who became enough of a woman lawfully to marry—but whose marriage was annulled on the ground that she (the wife) was a biological male. This decision by a Judge who is himself qualified in medicine showed that neither lawyers nor doctors have any real answers. We can try to fit people into cosy compartments—but neither the most compassionate of Judges nor the most patient of doctors can bring true certainty to those who live on the borders between male and female.

Then what (as the Israeli courts asked) is a Jew? The Rabbis reply without hesitation—the child of a Jewish mother, who does not possess some other religion. But biologically . . . legally . . . scientifically . . . there is no easy answer. Just for once, religion provides more certainty than science.

As for the doctor, there are diseases which are easily recognised. Some are contractable, others impervious to therapy. Some patients are terrified because they know the nature of their illness. But compared to the frightening and unknown, the really terrible afflictions of mankind are mercifully rare. The man with an unknown pain in his chest may, heaven forbid, be suffering from cancer or heart disease. But with any reasonable good fortune, his symptoms indicate nothing worse than infection, indigestion or some psychosomatic malady. Similarly, for the lady with a lump in her breast, it is those terrible days before the results of the biopsy come through that create havoc with life. 'If only I knew. . . .'

Or take the surveyor who looks over your proposed new premises. He notices a crack in a wall or a blockage in a drain. He may be able to say at once: 'We know the origin of this. . . .' Equally, it may take testing or involve surmise, if the appropriate label is to be placed on the architectural ailment.

Or suppose that you go to your accountant. You wish to claim certain expenses. Some he will quickly categorise as deductible or non-deductible as the case may be. Others he will say: 'Well, you never know. . . . The Revenue may wear it. . . . We'll put it in and hope for the best. . . .'

You want to go to a trade fair, industrial exhibition or professional conference overseas ? You could not afford the journey, if the cost must come from your taxed income ? 'Would the expenses be allowable ?' you ask your accountant. 'I hope so,' he replies. 'But I can't guarantee it.'

Everything depends on all the details . . . on whether the particular Inspector who peruses the account regards the expenses as 'wholly and necessarily incurred for the purposes of your profession' (see Chapter 6). If you do not like his decision, then you can appeal to the Commissioners of Inland Revenue—at no cost other than the expenses of your professional advisers. If you win there, the Inspector may appeal to the High Court—and if he wins there, you will have to bear the costs of your journey out of your taxed income—and probably the costs of the appeal as well. Were those costs incurred 'for the purposes of your profession ?' Once again, we enter the realms of doubt.

So the patient or client who knows where he stands is usually fortunate. It is recognised by doctors, surveyors, accountants and the rest, when it comes to the affairs of their own patients or clients. Then why do they expect certainty from their lawyers ?

'If we fight, will we win ? How much will the case cost me if I lose ?* When will we get to trial ?' asks the client. 'Everything depends on how the case develops . . . on the view taken by the court . . . on whether the lists are full . . . on the attitude and actions of the other side . . .' says the unhappy solicitor, 'iffing and butting' with great vigour. The client groans, 'There he goes again,' he thinks to himself. 'These lawyers are always prevaricating. . . .' Not at all like those dogmatic, accurate, reasonable, sensible doctors, surveyors, accountants, architects, engineers and the rest. . . .

* More on cases and costs in Chapter 111.

" NO, NO, MR JONES . . . YOU HAVE FORGOTTEN . . . . A DIRECTOR
HAS _NO_ RIGHT TO REPRESENT HIS COMPANY IN COURT————! "

Part three

Companies and Directors

Chapter 24

The Director's Personal Liabilities

A COMPANY has no human existence. Its operations are directed by its Board, controlled by its executives and managers and carried on by its staff and agents. The benefits of limited liability flow directly from the separation of private and corporate existence. But equally, the company as such may commit 'torts'—or civil wrongs. And those who administer the business may sometimes be held personally responsible.

An employer is 'vicariously liable' for the sins of his servant. If a director is negligent in the course of his duties and a third party suffers damage, the company can be made to pay. But when can the director be held personally liable? The higher your level in the company, the greater the mistakes you are liable to make—and the more important it becomes to know the legal answers to this major problem.

*   *   *

A Mr Feldman and a Mr Partridge were sued for damages resulting from an explosion caused by negligence, on land on which a company formed by them was manufacturing explosives. 'If the company was really trading independently on its own account,' said Lord Buckmaster, when the case reached the House of Lords, 'the fact that it was directed by Messrs Feldman and Partridge would not render these directors responsible for the company's tortious acts, unless indeed these acts were expressly directed by them.'

Then Lord Atkin: 'Prima facie, a managing director is not liable for tortious acts done by servants of the company unless he himself is privy to the acts—that is to say, unless he ordered or procured the acts to be done. . . . If the directors themselves directed or procured the commission of the act, they would be liable in whatever sense they did so, whether expressly or impliedly.'

So if a wrongful act is committed by one of the company's

employees, you (as director, manager or executive) will only bear personal responsibility if you 'ordered or procured' the commission of the wrongful act. If you were privy to it—if, in any sense, you expressly or impliedly authorised its commission—then you can be held personally liable.

A director, on behalf of his company, employed a band which which performed a musical work in breach of copyright. The director knew absolutely nothing about their doing so. He was held in no way responsible for the wrong that was committed and could not personally be held to account for it.

Then there was the director who joined in an authority to brokers to obtain subscriptions. There were mis-statements of fact in a prospectus issued by those brokers. The director was held not liable in an action for deceit. He did not authorise or know of the mis-statements. A director is only liable in respect of false representations in a prospectus, even if this is issued by his co-director or some other agent of the company, if he expressly authorised or tacitly consented to its issue.

What, then, if one director commits a wrongful act with the knowledge of another? Both directors will be responsible. Judgment may be obtained against either of them, but each may seek a contribution or even an indemnity from his fellow. The chances are that each could be made to shoulder 50 per cent of the liability.

So, in so far as the 'torts' of company's servants are concerned, provided that you are never privy to any irregularity, even if wrongful acts are done in the name of your company, you yourself will not be held liable for them. Conversely, if you clap your corporate telescope to your blind eye . . . if you deliberately avoid seeing the wrongs committed by others in the company's name . . . if you direct the commission of a tort (expressly or by implication) . . . then and only then can you be brought personally to book by those who suffer. Otherwise, they must look to the company.

Of course, if you yourself commit the wrongful act in the course of your employment, the situation is quite different. Then you may well get an indemnity from your company, but you will remain personally responsible.

In practice, the company's rights against its executives and employees are seldom exercised. The insurers pay up. The policy covers both corporate master and individual man, so no useful purpose is served by clutching at the private bank account. But make no mistake about it—the individual director is just as responsible for his own misdeeds as any other person by whom the company lives and earns its living.

Chapter 25

A Director's 'Fiduciary Relationship'

AN ARCHITECT was managing director of a company which carried out construction services for large concerns, both private and public. His duties included the procuring of new business, especially in relation to the gas industry. He looked after the interests of industrial development consultants when negotiating with the Eastern Gas Board, who wanted to build four depots. Unfortunately for the company, the negotiations proved abortive.

Not long afterwards, the architect (says the Law Report) obtained his release from his employment by Industrial Development Consultants 'by representing dishonestly that he was in bad health'. It later transpired that he had been approached 'in his private capacity' by the Deputy Chairman of the Gas Board. He then obtained for himself the contract which his former employers had been after. This, we are told, resulted from work which he had done, unknown to them, while he was still their managing director.

The ex-employers sued the architect, claiming that he should account to them for all benefits which he had received under the contract, including all remuneration and fees. And even though it appears that the plaintiffs would not have got the contract in any event or at any time, they won their case.

Where an agent acts for a principal—or a director for his company or a partner for his firm—there exists a so-called 'fiduciary relationship'. There is a duty to exercise the utmost good faith.

If you sit on the opposite side of a bargaining table, you must not tell lies. You are not entitled to defraud the other contracting party. But you are not under any duty to disclose to him the profits which you may make from the deal, either personally or for your principal.

However, as between your company or firm or employer and yourself, you must (as one judge put it) 'disgorge your profits'. You must not make a 'secret profit' from the exercise of your duties.

Further, every principal is entitled to an account from his employee or other agent. Whether it is your partner, your manager, your fellow director or your foreman or secretary, he must account to you for any financial advantage which he obtains, as a result of his employment with you.

Note; This duty does not cease along with the employment. The director had left his company before he made a penny out of the Gas Board. But the judge still ordered an account.

Note, too, even though the company itself would not have made anything out of the deal, the director was not entitled to benefit from the arrangement that he later made on his own account. A man who works for you is not entitled to turn that work to his profit, merely because he cannot turn it to yours. He is not entitled to say to a prospective client or customer: 'Very well—you will not do the deal with the company—so why not do it with me personally?'

The same principle applies to a trustee, who must not make any profit out of his relationship with the beneficiaries. Unless there is some express provision to the contrary it is 'an inflexible rule' of court that a person in a fiduciary position may not make a profit out of his duties. Nor is he allowed 'to put himself in a position where his interest and his duty conflict'.

You are entitled to insist that your employees, your partners or the directors of your company give faithful service. Because of their 'fiduciary relationship', they are trustees for you (or for your firm or company as the case may be) of any money or goods, profits or benefits, which they receive as a result of that relationship. A court will force them, if necessary, to give an account of such money or benefits. And if the account shows any secret profit . . . any benefit received as a result of work done as an agent but unknown to his principal . . . then an order will be made, requiring payment.

Conversely, you (like the unfortunate architect) stand in a 'fiduciary relationship' towards your principals. So it is as well to appreciate the grim strictness of these legal rules.

Chapter 26

A Director's Title

THE TITLE 'director' is an artificial creation. It leads to complications. On the one hand, a person who is not called a director, and, indeed, who does not even sit at the Board, may bear responsibilities in law which are identical with those carried by an executive who has the name 'director' conferred upon him. On the other hand, people may be called 'directors' who are not on the Board and may involve the company in exactly the same liabilities and responsibilities as if they were actually mighty Board members.

The Companies Act, 1948, defines director as including 'any person occupying the position of director by whatever name called'. The affairs of the company may be conducted by 'trustees', 'members of the council' or 'governors'. A director, by any other name, will still come within the definition.

Once appointed (by the Articles or some alternative method provided by them or by the shareholders in General Meeting), the directors assume grave responsibilities. They must carry out their duties fairly and responsibly and in the best interests of the company. Their names must appear, in most cases, on stationery, trade catalogues, circulars and the like—and so must their nationalities, if they are not British. Their positions must be registered, so that anyone who makes the appropriate company search will know who is at the helm. They are directors in fact, even if they only take a nominal part in the running of the business.

Note that a director will be an officer but an officer will not necessarily be a director. 'Officer', says the Act, includes 'a director, manager or secretary'. And the liabilities of each (as we shall see) may differ.

What matters, though, is that 'the law looks at the reality and not at the form'. A court would be concerned with the function of the officer and not with the name which the company has seen fit to bestow upon him. You cannot appoint a man to your Board and by calling him something other than a director remove his responsibilities and duties. Conversely, the mere fact that you deny a seat on your Board to someone who in fact manages or directs the activities of your company will not mean that he can avoid playing the commercial game, in accordance with the rules laid down by statute.

Now suppose that you call an official, 'marketing director', 'merchandising director', 'director of personnel' or some other grandiose title which suggests that he is on the Board, but you do not in fact admit him to your inner cabinet.

Anyone who is sufficiently curious can make a company search and discover that the employee is not a Board member. But only if disaster strikes is anyone likely to take that sort of trouble. In fact, the 'director' will deal with third parties (including both employees of the company and outsiders) on the basis of the title given. And they will be entitled to accept the man's position at its face value.

It follows that a company is not entitled to squirm out of its responsibilities by saying: 'The man who made the arrangements or entered into the purported contract on our behalf was not a member of the Board. And the Board have declined to approve or to ratify his action.' Even if the man had in fact no actual authority, the company 'clothed him with its ostensible authority'. It saw fit to give the man its apparent authority to act on its behalf in the capacity of director and anyone with whom he deals in that capacity may take the company's action at its face value.

If you wish to dignify an employee with the title of director, the fact that you do not put him on your Board will restrict his powers, authority and status within the company itself, but it will not prevent him from exercising the power which third parties are entitled to presume that he has by virtue of his title.

So if you dub a man director, you must take the consequences. The company will normally be bound by his contracts whether or not he is on the Board. If he is negligent, the company will be liable to pay for his carelessness. And, of course, looking on the profitable side, the company will also be entitled to benefit from his good work. For better or for worse, the man who directs, normally assumes the burdens and responsibilities of a director. And the man called 'director' is given responsibilities and status which the company must honour.

Chapter 27

Must You Supervise Your Colleague?

'IT IS not the duty of each director to supervise the running of a company,' said the Lord Chief Justice in the recent case of *Huckerby* v. *Elliot*. He is not even bound 'to exercise some degree of control over what is going on'. Nor is he bound to supervise his co-director, whom he has no reason to mistrust. With those wise words, the learned Judge lifted at least part of the burden that rests upon the bowed shoulders of the director of the industrial concern.

The Windmill Clubs Limited ran a gaming club in Leeds called the New Embassy. Chemin-de-fer was played by the guests. The company did not hold the appropriate licence.

Now, *The Customs and Excise Act, 1952*, provides that where a company does not hold the correct gaming licence and the offence is 'proved to be attributable to any neglect by a director', then the director as well as the company 'shall be deemed guilty of the offence'. Mrs Mavis Huckerby, one of the directors of the Windmill Clubs, was charged with an offence and convicted by the Leeds Stipendiary Magistrate. She appealed. The case came before a Divisional Court of three Judges of the Queen's Bench Division, presided over by the Lord Chief Justice, Lord Parker.

The Judge first set out the facts. Then he said this: 'At the trial, no evidence was offered other than agreed statements of fact . . . which disclosed that although the appellant was a director of the company, she knew little about the conduct of the club. This she left to her co-director and to the manager.'

We pause to wonder how many wives are nominally on the Boards of industrial concerns—and who think that a Board is a utensil, used in the kitchen. Wives, of course, are made directors so as to provide their husbands with votes, and also with fees and with tax advantage. Whether or not Mrs Huckerby came within that category, we do not know. All that is certain is that she took no active part in the running of the club. Her co-director and the manager were in charge.

When the case had come before the Stipendiary, said Lord Parker, he had held 'that it was for a director of the company to exercise some degree of control over what was going on'. These words were 'too wide. It is not the duty of each director to exercise some degree of control over what is going on, nor is it right to say that there is a duty on a director to supervise the running of the company and, in particular, to supervise a co-director who is secretary.'

I repeat that magic formula because it may work wonders if ever you (or your wife) get prosecuted for the sins of others on the Board. The fact that your name is on the notepaper or even that you attend Board meetings will not of itself make you responsible for exercising control over the running of the company—or, to be more precise, over the way in which others run it.

Or suppose that you decide that you want to get a distinguished name on to your Board. You approach a man, well known in the City? You tackle a titled gentleman, whose breeding and lineage exceed his knowledge of industrial affairs? He is unwilling to join you because he is afraid that he may be responsible if you go off the rails? Then read him the words of the Lord Chief Justice.

Anyway, Lord Parker continued as follows: 'I know of no authority which says that it is a director's duty to supervise a co-director or to acquaint himself with all the details of running the company. The prosecution evidence disclosed that the appellant was leaving matters such as licences to a co-director and to a secretary who was fully acquainted with the business.' So the prosecution had not proved their case and the appeal was allowed.

Mr Justice Ashworth said: 'I cannot accept that there is a duty on a director to see that the law is observed.' The Section concerned does not create 'an absolute offence.'

There are some offences which you commit even if you did nothing negligent or improper. If, for example, you fail to give preference to a pedestrian on a zebra crossing, you break the law. Even if the pedestrian ran out under your wheels, giving you no opportunity to stop, you have still offended, because the offence is 'absolute'. Of course, the fact that you could not avoid an accident, and that the pedestrian was in fact at fault, will provide your solicitor or counsel with marvellous material for a plea in mitigation. But it is no answer to the charge.

What matters to directors, though, is that unless an offence is absolute, we now know that one director cannot be made criminally liable merely because his colleague failed to carry out his obligations. We now have a loophole through which directors may leap, if charged with offences (for instance) under the Trade Descriptions Act, The Health and Safety at Work etc. Act, or the Factories' Act. If you are charged and are a director in name alone—or a boardroom director, with no control over the day-to-day running of the factory or works—then do not plead guilty. Thrust the case of *Huckerby* v. *Elliot* before the eyes of your solicitor. And then let him fight for your good name. With fortune (and the facts) on his side, he should win.

Anyway, prosecuting authorities learn their lessons. So we can now hope that inactive or boardroom directors will avoid prosecutions for company offences which were in no way caused by their neglect. And it is not 'neglect' (we now know) to leave the job of complying with statutory obligations to those whose business it is to do so.

So the Court has placed a benevolent limit on the ancient rule that each director is his brother's keeper. The case of *Huckerby* v. *Elliott* should bring joy to many an anxious boardroom.

Chapter 28

Take-overs, Mergers – and Self-protection

WHEN TAKE-OVER time arrives, heads may roll—for executives as much as the men on the shop floor. But a director is in a better position to see the blow coming and to try to feather his nest in anticipation of possible redundancy. How far can he go before personal interest conflicts with company responsibilities?

*   *   *

A company, of course, is a separate legal entity. So even if a director owns a substantial proportion of the shares, his first duty is to act in its best interest.

To prepare a new and long term service contract for himself shortly before a take-over—so as to ensure a handsome golden handshake if and when the take-over materialises—is not an act likely to benefit the company. On the contrary; the company will not have to pay, and there is rarely any good reason why it should do so.

Conversely, the director is fully entitled to make appropriate arrangements with the acquiring concern for his own protection. He can join its board or enter into a contract of service. He can do a deal with that company, whereby he is to be paid compensation when the take-over occurs—as long as the payment comes from the coffers of the acquiring concern and not from those of the company which is to be swallowed. But if there is any such arrangement, it must be revealed to the shareholders, as it is one of the factors to be borne in mind when deciding whether or not to vote in favour of the take-over.

An extremely useful guide to conduct during take-overs and mergers is contained in 'The City Code' prepared by the Issuing Houses Association in co-operation with the Accepting Houses Committee and various other bodies. This code, written at the suggestion of the Governor of the Bank of England, was revised in 1974 and although it relates primarily to companies whose shares are publicly held, it is also relevant to transactions in respect of private companies.

'The boards of an offeror company and of an offeree company,' the rule book says, 'have a primary duty to act in the best interests of their respective shareholders. . . .' A basic principle of law.

When approached with an offer, or with a view to an offer being made, the board must consider 'whether in the interest of its share-holders' competent outside advice should be sought. Above all, 'directors of an offeror or an offeree company shall always, in advising their shareholders, act only in their capacity as directors and not have regard to their personal or family shareholdings or their personal relationship with the companies. It is the shareholders' interests taken as a whole which should be considered, together with those of employees and creditors.'

To ask a man to put on one side 'personal or family shareholding' or 'personal relationship with the companies' is feasible for the director who is wealthy, but for the individual whose daily bread depends either upon his position on the board or his shareholding, it is often an impossibility.

There may be good reasons for a board preferring a lower offer or rejecting an attractive offer. Nevertheless, where acceptance of the lower of two offers is recommended or a controlling board accepts such a lower offer or rejects a more attractive one—frequently forcing the minority shareholders to act similarly—it must be prepared to justify its good faith.

'Good faith' are the operative words. A director has a 'fiduciary duty' in law towards the company to exercise his powers honestly and in the interests of the company and the shareholders.* In practice, of course, conflict often arises when there is a take-over. It is because directors owe a fiduciary duty that they are not permitted to make a secret profit out of their position.

'Directors whose shareholdings, together with those of their families and those held on trust effectively control the company, or shareholders in that condition who are represented on the Board of a company, who contemplate transferring control,' says Rule 10, 'should not, other than in very exceptional circumstances, do so unless the buyer undertakes to extend a comparable offer to the remaining shareholders.'

In such very exceptional circumstances the panel on take-overs and mergers set up at the request of the Bank of England should be consulted in advance.

A take-over bid is made for a company where the directors have only six months to go before expiry of their contracts of service. They know perfectly well that if the company remains independent, with themselves in control, new contracts on improved terms will be made. But if the small company is to be embraced in the grasp of a larger outfit, their services may not be required. Alternatively, they may be retained on sufferance, for a limited period, to ensure a smooth change over. Or maybe they will not want to remain as subordinates. Naturally, the first reaction is to move the clock forward—very fast—and enter into new contracts with the company.

'The take-over is still far away and may never transpire. . . . If the company remains independent, as seems likely, it will need our services and if we are not to be enticed away by other concerns, the company must be competitive in the remuneration and conditions and security it provides. . . . We would have made these arrangements, even had there been no question of take-over. . . . It would have been stupid for us to wait until the last minute.'

Some or all of these excuses may be justified. But the odds are that

* See also Chapter 25, for later case on 'fiduciary duty'.

they are nothing more than a mask for what is, in strict theory, an improper practice to ensure that if there is a take-over or merger the golden handshake will be a firm one.

What protection does a director have? Section 184 of the *Companies Act, 1948*, states: 'A company may by ordinary resolution remove a director before the expiration of his period of office notwithstanding anything in its Articles or in any agreement between it and him.'

With certain exceptions such as life directors of private companies —a simple majority is enough to shift a director, provided only that special notice is given of the resolution to remove him, giving the man concerned the opportunity to reply.

If removed before his period of office expires, the director has the same rights as any other servant or agent of the company, when it comes to claiming damages for wrongful dismissal.

In general, this means compensation for loss of office by a tax free golden handshake. The longer the period of office which he loses, the higher the pay which he would have received and the more the company will have to contribute. It will be his company and not the acquiring company which will do the paying.

Section 193 of the Act applies 'where, in connection with the transfer to any persons of all or any of the shares in a company, there is to be a transfer resulting from an offer made:

(*a*) To the general body of shareholders;
(*b*) By or on behalf of some other body corporate with a view to the company becoming its subsidiary or a subsidiary of its holding company;
(*c*) By or on behalf of an individual with a view to his obtaining the right to exercise or control the exercise of not less than one third of the voting power at any general meeting of the company;
or (*d*) Conditional on acceptance to a given extent.'

In any such case:

'If a payment is to be made to a director of the company by way of compensation for loss of office, or as consideration for, or in connection with, his retirement from office, it shall be the duty of that director to take all reasonable steps to ensure that the particulars shall be included in or sent with any notice of

the offer made for their shares which is given to any shareholders.'

Section 193 continues by saying that 'if any such director fails to
take reasonable steps as aforesaid . . . or any person who has been
properly required by any such director to include the said particulars
in or send them with any such notice as aforesaid fails so to do . . .'
he may be fined up to £20.

Worse, if he does not comply with his duties of disclosure, any
sum received by him will be held in trust for any persons who have
sold their shares as a result of the offer made. Indeed, the expenses
incurred in distributing that sum amongst those persons shall be
borne by him and not be deducted from the sum.

Still, practice tends to be far removed from theory. There appears
to be no trace of any case where Section 193 has been put into effect.
But there are two recent reports which throw light on these vital
rules.

In *Lindgren and Others* v. *L. & P. Estates Limited*, the question of
the fiduciary duty of a director was considered by the Court of
Appeal.

'A trustee cannot in general deal with himself or obtain an advantage himself in a transaction in which he is on both sides of the
table,' said Lord Justice Harman, pointing out that a director must,
'consider the interests of the company' before taking a decision.

Lord Justice Winn held that on the particular facts, there had been
no 'breach of an equitable duty' by the director to the company. The
director had, 'independently considered the commercial merits' of
the agreement in question. That is all that the law requires—that,
and proper disclosure.

Finally, the judgment of Mr Justice Ungoed Thomas in *Selangor
United Rubber Estates Limited* v. *Cradock*—a case which was argued
before him for over four months.

The Judge considered the alleged misapplication of the plaintiff
company's monies by a director, 'in bad faith and in breach of his
duty as director and in furtherance of an arrangement' with another
defendant. The complications which can arise from such arrangements emerge as the most frightening moral of this massive, legal
tale.

If your company is to be taken over, mind what you do for your
own protection—and preferably do it on the advice of your lawyers,

as well as your accountants. Ignore the rules and you may get away with it. At worst, you may find yourself in the midst of a High Court legal battle.

Chapter 29

Battles in the Boardroom

A LARGE industrial concern recently sacked its managing director. Sensibly, he consulted his solicitor. 'We quarrelled over policy,' he said. 'I want to expand . . . to modernise . . . to build for the future. . . The rest prefer to sit back on their uninspired haunches. "Consolidation", they called it. "Stagnation" was my word. Anyway, they conspired to sack me. I want to sue for conspiracy.'

Now, it is a civil offence ('tort') to conspire to defraud. Damages may be obtained against those who put their heads together in an attempt to rob you or your business of its money. But if an act is lawful, it does not become improper because several people combine to do it.

Suppose, for instance, that Mr X decides that the head of his department (a Mr Y) should be elbowed out of the way. Mr X hints to the chairman that Mr Y is inefficient. He lets it be known that he (Mr X) would do the job much better. And he says quite openly that some of the recent disasters have been caused through Mr Y's dereliction of duty, advancing senility or galloping incompetence. The chairman sacks Mr Y.

Now, if Mr Y gets his proper notice or pay in lieu, he will probably have no lawful complaint except a possible claim for compensation for unfair dismissal (see Chapter 52)—even if he happens to be on the Board. However immoral the behaviour of Mr X and however ungrateful the sacking by the chairman, Mr Y has got his desserts—the money to which he was lawfully entitled under his contract of service. He would therefore recover no further damages either against the company or (still less) its chairman or against Mr X.

Now suppose that Mr X was not alone in sharpening the knife which he was to drive into Mr Y's back. He was ably assisted by Mr Z and Mr A, who both felt that the elbowing out of Mr Y would make room for their advancement. The three men conspired against the fourth. But there was no question of fraud. Mr Y would get no damages. 'The Dirty Tricks Act is not yet on the statute books,' a Judge proclaimed a short time ago.

He could then sue the company for damages for wrongful dismissal. And if he happened also to be a shareholder and could show that Messrs X, Z and A (and possibly the chairman) had put their crafty heads together in order to defraud him of the value of his shareholding, then a claim for conspiracy might arise.

'A conspiracy consists in the agreement of two or more to do an unlawful act, or to do a lawful act by unlawful means,' said Mr Justice Willes. The real purpose of the conspiracy must be 'the inflicting of damage on A as distinguished from serving the bona fide and legitimate interests of those who so combine', with the result that A suffers damage.

So to succeed in a conspiracy action, the dismissed director (or other executive) must show that former colleagues or superiors combined to cause him an unlawful injury.

Of course, if you can prove fraud by one person, that should be quite enough. And remember that fraud consists either of the making of a false statement in the knowledge that it was untrue or 'recklessly, careless whether it be true or false'. Commercial fraud does not necessarily involve knowledge of the untruth. Recklessness is quite sufficient.

So now put yourself in the unhappy position of an industrial executive or director, shown to the door. The first question to ask is— have I been lawfully wronged? The fact that there has been a moral injury is normally irrelevant. There are many injuries for which the law provides no recompense.

Next, is there a good claim for damages for wrongful dismissal? If so, then remember to mitigate your loss.

If the removal was from the Board of the company, was it in accordance with the company's Articles—or in compliance with the Companies Act? The director who has become bankrupt or of unsound mind or who has committed an indictable offence against the company will have no complaint if he is sacked.

Then what about fraud or conspiracy? Could this provide the level for the extraction of a sensible compromise settlement?

They say that you may judge a man by the company he keeps and the books he reads and the executive by the subordinates whom he employs. You may also judge the wisdom of an industrial executive by the experience and sagacity of the solicitor he employs. If disaster comes your way, then the sooner you get to your lawyer the better.

Conversely, if you are considering ousting an executive or a colleague, then ask yourself: Will I give him any rights against the company or myself? And if you are not sure of the answer, then you too should make your way with speed to your man of law—before you take an irreversible step in the wrong direction.

Chapter 30

Oppressed Minorities

THE WORLD of industry is beset with strife. The chairman of a great complex is fired by his colleagues on the Board. The managing director of an industrial giant is consigned to the scrap heap. One of the three founders and shareholders in a manufacturing company is turfed off the Board. So what happens? The miserable outcast rushes hotfoot to his lawyers. 'I am an oppressed minority,' he says. 'They have conspired against me. I want my rights.'

What rights has the member of the Board, ousted from his seat of office? If you are in that unhappy non-position, what can the law do to help you? Conversely, what are the risks for you, if you heave an aggravating rival or a non-productive fellow director out of his office?

*   *   *

First, the dismissed director may have rights as an employee. He may work under a contract of service, in the same way as any other servant of the corporation. If his dismissal is in breach of his contract of service, then he is entitled to damages. Because the Board are mighty, they do not lose their rights as servants.

Conversely, a director who misbehaves may be sacked in the same way as anyone else. The Board member who persistently fails to turn up for meetings . . . who neglects his duties . . . who enters into competition with his own company . . . who 'repudiates' his contract of service . . . is asking for the sack. If he gets it, the law will give him no special rights.

So the dismissed director's first duty to himself is to attempt to obtain compensation for loss of office. This (says *The Companies Act, 1948*) must be disclosed to the members and approved by the company. If it does not exceed £5,000, it is a golden handshake and marvellously free of tax. So the clouds of fraternal disapproval may have a golden lining.

But what about 'oppression of minorities'?

This protection (which is not very powerful) applies to shareholders and not to Board members. In theory at least, a Board is a democratic body and the minority must bow, if necessary. But what of the shareholders?

For the smooth functioning of a company, says one expert, 'a proper balance of the rights of the majority and minority shareholders is essential'. The law 'attempts to maintain that balance by admitting on principle the rule of the majority but limiting it, at the same time, by a number of well defined minority rights'. If you hold shares in the company which employs you, then you should know these rights. Equally, if you are thinking of evicting a director who is also a shareholder, pause and consider.

First, there are occasions when the act of a company must be approved by the members—and sometimes special resolutions must be passed, requiring a three-quarters majority. For instance, in general the Articles of Association (which govern the internal regulations of the company) can only be altered by special resolution.

Next, there are occasions when individual shareholders may be able to recover the company's property from those who have taken it and who, by their voting power, have prevented the company itself from suing. This is an example of a 'fraud on the minority'. Majority shareholders must not milk the company for their own benefit in a fraudulent manner.

Next, under Section 210 of the Act, a member can petition the court for relief where the company's affairs are being conducted in a manner 'oppressive to some of the members', including the petitioner. But the fact that you do not like the way in which the company is being run will not of itself give you the right to make the running. Even if the majority happens to be mistaken, if it is acting bona fide—out of a genuine desire to benefit the company's business—you are out of luck. Unless you can get yourself into a majority—either by buying more shares or influencing other shareholders in your direction—you are out of luck.

If you can gather together 200 members or the holders of one-tenth of the issued shares, you could apply to the Department of Trade and Industry for an investigation of the company's affairs or of the ownership of the company. Again, if there is an attempt to alter the objects of the company, dissentient holders of 15 per cent of the issued shares could apply for cancellation of that alteration. But generally, the majority rules.

In practice, though, the director who is also a contributory to the company holds one major card, which may be withdrawn from his sleeve at any time. He may apply to have the company wound up. Even if this application fails, the moment it is advertised the company is likely to be in trouble. Its creditors will become restive and its credit may dry up. Even if the petition is thrown out by the court, it may cause very great harm. So in the next chapter we will consider some of the grounds for winding up—both those which are notorious and those which are scraped by lawyers off the bottom of the barrel on more occasions than most people realise.

Chapter 31

Winding up the Company

THERE ARE many reasons for winding up a company, some a good deal more laudable than others. As we have seen, the threat of winding up may cause chaos on the Board. So whether you are yourself a director with a massive shareholding or a more minor executive who has seen fit to acquire a share or two in the business, you should know the basic grounds for thrusting a company out of business.

First, the main rules, as you need to know them. The company itself may by special resolution resolve to be wound up by the court. The members may petition for the throttling of their own corporation.

Next, if a company fails to deliver its statutory report or to hold its meeting, then application may be made to the court to wind up the business.

Third, if the company has no intention of carrying on busines, it may be wound up. Note: The fact that the company is not actually trading will not be enough to prevent it from doing so in the future. In one case, a company satisfied the court that it intended to continue its operations when trade prospects improved. A petition to wind it up was dismissed.

The most common ground for compulsory winding up? That the company is unable to pay its debts.

A company is deemed (or presumed) to be insolvent: (i) if execution issued on a judgment in favour of a creditor is returned unsatisfied in whole or in part; (ii) if it is proved to the satisfaction of the court that taking into account its contingent and prospective liabilities it is unable to pay its debts; or, most commonly, (iii) if a creditor for more than £50 has served on the company a demand requiring payment and the company has neglected to pay the sum due for three weeks.

If there is a bona fide dispute over a debt, the company has not 'neglected to pay' because it exercises its rights in law. But where the company is 'commercially insolvent in that it does not have assets presently available to meet its current liabilities', it is in trouble. And just think how many industrial concerns would be unable to meet their current liabilities, if their credit were to dry up.

The fact that your company is carrying on a business which is losing at the moment will not make it 'unable to pay its debts', if its assets exceed its liabilities. But even where assets do exceed liabilities, if those assets are not 'presently available to meet its current liabilities', the company may be insolvent.

The disgruntled director, dismissed from his post, may well know the state of the company's finances. If these are presently shaky even if there are great hopes for the future, the director may have to be assuaged, if only to stave off a petition.

Finally, an order for winding up will be made 'where the court thinks winding up just and equitable'. But this ground is not as wide as it sounds. In the course of time, courts have defined what is 'just and equitable'.

Where there is deadlock in the management, it may be 'just and equitable' for the company's business to be wound up. But deadlock usually applies only where the company is in substance a partnership and there are grounds for dissolving a partnership.

In one case, a director behaved in a thoroughly irregular manner, excluding other directors from the management of the company and acquiring complete control of its operations. As there was a fairly even holding of shares amongst the directors, and as the business was in reality a partnership even though it was cast in the mould of a company, winding up was ordered.

In another case there was an unjustifiable exclusion of a working director from the 'partnership' business. A winding-up order was made.

Two men were the sole shareholders and directors of a company, with equal rights of management and voting power. They quarrelled bitterly. They could not agree on the appointment of important executives. They communicated through the company secretary. Although the company made large profits in spite of a disagreement, it was held that there was a complete deadlock in the management. It was a proper case for a winding-up.

Then there was the private company which consisted of three shareholders only. They held all the issued shares and were the original allottees. The shares were fully paid in equal proportions. One shareholder was resident in America and the other two were the present directors of the company. They could not agree. The affairs of the company were now in deadlock and there were pending actions between the shareholders of the company.

The Articles of Association provided that when a shareholder wished to withdraw from the company, he should offer his shares to the others in the event of neither of them purchasing those shares the shareholder who wanted to withdraw should be entitled to have the company wound up. One of the directors offered his shares to the two other shareholders. Neither of them agreed to buy. He presented the petition for the compulsory winding up of the company, which the other two shareholders opposed. The court held that it was 'just and equitable' that the business should be brought to an end.

The managing director of a company had 'a preponderant voting power'. He failed to hold meetings or to submit accounts or to recommend dividends. He 'laid himself open to the suspicion that his object in so doing was to acquire the minority shares at an under-value'. The Judge made a winding-up order.

In other cases, companies have been wound up where they were held to be 'bubbles'—to have had no business or assets; or where the company was 'formed to carry out a fraud' or to 'carry on an illegal business'.

So the court does have wide powers. But these will not be exercised merely because a director is dismissed or a shareholder is disgruntled. Still, the director spurned may be in a stronger position than he realises. Next we consider ways in which he can prevent himself from being removed from the Board.

Chapter 32

Checklist for Closing Down

CALL IT 'rationalisation', 'consolidation' or disaster—when you close a branch or a business, there are legal complications to be recognised in advance. Check the list, before taking your decisions.

There are four main areas of potential trouble: premises, employ-ees, suppliers and creditors.

* * *

1 Are you a freeholder or a tenant? If you own the freehold, then you are fully entitled to sell it, as and when you wish, provided that you can find a buyer. If you are short of cash, you may still be able to sell and then to lease back the premises from the buyer. But there is no legal reason why you should not dispose of your asset.

2 Are you a tenant? If so, then carefully examine your lease or tenancy agreement to see whether there is any term affecting assign-ment or sub-letting. These may be absolutely forbidden—in which

case you are in the hands of your landlords. They may waive the prohibition, probably in return for payment, but possibly with some relief if your business is in trouble and you can find an assignee or sub-tenant in a stronger business position.

3   Do you need your landlord's consent to assignment or subletting? If so, the law implies a term that such consent shall not be unreasonably withheld. If you find a responsible and solvent assignee or sub-tenant who can provide adequate references, you should be in the clear.

4   Have you given any personal guarantees? If you are the original tenant under a lease, the landlords may have a comeback against you if your assignee does not comply with the covenants. So *you* may need a personal guarantee from an individual before you assign to a limited liability company.

5   Check the curious rules on redundancy. For instance, if you make an employee redundant, then you will have to find half the redundancy pay (maximum total: £2400; your share: £1200) out of your own business pocket (or, in the case of an individual trader, out of his assets). If you put your company into liquidation, then the entire redundancy pay comes from public funds—and the Revenue proves in the liquidation for the half which the company should have paid—but its claim goes into the pool along with other non-preferential creditors. Also: under the Employment Protection Act (Part 5) you must (if possible) give prescribed warnings of major redundancies or face potentially massive penalties.

6   Have you outstanding orders with suppliers for goods or for equipment? If these are already purchased, you may dispose of them as you wish. But even if they have not been delivered, the closing of a business or branch or unit will not give you any right to cancel orders.

7   All contractual documents should be handed to your solicitors. They may find loopholes—maybe some element of a binding contract was missing. Perhaps your unconditional order was not 'accepted' by the supplier, who only agreed to deliver on terms substantially different from yours (hence making a 'counter-offer').

8 If a deal is firm, you have no right to cancel because you have decided to go into a different line of business, to move your premises, to sell or to close down. If you refuse to accept delivery, you will have broken the contract and your supplier will be entitled to damages. Therefore:

a   Can you induce your supplier to let you off the hook—for the sake of goodwill; because you can promise further orders in the future; or because of your difficulties in paying for the goods if they are delivered?

b   If you are selling, can you get the assignee to take over your obligations?

c   If you are going to have to pay damages, then check on the profit which your supplier will not now make on the deal. But can he mitigate his loss by selling elsewhere? If so, then he must do so. Note: there is no need for a term in your contract with the supplier giving him the right to damages. Such a term is inevitably applied into a contract for the supply of goods or services of any sort, in the absence of some agreement to the contrary.

9 Have you consulted your solicitor and your accountant, so as to sort out all the legal and tax angles (including possible tax losses)? It is vital that you should know both the strength and the weakness of your position.

10 Anyone who considers buying your business will wish to inspect the books and to know the precise trading position. Are your records in order?

11 If you close down the business, then you will have to make your peace with the creditors. Among factors affecting the strength of your bargaining position will be the following:

a   Liquidity of the business.

b   Whether it has been trading as a separate company or as part of a major enterprise.

c   The extent of the limitation of its liability—as opposed to the existence of personal guarantees from you, your family or others.

d   The reasonableness of any offers which you can make to those who are owed money.

e   The answers to the problems posed in points (1) to (10) above.

Chapter 33

Removing a Director

THE VAST bulk of modern businesses are operated through limited liability companies. Every company is run by directors—and a seat on the Board is the ambition of most executives. But once you are appointed to chair at the table of power, what are your prospects of staying there? When and how may a director be removed?

The Companies Act, 1948, says that (with very few exceptions) any director may be removed by an ordinary resolution passed at a general meeting of the company. A simple majority is enough to shift a director, even if his period of office has not expired. And this applies notwithstanding anything in the Articles or in the agreement between him and the company. Provided that special notice is given of such a resolution, it will be upheld by the courts.

The director is entitled to receive a copy of the notice of the intended resolution. He may have his own representations set out in writing at reasonable length and sent to the members of the company. Only if he sees fit to use his right to make written representations for the purpose of 'securing needless publicity for defamatory matter' may he lose it. But in any event, he must be given the right to speak out at the company meeting.

The Articles of Association of one family company provided that each of the three directors was to have one-third of its shareholding. But on any resolution to remove a director from office, that director's votes were to treble in power. So instead of having one vote for this purpose, he would have three—and hence he could keep himself permanently in office.

The family quarrelled. Two of the directors wished to oust their relative. And they maintained that the Article which prevented them from doing so was unlawful and contrary to the rule in the Companies Act that any director could be removed by an ordinary resolution.

Unanimously, the Court of Appeal upheld the right of the company to provide special weight to its members' votes. So if you wish to ensure that you cannot be thrown off the Board, you should create (or amend) your Articles accordingly. Until the law is changed, the Court of Appeal has provided a safety belt for directors with sufficient power to instal it.

In practice, of course, general meetings normally vote on resolutions placed before them by the Board. The Board itself operates on a majority system (subject only to the chairman's casting vote). If you wish to remain in power, then you should pack the Board with as many of your own supporters as you can decently muster.

Now suppose that you are heaved out of the boardroom. What can you do? You may claim damages for breach of your contract of service. But you must mitigate your loss by trying to find suitable alternative employment. Your damages will be the amount which you would have received had you retained your job for the specified period, minus anything which you actually managed to earn during that period. And a further deduction will be made in respect of the tax which you would have paid had you not been removed.

If a director receives a golden handshake, then the first £5000 is tax free. He is better off, then, with compensation then he would be with damages. So the Revenue has provided one of the most satisfactory ways of settling this sort of claim. The ex-director drops his action. The company votes him a golden handshake. He receives more than he would have got, had he won his case.

Apart from removal, a director must retire at the end of the first annual general meeting after he reaches the age of 70. There are exceptions. First, if the company is a private company which is not the subsidiary of a public company, this rule does not apply. The articles of the company may themselves otherwise provide. Or the director may have been appointed or approved by the company in general meeting by a resolution of which special notice stating his age was given.

In practice, if a director does have to retire because of age, he may be reappointed by a resolution, stating his age. And the rule that the articles may alter the age limit or provide that the director shall not be obliged to retire on reaching any age, enables many a wise beard to hobble into the boardroom, supported by arthritic shoulders.

Normally, a company's articles provide for directors to vacate offices on the happening of certain specified events. Table A of the Companies Act provides draft articles which are commonly incorporated into those of a company. Article 88 provides that the office of a director shall be vacated not only if he ceases to be a director because he is dismissed but also (among others) in the following cases:

1 If he becomes bankrupt or makes any arrangement or composition with his creditors generally; an undischarged bankrupt may only act as a director of a company or be concerned in its management with the leave of the court—for breach of this rule he may be imprisoned for up to two years or fined £500.

2 If a director is convicted of an offence triable by jury, in connection with a company—or if it appears in a winding up that he has been guilty of fraudulent trading or of some fraud or breach of duty in relation to the company—then the court may order that he shall not be a director or concerned in the company's management for up to five years; in that case, he automatically vacates his seat. So he does if:

3 He becomes of unsound mind; or if he

4 Resigns his office by notice in writing to the company; or if he

5 Is absent from meetings of the directors for more than six months without their permission.

If a director is ill and unable to travel, then his office is not automatically vacated. But in one case a director was advised by his doctor that his health 'would be benefited by going abroad'. He was away for over six months and his office was held to have fallen vacant.

So directors should not regard themselves as appointed for life. They may be removed for bad behaviour—or for no reason at all. In the former case, they may still receive compensation for loss of office—but if the company tightens its fists, the law cannot help. In the latter case, the director's scorn may unleash a legal fury.

Chapter 34

The Protection of Depositors and Investors

'FIFTY PER CENT interest per annum—and your money back at any time, on demand!' The impossibility of this sort of advertiser living up to his promise ought to be obvious to everyone. It is not. Ever since the gay old days of the South Sea Bubble, greed or gullibility, has overcome good sense. And investors and depositors have tumbled over themselves to lose their money.

From time to time, Parliament has stepped in to try to protect the unwary. First came *The Prevention of Fraud (Investments) Act, 1939.* Then there were sections in the Companies Acts of 1947 and 1948. In 1958, these provisions were consolidated into *The Prevention of Fraud (Investments) Act, 1958.* And following the fiasco of the State Building Society, *The Protection of Depositors Act, 1963,* tightened up the law still further.

Under the 1958 Act, dealers in securities must, in general, be licensed. This does not apply to members of recognised Stock Exchanges, to the Bank of England, or, among others, to any person acting in the capacity of manager or trustee under an authorised Unit Trust scheme. But those who are licensed have to put down deposits or give guarantees, in order that their solvency be assured. Licences can be refused or revoked. The Department of Trade and Industry has to be kept in touch by holders of licences with any changes in their addresses and the Department of Trade and Industry was given power to make rules as to the conduct of business of licensed dealers. Licence holders' names are published and, in general, to prevent the public being defrauded, those who sell them shares are controlled.

Section 11 gives power for Orders to be made with the approval of the Treasury that a Building Society might issue 'no invitation to subscribe for, or to acquire or offer to acquire, securities or to lend or deposit money. . . .' And by Section 12, the DTI is empowered to 'appoint one or more competent Inspectors to investigate and to report on the administration of any Unit Trust scheme, if it appears to the DTI that it is in the interests of Unit holders so to do and that the matter is one of public concern'.

And then comes the Section that is strengthened by the 1963 Act. 'Any person, who by any statement, promise or forecast which he knows to be misleading, false, or deceptive, or by any dishonest concealment of any material facts, or by the reckless making of any statement, promise or forecast which is misleading, false or deceptive, induces or attempts to induce another person . . .' to agree to acquire securities or to share in the 'profits or income alleged to arise from the acquisition, holding, management or disposal of any property other than securities . . .' or to 'secure a profit to any of the parties by reference of fluctuations in the value of any property other than securities', is made liable to be imprisoned for up to seven years. And, in general, restrictions were placed on the distribution of circulars relating to investments.

Here, then, was a massive restriction on smooth-tongued operators preying on the share-buying public. But it was clearly not enough. There was still no sufficient restriction on the issue of advertisements inviting the public to invest money by way of deposit and no sufficient control by the public over companies whose businesses were financed by such money. And so came *The Protection of Depositors Act, 1963.*

Where companies are incorporated in Great Britain or have a place of business there, the Act in general requires them to lodge special accounts with the Registrar of Companies and the DTI first before any advertisement for deposits is issued and thereafter from time to time. Strict limits are placed on the nature of such advertisements. And anyone who dishonestly or recklessly makes false statements, promises or forecasts, or conceals material facts and so induces or attempts to induce someone else 'to invest money on deposit with him or with any other person, or to enter into or offer to enter into any agreement for that purpose' is liable to be imprisoned for up to seven years or to a fine of an unlimited amount, or to both.

Once again, information has to be supplied by such companies and the public and the DTI has to be kept in touch over any changes.

The result? Depositors and investors may nowadays be reasonably confident that if someone swindles them, the law will have the power to deal with the swindler. But in a world where the criminal lawyer will never be out of a job nor the confidence trickster short of new ideas, the investor and the depositor must still keep a wary eye on his own interests. If he loses his money, then it will be small satisfaction to him if the crook is convicted of an offence under one of the above Acts. The consignment of a swindler to a spell in one of Her Majesty's prisons will not bring back the money of the person swindled.

On the other hand, the swindler's task is harder and his precautions have to be more careful. No longer can he blatantly appeal for funds and, if pinned down, reply that he was only indulging in 'commercial puffing'. Today he must side-step the law when seeking his money. And, with a little bit of luck, he will land in the trap which Parliament has set for him, before his victim lands in the trap which he has laid.

Chapter 35

Changing Your Line of Business

WE ARE all agreed that the object of a business is to make a profit. But how to do it, that is the question.

'Well,' you say, 'first you decide what your line's going to be . . . and then you follow it. Too simple. And if you're a partnership or a one man firm, you can do what you like, and if things don't go well, you can just change course and head for something better. But if you're a company, all your objects have to be written into its Memorandum of Association—and once that's done, you've had it. Those are your objects and you've got to stick to them.'

Nonsense. You can change them any time you like.

'Really? Still, I would like to know just how broadly a company's objects clause is interpreted, and whether and how it can be altered.'

The acts of a company only have legal effect if they are *intra vires*—that is, if they come within the scope of the objects clause of its Memorandum of Association. That is its charter. That document gives it life and a purpose for its existence. Outside the bounds of that purpose, it is quite ineffective.

'Does that mean that if my company is empowered to engage in the sale and manufacture of clothing and it enters into an agreement to take over a colliery, then that agreement is so ineffective that even if the objects clause is amended later on to include a power to purchase and operate collieries, that won't bring my contract to life?'

Absolutely.

'Which explains why this clause is so important?'

Quite so. The objects clause should be most carefully drafted, to incorporate in the most specific terms possible, all the lines of business in which the company intends to engage. But even then, not everything can be thought of, and so most of these clauses end with words like this—'and to do all such other things as are incidental or conducive to the attainment of the above objects, or any of them'.

'And that could mean anything or nothing. What does it mean?'

That is a very difficult question. Some lawyers believe that it means very little. As one learned gentleman put it, a company has, anyway, 'implied power to do whatever is fairly and reasonably necessary to effectuate its specified objects. In each case the question depends on the specified objects of the company.'

So a company formed to carry on the business of a colliery proprietor might no doubt acquire and work collieries; have a banking account; for the purpose of its business borrow money on mortgage or otherwise, and draw, accept, and endorse bills of exchange, compromise claims made against it; remunerate its employees; pay dividends to its shareholders; advertise its products; establish branch offices; acquire rolling stock; and machinery, and vessels for conveying its coal—for all these things and many others are reasonably implied by the words used.

Of course, the difficulties arise when the directors want to know what is 'fairly and reasonably incidental' to the objects. It is much more convenient for businessmen not to leave to implication powers with which it is clearly desirable specifically to invest the company.

'All of which really means, I suppose, that if a particular operation is not specifically mentioned in the objects clause as coming within the powers of the company, then you must look carefully to see whether or not it is "*intra vires*", i.e. within the company's powers. You must ask yourself, using your common sense, whether that particular operation is 'reasonably incidental' to the main purposes of the company. Having asked yourself, if you don't give yourself a clear answer you'll have to ask a lawyer!

'And to avoid having to do that, you're much better off if you draw your objects clause in the widest way in the first place.'

Yes, indeed. But 'widest' is not the same as 'vaguest'. If a clause is too vague, the Registrar of Companies can refuse to register it.

'Suppose that my company was incorporated for the manufacture of ladies' clothing, would I need a special power to take over a similar business—to buy out someone else in the same line?'

Yes. But that's the sort of additional clause that's normally in a Memorandum.

'And could I use my machinery to manufacture men's clothing if I felt like it?'

Again, no—unless your objects clause provided for it. But why should it not do so?

There is no point in not putting it in. If your objects clause specifies that you may make men's clothing, this does not mean that you have to do so if you don't want to.

'What about extending or altering the objects clause? When can that be done?'

In the old days, it could not be done at all. Later, it could only be effected by applying to the Court. But today a company may alter the objects clause of its Memorandum by special resolution (see Chapter 36.

'Always?'

Always—insofar as the changes are required to enable the company:

1 To carry on its business more economically or efficiently.
2 To attain its main purpose by new or improved means.
3 To enlarge or change the local area of its operations.
4 To carry on some business which under existing circumstances may conveniently or advantageously be combined with the business.
5 To sell or dispose of the whole or any part of the undertaking of the company.
6 To amalgamate with any other company or body of persons.

Item (4) is the main one. You can now alter your objects so as to carry on almost any other trade or business. But you must remember to make the alteration before and not after you branch out into fresh fields of commerce, or you may find that the grass is greener where you were.

A reminder. Application can be made to the Court by shareholders with a big enough holding to have the alteration cancelled (for details, consult your solicitor). This application must be made by petition, within 21 days after the date when the special resolution concerned was passed. But if 21 days go by and no such petition is filed, then you have just 15 days to deliver to the Registrar of Companies a printed copy of your Memorandum as altered.

If you do not, then you, your company and every one of its officers is liable to be fined £10.

Chapter 36

Company Meetings

WHAT MEETINGS must a company call? What meetings may it call? And when may members of a company themselves requisition a meeting—either directly or with the help of the court?

*   *   *

Within a period of not less than one month not more than three months from the date at which a public company is entitled to commence business, a general meeting of members must be called. This is known as 'the statutory meeting'.

Thereafter, a company is bound to hold an annual general meeting every year, and notices calling the meeting must specify it as such. Not more than 15 months may elapse between the date of one annual general meeting and the next—subject only to the proviso that a new company has eighteen months from the date of its incorporation within which to hold its first AGM.

If a company in which you are interested has not held its AGM, and you can get satisfaction no other way, you should (either directly or through your solicitor) contact the Department of Trade and Industry. The DTI may then itself call or direct the calling of a general meeting 'and give such ancillary or consequential directions as the DTI think expedient. . . '.

Suppose, now, that a member wishes to call a special meeting of the company to discuss some particular matter. To get results, he must either himself hold at least one-tenth of the paid-up capital of the company or must be able to get the backing of enough shareholders to make up that proportion. Under Section 132 of *The Companies Act, 1948* (which we shall call 'the 1948 Act'), 'the directors of a company, notwithstanding anything in its Articles, shall, on the requisition of members of the company holding at the date of the deposit of the requisition not less than one-tenth of such of the paid-up capital of the company as at the date of the deposit carries the right of voting at general meetings of the company . . . forthwith duly proceed to convene an extraordinary general meeting of the company.'

The requisition must state the objects of the meeting and must be signed and deposited at the registered office of the company. The requisition itself may be in a single document or it may 'consist of several documents in like form each signed by one or more requisitionists'. The directors than have twenty-one days from the date of the deposit of the requisition in which to convene the meeting. If they fail to do so, the requisitionists or any of them who represent more than one-half of the total voting rights of all of them, may themselves convene a meeting. But this may not be held after the expiration of three months from the date of the deposit of the requisition.

The Act lays down the length of notice which must be given before meetings are called. Twenty-one days' written notice is required for the AGM. Meetings other than the AGM, or those called for the passing of a special resolution, require fourteen days' written notice.

If insufficient notice is given, the meeting may still be valid. If, in the case of a meeting called as the AGM, all the members entitled to attend and vote agree that the meeting shall be treated as validly convened, all will be well. And in the case of any other meeting, if there is a majority who together hold not less than 95 per cent in nominal value of the shares giving a right to attend and vote at the meeting and if they resolve that the meeting was properly convened, then once again the irregularity is waived.

So if ever a shareholder wishes to call a meeting, he should check the articles of the company to see what provision they make as regards procedure and voting. In the absence of anything to the contrary in the articles, he should look at the 'Table A' clauses, which are usually made to apply where there are no special, contradictory articles. For instance, 'two or more members holding not less than one-tenth of the issued share capital . . . may call a meeting. . . . In the case of a private company two members, and in the case of any other company three members, personally present shall be a quorum. . . . Any member elected by the members present at a meeting may be chairman thereof. . . . In the case of a company originally having a share capital, every member shall have one vote in respect of each share or each £10 of stock held by him, and in any other case, every member shall have one vote.'

Suppose, now, that the company will not call a meeting which a member believes is necessary, though he cannot himself muster sufficient share power to requisition it. All is not necessarily lost. Under Section 135 of the 1948 Act, 'If for any reason it is impracticable to call a meeting of the company in any manner in which meetings of that company may be called, or to conduct the meeting of the company in the manner prescribed by the Articles or this Act, the court may, either on its motion or on the application of any director of the company, or of any member of the company, who would be entitled to vote at the meeting, order a meeting of the company to be called, held and conducted in such a manner as the court thinks fit. Where any such order is made, the court may give such ancillary or consequential directions as it thinks expedient. . . . Any meeting called, held and conducted in accordance with an order under the foregoing sub-section shall for all purposes be deemed to be a meeting of the company duly called, held and conducted.'

It is not often that the court can be convinced or cajoled into calling a meeting. But there is a powerful, residuary right given to investors who feel that otherwise they are not going to have the opportunity to ventilate their grievances.

Finally, a word about voting at meetings. If a member believes that a proper poll ought to be taken, then he is entitled to demand one. 'Any provision contained in a company's Articles shall be void,' says the 1948 Act, 'in so far as it would have the effect either of excluding the right to demand a poll at a general meeting on any question other than the election of the chairman of the meeting or the adjournment of the meeting; or of making an effective demand for a poll on any such question which is made either by not less than five members having the right to vote at the meeting or by a member or members representing not less than one-tenth of the total voting rights of all the members having the right to vote at the meeting, or by a member or members holding shares in the company conferring a right to vote at the meeting, being shares on which an aggregate sum has been paid up equal to not less than one-tenth of the total sum paid up on all the shares conferring that right.'

Five members with the right to vote at the meeting may demand a poll. So may those holding one-tenth of the total voting rights or one-tenth of the paid-up share capital.

Parliament, then, has done its best to see that company meetings are properly conducted and members' grievances properly aired. But that is hardly surprising. Who does not wish to encourage self-imitation?

"OUR INCENTIVE SCHEME IS SIMPLE — MAKE A MISTAKE AND YOU'RE FIRED...!"

Part four

Employment Law

Chapter 37

Your Contracts of Employment—a Checklist

WITHIN thirteen weeks of the commencement of employment or within four from any variation, an employee must be given written particulars of his main terms of service. Some terms are obvious; others often get left out.

First, the basic requirements. Make sure that you include them all:

1   The scale or rate of pay or how it is calculated—and whether it is paid weekly, monthly or by some other period.
2   Hours of work, including normal working hours and any required overtime.
3   Holiday entitlement and holiday pay—and how holiday entitlement is calculated, e.g. whether an employee who leaves in the middle of the year is entitled to a proportion of a full year's holiday pay.
4   Any agreement about the employee's rights to pay when off work through sickness or injury.
5   Any applicable pensions or pension scheme.
6   The length of notice that the employee is obliged to give and entitled to receive—which cannot be less than the statutory minimum periods but may be much more. Minimum periods for the employee to receive are now 7 days after 4 weeks; 2 weeks after 2 years; 3 weeks after 3 years; 4 weeks after 4 years; and so on, one week for each year's service, up to 12 weeks for 12 years. He must *give* a minimum of 7 days notice after 6 months service.
7   The person to whom the employee can apply in case of grievance, and other steps in grievance procedure.
8   The name of the employing individual, firm or company—especially important in cases of insolvency.
9   The date when the employment began. You must state whether the current job is or is not continuous with any previous employment and, if so, then when that employment began (Employment Protection Act).

10 The employee's job title (new—under the Employment Protection Act).

11 Any disciplinary rules applicable to the employee, or referring to an easily accessible document, specifying such rules (also under the Employment Protection Act).

In addition to the *required* information and terms, every business or professional man should *consider* including the following terms in each contract:

1 A restraint clause, i.e. a term restraining the employee from competing against the business, when his employment ends. No restraint clause means no restriction on competition. But these clauses are complicated and if you wish to insert them, you should consult your solicitor.

2 Right to search. To search a suspect's person without his consent is an assault; to search his property is a trespass. Many employers include a term in contracts of service saying: 'The employee agrees to submit to the search of his person or property at the request of the management'. If an employee then refuses to be searched, you should refer him to his contract of service—but if he persists in his refusal, call in the police.

3 Do you have office, business or works rules? If so, these should be specifically incorporated into each contract. A misunderstanding is avoided; and the specific terms of the rules will without doubt be applicable to the individual employee.

4 Moonlighting—which becames more frequent as times grow tougher. Are you prepared to allow your employees to take other jobs in their spare time or at weekends—if not, then specify that the employee shall not engage in other employment without your consent. There is an implied term in any event that the employee will not compete against you; but include an express one which leaves the decision as to what is or is not competitive to you.

5 If your employee draws sick pay plus national insurance benefits, he may be better off financially in illness than he is in health. To avoid this anomaly, include a term that specifies that from any sick pay entitlement you will deduct a sum equal to national insurance benefits.

6 No employee is entitled to 'stationery or other materials',

franking facilities for private mail or anything else as a 'perk', without his employer's consent, express or implied. Do your employees, though, take certain privileges for granted? Are they likely to help themselves to unauthorised 'perks'? Then why not set out precisely those privileges to which they are entitled—and those which are forbidden.

If you find on checking this list that there are items that you have not included in the contracts of present employees but which you would like to insert, here is how to do it:

1   You must vary the present contracts.
2   Variation is only lawful with the employee's consent.
3   If the term is not to the employee's benefit, he is likely to agree to the variation only as part of a larger deal which is beneficial to him.
4   So when you grant an increase in pay, inform your employees; 'We are taking this opportunity to revise our employees' terms of service. Please read the enclosed documents; if you have any questions about it, Mr—— will be pleased to discuss them with you; and please sign at the foot of the document, to indicate your agreement'.
5   Signature is not necessary—but once an employee has signed, he cannot then successfully claim that he did not read or understand the revised terms; he will be bound by them.

Note: A contract of service—or written particulars of main terms—may be contained in a number of documents—or even may be partly oral or partly in writing. The fewer the documents and the more complete the writing, the less the chance of disputes—and that is the object both of the rules laid down by the Contracts of Employment Act, and of this checklist.

Chapter 38

Varying Your Contract

THERE ARE many reasons why you may wish to vary the terms under which you serve your company. Maybe there is to be a merger or take over, so that the company will no longer be under your control and you wish to protect your future. But equally, you may simply wish to better yourself . . . to improve the conditions under which you work . . . to raise your pay, secure your future, make up for underpayments in the past whilst the business was being put on its feet.

So let us consider how, when and where these happy ends may be lawfully achieved—and when any contract, in fact, may be varied.

*   *   *

The ordinary rules for the variation of a contract may be stated simply: With the consent of the parties, any variation is possible, at any time. Suppose, for instance, that you are a purveyor of goods or services and have agreed on a price. It turns out that your expenses rocket sky high. In theory, you could be held to your price. But in practice, you might well say to the other party: 'Look, if I have to abide by the agreed price, there is no question about it—I shall have to skimp . . . it would be most unfair, under the circumstances. . . . I would be grateful if you would agree to increase the rate for the job, to make it an economic proposition. . . .'

The other party may decline to oblige. He is fully entitled, within the terms of his contract, to do so. But then he may not wish to see your company become insolvent, in the middle of doing a job for him. He may think that your request is reasonable. He may agree to the variation of the contract, so as to comply with your wishes. In that case, the parties having consented, the changes can be made.

Again, you may have agreed on a date for delivery. Time of delivery may be 'of the essence' of the deal. You may be entitled to call off the entire arrangement if the goods do not arrive on the due date, and then to sue for damages, to compensate you for any loss that you may have suffered as a result of the breach of contract. But you may decide to hold your hand . . . to give the other party additional time, to carry out his obligations. . . . You may waive the right to obtain delivery on due date—and, in the process, vary the contract.

Of course, unilateral variation of a contract, without the consent of the other party (or contrary to his wishes), is a breach of contract. It may amount to a repudiation of the entire deal. The other party may be entitled to regard the agreement as at an end. Just as no original contract can be made without agreement, so no lawful variation may be achieved otherwise than by consent.

Now apply these ordinary contractual principles to those extraordinary contracts—agreements for service or employment. There is normally no reason whatever why these should not be varied, by agreement between employer and employee.

Suppose, for instance, that your assistant asks for a rise. 'I know that I am on a sliding scale,' he says, 'and my next rise is not due for another twelve months. But I have had to do a vast amount of additional work . . . to assume responsibilities never contemplated between us . . . and my finances are in a bad way. . . .' You may well oblige him and put forward his rise.

Alternatively: 'I am afraid I can no longer cope on the salary you are giving me. I appreciate that I must give you six months' notice—but I cannot survive that long, without receiving better pay.' You have the choice. You can either tell the man that you insist upon his keeping to the terms of his contract—in which case, he will doubtless walk out on you and you will be able to do nothing whatsoever about it (other than to enforce any binding restraint clause which may exist in his contract—see Chapter 42)—or you can agree to a variation.

Now look at your own contract—the agreement under which you serve your company. This may have years to run—but there is no reason, in law, why it should not be varied in order to comply with your wishes—provided, of course, that no one is going to be defrauded or that you are not using your position so as to take unfair advantage of the shareholders.

'No man can . . . acting as an agent,' said a Lord Chancellor, many years ago, 'be allowed to put himself into a position in which his interest and his duty will be in conflict.' So under Section 199 of the

Companies Act, a director who is in any way interested in a proposed or actual contract with the company is bound to declare the nature of his interest at the board meeting at which the question of entering into the contract is first considered—or otherwise at the first meeting after he becomes interested in the contract in question. And the company's articles usually provide that he shall not vote on any such contract or that if he does vote, the vote shall not be counted.

Again, he must not take a secret benefit as a result of his office. He may not accept (for instance) any money, shares or other benefit from a promoter, either while negotiations between the promoter and the company are still going on or after they have been completed. Nor can a director obtain some benefit for himself and then authorise himself to retain it as a result of the use of his voting power.

But what about a contract of service? No secrecy arises here—and the director's interest could not be more direct, declared or apparent.

Article 76 of Table A provides: 'The remuneration of directors shall from time to time be determined by the company in General Meeting.' Usually, then, any variation in remuneration to be paid must be as a result of a vote at a general meeting. If you want a variation, you must call your general meeting—and vote yourself your money. In any event, check the articles.

Note, too, that Section 189 of the Companies Act prohibits tax free payments to directors—the only way to achieve that sort of happy result is through a 'golden handshake' of up to £5,000. This, too, can be voted to you—even if it forms no part of your original contract. Indeed, it is almost certainly a variation. In consideration of your being paid the money in question as compensation for loss of office, you agree to shake the company's hand and depart.

Subject, then, to the rules which (in theory at least) require a director to make a clean breast of any benefits which he will require as a result of a merger or take-over, variations of the original contract are perfectly in order—provided that they are made in accordance with the articles and with the Companies Act.

My advice? Have the varied contract of service tailored to your needs, in the same way as the original—and this time, make sure that you have it properly vetted by a solicitor, fully instructed by you as to your requirements. That is very often the only way to make certain that you are getting what you want, in a thoroughly lawful (and hence enforceable) manner.

Chapter 39

Attachment of Earnings

The Attachment of Earnings Act, 1971, is beginning to bite. It consolidates all previous enactments under which wages and salaries could be 'attached', for the payment of debts. But it also added new and important rules, which every office proprietor and manager needs to know.

*　　*　　*

In the past, if a debtor failed or refused to meet his obligations, when he was in a position to do so, a judge would eventually send him to prison. There was no alternative. The result? The man was rendered at least temporarily incapable of meeting his obligations, even if he would otherwise have been prepared to do so. No one benefited—least of all the public, who had to provide the debtor with full board and lodging.

The Act enables creditors to lay hold of at least part of a man's earnings. By making the appropriate deductions at the source of his income, the debtor will not have the opportunity to avoid his obligations.

The Act applies to civil debts, resulting from judgments in the High Court (for sums, in general, of over £750) or the County Court (in less substantial cases). Provided that the sum involved is £5 or more, application may be made for an 'attachment order'.

A Magistrates' Court, too, may make an order in respect of 'fines, costs, compensation or forfeited recognisances'. But most important of all, in practice, any court may make an order attaching an employee's earnings, to secure payment 'under a maintenance order'— and that means not only an order for alimony or maintenance payable to a wife, but also one to provide maintenance for children.

If an Attachment of Earnings order is made, it will be 'directed to a person who appears to the court to have the debtor in his employment'. If you are the employer, it will 'operate as an instruction' to you, to make periodical deductions from the debtor's earnings. And at such times as the order may require, you will have to pay the amounts deducted not to the creditor but to the collecting officer of the court.

Once an order is served on you, then you must comply with it within seven days. And you may also deduct the magnificent sum of five new pence 'or such other sum as may be prescribed by order made by the Lord Chancellor', towards your clerical and administrative costs. You must also give to the debtor a statement in writing of the total amount of the deduction, although this may be included in your ordinary wages slip.

The order will specify 'the normal deduction rate, that is to say, the rate (expressed as a sum of money per week, a month or other period) at which the court thinks it reasonable for the debtor's earnings to be applied to meeting his liability under the relevant adjudication'. It will also specify a so-called 'protected earnings rate'. This will be the rate below which 'having regard to the debtor's resources and needs, the court thinks it reasonable that the earnings actually paid to him should not be reduced'.

If an employee's earnings are the same each week, all this will present little difficulty. Assuming that when you deduct the appropriate money at 'the normal deduction rate', the balance left to be paid to the employee is at least as great as 'the protected earnings rate', there are no problems. But if earnings fluctuate and you find that by deducting the 'normal deduction' you would leave the employee with less than his 'protected earnings', the judgment debtor will get less than the 'normal deduction' for the week in question.

So you take the employee's 'attachable earnings'—that is, the gross sums payable by the employer to the debtor as wages or salary —including overtime pay, bonus, fees, commission 'or other emoluments payable in addition to wages or salary or under a contract of service'—plus 'pension, or periodical payments by way of compensation for loss of office'.

You deduct PAYE and National Insurance and Health Service contributions as usual, and also contributions to any 'regular superannuation scheme'. You do not take off any other sums which you may ordinarily deduct from the debtor's earnings, such as National Savings contributions.

From the 'attachable earnings' you deduct the employee's 'protected earnings'. If the balance does not exceed the 'normal deduction' you ship off that balance to the court. If there is a surplus, you pay that to your employee, along with his 'protected earnings', If the balance is less than the 'normal deduction', then the judgment creditor is out of luck—all he will get is the balance.

If there is an underpayment one week, you will have to make it up in a future week which produces a surplus. And if the debtor's 'attachable earnings' are less than his protected earnings, he must be paid the full amount—and you are not even allowed to deduct your 5p. Well, you have made no deduction so you incurred no clerical expenses.

The Home Office and Lord Chancellor's Office have between them produced a useful explanatory booklet. It is available from HMSO or your local bookseller at 15p—and, contains some useful mathematical examples. I recommend it.

So you now have an outline of the new rules as you need to know them. Even if their operation comes within the domain of the company accountant, you will probably have to explain the rules to your employees—in which case, it is a very good idea to know them yourself.

Chapter 40

A Servant's Inventions

AN EMPLOYEE with an inventive mind is a blessing to his boss. But who owns the inventions he makes during the eourse of his employment? And how far is a servant entitled to use the skill, knowledge and technical know-how obtained in your service when he leaves to work for someone else? These are questions that Courts have had to consider, time after time.

*　　*　　*

In 1937, the Triplex Safety Glass Company Limited, sued an employee named Scorah, who had discovered a method of producing acrylic acid. They wanted a declaration that he was 'a trustee of the invention' for them and 'was bound to assign the rights therein when requested to do so by the Company, subject to his being indemnified against costs to which he might be put'. The case came before Mr Justice Farwell in the Chancery Division, and he summed up the law in two clear paragraphs. He said:

'It must . . . be remembered that no employee is entitled to filch his employer's property in whatever form that property may be, whether it is in the form of a secret process or whether it is in some other form. That is, and remains, the property of the employer, and must not be wrongfully used by the employee in any way. On the other hand, no employer is entitled to prevent his employee from making use, in the service of any persons or in his own business, of any knowledge or skill which the employee has gained by his term of service with the employer.

'It would obviously be very injurious to the public as a whole that a man who had learned his business, or a large part of his business, in the workshops or laboratories of an employer should not be entitled to make use of that in any other way, and, therefore, any information or skill or knowledge which he has acquired in the business of the employer, apart altogether from secret processes or any suchlike property, is something which the employee is entitled to use in any way he pleases after the employment has ceased.'

So if a process is secret, your servant cannot 'filch it' and use it for his own benefit. But any general knowledge or skills he can take away with him and use as best he can.

A warning. Do not expect your servants to know what you regard as secret or confidential, without being told. If you wish some process or scheme to be regarded and treated as confidential, it is up to you to inform your employees—in no uncertain terms. If you do not, you may not be able to prevent them from passing on the information, or using it as they see fit, when they leave you.

Returning to the Triplex case, the Judge held that the discovery had been made by Mr Scorah on behalf of his employers, who were therefore entitled to the declaration they sought.

'But was the invention automatically the property of the employer', you ask, 'even though nothing was expressly said about it in the contract of service?'

In the leading case of *Sterling Engineering Company* v. *Patchett*, the House of Lords gave the answer. 'It is an implied term . . . in the contract of service of any workman,' said Viscount Simonds, 'that what he produces by the strength of his arm or the skill of his hand or the exercises of his inventive faculty shall become the property of the employer. If the employment is of a designer, that which he designs is thus the property of the employer, which he alone can dispose of. If it is patentable, it is for the employer to say whether it shall be patented, and he can require the employee to do what is necessary to that end. And if it is patented in their joint names, the employee holds his interest as trustee for the employer. If this is, as I think it clearly is, the law, it can only be excluded by an express agreement that it shall be varied and some other legal relationship created.'

So if you are an employee, and you do not want your boss to have the unchallengeable right to the benefit of any patentable inventions you make while in his service, then your contract of service must clearly say so.

Lord Reid, in the same case, put the law a little differently. 'In the ordinary case,' he said, 'the benefit of an invention belongs to the inventor. But if at the time when he made these inventions, he was employed by the company as their . . . designer . . . it is, in my judgment, inherent in the legal relationship of a master and servant that any product of the work which the servant is paid to do belongs to the master: I can find neither principle nor authority for holding that this rule ceases to apply if a product of that work happens to be a patentable invention. Of course, as the relationship of master and servant is constituted by contract, the parties can if they choose, alter or vary the normal incidence of the relationship, but they can only do that by express agreement, or by an agreement which can be implied from the facts of the case.'

Mr Justice Roxburgh applied these principles in 1956. A man called Homewood was employed by the British Syphon Company Limited as their chief technician, to advise them on all technical matters relating to their business, which included the manufacture of soda-water syphons. He was in charge of design and development. While in that employment he designed an improved form of soda-water syphon. His company had not asked him 'to design a new method of dispensing soda water' nor had he been requested to give any advice in relation to such a problem. So he considered that the invention was his own. He applied for letters patent relating to it. His company sued, claiming an order that Mr Homewood assign to them his interest in the application.

Mr Homewood, said Mr Justice Roxburgh, 'was employed to give the Plaintiffs technical advice in relation to the design or development of anything connected with any part of the Plaintiffs' business. No particular problem had been put before him, but if, and as often as, any problem of that kind was put before him, it was his duty to be ready to tender his advice and to assist in any matter of design or development. He was paid to stand by in that respect. He had other functions, but those are not material to the present case.

'Would it be consistent with good faith, as between master and servant, that he should in that position be entitled to make some invention in relation to a matter concerning a part of the Plaintiff's business and either keep it from his employer, if and when asked about the problem, or even sell it to a rival and say: 'Well, yes, I know the answer to your problem, but I have already sold it to your rival'? In my judgment, that cannot be consistent with a relationship of good faith between a master and a technical adviser.

'It seems to me that an employee has a duty not to put himself in the position in which he may have personal reasons for not giving his employer the best advice which it is his duty to give if and when asked to give it.

'What I am saying only relates to matters concerning the business of his employer. That, of course, is quite clear, but, in matters of that type, it seems to me that the employee has a duty to be free from any personal reasons for not giving his employer the best possible advice. . . . He is not entitled to put himself in the position of being able to say: "You retained me to advise you, and I will tell you what I advise. Do it this way, but you will have to buy the method from your rival, because I have just sold it to him, having invented it yesterday."

'That seems to me to be reasoning which . . . makes it right and proper for me to decide that this invention (which, in my judgment, plainly relates to and concerns the business of the Plaintiffs, viz., the distribution of soda water to the public in containers of a satisfactory character) if made during a time during which the chief technician is standing by under the terms of his employment, must be held to be the property of the employer. Accordingly, my decision is for the Plaintiffs.'

In the absence of any express agreement to the contrary, an invention made by your employee, and connected in some way with his employment, belongs to you. If the employee wants some other arrangement, that must be included in the contract of service. But what if you wish to restrict your employee's freedom still further, so as to make sure that he does not impart information learned while in your service?

'Prima facie,' said Mr Justice Farwell in the Triplex case, 'every contract which is in restraint of trade made between an employer and an employee is illegal as against public policy, and is not enforceable in these Courts, and the onus is on an employer to show that the terms of the contract are not more than are reasonably necessary for the proper function of himself and his business and are not injurious to the public as a whole.' Restraint clauses are disliked by the law— as we shall now see.

Chapter 41

Is Moonlighting Legal?

TIMES are tough and many employees are prepared to work evenings, weekends and holidays in order to make both ends meet. 'Moonlighting' is becoming increasingly common. But is it legal? If you 'moonlight' and your employers find out about your activities, are they entitled to dismiss you?

Conversely: If you discover that your employees are making an honest outside living, are you entitled to insist that they either give up that activity or leave your service? And what difference does it make if a contract of service contains the sort of clause that is common in contracts of service of many people: 'You will be expected to devote your full time to the service of the company . . .'. Or 'You will not engage in any other employment, during the subsistence of this contract . . .'?

*   *   *

All contracts—including contracts of service—contain two types of term: 'express' and 'implied'. A term specifically banning alternative or additional employment is 'express'; a term preventing an employee from competing with his company or firm is invariably implied.

A term in a contract for personal service that places an unreasonable restraint on the individual's freedom to earn his living is usually void and 'contrary to public policy'. A clause in your contract, for instance, preventing you from competing with your company or firm on leaving its service will only be upheld if it is reasonable in all respects. But there is nothing 'unreasonable'—in law at least—in saying: 'We employ you full time and object to your engaging in any other lucrative employment. We want you to be free to do your work for us, as and when required . . . We do not wish to run the risk of your engaging in other gainful activities. . .'.

Naturally, you do not have to agree to this term. It is open to negotiation, in the same way as any other. And even if you have an express term in your contract which forbids 'moonlighting', your employers may close a blind eye, if they wish. If in doubt, ask. They will recognise the problems of keeping up your standards when cash is tight and may even be glad that you can earn money elsewhere so that they do not feel that they are bound to increase your pay—a step which they may or may not be able to afford.

So much for the express term. What of the more common case where nothing is said?

An employer does not buy his employee's time, twenty-four hours a day, three hundred and sixty-five days a year. So we start from the basis that an employee is free to spend his spare time as he wishes. And if he prefers to take on additional lucrative employment— instead of playing with his children or watching television—then (says the law): 'Good for him'. But he must not compete with his full-time outfit.

Obviously, you would not expect to be entitled to take business from your company. You cannot use your contacts and knowledge in order to acquire for yourself work that should go to your employers. You must not compete with those who provide your daily bread by your activities on behalf of others who provide you with some extra cake.

In practice, difficulties arise in the borderline cases. There is no direct competition—but could problems arise in the future?

Some years ago, a company of instrument makers employed six men at weekends who worked as glass grinders for a different company during the week. Their full-time employers obtained an injunction, restraining the employment of the men at weekends. The Court recognised that there was no direct or immediate competition because the companies were in different lines of business. But competition could arise in the future. One day, the employee might have to say: 'I'm sorry, I cannot answer your question because to do so I would have to reveal a process or a secret which came to me in the course of my part time working'.

The Court granted the injunction with obvious reluctance. It said, in effect, the lower down the scale the employee comes, the less likely it is that the Court would interfere with his freedom to use his spare time as he wishes. Conversely: The more experienced, skilled, professional, responsible and highly paid you are, the more readily the Court would intervene, to prevent any conflict between your full time and your spare time working—even if that conflict is future and potential rather than present and immediate.

As usual, these general rules are subject to agreement to the contrary. There is nothing to prevent you, for instance, from saying to potential employers: 'I will gladly come to work for you, but only provided that you do not object to my carrying on my own, private business in my own spare time'. If they are prepared to take you on upon that basis, then so be it—provided, of course, that even then you do not abuse your position as an employee for your private benefit. There is all the difference in the legal world between honest 'moonlighting' and making secret profits as a result of your privileged position in your firm or company.

The same rules that apply to you apply in reverse to those whom you employ. They may not compete with you; dishonestly steal your goodwill; or make secret profits—and the fact that they may be doing so in their own spare time will in no way make the practice lawful. They must not break express or implied terms in their contracts—however rough their financial weather.

Chapter 42

Restraint Clauses – and Unfair Competition

THE COMPETITION most to be feared is that from a former employee, partner, assistant or fellow executive. He (literally) knows your business. Conversely, if you switch jobs, what can you take with you when you go? Are you entitled to use the knowledge and know-how, skills, specialities and contacts that you acquired in your present post, for some competing outfit—or for yourself?

* * *

In general, an ex-employee may compete to his heart's content. He may set up in exactly the same line of business, in adjoining premises, the day after he leaves. Only if there is a valid, binding restraint clause in his contract of service can he be prevented from doing so. And as the law seeks to preserve a man's freedom to earn his living where, when and how he sees fit, restraint clauses are, on the face of them, void as 'contrary to public policy'.

A restraint clause will only be upheld if it is reasonable from everyone's point of view. It must not be more extensive than reasonably necessary for the protection of the employer's business. It must not put an unreasonable restraint on the employee's freedom to earn his living. And it must not be unreasonable from the viewpoint of the public.

Some restraint clauses are a nullity because they are too wide in time. Others cover too wide an area. Yet others are worthless because they include too wide an area of business activity.

Normally, a restraint clause that is too extensive can seldom be 'severed'. Like every egg except that of the renowned curate, a restraint clause is usually either all good or all bad. A restraint clause *will* be severed, however, provided that the following conditions are satisfied:

a   The parts to be severed are independent of one another and are substantially equivalent to a number of separate restrictions;
b   The severance can be affected without affecting the part remaining; and
c   The excess to be severed is not a part of the main purport and substance of the clause.

For instance, it was held that a restriction imposed upon an estate agent's clerk and negotiator which prevented him from carrying on or working in a similiar business within five miles of the branch office which he managed or the head office at which he had not worked was severable. The restriction regarding the head office was deleted from the clause.

But suppose that the clause simply provides that the former partner will never solicit business from the firm's clients. This is undoubtedly too wide. Had it been restricted to those people who were clients during the period whilst he was in the firm's service, then he would probably have been bound. As it is, the clause need not trouble him.

The drafting of these clauses, then, is a highly skilled occupation. Only someone with specialist knowledge of the sort of clauses which courts have upheld in similar circumstances will be able to judge the chances of a particular restraint being upheld. If you want to prevent competition from those whom you employ today when they leave you tomorrow, you should get your solicitor to draft a restraint clause, tailored to your particular needs. And have it incorporated into the service contracts of your employees.

Conversely, if you wish to compete with your present or former outfit, look at your contract of service. If there is no restraint clause at all, then all is well. If there is such a clause, all is not lost—take it to your solicitor to see whether a court would be likely to enforce it. You may be luckier than you think.

Chapter 43

Who Gets a Share in the Bonus?

BONUS, commission or profit-sharing schemes are common in the business world—and so is the unnecessary misunderstanding and ill-will created by that most common question: What are the rights of the employee who leaves (for whatever reason) during the course of the year? Is he entitled to a pro rata share, or to nothing?

The manager of a travel business was employed on the basis of a letter of appointment that set out his annual salary, holiday arrangements and duties and added: 'You will be entitled to participate in our profit-sharing scheme'.

Six months later, he was offered a better post elsewhere and he handed in his proper notice, which was duly accepted. But when he was paid off, he received no commission. He wrote to complain.

The employers replied: 'As we explained to you at the interview, profit is shared among the staff with us at the end of March, when the year's accounts are done. We cannot know our profit before that date'.

The legal position depends upon the contract made between the parties. What was agreed—expressly or by implication?

Contracts of employment or of service (like any other contract) may be made orally or in writing or partly orally and partly in writing. To spell out the agreement, a court would look first at any written terms.

The travel agent's letter of appointment made it plain that the employee was entitled to participate in the profit-sharing arrangement. But it left open the question: What was that arrangement? On the face of the letter, the employee could reasonably expect to obtain a share in the profits. In the absence of some other express term, a court would be likely to hold that once you have given service, you are entitled to a share; and if your service does not last a full year, then you should get a proportionate amount.

After all, otherwise a man might serve 51 weeks and then be dismissed, perhaps as redundant. Why should the law put a bonus on employers' engaging in dismissal operations immediately before their accounting year comes to an end?

Still, the law will not *require* employers to give any commission or bonus at all, nor any share in the profits—and if the employee has agreed (however unwisely) to limit his rights, then he cannot afterwards obtain a legal remedy.

The travel agents maintained that they explained the details of the profit-sharing arrangements to their prospective employee when they interviewed him for the job. They said that they told him that only those staff who were actually on their books when those books were totted up would be entitled to a share in the profits shown. They argued that no one who leaves before the profits are assessed can obtain a share because the firm will not know what profits (if any) are available for sharing; that employers cannot be expected after the profits are made up to check on each employee who left during the course of the previous accounting year (even people who may have served only a few days, at the start of that year) and send them a share in the money; and that the arrangement was not only agreed but one which is common practice and extremely reasonable.

Once again, a Court would not be concerned at the *reasonableness* or otherwise of the arrangement, except in so far as it might shed light on the likelihood of the employee having agreed to it. The question that a judge would, if necessary, have to determine is this: In the light of the letter of appointment of all the circumstances of the case, what probably happened at the interview?

The employee will undoubtedly say that it was not made clear to him that he had to serve a full year or he would get no share in the profits; the employer's representative would (with equal certainty) say that he told the prospective employee of the circumstances and moreover it is his invariable practice so to do.

The employee will retort: 'I am not interested in your invariable practice—you did not follow it in this occasion—otherwise I would not have worked for you. The salary on its own was not enough . . .'.

This would probably receive the retort: 'We would not have employed you on any other basis than that now stated. Nor have we ever employed anyone else on any other basis than that, since our profit-sharing scheme was initiated'.

After looking at the documents and considering the evidence, the Judge would have to piece together the probabilities of the past in order to do justice in the present. And no lawyer, however wise, can guarantee the outcome of that battle.

Like most cases of this sort, the travel agent's dispute was compromised. Neither side wanted to get involved in the miseries or the expense of litigation which is uncertain in its outcome. But the morals of the tale are clear—for employed businessmen and professional men and those who employ them alike.

Make your agreement sufficiently clear at the beginning and you will avoid miseries at the end. When dealing with profit-sharing or bonus schemes, make it plain that only employees on the books on a specified date will be entitled to the money—or that bonus, commission or a share in the profits will (like holiday money) be paid on a pro rata basis.

It is precisely to avoid this sort of frequent dispute over holiday pay that *The Contracts of Employment Act, 1973* (repeating a provision in *The Industrial Relations Act, 1972*) provides that written particulars of holiday entitlement should specifically set out the manner in which holiday pay is to be calculated. There is no similar law applying to profit sharing and the like. There should be; no doubt in future there will be; but meanwhile, it is for the parties not only to make their deal but to be sure that they can prove it, in case of dispute. A little care in specifying the terms in writing at the start of the relationship will make the ending of that relationship a lot less harrowing.

Chapter 44

Absenteeism – and Pay when Ill

'WE'VE BEEN suffering from absenteeism. So we decided to put an end to it. We informed all our employees that, in future, overtime would be paid at the end of the month—rather than at the end of the week after that in which it was earned—and that we would deduct from that overtime pay, money for any time lost during the month due to absence from any cause whatsoever.

'The result? Absenteeism cut by nearly half. But when we deducted four days' pay from the money due to one of our foremen, who had been absent from work through illness covered by a doctor's certificate, he went to see his lawyer. And we've received a threatening letter.

'What is the legal position, please? Is a man entitled to be paid while he's off work—no matter what the reason for his absence? And is there any reason why we shouldn't pay overtime at the end of the month?'

*   *   *

As usual, the answer depends in each case on the contract of service. If an employee has agreed to be paid overtime at the end of the month, then there is no reason why he should not be paid in that way. But if you engaged him upon the basis that he was to receive his overtime pay the week after he earned it, you have no right to change the system without his consent. If you do, you are in breach of the contract of service. And he is entitled to shout about it.

You may, of course, invite the man to agree to a change. Contracts may always be varied—with the consent of both sides. But just as it takes at least two to make a quarrel, so it does to make or to vary a contract. One person may break it—but it takes two or more to make or to alter it. So it is wrong to change the mode of payment without your employees' consent.

Now for payment during illness. If the contract of service includes some specific agreement on the point, all is clear. You may say: 'You'll find us a good firm to work for. If you're ill for any period not more than four weeks, we give you your pay in full. And for the next month, you'll get one half.' If that is the basis on which you engage staff, fair enough—assuming that there are no trade union objections.

Equally, there is nothing to prevent your saying to your staff when you take them on: 'We only pay for time actually spent on the job. If you're not here, you get nothing.' The man knows his position? He agrees to it before he comes on your payroll? Then he will be bound by his agreement.

On the other hand, if nothing is said, what is the situation? Here you must make a clear distinction between absence through illness and absence for a day at the races or through avoidable causes. In the latter case, a servant will not generally be entitled to pay while away. In the former, he usually will.

Not long ago an executive of a clothing business found himself in the High Court, sued for sick pay. The Court ruled that in the absence of some term (express or implied) to the contrary, a servant is entitled to his pay, even though ill, for so long as the contract of service remains in effect. 'If the employer,' said the Judge, 'seeks to establish an implied condition that no wages are to be paid, it is for him to make it out.'

So, if a person is ill, you may dismiss him. But he will be normally entitled to his proper notice or wages in lieu.Until the contract comes to an end, the man is entitled to be paid, even though he is so unwell as to be unable to do his job. If you think that in some particular case the employee should not be paid while ill, the burden of proof is on you to show why not. In addition, remember that temporary illness will seldom entitle you to dismiss a man 'fairly'.

The only exception? An employee who has become permanently incapacitated. He is quite unable to carry out his contract of service and will not be able to do so again within a reasonable time? His incapacity may put an end to the contract. But—morality on one side—an employer would be wise to have a word with his solicitor before stopping the pay of an injured employee and throwing him off the payroll, with neither notice nor wages in lieu. Note, too, that severe or prolonged illness may make a dismissal 'fair'.

Chapter 45

The Stealing of Staff

WHAT CAN the law do to prevent your competitors from stealing your staff? Conversely, if you prefer to acquire your skilled help, ready trained, are there any legal limits on your right to fish them out of your competitors' pool? Every businessman needs to know the legal rules on the poaching of staff. Here they are.

*   *   *

The law insists on a person's right to improve himself. He is entitled to change jobs as often as he sees fit, so as to improve his pay or conditions of work. Provided that he gives proper notice, the law wishes him the best of good fortune in his climb to the top.

Conversely, every employer is entitled to attract to himself the best staff available. If, in the process, he strips competitors' businesses of their most valued employees, well—that's business, isn't it? If you cannot offer sufficiently attractive pay or conditions to keep your staff happy, that will be your misfortune.

It follows that there is no law against the poaching of staff. You are entitled to fish in any waters you please, to hook for yourself the finest, best trained, most efficient employees. And if the treasures from your payroll are slipping into other people's pockets, what can you do? Usually, your only hope will be to meet the competition by raising levels of pay and/or by improving conditions of work. You must be as competitive in the labour market as in any other, if you are to administer an efficient business.

But there is one major exception to this rule. Would-be employers must not induce prospective staff to break their contracts of employment. They must not entice new employees to leave their old employment without giving proper notice. Failure to give due notice is a breach of contract. Procurement of such failure is a 'tort'—a civil wrong, giving rise to a good claim for damages.

Suppose, then, that you cast covetous eyes upon your competitor's office manager, personal assistant or sales director. By all means invite him to join your ranks. Inveigle him away from his present post with higher pay for now, better prospects for later, grim comments on the lack of future in his current employment. But do not let your need or greed for his services induce you to encourage him to leave without giving and serving due notice.

Of course, the mere fact that an employee does not give the notice he should will not of itself give his jilted ex-employer any rights against the new boss. It is not enough to show that your employee broke his contract. You must also prove that the breach was procured.

If, then, you set out on a staff-hunting foray, there are two rules to remember. First, if you can snatch staff from another man's table, the law allows you to help yourself. Law and morality are seldom synonymous. Second, provided that you do not procure a breach of contract by your new employee, the law will give his former boss no remedy whatsoever against you.

On the other hand, if you are losing employees, here are two rules for you. First, to staunch the flow of the lifeblood of your business, you will amost certainly have to apply greater quantities of cash. But second, if you can prove (*a*) that an employee has left you without giving proper notice; (*b*) that he has taken another job with a particular employer; and (c) that the employee did not break his contract of his own volition but as a result of some procurement or enticement by the new boss—then and only then will you have a good 'cause of action' against your successor. The difficulty, in practice, of proving these cases explains their rarity.

Incidentally, you may find your competitors actually coming on to your premises to seduce (metaphorically, in most cases) your staff. Ask them to go, and if they refuse, then throw them out. They are trespassers and you may use reasonable force to eject them. But if they rendezvous with your executives in the local bar, restaurant or hotel, you had best rely on their loyalty, and your excellence as an employer, to keep them on your payroll.

Chapter 46

Go – in Good Health!

EXECUTIVES TEND to be no more static than the products their businesses produce or sell. Problems of dismissal and redundancy arise from the highest level downwards. One way or another, the law on the subject is well worth some careful thought.

*   *   *

'It was a good job, as good jobs go,' said the executive on the street, 'and as good jobs go, it's gone.' Maybe he should have gone first. One tactic if you suspect that your position is likely to be taken away is to hang on as long as possible. The other is to choose your own time to move. There are, as usual, legal considerations to be weighed in the balance before making your decision.

Just as your employer is bound to give you proper notice to terminate your contract of service, you must do the same by him. If you have been continuously employed for thirteen weeks or more, then *The Contracts of Employment Act, 1972* (see Appendix 2), says that your notice must be 'not less than one week'. But your contract may itself provide for a longer period of notice. Or if it is silent on the point, then you are bound to give 'reasonable notice'—which may be far more than the statutory minimum.

That is the theory. The practice is very different. If an employer wrongfully dismisses, then the employee's loss is reasonably simple to calculate. But what is the employer's damage if his manager or assistant leaves without giving proper notice? How much money does the company lose if a director, research chemist, accountant or operative leaves without any notice at all? What is the firm's financial loss if a salaried partner, a bookkeeper, a clerk or a secretary simply fails to return from holiday? 'Incalculable,' you say. Precisely. It may be large or small, but either way you cannot tot it up in terms of hard cash. And no calculation means no effective legal claim.

Suppose, then, that you are offered a better post at a higher salary. But they need you now. If they induce you to break your present contract of service by not giving proper notice, then (once again in theory) your present employers may have a good claim against the procurers of your contractual breach. But their chances of getting any money out of you are remote in the extreme. However great the chaos caused by your departure . . . however much harder your colleagues may have to work to make up for your absence . . . . however scandalous your behaviour . . . the odds are that your foul play will not give rise to any penalty.

'But surely my employers could get an injunction, requiring me to serve out my period of notice or at least not to work for others during that period?' you say.

Not so. Courts dislike making orders which they cannot enforce. And who is to judge whether the employee who is forced back to the grindstone is bringing his nose anywhere near it?*

The sad fact (for the employer at least) is that the theory and the practice of this branch of the law are completely at odds. If the employee is both knowledgeable and unscrupulous, he can probably walk out at any time without fear of legal retribution. But maybe this is not as unfair as it seems, in a world in which almost any employee may receive his notice or pay in lieu at any time to suit the employer.

So if you decide to beat the boss to the draw, the law usually says: 'Go—in good health.' But there are hazards. Naturally, you must be sure not to leap into the fire or you may be homesick for the frying pan. Perhaps a negotiated withdrawal might produce some form of golden handshake. Maybe your employers have some hold over you

---

* The converse does not necessarily apply—'orders for reinstatement' may now be made if an employee is unfairly dismissed.

through your overdrawn commission account. And have you
checked your contract of service to ensure that there is no binding
restraint clause,* to prevent you from taking on the new post which
you have in mind?

Above all, make sure that you are not going to lose your redundancy pay or pension benefit without adequate return. In one recent
case, a company warned its staff that a particular section of the
factory would have to be closed down before too long. An executive
who saw his job going up in smoke found an alternative appointment.
He left and then requested his redundancy pay. As an employee of
very long standing, this would have amounted to some hundreds of
pounds. But because he had left before he was actually dismissed, he
completely lost his entitlement to redundancy pay. You are only
entitled to redundancy pay if you are actually dismissed because of
redundancy (as defined by the Redundancy Payments Act). You
normally get no redundancy pay if you leave prior to dismissal†. So
more haste may mean less money. If you've got to go, you've got to
go—but do try and wait until you are actually dismissed.

Once you are dismissed, then you may give written notice to your
employer that you want to terminate your contract on a date earlier
than the date on which your employer's notice is due to expire. Then,
unless your employer gives you a counter-notice in writing, within
the specified time, you will normally be entitled to your redundancy
pay even if you do not work out your notice. Redundancy is a complicated concept. So words with your solicitor before you take the
plunge are unlikely to be wasted. If you must leave, then mind how
you go, won't you? A false step may prove extremely expensive.

---

* Chapter 42

† But see Chapter 54 for the new rules on 'constructive dismissal'.

Chapter 47

References – and the Cost of Free Advice

WHAT ARE the real risks in giving a reference? Are you liable to be sued for libel? What if the reference is incorrect? Are you bound to give a reference? How can the reference giver protect himself? Important questions these for the commercial employer—but even more personally vital to him if he decides to seek fresh outlets for his talents. What, for instance, are your rights if your company declines to supply a reference? Or maybe you are in line for a series of posts, and each time something goes wrong. You suspect that you are getting bad references. What should you do?

Finally, if you want a reference—either for an employee, or, perhaps, for a business concern to which you are considering giving credit—how best should you handle the situation, from both a legal and a tactical viewpoint?

* * *

No one is bound to give or entitled to receive a reference. There is no law which requires businessmen to oblige by helping each other to decide whether to grant employment or loans. References, in the main, are commercial courtesies. But once given, they carry legal consequences in their wake. Their two main sources? Defamation and negligence.

Naturally, there is nothing defamatory about a good reference. But as soon as you give a bad one, you speak ill of your fellow man. You tend to 'lower him in the eyes of right thinking people' or 'to bring him into hatred, ridicule or contempt'. If the unkind words are written, they are libellous; if spoken, slanderous. In either case, they are defamatory.

The fact that the bad reference is true will provide a defence to a defamation action, brought by the person named and defamed. But if a plea of 'justification' fails, the damages will be far greater. After all, you have then repeated the defamatory statement, before another (and probably much wider) audience. If you stand your ground and the law pushes you into retreat, the result may be extremely expensive.

Quite apart from defamation, the reference giver must take care. If, for instance, you say that James Smith was an honest clerk or book-keeper, who left of his own accord—whereas in fact you muddled him with another man of the same name who was sacked for 'fiddling the books' you may be in trouble.

In a recent case in the House of Lords, Lord Reid put the rule like this: 'A reasonable man, knowing that he was being trusted or that his skill and judgment were being relied on would, I think, have three courses open to him. Keep silent or decline to give the information or advice sought; or he could give an answer with a clear qualification that he accepted no responsibility for it or that it was given without that reflection or enquiry which a careful answer would require; or he could simply answer without any such qualification. If he chooses to adopt the last course, he must, I think, be held to have accepted some responsibility for his answer being given carefully, or to have accepted a relationship with the enquirer which requires him to exercise such care as the circumstances require.'

Lord Morris of Borth-y-Gest, in the same case, said: 'If A assumes her responsibility to B to tender him deliberate advice there could be a liability if the advice is negligently given. I say "could be" because the ordinary courtesies and exchanges of life would become impossible if it were sought to attach legal obligations to every kindly and friendly act. But the principle of the matter would not appear to be in doubt. If A employs B (who might, for example, be a professional man such as an accountant or a solicitor or a doctor) to give advice, and if the advice is negligently given, there could be a liability in B to pay damages. The fact that the advice is given in words would not, in my view, prevent liability from arising.

'Quite apart, however, from employment or contract there may be circumstances in which a duty to exercise care will arise if a service is voluntarily undertaken. A medical man may unexpectedly come across an unconscious man, who is a complete stranger to him, and who is in urgent need of skilled attention: if the medical man, following the fine traditions of his profession, proceeds to treat the unconscious man he must exercise reasonable skill and care in doing so.'

Whether dealing with references or with ordinary advice, the law may be summed up like this: 'In the ordinary course of business or professional affairs, a person may seek information or advice from another, who is not under contractual obligation to give that information or advice. If the circumstances are such that a reasonable man so asked would know that he was being trusted—or that his skill or judgment was being relied upon—and he chooses to give the information or advice . . . then the person replying accepts a legal duty to exercise such care as the circumstances require in making his reply.'

Note that this applies not just to the giving of free references about people or the financial status of business concerns, but any other sort of advice. If you choose out of kindness to confer the benefit of your wisdom upon others, take care. That bad tip on the stock exchange . . . those unwise words on the building of a business or the liquidation of an enterprise . . . may cost you dear.

So we start with the proposition that the reference giver is a risk taker. Why, then, should he extend his commercial neck? Because he wishes others to do the same for him. He must do as he would be done by. And the law recognises that commercial wheels would cease turning if businessmen were to find it too potentially expensive and perilous to co-operate through exchanging information and advice.

So the law provides, first, a special and splendid defence to proceedings arising out of defamatory references. It says that these references are given on occasions of 'qualified privilege'.

Judges, advocates and witnesses in Court or parliamentarians speaking in the Lords or Commons are blessed with 'absolute privilege'. Whatever they say, however defamatory, unfair or malicious, cannot result in successful defamation proceedings. It is regarded as so important that Courts and Parliament should both operate without this sort of constraint that those who speak in either are highly privileged persons.

Similar privilege is granted to the givers of references. But it is 'qualified'. If it can be shown that the reference was given not out of a desire to assist the receiver but out of a wish to damage the person named, then the defence is destroyed. If the reference was given out of 'malice' it will fail. But even if the reference is unjustified and cruel, the non-malicious giver will be fully protected in law.

So the risks of defamation proceedings arising from unfavourable references are, in fact, quite small. And in practice, the person defamed seldom sees the document concerned—so even if malice exists, the chances are that he will not even be able to start to prove his case.

Note, in passing, that the subject of the reference has no right to see it. He is not entitled to a good reference, nor can he bring action against his former employers if they decline to give any reference at all. And if he loses jobs because the references are both untrue and to his discredit, he is generally powerless.

In practice, quite senior people often leave companies or firms after a splenetic row and then find it difficult to get another post, particularly if they were with the previous concern for a considerable period and can get no references elsewhere. My advice, if you are faced with this situation? Be completely frank with your prospective employers. Tell them the circumstances in which you left the other company. Point to your long period of loyal service with them. Say that it is hopeless to ask for a reference—or, if one comes, that it is unlikely to be favourable. Produce such references as you can (private ones, if necessary) showing your integrity and ability. And hope that your previous outfit will not succeed in ruining your prospects forever. Still, your desire for a good reference—which cannot by law be forced out of your present employers—may encourage you, if possible, to leave on friendly terms.

What, then, is the best tactic, if you require a reference for a prospective employee? Write, if you wish. Send a questionnaire, if you prefer. But precisely because business people are afraid of putting defamatory words onto paper, I suggest that whenever possible you obtain the reference orally. It is just as defamatory to speak ill of someone by word of mouth—but it is far harder for him to prove that you did so. And the commercial world tends to be a great deal more frank in person or by telephone than with pen in hand.

Now a cautious word on wise 'disclaimers'. In the House of Lords case from which we have already extensively quoted, one bank gave another a reference concerning a customer's credit-worthiness. It was incorrect—but it was headed with the following words: 'Confidential —for your private use and without responsibility on the part of the bank or its officials'.

The House of Lords unanimously decided that the reference giver was completely protected, even if those who suffered through relying upon the reference could prove negligence (as, indeed, they had done to the satisfaction of the original trial Judge).

'The bank,' said Lord Reid, 'which gave the reference, by the words which they employed, effectively disclaimed any assumption of a duty of care. They stated that they only responded to the enquiry on the basis that their reply was without responsibility. If the enquirers chose to receive and act upon the reply, they cannot disregard the definite terms upon which it was given. They cannot accept a reply given with this stipulation and then reject the stipulation. . . . The words employed were apt to exclude any liability for negligence.'

Lord Devlin put it this way: 'A man cannot be said voluntarily to be undertaking a responsibility if at the very moment when he is said to be accepting it, he declares that in fact he is not.'

So if you give a reference, you should take a substantial leaf from the book of every bank, by adding a disclaimer. 'Whilst every care is taken in the supplying of references,' you might say, 'no legal liability whatsoever is accepted in respect thereof by the company, its officers or staff.' Alternatively: 'We are pleased to provide information as a business courtesy, but it must clearly be understood that no responsibility is accepted in respect thereof.' Disclaim, loud and clear, and your words should bring no legal consequences in their train.

Of course, by disclaiming responsibility to the recipient, you do not cover yourself against a claim by the person named and defamed. But in the unlikely event of trouble arising, you should find 'qualifying privilege' coming to your rescue. And if the reference happens to be both favourable and inaccurate, at least there is no reasonable prospect of any resultant negligence action succeeding against you.

Chapter 48

Redundancy Payments*

MASS REDUNDANCY in the lower ranks of industry and commerce hits the headlines. Backed by their unions, the men can fight for their jobs or at least raise a public outcry if they are thrown out of work. Not so the executives and the men who manage. They must fight their

* Compare new definitions of 'dismissal', in Chapter 53.

lone battles for their livelihood. And while *The Redundancy Payments Act, 1965*, provides a cushion for all who are 'dismissed for redundancy', its provisions are not well enough known in the ranks of executives.

For instance, just when are you regarded as 'redundant'? If the company is cutting back on its senior, salaried staff, and you observe the way the wind is blowing, do you lose your right to redundancy pay if you move out before you are thrown out? How is redundancy pay assessed and what is the most you can get? Is redundancy pay taxable? If a dispute arises over redundancy money, who decides it? And what decisions have already been given on the meaning of the Act, which you should know?

Here, then, are the legal rules as you are most likely to meet them— either on your own behalf or as an employer of others.

*   *   *

You can only claim redundancy pay if you are dismissed by reason of redundancy. You must be 'dismissed'; and you must be 'redundant'. These words are not as simple as they sound.

R. H. McCulloch Limited issued a notice addressed 'to all personnel in Sussex'. It informed them that after a certain date 'we shall have no further work in the Sussex area. But we can offer you continuation of your employment with similar conditions' in other areas. And it asked for an answer by return of post.

Mr J. W. Moore regarded himself as dismissed and took another job elsewhere. He claimed his redundancy money.

'The notice amounts to a dismissal,' said the Lord Chief Justice. An employee is 'taken to be dismissed by his employer if, but only if . . . the contract under which he is employed by the employer is terminated by the employer, whether it is so terminated by notice or without notice . . .', so says the Act. In this case, the notice given to Mr Moore and his colleagues 'amounted to a dismissal . . . it was plainly saying: Your work in the Sussex area has come to an end, we cannot afford to employ you doing nothing, and accordingly our contract with you will be terminated on that date.' The fact that it then goes on to offer in effect a new contract of employment elsewhere in no way meant that Mr Moore was not dismissed as redundant.

On the other hand, a Mr Shaw lost his case against Morton Sundour Fabrics. They informed him that he would shortly be redundant. He found himself another job almost at once and gave in his notice. He claimed his redundancy pay, but the court held that for notice to terminate an employee's employment, there must be date of termination—or at least facts from which that date could be inferred. Simply to indicate that redundancy is on its way will not amount to a dismissal.

So be patient. If you see a merger or a take-over in the offing or redundancy coming over the horizon, do not jump the gun. If you have been continuously employed by the same concern for over two years, you will lose your redundancy pay. And that may be worth far more than your pay in lieu of notice. What is more, like the fabled golden handshake up to £5,000, it is tax free.

So you wait until you are dismissed. But are you 'redundant'?

'An employee who is dismissed shall be taken to be dismissed by reason of redundancy,' says the Act, 'if the dismissal is attributable wholly or mainly to:

(a) The fact that his employer has ceased, or intends to cease, to carry on the business for the purposes of which the employee was employed by him, or has ceased, or intends to cease, to carry on that business in the place where the employee was so employed; or

(b) The fact that the requirements of that business for employees to carry out work of a particular kind, or for employees to carry out work of a particular kind in the place where he was so employed, have ceased or diminished or are expected to cease or diminish.'

It follows that if you are sacked because your employers are not satisfied with your work . . . because the company feels that you are not keeping up with developments in the industry . . . because of any reason other than redundancy, as defined—you get no redundancy pay.

Not surprisingly, there are countless disputes over redundancy money. Initially, these go to industrial tribunals, whose procedure is comparatively swift and informal. But their decisions can be (and often are) challenged before an Appeal Court of three Judges. Here are some cases in which the employee got no redundancy money:

A man was dismissed because of his employer's 'genuine suspicions of irregularities': an employee declined to carry out work which was outside the scope of his normal duties but within the terms of his contract of employment; a workshop manager had extra responsibilities heaped on his shoulders, but his employers found that he was 'inefficient and incompetent' and appointed someone else to his position. None of these men got redundancy pay.

On the other hand, here are some decisions to the contrary:

At the time of a man's dismissal, there was insufficient work; a manager went on holiday and the company found that it could manage without his services, so he was dismissed on his return; employers engaged on secret Government work failed to show that dismissal of an employee was 'necessary for security reasons'; an employee was replaced by his lower paid female assistant. All these staff received redundancy pay.

Complications arise where there is an offer of alternative employment. Provided that the new contract would take effect on or before the date when the former contract came to an end and the terms and conditions of the new employment would not differ from the corresponding provisions of those in force immediately before his dismissal, an employee must not unreasonably refuse the offer or he will lose his right to redundancy pay. An employee must also not unreasonably refuse an offer of alternative employment which is different in its terms if that offer has been made in writing. In this case, the new employment can take effect immediately on the ending of the old job or after an interval of not more than four weeks.

Again, merely because the company changes hands or the business comes into new ownership will not give you any claim to redundancy pay if the new employer re-engages you or you unreasonably turn down an offer of similar employment from new proprietors. Remember, too, that if control changes merely because shares change hands, in law you will still be employed by the same company. You leave them at your own financial risk.

If by any chance you are nearing retirement, bear in mind that once you are over 65 (or 60, if you are a woman), you get no redundancy pay. If you are to be dismissed for redundancy, try to encourage your employers to do so before your appropriate birthday. But note that the Act specifically allows employers to terminate contracts in case of misconduct. So no useful purpose is served by courting the sack through active discourtesy, disobedience or other breach of express or implied terms in your contract of employment.

Now suppose that redundancy money is payable. How much will

you get?

Schedule 1 of the Act lays down the method of calculation of redundancy payments. In brief, taking into account only the theory of employment over the age of 18, you should get:

1 One and a half weeks' pay for each year of employment in which you were aged 41 or over.
2 One week's pay for each year of employment when you were aged between 22 and 40 inclusive.
3 Half a week's pay for each year of employment when you were aged between 18 and 21 inclusive.

If in doubt as to whether you are entitled to redundancy pay, ask for it. If it is not received, consult your solicitor. And remember that the burden of proving that a dismisssal was not due to redundancy lies firmly upon the employer.

Equally, if in doubt as to the amount of your redundancy pay, ask a solicitor (or your local office of the Department of Employment will help your calculations). The longer your service and the greater your age, the more redundancy pay you will get—provided that you do not exceed the upper age limit, even by one day—in which case, you would get nothing.

Those, then, are the basic rules as the manager needs to know them for his own purposes. Naturally, to discover the position for your employees, you simply apply those same rules in reverse. While staff at lower levels receive less remuneration and therefore less redundancy pay, the grounds for claiming redundancy money are precisely the same, whether you sit at the head of the Board room table or at the foot of the filing cabinet. Either way, redundancy could mean disaster. But the law provides a cushion which you should know how to wield.

Now consider Section 3 (2) of the Redundancy Payments Act.

'An employee shall not be taken . . . to be dismissed . . . if his contract of employment is renewed, or he is re-engaged by the same employer under a new contract of employment, and

(*a*) in a case where the provisions of the contract as renewed, or of the new contract, as the case may be, as to the capacity and place in which he is employed, and as to the other terms and conditions of his employment, do not differ from the corresponding provisions of the previous contract, the renewal or re-engagement takes effect immediately on the ending of his employment under the previous contract, or

(b) in any other case, the renewal or re-engagement is in pursuance of an offer in writing made by his employer before the ending of his employment under the previous contract, and takes effect either immediately on the ending of that employment or after an interval of not more than four weeks thereafter.'

Briefly, you may dismiss a man and then re-engage him and he does not become redundant. There may even be a four-week interval if you offer to take the man on, before his present employment ends. Section 4(1) adds:

(c) If the employee anticipates the expiry of the employer's notice, then he may still be taken to have been dismissed. 'The employee himself must give notice in writing to terminate the employment on the date earlier than that in which the employer's notice is due to expire'—once notice is given the employee does not necessarily have to work it out or lose his redundancy pay. But:

'If, before the employee's notice is due to expire, the employer gives him notice in writing—

(a) requiring him to withdraw his notice terminating the contract of employment . . . and to continue in the employment until the date on which the employer's notice expires, and

(b) stating that, unless he does so, the employer will contest any liability to pay him redundancy payment in respect of the termination of his contract of employment, but the employee does not comply with the requirements of that notice, the employee shall not be entitled to a redundancy payment . . .' subject to a ruling by the Tribunal to the contrary. So make sure that you serve the required notices—whether you are acting in the capacity of employer or employee at the time.

(c) Where a change occurs in the ownership of a business (is your company selling out?) then 'if, by agreement with the employee, the person who immediately after the change occurs becomes the owner of the business or part of the business in question . . . renews the employee's contract of employment (with the substitution of the new owner for the previous owner) or re-engages him under a new contract of employment . . .', then the employee is taken to be re-engaged and will get no redundancy pay. Moreover, if the employee unreasonably refuses an offer of employment by the new owner, he forfeits his right to redundancy money. He is out of work through his own choice.

If the business changes hands and employees are dismissed, we have the classic redundancy situation. They are entitled to their redundancy money. But if they are offered new employment by the successors to the business and in all the circumstances it would be unreasonable for them to refuse that offer, they get no redundancy money.

So if you see a take-over in the offing, take care before you leave—and conversely, if you are advising your company in connection with a sale—before redundancy pay is taken into account as one of the expenses of the change, ensure that the purchasers will not be willing to make the appropriate offers to your staff.

In the old days, redundancy situations tended to be as uncomplicated as they were disastrous (for the employees, at least). Nowadays, their complication is matched by the benefits which can be acquired by the employees who know their rights. And employers who know their basic redundancy law can save themselves a good deal of money. Executives and professional men, who often have dual capacities, can serve themselves and their employers best by knowing the rules.

Note: Until 1976, the employer could normally reclaim 50 per cent of any redundancy payment from the Redundancy Fund. This is now to be reduced to 40 per cent.

Chapter 49

Part-Time Problems

Do YOU employ part-timers? If so, then how safe are you in sacking them? Are they entitled to redundancy pay or compensation for unfair dismissal, in the same way as people who work full-time?

*　　*　　*

Redundancy pay is designed as a cushion, to help people who are thrust out of work because their jobs have gone by the board. If you dismiss your assistant, manager or secretary, because you move or close your business or works, your office, shop or studio, or because you no longer require a person to do that job, then you have created a redundancy.

To be entitled to redundancy pay, the employee must be over 20 and under 65 (60 is the age for women)—and he must have worked at least 21 hours per week for a continuous period of 104 weeks.

Assuming that a part-timer's age is below the upper limit, then if he is made redundant he is entitled to his redundancy pay, provided that he has worked the necessary number of hours.

What, then, of 'compensation' for 'unfair dismissal' under the Trade Union and Labour Relations Act?

If you fire a part-timer, then he is 'dismissed' and while he cannot get 'damages' for 'wrongful dismissal' if he receives his proper notice, he may still be dismissed 'unfairly', even if he gets far more notice than his minimum legal requirements.

The fact that your employee is a part-timer gives you no right to sack him either 'wrongfully' or 'unfairly'. A man is dismissed 'wrongfully' if he is not given his proper notice or pay in lieu. He may be fired 'unfairly' even if he receives more than his proper notice.

If you give your employee agreed notice or, in the absence of agreement, reasonable notice, or in any event not less than the statutory minimum—then you will not have dismissed 'wrongfully'. But give a full-timer or a part-timer less than his proper notice and you are in trouble—unless you can show that he has behaved so badly that he has 'repudiated' his own contract of employment. If he has destroyed the basis of his contract, then you may accept the repudiation and show him to the door.

So while a part-timer has the same rights to proper notice as a full-timer, he is just as bound to serve you faithfully, diligently, obediently, honestly and well.

Unfortunately for him, though, the part-timer is not protected by the Trade Union and Labour Relations Act against 'unfair' dismissal, unless he normally works twenty-one hours a week or more. The test is not how long the employee works in any particular week—he may for instance, take on extra tasks during the summer or the Christmas season. The question is: Does he normally work twenty-one hours or more? If so, then he is protected: If not, then he can get no help from the recent Act.

Anyway, the business or professional man who takes on part-timers for eighteen hours a week is fairly well protected—he has some leeway for overtime. But the man who does not know his law and employs people for twenty-one hours or more might just as well have full-timers on his books, insofar as redundancy pay and compensation for unfair dismissal are concerned. Once they work the magical twenty-one hours a week for the required period, they have the same protection as those who labour for forty hours or more.

Why should the law draw the line at twenty-one hours? Look not for logic. A line there must be—and a line there is. What matters is to recognise it, well in advance.

Note that these rules apply irrespective of the employee's age or status. To get redundancy pay, an employee must be at least twenty years old (that is, he must have served continuously for two years since reaching the age of eighteen) and he must be below 65 (60 if a woman). For protection against 'unfair dismissal', there is no lower age limit (apprentices, for instance, are well covered), but retirement age provides the upper limit.

So when assessing a part-timer's entitlement, you take the same age limits as apply in the case of a full-timer—but add on extra rules, to see whether the part-timer has the protection of the law.

Finally, these rules apply, of course, only to your actual employees. Many business and professional people use freelance help—they get assistance from self-employed men and women who are not protected against redundancy or 'unfair dismissal'. After all, if you make yourself redundant or put yourself out of a job, you have only yourself to blame.

So you can employ your helper for one hour, twenty-one hours or for his full working day and he bears his own risks on his own head.

The law is designed to protect the employees of others, and not those who see fit to employ themselves.

Note: The 21 hours referred to in this chapter is to be reduced to 16 hours a week (or 8 hours after 5 years service), probably from early 1977.

Chapter 50

Industrial Training

THE OBJECT of *The Industrial Training Act, 1964*, as amended by *The Employment and Training Act, 1973*, is basically 'to make further provision for industrial and commercial training'. If you are an employer of others you should know how the Act works. It may provide a source of revenue, an additional expense—or both.

After the appropriate consultations, the Manpower Services Commission, which was set up under the 1973 Act and is responsible for planning, developing and operating employment and training services, may make proposals to the Secretary of State for Employment (called 'the Minister' in the Act) that an Industrial Training Board should be set up. If such proposals are made, the Minister is empowered to make an order setting up an Industrial Training Board 'for the purpose of making better provision for the training of persons over compulsory school age . . . for employment in any activities of industry or commerce'. Check with the Commission to find out if there is such a Board in the industry with which you are concerned.

A Board is given seven main functions 'for the purpose of encouraging adequate training of persons employed or intending to be employed in the industry'. It may provide or secure the provision 'of such courses and other facilities (which may include residential accommodation) for the training of those persons as the board considers adequate, having regard to any courses or facilities otherwise available to those persons'. If there are any other courses or facilities so available, then it 'may approve such courses and facilities'; from time to time, it may consider 'such employments in the industry as appear to require consideration' and may make recommendations about 'the nature and length of the training for any such employment and the further education to be associated with the training, the persons by and to whom the training ought to be given, the standards to be attained as a result of the training and the methods of ascertaining whether those standards have been attained'.

Then the Board may apply or make arrangements for the application of 'selection tests and of tests or other methods of ascertaining the attainment of any standards recommended by the Board and may award certificates of the attainment of those standards'. It may assist people to find facilities for training for employment in the industry; it may carry on or assist other people in carrying on research into any matter 'relating to training for employment in the industry' and, finally, it may provide 'advice about training connected with the industry'.

In other words, a Board is clothed with immense responsibility for ensuring that there are proper facilities for training in a particular industry, setting up proper standards, and seeing that those standards are adhered to. What is more, it is entitled to enter into contracts of service or apprenticeship with people who intend to be employed in the industry and to attend courses or avail themselves of other facilities provided or approved by the Board. It may itself, then, take on the role of employer or apprentice-master. And one Board may help another by providing courses or other facilities; it may provide advice both to the Commission and to an employer in the industry when requested to do so; it can enter into agreements with people 'for the making by them of payments to the Board in respect of the exercise by the board of any of its functions'; and it may take part in any arrangements 'for persons to select, train for and obtain suitable employments and to obtain suitable employees'.

Finally, a Board is empowered to pay maintenance and travelling allowances to people attending courses it provides or approves, to make grants or loans to people providing such courses and facilities, to pay fees to those providing further education in association with training courses provided or approved by the Board, and to make payments to people 'in connection with arrangements under which they or their employees make use of courses or other facilities provided or approved by the Board'.

'But how does it carry out its functions?'

It is empowered to appoint committees, either on its own or in conjunction with other industrial training boards, and the committees (whose members may receive expenses and whose chairman may be paid) will act as the executive arm. 'More important, perhaps, how do they get their money?'

The Minister may make a 'levy order' and in accordance with it the Board may impose a levy on employers in industry (other than employers who are specially exempted).

'How is an employer's liability assessed?'

The manner of assessment is laid down in the particular levy order. If you do not think a particular order is fair, then you have a right to appeal to a special tribunal set up under the Act.

Happily, the industry does not necessarily bear the whole burden. The Commission, with the approval of the Minister, may 'make grants and loans' to a Board. What is more, a Board may, with the Commission's consent or on its authority, 'borrow temporarily from any other person by way of overdraft or otherwise such sums as it may require'.

The Board may require employers in the industry to furnish returns or information and to keep records and to produce them for examination. But these details may not, without the employer's consent be disclosed to anyone other than to the Minister or one of his officers or to a Board or its committee or officer or to the Commission. This is not intended as a statutory outlet for confidential information which your competitors would dearly love to possess. But if legal proceedings have to be taken as a result of the Act, or indeed 'any criminal proceedings' at all, disclosure may result.

'What if you do not want to reveal the information?'

In that case, you may be fined up to £100 by a Magistrates Court—or £200, on a second conviction. And for any person who may 'knowingly or recklessly' make false returns or false records or discloses information which is provided confidentially to the Board or the Minister or his officers or the Commission, the maximum which a Magistrates' Court can impose is three months imprisonment or £100 fine or both. But if a jury convicts, then the maximum is two years imprisonment or a fine of unlimited amount, or both. The law is given a very strong arm. And if one of these offences is committed by a company 'with the consent or connivance of, or attributable to any neglect on the part of, any director, manager, secretary or other similar officer' or anyone purporting to act in the capacity, then he may be punished, as well as his company.

Industrial training boards are responsible to the Commission and must report to it. They must keep proper accounts and, if things go wrong, the Minister is entitled to amend an industrial training order or to revoke it altogether.

After giving power to industrial training boards to provide for training for overseas employment, the 1964 Act then sets out the constitution of a Board. Its members are appointed by the Minister. It must have a chairman with industrial or commercial experience, an equal number of representatives of employers' and employees within the industry, plus people appointed by the Minister (presumably educationalists). A deputy chairman may be appointed, and various departments are empowered to send one person to meetings of the Board, with the right to take part in its proceedings.

These, then, are the bare bones of the Act. As time goes on, the Commission and employers alike are fleshing it out, in its full educational glory—and expense.

Part Five

Labour Relations, Employment Protection and Unfair Dismissal

Introduction

In the old days, a man used to talk about 'his job'—but in fact it belonged to the boss—to give or to take away, as he saw fit.

Then came the rules on 'wrongful dismissal', which at least ensured that a person was entitled to his proper notice or pay in lieu. And increasing minimum periods of notice were introduced by various recent statutes.

Next: In its only truly uncontroversial Part, the Industrial Relations Act provided that an employee who was dismissed 'unfairly' had a claim for compensation, even if he received his notice or pay in lieu.

Finally: The Employment Protection Act has provided a whole series of additional rights and remedies, designed to buttress employees in 'their' jobs. And women are not to be treated less well than men in like occupations—so rule the Equal Pay Act as strengthened and amended by the Sex Discrimination Act (often affectionately known in Parliamentary circles as 'The Sex Act').

This Part of the book explains the main rules on dismissals, new and old; the protection now enjoyed by most employees, thanks in the main to the new legislation; and the new status of women workers—with hints on its hidden perils, for them.

Chapter 51

The Industrial Relations Act—and After

IN 1974, the Government's programme for industrial relations reform was divided into three steps. First, the Trade Union and Labour
Relations Act repealed the bulk of the Industrial Relations Act;
second, the Employment Protection provisions introduced new
rights for employees at every level; and third, arrangements for
employee participation in management are in the melting pot.

To understand and to cope with the current industrial relations
set-up, it is vital to understand the effect of the repeal of the Industrial Relations Act—both what that repeal achieved and what
was left undone or unaltered. And enough time has now passed for
rational assessment to be substituted for blind misery.

Paradoxically, the removal of many specific provisions of the Act
has had little practical effect; the major change has been one of
atmosphere. Conversely, the unmaking of the law by Parliamentary
decree has left some permanent sediment—some beneficent, much
not.

What remains on the credit side?

First: the old Act raised industrial relations up from the level of the
shop floor, into the laps of the board. The Code of Industrial Relations Practice (which remains in force, unless and until it is replaced by guidance from the Advisory, Conciliation and Arbitration
Service) became the centre of argument for top management. The
importance of industrial relations was realised. Complacency on that
topic will never be the same again.

Second: the unfair dismissal rules contained in the Industrial
Relations Act were re-enacted almost unchanged in the Trade Union
and Labour Relations Act. These have now been strengthened by the
Employment Protection Act. They provide a permanent cushion for
the employee, unreasonably deprived of his livelihood. The answer
to the question: 'To sack or not to sack?' is now almost invariably
provided by middle or top management. To their frequent chagrin,
supervisors and charge-hands have almost always been deprived or
their right to fire—the cost of a mistake is far too great.

On the debit side, what is left of the old Act?

First: the cloud of industrial suspicion has only partially lifted. Trade unions will not forget the Act—and management still must contend with the residue of suspicion.

Second, and more important, when fighting the Bill and later the Act, unions learned that it is possible to flout the law with impunity. Mr Bernie Steeer, the dockers' leader, complained bitterly—not when he was put into prison but when he was released. Those who wish to change our social and industrial system are well served by martyrdom.

Again: the AUEW engineers refused to pay the £60,000 fine imposed on them by the Industrial Court. To counter their threat to down tools throughout the land, their fine was paid by anonymous donors.

Anyone who wishes to understand the importance (and the difficulty) of harnessing trade union support to any government policy in time of economic woe must never forget the Industrial Relations Act backwash. Like the Jarrow hunger march, it is deeply embedded in trade union attitudes—for ever.

Strangely enough, it is these less obvious results of the Act and of its repeal which are of paramount importance. The removal of the Act itself from the Statute Book has had surprisingly little effect. Consider:

The Act banned most *closed shops*. Neither management nor unions in general took any notice of the ban. Its removal has merely legalised the existing situation.

Agency shop agreements (post-entry closed shop agreements, with exceptions) scarcely existed—they were available, in any event, only to unions on the register. Their abolition goes unmarked and unmourned.

Unions were *registered* before the Act; they remain registered now; and the Registrar of Trade Unions had little useful work to perform. The removal of the Registrar and his powers have had no practical effect.

Bargaining remained unchanged during and after the Act. The new procedures were largely unused.

The *emergency powers* (up to 60 days cooling-off period and compulsory strike ballots) were used only once, during a railway strike. They were ineffective and their abolition is unnoticed.

Trade unions and their offices are again protected by cover

equivalent to that provided by the Trade Disputes Acts. The Industrial Court had in any event proclaimed that (having learned from the episode with the dockers) it did not intend to punish individuals. Which was (and is) just as well.

The *legally binding collective bargain* was a dead letter. The parties were given the right to contract out—which they almost always did. Today, parties may contract in, if they wish—which they do not.

The *legal framework* has theoretically gone. The Industrial Court has been abolished—but in any event, it spent the bulk of its time dealing with appeals from Industrial Tribunals, on points of law. Its functions (and its procedures) have now been transferred to the Employment Appeals Court. But the regulation of industrial relations will never again be moved from the shop floor to the court room.

It is vital, then, for all employers to look at the realities of industrial relations law if he is to cope with changes both new and in the pipeline. That reality is comparatively simple to state. The old Act has gone and its repeal has left a remarkably small imprint on industrial law. But is has stamped its impact on labour relations, for generations to come.

Finally: the rules requiring employers to provide information to employees during the course of collective bargaining and in annual reports (subject in each case to massive exceptions) were never activated. Those concerning collective bargaining have returned, word for word, in the Employment Protection Act.

Chapter 52

The Laws on Dismissal

IN THE OLD days, however short the notice, however unfair the dismissal, the employee could only claim damages if he did not get what he contracted for.

Today, a dismissal remains 'wrongful' if the employee does not receive his agreed notice (for details, see his contract or the written particulars supplied under *The Contracts of Employment Act, 1972*);

in the absence of agreement, 'reasonable' notice—depending upon all the circumstances of the case; and in any event, not less than the statutory minimum (see Chapter 37).

In addition, an employee who is dimissed 'unfairly' may claim up to £5200 (or £50 a week for two years) under the Trade Union and Labour Relations Act (replacing the Industrial Relations Act—see Chapter 53), plus new Employment Protection Act remedies (see Chapter 55).

For an employee to obtain damages for wrongful *dismissal*; compensation for unfair *dismissal*; or redundancy pay—receivable if he was *dismissed* as redundant—he must prove that he was 'dismissed'. If he left voluntarily—or before he received his notice, he was not 'dismissed' (even if he was warned that a dismissal was on the way).

Dismissal may be *actual*—with or without notice; the employer may 'repudiate' the contract—smash it—by not paying salary, wage or commission due or (more likely) by a reduction in status or pay; or it may be 'constructive'—where the employee is forced out of his job through bad treatment by his employers.

If an employee resigns, then he will still be 'dismissed' if he can show that his employer made it impossible for him to stay on at his job or otherwise smashed the contractual agreement.

Conversely: if you can prove that there was no 'dismissal', your employee remains entitled to every penny that he has earned up to the date when his employment came to an end—but to nothing more.

If you 'dismiss', the next question is: Did the employee get his proper notice or pay in lieu? If so, then he cannot get damages for 'wrongful dismissal'—his only possible claim will be to an Industrial Tribunal for compensation for 'unfair dismissal'.

You may decide to dismiss an employee without his normal notice or pay in lieu. You will be justified in doing so only if he has 'repudiated' his contract. He may smash it by one really serious act—like the assistant who smokes near inflammable goods or the manageress who steals; or as a result of habitual or persistent minor acts—disobedience, discourtesy, lateness or absenteeism, for instance. If you wish to show that the employee has repudiated, the burden of doing so will be on you. Summary dismissal is seldom warranted—and employees should be given their notice or pay in lieu and the benefit of the doubt.

If you are afraid that the giving of notice or pay in lieu may provide a weapon in the employee's hands if he claims compensation for unfair dismissal and you say that you regarded his conduct as serious, then send a letter along with the money; Say: 'This payment is made without prejudice to the company's right to dismiss summarily': add, if you wish, that you appreciate the employee's previous service . . . that you do not want to cause hardship . . . whatever other reason is correct.

Whether the employment was terminated with or without notice, the next question is: Was the dismissal 'fair'. Once the employee has proved that he was dismissed, the burden of proving fairness rests upon the employer.

Exceptions: Employees are not covered if:

1 They have been in the employer's continuous service for less than 6 months (note the reduction from previous longer periods).
2 They are over retirement age, or part-timers—normally working less than 16 hours a week, or 8 hours after 5 years' continuous service, (Employment Protection Act).
3 Employees who are genuinely redundant, i.e. not made redundant unfairly as an excuse for dimissing them, rather than others.

If an employee claims compensation for unfair dismissal and can show that he was 'dismissed', unless he comes within one of the above exceptions, you will have to show the reason for the dismissal and that you acted reasonably in treating that reason as sufficient to warrant depriving the man of his livelihood.

Reasons given by the Act include: lack of capability, skill, technical or academic qualifications; conduct; redundancy; illegality, e.g. where foreign employee's work permit has expired. A person may be 'incapable' of doing his job because of ill health or old age.

Establishing a 'reason' for a dismissal is easy. The burden of showing that the dismissal was 'fair' now rests on the employer. So:

1 Never dismiss in anger.
2 Always get a second opinion before dismissing any employee (not covered by above exceptions). And
3 Always follow dismissal procedure recommended by the Code of Industrial Conduct—including especially the giving (wherever possible) of at least one written warning before sacking.

Most employees whose claims for compensation succeed only obtain less than £200 compensation—often much less. They must prove their damage. No loss means no compensation; and where the employee has contributed towards his own dismissal by his conduct, his compensation will be reduced accordingly.

If in doubt as to likely result of claim or as to probable amount of compensation, consult your solicitor. The employer who dismissed an employee in the past could generally do so very cheaply; today, the cost of a dismissal may be extremely high. Details now follow.

Chapter 53

Dismissal—and the Trade Union and Labour Relations Act

THE Trade Union and Labour Relations Act retained and strengthened the unfair dismissal rules—which were incomparably the most important and lasting part of the Industrial Relations Act. The employee's position is now greatly improved.

In the past a sacked employee normally had to bring his claim for compensation for unfair dismissal in writing and within 28 days of the termination of his employment. This period has now been extended to three months.

The maximum comepnsation that could have been awarded *was* £4160—or 104 weeks at £40 per week. These maximum figures have been raised to £5200—or 104 weeks at £50 per week.

Before an employee can obtain any compensation at all for unfair dismissal, he must prove that he was 'dismissed'. He must show that he did not leave voluntarily without being actually or 'constructively' fired.

In most cases, this presents no difficulty. But there are sometimes battles over whether the employer forced the employee to quit—or whether the employee had been driven out by his employer's behaviour.

The 1974 Act defines 'dismissal' as including a case where 'the employee terminates the contract of service with or without notice, in circumstances as such that he is entitled to terminate it without notice by reason of the employer's conduct'.

An important employee's maxim has always been: 'Never resign —unless you have a better job to go to'—or you will not be 'dismissed'. Today, the Tribunal will look at all the facts to see whether the employee was entitled to resign without notice. Had the employer treated him so badly as to show that he did not intend to be bound by the arrangement? Was the man, in effect, sacked by implication . . . 'constructively' . . . without just cause. . .? If so, then the man is 'dismissed' quite as effectively as he would have been, had the employer specifically sacked him.

The 1974 Act shifted the burden of proof onto the employer who wishes to show that a particular dismissal was 'fair'. In the past, the employee had to show that he was dismissed; the employer was then required to prove the 'reason' for the dismissal—in practice, an extremely simple task; and the Tribunal had to weigh up whether or not the dismissal was 'fair'. Today, the employer must prove 'fairness' in the same way as in the past if he wished to avoid making a redundancy payment it was up to him to prove that the dismissal was due to a cause other than redundancy.

'The determination of the question of whether the dismissal was fair or unfair, having regard to the reason shown by the employer', says the Act, shall in most cases 'depend on whether the employer can satisfy the Tribunal that in the circumstances (having regard to equity and the substantial merits of the case) he acted reasonably in treating it as the sufficient reason for dismissing the employee'.

A dismissal is 'fair' if it is 'reasonable'. Conversely, if the employer acted unreasonably in treating the reason as sufficient to warrant depriving the employee of his livelihood, then he acted 'unfairly' and will be liable to pay compensation.

As under the 1971 Act, the Tribunal will take into account the extent to which the employee contributed towards his own dismissal; and he must do what he can to 'mitigate his loss', i.e. to keep it to a minimum by finding other employment as soon as he reasonably can.

In the past, nearly 65 per cent of all claims for compensation for unfair dismissal which eventually reached Tribunals failed. Only about 35 per cent succeeded. The percentage of successes is now greater.

On the other hand, in spite of the increase in the maximum sum awarded, claimants are not getting much more money than before, when the majority of successful claims result in awards of less than £200. This is starting to change, thanks to the Employment Protection Act.

The real problem for the successful claimant remains: How does he prove his loss? If his case comes before the Tribunal only two or three months after he has lost his job, and he has not obtained other work, he can only prove actual loss of earnings up to the date of the hearing. The rest is speculation. The Tribunal will not adjourn the case; make an interim award; and tell the claimant to come back if he does not obtain other work.

So even after further changes in remedies for successful claimants, resulting from the Employment Protection Act (see Chapter 55), businessmen will not have as much to fear from the law as many believe—but equally, none should spend his own tax-free compensation, until it is safely in his pocket.

Chapter 54

Constructive Dismissal

THERE IS more than one way to operate a filing system or to run a business—or to dismiss an employee. To avoid all doubt, the Trade Union and Labour Relations Act defines 'dismissal' in three ways. Thus:-

'An employee shall be treated for the purposes of this Act as dismissed by his employer if, but only if:-

(*a*) The contract under which he is employed by the employer is terminated by the employer, whether . . . by notice or without notice, or,

(*b*) Where under that contract he is employed for a fixed term, and that term expires without being renewed under the same contract, or,

(*c*) The employee terminates that contract, with or without notice, in circumstances such that he is entitled to terminate it without notice by reason of the employer's conduct'.

As discussed in Chapter 53, an employee who is not 'dismissed' cannot have been 'dismissed', as redundant, so he will get no redundancy pay; he is not 'wrongfully dismissed'—that is, without his proper notice or pay in lieu—so he has no claim in damages in a civil court; nor is he 'unfairly dismissed'—any hope of getting £5200 (two years at £50 a week) or any part thereof, is lost, or an order for reinstatement or an 'additional award' for the breach.

A company called a meeting of its employees and informed them that a department would, alas, shortly have to be closed down. The employees were advised to find other work elsewhere. A senior manager obtained another job; left the company; and claimed redundancy pay.

It was held that the unfortunate man had jumped the legal gun. He had left before he was fired. He was not 'dismissed'.

Another manager quarrelled with his boss and said: 'If you go on treating me like this, I'm off'. The boss said: 'Go then'—and gave him his cards. Held: He was 'dismissed'—this time it was the employer who had acted too fast.

Now suppose that you know your law and are determined not to risk 'dismissing' your employee. But he declines to resign.

Shrewdly, you apply pressures. You give him jobs that you know he does not like, but which come within the scope of his normal duties. You require him to work together with (or under) people with whom he tends to clash. Properly (but unkindly) you jump on him, for minor infractions of the rules—or refuse to bend them a little, so as to make his working life more pleasant. Eventually, when he has 'had enough', he leaves.

Has the man been 'dismissed' then, when he has taken himself off your payroll?

'Yes', says the law. Dismissal was not 'actual', because you did not sack the employee. But it was 'constructive'—and just as real, in common sense and legal fact.

'Dismissal' was defined by the Industrial Relations Act as including the termination of the contract by the employer or the expiry of a fixed term without its being renewed [in other words, paragraphs (*a*) and (*b*) above]. No reference is made to the employee terminating his contract, when he is entitled to do so 'by reason of the employer's conduct'.

There has been much argument as to whether or not 'constructive dismissal' is impliedly covered by the present rules. In future and (in legal jargon) 'for the avoidance of doubt', we shall know for certain that where you dismiss an employee 'constructively', this right to compensation will be precisely the same as it would be if you sacked the man formally.

In practice, for every past argument on law there will be fifty future ones on fact. Suppose, for instance, that your employee believes that you are making life impossible for him. He takes offence unnecessarily. Or maybe he is genuinely paranoid.

So the man says that he is dismissed. You deny it. The Tribunal must look at all the facts and decide. The employee has 'terminated his contract'—with or without notice. But were the circumstances such that he was 'entitled to do so without notice by reason of your conduct'? Had you treated him so badly as to show that you did not intend to be bound by the arrangement? Did you, in effect, sack him—by implication . . . constructively . . . without just cause. . . ? Upon the answer to that question may depend, in the near future, several thousand pounds of your money, or that of your firm.

Indeed, the dangers of your having to pay out a large sum are greatly increased by other Sections in the Act—which put the burden of proving 'fairness' on to the employer; which decrease the time that an employee has to be on the books before he can get compensation from two years to one; which increase the time for application for compensation from twenty-eight days after the termination of the employment to six months; and which increase the maximum compensation.

Chapter 55

How to Lose £11,760 Through One Angry Moment

THANKS TO the Employment Protection Act, an employee who is unfairly dismissed may, in some cases, recover over £10,000. While the rights of an employee who is dismissed 'unfairly' remain largely unaffected, his remedies are radically changed. Under the Act Industrial Tribunals acquire a remarkable new power, never previously granted to any court. Previously, they were entitled to 'recommend' that an unfairly dismissed employee be 're-engaged', on appropriate terms—an entitlement which they only exercised in less than 5 per cent of successful claims. Under the new Act, they may '*order* reinstatement'—and failure to obey that order may lead to the employee receiving an 'additional award' of up to 6 months' pay in normal cases or one year's pay where the employer has unfairly dismissed because of his employee's proper attempts to take part in trade union activity or as a result of racial or sex discrimination.

In the past, even the most unfair dismissal could only lead to a penalty of £5200 or two years' pay at £50 a week. As only about one third of all claims succeeded and only a tiny handful came anywhere near the maximum; as, indeed, the majority of the minority of successful claimants recovered less than £200; and as the awards took into account, in any event, only the employee's actual or prospective loss—some employers have come to regard the law as weak. But now the first remedy to be considered is reinstatement, rather than compensation; and as there is inevitably a 'basic award' as well as a 'compensatory award'—the time has certainly come for a drastic re-assessment of disciplinary and (in particular) dismissal procedures.

Assume, now, that an employee is held to have been dismissed 'unfairly'. Instead of compensation being the first problem, it has become the last. Now the Tribunal is required to ask the employee: 'Do you wish the Tribunal to make an order, requiring your employers to reinstate or to re-engage you?'

If the employee does not wish to return to his old company or firm, then the Tribunal will assess compensation. If he does wish to go back, then the Tribunal must ask the employer whether he is prepared to take the man back. If so, then there will no doubt be a discussion about terms—but the matter will be duly settled.

If the employer says that he does not wish to retain the employee's services, then the Tribunal must consider whether or not to make an 'order for reinstatement' or 're-engagement', and if so, then on what terms. If it decides not to make an order, then (once again) compensation becomes the sole question.

If an 'order for reinstatement' is made, then the employer must decide whether or not to comply with it. Unreasonable failure to comply is not a contempt of court leading to possible imprisonment. But where 'the terms of the order are not fully complied with, the Industrial Tribunal shall make an award of compensation . . . of such amount as the Tribunal thinks fit, having regard to the loss sustained by the claimant in consequence of the failure to comply fully with the terms of the order'.

Subject to the above, the Tribunal awards compensation for unfair dismissal on the normal basis (details follow). In addition, unless the Tribunal considers that it was 'not practicable to comply with the order' an *additional* award will be made, as follows:

1   If the dismissal was unfair because it arose from the employee's desire to be a member or to take part in the activities of an independent trade union, or because the dismissal was 'an unlawful act of discrimination' under the Race Relations Act (shortly to be strengthened) or was 'a dismissal which was an act of sex discrimination' then the award will be not less than 26 or more than 52 weeks' pay, at a maximum of £80 a week, i.e. up to £4000.

2   In any other case, the award will be 13 to 26 weeks' pay; again. £80 a week, up to £2000.

Where a Tribunal makes an award of compensation for unfair dismissal, that award now consists of (*a*) a basic award and (*b*) a compensatory award. The first job of a basic award is to provide some solace in cases where the employee is unfairly dismissed but gets neither redundancy pay nor compensation. In that case, he is now entitled to two weeks' pay.

Otherwise, the amount of the basic award is calculated on a sliding scale, depending upon his length of service, up to a maximum of 20 years*. Details from the local office of the Department of Employment or from any Industrial Tribunal or from your solicitor.

In addition, the Tribunal continues to award 'compensation'— being such amount as it considers 'just and equitable in all the circumstances, having regard to the loss sustained'. As before, such loss includes expenses and benefits, unfairly taken from him.

Finally, tucked away in a Schedule, the Act contains an important new protection. An employee *must*, where practicable, still apply within three months of the termination of his employment; but he *may* now do so at any time after he is given his notice.

This provision should make it easier and more likely for Tribunals

* It amounts to the same as the employee's lost redundancy entitlement. Maximum: £2,400.

to order re-instatement or re-engagement. The unfairly dismissed employee who does not wish to return to his job and who must show the maximum loss if he is to obtain the maximum compensation may still benefit from delay in lodging his claim. But the employee who wants to sit tight—like the difficult shop steward whom the company is anxious to dislodge—need wait to complain no longer than the day on which he receives his marching orders. The Tribunal may hold an interim hearing and suspend the operation of the dismissal until the case is heard. The employee is, indeed, well protected.

Chapter 56

Information and Collective Bargaining*

BEFORE THE demise of the Industrial Relations Act, one of our top trade union leaders was asked: 'What do you want in its place?'

He answered with one word: 'Information'.

Curiously, the requirement to give information was originally contained in the Industrial Relations Act; in the course of collective bargaining (although not in annual statements by companies); it has been repeated in almost identical terms in the Employment Protection Act; and it is likely to have far more impact than most of the sections which have received most of the publicity.

There are, of course, some companies that already provide substantial information to trade unions. On the other hand, there are some trade unions which simply do not want to know: 'How you cope with the company's problems is your affair', they say. 'Our job is to look after our members. . . .' The industrial world is full of strange problems.

Again, trade union members often work in the accounts department; in every plant there is a grapevine; and sometimes the unions know far more than the management realise. Still, the information provided through hearsay often becomes rumour and the management may be well advised to translate that rumour into fact.

* Probable implementation: by end of 1976.

Consider, then, the new 'general duty of employers to provide information'.

'For the purposes of all the stages of . . . collective bargaining between an employer and representatives of an independent trade union . . . it shall be the duty of the employer . . . to disclose to those representatives on request all such information relating to his undertaking as is in his possession, or that of any associated employer, and is both

(a) information without which the trade union representatives would be to a material extent impeded in carrying on within such collective bargaining, and,

(b) information which it would be in accordance with good industrial relations practice that he should disclose to them for the purposes of collective bargaining'.

Note:

1   Only 'independent' trade unions will benefit. A union is not 'independent' if it is controlled or financed by the employer. TUC unions are in; 'tame' staff associations and the like are out.

2   Information need only be provided 'on request'. If the union does not want it, it need not have it.

3   Only 'collective bargaining'—as opposed to bargaining over individual contracts—is affected.

4   The information to be provided is that which concerns the employer's 'undertaking'—which means, his entire business and not merely that part of it where the particular employees work. And the employer may have to provide information not merely regarding his own circumstances but also that of any associated company or 'employer'.

Now take the ordinary bargaining situation. The trade union representatives will no doubt want to know the state of the order book; whether the company as a whole or the unit in particular is making (and expects to make) a profit or a loss—and to be supplied with details; and if (as is almost inevitable) the employer declines to accept the wage claim in full, saying that it could not afford to do so, then the trade union would demand what lawyers call 'further and better particulars' of that allegation.

All that information is likely to come under (*a*) and (*b*) above. Surely the trade union representatives must be 'to a material extent impeded' in carrying on the collective bargaining if they do not know all the facts? And surely it must be 'in accordance with good industrial relations practice' that the employer should make full disclosure?.

However, the new Act provides precisely the same exceptions to the swingeing general rule as did the 1971 Act. Here they are:

'No employer shall . . . be required to disclose—

(*a*)   any information the disclosure of which would be against the interests of *national security*, or

(*b*)   any information which it could not disclose without contravening a prohibition imposed by or under an *enactment*, or,

(*c*)   any information which has been communicated to the employer *in confidence*, or which the employer has otherwise obtained in consequence of the confidence reposed in him by another person, or,

(*d*)   any information relating specifically to an *individual*, unless he has consented to its being disclosed, or,

(*e*)   any information the disclosure of which would be *seriously prejudicial* to the interests of the employer's undertaking for reasons other than its effect on collective bargaining; or,

(*f*)   any information obtained by the employer for the purpose of bringing, prosecuting or defending any *legal proceedings*'.

Sub-paragraph (*e*) is crucial. Almost any employer can avoid giving almost any information by alleging that it would be 'seriously prejudicial' to his business if he were to do so. Competitors must not know the state of the order book nor creditors that of the bank account. . . . If times are bad and the word gets out, the very jobs which the men are trying to protect will be at risk because, as everyone knows, 'to him that hath shall be lent . . . from him who has not shall be taken away . . . ?

How, then, can these two, apparently conflicting sections be reconciled, in daily industrial practice? That was the question asked of the Commission on Industrial Relations, in connection with the same provisions in the Industrial Relations Act. The Commission's answer was contained in a substantial document which may be summed up in a sentence: 'We don't understand it either . . . but the courts will have to interpret the clauses, in the light of experience. . . .'

Armed with that inconclusive report and under pressure from employers' organisations, the (then) Government procrastinated; when asked when it was proposing to implement the sections it replied: 'Consultations with interested parties are still continuing'; and was happy to allow the sections to lie fallow.

When drafting the Employment Protection Act, the successor Government shrewdly left the wording of the sections as it was, so as to leave the (now) Opposition very little ground for plausible complaint. And instead of placing responsibility on the Commission on Industrial Relations (now disbanded) for advising in advance, it requires the Advisory Conciliation and Arbitration Service (ACAS) to prepare a Code of Practice relating to the disclosure of information. When so doing, the ACAS must (says the Act) have regard not merely to the duty of employers to disclose but also to the exceptions to that duty.

Industry now awaits expectantly for the Code, which will probably be laid before Parliament for approval early in 1977. Then (and only then) will these sections be activated.

At that stage, it will become an offence against the Act not to disclose the required information. An independent trade union which has unsuccessfully requested disclosure may complain to the (new) Central Arbitration Committee, in writing and giving particulars. An attempt will then be made by the ACAS to conciliate but if that fails, the Committee will hear the complaint and make an appropriate declaration.

If the Committee certifies that information should be given, then no doubt the employers concerned will comply. Failure to do so would lead to a further complaint which would again be considered by the Committee. If considered wholly or partly well founded the Committee will make a further declaration, setting out the terms and conditions of an award which the employer is then required by the Committee to observe. These terms and conditions 'shall have effect as part of the contract of employment' of any employee concerned.

It appears that the sanction for failing to comply with the award of the Committee will be proceedings (probably before an Industrial Tribunal) alleging breach of the employee's contract of service. The distance in time between the original request for information and the final proceedings before a Tribunal or Court is likely to be long and tortuous. The implementation arrangements under the Industrial Relations Act were speedier—and probably more offensive to both sides.

Instead of relying on goodwill or common sense, then, the law will soon impose a duty. If there is a failure to comply with that duty, the ACAS will no doubt settle the bulk of the claims and the Committee's Order will produce results in almost all the rest.

After all, if you are required to give information and persistently fail to do so, all those who would most appreciate a leak will scarcely need one. Your dogged determination to keep silent will be enough indication to creditors or competitors of the unpleasantness or otherwise of the matters which you are trying so desperately to hide. Indeed, because they may misread your silence or exaggerate its importance, you may well have been better off to give the information in the first place. And that is precisely what the trade union leader whom I mentioned at the start was after.

All employers who engage in collective bargaining with independent trade unions must watch carefully for the promulgation of the new Code of Practice on the giving of information. Meanwhile, the more they get into the habit of disclosure, the less of a shock they are likely to suffer when the wheels are finally implemented.

Chapter 57

Guarantee Payments*

TOO MANY companies and firms are forced onto short-time working or even to lay off valued employees. In general, salaried staff continue to receive their pay as before. Unless they are made redundant, they continue to earn. They are not paid by the hour or (subject, of course, to possible bonuses and the like) on the basis of production achieved.

Hourly paid workers, on the other hand, must put in their hours or they will take out no pay. Thanks to the Redundancy Payments Act and to a combination of laws which ensure that they receive proper notice or pay in lieu, most have a reasonable cushion against dismissal. But while still employed, they have no guarantee of the

* Probable implementation: April 1977.

opportunity to earn their pay. One object of the Employment Protection Act is to meet this anxious problem of millions of workers—a problem which is particularly acute, of course, in times of economic recession and depression.

Employers in any industry are faced with cash shortage and shrunken order books while understandably anxious lest the new Act will add a further (and this time an unbearable) burden to their already bowed backs. They need scarcely worry. The protection guaranteed to employees is indeed minimal. And it cannot be more (unless and until the rules are changed, at least) than £6 a day for 5 days in each of the specified calendar 3 months periods.

Who, then, will qualify for the protection? And how will it be secured?

'Where an employee throughout the day during any period in which he would normally be required to work is not provided with work by his employer by reason of:

(*a*) a diminution in the requirements of the employer's business for work of the kind which the employee is employed to do, or,

(*b*) any other occurrence affecting normal working of the employer's business in relation to work of the kind which the employee is employed to do,

he shall be entitled to be paid by his employer . . . a "guarantee payment", in respect of that day. . . .'

Exceptions: he will be entitled to no guarantee payment in respect of the 'workless day' if the failure to provide him with work results from a 'trade dispute involving any employee of his employer or of an associated employer'; nor if:

(*a*) his employer offers to provide alternative work for that day which is suitable in all the circumstances, whether or not work which the employee is under his contract employed to perform, and the employee has unreasonably refused that offer; or,

(*b*) he does not comply with reasonable requirements imposed by his employer with a view to ensuring that his services are available'.

Finally: the employee must have been 'continuously employed for a period of four weeks ending with the last complete week' before the 'workless day'.

So any employee who has been continuously employed for four weeks before the day when he is given no work at all will, in general, be entitled to the payment—provided that the absence of work is not due to a trade dispute involving employees in the same business —and provided that he has not been offered and unreasonably refused other work nor refused to make himself available.

Next: how much and for how long?

In general, the employee will be entitled to the guaranteed minimum remuneration which he would have received, had he been so employed—with a maximum of £6 in respect of any day. And 'an employee shall not be entitled to guarantee payments in respect of more than the specified number of days'—normally five—'in any of the relevant periods'. These are 'the periods of 3 months commencing on the 1st February, 1st May, 1st August and 1st November in each year'.

Those are the broad provisions. For details, if you are unfortunate enough to need them, consult your local office of the Department of Employment. And do so before you run into disputes.

The Act recognises that (alas) disputes are inevitable. For instance, did a particular employee unreasonably refuse alternative employment? Was the workless day due to a trade dispute in which employees of an associated company were 'involved'? Was the amount of the payment correctly assessed?

Any employee who considers that his employer has refused to pay the whole or any part of a guarantee payment to which he was entitled may present a complaint to an Industrial Tribunal. As usual, he has three months from the relevant date (in this case, the workless day) within which to start his proceedings. And where a Tribunal finds a complaint well founded, it will order the employer to pay the complainant the amount of the guarantee which it finds is due to him.

If you have a collective agreement in force in your outfit under which employees are guaranteed remuneration which is at least equivalent to that provided by the statute, then you may apply to the Secretary of State for Employment for an 'exemption order'. Details of applications and qualifications are in the Act.

Hopefully, you will not have to worry about these payments. But if the workless days are endured and payments must be made, until the workings of the Act become clear, do not hesitate to take advice from the Department of Employment or, where necessary, from your lawyers. If disaster strikes and your business goes under, then the Act now ensures that the employees concerned will receive their guarantee payments. These join the list of preferential debts at the head of the queue, where a company goes into liquidation. And if there is not even enough money for the preferential creditors to receive their due, guarantee payments will be payable out of the (bolstered and reinforced) Redundancy Fund. Details in Chapter 61.

Chapter 58

Equal Pay, Sex Discrimination and Maternity Rights*

THE combination of the Equal Pay Act, the Sex Discrimination Act and the Employment Protection Act has produced a mixed blessing of staggering proportions to working women. Many of those who have jobs and can hold them are better off. But in times of unemployment, the rest must beware. Since 29 December 1975 every incentive to employ a woman in preference to a man has disappeared—except, of course, in those jobs in which employers discriminate against men because women tend to do them better. Instead, it will often be far less expensive to employ a man.

On 29 December 1975 the Equal Pay Act came into full force. It became unlawful to pay less to a woman than you would to a man in the same or like employment or whose jobs are rated on an equivalent basis. There are, of course, disputes as to whether or not the particular job is equivalent to that done by men—and any disputes are sorted out by industrial tribunals.

Whatever the expense, these rules are undoubtedly accepted by men—employers and employed—and before long people will doubtless wonder how the situation could ever have been any different. Meanwhile, the cost of employing some ladies will undoubtedly increase; some women of the more old-fashioned variety will continue to feel that the husband is the breadwinner and should get more—and some men will agree; and those who deal with

* Maternity pay date: 1 April 1977. Otherwise legislation is in full force.

pensions will regard the situation as increasingly anomalous.

After all: women may reasonably expect to live into their seventies while the expectation of life for a male is only sixty-eight; yet women can retire and receive their pensions at the age of sixty while men must wait till sixty-five. So the cost of equivalent pensions for women will, of course, be higher because they receive them earlier.

No amount of feminine logic can explain this one. I asked a certain very prominent woman politician why women should be entitled to retire at a younger age than men and she replied: 'Because, dear, they live longer'. Now, you work that one out.

As if all this were not bad enough, the Sex Discrimination Act introduced powerful amendments to the Equal Pay Act. Not surprisingly, the Act made it unlawful for anyone to discriminate against those who seek to exercise their rights under the Equal Pay Act. No one must be discriminated against 'on the ground of her sex'—nor victimised because she seeks to exercise her rights.

Again, married people of either sex are not to be discriminated against in the employment field. And (theoretically at least) the new protection will also apply to downtrodden males. Men are (for instance) now entitled to equal treatment as 'midwives'.

There are exceptions—the most important, that undertakings with five or less employees are, in general, not included. And it is only unlawful for a firm which consists of six or more partners to discriminate against a woman in either the membership of that partnership or in the terms offered to members.

All other businesses must not discriminate against females in connection with their hiring, firing, training or promotion. And the same rules protect 'contract workers'—people not employed by you but supplied by others for your business purposes.

The second exception is charmingly described. It applies 'where sex is a genuine occupational qualification'—a term which only a Parliamentary draughtsman could have produced with a straight face. 'Being a man is a genuine occupational qualification for a job', we are told, 'only where the essential nature of the job calls for authentic male characteristics, so that it would be wholly different if carried on by a woman' or where 'the job needs to be held by a man to preserve decency or privacy because it is likely to involve physical contact with men in circumstances where they might reasonably object to its being carried on by a woman'. Also, where 'the holder of the job is likely to do his work in circumstances where men might reasonably object to the presence of a woman because they are in a state of undress or are using sanitary facilities', then discrimination is permitted.

Happily, there will be no need to employ male bunny girls—nor female Catholic priests (further exception, of course, is made for religious employment). And the right not to make schools co-educational is specifically preserved.

Equal pay . . . equal rights at work . . . no discrimination or victimisation because of sex. . . so there are no financial incentives to employing women. The question: 'Whom shall I take on to fill a vacancy?' or 'Whom shall I promote?' will be answered (hopes the law) in accordance with merit and not on grounds of sex.

However: the Employment Protection Act provides special privileges that—at least in the case of women of childbearing age—may make it considerably more burdensome and expensive to employ a women than a man in the same or in an equivalent job. Breach of the Sex Discrimination Act may lead to a claim in the Industrial Tribunal which (in theory at least) could provide the successful claimant with up to £5200 compensation. But no such claim will be necessary for the lady who becomes pregnant.

The Employment Protection Act provides that 'an employee shall be treated . . . as unfairly dismissed if the reason or principal reason for her dismissal is that she is pregnant, or is any other reason connected with her pregnancy'—with two exceptions. It is not 'unfair' to dismiss a woman who 'because of her pregnancy is incapable of adequately doing the work which she is employed to do'. Second: if because of her pregnancy the employee 'cannot or will not be able to continue . . . to do that work . . . without contravention . . . of a duty or restriction imposed by or under an enactment', then it remains fair to dismiss her.

However: if there is a 'suitable available vacancy', then the woman must be offered that vacancy before or on the effective date of termination. And the new contract must take effect immediately on the termination of the previous one; the work to be done under that contract must be 'of a kind which is both suitable in relation to the employee and appropriate for her to do in the circumstances'; and the terms and conditions of that employment must not be 'substantially less favourable to her than the corresponding provisions of the previous contract'.

So you decide not to dismiss an employee (married or unmarried—

that is a question of morality or preference, not of law). Watch out. If she is 'absent from work wholly or partly because of pregnancy or confinement' then (assuming she qualifies—and probably from 1 April 1977) you must pay her 'maternity pay'. This will be 9/10ths of her normal money, minus maximum state maternity benefits. The money will be payable on usual pay days but recoverable in full from the Maternity Fund.

To qualify for maternity pay, the woman must have been 'continuously employed' for two years by the beginning of the eleventh week before the expected date of her confinement—unless you have previously dismissed her because she was incapable of doing the job as a result of her condition. If she leaves voluntarily before that date, she loses her rights.

In addition (since 1 June 1976), the qualified mother has been entitled to her job back at any time within 29 weeks of the date of her confinement—with a possible extension of four weeks, if she is unfit at the end of the 29 week period. In addition to the same qualifications as for maternity pay (two years continuous employment by start of eleventh week before confinement and staying on until that time, unless previously dismissed), she must 'where reasonably practicable' notify her employer of her intention to return, not less than three weeks before she departs. That notification must be in writing, if (but only if) the employer so requests.

In practice, you should always request that notice be given in writing. At best, put a requirement into every woman's contract that if she is absent due to pregnancy or confinement and intends to return to her job, she is requested and required to say so in writing, where reasonably practicable at least three weeks before she leaves. In any event, when a woman is leaving to have her baby, she should be seen by the appropriate supervisor and asked to sign a standard form saying that she does or does not intend to return to work.

If the mother states that she does not intend to come back, you can hire a replacement without worry. Otherwise, you are in difficulty. The Act says that the dismissal of a replacement (who will normally be protected by the unfair dismissal rules after 6 months service) may be fair if (but only if) the replacement is told that he (or she) may have to go, if and when mother returns. Naturally, it will not be easy to find a replacement who is willing to serve on that basis. Nor will you be likely to wish to appoint anyone on those terms.

These rules are unlikely to cause trouble for employees on the shop floor or in the typists' pool. If and when a mother decides to return, room can no doubt be made for her. But there is certainly a new and powerful disincentive to the employment of women in executive or managerial posts. After all, they may be incapable of doing their job for months before the birth of their babies; they could be away for at least a year—and you will have to keep their jobs open; so who now will employ a woman when a man can do the job equally well?

The Sex Discrimination Act, of course, makes it an offence to discriminate against a woman on the ground of her sex—in connection with appointment, transfer, training, promotion or any other benefits in the employment field. Unfortunately, the stringency of the new rules puts the employer on the legal spot. Comparatively few mothers do come back after childbirth—but most who know their rights now state an intention to return. After all, if they change their minds and decide not to come back, they lose nothing; but if they burn their boats by stating an intention not to return, they lose their statutory rights, however good a reason for their alteration of intent. It remains a woman's privilege to change her mind—even though the cost for the employer may be extremely high.

Chapter 59

Time off – for Trade Union and Public Duties*

ADLAI STEVENSON once remarked: 'The worst sort of thief is the man who steals my time – I can never get it back'. You can never get back the time which your employee spends on public or trade union duties —but the Employment Protection Act now recognises that—where reasonably practicable—the employee should not have to steal that time, in order to serve the interests of good industrial or public relations. Whether you like it or not—and many employers already accept the inevitable, with excellent grace—employees may often now be entitled to time off in working hours.

First, public duties.

'An employer shall permit an employee of his who is a Justice of the Peace, a member of the local authority, a member of a statutory tribunal, a member of (in England and Wales) a regional health authority or area health authority (or, in Scotland, health board)', or a manager of a local education authority, educational establish-

* Probably in force by mid-1976.

ment (or, in Scotland, a school or college council or the governing body of the central institution or a college of education), or a member of a water authority or river purification board—to take time off during the employee's working hours. The object of the time off? 'The performance of any of the duties of his office or, as the case may be, his duties as such a member.'

The duties referred to are:

'(*a*)   Attendance at a meeting of the body or any of its committees or sub-committees; or

(*b*)   The doing of any other thing approved by the body, or anything of a class so approved, for the purpose of the discharge of the functions of the body or for any of its committees or sub-committees.'

How much time must an employee be permitted to take off and on what occasions and subject to what conditions?

The answer depends in each case upon what is 'reasonable in all the circumstances'. Special regard, says the Act, must be had to the following:

'(*a*)   How much time off is required for the performance of the duties of the office or as a member of the body in question, and how much time off is required for the performance of the particular duty;

'(*b*)   How much time off has the employee already been permitted, either for public duties or for trade union work (see later); and

'(*c*)   The circumstances of the employer's business and the effect of the employee's absence on the running of that business.

For the larger firm with many employees, the absence of one man or woman for an occasional public duty will go almost unnoticed. Remove the same employee for the same time from a small outfit and it may grind to a temporary halt. Again, the employee must not be unreasonable in his demands for time off, while the employer must be reasonable in acceding to his sensible requests.

Of course, the list of public duties is limited—and the Employment Secretary may add to it. And although jury duty is not included, it need not be—you cannot refuse to permit your employees to sit on juries. They may, though, ask for their jury duty to be postponed if it would create difficulties for the business for them to be away, and courts do try to oblige in cases of that sort.

Next, if any of your employees are officials of independent trade unions, recognised by the company or firm for the purposes of collective bargaining, they are to be entitled* to time off—during working hours—for two purposes:

1   To carry out official duties 'concerned with industrial relations between the employer and any associated employer and their employees' or

2   To undergo 'training in aspects of industrial relations relevant to the carrying out of those duties.'

Again, the amount of time off which must be allowed will be that which is reasonable in all the circumstances—and in considering reasonableness, regard will be had to any current Code of Practice issued by the Advisory, Conciliation and Arbitration Service.

A trade union official given time off for industrial relations purposes (as opposed, for example, to engaging in general organisation for his union) will be entitled to his normal remuneration. But the law will not require you to pay employees who take time off for public duties.

Third: 'An employee who is given notice of dismissal by reason of redundancy shall . . . be entitled before the expiration of his notice to be allowed by his employer reasonable time off during his working hours in order to look for new employment or to make arrangements for training for future employment.'

Once more, the employee is only entitled to time off as and when it is 'reasonable' for him to take it.

What happens, then, if an employee does not get the time off to which he considers that he is reasonably entitled—for trade union or public duties or to replace the job which is about to disappear? As usual nowadays, he may complain to an industrial tribunal. Where reasonably practicable, the employee (again, as usual) has three months from the date when the complaint arose within which to bring it to the notice of the tribunal.

In the case of time off for public or trade union duties, the tribunal may award a successful claimant such compensation as it considers 'just and equitable in all the circumstances, having regard to the employer's default in failing to permit time off to be taken by the employee and to any loss sustained by the employee which is attri-

* Expected to be in force by the end of 1976.

butable to the matters complained of'. In addition, if the employer has failed to pay the employee the whole or part of any amount required to be paid as remuneration, if he properly took time off for trade union duties, then the tribunal may order the employer to pay the employee the amount which is due to him.

Where a redundant employee is not given time off to hunt or make arrangements for training for other work, then he may be awarded up to two-fifths of a normal week's pay.

If yours is a company or firm which already gives reasonable time off to employees for public or trade union duties or to search for other work when made redundant, these new rules will not affect you. But if you are an outfit which is mean in any or all of these respects, the law may now force reasonable generosity upon you.

Chapter 60

Employee's Rights in an Insolvency

UNTIL THE Employment Protection Act, anyone employed by a business which went bust was in deep trouble. He would receive his redundancy pay—all of it—from public funds. If there was a little money in the kitty, then he had certain, pathetic, preferential rights. But if the cupboard was bare, he would get no crumbs. The Employment Protection Act changes this intolerable position by increasing preferential rights to such monies as are available and by enabling any balance unpaid to come from the (suitably buttressed) Redundancy Fund. Buttressed, of course, by big additional payments to be made by solvent employers which are likely to amount to about 1 per cent of the payroll.

Preferential treatment in the winding up of a company or firm is now given to guarantee payments; remuneration on suspension on medical grounds—due to the employer's failure to comply with the rules; maternity pay; payments for time off for trade union or public duties; or remuneration under a protective award (where no sufficient warning of or consultation about proposed redundancy).

All those amounts will be recoverable by the employee from the Redundancy Fund, if the Secretary of State for Employment is satisfied not only that the employer is insolvent but that the money is not available. In addition, the following debts will also be payable from the Redundancy Fund. These additional debts are:

1   Arrears of pay for up to eight weeks.*
2   Pay in lieu of notice.*
3   Holiday pay for up to six weeks.*
4   Basic award of compensation for unfair dismissal (but not any compensatory or additional award).* And
5   Reasonable reimbursement for the whole or any part of a fee or premium paid by an apprentice or articled clerk.

In general, then, all preferential debts may (if necessary) be recovered from the Redundancy Fund; but not all money recoverable from that fund, e.g. pay in lieu, holiday pay or basic award of compensation for unfair dismissal, are preferential debts.

Chapter 61

New Redundancy Rights

THE REDUNDANCY PAYMENT ACT, 1965, took some of the sting out of being industrially unwanted. But no one with less than two years service had (or has) any right to redundancy pay; that pay is itself on a sliding scale and only the long service employees get big money (maximum today: £2400—40% of it from the Redundancy Fund); and until the Employment Protection Act no employer was bound to give any prior warning of redundancy to any employee. To this latter inequity, the Employment Protection Act has turned its attention.

In a well-known Leicester factory the management discussed a rise in pay with workers' representatives on the Thursday. They called in the Receiver on the Friday. Eighteen hundred men were put out of work—with no warning.

The directors of a northern works knew that they would shortly have to close down an entire department. Hoping, perhaps, that something would turn up, they said nothing to anyone. Three hundred men were left stranded, without notice—and, of course, with no opportunity to find alternative work.

* Up to a maximum of £80 per week.

To meet these regrettably typical cases, the new Act provides that in all large-scale redundancies where there are no 'special circumstances', the employers must inform the Secretary of State and (where appropriate) trade union representatives. Failure to do so will lead to the making of a very expensive 'protective award'. The redundant employees will be entitled (in broad terms) to be paid by the employers the same money that they would have received for the required period of warning—in addition, of course, to their redundancy pay.

An employer who proposes to dismiss as redundant an employee who belongs to a 'recognised trade union' is bound under the Act to consult representatives of that union about the dismissal. The trade union representative means an official or other person 'authorised to carry on collective bargaining with the employer in question by their trade union'.

So where the union is both independent and recognised for bargaining purposes, a representative must be 'consulted'—not merely to give its members the opportunity to look for other work but (hopefully) so that the consultations may provide suggestions from the workers' side which may help to keep the jobs alive.

Employers must consult 'at the earliest opportunity'. In any event, the Act lays down minimum consultation as follows:

1   Where the employer is proposing to dismiss as redundant a hundred or more employees at one establishment, within a period of 90 days or less, then at least 90 days before the first of those dismissals takes effect. Or

2   Where the employer is proposing to dismiss as redundant ten or more employees at one establishment, within a period of 30 days or less, then at least 60 days before the first of those dismissals takes effect.

The 'consultation' required involves disclosure in writing to the trade union representatives concerned of the following:

1   The reasons for the employer's proposals.
2   The numbers and descriptions of employees whom it is proposed to dismiss as redundant.
3   The total number of employees of any such description employed by the employer at the establishment in question.

4 The proposed method of selecting the employees who may be dismissed.
5 The proposed method of carrying out the dismissals, with due regard to any agreed procedure, including the period over which the dismissals are to take effect.

Delivery of the information must be by post to the address notified by the trade union to the employer or else to the head or main office of the union.

If there are 'special circumstances which render it not reasonably practicable for the employer to comply' with any of the above requirements, then the employer shall 'take all such steps towards compliance with that requirement as are reasonably practicable in those circumstances'.

A similar duty is imposed on all employers intending to dismiss the same number of employees at any one establishment to give the same period of notice, in writing, to the Secretary of State. And where there is a recognised, independent trade union representing the men, then he must also give a copy of the notice to representatives of that union.

A trade union that does not receive proper notice may complain to an industrial tribunal. If the employer's defence is that there were 'special circumstances' which rendered it 'not reasonably practicable for him to comply' with the rules, then the burden of proving that he comes within the exemption rests on him. And he must also prove positively that 'he took all such steps towards compliance with the requirement as were reasonably practicable in the circumstances'.

If a tribunal finds a union's complaint to have been well founded, then it will make a declaration to that effect and 'may also make a protective award'. A protective award, in effect, is an order that the employer shall pay remuneration to the employees in respect of whom notice should have been given, for a 'protected period'. This is a period beginning with the date on which the first of the dismissals to which the complaint relates takes effect or the date of the award, whichever is the earlier—and ending on such date 'as the tribunal shall determine to be just and equitable in all the circumstances, having regard to the seriousness of the employer's default'.

Maximum protective awards: where 90 days notice should have been given—90 days pay; where 60 days notice should have been given—60 days; and in any other case: 28 days.

Note the last period. Consultation is required not only in the case of large scale dismissals but in every case 'at the earliest opportunity'. The specified periods apply 'in any event'—and they are also minimum and not maximum periods. Where it is possible to give more notice, then the unfortunate employee must have longer notice of the industrial Sword of Damocles.

The rate of remuneration payable to any employee under a 'protective award' will be 'a week's pay for each week of the protected period'—or proportionately for periods of less than a week. The employee will get the same normal pay as he would have received during that period. If an employee considers that he has not received proper payment under the protective award, then he may complain to an industrial tribunal which may order the employer to pay the appropriate sum.

An employer who fails to give notice to the Employment Secretary is liable to be fined up to £400. In addition, failure to notify unions or the Secretary of State will give the Secretary of State power to reduce the amount of the rebate which would normally be payable from the Redundancy Payments Fund 'by such proportion (not exceeding 1/10th) as appears to the Secretary of State to be appropriate in the circumstances'.

It follows that redundancies must be planned and notified as far in advance as possible. Failure to do so where there is no recognised trade union and which results in failure to notify the Secretary of State may lead to a comparatively small fine, and/or the loss of up to 1/10th of the redundancy rebate. Failure to notify the appropriate union may cost a small fortune—the employer will have to produce not merely his share of the redundancy payment (plus, where the Minister sees fit, up to 10 per cent of that proportion of the payment which would normally come from the Redundancy Payments Fund). He may also have to pay employees their normal remuneration—with no upper limit—and up to a maximum in some cases of 90 days.

Naturally, if the employer is insolvent, the various penalties will become irrelevant. It is businesses that stay alive which will suffer. And protective awards join the category of 'preferential debts', where the employer is insolvent; and if there is insufficient cash in the (extinct) employer's kitty to pay the award even though it has been given preference, the entire award will be produced by the Redundancy Payments Fund.

So if redundancies are in the offing, you should anticipate them as far ahead as reasonably possible—and give notice accordingly. Undue delay may now prove more painful for you than for your dismissed employees.

"DEAR SIR, WITH REGARD TO YOUR NEGLIGENCE CLAIM AGAINST YOUR EMPLOYERS, OCEAN LINERS LIMITED . . . . "

Part Six

Health, Safety and Pollution

Chapter 62

Duties To Employees

EVERY year, over 500 lives are lost and over 500,000 people are injured in industrial accidents. The object of the Health and Safety at Work Act is to combat this carnage. The industrial hazards that will (everyone hopes) be avoided by employees are matched by the hideous consequences that may flow from the Act, for employers —including Board members—who either do not know or who ignore the law.

Section 36: 'Where an offence . . . committed by a body corporate is proved to have been committed with the *consent* or *connivance* of, or to have been attributable to any *neglect* on the part of, any *director, manager, secretary* or other similar officer . . . or a person who is purporting to act in any such capacity, he as well as the body corporate shall be guilty of that offence and shall be liable to be proceeded against and punished accordingly.'

So the company may be prosecuted—and if convicted on indictment (by a jury) may be fined an unlimited sum. The guilty executive may not only be fined an unlimited sum but also (in some cases) imprisoned for up to two years.

The main effect of the Act is to transfer the civil law on industrial injuries into the realm of crime. You can insure against your civil liability to injured employees—but no insurer will stand in your place in the dock, nor vegetate on your behalf in your prison cell.

Section 2 creates the main general duties. Every employer must 'ensure, as far as is reasonably practicable, the health, safety and welfare at work of all his employees'. At civil law, he must not submit his employees to unnecessary risk. In criminal law, he may be prosecuted if he does not take 'all reasonably practicable steps' to look after his employees at work.

To make sure that there is no doubt as to the breadth of the employer's duty, the Act spells it out. Among the matters to which the duty extends are:

> 'The provision and maintenance of *plant* and *systems of work* that are, so far as is reasonably practicable, safe and without risk to health . . .

Arrangements for ensuring, so far as is reasonably practicable, safety and absence of risks to health in connection with the *use, handling, storage* and *transport* of articles and substances . . .

The provision of such *instruction, training* and *supervision* as is necessary to ensure so far as is reasonably practicable, the health and safety at work of his employees . . .

The maintenance of any *place of work* in a condition which is safe and without risk to health . . .

The provision and maintenance of a *working environment* that is not only so far as is reasonably practicable, safe and without risk to health, but also 'adequate as regards facilities and arrangements for their *welfare* at work.'

Note that last phrase. If you do not take reasonable steps to provide adequate facilities for your employees' welfare at work, you may be convicted of a criminal offence, and (in theory at least) severely punished.

Nor must you keep your duty secret. You must prepare and, when necessary, revise 'a written statement of your general policy with regard to the health and safety at work of your employees and the organisation and arrangements for the time being in force for the carrying out of that policy'—and you must bring that statement and any revision to the notice of all your employees.

Regulations have been made to provide for the appointment of representatives by 'recognised trade unions', to represent employees in consultations with employers. It is now every employer's duty to consult such representatives 'with a view to the making and maintenance of arrangements which will enable him and his employees to co-operate effectively in promoting and developing measures to ensure the health and safety at work of the employees and in checking the effectiveness of such measures'.

The protection of the Act goes beyond employees. 'It shall be the duty of every employer', says Clause 3, 'to conduct his undertaking in such a way as to ensure, so far is reasonably practicable, that *persons not in his employment* who may be affected thereby are not thereby exposed to risks to their health or safety'.

Suppose that you create noise, vibration, smoke or dust from your factory. Your neighbours are affected? There is a risk to their health? Then you are liable to be prosecuted—along with your company. (For duties to visitors, see next chapter.)

Non-domestic premises are covered. Where you have a place

of work used by people not employed by you or used as a place where people not in your employment 'may use any plant or substance provided for their use there', then you must take all due care for their health and safety.

Launderettes are covered. So (for example) are car parks, social and sporting clubs, sites and other premises which you provide but others use. You are required by law to keep your visitors to your premises safe, on pain of potential prison.

Now for real trouble: 'It shall be the duty of any person who *designs, manufactures, imports* or *supplies'* any article or substance 'for use at work' to take all reasonably practicable steps to ensure that the article or substance is safe. He must carry out any necessary testing, research or examination. If he does not 'eliminate or minimise' risks, so far as he can, he may be prosecuted.

At present, a manufacturer, designer or importer owes a duty of care at common law, not to cause injury, loss or damage to 'the ultimate consumer' of his product. But that is a duty enforceable only by bringing a claim for damages in a civil court. The new duties may now be banged home by the criminal courts.

One way of discharging the duty is for the designer, manufacturer, importer or supplier of an article (as opposed to a substance) to obtain a written undertaking from his immediate supplier that the supplier has taken steps sufficient to ensure that the article will be safe.

Happily, others must still take care for themselves and for the safety of others. Every employee must avoid negligent acts, liable to harm the health or safety of himself or of others. And he must 'co-operate . . . so far as is necessary' to see that the new rules are complied with.

If an employee refuses to use safety clothing or equipment, you may be entitled to dismiss him, If he is injured, you may prove contributory negligence—alleging that his own stupidity was the whole or partial cause of his own misfortune. If you have used sufficient 'publicity, propaganda and persuasion' to induce him to make use of the clothing or equipment provided, then you should be in the clear. This is old law. Now, in addition, the employee may himself be prosecuted.

Those are some of the main rules, laid down by the Act. Other hideous possibilities lie lurking in new powers given by the Act to the Government of the day. These come into two categories:

Regulations and Codes of Practice.

The power to make health and safety regulations is almost unlimited. These may cover almost any area of industrial or commercial life where there are any worries about the health and welfare of workers. Without Parliament having the chance to amend these rules, they will create new crimes with major penalties.

When an Act goes through Parliament, it may be amended—and usually is. MPs may accept one part and reject another. The public has reasonable protection against parliamentary mistakes.

Not so with regulations. Delegated legislation is a potential menace of the first order. Parliament may consider the regulations; it may have the opportunity to reject them; but it will have no power to amend. Instead, Parliament has created a 'comprehensive and integrated system of law', with new powers of delegated legislation attached to it.

A 'Health and Safety Commission' and 'Executive' have been created. The job of the Commission includes the duty to 'assist and encourage' . . . to make 'such arrangements as it considers appropriate' for the carrying out of research and for the provision of training and information . . . to institute enquiries into accidents . . . and to keep all interested parties properly informed as to the law—and above all, to submit to the Government of the day 'such proposals as it considers appropriate for the making . . . of regulations. . . .'

You may be prosecuted, fined or imprisoned even if no accident takes place. But if your business is afflicted by a disaster, you may expect the new Commission to descend upon you and to carry out enquiries. The powers of prosecution, though, rest with the new Executive, through the factory inspectors and, generally, via legal authorities.

The Commission has begun to issue 'Codes of Practice'. Like the Highway Code and the Code of Industrial Practice, the Health and safety Codes have powerful persuasive force. You cannot be either prosecuted or sued for breach of the Highway Code—but any breach may be quoted in evidence against you in a civil or criminal action. The same applies to the Health and Safety Codes. You contravene them at your peril.

It is the duty of the executive to make 'adequate arrangements for enforcement'. Normally, the local authorities have the delegated delight of keeping you in line with the new regulations. Intention? To establish an integrated inspectorate. In the past, a machine or system may be approved as safe in one part of the country and proscribed in another. Now, there should be one standard for all.

Happily, it is unlikely that the offender will be clobbered by the law, without due warning. An inspector comes onto your premises and decides that some arrangement is unsafe or some facility inadequate? Then he will probably serve an 'Improvement Notice', requiring you to put matters right within the period specified.

Alternatively, if the inspector considers that the activity concerned involves a 'risk of serious personal injury', he may serve a 'Prohibition Notice', requiring the activity to be discontinued forthwith. Only if one of these notices is flouted will the offender be likely to find himself—personally and/or his company—literally as well as metaphorically in the dock.

General rules apply, then, to all employers—as well as to manufacturers, designers, importers, suppliers—and those who erect or who install machinery or equipment. But the Act also extends the scope and coverage of building regulations. If construction comes within the activities of your company, you should take special advice on the new arrangements. Equally, if you provide materials for building, prepare for new controls.

Where you can show that an offence is 'due to the act or default of some other person', you may wriggle off the legal hook and leave that 'other person' dangling. Thanks to a peculiarly unfortunate House of Lords decision in the case of *Tesco* v. *Nattrass*, an 'other person' may be a member of your own staff. In other words, if you can show that you set up a proper system but someone whom you employ failed to carry that system into full effect, then he may take the blame and you and your company will escape. Details in chapter 66.

The present statutory rules remain in force. The Factories Act and the Offices, Shops and Railway Premises Act—and the regulations made under them—have lost none of their force. But they are now supplemented by a mighty edifice of almost unlimited extent. And while it is splendid to be provided with defences, so that you may be acquitted once you are charged, it is infinitely better not to be charged at all.

The Act specifically stated that it was not intended to change the civil law. Whatever its intentions, the changes are mighty. If one of your employees is injured due to a breach of your duties under (say) the Factories Act, he will claim damages for breach of statutory duty. The new Act provides a mass of novel 'statutory duties'. Break them and you may be prosecuted. But if the breach causes an accident, you may also be sued. A conviction will almost certainly lead to civil liability. At worst, you had better hope that your insurers will foot the new Bill.

Chapter 63

Duties to Contractors and Other Visitors

SECTION 2 of the Health and Safety at Work Act imposes responsibilities on *employers* for the health and safety of their *employees* at work. Whether those employees are at work in your plant, office or workshop; travelling in their cars or yours, but about your business; or working for you on someone else's premises—you must take such steps as are 'reasonably practicable' to keep them safe and well.

An employee on what lawyers charmingly call 'an independant frolic' is unprotected. He is not then 'at work'—even if he happens to be on your premises.

Conversely, the Act defines premises with remarkable width. The word includes not only your buildings and your site but also (*inter alia*) your vehicles. Provided that your employee is doing your work (even in an improper, unauthorised or forbidden way), you must do what is 'reasonably practicable' to look after him.

Naturally, the further your employee wanders from your supervision, the less 'reasonably practicable' it is likely to be for you to look after him. In general, though the less the supervision the greater the training; the greater the responsibility shouldered by the employee the more careful the employer must be in selecting him for the work.

Section 3 is brief. Its major clause reads: 'It shall be the duty of every employer to conduct his undertaking in such a way as to ensure, so far as is reasonably practicable, that persons not in his employment who may be affected thereby are not thereby exposed to risks to the health or safety'. Your undertaking is your business—whether you are an industrialist, a trader or a professional advisor. You are now required by the criminal law to take such steps as are 'reasonably practicable' to protect not merely those who you employ but others who are affected by your business or profession.

Take, first, those who visit your premises in what the Occupiers' Liability Act describes as 'the exercise of their calling'. The contractor and the sub contractor; the insulator and the window cleaner; the erector and the installer . . . the architect, surveyor or doctor . . . the representative coming to sell or the buyer to purchase. All visit in the course of their jobs.

The civil law has long required that you comply with a 'common duty of care' to all of them. You must take such care as is reasonable in all the circumstances for their safety. And the civil law expects that these experts will take reasonable steps to guard themselves and their employees against risks 'ordinarily incidental to their calling'.

The fact, then, that someone is on your premises to do his job does not free you from your responsibility to take such care as is reasonable for his safety and that of those whom he employs. But he has duties (in civil law, to avoid negligence, and in criminal law to comply with Section 2 of the new Act) to do what he reasonably can for their safety. The master owes a duty to his servants—and the occupier to his visitors.

Happily, your visitors owe like duties to you and to your employees. In civil law, they are required to avoid negligence. And under Section 3 of the Act, just as you owe a duty to them, so they owe an equivalent duty to you—and breach of that duty may render them liable to precisely the same, tough penalties as your breach of your obligations to them and theirs.

Or take children. The Occupiers' Liability Act says that you must expect them to take less care of themselves than would adults in similar circumstances. And recent court rulings have made it plain that visitors in general and children in particular may be regarded as lawful guests, even when you would consider them to be trespassing. You owe both a legal and a moral duty to those whom you ought reasonably to expect will be on your premises.

In criminal law, now, that duty becomes more pronounced and

far more dangerous to flout. You must take care for the safety of all your visitors—and they must reciprocate—on pain of potential penalties.

How, then, should you cope in practice with the contractor or sub-contractor who erects an unsafe scaffold, leaves wiring, tools or boxes lying around or behaves in some other way which you regard as a danger—either to himself or to your employees?

No longer can you afford to turn a blind eye and hope for the best. If you observe the danger and do nothing about it, then you may be 'consenting' to its continuation. Any active participation in the misdeed is 'connivance'. Any failure to take proper steps is 'neglect'—and any director, manager, company secretary—or, indeed, any individual—who consents to, connives at or neglects to cope with a hazard is liable not only to the same indeterminate fine as the company which employs him—but (as an individual—however mighty) to a maximum of two years imprisonment.

So complain about the hazard to the visitors; remonstrate with the boss; and if special tact is required, then telephone and speak to someone at the top of the visiting outfit. Refer to the duties under the Act; whisper a warning that the factory inspector is expected at any moment—and you are almost certain to get both results and thanks, speedily and in a way which should remove the hazard to the benefit of all at risk.

Today, then, each of us is his brother's keeper—at least in the eyes of the criminal law on health and safety at work.

Chapter 64

Duties to Customers and Clients

ALMOST every manufacturer has vessels or substances on his premises that could explode or ignite—and any such explosion would probably cause havoc and potential death. With the echoes of Flixborough ringing in all our ears, we now ask: who would today be responsible if an accident is caused through faulty design or manufacture? Section 6 of the Health and Safety at Work Act provides (in effect) that the blame will lie on the guilty party.

'It shall be the duty of any person who designs, manufactures, imports or supplies' any *article* for use at work, to take such steps as are reasonably practicable—through research, testing and examination and the provision of adequate information which will allow the article to be properly used—to ensure that it will not cause damage. And similar rules cover those who manufacture, import or supply *substances* for use at work.

The Act only applies (with some probable extensions beyond territorial waters) within the jurisdiction of the courts of the United Kingdom. Designers, manufacturers and suppliers within that territory are covered.

However: those who import their plant or machinery are equally at risk from the new criminal law. As the tentacles of the courts cannot extend to the lands of manufacture, they catch hold of the goods—and those who import them—when they cross our frontier.

Who is an 'importer'? If you import through an agent, for example, who bears the new burden? That is a pure question of fact. If the agent is acting for you—if he is your agent—then you are the principal—and hence the importer. If, on the other hand, the import agent is in reality the principal in the transaction and is selling you the goods, then the responsibility will be his.

Now suppose that a disaster occurs in your plant. A vessel explodes and an employee is killed. Who bears the responsibility?

In civil law, there are numerous potential defendants to an action. The following questions would be asked:

1   Did you fail in your duties as employer, sufficiently to instruct or train the people dealing with the vessel to ensure that they did their job in a safe manner?

2   Was the erector or installer at fault—perhaps because he failed to pass on proper instructions or because he sealed off a safety valve?

3   Was the real responsibility that of the manufacturer, because he produced defective goods—or provided insufficient instructions in their use or operation?

4   Was the defect one of design—in which case, had the designer carried out adequate research or testing, to ensure (insofar as he reasonably could) that the vessel was safe? Had he failed to do his job in a proper and workmanlike manner and in accordance with standards which one would expect of the person of his

standing, skill training and experience?

5   Was the fault that of the person harmed? Was he wholly or partly responsible for his own disaster, through his 'contributory negligence'?

The blame, then, may be that of one party—or it may be shared between two or more. And the damages will be sorted out between the parties—or, to be more precise, between their insurers.

Today, identical questions will be asked by the factory inspector or, where appropriate, by those who take part in an enquiry, set up by the Commission on Industrial Relations. Upon the answer to those questions will depend not merely which insurers (if any) are likely to pay (and how much and to whom)—but also: Who will be prosecuted and with what result?

Today, then, there is a mighty new duty imposed not merely on employers for the health and safety of their own employees and that of others—visitors, passersby, neighbours and strangers alike—who are affected by their 'undertaking'. The legal (and criminal) duty stretches also to all those who design, manufacture, supply, import, erect or install industrial plant or machinery or substances intended for use at work.

Chapter 65

Your Personal Liabilities

THE OBJECT of the Health and Safety at Work etc. Act? To save lives and limbs . . . to cut down the rate of industrial injuries, physical and mental—caused by over a quarter of a million accidents at work, each year.

No one enjoys imposing fines on business enterprises or on their executives nor, still less, sending company directors or secretaries, managers or executives, shop stewards or workers to prison. Punishment is a last resort—but if making an example of a few will save the lives of many, then watch out. The Act puts everyone in peril, from the bottom of the industrial or commercial heap to the peak of achievement.

The company itself may be fined but it can scarcely languish behind the wrong sort of bars. That privilege is reserved for those by whom it acts.

Section 37: 'Where an offence committed . . . by a body corporate' —that is, a company, statutory or local authority or anyone other than an individual or a firm—'is proved to have been committed with the consent or connivance of, or to have been attributable to any neglect on the part of' the individuals named, they will be guilty of the offence.

'Consent' . . . 'connivance'. . . . 'neglect'—those are the key words. The individuals? 'Any director, manager, secretary or other similar officer of the body corporate or a person who was purporting to act in any such capacity.' Any executive, then, or anyone who is acting in an executive role.

The company may still be convicted, but the individual himself will be guilty and 'liable to be proceeded against and punished accordingly'.

'Where the affairs of the body corporate are managed by its members, the preceding . . . shall apply in relation to the acts and defaults of a member in connection with his functions of management as if he were a director of the body corporate. Members of boards, of corporations and of other 'bodies' must watch out.

Naturally, the mere fact that you are a servant or agent, an executive or officer of a company will not of itself make you criminally liable—under this Act or any other—for its wrong doings. You must have played some personal part in the affair.

A woman was chairman of a company which operated gaming establishments. The company failed to obtain appropriate licences and she was prosecuted and convicted.

The conviction was set aside on appeal. The chairman was non-executive; she had no knowledge of the offence; she had played no part in it—and on the wording of the statute concerned, she was not to be held personally liable merely because she held office.

In the new Act, the prosecution must prove 'consent', 'connivance' or 'neglect'.

To 'consent' means to agree to the commission of the offence. To 'connive' at its commission imports not merely a positive approval but some sort of active role—perhaps a deliberate closing of both eyes.

It is the word 'neglect', though, which provides wider scope. You 'neglect' your duties if you are guilty of some act of omission which has led, directly or indirectly, to the commission of the offence.

If you are a mere non-executive director, then 'neglect' may not bother you. But if the Act is flouted and you should have done something to ensure that it was complied with—either through training, supervision . . . personally or by delegation . . . then you are one of those at whom the Act points an accusing finger. You may find yourself (literally as well as metaphorically) in the dock.

Chapter 66

Passing the Buck

WITH maximum penalties as hideous as two years' imprisonment and an unlimited fine, the Health and Safety at Work Act places a new and shining premium on passing the legal buck. 'It weren't me what done it' has made a quick (but not unique) shift from class-room to court.

The famous case of *Tesco Supermarkets Limited* v. *Nattrass* pointed the way to the successful blaming of managers for the faults of the company. Potential defences open to those charged with 'applying false trade descriptions' to goods or services are much the same as those provided for people who fail to take reasonably practicable steps to protect the health, safety or welfare of employees at work or of others affected by that work.

Washing powder was displayed at a Tesco Supermarket at a reduced price. A pensioner tried to find a packet at the special offer rate but was told that there were none in stock. She bought one at the higher price and reported the company to the Weights and Measures Authorities, who prosecuted under Section 11 of the Trade Descriptions Act, which makes it an offence to offer to supply goods after giving 'by whatever means, any indication likely to be taken as an indication that goods are being offered at a price less than that at which they are in fact being offered'.

There was no dispute on the facts, but Tesco's relied on a special defence. They claimed 'that the commission of the offence was due to a mistake or to reliance on information supplied to them or to the act or default of another person, an accident or some other cause beyond their control'—and maintained that they 'took all reasonable precautions and exercised all due diligence to avoid the commission of such an offence by themselves or any person under their control'.

They proved that they had set up an excellent system and that the offence resulted from the failure of their manager properly to operate that system. He (they said) was 'another person'.

The magistrates held that the manager was not 'another person' but was acting as servant or agent of the company and that therefore the company could not rely on his failure to do his job. The prosecution appealed and the Divisional Court held that the manager was 'another person' but that as a person 'acting in a managerial or supervisory capacity' had failed to exercise due diligence, the company must take the legal responsibility. Tesco's appealed to the House of Lords.

'I find it almost impossible to suppose', said Lord Reid, 'that Parliament or any reasonable body of men would as a matter of policy think it right to make employers criminally liable for the acts of some of their servants but not for those of others. I find it incredible that a draftsman, aware of that intention, would fail to insert any words to express it . . . I think that it was plainly intended to make a just and reasonable distinction between the employer who is wholly blameless and ought to be acquitted and the employer who is in some way at fault, leaving it to the employer to prove that he is in no way to blame.

'What good purpose would be served by making an employer criminally responsible for the misdeeds of some of his servants but not for those of others? A board of directors can delegate part of their functions of management so as to make their delegate an embodiment of the company in the sphere of the delegation. But here the board never delegated any part of their functions. They set up a chain of command through . . . supervisors, but they remained in control. The shop managers had to obey their general directions and also to take orders from their supervisors. The acts or omissions of shop managers were not acts of the company itself'.

This remarkable view—that the acts of managers, supervisors or other executives are not in the circumstances 'acts of the company itself'—was supported by all the other law lords. Lord Dilhorne, for instance, said that managers in a large business 'cannot properly be regarded as part of the company's directing mind and will and so can come within the reference to "another person".'

'To treat the duty of an employer to exercise due diligence as unperformed unless due diligence is also exercised by all his servants to whom he has reasonably given proper instructions and on whom he could reasonably rely to carry them out', said Lord Diplock, 'would destroy the power of the defence provided and thwart the clear intention of Parliament.'

There are those who maintain that it could not have been 'the clear intention of Parliament' that managers should be prosecuted in place of men. But while there is considerable variation of approach and system as between enforcement authorities in various parts of the country, managers—sometimes together with their companies, sometimes on their own—are feeling the full force of the old law. They must now beware of further miseries.

Section 36 of the Act provides that where 'the commission by any person of an offence under any of the relevant statutory provisions is due to the act or default of some other person, that other person shall be guilty of the offence, and a person may be charged with and convicted of the offence by virtue of this sub-section whether or not proceedings are taken against the first mentioned person'.

Whether or not the company is prosecuted, the executive is at risk. The company which wishes either to preserve its high reputation for looking after the health, safety and welfare of its employees—or which is merely mean and nasty and ready and willing to cast off the blame on individuals, when it can—may certainly rely upon this section which, in combination with the decision in Tesco's case, will provide it with a let out—provided, of course, that the company—like Tesco—had set up a first-class system and that it was the manager who was himself at fault.

So while the company may elbow its way out of trouble by legal buck-passing, the executive may himself be in the front rank of the accused.

Chapter 67

Inducing Employees to Obey the Safety Rules

IT IS NOT enough for the business or professional man to supply employees with all necessary plant, materials and appliances, including safety equipment. He must also do his best to ensure that his employees make use of that which he provides.

If an employee fails to take the precautions specified by you, then you may still be held liable (in whole or in part) if he is injured as a result. Courts have held that in addition to providing safety guards and equipment, the employer must 'use all reasonable persuasion and propaganda' to induce his employee to use that equipment.

Under the Health and Safety at Work Act the employer's civil liability for the safety of his employees is turned into a criminal responsibility. Fail to take all steps that are reasonably practicable to ensure that your employees are safe in and about their work and your company or firm may be fined an unlimited sum and/or you and any other director, manager or other officer may be fined and imprisoned for up to two years. It is therefore vital not to be legally guilty of any 'consent, connivance or neglect'.

It follows that—for the safety and welfare both of your company, its employees and yourself—you must 'persuade and propagandise' your employees—whether in shop or works—to take proper care for themselves. They may prefer not to use guards or equipment because these slow down their work and reduce their piece work earnings; because they find the equipment uncomfortable, guards clumsy; or out of laziness. Whatever the reason, here is a suggested procedure, designed to put the maximum, fair pressure on employees to look after their own safety—and so to avoid civil or (eventually) criminal liability which may otherwise fall on the company and/or on you.

1   Check that the system of working and the equipment concerned are really adequate and satisfactory.
2   Train, instruct and supervise the employees in the use of the system and/or equipment.
3   Consult any workers' organisation or committee, so that they fully understand the arrangements and approve of them—and

seek their help in the enforcement of the rules.

4   Speak personally to the employee who is not complying with the rules; emphasise the importance of doing so; and warn him of the consequences of failure.

5   Refer the employee to Sections 7 and 8 of the Act which required the employee to take proper care of his own safety and not to interfere with safety equipment and the like—and which (theoretically, at least) render him liable to the same penalties for breach as the employing company or managers.

6   If the oral request to reform fails, deliver a written one, preferably by hand. If possible, obtain a signed receipt, acknowledging the warning.

7   If danger (actual or potential) is being caused to fellow employees, emphasise the unfairness of the conduct to others.

8   If dangerous behaviour persists, consider dismissal. Factors to be taken into account include:
   (a) the nature and extent of the danger—to the employee himself and to others;
   (b) the effect of dismissal on good industrial relations;
   (c) the employee's length of service, degree of responsibility and general conduct; and,
   (d) all the other circumstances of the case which might make the dismissal 'unfair', so as to give the employee a right to compensation.

9   Collate documentation—including records of efforts to persuade employees to take care; discussions with safety representatives, trade unions and/or fellow workers.

10   Deliver a second written warning, stating:
   (a) if applicable, that further non-compliance will leave you with no alternative other than to dismiss; and in any event,
   (b) drawing attention to previous warnings and to Health and Safety at Work Act rules; and stating that no responsibility can in any event be accepted by the company in the event of the risk giving rise to injury loss or damage to employee. (*But note*: This disclaimer may be of help in a civil action but it will not necessarily free the employers from liability).

11   Consider whether equipment or system of work requires redesigning, either to remove employees' objections or so as to make it impossible for the machine or equipment to be used in

the dangerous manner complained of.

You will not necessarily wish to use the above steps in the order given. Adapt them, as best suited to your business and circumstances. But follow the rules and it can hardly be said that you did not take 'reasonable steps' to influence your employee.

In the event of an accident, you would probably avoid liability— the employee's responsibility would be 100 per cent. He knew of the dangers; you could prove your case; and the responsibility would be his.

Equally, if you are prosecuted either under the Factories Act, the Offices, Shops and Railways Premises Act, or under the 1974 Act, your defences would be well prepared.

Chapter 68

New Procedures for the New Act

FACED with the stark prospect of huge penalties under the Health and Safety at Work etc. Act, all business and professional men must brush up their procedures and prepare to avoid legal battle. The main problems can be broken down into 11 areas of concern. Here is a checklist. Cover each point and—with luck—you should be safe.

* * *

1 Contracts of Employment
What changes should you make in your employees' contracts of employment or service, so as to take the new Act into account? Consider especially the following:

1   Should you include a term that employee will submit to medical examinations at the request of the management. A refusal to accept this term will cast inevitable suspicion on the person's health.
2   A requirement that the employee will wear protective clothing

and/or make full use of all guards or other equipment provided for his safety.

3   A requirement that the employee will co-operate in all safety procedures.

Your new contracts may provide that failure to comply with these rules may result in dismissal. The employee will then at least know where he stands and be unable to allege that you have sprung a legal surprise upon him.

2   Medical Examinations

Do you arrange medical examinations (1) for existing employees; or (2) for prospective employees? If so, are you satisfied that these are sufficient? Have you made adequate arrangements for resident or consultant doctors—with job specifications for them to include the requirement that they supervise your compliance with your duties under the Act. They should equip themselves with the rules; make any necessary inspections within your premises or concerning your processes. The Act does not specifically require medical examinations, although Regulations to do so may be made under the Act. But are you taking all 'reasonably practical' steps to protect employees if you do not provide medical testing?

3   Employers and Safety Measures

Do you operate a sufficiently firm and safe procedure to deal with employees who fail or refuse to make use of safety clothing, equipment or procedures? You must plan methods; establish procedures; insist that these be followed with as much firmness as those established in accordance with the Code of Industrial Relations for dismissal purposes; and you must decide whether and when to dismiss employees who refuse to take sufficient care for the safety of themselves and for that of their colleagues.

4   Bomb Warnings

The Industrial concern which does not suffer from 'bomb scares' is extremely fortunate. You will already have and (hopefully, keep well oiled) procedures to deal with fires or fire alarms. Similar procedures are essential for bomb scares.

Consult your local police; if co-operation from authorities is inadequate, either in connection with advice or search, then consider seeking pressures from your trade association or chamber of commerce. Also: Are you satisfied that your security arrangements are sufficient to deter would-be bombers? And have you arranged for your mail to be scanned, when letter bomb outrages are in vogue?

5 Insurance

Most insurance policies contain exclusion clauses. Check your policies with care, to ensure that you will remain insured, in spite of the Act. If there are exclusions in respect, for example, of breaches of the Act or damage, etc., caused by bombs, then you may have to pay an additional premium in order to exclude the exclusions. If in doubt, consult your insurance brokers or your insurers.

6 Written Statements

The Act requires all employers to prepare and, where necessary, to revise written statements of the policy, organisation and arrangements they made for the safety and health of their employees. The statements must be brought to the notice of all employees.

Do you provide a statement to all employees, separately or as part of your works or organisational rules? If so, then you may be left with the problem of providing detailed instructions for each process or job. Guidance from the Health & Safety Commission requires you to identify the main hazards affecting each job and to state how these hazards may be avoided. Details in Chapter 69.

7 Documentation

Breaches of the Act may prove extremely serious. It is therefore vital for you to prepare your defences in advance. This may best be done by a careful system of documentation.

The object of the documents: to show that your safety, health and welfare arrangements are in accordance with the Act and any default is that of 'some other person' and is not your fault.

Management at every level must be prepared to prove that they prepared and passed on adequate instructions to the next level down. Where sufficiently important, documents should be not only provided but signed copies obtained and filed.

Alternatively, documents may go up the line. For instance, you may consider that certain procedures require improvement; that machinery should be adapted or changed; or that more employees are needed for a particular operation, in the interests of safety. If you wish to be able to prove that you passed on this advice to higher authority, then put that advice into writing and keep a copy.

8 Warning the Board

Are the company's top executives aware of the new legal risks to them personally? Directors, secretaries, managers—all are equally in peril. So everyone from the chairman down should be warned of his responsibility under the new Act.

Conversely: has adequate training—including instructions and warnings arising from the new Act—reached down to foremen, shop stewards and operatives? Do your procedures for establishing or maintaining communication between various levels of management of safety, health and welfare matters require overhaul?

9 Training

The Act specifically requires adequate training, in the interests of safety and health. Are your current training methods adequate at every level and are you giving sufficient authority to your training, personnel or safety officers or managers?

10 Consultations and Committees

Responsibility on safety matters is spread over every level. Consultation should be aimed at ensuring that better and not worse relations are created due to the inevitable shared responsibility.

Regulations have been made, requiring consultation with workers through their 'recognised trade unions'. Have you established sufficient consultation'? Are your 'safety watchdogs' properly trained?

Safety committees should be set up. If you already operate a safety committee, are you satisfied that it meets sufficiently often; that there is sufficient involvement of both management and workers in its efforts; and that it has sufficient backing from the Board?

11 Supplying Information

The Act recognises that those fully informed on safety and health matters are least likely to suffer injury. Specific information is required under four heads. Do you supply it?

1 Employers are required by Section 2 to provide all necessary information to employees; this will be set out in the written statements and also in instructions concerning specific machinery or equipment.

2   Section 3 requires occupiers to provide adequate information to visitors, neighbours and the general public. Take special care to ensure that visiting children and those who have charge of them (including cleaners and lorry drivers) are fully and carefully warned of any special dangers to children in their care.

3   Section 4 requires occupiers and those in control of non-domestic premises to provide adequate information to those who use equipment provided by them on such premises—which include not only launderettes and car parks but also social and sporting clubs, provided or operated as part of the employer's undertaking.

4   Section 6 requires many factories, designers, importers and suppliers of plant, components and substances designed or intended for use at work to provide all necessary information to users.

The information should be supplied, wherever necessary, in writing. Is your documentation sufficient?

12   Problems for Buyers

Section 6 (6) provides that there is no need to repeat testing or examination carried out by others; and where the buyer is supplied by a written undertaking by the seller, he is freed from his responsibility. Therefore all buyers and purchasing departments should reconsider their procedures to ensure that they require details of testing and examination carried out by their suppliers; and further to require the provision of written undertakings by all suppliers.

Conversely, sellers must be prepared to provide details of testing and of examination, plus written undertakings. Are these available for your customers.

*   *   *

Most industrial and commercial concerns already operate excellent procedures in some of the above respects. Thanks to the new Act, all these procedures must be complied with by those who wish to avoid the risk of infringing the rules and suffering heavy penalties. As always, Parliament hopes that the existence of the penalties will avoid the necessity for their use. So check the above list with care and get your procedures and documentation into first-class order.

Chapter 69

Written Statements of Policy, Organisation and Arrangements

COMMENTING in the House of Commons on the Flixborough disaster, Harold Walker MP (the then responsible Minister) said: had the Act been in force at that time, there would have been no hesitation in bringing prosecutions before Crown Courts ('on indictment')—Maximum penalties: 2 years' imprisonment and/or unlimited fines. He also emphasised the responsibility of every level of employer, from Boardroom downwards, for ensuring compliance with the rules.

One of the first requirements which every business or professional man should by now have complied with? The issuing of a written statement of his health and safety policy, organisation and arrangements—on his own behalf and, where appropriate, on behalf of his company or firm. The Inspectorate has allowed latitude to those who are taking time so as to produce a statement properly. But the Act provides no time limit—and the sooner your statement is prepared and 'made available' to all your employees, the better. Here, then, are the rules, together with guidance (from the Health and Safety Commission and from experience) on how to apply them.

*　　*　　*

Section 2 (3) of the Act reads: 'Except in such cases as may be prescribed, it shall be the duty of every employer to prepare—and as often as may be appropriate, to revise—a written statement of his general policy with respect to the health and safety at work of his employees'.

Exceptions: undertakings with less than five employees. If you employ four or less people in your entire company, firm or undertaking, then you are excluded. The fact that each office may have a small staff is irrelevant. The law looks at the totality.

So you must prepare, as soon as possible—and, where necessary, revise—a written statement of your general policy on health and safety.

So far, no difficulty. 'Our company gives paramount importance to the health and safety at work of employees. . . .' 'The Health and Safety at Work Act enables us to restate our company's policy: that every level of management is expected to give top priority to the health and safety at work of all employees. . . .' 'The health and safety at work of employees is a major concern of your Board. . . . Our policy is to take all reasonably practicable steps for the protection not only of employees but all others affected by our undertaking. . . .'

In business, as in Government, it is far easier to state a policy than to carry it out. The sub-section therefore requires the written statement to include details of 'the organisation . . . for the time being in force for carrying out that policy'.

What is your safety organisation? Do you have one? Is there a safety officer in your outfit—and if so, then is he properly trained?

To whom should your employees turn if they consider that a particular practice is unsafe? If yours is a larger outfit, do you have a safety committee? What steps do you take to enable your employees to make their views felt on safety and health matters?

The Health and Safety Commission has issued regulations, requiring you to consult with appointed representatives of recognised trade unions. If you deal with trade unions for the purpose of collective bargaining, you must consult them—as part of your safety 'organisation'. As a result of the Employment Protection Act, you are not forced by law to consult with elected representatives of non-unionised employees.

Every business or professional man who employs five or more people must arrange such 'organisation' as best suits his business and as is most likely to produce results. Once your organisation is worked out, you can then put it onto paper.

Finally, the sub-section requires the written statement to specify the 'arrangements for the time being in force' for carrying out the health and safety policy. This means that the notice must set out the main risks which any particular employer faces and how to deal with them.

The Health and Safety Commission has produced guidance for employers. It says: 'The main hazards should be identified and reference made in a statement to additional rules and regulations which must be observed'.

So set out your safety 'arrangements', briefly and clearly. And refer employees to additional rules—such as 'the dangers of untidy working areas or, of the failure to use guards or to wear protective clothing, the introduction of new machinery or substances; maintenance work, etc., . . . Procedures should be laid down for accident reporting and for the results of accident analysis to be made available to all management levels and to the Safety Committee'.

It is up to each business or professional man, then, to prepare his own statement—or to get together with colleagues in the same trade or business, with similar set-ups and to share ideas. When the Inspector next visits your outfit, his first question is likely to be: 'Have you prepared your written statement'? If you have not, then you will need a good reason for your failure. You are, after all, breaking the new law.

Once your statement is prepared, you must 'make it available' to each individual employee. At best, give every employee a copy. Or maybe each employee will get a copy of the main statement on policy and organisation, while details of 'arrangements' are put on a notice board in a prominent position. How you make statements available is a matter for you. That you must now do so as a matter of urgency is a specific and extremely important requirement of this new and vital statute.

Chapter 70

The Control of Pollution

PARLIAMENT steps in where voluntary effort and the civil law have failed to achieve acceptable minimum standards. In the field of pollution, neither public realisation of the perils to our environment nor civil remedies sometimes available to those whose environment is threatened or destroyed (nuisance actions, in particular) have been sufficient to induce industrialists to conform.

So there has been a burst of statutory effort, designed to clout the polluter into reasonable submission—often on pain of mighty penalties from the criminal law.

Section 5 of *The Health and Safety at Work etc. Act, 1974,* came into force on 1 April 1975. It deals solely with emissions into the atmosphere and, like the rest of the Act, is in addition to and not in substitution for existing legislation. It immensely strengthens the hand of the public health authorities, and is enforceable through the use of 'prohibition notices' (appeal to the Industrial Tribunal by all means—but meanwhile, comply—the appeal does not suspend the operation of the notice) and by 'improvement notice' (appeal carries suspension, pending withdrawal or decision).

Above all: Section 5 may be enforced through the imposition of the usual penalties available under the Act. Any director, manager or company secretary (for instance) through whose neglect or with whose consent or connivance the offence has been committed may receive up to two years' imprisonment and unlimited fine for his efforts—with an unlimited fine available for his employers.

Section 5: 'It shall be the duty of the person having control of any premises of a class prescribed . . . to use the best practicable means for preventing the emission into the atmosphere from the premises of noxious or offensive substances and for rendering harmless and inoffensive such substances as may be so emitted'.

As we go to press, the 'classes of premises' have not yet been defined—but definition may have arrived by the time you read these words. And it will no doubt include all those premises from which the air which people breathe is polluted in the name and for the purposes of commerce or industry, public or private.

Note, first, that there is no absolute prohibition against polluting the atmosphere. All that is asked is the use of the 'best practicable means'. If it is reasonably practicable to avoid any pollution at all, then pollution must be avoided.

If pollution there must be, then (once again) 'the best practicable means' must be used to 'render harmless and inoffensive' those substances which are so emitted. The Act does not define the words 'reasonable' or 'reasonably practicable'. But Section 40 provides that if there is a contravention of the Act and the accused maintains that he did in fact use 'the best practicable means' to avoid that contravention—or that he did what was 'reasonably practicable' to comply—then it shall be for him to prove his innocence.

The shifting of the burden of proof onto the accused is comparatively rare in criminal law—and should be causing grave concern to the polluters of the air*. Suppose, for instance, that it would be possible greatly to reduce the harmful or offensive effects of the pollution if enough money were available to instal machinery or devices—or to alter systems—but that 'in the current economic

* This rule applies throughout the 1974 Act. He who relies on his having done what was 'reasonable' must prove it.

climate' the 'body corporate' concerned may feel that the cash should not be laid out for the venture.

Is it, then, in those (sadly common) circumstances 'reasonable' not to take means which are available because cash is tight? Could it be said that it is 'practicable' to use 'means' to avoid or cut down pollution, when you do not have the financial means to make any necessary purchase or changes?

The Inspector will decide on whether or not to serve a notice and, if that notice is breached, then to prosecute—or, indeed, whether to institute proceedings at once. And if a prosecution is launched, then it will be for the appropriate court (Magistrates' Court, where trial is to be 'summary'—otherwise a Crown Court) to consider the question of 'reasonableness' along common sense lines. The greater the pollution and/or the smaller the cost of the remedy, the greater the burden on the accused. Conversely: the less harm that is actual or imminent or prospective and the greater the cost of its remedy, the more reasonable it will become not to take otherwise available means.

Note: Section 5 (2): 'The reference in sub-section (1) above to the means to be used for the purpose there mentioned includes a reference to the manner in which the plant provided for those purposes is used and to the supervision of any operation involving the emission of the substances to which that sub-section applies'. 'Operation of plant', then, and 'supervision' are specifically covered.

'(3) Any substance or a substance of any description prescribed for the purposes of sub-section (1) above as noxious or offensive shall be a noxious or . . . offensive substance for those purposes, whether or not it would be so apart from this sub-section'. Once again, regulations will undoubtedly be made under this 'enabling statute'—watch out for them.

Finally: '(4) Any reference in this section to a person having control of any premises is a reference to a person having control of the premises in connection with the carrying on by him of a trade, business or other undertaking (whether for profit or not) and any duty imposed on any such person by this section shall extend only to matters within his control'.

Matters under the control of others come outside the section. And so do all domestic premises.

What of other new law on pollution? In particular: what has happened to *The Control of Pollution Act, 1974*?

On 24 July 1975, the responsible Minister, Mr Denis Howell, said that he hoped that it would soon be possible to reach decisions about the implementation of the Act.

At present, *The Disposal of Poisonous Wastes Act, 1972,* still reigns supreme. No waste may be removed from any premises unless notices have been served containing particulars specifying the premises from which the waste is to be removed; the land on which it is to be deposited; the chemical composition and the nature of the waste; the quantity to be deposited; the description, number and size of any containers to be used; the name of the person to move the waste.

This information must be sent to the County Borough Council or County District Council; to the River Purification Board or River Authority; and to the person who is undertaking removal for both the area in which the waste is to be deposited and that in which the premises are situated.

The Control of Pollution Act will provide far firmer measures. But with current economy drives, what hope is there that the Act—which 'shall come into force on such day as the Secretary of State may by Order appoint'—will become effective? When the Minister talks about reaching decisions about implementation 'shortly', when will that be?

A wit remarked that 'in the long run', we are all dead. The same may apply 'in the short run', if disasters occur such as that of the lorry driver Mr Tom Carroll, who died when he was poisoned by fumes on Britain's biggest rubbish dump at Pitsea, Essex. He discharged a load of sulphuric acid at the wrong part of the tip; the slip trench already contained polysulphide waste; the two chemicals reacted to produce hydrogen sulphide—and Mr Carroll was overcome by the fumes and died before he reached hospital.

Under the 1974 Act, local authorities will have to provide their own disposal sites. How long are they to wait?

It is expected that before long all private operators who wish to use sites for the dumping of noxious wastes will have to apply for and obtain licences. Local authorities will have power to withhold or to remove licences and to prescribe Codes of Practice. And while the Disposal of Toxic Wastes Act lays the burden of proving damage to the environment on the local authority bringing the charge, the new Act removes this requirement.

Each local authority will have to make a survey of all domestic and industrial wastes in its area. In addition to detailed plans for disposing of all wastes, they will have to bring in a system for the licensing of both waste disposal operators and of landfill disposal sites. Equivalent conditions will be required for the authority's own refuse disposal operations.

Meanwhile, we can hardly expect the existing means for the disposal of toxic waste to go out of use. But while new disposal methods may be expensive, the implementation of those parts of the new Act which require local authorities to carry out surveys —and those which increase penalties for existing pollution offences —cost little and may do much good.

The whole of Schedule 2 of the new Act is concerned with the increased penalties—generally four or five fold—under existing legislation: *The Public Health Act, 1936; The Public Health (Scotland) Act, 1897; The Water Act, 1945; The Clean Air Act, 1956; The Radioactive Substances Act, 1960; The Clean Air Act, 1968;* and others. And those who break the licensing rules concerning the disposal of controlled waste under the new Act may (like offenders against the Health and Safety at Work Act) be fined up to £400 by a Magistrates' Court or an unlimited amount—plus up to 2 years' imprisonment—by a Crown Court.

Once again, of course, there are defences. Can the accused prove that he 'took care to inform himself, from persons who were in a position to provide the information, as to whether the deposit or use to which the charge relates would be a contravention' of the Section? Maybe he 'did not know and had no reason to suppose' that information given to him was false or misleading and that the deposit or use might be in contravention of the law? Or did he act 'under instructions from his employer' without either knowing or having reason to suppose that there was to be a breach?

If charged with 'making, causing or permitting' an unlawful deposit or use, then he may have taken 'all such steps as were reasonably open to him to ensure that the conditions were complied with'. And if the acts were done 'in an emergency, in order to avoid dangers to the public', then he should be in the clear.

There are some who fear that the Health and Safety at Work Act will not be enforced because of its cost to industry. In practice, though, most accidents are caused through lack of care, concern and foresight, not through the absence of equipment. In the same way, there is much that could be done to control pollution, without undue expense. Anyway, who is to measure or to count the cost of lives and limbs—or, for that matter, of caring for the limbless or the families of those who were deceased? And how many pennies saved today will cost how many pounds (however devalued) tomorrow?

While the future implementation of present legislation remains in doubt, two facts are present certainties. First: the concern of the public—and of Parliament—is assured and powerful. Second: unless and until pollution measures are made more vigorous and effective, we shall continue to have disasters—whether major, from a lead factory or minor (except, of course, to the individuals concerned) in cases such as that of the Pitsea lorry driver. And each disaster will produce a call for implementation of the measures which are now on the statute book; which provide the raw material for future action of the most vigorous kind—and which bring the criminal law into play, to bolster up the inadequacies of the civil law.

"THAT'S ONLY THE WINDSCREEN — THE REST OF THE CAR'S DONE A BIT MORE."

Part seven

Contracts and Contractors

Chapter 71

Have You Made a Contract? A Checklist

BUSINESS and professional men are constantly making contracts. Every agreement to buy or sell anything—goods, equipment or services, including your own—creates a contract, once it becomes binding.

But the crucial question is: how binding is your agreement? Upon the answer depends your right to cancel the deal as opposed to the right of the other party to force you to go on with it. Conversely, you need to know when you can force the other party to comply with his side of the bargain.

The tougher the times, the more vital it becomes to know the answers to these questions. Here, then, is a contractual check list.

* * *

1   Has anyone made a firm offer or are you still at the stage of 'ifs' and 'provided thats'? The goods on display in the shop window or trade exhibition, or advertised in the paper, are not 'offered'. Offers are invited. Equally, an offer which is conditional upon something or someone else approving is no offer at all—and may be 'accepted' without risk. The acceptance will itself constitute the 'offer'.

2   If there has been an offer, has it been unconditionally accepted? If you receive an offer and reply by sending the 'acceptance' subject to your terms, then if those terms differ substantially from any in the offer, yours is merely 'a counter-offer' and not an 'acceptance' at all. At that stage, you are still negotiating—even if the other party thinks that the deal is sewn up.

3   Has anyone accepted the 'counter-offer', either formally or, more likely, by delivery of the goods or provision of the services? If not, then at any time before action completes the deal, either party (if he knows it) may take advantage of the situation. The buyer may cancel or go elsewhere. The supplier may put up his prices or withdraw the goods or services from the market.

4   Have you agreed on all the main terms? If not, then the contract is probably 'too vague to be enforceable'. Exception: if you have

agreed on the way in which future agreement can be arrived at, thus: 'The price to be agreed or, in the absence of agreement, to be such price as is fixed by the Chairman of the Chamber of Commerce'. Only in the rarest cases will the Court decide on major terms. Example: where contractors do 'extras' on your property, with no price agreed in advance. The law then implies a term into the contract that you will pay a 'reasonable price'—that the contractor will be paid on a so-called *quantum meruit* basis.

5   Is the contract one which needs to be made in or evidenced by writing, if it is to be effective? These exceptional deals include: Contracts for transfer of interest in land, for insurance or HP or for the transfer of shares; and contracts of guarantee. If it comes within these exceptions then no writing means no deal. Otherwise, the fact that you made your arrangement orally is legally irrelevant.

6   Could you prove that the above main essentials of a contract are all present? Writing, of course, is a great help—most contested cases are eventually decided largely on the documents. But the absence of writing (in all cases other than the above exceptions) does not turn a legally binding contract into a mere 'gentleman's agreement'. In law, if you only have a 'gentleman's agreement'—then you or the other party may break it with impunity.

7   Is there any element of illegality in your deal? Conspiracies (for example) to contravene the tax laws or the Customs and Excise Authorities—for gaming transactions—are void.

8   Have both parties 'capacity to contract'? Minors (aged under 18) can avoid any contracts which are not for 'necessaries'—goods reasonably necessary for them at the time when the deal is done—and that includes all business contracts and contracts of loan. But note: Contracts which are 'ultra vires' a company—that is, which go beyond the powers contained in the objects clause in the company's memorandum of association—are now enforceable against it.

9   Can you identify the other contracting party with certainty? Take particular care to avoid dealing with or, later, billing a small or rocky company instead of the (hopefully) completely solvent parent company or outfit with which you believed that you are doing business. Watch out especially for changes in name or notepaper.

10   Are there any 'post-contractual documents'—like receipts or delivery notes—which seek to add terms or conditions which were not contained in the original arrangement? Initially, these have no effect and can be ignored—they come after the contract. But if either

party knows from previous experience that the other side invariably does business only on those terms, then they may become incorporated into future arrangements.

11 If you find that you have a binding contract on your hands and it includes exclusion clauses, are those clauses or any of them 'unfair and unreasonable' in all the circumstances of your case? If so, then a Judge would probably be prepared to declare them void—a power given to him by the Supply of Goods (Implied Terms) Act. This statute also removes the effect of any exclusion clauses dealing with quality ('merchantability') or suitability for use, in contracts made with private buyers. So when you sell to the public, recognise that these clauses are now useless.

12 If you are liable under the contract, can you pass the buck back to anyone else? Have you retained a 'right over' against your supplier, so as to obtain an indemnity from him?

13 Have you obtained any necessary insurance—to cover you, perhaps, if you must bear the loss if the goods disappear or are damaged in transit?

IF YOU CANNOT ANSWER ANY OF THESE QUESTIONS, THEN THE TIME HAS PROBABLY COME TO SEE YOUR SOLICITOR.

If the answers are not obvious, then they may be extremely complicated. To save the solicitor's time (and hence your money) remember to bring with you all letters, order forms, acceptances or other relevant documents when you see the solicitor and also, if you can, a typed statement, clearly setting out the facts as you remember them—and, preferably as you would be prepared to prove them.

Chapter 72

Buyers' Rights—a Checklist

EVERY business or professional man who buys materials or equipment for his office, shop or factory, needs to know how the effect of the old rule 'caveat emptor' has been whittled down. It is vital for him to understand the modern protection provided by a combination of *The Sale of Goods Act, 1893*; *The Trade Descriptions Act, 1968*; *The*

Misrepresentation Act, 1967; *The Supply of Goods (Implied Terms) Act, 1973*; and *The Fair Trading Act, 1973*. He must also know the limitation on that protection as it applies to business buyers of goods —as opposed to services. Check this list and it will guide you to your rights as a buyer and to those of your clients and customers, insofar as they buy goods—as opposed to services—from you.

*   *   *

1   The Sale of Goods Act—Defects and Uselessness
Section 14 of the Sale of Goods Act—which applies to both business and private buyers—requires (in general) that goods supplied shall be (*a*) 'of merchantable quality', i.e. not suffering from any defect which would make them 'not reasonably saleable'; and (*b*) reasonably suitable for the purpose supplied. This protection applied, though, only 'in the absence of some agreement to the contrary'. Agreements to the contrary were generally contained in 'guarantees', 'warranties', order forms or other contractual documents. Wise and wily sellers too frequently attempted to exclude or restrict the customer's Sale of Goods Act rights—which lie against the seller (manufacturer, wholesaler, retailer or as the case may be).

2   The Supply of Goods (Implied Terms) Act—Excluding the Exclusions
Primarily designed to protect 'consumers' (that is, private buyers), the Supply of Goods (Implied Terms) Act effectively disposed of exclusion clauses in 'consumer' contracts by declaring them to be void. Equally vital: a court is given power to declare any similar exclusion clause in a business contract to be void if the judge considers that it would be 'unfair and unreasonable' to enforce that clause, in all the circumstances of the case.

Note: this Act does not apply to services—which are likely soon to be the subject of new legislation.

3   Misrepresentations
Thanks to the Misrepresentation Act, anyone who enters into a contract after a false statement of fact has been made to him may avoid the deal and get his money back *or* regard the contract as subsisting and claim damages to compensate him for any loss which he has suffered as a result of the misrepresentation. He need not

prove fraud—that is, intention to deceive or 'recklessness'. But the buyer must still beware of 'mere commercial puffs'—statements of opinion which do not bind the maker.

4 The Fair Trading Act

The Director General of Fair Trading now has remarkable powers under the Fair Trading Act, all designed to protect 'consumers' against actions on the part of sellers which are 'contrary to the economic interests of consumers in the UK'. An offender may be asked to give a written undertaking not to repeat his wrongful behaviour. If he gives the undertaking and breaks it, then he may be taken to the Restrictive Practices Court which may grant an injunction against him—breach of which is a contempt of court. If he refuses to give an undertaking in the first place, he may be taken straight to the court.

The Director General also has the power to recommend the making of Statutory Instruments, to curb economic practices which are unfair to consumer interests—business and professional men should watch out for action from the Director General—in co-operation with the Consumer Protection Advisory Committee and the Government. Regulations are on their way.

5 The Trade Descriptions Acts

The civil law is designed to provide remedies as between citizens—individually or in firms or companies or other bodies. The criminal law sets minimum standards by which all must comply for the benefit of society. *The Trade Descriptions Act, 1968*, makes it a criminal offence to 'apply a false trade description' to goods or services. A description is 'false' if it is misleading. And the culprit may be both fined and ordered to pay up to £400 compensation to the innocent victim.

The Trade Descriptions Act, 1972, requires imported goods to be fully marked. Like its predecessor, it is administered by the Consumer Protection or Weights and Measures Authorities.

6 Remedies

It follows that the customer has a claim in the civil law of contract against the seller. If there has been a false trade description, he may also report the offender to the authorities who may prosecute; and if the prosecution is successful, there will be no need to take civil proceedings.

Note: the seller has a contractual relationship with his customer. So if the business or professional man sells goods which are defective in manufacture, the buyer's rights are as against him as retailer; he, in his turn, can claim in contract against his wholesaler—who, in his turn, will have a right to be indemnified by the manufacturer. But while the private customer is usually wholly protected against exclusion clauses which remove his rights to acquire goods which are not defective and which are reasonably suitable for the purpose supplied, the business buyer can only exclude the exclusions if he can prove them to be 'unfair and unreasonable'.

*   *   *

So the business buyer must still beware of exclusion clauses. But the law is increasingly designed to protect the 'consumer' against the perils caused by his own inexperience. The business or professional man who makes deals as part of his livelihood is also a 'consumer' in his private capacity—and should know the rules for his personal protection, when he is buying for his home or family.

Chapter 73

The Fair Trading Act

THE Fair Trading Act is like a Parliamentary cannon. It has enormous potential destructive power if aimed correctly and fired with determination.

In theory, it is the 'consumer trade practice' at which the Act is mainly directed. This means any practice 'carried on in connection with the supply of goods (whether by way of sale or otherwise) to consumers or in connection with the supply of services for consumers', and which relates to terms and conditions of sale, promotion 'by advertising, labelling or marking of goods, canvassing or otherwise'; 'methods of salesmanship'; packing and get up; and even 'methods of demanding or securing payment for goods or services supplied'. The range, then, is total—from the birth of a deal until its final end.

Nor can the industrial or commercial supplier of goods or services simply shrug off the Act by saying: 'We don't deal with consumers'.

The consumer comes at the end of the line. If a practice 'adversely affects his economic interests', then he will blame his immediate supplier—who will certainly try to pass the legal buck back where it belongs.

Once a complaint is made to the Director, he will normally refer it to the Consumer Protection Advisory Committee which (in its turn) will report back. If both the Director and the Committee consider that the advertising or debt collecting or marketing method concerned or the terms of trading are 'unfair' then there will be trouble. In particular, the Committee will normally consider whether the practice concerned 'has the effect or is likely to have the effect of misleading consumers . . . of withholding from them adequate information . . . confusing them . . . or subjecting them to undue pressure . . . or of causing the terms and conditions on or subject to which they enter into the transactions to be inequitable'.

Once a trade practice is condemned, then the Minister may be invited to make a Statutory Instrument, to curb or to ban that practice. If he does so, this document will be laid before both Houses of Parliament, but neither has the power to amend it. A Statutory Instrument is one of the most potentially powerful (and potentially pernicious) means of passing law, precisely because Parliament can only accept or reject. It will be a rare Instrument banning an alleged 'unfair consumer practice' which will be thrown out.

Once a Statutory Instrument is passed, anyone who offends against its terms is liable to heavy fines or even, in theory, to imprisonment. A new and serious offence will have been created without having had to go through detailed Parliamentary scrutiny.

The Director has an even straighter route to Court. If he considers that a particular trade practice is 'unfair', then he may ask the offender for a written assurance that the practice will be discontinued. If the offender declines to give the assurance or if, having given it, he breaks his word, then the Director may bring him before the Restrictive Practices Court.

At that stage, the Court may invite the offender to give an undertaking not to repeat his wrongful behaviour. Alternatively, it may impose a restriction by order. If there is a breach of either undertaking or order, the offender is then 'in contempt of court' and liable to be fined, imprisoned or both.

The application of these rules will soon have enormous impact over an entire range of operations. Pyramid selling . . . double pricing

. . . misleading (although at present lawful) advertising . . . undesirable labelling . . . all are covered. So is the marketing of goods (cosmetics and cream are obvious examples) in containers which give a false impression of quantity. So is debt collection by methods which do not amount to 'harassment' in law, but which may be regarded as undesirable.

As for the contractual documents which contain 'terms and conditions of trading', designed to remove consumer's rights—these are likely to come up for the chop. Fraudulent, spurious 'guarantees' and 'warranties' have already taken a beating under the Supply of Goods (Implied Terms) Act (Chapter 72). But even without any new legislation, similar terms in contracts for the provision of services could be banned.

The big question now is: How will these new rules be applied in eventual practice? Already, undertakings to reform have been extracted from erring businessmen—and published. How many Statutory Instruments will Parliament have placed before it, turning activities which were previously lawful into criminal offences? And who will be referred to the Restrictive Practices Court?

The Director General of Fair Trading is making energetic use of his new powers. As the months go by, their effect is becoming increasingly crucial.

Chapter 74

Trade-ins and Trade Descriptions

THE Appeal Court decision in the case of *Fletcher* v. *Budgen*—in which it was held that the Trade Descriptions Act applies to buyers as it does to sellers—has turned the law on its learned head. Those who sell and at the same time buy in secondhand goods must take great care to tell the truth when they buy as they do when they sell.

First, the facts: Howard Budgen is a car dealer who inspected a vehicle offered to him on a trade in. He convinced the seller that there was no possibility of repairing it; that repairs would not make it safe; and that the only possible course of action was for the car to be written off and scrapped. As a gesture, he paid £2 to the owner.

Shortly afterwards, the owner was staggered to see the car advertised for sale at £136—complete with MOT certificate. Mr Budgen had carried out repairs costing about £56 which had in fact made the vehicle safe and roadworthy.

Mr Budgen was prosecuted under Section 1(1)(a) of the Trade Descriptions Act, for applying a false trade description to the goods which he was buying.

York Justices found that Mr Budgen's statements about the car were to his knowledge untrue. But they held that there was no case to answer because (they said) the Act 'has no application when the descriptions are applied to goods in the course of their acquisition'. The prosecutor appealed—Mr Budgen neither appeared nor was represented at the hearing.

The Lord Chief Justice delivered the decision of the Appeal Court. He referred to the well known case of *Hall* v. *Wickens Motors (Gloucester) Limited*. There the Court considered the case of the seller who, some weeks after the vehicle had been bought, inspected it and honestly (but incorrectly) certified that the vehicle should not receive an MOT certificate because of a fault in a tyre. He was acquitted because he had not applied the Trade Description 'in a transaction associated with the sale or supply of the goods'.

Section 1 (a) of the Act bans the application of any false trade description to goods 'in the course of a trade or business' and in connection 'with the sale or supply of the goods'. Reading the Act as it stands and 'looking at the language used in giving it is natural consequences', had Mr Budgen broken the law?

The Lord Chief Justice admitted that he had previously 'subconsciously thought that the Act only applied to false trade descriptions used by sellers'. He had 'never before been required to think about circumstances in which the public need to apply restrictions to a buyer was very much the same as the public need to apply them to the seller'.

Still, while the Judge 'confessed to being surprised at the conclusion to which he had ultimately come', he ruled that the Justices were wrong; the case must be sent back to them with the direction to conclude the hearing; and unless and until parliament overrules this decision (which is incredibly unlikely), dealers who buy in must not mislead the seller by falsely running down the state or value of the goods.

'Surely,' you say, 'this destroys the whole basis of bargaining'?

It undercuts the basis of dishonest bargaining—but it does not interfere with the honest haggle.

After all, the dealer is an expert who (as the Act requires) is engaging in a transaction which comes within the scope of his own business. 'The potential buyer', said the Judge, 'was engaged in the trade or business of buying cars', and it is not 'in any sense illogical and is not likely to run counter to any intention that Parliament might have had' to extend the prohibition of falsehood to the buyer.

On the contrary. 'It is perfectly reasonable and logical that when the buyer is the expert and the seller might be the amateur, and the buyer makes an examination of the goods in his capacity as an expert and then proceeds to pronounce on the quality or otherwise, he should be as much liable to be restricted in his language as is a seller who, in the normal course of events, knows all about the goods and has to be restricted in any temptation to make false and misleading statements about them.'

After all, if you are selling, in the course of your business, you must not falsely describe your goods or services—whether by word of mouth or otherwise. Equally, if you are buying when conducting your trade or business, why should you be allowed to tell lies? You negotiate a sale, without engaging in falsehood? Then you must do the same when you make a purchase.

This does not mean (as the Lord Chief Justice made clear) that every buyer runs a risk of committing a criminal offence merely because he deprecates or makes 'somewhat derogatory remarks about goods offered to him. 'It would be sad', said the Judge, 'if such a situation arose.' But when you remember 'that it is only a buyer conducting a trade or business and therefore in most instances himself an expert who could fall foul of the Act', to hold that a buyer must tell the truth would be 'in accordance with the language of the Act . . . and would also make very good sense, in view of the fact that its effect is to restrict those who carry on a trade or business.'

So you must be careful not only when you sell but also when you buy. The expression *caveat emptor*—let the buyer beware—has acquired a new and potentially perilous meaning for all purchasers.

Chapter 75

Hiring and Leasing

IF YOU hire or lease vehicles or equipment, how far will the law protect you against contractual terms, set out in the suppliers' documents? *The Sale of Goods Act, 1893*, and *The Supply of Goods (Implied Terms) Act, 1973*, are both designed to protect buyers. But what protection will the law give you, if you merely hire?

First, you must expect to be bound by your deal—especially if you have added your signature. *Caveat emptor*, thunders the law—'let the buyer beware'. 'Let the hirer beware' is an extension. The owner (or lessor) of the equipment provides a service. And none of the legislation intended to protect buyers spills over for the benefit of hirers*—with the limited exception of *The Fair Trading Act, 1973*.

So when you are considering hiring, check the terms with care. You will probably be bound by them—even if you had not read them or did not even know of their existence.

An accountant agreed to rent office equipment for 14 years. The hiring agreement gave him a right to cancel, but only on payment of the remainder of the 14 years rental, minus a quite small sum attributed to cost of servicing the equipment.

Before the equipment had even been delivered, the hirer cancelled. The owners sued for the rental—and won their case. The clause specified what lawyers call a 'genuine pre-estimate of damage' and the hirer could not avoid his responsibilities by alleging that the sum claimed was an unenforceable penalty. He had no benefit from the deal but the hirers had lost money as a result of his breach of contract. Therefore they were entitled to their damages as set out in their contract.

On the other hand, because you are presented with so-called 'standard terms', do not be fooled. These terms may always be varied, provided that the owners' wish for your custom is sufficient to induce them to be reasonable.

For instance, if you are renting equipment and a minimum term is specified, you could always try your hand getting that term reduced—and you will probably succeed—often without even having to pay a higher charge.

Or consider this typical clause: 'No statement, description or condition contained in any catalogue or advertisement issued by the

* There are, of course, many rules to protect private individuals who enter into *hire purchase* contracts.

owners or in any communication from the owners—whether made verbally or in writing by any of the owner's agents or employees—shall give or imply or be construed as giving or implying any warranty or in any way enlarging varying or overriding these terms or conditions.'

On the one hand, no term of this sort could free the owners from their duty to avoid misrepresentation. If you have been induced to enter into the deal by any false statement of fact made by any of the owner's representatives that representation cannot be excluded through any such contractual term.

On the other hand, if you have agreed to the clause, then, however unreasonable your agreement may be, you will be bound by it. But if you have actually signed an agreement, it is absolutely hopeless to say that you did not understand or know of the existence of any particular term.

Some hiring contracts contain exclusion clauses that are monstrous. So you may confidently expect legislation before long, making those terms just as void as the Supply of Goods (Implied Terms) Act has made them in contracts for the supply of goods.

At present, though, if you leave the clause like that in your contract with the people who supply you with your equipment, you must expect them to be able to rely upon it.

The exception? Fraud or misrepresentations. Even today, the supplier cannot get rid of his obligations if he tells untruths.

Finally, the Fair Trading Act. This gives the Director General of Fair Trading the power to curb any commercial practice which he regards as 'unfair to the economic interests of consumers in the UK' —but it bears no relation to contracts for hire, in the world of commerce.

Happily, many suppliers do not rely on their exclusion clauses. But those who hire equipment or vehicles should do so in the full knowledge that the owners are entitled to rely upon their rights, if and in so far as they see fit to do so.

Chapter 76

Your Servants – Your Agents?

THE LAW makes an important distinction between 'servants' and 'agents'. A servant is a person who works under a contract of service (see Part Four). An agent is one who acts for you and on your behalf, whether or not his name appears on your payroll. And to every employer, the vital question is: Are we entitled to avoid the consequences of the acts of the individual concerned?

Suppose, for instance, that a senior employee attends a trade fair and sees fit—probably in a burst of misguided enthusiasm—to place an order for machinery, equipment or supplies which the company does not require. Is it entitled to cancel the order or is it bound by the unwanted deal?

Or you give authority to your employee to do a particular job on your behalf. He sees fit to exceed that authority. What are the legal consequences?

How far, then, must you go in limiting your employees' authority, if that limitation is to affect others? Conversely, to what extent need you inform others of the limits you place on the authority of your staff? And how far can the erring employee who oversteps the limits of his responsibilities be made personally liable for the results? Could he be sacked? Could he be forced to pay the losses out of his own pocket?

Important—and everyday—problems, these, in the world of industry and commerce. So here are the legal answers.

* * *

However small the business, the boss will not be able to do it all himself. Indeed, if he happens to operate through a company, all business has to be done by 'servants or agents' on its behalf. Whether the employer is an individual, a firm or a company, he (or it) is almost always bound by deals, made on behalf of the business—and it is irrelevant whether the person who actually makes the bargain happens to be on the payroll, and whether or not the deal is actually a 'bargain' at all.

When someone acts on your behalf, he may have your actual

authority. If you come to regret the authority you have given to your employee or agent, that will be your misfortune.

Troubles usually come when the employee or agent oversteps his authority. Whether he is a buyer or representative, a seller or stand-in, it matters not. His power is limited by his instructions; he ignores his orders; he places his employers or 'principals' in difficulty. What then?

There are two angles to this one—that of the third party and that of the individual. From the viewpoint of the other man—the person who has relied upon statements made by the individual on the organisation's behalf—it is irrelevant whether the authority displayed was actual or only apparent. If the person representing the business had the 'ostensible' authority to make the deal, then the business is bound by it.

It follows that you must take care not to 'hold out' your servants or agents as having more authority than they actually possess. If you 'clothe your servants with apparent authority', then even if their clothing is deceptive . . . even, indeed, if you stripped them of authority which they held in the past . . . those who deal with them are entitled to consider the appearances. If these are deceptive, then it will be the employers or principals who suffer, not those who are taken in.

Your assistant or stand-in, representative or agent, places or accepts an order? An ordinary, sensible, reasonable man dealing with him and knowing the position that he holds with your outfit—or the position which he appears to hold, thanks to the apparent authority which you have given him—would take it that he is acting within his instructions? Then however unsatisfactory the deal, it cannot be avoided because of any lack of actual authority. The commercial sheep in wolf's clothing may eat into the profits of the business which employs him, whether as servant or agent or both.

If, then, you wish to place really effective limits on the authority of those whom you command, you should inform those with whom they deal. 'Mr Smith is entitled to place orders up to £X, on the company's behalf . . .', 'You will appreciate that Mr Y's authority is limited to . . .', 'We shall be obliged if you will assist Mr Z to buy/sell . . . in connection with the above department only . . .', 'I am pleased to introduce Miss A, who is our newly appointed ——, fully entitled to . . .'. Provided that the limits are set out clearly, anyone who sees fit to assist your representative (in the widest sense of that word) to exceed those limits does so at his own risk.

Second, it is essential to emphasise to the representative himself that he must not exceed his authority—and that if he does so, he is asking to be dismissed. There is, of course, an implied term in the contract of service of an employee and in the contract of agency of any other sort of representative that the authority given will not be exceeded. If that term is broken either in a major respect or persistently, then the person concerned may be sacked.

Finally, what if you attempt to repudiate a contract on the ground that your employee had no authority to make it? The other party will doubtless rely upon the agent's 'apparent' or 'ostensible' authority. He may bring the agent into any legal action which results, as a 'second defendant'. Damages may be claimed against him for 'breach of warranty of authority'. He has warranted that he had the authority to make the deal? Then in the unlikely event of the action failing against the employer or principal, the agent may be made personally liable under the contract.

Conversely, if your employee or agent lands the business in trouble through exceeding his authority, he has broken his contract and (in theory at least) he may be forced to indemnify the business for any resultant loss.

In practice, of course, the erring servant or agent is seldom made to pay for his sins out of his own pocket. His employers or principals (or their shareholders) are the sufferers. So the clearer the limits placed on the authority of their servants or agents—and the more those limits are made known both to the individuals concerned and to others with whom they deal—the less that loss will be.

This advice has become doubly important since a company secretary landed his outfit in huge expense. He hired cars at his company's expense for his own use and was clearly guilty of a criminal offence. His company was held liable to pay every penny of the account submitted by the owners of the cars. They had 'held out' their secretary as having the power to order the cars. He had the 'ostensible' or 'apparent' authority to place the orders—and from the point of view of the innocent third parties, that was as good as actual authority.

Even if your employee is a criminal, you may be liable in a civil court for the results of his misdeeds. Happily, you will only be liable in criminal law for the crimes of your servant or agent if you were in some way at fault.

Chapter 77

When You are Mistaken

MOST NOTORIOUS mistakes are, of course, made by other people.

Suppose that a customer notices an item marked with a £10 price tag. 'I'll have it,' he says. 'Terribly sorry, Sir,' you answer, 'but there's been a mistake. Someone left a nought off the ticket.'

'Your mistake,' he says, triumphantly. 'You put the goods up for sale at the marked price—and I'm entitled to buy at that price.'

'Wrong,' says the law. 'No one is entitled to buy goods on a display in a trade or industrial exhibition or in a shop window or showcase or on the counter. By putting the goods on display, the seller is not "offering" to sell them, in the legal sense of the word. He is simply issuing an "invitation to treat"—he is inviting you to make an offer for the goods. When you do so, he can either accept or refuse it, as he sees fit.'

It follows that the seller is not bound to dispose of goods to any particular customer or to anyone at all, either at the marked price or at any price. Unless and until there is an unconditional offer, unconditionally accepted, there is no deal.

Not long ago, an executive saw a magnificent office machine in a shop window, with a nought left off its price. He went inside and bought it at the price marked. He thought he was getting a great bargain—and he was right. The shop did not discover its mistake until after the deal was done. By that time, the error could not be undone. The customer had made his offer. The shop had accepted it. The price was agreed—and the fact that there was a 'unilateral mistake' on the part of the shop did not destroy the effect of the contract.

The essence of a binding agreement is that the parties are *ad idem*—that their minds are at one. By definition, no agreement means no contract. If one party makes an offer to the other which the other party accepts in quite a different sense from that intended by the offerer, there is probably no deal. Where the parties are at cross purposes, there tend to be bitter arguments as to whether or not there is any agreement at all.

There is seldom room for argument where a party has signed a deed or document. 'I didn't realize that there were conditions on the back,' says the startled purchaser. The front of the document read: 'For conditions, see reverse.' The fact that the signatory did not read the terms . . . could not have understood them had he done so . . . was ignorant of their very existence—that is his misfortune.

In general, only if you did not know the nature of the document you are signing will you be able to avoid the transaction because you were mistaken as to its contents. A man who was told that he was signing a guarantee similar to that signed on a previous occasion but in fact put his signature on to a bill of exchange escaped from liability.

Where both parties are mistaken, the contract is normally *void ab initio*—stillborn. Although both parties are agreed (so there is *consensus ad idem*), the law will usually let both parties off the contractual hook. And there is a possibility of having contractual documents 'rectified', so as to express the intentions of the parties.

Now suppose that you get a bill for rent, light, heat, telephone—or anything else for that matter. You pay. A few weeks later, you receive a letter: 'We very much regret that due to a clerical error, you were undercharged. We enclose a revised statement herewith and shall be pleased to receive the balance due at your earliest convenience.' 'The matter is concluded,' you reply. 'You have received the sum demanded in respect of the goods or services provided. You are entitled to no more.'

You are wrong. In consideration of your agreeing to pay the contractual price, the other party undertook to provide the goods or services. He carried out his side of the bargain. You will not be allowed to take advantage of the error in his accounts department.

The converse applies. Due to a mistake in your accounts department (or of the young lady who happens to be that department), a customer is undercharged. When the mistake is spotted, you write asking for the balance of your money. Your customer cannot rely on your mistake to avoid paying the money which he properly owes.

Again, suppose that you owe £500. By mistake, you send a cheque for £5,000. Clearly, you are entitled to the return of the excess and if you do not get it you would have a good claim for 'money received to your use'.

But note: while money paid under a mistake of a fact 'or through excusable forgetfulness of a fact' may normally be recovered back, the same does not apply to money paid under a mistake of law.

Where the plaintiff paid money volutarily and with full knowledge of the facts to satisfy a claim which he could successfully have resisted, it was held that his funds were gone for ever. In the eyes of the law, ignorance of the law is usually inexcusable. It is more tolerant of errors of fact.

The law on mistakes, then, is miserably complicated. And about the only errors which bring real joy are those perpetrated in print and discovered by the hawk-eyed reader.

Chapter 78

Collecting the Money You are Owed—a Checklist

THE MORE money you are owed the more vital the need to know how far and when the law can help you to recover your debts. 'To sue or not to sue?' That is the first question. Allied to it: 'If you obtain a judgment, how can you best enforce it?'

*   *   *

Steps Before Action
Litigation is a luxury and a last resort. Normal preliminaries are the following:

1   Submission of accounts; statements; polite reminder (oral, by all means—but confirmed in writing, especially if debtor's representative promises payment).
2   Stiff written demand; then threat to place matter in hands of lawyers or debt collecting agency.

Professional Help
The business or professional man who is his own lawyer has a fool for a client. If your efforts to get in the money you are owed all fail then—unless the debt is very small—you should put it in the hands of your solicitor for collection. But it is essential for you to understand the basics of collection so as to provide him with the information that he requires; to issue appropriate instructions so as to ensure that you are not simply throwing good money after bad; and so that you can assess tactics, together with him.

The alternative—which requires at least equal knowledge—is to consult professional debt collectors. The basic principles which now follow remain the same. But unless you know of or are recommended to a thoroughly reliable debt collecting agency of excellent repute, or unless your solicitor recommends the use of such an agency having regard to the nature of the debt concerned, you are better off to leave the collection to your lawyer.

Legal Preliminaries to Action
Before starting proceedings, your lawyer will normally write a 'letter before action'. He will inform the debtor that unless payment is made forthwith (or within such time as is stated), proceedings will be commenced.

If oral pressure is required—or especially if a debtor has indicated intention to defend proceedings and has himself appointed solicitors —direct approach (oral and/or writing) will be made to them.

To Sue or Not to Sue?
Before suing, the following must be taken into account:

1   Amount of the debt. The smaller the sum, the greater the temptation to write it off.
2   Solvency of the debtor. Suing a man (or a company or firm) of straw is throwing good money after bad.
3   Availability of debtor. If he has 'done a midnight flit' or gone abroad, the cost of employing process servers, enquiry agents or others to serve the writ or summons is probably not worthwhile.
4   Nature and strength of defence. The more real the defence and the more likely the prospect of the debtor pursuing it, the greater the incentive to compromise or (at worst) to write off.

Defences
Likely lines of defence would probably have been disclosed in the pre-litigation discussions and/or correspondence. Unfortunately, a determined debtor (or one who is fending off the day of payment as best he can—probably because of his own poor cash flow position) has many possible answers. Common examples include:

1   No contract, i.e. denial of agreement to supply goods or services charged for.

2　Defective goods or services: (*i*) breach of express term, e.g. goods or services not in accordance with specification or quotation, and/or (*ii*) breach of implied term, e.g. that goods will be 'of merchantable quality' as services carried out 'in a workmanlike manner and with reasonably suitable material'.

The cost of proceeding

The vast majority of legal actions never reach trial. Either the defendant pays or there is a compromise. But the most unlikely defendants fight—and before proceedings start, you must either place a limit on the sum which you are prepared to spend in the hope of recovering the debt, or you must be prepared to go the whole way—or you must take a preliminary view. In any event, you must ask your solicitor to estimate the cost involved.

A business or professional man may (with allowances for contingencies) estimate with some degree of certainty the sum likely to be involved in a project. A solicitor can rarely give more than an interim and provisional estimate. The following items are seldom possible to assess precisely in advance:

1　The vigour with which the defence will be pursued and in particular, the number and nature of interim applications or summonses—and/or the appeals which it will be necessary to make —or to defend.

2　The extent of 'discovery'—that is the cost of inspecting and, where necessary—copying relevant documents.

3　The experience and eminence of Counsel who will be employed by the debtor—and which will of itself often dictate which Counsel are engaged on your behalf. (For example, will the debtor employ leading Counsel?)

4　The eventual length of the trial—which will depend not only on the complexity of the issues and the extent of the dispute between the parties, but also upon the number and nature of the witnesses and upon the personality and patience of the Judge.

*　　*　　*

Into the scales go all the pros and cons—and whichever course you choose—to sue or to write off—you make your choice in full knowledge of all the facts and with your eyes wide open to the potential risks and results.

Chapter 79

Fending Off Your Creditors—a Checklist

OBVIOUSLY, the best way to get rid of your debts is to pay your creditors. And I am certainly not advising non-payment. But when times are rough and business and professional people cannot themselves get in the money they are owed, they may be forced to use the law so as to beat the great enemy—time.

Here is a summary of how the law can help you to preserve your cash flow—or that of your company or firm—together with the limits on that help.

* * *

1 Check that the sum claimed is indeed due. In a computerised age, bills, accounts, invoices and statements are frequently incorrect. Further: ensure that you have not already paid the sum concerned. Are you satisfied that your own accounting system—which may have been quite adequate when cash flowed readily—gives you sufficient control now?

2 If the claim is prima facie correct, i.e. the goods or services are accurately stated and the sum specified is the contract price, have you a legal defence to the claim—and if so, then what is its strength? Typical defences include the following:

(*a*) That the goods, materials or equipment were not in accordance with contract. Check:

  (i) Was there a breach of an express term in the deal? Were the goods (or any of them) different to those ordered?

  (ii) Was there a breach of an implied term; were the goods defective (and hence not 'of merchantable quality' or not 'reasonably suitable for the purpose supplied') so that there was a breach of *The Sale of Goods Act, 1893*?

  (iii) Were the services supplied in accordance with contract? Or was the work done in a manner—or with materials other than those demanded?

  (iv) Was the work defective? Is the creditor in breach of an implied term in the contract; That the work will be done in a proper and workmanlike manner and with reasonably suitable materials?

(b) That the goods were delivered—or the work done—late. Check:

(i) Was there an express term making time an essential of the deal?

(ii) Was there some obvious implication which would show that the parties must have intended time to be 'of the essence' of the arrangement?

(c) That the contract itself was not completed—probably through the absence of some essential term. Check:

(i) Was there an *unconditional offer*, as opposed to (1) a mere 'invitation to treat'—or (2) a 'conditional' offer perhaps dependent upon someone else's consent?

(ii) Was there *unconditional acceptance*—as opposed to (1) acceptance subject to a condition or, more likely to (2) 'a counter offer'—usually contained in a document which may be called an 'acceptance' but which in fact attempts to impose terms which contradict those contained in the offer?

(iii) Was there 'consideration'—normally the price or some other *quid pro quo*?

(iv) Was there sufficiently clear agreement on all essentials—price, quantity, quality etc.? (Exception: Where services are carried out and the claimant is entitled to reasonable payment on a *quantum meruit* basis).

(v) Was delivery of the goods or the carrying out of the services accepted by the other party?

3 Next: double check all contractual documents; do they provide you with any other technical defence? If in doubt, consult your solicitor.

4 When taking legal advice, to save time and money, bring with you all relevant contractual documents, including all correspondence; and also bring full statements as to circumstances—so as to prevent solicitors having to prepare those for you—in their time and at your expense.

5 By this stage, you should be able to assess your prospects of fending off a legal action by your creditors—and you can then decide on tactics. Considerations include the following:

(*a*) Whatever the nature of strength of your defence, are your creditors likely to be fair, reasonable and helpful—bearing in mind their own cash flow difficulties and their assessment of the advantages or otherwise of pushing you? They will consider the value of (hopefully) past and (certainly) future business from you;

(*b*) Whether suing you would or would not be likely to produce a speedy outcome. If you have no *prima facie* defence then they might well obtain summary, i.e. swift and cheap, judgment. Conversely: if you have at least an arguable defence which is visible on the correspondence, suing may not be worthwhile. Also: if they push too hard, will they be likely to make you insolvent and hence produce exactly the opposite result to that which they require, i.e. payment of money due.

(*c*) Correspondence: and how it will appear to a court—including your apparent defences. Note: 'without prejudice' letters will not normally be disclosable.

6   Lawyers can normally fend off the day of judgment—or the payment of a debt—for a considerable time. The length of that time depends upon the strength of the defence; the vigour and efficiency of the creditors or their lawyers; and whether or not they can rake together a counter-claim, for loss suffered e.g. as a result of defective materials or work or due to delay. But lawyers are entitled to their proper costs. So when assessing need for their help, consider the following:

(*a*) Would a satisfactory compromise on the amount of the claim be more or less likely to be obtained with the lawyer's help?

(*b*) In so far as there is no adequate defence or no defence which you would wish to argue to what extent would your prospects of obtaining reasonable terms for payment be more likely to be achieved with a lawyer's help—as opposed to a direct (and probably totally frank) approach by you to the appropriate creditor's representative?

(*c*) What delay do your lawyers believe that they would be able to obtain from you—and what would be the likely legal cost?

*   *   *

Interest rates are high; a premium is placed on non-payment; and one branch of the legal profession which is burgeoning is that concerned with the collection of debts—and the fending off of debtors. The law is not always a moral instrument. But business and professional people who wish to survive must know how best to use it.

Chapter 80

Time

IF YOU agree to carry out the terms of a contract, when must you do so? If you submit an estimate, how long will it remain open? And if goods are sent to you for a job to be done on them, how long may you allow before you submit an estimate?

*   *   *

An expensive appliance was handed in for repair at a branch of a nationalised undertaking, at the beginning of December. The customer asked for an estimate of the cost. The appliance, according to the Board, at the end of March, 'was returned to the manufacturers on 23 December . . . and since then we have written to them on two occasions and also telephoned them requesting the estimate which was eventually received and duly forwarded . . . on 3 March'. Nearly three months to provide an estimate for a small job. We 'must apologise on behalf of the manufacturers for the delay . . .', said the Board.

The 'manufacturers' took a different line. They wrote to the customer—after she had written to them three times inviting a reply —stating that 'it would appear that the delay in dealing with your appliance was due to the delays of the Board'.

Well, we hold no particular brief for Boards. But let us give credit where credit is due. The Board did all it could—and the manufacturers took months to deal with the customer, and then tried to put the blame on the Board. And, incidentally, when the estimate did arrive, it was so high that the customer decided not to accept it and to use the money to pay a substantial part of the cost of a new machine produced by rival manufacturers.

'But what were the legal rights on each side?'

When the customer asked for an estimate, she was simply inviting the firm to make an offer to repair the goods. When that offer—in the estimate—was given, she could either accept it or reject it. She rejected it.

What about the time taken in giving the estimate?

The manufacturer would be allowed 'a reasonable time'. In theory, if that were exceeded the customer could sue for damages, to compensate her for the time—or, at least, the unreasonable time—that the goods had been out of her hands. In practice, this is hopeless. If no financial loss is suffered, you might get a few pounds for the inconvenience caused—but court proceedings would hardly be worthwhile. The customer's remedy is to take his custom elsewhere.

'What if the estimate had been accepted—when should the job have been finished?'

If a time was specified in the acceptance and it was clearly a matter of importance to the customer that the job be finished within that time, then the date fixed would be the required date of completion. But if no date was specified, then once again the firm would have 'a reasonable time'.

The leading case on this branch of the law is *Charles Rickards Limited* v. *Oppenheim*. Rickards agreed to supply a car chassis to Mr Oppenheim and have a body built on to it within seven months. It was made quite clear that the work had to be finished on time— that 'time was of the essence of the contract'. But seven months passed and the car was not ready. Rickards themselves were not personally at fault. Their subcontractors had let them down. In any event, Mr Oppenheim was told that the car would be ready in two weeks and he gave a written notice to Rickards' sub-contractors saying that unless he received the car within four weeks, he would refuse delivery. This notice was duly passed on to Rickards.

The car was not delivered within four weeks, and when eventually it did turn up, Mr Oppenheim refused to accept it. The company brought an action against him; claiming the price of the body work. He counter-claimed for the chassis or its value.

The first question for the Court? Whether or not time was 'of the essence of the contract'. It was. The customer had picked a date and made it clear that this was to be an essential term.

Next question: after that time had passed and the customer still said that he would give extra time, could he still rely on the set period? No, said the Court, he could not. He had 'waived' the stipulation as to time. He was 'entitled to give reasonable notice', reintroducing time as 'of the essence of the matter, whether the contract was for the sale of goods or for work and labour. The reasonableness of the notice had to be judged at the time at which it was given . . .

There had been a waiver—but when Mr Oppenheim said, 'I'll give you four more weeks', he was attempting to reintroduce the period of time. Was this a successful attempt? That would depend on whether or not the new period was 'a reasonable one'. Was it? 'Yes', said the Court. 'On the facts of the case it was reasonable . . . and it was a good notice to the Plaintiffs, even though it was given by Mr Oppenheim only to the sub-contractors.'

So if you are going to be late in delivery, do not think that you can get away with it simply by getting your customer to grant an extension of time. If that, too, were to pass, he would be entitled to refuse delivery and to claim damages from you—as Mr Oppenheim did from Charles Rickards.

You will have noticed that the same rule about waiver applies both in contracts for the sale of goods and those for work and services. In general, in this respect, the law does not make any difference between them. But *The Sale of Goods Act, 1893* (reproduced in Appendix 4) does give us a little special help with regard to contracts for the sale of goods.

'Unless a different intention appears from the terms of the contract,' says Section 10, 'stipulations as to time of payment are not deemed to be of the essence of a contract of sale. Whether any other stipulation as to time is of the essence of the contract or not depends on the terms of the contract.' So unless you make it clear that if you are not paid by a certain date, you are not going on, the time that you are to be paid is not regarded as an essential part of the contract.

Otherwise, the section is clearly of no assistance at all. All it says is that if you want to find out whether or not time is 'of the essence' in any particular case, you must look at the terms of the particular contract. Nevertheless, as one learned authority puts it, 'as regards stipulations other than those relating to the time of payment, time is usually of the essence of the contract, at any rate in mercantile transactions'.

If you are anxious to have something done on time, then say so. If you are doing the job, then try not to be tied down as to time. And remember that the fact that your lateness—like that of Charles Rickards—may be due to factors entirely beyond your control, won't help you at all. This is one occasion where it may not be better to be late than never. Late and never may be synonymous.

Now another, but equally common, contractual problem involving time. There are a number of good firms that provide excellent equipment for businessmen, their factories and offices. And they do so on a rental basis. You hire the machinery, you pay a comparatively modest price, the owners do the servicing for you—but the contracts usually provide that the machinery shall remain something like fourteen years from the date of installation.

This is not an unreasonable stipulation in most cases. The machinery—telephone installations or what-have-you—must be manufactured and the owners will probably make a loss over the first few years. Their profits come later on. But please do not think that you will be able to opt out of your obligations in those few years, if you decide that you do not like the machinery . . . if you want something new . . . if you go out of business or change your line . . . if you move into other offices, which are already equipped. . . . You will be bound by your agreement.

Still, if you do not like the period set—or any other clause in the proposed agreement—then do not agree to it.

'But that's no good,' you reply. 'They'll never agree to instal them for less than fourteen years—or whatever the particular period is.'

Wrong. To avoid losing your business, the company may well relent on the time period. They do not wish to lose their profits. They will simply drive the best bargain they can. So read the agreement, discuss it with the representative, see if you can get his company to budge. If you can and are happy, then rent their equipment. If you cannot, then you must decide whether or not it is worth your while to accept their terms. But what you must not do is to make an agreement and then expect to get out of it.

Chapter 81

Import/Export – and Foreign Accounts

IT IS all very well to be patriotic and to help the export drive by building up your foreign accounts. But what happens if the accounting parties fail to pay up? Equally, it is splendid for international good-will that you should buy goods from abroad. But what happens if they are defective or you lose money because they do not arrive, as contracted for or at all? After all, if the deal involved UK firms, you could sue them soon enough. But what of foreign contractors?

* * *

If the overseas contractors come to England or maintain a registered office here, you can slap a writ on them and treat them like Englishmen. All being well, you will get your judgment. If they have property over here, you will then be able to force your judgment against that property. You can levy execution upon it . . . send in the bailiffs . . . or if the deal was done through an English affiliate, you may be able to wind it up.

But even if you can serve the proceedings in this country and even if you get your judgment, that will not be the end of the matter if the foreigner has no property here which can be reached to satisfy the judgment. In that case, the judgment may not be worth the paper it is written on. If you want your money, you have to start all over again, suing in the court of the foreign country concerned.

There are exceptions. For instance, there are arrangements made under *The Administration of Justice Act, 1920*, under which countries in the Commonwealth mutually agree to enforce each other's judgments. And under *The Foreign Judgments* (*Reciprocal Enforcement*) *Act, 1933*, similar arrangements have been made with certain non-Commonwealth countries—Austria, Belgium, France, the Federal Republic of Germany, the Isle of Man, Israel, Italy and Norway in particular. So, of course, trading with individuals or companies in those countries is safer than dealing with people elsewhere.

All this presupposes that you can serve your writ within the jurisdiction of our own courts. But what happens if you cannot do so? The answer lies in Order 11 of the Rules of the Supreme Court. This sets out a number of cases in which leave will be given by the High Court to a plaintiff in this country to serve his writ or notice of his writ outside the jurisdiction. Here are the cases:

'*a* If the whole subject matter of the action begun by the writ is land situate within the jurisdiction . . .' The English courts will exercise jurisdiction over anyone where there is a battle concerning English land.

'*b* If an act, deed, will, contract, obligation or liability affecting land situate within the jurisdiction is sought to be construed, rectified, set aside or enforced in the action begun by the writ.'

Once again, it is the land within the court's jurisdiction which attracts the court's power to grant leave to serve outside it.

'c If in the action begun by the writ, relief is sought against a person domiciled or ordinarily resident within the jurisdiction.' This one is designed to catch the Channel hoppers, international travellers and others who do midnight flits over the water to avoid the process servers. If such persons usually live here or are domiciled here (this country being a permanent place of abode), then they can be reached, wherever they fly.

'd If the action begun by the writ is for the administration of the estate of a person who died domiciled within the jurisdiction or if the action begun by the writ is for any relief or remedy which might be obtained in any such action as aforesaid.' Someone dies here. His property lies here. And the court will ensure that it can consider here matters arising out of the death.

'e If the action begun by the writ is for the execution, as to properties situate within the jurisdiction, of the trusts of a written instrument . . . it ought to be executed according to English law. . . .' Once again, it is the property within the jurisdiction which matters.

'f If the action begun by the writ is brought against a defendant not domiciled or ordinarily resident in Scotland to enforce, rescind, dissolve, annul, or otherwise affect a contract, or to recover damages or obtain other relief in respect of the breach of a contract, being (in either case) a contract which: .

(i) was made within the jurisdiction, or
(ii) was made by or through an agent trading or residing within the jurisdiction on behalf of a principal trading or residing out of the jurisdiction, or
(iii) is by its terms, or by implication, governed by English law.'

To sue a Scotsman (or a Scottish company) upon a contract made here or through an agent here or which is governed by English law, you must still go to Scotland. But otherwise, you may serve abroad. It is this rule which is relied upon in most commercial cases in which leave to serve out of the jurisdiction is obtained. If the deal is made in England, you may enforce it in England. If the person who made it was an agent trading or residing here on behalf of a foreign individual or corporation, a foreign contractor may be served with a writ. And if, expressly or by implication, it is the law administered by our courts which will apply, our courts will give leave to serve the foreigner abroad.

> '*g* If the action begun by the writ is brought against a defendant not domiciled or ordinarily resident in Scotland or Northern Ireland, in respect of a breach committed within the jurisdiction of a contract made within or out of the jurisdiction, and irrespective of the fact, if such be the case, that the breach committed out of the jurisdiction that rendered impossible the performance of so much of the contract as ought to have been performed within the jurisdiction.'

Never mind, then, where the contract was made. If it was broken by some act committed in this country, leave will be given to serve the foreigner abroad.

> '*h* If the action begun by the writ is founded on a tort committed within the jurisdiction.'

If a foreigner is guilty of negligence, nuisance, making a defamatory statement—and the civil wrong is committed in this country—then he may be followed abroad by the long arm of the law.

> '*i* If in the action begun by the writ, an injunction is sought ordering the Defendant to do or refrain from doing anything within the jurisdiction (whether or not damages are also claimed) in respect of the failure to do or the doing of that thing.'

Foreigners, then, may have their behaviour within the jurisdiction controlled, even though they have gone outside it. They may, after all, return. . . .

> '*j* If the action begun by the writ being properly brought against a person duly served within the jurisdiction, a person out of the jurisdiction is a necessary or proper party thereto.'

The foreigner may be joined as a party in the English proceedings. Even if he could not have been a sole defendant, he may be made a co-defendant.

'*k* If the action begun by the writ is either by a mortgagee of property situate within the jurisdiction (other than land) and seeks the sale of the property, the foreclosure of the mortgage or delivery by the mortgagor of possession of the property but not an order for payment of any monies due under the mortgage or by a mortgagor of property so situate (other than land) and seeks redemption of the mortgage, reconveyance of the property or delivery by the mortgagee of possession of the property but not a personal judgment.'

Actions on mortgages within the jurisdiction may be brought against people outside it.

Finally,

'*l* if the action begun by the writ is brought under *The Carriage by Air Act, 1932.*'

Air accidents are in, even if those who cause them are out.

That, then, is the Rule. English courts have given themselves considerable powers in bringing foreign contractors within their grasp. Once leave to serve has been given, service can usually be effected through the British Consulate in the country concerned or in accordance with the law of the country where the service is to be effected. But in Commonwealth countries, service may be effected without the intervention of the British representative. And there are detailed rules relating to certain other countries with which we have Conventions.

So while suing in this country may be an expensive operation, suing abroad or suing those who are abroad is inevitably even more so. Happily, where the foreigners have a place of business in this country, they can be served at that place of business. But conversely, you may find yourself sued in a foreign court and the foreign judgment enforced in this country, if you are in the wrong. Equally, if you sue a foreign defendant in our courts, he may counter-claim here against you. And if you sue abroad, you may be faced with a counter-claim there.

All these are unhappy rules, dealing with deals which have gone sour. But then, it is not from the sweetness of satisfied customers that lawyers who deal in litigation make their living. . . .

Chapter 82

Common Market Law

WHETHER YOU launch yourself or your business or profession into the European Community, you need to know the areas in which new law is likely to affect you. And even if you remain firmly at home, you may find new troubles to contend with. Here is a review of some of the legal perils and pitfalls—some you will have to meet; others you can side-step, if you only know of their nature and existence.

* * *

Rule one: Avoid panic. We will not get swamped by the Code Napoleon or any other foreign law. Repeatedly, the Government has reassured us: 'All essential features of our law will remain', it says. Our court systems; trial by jury; habeas corpus—all will be as before.

The rules on 'tort' will remain unaltered. For instance, the rules on negligence remain the same. The man who causes injury, loss or damage to his employee will still only be liable to pay compensation if the employee can show that the trouble was caused as a result either of a breach of statutory duty (such as that created by the Offices, Shops or Railway Premises Act, the Health and Safety at Work Act, or by the Factories Act) or through some lack of due care on the part of the employer or another member of his workforce.

Above all, contractual rules will remain the same. Whether you are contracting in Britain or abroad, the rules of the deal will be as now.

It follows that whether you are buying or selling plant, equipment or services, you must not presume that your legal protection will be better because of Common Market entry. You must, for instance, make sure where possible that your contract is governed by English law—at least if you want our courts to retain their jurisdiction. You must not presume that you will be able to serve a Common Market debtor with your writ or summons outside the UK, merely because we share membership in the Community; and even if you obtain a judgment, you will not necessarily find it any easier to enforce.

Still, there have been many changes since we entered the EEC. First, mobility of labour. On the one hand you may have talents, experience and knowledge of international use. You are entitled to live and to work in any of the Common Market countries you choose, as and when you see fit. Once there, you will be free to enjoy all the benefits of that country's social service system.

Conversely, you may wish to import specially skilled labour from (say) France or Germany. You are free to do so. Your new employees will have a complete right to live, to settle and to work here—without permits or problems.

There may, of course be tax difficulties. With the exception of Italy, all the existing Community Members enjoyed the miseries of VAT for some time before it came our way. And you must watch out for problems of exchange control. There is freedom of movement of capital within the Common Market, under EEC law. So if you export capital, consult your bank or your accountant.

* * *

You should also take specialist advice on tax problems. We retain (in the main) our own tax system, as before—as do each of the Common Market countries. Harmonisation of law is a long, gradual and uncertain process. Meanwhile, in so far as you retain your residence and your work within the UK, you will have to put up with our own laws; and in so far as you move out into Europe, you must expect to have to deal with their home-grown law and lawyers.

If you operate through a company, you may one day have to adapt your rules very considerably. The EEC Commission is studying the possibility of a European Company (to be known as 'Societas Europea'—or 'S.E.'). This new international creature will have rules superimposed upon those of the country concerned. But this lies well in the future. At present, company law has been altered only in minor respects.

First, every company must re-examine its order forms, business letters and stationery. Normally, these must state 'in legible letters' the company's place of registration; its registered number; and the address of its registered office. And any reference made to share capital on any such documents must refer to paid-up share capital only.

In addition, an up-to-date, printed copy of the Company's Articles should have been sent to the Registrar. In the old days you did not have to reprint your Articles, merely because you made some alteration. All you had to do was to file a copy of the alteration itself. Now many companies have had to have their Articles reprinted.

Finally, the *ultra vires* rules are altered. Your company's powers are contained in the Objects Clause of its Memorandum of Association. The company was only entitled to operate within the scope of the Objects. Any contract made outside the powers contained in the Memorandum was *ultra vires*—beyond the company's powers and hence a nullity. Indeed, an *ultra vires* act was not even capable of subsequent ratification. It was dead and useless.

This rule has gone where the other party acts in good faith and without knowing of the lack of power in the objects clause. Now and in future, those who deal with your company in good faith are entitled to presume that the company is acting within the scope of its lawful powers. And if the deal is made before the company actually has any powers at all—prior to its formation or registration—then the person making the contract is personally liable. So mind what deals you make on behalf of unborn corporations.

Once you or your company enters into any business within the Community, you must carefully avoid restrictive practices. The law forbids the making of any arrangement 'the object or effect of which is to prevent, restrict or distort competition within the Common Market'.

Again, many British outfits tender for business. If public tenders are a substantial part of your work, then check on the extent to which the EEC companies have harmonised their law on public tendering. Discussions are going on regarding tendering, and also on the harmonisation of technical and industrial safety standards and industrial training.

It is unlikely that you will have to make any immediate changes in your safety precautions or provisions or in the technical standards required of you. But it is vital that you keep a weather eye open for changes.

The EEC Commission is hard at work in the technical, safety and training fields, co-ordinating, encouraging and financing research. As long ago as 1970, it published a document entitled *The Industrial Policy of the Community*, showing the lines of advance. These will almost certainly lead to specific legal instruments and requirements. You should watch out for advice, guidance and suggestions within your own fields. In due course, these are likely to lead to enforceable legal rules.

In so far as we harmonize our laws with those of other EEC countries, new legislation will have to be passed by our own Parliament. Just as it is Westminster which has introduced VAT, so our own Parliament will be obliged to change our own laws, to accord with Common Market policy and decisions. To that extent, you need not worry about foreign jurisdictions—changes will come from home.

On the other hand, if you live or do business in another EEC country, you will have to comply with that country's internal laws. Like our own country, it retains most of its sovereignty and the right to regulate relations between individuals and businesses within that country—through its own criminal and civil laws. Its rules on negligence and on contract, for instance, will remain unaltered—like our own.

So we end where we began—with the *status quo*. Most British business and professional people have found little change in the law as it affects them. But as the Community grows and as we become more deeply embedded into it, alterations will gradually appear. To keep out of trouble in future, you should keep a careful watch for trouble in the offing. And if that trouble comes, you should employ the best lawyer you can find.

Finally, remember that just as most laws will remain the same, so most lawyers will retain their previous specialization. Do not expect (for instance) a lawyer in London, Loughborough or Leith to be an expert in Italian, French or German law. If you are launching into the Common Market and require legal advice in this country, you will have to seek out a specialist. And if you operate abroad, you must find a lawyer to help you, in the country of your choice.

With an eye on the future; a good lawyer; and good fortune—all should be well. He who lacks any of those three essentials may find himself in Common Market trouble.

Chapter 83

Some Principles on Interest

'IT HAS been our custom for some years now to charge interest at 6 per cent per annum on accounts which are over three months overdue for payment, and this is clearly stated at the bottom of our invoices and statements. It has been suggested to us that we have, in fact, no legal right to charge this interest, and that there is no obligation on the part of the debtor to pay it, should he settle his account voluntarily or, alternatively, be sued for payment.

'Many of our customers are notoriously slow payers and use their supplier as a cheap way of getting the use of money. We have always felt that the 6 per cent charge was some recompense for the facility. What is the legal position?'

*   *   *

The essence of the question? If you are not paid when you should be, can you charge interest? The essence of the answer? Only if there is an agreement, express or implied, between you and your customer, which allows you to do so.

Express agreement is simple to make and to understand. If you want to charge interest on overdue accounts, then you should tell your customer that this is one of the terms upon which you trade. Just as you specify a price, a delivery date, a period within which payment must be made, so you may specify an interest charge if payment is late.

It is much too late to attempt to do this in an invoice or a statement. Terms printed on these documents are no part of the contractual agreement. That was concluded days, weeks or even months before these documents were drawn up or received. Businessmen have a peculiar idea that they can introduce new terms into an agreement by printing them on demands for payment, confirmation slips, delivery notes and the like. In law, this is not permitted.

On the other hand, if you have traded for a long time with a particular firm or individual and you have brought your interest charge on late payments to his notice, it may be that you will have his implied agreement to pay them. True, the first time that he is late in payment and you bang on the 6 per cent he can refuse to pay the interest. But if he pays it and still carries on trading with you, a Court might be prepared to accept that he knew of your system and had consented to it. In that case, the fact that he had not expressly agreed would not matter. An implication will do.

'Unless a different intention appears from the terms of the contract,' says section 10 of *The Sale of Goods Act, 1893*, 'stipulations as to time of payment are not deemed to be of the essence of the contract of sale.' So if a customer owes money for some goods which you have sold him, then even if you have stipulated a certain time for payment, this term will not be 'of the essence' of the agreement, unless you have expressly made it so.

It follows from this that in contracts of this kind you most certainly cannot charge interest if payment is late. It may be a breach of contract, but it is not normally an essential one. You may give your customers more time to pay, or agree to accept payments by instalments, if he will agree to pay you interest. Then a new agreement is created, and your customer is bound by it.

If the time comes that your patience is exhausted and you decide to sue for your money, the situation as to interest changes. Three Acts of Parliament may come to your rescue.

First, Section 3 of *The Law Reform (Miscellaneous Provisions) Act, 1934*, says that: 'In any proceedings in any Court of Record for the recovery of any debt or damages, the Court may, if it thinks fit, order that there shall be included in the sum for which judgment is given interest at such rate as it thinks fit on the whole or part of the debt or damages for the whole or any part of the period between the date when the cause of action arose and the date of judgment.'*

The High Court, as well as your local County Court, is a Court of Record. So if you sue for your money and win, the judge will be able to order that interest be paid on the debt concerned from the time the debt arose until the date of judgment—or any part of that time which the judge considers to be just.

In practice, if the Court takes the view that you have been wrongfully and unnecessarily deprived of your money, it may well grant you interest. Usually, this will be at 4 per cent. But the Act gives the Court a complete discretion both as to the rate of interest—and as to whether or not to grant any at all.

The second Act which may help you applies where cheques bounce. Section 57 of *The Bills of Exchange Act, 1882*, provides that: 'The holder may recover from any party liable on the bill, and the drawer who has been held to pay the bill may recover from the acceptor, and an indorser who has been compelled to pay the bill may recover from the acceptor or from the drawer or from a prior indorser . . . (*a*) the amount of the bill; (*b*) interest thereon from the time of presentment for payment if the bill is payable on demand, and from the maturity of the bill in any other case. . . .'

*The 1934 Act does not apply to Scotland but by virtue of *The Interest on Damages (Scotland) Act, 1958*, a court in Scotland may order that interest shall be payable from the date that the action for the recovery of the money was commenced in the court until the date of judgment.

So if a customer's cheque is dishonoured, take heart. Here at least the law takes an interest in your problems and gives you interest on the money you're owed. Assuming, that is, that the customer concerned is worth suing, even for the principle.

Third, *The Judgments Act, 1838*, provides that in any action in the High Court every judgment debt carries interest, now at the rate of $7\frac{1}{2}$ per cent, from the time of entering the judgment until the debt has been paid. Note, however, that this provision does not apply to the County Court judgments, so in the County Court you will only be able to get interest for the period up until the date of the judgment.

Chapter 84

The Cost of Contractors

LIKE ALL businesses, we employ contractors to maintain, convert, insulate or to do other work on our premises—or, for that matter, on our vehicles. We have far too many disputes with them over prices and quality of work. What are our rights, please?

Conversely, what are we entitled to charge when we carry out work for our customers? And what sort of standards are they entitled to demand from us?

*   *   *

First, consider the situation when you are the customer.

Contractors (by definition) are those whom you employ under contract. If the terms of that contract are agreed, both sides are bound.

Suppose that you book a builder and agree his price. You then discover some 'little man' who will do the job for you for much less money. Too bad. You have no right to avoid your bargain. If the contractor is prepared to let you off the legal hook, you are lucky.

Conversely, suppose that your contractor underestimates. He holds down his price to some uneconomic level so as to get your job. He is not then entitled to say: 'I can't do it for the agreed price.' As with most other contracts not made by infants, they either bind both sides or neither.

'But what happens where no price has been agreed in advance?'

you say. 'Is the man entitled to demand whatever the market will bear?'

Certainly not. He may charge only on a so-called *quantum meruit* basis—what the job is worth . . . a reasonable charge . . . and what is 'reasonable' depends on all the circumstances of the case including the standard of the work, the time taken and by whom, the skill and cost of the labour used and the nature and cost of the materials.

In practice, 'extras' usually cause the trouble. 'Let's have an extra shelf over there,' you say. 'While you're here, would you mind fixing our damaged floorboards, repainting the corridor. . . .?' You've accepted the contractor's firm estimate for the main job and you do not trouble to get estimates for the extras.

Maybe the contractor has discovered that he will be out of pocket on the estimated work. He knows that he cannot raise his agreed price. So having undercharged on the contract, he overcharges on the extras. Alternatively, you simply do not realise how the extras are mounting up so when you receive the bill you retire to bed with a migraine and a tranquilliser. Your magnificent afterthoughts and changes-of-mind (or, of course, those of your managerial staff) are costing you a fortune.

If this happens to you, don't panic. Take stock, if necessary with the help of a surveyor, of the work done and the prices charged. If they are reasonable, you will just have to pay. But if the prices are unreasonable, refuse to pay them. Offer a reasonable price and no more.

The obvious way to avoid this sort of trouble is to tie down every contractor to precise figures on every item of work done, including all the extras. Reputable contractors would rather be at work than in court and realise that prior agreement on prices (preferably confirmed in writing) would help both sides to keep clear of lawyers. So they provide written estimates on request. Conversely, if a contractor refuses to give an estimate for an extra, this (in most cases, at least) is a pretty clear hint to you to take your work elsewhere.

If, then, you obtain your estimate and the asking price is too high, bargain. If haggling proves hopeless, then you can either order the work with both your eyes and your pocket book wide open—or refuse to accept the estimate.

But what if the job is defective? Suppose that the pipes leak . . . the paintwork blisters . . . the building subsides . . . the roofing falls . . .?

Every contractor impliedly promises that he will do your work in a proper and workmanlike way and with reasonably suitable materials. If either his work or his materials are defective, he has broken his contract. You are entitled to claim damages, to compensate you for your loss. In practice, this means that you are entitled to deduct from his bill the reasonable cost of putting his work into proper order.

Note that you are not bound to allow the contractor a second try. You can drive him forth from the site and call in someone else to put things right. But in general, wisdom demands patience because experience tells that impatience leads to litigation, and any sort of court action involving the work of contractors should be regarded as a luxury to be indulged in only where there is no reasonable alternative.

When a contractor's case does get to court, the proceedings tend to be lengthy and costly. Usually, a schedule is drawn up showing all the work alleged to be defective, all the prices charged and in dispute, the comments of both sides and the bare bones of the argument. By the time that experts have given evidence on both sides, counsel have examined and cross-examined the witnesses and addressed the judge, wrangling and haggling has proceeded in the corridors and all the documents have been copied, produced, read out . . . the odds are that the legal costs exceed the amount in dispute between the parties and whoever wins the case, both sides lose.

The best way to avoid litigation is to pick the right contractor at the start and to agree all prices in advance. Impossible? Then if you see a dispute in the offing, try to head it off with any sort of reasonable compromise. If that fails, then call in your lawyer and your surveyor at the earliest possible stage. They may achieve a compromise where you have failed. But if the worst comes to the worst, then at least you will know that your case will be properly prepared and your chances of winning it greatly improved. Most losing litigants have destroyed their own cases long before trial. And then the true meaning of the word 'trial' becomes all too expensively obvious.

In your capacity as a contractor for others, apply the above rules in reverse. You may charge the agreed price or else a reasonable sum. And you must do the job in a proper and workmanlike way and with reasonably suitable materials.

Chapter 85

What Can Repairers Charge?

VEHICLES, ADDING machines, computers, typewriters and all the rest of the modern allegedly-labour-saving devices dominate the world of the efficient business or professional man. The trouble is, of course, that machines are like people—they break down, for good reason or none. They must then be repaired.

So consider: What is a repairer entitled to charge? If he takes your car or computer into his premises, is he entitled to keep it until you have paid his bill—however exorbitant that bill may be? And what are your rights if the job is bungled?

* * *

Whenever you arrange for your machinery to be fixed, you enter into a contract with the repairer. In return for his undertaking to do the job required, you agree to pay his proper price. The rules are almost exactly the same as they would be if you arranged for your premises to be repaired or maintained and as explained in the previous Chapter, the contractor is entitled to the agreed price or, in the absence of agreement, to a reasonable price. The danger of not fixing a price in advance? That the contractor will tend to underestimate on the main job, so as to have his price accepted—and then try to make up his money by overcharging for the extras. If you give the contractor extra work, then my advice is: Get a price for that, too, before you give the go ahead.

Still, the one advantage you have when a contractor is working on your premises is that (literally) he cannot take them away. If there is a dispute, he cannot (for instance) remove parts of your building or items of your machinery, until he receives his money—even if his claim is fully justified. But when you put your car or equipment into his hands, the law gives him a special advantage. He then has what is known as a 'lien'—the right to hold the property upon which he has done work until you pay him his proper charges.

'But what if we say that his charges are not proper?' you ask, with justification.

What, indeed? He says: 'My charges are reasonable and right. Until you pay them, I will not release your property.'

You probably need your vehicle or equipment very urgently. If you want it back, then you will either have to pay—or to sue. As suing will take a very long time indeed, the chances are that you will give way to the financial blackmail and pay up. You may then have to sue for the overcharge—which is probably not worth doing.

What, then, if the work is defective?

There is an implied term in every contract under which services are performed that 'in the absence of agreement to the contrary' the job will be done in a proper and workmanlike manner and with reasonably suitable materials. Assuming that you have not signed an order freeing the repairer from liability for defects, you are entitled to have the job done properly.

If the vehicle or equipment does not work, when the repair job is completed, the odds are that the repairer has not earned his money. You have then suffered damage—and are legally entitled to damages—these being designed to put you in the same financial position as you would have been in, had the work been carried out in accordance with contract. Normally, you may deduct from the repairer's bill the reasonable cost of putting the work into proper order.

In theory, you are not even bound to allow the repairer a second chance. In practice, it is normally wise to give the contractor the chance to fix his own work—if only because otherwise you are not taking reasonable steps to 'mitigate your loss'—you must do what you can to keep your loss to a minimum, and if you rush off to some other repairer, it may be said that you are incurring unnecessary charges. Still, by that time you will have your equipment (or vehicle) back in your possession—and at least you will not have to battle against a repairer's lien—not, that is, until the second repairer takes over where the first left off. And I hope that he will do a better job!

Chapter 86

Rights of the Unpaid*

IF YOU remain unpaid, you may sue for your money. Conversely, the moment that you owe a debt, your creditor may issue legal proceedings. Whether or not legal battle is worthwhile is a problem that was considered in Chapter 78. Now, consider the other rights of the unpaid seller.

Not long ago, a contractor installed heating plant in business

* See also Chapter 117, for Legal Aspects of Billing.

premises. It never worked properly, so the proprietors declined to pay the bill. They received a letter in the following terms:

'We would refer to our accounts rendered. Unless these are paid in full within seven days hereof, we shall return to the premises, dismantle the plant, hold you responsible for the cost of the dismantling, and claim such damages for breach of contract as we may be advised.'

Not every unpaid contractor puts his demands quite so blatantly, nor his threats in such extravagant form. Still, this sort of arm twisting by the unpaid seller of services is remarkably common. But how far are such threats enforceable at law? What are the rights of those who sell their time and skill, either as such or in combination with the supply of materials?

If the contractor has carried out his job properly, then he is entitled to his money. If you fail or refuse to pay the money when it falls due, you are in breach of contract. You may be sued for damages—but the only damage suffered will be the amount due but unpaid under the contract. If there was some express term that interest would be chargeable if the debt was overdue, then this could be added on to the unpaid capital. If legal proceedings are actually commenced, then interest may be claimed. That is all.

It follows that the contractor has no right to claim the return of 'his' materials. Once he has affixed them to your premises, they undoubtedly become yours. Parts used to fix the boiler . . . radiators installed as part of a new central heating plant . . . insulation materials, nailed to the roof or walls—these 'adhere to the freehold'. They become part of your property. The contractor has no right whatsoever to their return. If he were to sue for them, he would fail. It follows that he has no conceivable right to snatch them back. That which he cannot obtain through legal action would be doubly unobtainable by the use of 'self help.'

In any event, ownership in goods passes when the parties intend it to pass; in the absence of express agreement to the contrary, the rules as to intention are laid down by the Sale of Goods Act (Appendix 4). In the broadest terms, ownership generally passes when goods are set aside by the seller for the buyer, even if they have not yet been paid for or delivered. By the time the contractor has used his spare parts or his appliances for your needs, ownership has passed—and the contractor cannot possibly recover the items. They are no longer his.

Anyway, even had the contractor the right to the goods (which, I repeat, he most emphatically has not), if he were to enter your premises without your consent in the hunt for his own property, he would be a trespasser. Even if you were wrongfully detaining his goods, that would give him no right to invade your territory. The moment he did so, you could ask him to go and if he refused you would be entitled to use reasonable force to eject him. There are many business people who are ignorant of the law and trespass upon the land of others. They are liable to find themselves in very deep trouble (details in Chapter 98).

It follows that the man who sells services and is unpaid for them should put his lawyers on the trail. Like a pea in a biscuit tin, an empty threat may rattle loud but strikes no fear into the soul of the knowledgeable.

As for the unpaid seller of goods, his rights are specifically laid down in Part 4 of *The Sale of Goods Act, 1893*. The seller of goods is deemed to be 'an unpaid seller', for the purposes of the Act—

'*a* When the whole of the price has not been paid or tendered:
'*b* When a bill of exchange or other negotiable instrument has been received as conditional payment, and the condition on which it was received has not been fulfilled by reason of the dishonour of the instrument or otherwise.'

So tender of only part of the price—or payment of only a proportion—will not prevent the seller from being 'unpaid', and hence entitled to exercise his Sale of Goods Act rights. What are they?

First, Section 39: In general, even if ownership of the goods has passed to the buyer, the unpaid seller has 'by implication of law—

'*a* A lien on the goods or right to retain them for the price while he is in possession of them;
'*b* In case of the insolvency of the buyer, a right of stopping the goods in transit after he has parted with possession of them;
'*c* A right to resale as limited by this Act.'

If you are a manufacturer, wholesaler or retailer and goods have been set aside for the buyer, ownership in the goods may have been transferred. But this does not mean that you will be forced to deliver if you are unpaid. You are free to say: 'Until I am paid the price, I will not disgorge the materials—however much you may need them.'

Conversely, if a supplier says: 'Not having done business with you on any previous occasion, we regret that we must insist upon payment prior to delivery', he is fully entitled to do so. By Statute, he may demand payment before he releases his lien on the goods. 'While he is in possession of them' he has a 'right to retain them for the price'.

Naturally, if there were some agreement to the contrary, the situation would be different. Maybe you arrange with a supplier that he will give you credit?

You are to pay at the end of the month following delivery perhaps? Then the Act (as always) in no way interferes with the contractual bed in which you have seen fit to lie. But otherwise, I repeat, the unpaid seller's first right is to exercise a lien on the goods, if they remain in his possession.

Now suppose that you sell goods and the buyer becomes insolvent before he acquires possession of his property. Even if the property has left you . . . even if it is in the hands of a carrier, perhaps, on its way to its destination . . . you may stop it in transit.

What, then, of the right of resale? Section 48:

'Subject to the provisions of this Section, a contract of sale is not rescinded by the mere exercise by an unpaid seller of his right of lien or retention or stoppage in transitu. Where an unpaid seller who has exercised his right of lien or retention or stoppage in transitu resells the goods, the buyer acquires a good title thereto as against the original buyer. Where the goods are of a perishable nature, where the unpaid seller gives notice to the buyer of his intention to resell, if the buyer does not within a reasonable time pay or tender the price, the unpaid seller may resell the goods and recover from the original buyer damages for any loss occasioned by his breach of contract.'

So if the unpaid seller exercises his lien or stops goods which have left his possession and are in transit to the buyer, the contract of sale remains alive.

An unpaid seller is not entitled in all circumstances to resell property. But if it is perishable—or if he gives notice of his intention to resell—then unless he is repaid within a reasonable time, he may consign the goods to another buyer, who will acquire a good title to them. The law expects sellers to be reasonably patient, where the goods will not perish as a result. Again, where the buyer is not informed of the intention to resell, to resell is to break the contract, unless the goods are perishables. So sensible sellers who are unpaid will give notice of intention to resell. They will discuss with their lawyers how long a time would be 'reasonable'—and when that time has passed, if they have not received their money they will mitigate their loss by finding some other buyer who is more likely to produce the money.

Even where a lien is exercised or goods are stopped in transit, the contract remains alive. Even where the original buyer does not pay when he should, and the goods are sold elsewhere, damages may still be claimed from the man who should have paid them. As usual, these will be designed to compensate the seller for any loss which he suffered as a result of the breach of contract. They will be the difference between the price which the original buyer was to have paid and that which the seller eventually managed to get from the people who did pay for the property. The original buyer's best hope? That maybe the seller will break even or even make a profit on the deal, second time round—in which case the buyer will pay no damages whatsoever.

'Where the seller expressly reserves a right of resale in case the buyer should make default, and on the buyer making default resells the goods, the original contract of sale is rescinded—but without prejudice to any claim the seller may have for damages.' Some sellers specifically state in their contracts that if the buyer does not pay on a specified date, he shall be entitled to resell the goods. If that happens, the contract of sale dies—but the seller may still have a claim for damages.

Section 46 lays down how stoppage in transitu is effected. The seller may exercise his right of stoppage in transitu 'either by taking actual possession of the goods, or by giving notice of his claim to the carrier or other bailee or custodier (*sic*) in whose possession the goods are. Such notice may be given either to the person in actual possession of the goods or to his principal. In the latter case the notice, to be effectual, must be given at such time and under such circumstances that the principal, by the exercise of reasonable diligence, may communicate it to his servant or agent in time to prevent a delivery to the buyer.'

Very sensibly, the law says that you have a choice: You may inform the head office of the carrier or the boss of the firm which has the goods in its care, or the actual person who holds the goods at the particular time. Telephone the head office of the carriers, if you wish —or inform the driver of the vehicle with your goods on board. Either will do.

'When notice of stoppage in transit is given by the seller to the carrier, or other bailee or custodier in possession of the goods, he must redeliver the goods to, or according to the directions of, the seller. The expenses of such redelivery must be borne by the seller.' So the carrier must do as you ask. He must comply with the notice you give to him. You will have to bear the expense of the redelivery—but, of course, this will be added on to your claim for damages against the buyer.

'Goods are deemed to be in course of transit,' says Section 45, 'from the time when they are delivered to a carrier by land or water, or other bailee or other custodier for the purpose of transmission to the buyer, until the buyer, or his agent in that behalf, takes delivery of them from such carrier or other bailee or custodier.' The transit is at an end 'if the buyer or his agent . . . obtains delivery of the goods before their arrival at the appointed destination'.

From the time that you deliver goods to a carrier or other bailee until the buyer obtains delivery or possession, you may stop them if you are unpaid and the buyer becomes insolvent. You do not have to allow your goods to be amongst the assets to be used to pay off the buyer's creditors, whom you will then join.

In practice, what matters is to move swiftly. If you are not only unpaid but suspect the buyer's solvency, you can still jump the queue if you retain the goods in your possession (and hence can exercise a lien) or if they have not yet reached the hands of the buyer (in which case they may be stopped in transit). But please note: These rights are only exercisable where the buyer is insolvent—and not, for instance, because you find that you can obtain a higher price elsewhere.

When understood, the rights of the unpaid seller are comparatively simple. But fail to understand them and exercise rights which you do not have and you are asking for problems. And that is precisely what the contractor discovered, when he attempted to recover parts of the central heating installation which he had put in. His clients had been to their lawyers; and the police awaited the contractor at the door of the premises.

Chapter 87

Unsolicited and Uncollected Goods

IT IS a rare business or professional man who does not from time to time receive unsolicited goods.

The Unsolicited Goods and Services Act, 1971, was designed to deal with these problems. So consider: What does this important statute really say? What are you entitled to do with goods which arrive in your hands, uninvited and unwanted? And can the sender be prosecuted?

* * *

In general, the recipient of any goods is their 'bailee'. Whether he asks for them or not . . . whether he is paid to look after them or receives them gratuitously or as a favour . . . he is bound to take reasonable care of the goods placed in his charge.

The Disposal of Uncollected Goods Act attempted to give repairers the right to sell goods which were not picked up. But in practice, the Act requires so many formalities from the trader that it is almost useless.

As for the receivers of unsolicited goods, they were in a hopeless position. They were bound to take reasonable care of the unwanted property. Hence the 1971 Act.

A person who now receives unsolicited goods 'with a view to his acquiring them' may, in many cases, 'use, deal with or dispose of them as if they were an unconditional gift to him, and any right of the sender to the goods shall be extinguished'.

Note, first, that the law is in no way altered if you asked for the goods to be supplied to you on sale or return or on approval. The Act deals with goods sent 'on spec'.

Second, the recipient must have 'no reasonable cause to believe that the goods were sent with a view to their being acquired for the purposes of a trade or business'. So this section is not designed to protect traders. It is there for the benefit of the public at large.

If, then, you receive unsolicited goods which are intended for you to sell, I suggest the following:

1 Write to the suppliers forthwith, describing the goods; setting out the date when you received them; and requiring them to be collected forthwith.
2 If that does not do the trick, send a further letter, saying that you will charge for storage;
3 If you have space available, put the stuff out of reach—and try to return it to a representative of the suppliers, when next he calls—remembering, of course, to get a receipt;
4 Alternatively, see whether you can ship the goods back, letting the recipient meet the bill; and if this is impossible, then
5 Write to your Member of Parliament—he may take the matter up with the suppliers—perhaps hinting that he will try to have the Act extended to traders—in which case the senders may see sense.

Now assume that the goods were sent to you at your home and you 'have neither agreed to acquire nor agreed to return them'. When can you 'use, deal with or dispose of them' as if they were a gift? The Act provides two ways.

First, if you can show 'that during the period of six months beginning with the day on which you received the goods, the sender did not take possession of them and you did not unreasonably refuse to permit the sender to do so' then you can hold on to the goods as if they were a gift to you.

Second, if you do not want to wait for the end of the six months period you can serve written notice on the sender stating your name and address and 'if possession of the goods in question may not be taken by the sender at that address, the address at which it may be so taken'. The notice must also contain a statement that the goods are unsolicited and must be served 'not less than thirty days before the expiration of the six month period'. Provided that the sender does not take possession of the goods within thirty days from the date of the notice and you do not unreasonably refuse to permit him to do so you are entitled to keep the goods.

Now for Section 2—which protects traders, as well as private citizens:

'A person who, not having reasonable cause to believe there is a right to payment, in the course of any trade or business makes a demand for payment, or asserts a present or prospective right to payment, for what he knows are unsolicited goods sent . . . to another person with his view to acquiring them, shall be guilty of an offence and on summary conviction shall be liable to a fine not exceeding £200.'

So if suppliers send you unsolicited goods to your business, you will not acquire any right to them. But if he makes a demand for payment without reasonably believing that you had agreed to acquire the goods, then he may be fined up to £200 by a Magistrates' Court.

Further, if that sender 'not having reasonable cause to believe there is a right to payment' threatens to bring legal proceedings or places you on a list of defaulters or threatens to do so or 'invokes or causes to be invoked any other collection procedure or threatens to do so' he may be fined up to £400.

The senders of unsolicited goods take a very considerable risk. A person who sends unsolicited goods 'for the purpose of a trade or business' may be guilty of a criminal offence if he demands payment or makes threats, even if the recipient was a trader and could acquire no right to those goods, under the Act.

So anyone who sends goods to your business which you do not want should be warned: 'Do not try to extract payment from me, or you will fall foul of the law.'

Warning: Only after six years will the sender lose his rights to the goods sent to you for your trade or business; until then, they remain his—so if you use, sell, dispose of (or, for that matter, smoke, eat or otherwise consume) those goods, you will have 'acquired a property' in them. Then you will become liable to pay.

Meanwhile, the 1971 Act gives single protection to the trader and double to the ordinary consumer.

Chapter 88

Commission When the Deal Goes Off

EVERY business and professional man should know the rules on the payment of estate agents. Since the case of *Christie Owen and Davies* v. *Rapaccioli*, it has become all too easy to be forced to pay an estate agent even if he does not introduce the eventual purchaser.

There is no law which says that an estate agent is only entitled to his money if he introduces the eventual purchaser. There is nothing to prevent you from agreeing to pay your agent if he produces someone who is 'ready, able and willing' to buy. Indeed, vast numbers of estate agents' arrangements are on that basis—and their documents say so. But in the past, these arrangements have been interpreted as meaning: 'The agent is to be paid only if the deal goes through.'

Estate agents maintain that this is grossly unfair. After all, an architect may not get his whole fee if the building is neither erected nor completed, but if he has prepared the plans in accordance with instructions, then he is entitled to at least a proportion of the money. His earnings are not dependent upon the erection of the structure.

The answer to that one? That estate agents may effect a sale through one phone call, a single advertisement or a sign in window. If they are lucky, with minimal effort they will get the entire fee. They are not like architects who have to sweat over the original plans and then supervise, while those plans are put into operation.

To this background, Messrs Christie Owen and Davies were instructed by a caterer called Rapaccioli to help sell his restaurant. Mr Rapaccioli wanted £20,000 plus stock and valuation.

The agents were to be entitled to commission in the event of their 'effecting an introduction either directly or indirectly of a person . . . ready, able and willing to purchase at the above price . . . or for any other price' which Mr Rapaccioloi might be prepared to accept.

Christie's duly introduced a Mr Abbas as prospective purchaser and he telephoned to a director of the plaintiffs, offering £17,700 for the lease and goodwill, plus stock and valuation. Mr Rapaccioli agreed to accept the lower price and solicitors were instructed on both sides.

Draft contracts were approved; the deposit was paid—but Mr Rapaccioli, having apparently got a better offer, declined to go on with the transaction.

Question for the Court: was Mr Abbas a person 'ready, able and willing to purchase'? The trial judge held that he was not, because no binding contract had been entered into between him and the defendant. It was conceded that Mr Abbas was 'able' to purchase at the price mentioned. But was he 'ready and willing'?

Lord Justice Cairns set out three principles which now regulate the interpretation of 'readiness and willingness'.

1   The decision as to whether commission is payable depends on the terms of the contract and on the ordinary rules of interpretation. It follows that the client may make whatever agreement he likes with the estate agent, however unfavourable to himself, and he will be bound by it. To find out whether you or your client are bound to pay commission, look at the documents, or correspondence and interpret them according to their ordinary meaning. If that is impossible, then get the help of a lawyer to establish how courts have interpreted the phrase in question.

2   When the agreement between principal and agent is for commission to be payable on the introduction of a person ready, able and willing to purchase, the commission is payable if a sale actually results. Obviously. More important: it 'may become payable when the transaction becomes abortive'. So the mere fact that the deal goes off will not necessarily deprive the agent of his remuneration.

3   Commission is payable when a person who is able to purchase is introduced and expresses readiness and willingness by 'an unqualified offer to purchase', even though such offer has not been accepted and could be withdrawn. Assuming that this offer comes within the terms that the agent has been authorised to invite and that the offer is not withdrawn by the purchaser but is refused by the vendor, the agents will be entitled to their money.

Mr Rapaccioli had turned down a good offer made by a purchaser who was ready, willing and able to buy—therefore Christie Owen won their case and were entitled to £835 commission.

So the old rule that unless there was a contract of sale, the purchaser could not be 'willing' has gone. He may be forced to pay commission, even if there is never any contract.

Equally, you may find that if you are prepared to accept a certain sum; your estate agent finds you a buyer who is ready, willing and able to purchase at that price; that if you accept a higher price thereafter from someone else and call off the first deal, you may have to pay two lots of estate agents. The first man earned his money by introducing the contact, the 'ready, willing and able' purchaser, in accordance with his contract with you. The second one produced the purchaser who actually bought the premises.

So where a purchaser makes an unqualified offer at a specified or minimum sum as a result of the efforts of the estate agent concerned, the seller is not bound to accept that offer—but if he rejects it, he cannot prevent the estate agent from getting his money.

So nowadays, wise business and professional people who know the rules will do their best to enter into contracts which enable the estate agents to get their money only where a sale is *actually* effected as a result of an introduction made by those agents. It is bad enough to have to pay agents once—but far worse to have to produce twice the money, when one of the agents has earned it but in a way that is useless to you.

"WE NEVER HAVE ANY FUN LIKE WE USED TO — THE NEIGHBOURS HAVEN'T COMPLAINED FOR NEARLY A WEEK ——!"

Part eight

Negligence, Nuisance and Other Common 'Torts'

Chapter 89

Negligence – Gratuitous and Otherwise

THE MILK of human kindness can be a very expensive commodity. The law has no sympathy for those who do harm in the course of doing good. We all owe a 'duty of care' to our neighbours—whether or not we are paid for the jobs done.

Let us start with the snail that created legal history way back in 1932. It was quietly decomposing in the opaque depths of a ginger-beer bottle when it was rudely disturbed by a Miss Donoghue, who had been given the drink by a friend. She consumed the alleged beverage and as a result became seriously ill. She sued the manufacturers. 'Ridiculous,' they retorted. 'We don't know you. We owed no duty to you. Even if we were negligent* in our preparation of the ginger beer, you should have sued the person who gave you the drink.' 'Wrong', pronounced the House of Lords. Lord Atkin said this:

'You must take reasonable care to avoid acts or omissions which you can reasonably foresee would be likely to injure your neighbour. Who, then, in law is my neighbour? The answer seems to be—persons who are so closely and directly affected by my act that I ought reasonably to have them in contemplation as being so affected when I am directing my mind to the acts or omissions which are called in question.'

The most hard-hearted soft-drink maker must realise that the person likely to drink his poison is not the person who buys it from him, but 'the ultimate consumer'. Miss Donoghue was the 'neighbour' of the manufacturers. And she won a triumphant victory.

The next great leap forward came in 1963, in the House of Lords case, discussed in Chapter 18.

'If a reasonable man knows that he is being trusted or that his skill and judgment are being relied on,' said the learned Law Lords, in effect, 'and he gives the information or advice sought without that

* For the rules on professional negligence, see Chapter 18.

291

reflection or enquiry which a careful answer would require, and as a result of his negligent behaviour the enquirer suffers loss or damage, he will be liable in damages.'

The defendants in question wriggled off the hook thanks to their disclaimer. But we now know that anyone who gives advice, provides information or does any sort of service for anyone else is under a legal duty to take proper care. If he is negligent and his negligence causes damage, it will be no excuse to say: 'You didn't pay me . . . I only acted out of pure goodness of nature. . . .' Even a completely gratuitous kindness must be carefully performed.

So be sparing with your free advice. If you do not wish to deprive others of the benefit of your counsel, cover yourself by saying that the recipient of your wisdom follows it at his own risk . . . that you give your reference 'without responsibility' . . . that you can accept no liability if your recipe produces poisonous results, your old fashioned remedy paralyses the patient or your recommended short cut runs the car over a cliff. The odds are that you will be legally in the clear.

Chapter 90

Vicarious Liability

SIMON SMITH was worried. 'It's not that I object to smoking in itself,' he said. 'But it's dangerous and unnecessary while working. So I forbid it. I've always realised that this meant that some of my employees would sneak off to see a man about a dog-end, so to speak. But I'd never realised the real danger—that surreptitious smoking and the furtive stubbing out of tell-tale butts might lead to fire. And last week it did.

'The whole place caught alight—and the worst of it is that I'd only reduced my insurance cover a few months before. What's more, some valuable goods belonging to customers were damaged or destroyed, and I'm not covered at all for them.

'Now, what I want to know is this—am I liable to compensate the owners of those goods, when I'd taken every reasonable and proper care for their safety. After all, while they were damaged because of the negligent act of my servant, that act was forbidden by me. My man was disobeying my orders, and was doing something not only which he wasn't employed to do, but which was not permitted whilst doing the work for which he was employed.'

* * *

This common problem raises the whole question of an employer's liability for the wrongful acts of his servants—his 'vicarious liability', in lawyers' jargon.

The basic rule is simple. Each of us is liable to compensate people who suffer loss and injury due to our own personal negligence. And we are equally liable to pay up when damage is caused by the negligence of someone who is acting for us and on our behalf—that is, by our servant, acting in the course of his employment. That is where the troubles begin.

What is 'in the course of a man's employment'? To take Mr Smith's case, his servant was not employed to smoke, or allowed to do so while working. So was his wrongful and negligent act done 'in the course of his employment'?

Ask yourself, 'Was the man about his master's business? Was he doing something which he was employed to do, even if he was doing so in an improper or, indeed, in a forbidden manner?' If the answer is yes, the master is liable. If it is no, he is not.

Not long ago, a judge had to decide the case of two boys, who were stoking a fire on a building site. One of them pulled out a red-hot poker and waved it at the other boy's leg, to 'make him jump'. The lad jumped all right . . . but the poker set light to his apron and he was seriously burned. But was his boss liable in respect of those burns? Were they caused by the other boy's negligence 'within the scope of his employment'? The judge decided that they were. The boys were employed to stoke the fire and they skylarked around while doing so. To the extent that the injured boy was hurt by the negligence of his mate (and not, that is, through his own fault) the master was just as much to blame as the lad. And that was so even though the boys had been shown how to light and tend the stove, and warned not to skylark.

The test is not whether the wrongful act was forbidden—only whether it was done in the course of the employment.

A case similar to Mr Smith's problem concerned a petrol-station attendant who, in spite of being warned against smoking, caused an explosion by flicking a cigarette-end into some inflammable material. After long argument, the Court decided that he was doing his job, filling customers' tanks, and the fact that he did so negligently and dangerously and in a manner forbidden to him, did not take his act outside the scope of his employment. His firm would have to compensate the third party, injured in the explosion.

But Mr Smith's man had left his actual work when he caused the damage. He was, it might be argued on 'an independent frolic of his own'. An 'independent frolic' does take the act outside the scope of employment.

Suppose your van driver is delivering goods for you and causes an accident, you will have to pay up. If he goes off his route and races a friend down a new motorway and negligently causes damage while doing so, you will not be liable. The damage was not caused 'in the course of his employment'.

The difficulties arise in the borderline cases—where the driver goes off in your van to get a bite to eat, and deviates from his route, or where Mr Smith's employee leaves his work for a forbidden smoke, but does the damage on his master's premises and in working hours. Here one cannot definitely say whether or not the master will be found liable. The reason, of course, that most of such cases do not reach the Courts is that the employers (or their insurers) as well as the legal advisers of the injured person all realise the uncertainties . . . so the cases are nearly all amicably and sensibly settled long before they get to trial.

One of the comparatively recent changes in the law of vicarious liability has been the abolition of the so-called 'doctrine of common employment'. This excluded vicarious liability on the part of the master where the damage was caused to one servant by another in the same employment. Today, the employer may be vicariously liable to anyone, be he servant or stranger, negligently injured or damaged by an employee in the course of his employment.

This does not imply that the employee is not himself liable in law for the results of his own negligence. The fact that the boss may be responsible as well does not free him from liability. The reason why the boss gets sued is that the employee is so often not worth powder and shot. He is a 'man of straw', and as such, not worth going for. But he can be sued, and sometimes is.

Indeed, an employer is entitled (in theory at least) to be indemnified by his servant in respect of any losses suffered by him as a result of that servant's negligence. In practice, this is usually a hopeless proposition. But in a recent High Court case, a master's right to an indemnity was reaffirmed. So no employee should reckon on the certainty of not having to pay up if he causes damage by his negligence.

Still, do not try to recoup yourself by making deductions from your employee's wages, without his consent. This you may not be allowed to do. The Truck Acts forbid it, in the case of 'workmen'.

The act of negligence may be sufficiently serious to warrant summary dismissal. But if it is not, or if you decide to keep the negligent person on your staff, then you will probably have to forget about the damage. At least, that is what insurance companies usually do—they don't normally waste their time pursuing possible remedies against employees.

As for Simon Smith, he was advised that if his case came to court, he would probably lose—but that room for doubt would give good grounds for bargaining. In fact, he was let off lightly. The other side eventually agreed to take fifty per cent of what they might have won. It was a classic case of the bird in the hand.

Chapter 91

Neighbours and Nuisances

THE CLOSER you live to your neighbour, the less likely you are to love him. But the fact that he may be a nuisance to you in fact does not mean that he is creating a nuisance in law. It is a question of degree.

We must all expect to put up with a certain amount of disturbance as 'part of the give and take of neighbourly life'. For perfect peace, you must wait for the world to come. But if the degree of disturbance from which you suffer goes beyond that which the reasonable man should be called upon to endure, the law will come to his aid.

There are many forms of 'nuisance'. Noise, vibration, smoke, dust and fumes are the most common. If any of them emanate from your neighbour's home, what are your chances of acquiring comparative peace with the aid of the law?

The first question to ask is: should you reasonably put up with the disturbance in question? The sound of your neighbour's child practising her scales may drive you to distraction, but if she practises at reasonable times, you will just have to grit your teeth and bear it. Or you could leave the district. But if she destroys the calm of the night, you may obtain an injunction—an order of the court, forbidding any continuation of her nasty behaviour.

However much you hate the smell of a bonfire, your neighbours are normally entitled to incinerate their garden refuse. But if they choose only occasions when the wind will waft the smoke into your kitchen . . . if your windows must be kept permanently closed because their garden fire is the rule rather than the exception . . . if a person of normal sensitivity would consider that the nature, timing or volume of the smoke went beyond the bounds of reasonableness— then if you cannot get results through courteous requests or threats of legal action, you will have to let your solicitors get on with it.

It is always the standard of the average, healthy, normal person that the law applies in cases of nuisance. For instance, noise that would be quite unobjectionable to a woman in good health or to a man who works normal hours and sleeps through the night, may be torture for the woman who lies ill in bed or for the night-worker, trying to snatch some sleep while the sun shines. But they have no special rights or remedies in law. If you choose to deviate from the norm—or if you have no alternative—that is your bad luck.

Then again, in assessing the degree of disturbance, the court considers the area in which it takes place. Live in the country and you may reasonably expect to be fairly free from industrial noise, but you will probably have to put up with the ordinary smells of the farmyard. Take a flat in a busy, industrial centre and while you may legitimately complain if your neighbour keeps pigs or poultry in his backyard, you may have to suffer in dignified silence, whilst the machinery crashes and bangs across the street.

Occupy a home in semi-detached suburbia, and while you must expect a certain amount of family altercation through the party wall, if the do-it-yourself enthusiast engages in round-the-clock shift work, you will probably be able to prove a 'nuisance'. In other words, what is a nuisance in Bath may not be in Battersea.

Suppose that builders move in next door. They kick up a dust and din. Assuming that they have taken normal precautions to damp down the dust and to keep the noise to reasonable proportions and normal working hours, you will just have to endure with as much fortitude as you can muster, one of the miseries of life that has existed since time immemorial. But if the dust and the din make your life unbearable, you may not only obtain an injunction but also damages. Why should you have to bear the cost of having your spotless linen and upholstery dry cleaned?

Every case, then, is considered on its own facts. 'Reasonableness' is enthroned as the sole criterion. If you survey the wreckage of Guy Fawkes' night . . . look back with horror on noise that woke your children and caused the dog to howl . . . console yourself with the thought that it comes but once a year. So does Hogmanay . . . the Christmas dance . . . the birthday binge . . . after all, you probably have them yourself. And you may not always ask the neighbours to join you. But when it comes to persistent, all-night music from the café below . . . banging on the wall that wakes you, night after sleepless night . . . family rows that permeate your home from below . . . constant jumping of well-shod children on the uncarpeted floors above . . . then the time has come to take action. You too can make a nuisance of yourself. And the law will show you how.

Chapter 92

Coming to a Nuisance

DR STURGES built a consulting room next door to a factory. 'What better place for business?' he asked himself, rhetorically. The answer came in the form of bangs and hisses, squeals, rattles and clattering— all the row of particularly noisy modern machinery. The result? The doctor could not hear himself diagnose or prescribe, nor listen to the complaints of his patients. The time had come, he decided, to make his own complaints.

'Sorry,' said the factory people. 'We've been carrying on business in this industrial area for a long time. You decided to set up shop next door to us. That was your decision and not ours. We have to make a living. You will just have to put up with the noise and vibration as best you can—or move out to the foreign parts whence you came.'

But Dr Sturges was not a man to be easily moved (literally, if not metaphorically). Instead, he sued the proprietors of the factory.

Now, no one is allowed to use his land in such a way as unreasonably to disturb his neighbour's enjoyment of his property. But what is or is not 'reasonable' in any particular case is (as we have seen) a question of fact and often has to be hammered out with a great deal of (very dignified, of course) sound and fury in a court of law. And that is where the case of Dr Sturges ended up.

The doctor won his day. Lord Justice Thesiger held that the degree of disturbance caused to the good physician was more than that which an ordinary, reasonable individual would expect to have to endure as 'part of the give and take of neighbourly life'. Having regard to all the circumstances of the case, including the nature of the neighbourhood, the factory created a 'nuisance'. The doctor was entitled to an injunction, restraining the factory owners from continuing their unlawful behaviour.

Many morals may be drawn. First, the fact that you 'come to a nuisance' does not mean that you cannot complain of it. You are entitled to reasonable quiet for your work, no matter how new you are to a particular district. But the district you are in does matter.

As Lord Justice Thesiger said, 'Whether anything is a nuisance or not is a question to be determined, not merely by an abstract consideration of the thing itself, but in reference to its circumstances; what would be a nuisance in Belgrave Square would not necessarily be so in Bermondsey: and where a locality is devoted to a particular trade or manufacture carried on by the traders or manufacturers of a particular and established manner not constituting a public nuisance, judges and juries would be justified in finding, and may be trusted to find, that the trade or manufacture so carried on in that locality is not a private or actionable wrong.'

So you cannot expect the same quiet in your dockland office or surgery as you would in the hallowed precincts of Harrow or Harley Street.

Chapter 93

The Value of Life and Limb

THE MOST likely place for a businessman to suffer injury is on the road. But there are accidents in every place of work and even the most sedate and middle-aged executive may (literally) fall down on the job.

So assume the worst. You are injured. You are entitled to damages against the other driver—or against your employers—because you can prove that your injuries were (wholly or in part) the result of their negligence or breach of statutory duty. How much will you get?

First, there are those items which can be assessed in terms of hard cash. These include loss of wages or salary (minus the tax which would have been paid on it and also less one-half any National Insurance benefits received). There are convalescent and medical expenses, the cost of repairing or replacing a damaged vehicle—in fact, all those items which can be totted up in precise figures.

But what of your physical injuries? Who can put a price on human life or limb? You would not exchange your right arm for all the gold in Threadneedle Street? But if it has to be amputated because of someone else's negligence, you will require compensation—in pounds, shillings and pence. And if the case gets to court, a Judge will have to decide how much you receive. Your life and those of your family and friends could not be bought at any price. But where there is a fatal accident, caused by negligence, a Judge may have to assess the damages payable to dependants of the deceased. How? If you are involved in this sort of trouble, how much 'damages' will you get?

The answer depends on the sums awarded by courts in respect of similar injuries suffered by others as unfortunate as yourself. This is how insurers decide how much to offer to settle a case—and happily, the majority of claims are haggled to a satisfactory compromise, long before they get to court. This is how lawyers base their advice on the proper amount to accept—and the nearer the case gets to court, the more likely it is that lawyers have become involved.

The experts delve into the Law Reports and their own memories for awards in similar cases. Like as not, they discuss the problems with their colleagues—the more experience you can concentrate on the problem, the more likely you are to reach a sensible result.

But no two injuries are ever identical. And even if they were, people's reactions to pain differ enormously. If two people are knocked down the same way by a car, one may walk away with a shrug whilst the other dies. Everything depends upon the person's constitution. One man has a thick skull (literally). Another's is thin and brittle. One man can shrug off a severe shock with minimal after-effects. Another will suffer months of depression from a minor blow. In law, 'you take your victim as you find him'. Every case, like every victim, is different. And lawyers and insurers can never work out prospective damages for personal injuries with any absolute certainty.

Suppose, for instance, that a singer or a lawyer suffers damage to his vocal cords. He may lose his livelihood. But if the same man loses a leg, however mighty his misery, his loss of earnings may (if he is lucky) turn out to be minimal.

But suppose that the victim of the same accident was a labourer. His leg and his earning power go together. Even though his earnings may be a fraction of those of the limbless lawyer or artiste, his damages might be fifty times as great. But if the labourer lost his power of speech, his financial loss might be minimal. Lawyer, labourer, performer—and man of commerce—alike may obtain the same sort of award in respect of their pain and suffering. But there may be spectacular differences in their loss of actual and prospective earnings.

So reported awards cannot do much to help the layman to estimate what he would get for his injuries. There are too many variables. Newspaper summaries are too brief—or too full of the human interest angle which interests the reader but which may obscure the legal issue.

So if you get involved in a claim for damages for personal injuries, do not try to deal with it on your own. If you are at the receiving end of the trouble, then the odds are that your insurers will be behind you and you will have to do as they say. But if you are the claimant, it is most unwise to attempt to assess your own damages.

If your claim is to succeed, then you have nothing to fear from getting the help of a solicitor. The odds are that your case will settle and as part of the bargain your legal costs will be paid. If you are merely claiming lost cash (such as the cost of repairing your van, lorry or car), then you can probably assess the amount of that claim, without too much difficulty. But when it comes to personal injuries, the chances of your being able to assess the right answer are remote. The more serious the injury, the greater the claim, the more vital it is that you should consult an experienced solicitor at the first possible moment.

Solicitors' services are often dispensable—but never for the potential litigant with a serious, personal injuries claim. The lawyer will not only push for a quick settlement, where this is advisable, but (often equally important) not allow you to settle too early, when the course of the illness or injury and hence its after-effects are unclear. He will make certain that if you require Legal Aid, you will get it—and that if medical reports are necessary, they are obtained. If counsel's opinion is required, either as to your prospects of success or as to the damages you are likely to recover, he will obtain it. He will see that you do not lose your rights through suing too late, nor your money through settling too soon.

Chapter 94

Accidents and Injuries

Dangers are Divisible

MORE THAN one person may be injured in an accident. If, for example, you are a consulting engineer, both you and your client may be liable for its results. Consider *Driver* v. *William Willett (Contractors) Limited and R. G. Richardson-Hill & Partners.*

Rodney Driver sued his employers (Willett's) and Richardson-Hill (consultant safety and inspecting engineers). He had been employed as a general labourer on a building site. A scaffold board fell from a hoist and he was seriously injured.

The court held that the employers were negligent and in breach of their statutory duty because they permitted the hoist to be used in an unsafe manner. 'Not our fault,' they retorted. 'We contracted with the engineers, who had agreed to advise us on safety requirements and compliance with the relevant regulations. They undertook the duties of a safety officer under the Building Regulations then in force. They had not advised us to discontinue the unsafe use of the hoist.'

'It is plain from the evidence,' said Mr Justice Rees, 'that the consultants knew and could reasonably foresee that the employers' employees would be working on the site and that their safety would be endangered if the safety regulations were not observed or the work not safely conducted. In my judgment, the consultants also knew that the employers relied on them for advice as to the steps to be taken in relation to the safety precautions on the site generally and, in particular, as to the safety of the hoistway. . . .

'The Plaintiff fell clearly within the class of persons whom the consultants must have reasonably foreseen would be injured if they failed to give advice to the employers as to the safety precautions to be taken, and they therefore owed a duty to the Plaintiff. . . .'

'We were not in breach of that duty,' argued the consultants. The Judge disagreed. They had 'clearly failed in their duty to advise the employers to have the hoistway enclosed by wire mesh as soon as their site inspectors observed that the hoist was adapted for carrying scaffold boards and long timbers. They must have observed the state of affairs several months at least before the accident.'

'But even if we had complied with our duty and given the proper advice, that advice would not have been accepted and the precautions advised taken and the accident prevented,' said the engineers.

'I am satisfied on the balance of probabilities,' said the Judge, 'that the employers would have implemented that advice.' The result? Responsibility was apportioned in the ratio of 40 per cent to the employers and 60 per cent to the consultants. But the employers were entitled to recover from the consultants as damages for breach of contract such sum as the Plaintiff was awarded against the employers. Although the injured man could have recovered from either Defendants, for the 'tort' of negligence, the engineers were in breach of their contract and were liable to indemnify the employers in full. This was no joke. The trial Judge assessed the damages at £21,646.

Moral: Damages and responsibilities may be divisible—but are not necessarily payable in the same proportions. Watch out for the wording of contracts. Make sure that you are insured.

Damages

Damages for personal injuries are on the up and up. Here are some recent awards.

Mackrell v. *Patel*, a twenty year old unskilled labourer sued for damages following injuries to his left arm. There was continual wasting in the arm and this restricted him from doing heavier work. His ability to work as a lathe operator, which he had trained to do, was substantially impaired. He was unable to ride a motor cycle. He was awarded damages of £7500 comprising £3500 for pain and suffering and £4000 for present and future hardship in the labour market.

In *Franaszek* v. *Davis*, a sixteen year old lad suffered severe head injuries which caused a complete change of personality. He was no longer able to hold down regular employment although he was healthy. He was awarded damages of £15,000 for future loss of earnings and £10,000 for pain and suffering.

In *Fuller* v. *Another*, a boy aged 15 suffered severe burns from paraffin lamps and was in hospital for 11 months. He had 27 operations. Damages: £3500.

In *Coulson* v. *Another*, a 53 year old male who was a former coal miner developed a serious anxiety state after an accident in which he had to jump from the path of a railway engine which was showing no lights at night. He had to give up his pre-accident work. Now he was frightened of crossing the road on his own for fear of being knocked down. He was awarded damages of £5975.

Note that the range is enormous: the claims are common: and the amounts are constantly climbing. So check your insurance policy and make certain that you are properly covered, for all eventualities. And remember that interest is now added to the damages, along complicated lines recently laid down by the Court of Appeal.

Protect Your Staff

Of course, it is much better not to have to claim under your policy. If you become too bad a risk, your insurers will decline to renew your cover, when your present policy expires. Anyway, your premium is unlikely to remain where it is. So you must take care for the safety of those whom you employ—and not just when they are in your premises, either.

A Mr Bradford was sent by his employers on a 500-mile journey in a vehicle which was not only unheated but which 'had a defect necessitating frequent halts for "topping up" the radiator'. It was cold and (believe it or not) the man suffered frostbite. He sued his employers—and the judge decided that they had 'failed to take steps to protect him against the reasonably foreseeable hazards of weather conditions'. They were liable in damages.

Accidents to Others

Finally, note that you are responsible not only for your own personal due care. You get the benefit of the good deeds of your staff, in the course of their employment? Conversely, you are 'vicariously liable' for their sins, provided only that these are committed within the scope of the duties for which they are employed.

Messrs ITW Limited employed a Mr Kay. An employee got into the cab of a lorry, started the engine so as to move it out of the premises; it ran backwards down a slope and injured the chief storekeeper. The man who drove the lorry should have confined himself to driving fork lift trucks. His employers maintained that when he entered the cab of the lorry, he left the scope of his employment.

The Court of Appeal decided unanimously that once it was conceded that he was doing something in his working hours, on his employers' premises, and was seeking to act in his employers' interests, that 'his act had a close connection with the work which he was employed to do'. The burden of shifting responsibility was therefore on the employers to show that the act was one for which they were not responsible. This burden they could not discharge. So they lost their case.

Chapter 95

An Occupier's Liability

How FAR are you liable when someone is injured on your premises? Does it make any difference if it is a child or an adult? What about the window cleaner, the plumber, the insulating engineer—does he come at his own risk or at yours? And what about the traveller, the postman, the uninvited guest . . . are they in the same position as other visitors? *The Occupiers' Liability Act, 1957,** tells you all the answers.

*   *   *

In the old days, there were varying 'duties of care' depending on the capacity in which the visitors came on to the premises. There were 'licensees' and 'invitees'—and a forest of case law had been allowed to block the view of the basic essentials. But today there is a 'common duty of care' which an occupier owes 'to all his visitors, except in so far as he is free to and does extend, restrict, modify or exclude his duty to any visitor or visitors by agreement or otherwise'.

What is this 'common duty'? It is 'a duty to take such care as in all the circumstances of the case is reasonable, to see that the visitor will be reasonably safe in using the premises for the purposes for which he is invited or permitted by the occupier to be there'. So 'reasonableness' is once again made the criterion. The view and actions of 'the reasonable man' become the test.

But the Act helps a little more in telling us the sort of circumstances which a Court must take into account when seeing whether or not 'reasonable care' has been taken. 'Circumstances relevant for the present purpose,' it tells us, 'include the degree of care, and of want of care, which would ordinarily be looked for in such a visitor, so that (for example) in proper cases: (*a*) an occupier must be prepared for children to be less careful than adults; and (*b*) an occupier may expect that a person, in the exercise of his calling, will appreciate and guard against any special risks ordinarily incident to it, so far as the occupier leaves him free to do so.'

So there is a difference between children and adults. You may expect your visitors to take care of their own safety—but you must not expect children to have such a high standard as adults. You must take more care for their safety than you would for that of grown-ups.

Equally, you don't have to wet-nurse the window cleaner or pamper the plumber. In so far as their professions entail special risks, they will have to watch out for them—unless you make it impossible for them to do so.

* In Scotland the equivalent of *The Occupiers' Liability Act, 1957,* is *The Occupiers' Liability (Scotland) Act, 1960.* Under that Act, however, the question of reasonableness in the duty of care is left entirely to the courts.

'In determining whether the occupier of premises has discharged the common duty of care to a visitor,' the Act goes on, 'regard is to be had to all the circumstances, so that (for example):

(*a*) where damage is caused to a visitor by a danger of which he had been warned by the occupier, the warning is not to be treated without more (i.e. on its own) 'as absolving the occupier from liability, unless in all the circumstances it was enough to enable the visitor to be reasonably safe.'

On its own, then, a warning of danger will not free you from liability if it was not enough to amount to 'reasonable care' for your visitor's safety. And, we are told:

(*b*) where damage is caused to a visitor by a danger due to the faulty execution of any work of construction, maintenance or repair by an independent contractor employed by the occupier, the occupier is not to be treated without more as answerable for the danger if in all the circumstances he had acted reasonably in entrusting the work to an independent contractor and had taken such steps (if any) as he reasonably ought, in order to satisfy himself that the contractor was competent and the work had been properly done.

'The common duty of care does not impose on an occupier any obligation to a visitor in respect of risks willingly accepted as his by the visitor,' says the Act' And 'the question whether a risk was so accepted is to be decided on the same principles as in other cases in which one person owes a duty of care to another.'

Suppose, then, that you occupy a rickety building and a prospective buyer wants to look it over. If you warn him of the danger, that warning may or may not be sufficient to free you from liability. It will depend on all the circumstances. But if you have made it clear to him that he came in entirely at his own risk, and he willingly agreed to do so, then *volenti non fit injuria*—a volunteer has no remedy—and if the visitor tumbles down the stairs due to some defective treads, that will be, in all respects, his own downfall and not yours.

Now we come to the policeman, the man who inspects your meters, a person who enters premises for any purpose in the exercise of a right conferred by law'. These people 'are to be treated as permitted by the occupier to be there for that purpose,' says the Act, 'whether they in fact have his permission or not'.

What about the trespasser, the person who has come onto your land unlawfully? Although, as a general rule a trespasser trespasses at his own risk it has been held in a recent case in the House of Lords than an occupier may, sometimes, owe a duty of care to trespassers. If an occupier knows that there are trespassers on his land or that it is likely that trespassers will come onto his land and he also knows that there is something on his land which will be a serious danger to those trespassers then he is under a duty to take reasonable steps to enable the trespassers to avoid that danger. This duty will however, only arise where it can be said that by the standards of commonsense and common humanity, the occupier has been at fault in failing to take reasonable steps to avoid the danger.

Finally, remember: the above is *civil* law. Failure to comply may lead to a civil action for damages by the sufferer. The Health and Safety at Work Act is a criminal statute. The same careless act or omission may lead to a prosecution as well as to a civil action.

Chapter 96

Guard Dogs

BUSINESS and professional people frequently use guard dogs to protect their premises or property. So the decision of Mr Justic O'Connor in the famous case of the woman savaged by an alsatian is as important in law as it was vibrant with human interest. When the action was first heard, the plaintiff was awarded £2892 damages, to compensate her because she was savaged by a ferocious alsatian kept in a scrapyard. At the re-trial her damages were halved.

Section 2 of *The Animals Act, 1961*, provides that where you keep a dog then if that particular animal is likely to cause severe damage and this likelihood is known to you, you will only be able to avoid liability to someone injured by the animal in certain circumstances. Normally, you will have to prove that the animal was kept on the premises for the protection of persons or property and that keeping it there for that purpose was 'not unreasonable'.

A Mr Grainger had acquired an alsatian from the Battersea Dogs' Home. Everyone seemed agreed that alsatians are normally quite docile but that this animal was one of the odd exceptions—both vicious and nervous. Further, it 'disliked coloured people to the extent that it had to be locked up'.

The dog was kept in a scrapyard and was locked up during the day. A Mr Hobson was allowed to keep his stock cars in the yard and often came in, with helpers, in the evenings or at weekends. Miss Cummings was his friend and she was savaged by the dog. At the original hearing, the defendant did not turn up because he did not know the date and Miss Cummings satisfied the Judge that she was outside the scrapyard when the dog came and attacked her. At the re-hearing, an independent observer testified that Miss Cummings had in fact been in the yard and the Judge found that she had 'entered the yard as a trespasser'.

The first question: Did the defendant know of the dog's unusual characteristics—that it was likely to cause severe damage? Answer: Yes. Next: Had the defendant successfully shown that it was reasonable to keep the dog on the premises? 'The dog was untrained and ferocious', said the Judge. 'The defendant knew that. To keep such a savage dog in a built-up area where people can go, especially if permission is given to people to enter and to take other people with them, is wholly unreasonable'. So you must not keep a ferocious dog on your premises, even for the protection of property.

But Miss Cummings was a trespasser. She was partly to blame for the accident. She had not told the truth at the first hearing. She had gone into the yard 'in circumstances in which she did not need to go'. Therefore the damage was due partly 'to the fault of the person suffering it' so the damages were reduced by 50 per cent.

In law, you are not generally liable to compensate a trespasser. He enters your premises at his own risk. But you must not set a trap for him—whether a loaded spring gun or a pit by the door. And a savage dog will amount to a 'trap'.

A trespasser is a person who has neither your express nor you implied permission to be on your premises and it is certainly stretching that definition a long way to say that the girlfriend of a man who is permitted on to the premises is 'trespassing'. Still, the morals to be drawn from the case of *Cummings* v. *Grainger* are these:

1 You are entitled to keep a guard dog for the protection of your premises, provided that it is 'reasonable' to do so.
2 It is reasonable to keep a trained dog which will bring down—

but not 'savage'—people on your premises—lawfully or other-wise.

3 It is 'wholly unreasonable' to keep a savage, untrained dog in an enclosed area. Do so and you will have to take the legal consequences if that dog causes damage—and, of course, you should be insured in case the dog which you regard as trained and not abnormally ferocious in fact causes damage and the Court blames you for it.

4 Even a trespasser is entitled to some protection from the law. A ferocious dog may constitute a trap. However: even a trespasser may be held at least partially responsible for his own miseries and it is likely that the damages awarded to a trespasser for injuries caused by your ferocious dog will be halved.

Chapter 97

A Question of Contributory Negligence

I am a highly skilled and well paid executive—or, to be precise, I was. Unfortunately, I suffered a severe accident at work. I maintain that the company was entirely at fault and that I am entitled to heavy damages. They answer that the responsibility was mine.

Please explain how far an employee can be held responsible for his own accident.

* * *

To recover damages for negligence, you must prove that your mishap was caused through the failure of someone else to take due care for your safety. Before 1945, even if you could prove that the defendant had been negligent, he could avoid having to pay you any damages whatsoever by showing that your own lack of due care contributed to some extent at least to the accident. But since *The Law Reform (Contributory Negligence) Act, 1945*, this rule has been returned to the limbo where it belongs. The full extent of that return was shown by the House of Lords, in the very important case of *Smith* v. *National Coal Board*.

Section 1 says: 'where any person suffers damage as a result partly of his own fault and partly of the fault of any other person or persons, a claim in respect of that damage shall not be defeated by reason of the fault of the person suffering the damage, but the damages recoverable in respect thereof shall be reduced to such extent as the court thinks just and equitable having regard to the claimant's share in the responsibility for the damage.' In general, you can reckon that the damages recovered by the plaintiff will be reduced proportionately to his own share in the blame.

Suppose, for instance, that you are involved in a crossroads collision. Neither of you was taking proper care and you are each 50 per cent responsible. Before 1945, neither could obtain any damages from the other. But today the damage of each would be totted up and divided by two. Suppose, for instance, that the proper recompense for your pain and suffering, loss of salary whilst off work and repair costs for your vehicle amount to £1,000. Those of the other driver come to £500. You are entitled to 50 per cent of your £1,000 as against him and he to half of his £500 against you. Result? You are £250 in pocket.

In practice, you may not have to worry about this. Insurers on each side may settle on a knock-for-knock basis, leaving you without your no-claims bonus (if you had one) and with a real risk of an increased premium. But if the case comes to court, then if the liability was divided in that way, that is how the figures would work out.

Suppose, now, that you are injured at work. If the entire fault was that of your employer, you recover damages in full. If you were wholly to blame and your employers in no way negligent, then the fact that you suffered your injuries during the course of your employment would not make them liable in damages. And if they were partly at fault, then they (or their insurers) would doubtless do their best to attribute as much contributory negligence to you as reasonably possible.

The case of *Smith* v. *National Coal Board* arose from the tragic death of a shunter, run over by a train of three waggons being moved from one siding to another. The employers maintained that if the deceased had paid proper attention to his own safety, he would not have been killed. His widow contended that if the NCB had conducted their business with proper care, the accident would never have occurred and that they were entirely to blame. By a majority of three to two, the House of Lords found the deceased one quarter to blame and reduced his widow's damages by 25 per cent.

'An employer,' we are told, 'or those for whom he is responsible, must always have in mind not only the careful man but also the man who is inattentive to such a degree as can normally be expected.' You cannot expect your employees to be on the alert all the time. You are entitled to expect them to take proper care of themselves, but you must make allowances for normal, human failings. You are not responsible for the safety of others only in their brighter moments. Allowances must be made for their times of inattention. Once again, the law accepts that it is made for the protection of the fallible. And while a failing on the part of the sufferer may reduce the amount of damages awarded, it in no way absolves the other party from his duty of care.

So even if the injured party was asleep on the job, the law was not. In spite of the finding by a majority of their Lordships that the deceased was guilty of contributory negligence, the shunter's widow got £3,792. It would only have taken one more of their Lordships to have absolved him altogether of liability and the majority would have gone the other way. Do you wonder that lawyers are cagey when asked to assess the odds in litigation?

In practice, whenever there is an industrial accident, the employer's insurers ask themselves the question: 'Who caused the mishap?' If the answer is clear, then the only question that remains is: How much? If the answer is in doubt, then the haggling begins—and the injured man is certainly wise to put his own solicitors on the trail. If there is any sort of settlement, the chances are that his legal costs will be paid by the employer's insurers.

If no agreement can be reached, then legal proceedings are likely to be issued. Happily, the vast majority of cases settle long before they reach trial. But if there is no settlement, then a judge will eventually have to answer precisely the same question: who was negligent?

To the extent that the employee was careless and his carelessness contributed towards his accident, his damages will be reduced. Employers must not expose their staff to unnecessary risk. They must provide and maintain proper equipment. The workplace must be reasonably safe. And so must the system of work.

On the other hand, the employee must take care what he does. The employee who causes his own injuries entirely through his own stupidity will get no compensation from the company.

Chapter 98

Trespass – and Assault

UNOCCUPIED PROPERTIES are creating new law. Squatters move in one day, the law the next. Whatever your connection with the world of commerce, you need to know the rules on trespass—and assault. How far are you entitled to determine who may or may not be in your office or on your premises? To what extent is the occupier entitled to regulate his own visitors? If you are invaded by trespassers (singly or in numbers) are you entitled to use force to eject them?

* * *

In theory, your home is your castle. So is your shop, office, factory or farm. But the law lays down strict rules as to when and how unwanted guests may be evicted. And the laws on trespass and assault not only creep into the lives of us all, but are curiously interwoven.

We are all entitled to decide who may and who may not be on our property. With the exception of privileged persons (such as police officers with search warrants and men who arrive by statutory authority to read our gas and electricity meters) anyone on your land without your consent is a trespasser.

Consent may be either express or implied. You may invite representatives to try to sell, or clients to visit you for business discussions. But the postman does not require a gilt-edged invitation. Nor do your neighbours, whom you have long allowed to cross your yard or forecourt. The representative who arrives on the doorstep of your office, factory or home is normally a lawful visitor.

If you put up a sign saying: 'No hawkers or canvassers', the position might be different—just as it is when Americans erect their quaint signs: 'No solicitors'. But no invitation (express or implied) equals no right to be on your property.

Even if the visitor was entitled to come in, you are still free to turf him out. Ask him to go and if he refuses he becomes a trespasser. So it is with the customer or client who declines to leave your shop or office . . . the representative who declines to remove his foot from your door . . . the employee whose sit-down strike is on your factory floor. . . . 'It's a free country,' he says, refusing to budge. Not so.

You are entitled to demand that a trespasser leave your property. If he fails or refuses to do so you may use reasonable force to eject him. How much force will be reasonable would depend upon all the circumstances of the case. First, you must ask him to go. Then a firm frogmarch would normally be justified. But to cripple him with your paperweight, scalp him with a letter opener or pepper him with buckshot will seldom be appropriate.

Only if the trespasser offers real violence to you will the law smile upon your use of fierce force against him. As Baron Parke put it, in 1841: 'If a man finds another breaking into his house, he has a right to push him out and to use as much force as is necessary for that purpose.'

So it may often be a defence to a civil or a criminal charge of assault to show that you were acting reasonably in the defence of your rights as an occupier of property. And it is always a good defence to an assault charge to prove that you struck only in self-defence. But the force you use must bear reasonable relation to that offered against you. In a case where 'the prosecutor lifted up his staff and offered to strike the prisoner', that was sufficient justification for the prisoner to take avoiding action. 'He need not in such a case wait until the other has actually struck.'

But if you are provoked by words alone—however stinging, obscene or accurate—you commit an assault if you respond with sticks or stones. If you happen to kill your victim and can show that you were so provoked by his remarks as to lose your self-control, the jury before whom you appear when charged with murder may reduce the offence to manslaughter. If the provocation was enough to make a 'reasonable man' behave as you did, then you may avoid life imprisonment. 'But no provocation whatever can render homicide justifiable, or even excusable,' saith the law. Thou shalt not kill.

Again, the law insists that rather than strike, you must if possible retreat. Only when the trespasser on your property refuses to budge are you normally entitled to initiate the attack. The law is a cowardly creature.

In one recent case, a man who was charged with assult proved that he was gravely provoked, but the prosecution satisfied the court that had he wished to run away, he could have done so. He was convicted. The provocation, of course, was a very powerful portion of his Counsel's 'plea in mitigation'. But it provided no defence to the charge.

In practice, if faced with a trespasser who declines to move, the sensible step to take is a swift one, in the direction of the nearest policeman. Or dial '999'. If there is liable to be a breach of the peace, it is rare that the police will not intervene. If you suffer from a major invasion of squatters, then they may require an order of the court before they take steps to assist you. But as hordes of hippies have learned to their cost, such an order will be readily available. And in more minor incursions, the formalities are generally dispensed with. The law abhors assaults, deplores trespassers and does its best to allow the businessman to make his own rules on who may and who may not visit his premises.

Chapter 99

Remoteness of Damage

JUST AS you are not liable to pay damages merely because there is an accident in your office, shop, factory, works or other premises, so damages are not payable in respect of every injury for which you are responsible. Anyone who wants damages from you must prove that you were negligent or in breach of statutory duty and that the damages claimed are not 'too remote'.

So there is an accident. Question number one: Can the employee establish that the employer was negligent or in breach of his statutory duty? If so, then the action proceeds. If not, then it must be dismissed.

Next questions: What damage can the employee prove that he suffered as a result of the employer's wrongful act or omission? And how much of that damage is sufficiently 'foreseeable' to give rise to a claim?

Suppose that you yourself are injured. Perhaps you tripped over an obstruction which someone had carelessly left in a passageway or into a pool of oil, negligently allowed to accumulate alongside a machine. You break your leg; you are carted off to hospital; you are off work for a month, and return grinning bravely, supported by crutches.

Your company is insured against employer's liability and you claim. What would you get?

First, there is your actual provable, financial loss. If you were paid while off work, your 'special damage' would probably be quite small. Maybe there were medical or convalescent expenses. Next, there are damages for pain and suffering. Their amount would depend upon the nature and seriousness of the injury and whether or not you will suffer after-effects (quite minor injuries, for instance, may trigger off painful osteo-arthritic conditions).

Now suppose that the day following the accident you were due to attend an interview for another post. Had you been successful in your application, you would have improved your salary and working conditions. Instead of sitting in the interview room, you are lying on your hospital bed. You lose the job.

Immediately you can get to a telephone, you speak to your proposed interviewer. 'I am terribly sorry,' he says, 'but the matter was urgent. We have appointed another man. I'm sure that you would have had an excellent chance of obtaining the position . . . but . . .'.

'The company was negligent,' you tell your lawyer.

'I am therefore entitled to damages to compensate me in so far as possible for my financial loss.' Correct?

'Agreed.'

'I did not lose a mere few weeks' pay, but an immensely important opportunity to improve my financial position on a permanent basis.'

The lawyer shakes his head. 'The damage is too remote,' he says.

Unfortunately, unless you can show that the loss actually flowed from the accident as a reasonably foreseeable result, you get no damages.

In the Court of Appeal decision in the case of *Hinz* v. *Berry*, the Judges unanimously decided that, in certain circumstances, damages for 'nervous shock' arising out of an accident which occurred to someone are not 'too remote' to be recoverable.

The unfortunate Mrs Hinz had been married for ten years. They had four children and the lady was again two months pregnant. In addition, she was looking after four foster children. She and her husband drove in their Dormobile van down to Canvey Island. On their way back, they pulled into a lay-by and Mr Hinz was making the tea. His wife and one child walked across the road to pick blue-bells.

At this moment, a Jaguar car went out of control—a tyre had burst. The car crashed into the Dormobile. Mr Hinz was injured and a few hours later he died. The other children who had been in the Dormobile were injured.

Mrs Hinz heard the crash. She turned around and saw the disaster. She ran across the road and did her best to comfort her husband and care for her children.

In due course, Mrs Hinz claimed damages. She was awarded £15,000 in respect of the pecuniary loss which she suffered as a result of her husband's death. But what of damages for the shock she suffered 'by turning round and seeing her husband injured and the children strewn about'?

Damages, said the Court, could be given 'for nervous shock caused by the sight of the accident'. This is not too remote.

On the other hand, 'By English law no damages are awarded for grief or sorrow caused by another's death, or for worry about children, or for the difficulty of adjusting to a new life.' There are many wrongs for which the law provides no remedy.*

'Damages,' said the Master of the Rolls, 'are recoverable for medical effects, the nervous shock, and any recognised psychiatric injury. In some way the line has to be drawn so as not to give damages for grief and sorrow but for the medical consequences of the injury to health.'

There was 'telling evidence' that poor Mrs Hinz suffered 'far more than a widow would have done had her husband been killed in an accident 50 miles away'. A 'sound, level-headed, robust, hardworking capable woman', she might in the course of time have got over it. But in fact she was suffering from 'a morbid depression', two years later. She was 'physically ill'. And she was 'entitled to be compensated effectively for the extreme mental anguish that she had suffered during the past five years as a result of being present at the scene of the disaster.'

The trial Judge had awarded the lady £4,000 damages. Although this may have been a high figure, in the circumstances, it was upheld by the Court of Appeal.

* In similar circumstances in Scotland a widow would be entitled to claim damages in respect of the grief and suffering caused to her by her husband's death.

Chapter 100

No Loss, No Damage

IN THE recent case of *Sykes* v. *Midland Bank Executor and Trustee Company Limited*, a firm of architects and surveyors won a Pyrrhic victory, and in the process made new law. The Court of Appeal unanimously agreed that they had been negligently advised by their former solicitors, but the Judges were equally unanimous in their reduction of the £9,000 damages awarded by the trial Judge to a nominal, miserable, two pounds.

'A solicitor acting for a client in negotiations for a lease of premises,' said the Court, 'is under a duty to draw the attention of his client to any unusual clause that may affect the client's interest, even if the client himself is a professional man experienced in property transactions.' An architect, surveyor, builder, estate agent, property man or director in charge of his company's property, may himself be well acquainted with property transactions. He still has a right to receive the correct advice from his solicitor.

In Sykes' case, there was an underlease with some complicated and unusual clauses. The solicitor, said the Court, should have drawn their client's attention to the complications and, in particular, to have pointed out that the superior lessors were entitled 'arbitrarily to with-hold consent to a change of use'. The trial Judge described the clause as a 'trap' even for the 'careful lay reader'.

'When a solicitor is asked to advise on leasehold title,' said Lord Justice Harman, 'it is his duty to draw his client's attention to any clauses in a lease in an unusual form which might affect the client's interest.'

The solicitor had failed to warn the architects of the powers of their proposed superior landlords. He was therefore 'in breach of duty under his contract'.

Before anyone can obtain damages for breach of contract, he must show that 'loss flowed as a foreseeable result of that breach'. In one famous case, for instance, a man fell off a high scaffold and was killed. His employers had been negligent in failing to provide proper safety-belts. But the Court was satisfied that even if the man had been provided with a belt, he would not have used it. There was therefore no 'causal connection' between the negligence and the loss.*

In Sykes' case, the solicitor had in fact died before the matter got on for trial. But Counsel for his executors argued that 'there was no evidence that the failure to give proper advice to the plaintiffs made any difference to them'. At the trial, the Judge had 'pressed the sole witness for the plaintiffs on that point, very hard, but he answered that he really did not know whether warning of the trap . . . would have prevented the plaintiffs from taking the underlease at the same rent'.

In other words, even if the solicitor had given the correct advice, the architects might well have declined to act upon it.

'The probability was,' said Lord Justice Harman, 'that the warning which should have been given would have made no impact on the plaintiffs' minds and that they would have disregarded it.' So there was negligence—but no provable, financial loss flowing from it. So the 'nominal award of £2' was substituted for the £9,000 awarded by the trial Judge.

On the question of the solicitor's negligence, Lord Justice Salmon added this: 'Although there are no degrees of negligence, the negligence committed by the solicitor was slight and was such that many a professional man might commit on an isolated occasion in his career.' To err is human, and kindly Judges recognise the fallibility of lawyers.

Finally, the Judges said that 'there is no duty on a solicitor acting for a firm to communicate his advice to all the partners; it is sufficient if he tenders his advice to the partner dealing with the matter'.

So you are fully entitled to expect the correct advice—and all necessary warnings—from your solicitors. But if it is given to one member of your firm, that is sufficient. There is no duty on your solicitor to send a memorandum to every member of your firm—or, for that matter, to all those who sit on the Board of your company.

You must keep the appropriate lines of communication open within your own outfit.

Finally, let us look at the 'trap' in rather more detail. Clause 2 of the underlease provided that the tenants would 'not use the demised premises otherwise than as offices in connection with their business of architects and surveyors or as office and showrooms in connection

---

* There is, of course, no need for damage—nor even for an accident to occur—for there to be a successful prosecution under the Health and Safety at Work Act.

with any other business for which the permission in writing of the lessor and the superior lessors had first been obtained such permission by the lessor not to be unreasonably withheld.'

A further clause provided that the tenants would 'not assign or part with possession' without first obtaining the written consent of the lessor and the superior lessors, such consent not to be unreasonably withheld in the case of a respectable and responsible person.

'To a lawyer,' said Lord Justice Harman, the first of the two clauses, 'was perfectly clear—it distinguished between the lessor, who could withhold his consent to a change of user only if he had reasonable grounds, and the superior lessor, who had an absolute and arbitrary right to hold consent.' The second clause provided that both the lessors and the superior lessors could withhold consent to an underletting—but only if they had reasonable grounds. The architects 'were under the mistaken impression that in both clauses consent could not be unreasonably withheld and they executed the lease in that belief.'

The solicitor should have disabused them of that belief. He was negligent in failing to do so. Even though the negligence was 'only slight', it gave rise to a good claim for damages.

As we have seen, it was at the next stage that the plaintiffs' case fell down. The architects might well have taken the lease at exactly the same rent, even if proper advice had been given by the solicitors. So the plaintiffs emerged from the battle, theoretically the victors but in practice with nominal damages only. They applied for leave to appeal to the House of Lords. Leave was refused.

"I'M LOOKING FOR SOMETHING WITH A BIGGER BOOT____!"

Part nine

Crimes

Chapter 101

The Theft Act, 1968

The Theft Act, 1968, came into force on 1 January, 1969. It completely revolutionised the laws on stealing and kindred topics. As frequent prey to thieves (even, alas, on his staff) every business and professional man should know what the Act says—and how it has been interpreted. Whether you are dealing with 'con men' or common criminals, the rules are worth knowing. Here they are.

* * *

The offence of 'larceny' was abolished. In its place: 'A person is guilty of theft if he dishonestly appropriates property belonging to another with the intention of permanently depriving the other of it.' Whether the taking is made 'with a view to gain'—so that the goods may be sold—or 'for a thief's own benefit' is irrelevant.

'If he appropriates the property in the belief that he would have the owner's consent, if the owner knew of the appropriation and the circumstances of it', the taker has a good defence. Finally: 'If he appropriates the property in the belief that the person to whom the property belongs *cannot* be discovered by taking reasonable steps', he will not be guilty of theft. The converse still applies. Find goods and fail to take reasonable steps to trace the owner, but merely dispose of them or use them for your own purposes and you are guilty of theft.

In general, borrowing is still no crime. But a borrowing is illegal if the taker's 'intention is to treat the thing as his own to dispose of regardless of the owner's rights'.

Maximum penalty for theft? Ten years. For robbery (using force on a person, when stealing), the maximum is life imprisonment. 'Burglary' can now be committed at any time of the day or night and in any building. A trespasser who enters a building intending to or actually stealing in it or from it or causing damage to it or inflicting 'any grievous bodily harm' on anyone in that building is a burglar and may get fourteen years in jail for his trouble. If he 'has with him at the time any firearm or imitation firearm, any weapon of offence or any explosive', the maximum is life imprisonment.

It remains an offence to take a motor vehicle or other conveyance without authority (maximum penalty: three years), and to be a passenger in such a vehicle, knowing that it has 'been taken without lawful authority'. And the unlawful and unauthorised borrowing of bicycles now becomes subject to a £50 maximum penalty.

Fraud is newly defined: 'A person who by any deception dishonestly obtains property belonging to another, with the intention of permanently depriving the other of it', is liable to a maximum ten years' imprisonment. And 'deception' means 'any deception (whether deliberate or reckless) by words or conduct*, as to fact or as to law, including a deception as to the present intentions of the person using the deception or any other person.'

The various offences of 'demanding with menaces' are abolished. Instead: 'A person is guilty of blackmail if, with a view to gain for himself or another or with intent to cause loss to another, he makes any unwarranted demand with menaces.' A demand with menaces is unwarranted unless the person making it obviously believes that he has reasonable grounds for making the demand *and* that the use of the menaces is a proper means of reinforcing the demand.

It is not blackmail to demand that which you honestly believe to be yours, even if you reinforce that demand with threats—provided that you believe those threats to be proper. Maximum penalty for blackmail? Fourteen years.

One interesting by-product of this law has been an alteration in almost every form of property or household insurance. In some cases, insurers have issued endorsements to policies saying that they shall be interpreted as if the Act had never come into effect. In others, the alteration of definitions has completely changed the cover. If you are in any doubt whatsoever about your own insurance position, consult your broker or your insurers without delay.

Naturally, this is only the broadest outline of the main rules imposed by the Theft Act. If you get entangled with it, the sooner you see your solicitor the better. Meanwhile, those concerned with the law enforcement are pleased with the Act. It strengthens their hand—and is therefore most welcome to the business world.

* Including (according to the latest case) the fraudulent use of a credit card.

Chapter 102

A Criminal Mistake

IF YOU give your customer too much change and he knowingly keeps the extra, then he is guilty of theft. The Court of Appeal's decision in the recent case of *Regina* v. *Gilks* should be of great help to business or professional men who carelessly over-pay—and a warning to anyone who sees fit to hold on to money, overpaid in obvious error.

Donald Gilks, aged 35, went to a Ladbroke's betting shop in North Cheam. There he placed money on the noses of horses, including a creature called Fighting Scot. The race was won by a Welsh relative named Fighting Taffy.

By mistake, the relief manager paid Mr Gilks £106 over the odds, on the day's betting. 'At the moment of payment', said Lord Justice Cairns, 'Mr Gilks knew that he was not entitled to the money. But he kept it, contending that it was hard lines on Ladbroke's.'

In due course, Mr Gilks was convicted of theft. He appealed, arguing that the bookmakers had, in effect, 'made him a gift'.

Section 1 (1) of *The Theft Act 1968*, says (as we saw in the previous chapter) this:

'A person is guilty of theft if he dishonestly appropriates property belonging to another with the intention of permanently depriving the other of it, and "thief" and "steal" shall be construed accordingly'.

Where there is a 'dishonest appropriation' with the intention that the owner will never get his property back, that is stealing.

Section 2 (1):

'A person's appropriation of property belonging to another is not to be regarded as dishonest . . . if he appropriates property in the belief that he has the right in law to deprive the other of it . . .'.

If the person who has your property and keeps it honestly believes that he is entitled to it, then he is not a thief. Even if his belief is entirely unwarranted, provided that it is genuine he is entitled to be acquitted.

Suppose, for instance, that one of your employees believes that he is entitled to use your stationery and stamps as a 'perk' of his job.

Even if he is totally misguided and incorrect, he is not a thief—because of Section 2 (1).

'On the face of it', said the Judge, 'Mr Gilks' conduct was dishonest. The only possible basis on which the jury could find that the prosecution had not established dishonesty was if they thought it possible that the appellant did have the belief that he claimed to have.'

Mr Gilks had alleged that he thought that there was 'nothing dishonest about keeping the money'. But he did not say: 'I think that I am entitled in law to keep it.'

Under Section 2 (1), Mr Gilks would have been entitled to keep the money if he had a genuine belief that he had 'in law the right to deprive the other of it'. He had not even argued that he held such a belief. So he was 'dishonest', he was properly convicted; his appeal was dismissed.

The morals of this cautionary tale are abundantly clear. If you make an over-payment, you are entitled to the return of your money. Only when six years have passed will your claim in civil law have become 'statute barred'. In criminal law, the beneficiary of your mistakes is a thief.

Better still, thanks to Section 4 of *The Forfeiture Act, 1870* (as now amended), you do not even have to sue the offender in a civil court. If you apply to the criminal court which convicts the man and if you do so at the time of his trial, the Judge may order that the thief pay compensation to you. In a Magistrate's Court, this may not exceed £400.

'Upon the application of any person aggrieved and immediately after the conviction . . .' the court may . . . 'by way of satisfaction or compensation for any loss of property suffered by the applicant through or by means of' the crime order the criminal to make payment. 'The amount awarded for such satisfaction or compensation shall be deemed a judgment debt due to the person entitled to receive the same from the person so convicted.'

You will have what amounts to a judgment of the court, without having to spend time or resources on taking the criminal before a civil court.

So the victory of Fighting Taffy over Fighting Scot has led to new rights for the businessman—and new risks for the man who dishonestly takes advantage of his mistakes.

Chapter 103

Handling Stolen Goods

IT TAKES a tough man to turn down a big bargain. But when it comes to buying goods from strangers, the bigger the bargain, the greater the risk that the goods are stolen. As *The Theft Act, 1968*, provides a penalty of up to 14 years' imprisonment for 'handling stolen goods', here are some suggestions on how not to get wrongfully charged with that particular, nasty offence.

*　　*　　*

'A person handles stolen goods,' says Section 22 of the Theft Act, 'if (otherwise than in the course of the stealing), knowing or believing them to be stolen goods, he dishonestly receives the goods, or dishonestly undertakes or assists in their removal or retention, disposal or realisation, by or for the benefit of another person, or if he arranges to do so.'

In the old days, to convict of 'receiving' the prosecution had to show that the accused actually physically handled the goods. Nowadays, a man may be convicted of 'handling', even if he has never set eyes on the property. Anyone who dishonestly deals, directly or indirectly, with stolen property may find himself charged with 'handling' even if he never clapped a dishonest eye (still less, a thieving hand) on the 'hot' goods.

As the law seeks to knock down the dishonest fences (and so to see that robbery does not pay), it is inevitable that some foolhardy (and usually greedy) business and professional people get wrongly caught up in the web. And while it is a joy to be acquitted, it is much better not to get charged. So how do you achieve this careful result?

First, know from whom you buy. Even if goods turn out to be stolen, if you can both identify the seller and show that you have cause to trust him, you will be let off the legal hook. What then happens to him is his concern.

Next, look at the circumstances of the sale and see whether they are even apparently honest. If a fellow appears in the dead of night, for instance, send him on his way.

Then do make sure that you obtain a full receipt, setting out the name and address of the seller; identifying him, if possible (perhaps by the number of his car, van or driving licence); describing the goods; bearing the seller's signature—and also saying that the goods belong to the seller and (in appropriate cases) are not the subject of any charge or outstanding hire purchase agreement.

Naturally, all purchases should go through the books. But even if some escape the formal, accounting net, you must make absolutely certain that any casual purchase, the origin of which is potentially in doubt, is entered into your ledgers—and can be traced going out of them. The greater the bargain . . . the less you know the seller . . . the more suspicious the deal could look, to the trained police mind . . . the more vital it is that you can show that you dealt with the matter in an entirely normal way.

In fact, the police should be consulted before you buy, if there is ever any real doubt. Say to the seller: 'Look, I don't know you. I have an arrangement with the local police that when I buy in this way, I have them check their books on the goods beforehand. Have you any objection?'

If there is the least flinching on the part of the seller, do not buy. If he agrees, then you may still check with the authorities. By the time you come back from the telephone, the dishonest man will probably have disappeared.

Above all, remember that if the circumstances are sufficiently suspicious, a jury might well take the view that you must have known that the goods were 'hot' . . . that you were dishonest . . . that you either 'knew' or 'believed' that they were stolen. It is sometimes very difficult to believe that the honest businessman who falls for a dishonest bargain is as simple as he would like to seem. And when it comes to buying, it is up to you to see that you do not buy stolen goods. If in doubt, say no.

Naturally, it is up to the prosecution to prove beyond reasonable doubt that the accused 'handler' knew or believed that the goods concerned were stolen. A dishonest intent is not presumed against the purchaser. But where a purchase is made in suspicious circumstances; where the price is low and the buyer has taken insufficient precautions; where the books are inadequate and the buyer's excuses likewise—then it may take good fortune to be acquitted. To be tried and found innocent is excellent; it is much better never to be tried at all.

So when you are offered a bargain by a stranger, take care. You may find it much more expensive than it seems.

Chapter 104

The Trade Descriptions Act*– and the Employer's Liability

IN THE good, safe old days, provided that an employer guarded his machinery, deducted his PAYE and let his staff get on with their own criminal activities without his encouragement or support, he would keep out of the dock. And the chances of anyone making him criminally liable for the sins of his servants were remote. No more. Today the law requires the boss to exercise eternal vigilance—or take the consequences.

The Trade Descriptions Act, as everyone knows by now, is a criminal statute, imposing maximum penalties of two years' imprisonment and fines of unlimited amount, in suitably serious cases. But employers do not sufficiently realise that they may not be protected from prison because they happen to enjoy a cosy seat in the boardroom or a proud, executive position in the company. They may be 'vicariously liable' (see also Chapter 90), in a sense, for their employees' misdeeds—that is, liable personally to pay if their staff apply false trade descriptions to goods or services supplied by the company (or, for that matter, by the firm or individual employer).

Section 20: 'Where an offence under this Act which has been committed by a body corporate is proved to have been committed with the consent and connivance of, or to be attributable to any

* Appendix 1.

neglect on the part of, any director, manager, secretary or other similar officer of a body corporate, or any person who was purporting to act in any such capacity, he as well as the body corporate shall be guilty of that offence and shall be liable to be proceeded against and punished accordingly.'

So the company itself will be liable for the offence, but so will any guilty 'officer' (and in nationalised industries, members of boards of management are defined as 'officers'). What really matters is that, in order to obtain a conviction, the Crown (via the Weights and Measures authorities, whose duty it is to enforce the Act) do not have to show 'consent' or 'connivance'. If there has been 'any neglect' on the part of the individual, the crime of the company may be laid at his door.

In general, then, the law imposes a 'duty of care' on employers, for the safety of their staff and of the public. The boss must avoid negligence, if he wishes to avoid paying damages. But he must also take due care to ensure that the Trade Descriptions Act is complied with. Failure to do so may lead to jail.

On the other hand, if care is taken, the employer will be let off this particular legal hook. Section 24:

'In any proceedings for an offence under this Act, it shall . . . be a defence for the person charged to prove:

(*a*) that the commission of the offence was due to a mistake or to reliance on information supplied to him or to the act or default of another person, an accident or some other cause beyond his control;

(*b*) that he took all reasonable precautions and exercised all due diligence to avoid the commission of such an offence by himself *or any person under his control.*'

It is, of course, those last six words (italicised by me, not by the legislators) which employers must note. Assuming they can prove that the false trade description was applied by someone under his control, but despite 'all reasonable precautions' and 'all due diligence' on his part, directed towards the avoidance of the offence, he will be acquitted. He must also give (in general) seven clear days' notice to the prosecution that he intends to rely upon this defence— but subject to that, a good defence it will be.

So the Trade Descriptions Act does not establish 'absolute offences'.

If a prosecution is thrust at you, you may shield yourself with proof of your 'reasonable precautions' and 'due diligence'. But you will have to prove them. All the prosecution must do is to show that your employee applied a false trade description and the two of you are likely to find yourself side by side (and quite literally) in the dock—a thoroughly unhealthy and unpleasant experience. Only if you can prove no default on your part will you be acquitted.

Naturally, we may expect the authorities to wield their considerable power with a great deal of circumspection. While the livelihood of a Weights and Measures inspector does not depend upon all his prosecutions being made to 'stick', too many acquittals of too many important executives might well result in a well-merited rebuke. And, anyway, you will not be persecuted for your position. If you take 'reasonable precautions' and exercise 'due diligence', your chances of being prosecuted are remote. But connive at or assist in misleading the public through misdescribing the goods your company sells—or allow misdescriptions to occur through your lack of due care in directing your staff—and you are asking for trouble.

So if you have not yet applied your mind to the application of true and accurate trade descriptions, now is the time to do so—with new warnings to your staff of the perils that beset them—and of the dire consequences to them if they lead you into trouble with the criminal law. Help them to comply with the Act and you will do both yourself and them a good turn.

Finally, what of the civil law? In a recent case, it was held that while an employer cannot normally be held liable for the criminal acts of his servants, provided that he did not authorise or co-operate in their commission, yet if someone else suffers damage as a result of those acts, the employer will be 'vicariously liable'. If, for instance, one of your staff steals goods belonging to your customer, the chances are that you can be made to pay up. The answer, of course, lies in careful personnel selection and supervision—and adequate insurance. These are hard days for the soft employer.

* * *

Finally, note that the law on Trade Descriptions is being tightened up. Here's how:

(*a*) Under *The Criminal Justice Act 1972*, where a defendant is convicted of an offence under the Act, he may not only be fined and (theoretically at least) imprisoned, but required by the convicting court to pay compensation of up to £400 to the innocent party, deceived by the false trade description;

(b) Judges have warned that the Act will be enforced more rigorously—possibly by using the powers of imprisonment. Meanwhile, enormous fines have been levied, notably on tour operators;

(c) The Act may be amended further, so as to bring providers of services (car repair outfits and sellers of travel, for instance) within similar rules to those which apply to sellers of goods. At present, a seller of services is only liable under the Act if the prosecution can prove positively that he either knew that the statement he made was false or that he made it 'recklessly'. But to sell goods under a false trade description is an 'absolute' offence, and neither 'knowledge' nor 'recklessness' need be shown.

So watch out for new fireworks—and for firm enforcement of the old law.

Chapter 105

Bribery and Corruption

THE BORDERLINE between bribery and legitimate, business, greasing-of-the-palm is a narrow one. Ordinary business kindnesses are lawful and proper, but bribery and corruption are highly criminal.

Suppose, first, that you induce someone to work harder by offering an increased wage. That is not bribery. Equally, if you try to get people to join your firm by offering them better pay or conditions than they at present enjoy, that is not corruption. But if someone gives a gift to one of your staff in return for some special favour, then, unless the transaction is done with your knowledge and consent, this is both bribery and corruption. Moreover, although few employers or personnel managers seem to realise it, both the giver and the receiver are criminals in the eyes of the law.

'If any agent corruptly accepts or obtains, or agrees to accept or attempts to obtain, from any person, for himself or for any other person, any gift or consideration as an inducement or reward for doing or forbearing to do, or for having . . . done or forborne to do, any act in relation to his principal's affairs or business, or for showing or forbearing to show favour or disfavour to any person in relation to his principal's affairs or business', then he is an offender against the criminal law and is liable to a term of up to two years' imprisonment or to a fine of up to £500 or both imprisonment and a fine. These are the penalties which can be imposed 'on indictment'—that is, where the offender elects to be tried by jury. If he stands trial in a Magistrates' Court, then he is liable 'on summary conviction' to up to four months' imprisonment or a £200 fine or both.

That covers the 'agent'. Any person who acts on behalf of his employer is an agent. Any effort on an employee's part, successful or otherwise, to obtain some special benefit for himself in return for some act done in relation to his employer's business is a criminal offence, provided that it is done corruptly. So says Section 1 of *The Prevention of Corruption Act, 1906*.

But for a successful bribing operation, there must be two parties. And the Act goes on to deal with the corrupting giver.

'If any person corruptly gives or agrees to give or offers any gift or consideration to any agent as an inducement or reward for doing or forbearing to do, or for having done . . . or forborne to do, any act in relation to his principal's affairs or business, or for showing or forbearing to show favour or disfavour to any person in relation to his principal's affairs or business', then he is liable to the same penalties as the person bribed.

What is more: 'If any person knowingly gives to any agent or if any agent knowingly uses with intent to deceive his principal, any receipt, account, or other document in respect of which the principal is interested, and which contains any statement which is false or erroneous, or defective in any material particular, and which to his knowledge is intended to mislead the principal', then he, too, may find himself suffering the same penalties from the law.

Take an all too common example. Joe is a buyer. In order to induce him to purchase a certain line of goods, Mr X quietly offers him a commission of *y* per cent on all business accepted by his company.

At once Mr X is a criminal. As soon as Joe accepts the offer (even though he has not yet got the money), he too is an offender, just as much as he would have been if he had sought the bribe. And if, to cover the deal, Mr X supplies Joe with false receipts, then the giving of the false document is a further offence against the law.

But what does 'consideration' mean? The Act says that it 'includes valuable consideration of any kind'. Money, a right to buy goods at a discount, gifts in kind—all these are covered.

As for the word 'agent', this is very broadly defined. It includes 'any person employed by or acting for another'. And the expression 'principal', we are told, 'includes an employer'.

'But what about public servants?' you ask.

'A person serving under the Crown or under any corporation or any municipal borough, county or district council, is an agent within the meaning of this Act.'

Mind you, public employees are even more stringently restrained from bribery. Under *The Public Bodies Corrupt Practices Act, 1889*, the penalties for bribing, attempting to bribe, receiving a bribe or trying to get one when a public official is concerned are considerably higher than those where the public is not concerned. And under *The Prevention of Corruption Act, 1916*, where 'the matter or transaction in relation to which the offence was committed was a contract or proposal for a contract with Her Majesty or any government department or any public body or a sub-contract to execute any work comprised in such a contract', the offender is liable to a minimum of three years' and a maximum of seven years' imprisonment—in addition to any punishment which could otherwise have been imposed. Moreover: 'Where it is proved that any money, gift, or other consideration has been paid or given to or received by a person in the employment of Her Majesty or any government department or a public body, by or from a person, or agent of a person, holding or seeking to obtain a contract from Her Majesty or any government department or public body, the money, gift, or consideration shall be deemed to have been paid or given and received corruptly as an inducement or reward . . . unless the contrary is proved.'

The general rule in criminal law is that a person is presumed innocent until found guilty. But where there is any question of the bribery of a public servant, corruption is generally presumed, once a gift is shown to have been given or received, offered or requested.

True, there have been some Court battles over the meaning of 'public body'. If you are in doubt whether your own outfit comes within that definition, you should ask a lawyer. Nevertheless, the general rules are clear. Bribers and the bribed—givers and receivers of the 'dropsy'—those whose palms are greased and those who do the greasing—are often far more open to legal penalties than they realise.

This is not to say, of course, that the mere offering or receiving of a tip makes the offerer or recipient a criminal. If everything is done openly and with the knowledge of the employer, all is usually well. But if someone 'slips' one of your employees 25p or a £5 note, so as to jump the queue for the service you offer . . . if one of your staff takes a secret cut out of the proceeds of some operation in which the company is involved . . . if Christmas presents are kept hidden and unannounced . . . then the law has probably been broken, and if the offender replies that he 'did not know he was doing anything wrong', that will not save him from a possible heavy fine and/or prison sentence. Ignorance of the law, as usual, is no excuse.

Chapter 106

Murder, Manslaughter, Euthanasia

'IT IS possible,' said the distinguished committee of the Church Assembly Board for social responsibility, 'that there are circumstances in which the law itself would recognise that the best is to allow the end to come as quickly and as peacefully as possible.' As for professional ethics, 'In merely prolonging a travesty of life for the process of dying', the committee reported, 'it might be argued that the doctor would be passing beyond the role of the physician into that of the experimental scientist.' But where do you draw the line? How far will the law tolerate euthanasia? In what circumstances could it amount to murder or to manslaughter?

Murder was defined many years ago by the great Lord Coke like this: 'Where a person of sound memory and discretion unlawfully kills any reasonable creature in being and under the King's Peace, with malice aforethought (either express or implied)' then, if the death follows within a year and a day—the killing amounts to the crime of murder. And manslaughter is 'the unlawful and felonious killing of another without any malice, either express or implied'.

A murderer, then, must either have an intention 'to cause the death of, or grievous bodily harm to' the person actually killed or to some other person, or else 'knowledge that the act which causes death will probably cause the death of, or grievous bodily harm to, some person . . . although such knowledge is accompanied by indifference whether death or grievous bodily harm is caused or not, or by a wish that it may not be caused.'

As for manslaughter, there is no 'malice aforethought' necessary. It is enough if there is an 'unlawful killing'.

Now comes the nice point. If a doctor simply omits to give the appropriate treatment which could keep a patient alive, does he 'kill' his patient? If a person is in a deep coma but may be kept breathing almost indefinitely without hope of recovery, is it killing that person simply to allow his breathing to stop?

That the doctor who deliberately strangles a mongoloid baby, immediately after birth, is technically liable to be convicted of murder is clear. Equally, to allow the same baby to die through reckless lack of care for its well-being would be manslaughter (if not murder)—even though the doctor may feel that he is doing both the child and its parents a favour. The law will not allow a doctor to set himself up as the Almighty Judge.

On the other hand, simply 'to allow the end to come' might not amount to homicide at all. Where the death of a destitute person arose 'from neglect by a relieving officer to provide medical assistance', the officer was convicted of manslaughter. Where an apprentice died as a result of 'incautious neglect by his master . . . rather than from actual malice or wilful intention to injure', then the proper verdict was manslaughter. Where the accused 'neglected to buy food', the prosecutor had to show not only 'a duty in the prisoner to supply food, but also that the apprentice (or child) was of tender years, and unable to provide for himself'. So it would have to be shown that the doctor was under a duty to provide medical care to the person in question and that the patient was unable to obtain that care for himself.

Happily, this discussion is nearly always as academic (if as popular) as the old one about whether lawyers should 'defend people whom they know to be guilty'. There seems to be no case on record where a doctor was charged with either murder or manslaughter because he hastened the death of a mortally ill patient, either by giving too much treatment or too little—provided that the patient really could not be saved by the exercise of ordinary, proper care.

Equally, any lawyer who is told by his client that he is guilty must first satisfy himself that this guilt is real rather than imagined. For instance, the man who borrows goods and is charged with theft may not realise that he has a complete defence if the prosecution cannot show that he had no intention to return them. But that said, the person must either plead guilty or find himself another lawyer. In the much more common case, where the lawyer simply has his suspicions, it is not for him to set himself as judge. His duty is to present his client's case to the best of his (the lawyer's) ability.

Provided, then, that neither physician nor lawyer seeks to set himself up as judge, and provided that each does his duty with due care, the law requires neither more nor less of him. But the moment that either seeks to usurp the function of judge—heavenly or earthly as the case may be—potential trouble is on the way.

It would be pleasant, would it not, if all this were an academic matter? But what of the continental doctor who took the life of a thalidomide baby? Or the man you know who, at the behest of a weepy wife, killed for ever the pain of the cancer patient by an over-dose of pain-killing drug? Would you keep alive 'almost indefinitely' the man in the deep coma 'without hope of recovery'?

Be grateful that the law so often claps its telescope to its blind eye. The blindfolding of the figure of justice does not occur merely when a prosecution is brought and the scales are filled, but when the decision is taken that no prosecution be brought at all. What the law itself 'would recognise' if a case came to trial is not necessarily the same as its tacit recognition of the facts of life and death, given by a failure to prosecute in the first place.

Chapter 107

Race Relations

WHETHER race relations is a field in which Parliament can effectively interfere is a question of argument and philosophy. Employers must cope with whatever Parliament produces—and a new production is (as we go to press) on its way through Parliament.

The Race Relations Bill 'makes fresh provision with respect to discrimination on racial grounds and relations between people of different racial groups'. It amends and strengthens the Race Relations Acts of 1965 and 1968. And it establishes machinery for the enforcement of the race relations legislation which runs along very similar lines to that already existing under the Sex Discrimination Act.

'Discrimination', under the Bill, occurs where a person 'on racial grounds' treats another person 'less favourably than he treats or would treat other persons'. Part 2 of the Bill deals with discrimination in the employment field.

By Clause 4, it will become unlawful for a person 'in relation to employment by him at an establishment in Great Britain, to discriminate against another—

(a) in the arrangements he makes for the purpose of determining who should be offered that employment; or
(b) in the terms in which he offers him that employment; or
(c) by refusing or deliberately omitting to offer him that employment.'

Access to opportunities for promotion, transfer or training 'or to any other benefits, facilities or services' must not be afforded or withheld on grounds of racial discrimination. Nor must an employee be 'dismissed or subjected to any other detriment' on such grounds.

'Racial grounds' means: 'colour, race, nationality or ethnic or national origins'. The word 'nationality' is new. Under the old rule, you could discriminate against a person because of his current nationality although not because of his national origin. Note: Religion is not covered—although Jewish employees may be, on ground of their 'race . . . or ethnic . . . origin'.

Employment agencies, vocational training bodies, the Manpower Services Commission, the Employment Services Agency and the Training Services Agency are specifically covered. So is discrimination against contract workers—as opposed to people who are actually on your payroll.

It will be unlawful for a partnership of six or more partners 'in relation to a position as partner in the firm' to discriminate on racial grounds—although partnerships of one to five people may still select on whatever grounds they wish. Trade unions and employers' associations are also covered by the Bill. And it becomes unlawful for those who confer authorisation or qualification to discriminate in this way.

Matching the Equal Opportunities Commission, which already seeks to help women to get their rights, the 'Commission for Racial Equality' will establish Codes of Practice; conduct investigations; seek information; and assist those who are discriminated against.

Enforcement of the Act against defaulting employers will (as in Sex Discrimination and Equal Pay cases) be via complaints to Industrial Tribunals.

If a complaint of discrimination is established, the tribunal may make a declaration; it may order the payment of compensation; and it may make a 'recommendation' that the employer take within a specified period such action as the tribunal considers 'practicable for the purpose of obviating or reducing the adverse affect on the complainant of any act of discrimination to which the complaint relates'. Failure to comply with the recommendation may lead to further compensation.

There is much more in the Bill—including Part 9, making it an offence to 'incite to racial hatred'. There are exceptions to the rules— as where a person's race or colour is 'an essential qualification for the job' (Chinese cooks—but not Chinese waiters, it seems). And 'discriminatory advertisements' are outlawed.

By the time this book goes into its next edition, the next edition of the race relations legislation will have gone into law. Meanwhile, take care. Racial discrimination may be very expensive—especially as a person who is dismissed unfairly on grounds of his race may obtain his remedy even though he has not been employed for the usual six months qualification period.

Chapter 108

Prosecution Laws

To PROSECUTE or not to prosecute—that is the question which the business or professional man must frequently ask. Do you hand a suspected thief or pilferer—whether or not you employ him—over to the police? The decision is yours and the days are gone when keeping silent was itself a crime.

If the police decide to prosecute, then you are powerless to prevent the march of the law. But if they leave you to decide whether or not to sign the charge sheet, you have a tactical question on your hands of great importance. Before you make up your mind, check the following list. It sets out the main considerations to be borne most carefully in mind.

*   *   *

1   It is pointless to prosecute if the accused is likely to be acquitted. So have you obtained a written confession? If so, did you remember to caution the suspect, warning him that anything he said would be taken down in writing and might be used in evidence? No caution would probably mean that no mention could be made to the confession in court.

2   Could you prove beyond all reasonable doubt that the employee had acted dishonestly and that he intended 'permanently to deprive' you of the property taken? If he genuinely believed that he was entitled to the goods—perhaps as a 'perk'—or that if you had been asked for your permission to take it, you would have agreed, then prosecution would fail.

3   Assuming that you have a reasonable prospect of making the prosecution 'stick', but the accused is acquitted, could he show that you brought the prosecution out of 'malice'? If so, then he would have a good civil action for damages for 'malicious prosecution'. He would have to prove that you put him at risk out of desire to harm him or to some other unlawful motive, and not because of your wish to see justice done. The mere fact that the prosecution fails will not of itself give any rights to the accused.

4   Is the accused a member of a minority group, extra sensitive to any unfairness? If so, then be especially careful and tactful.

5   Have you enough evidence—oral or documentary—to prove your case? If it is your word against that of the accused, and the burden of proving the case rests upon you, then you would probably be wise not to proceed.

6   Are you sure that you wish to prosecute? A civil action may be withdrawn at any time on payment of the costs of both sides. A criminal prosecution may only be withdrawn with leave of the court —which will only be given for excellent reason and not (for instance) because you now feel sorry for the accused or because you realise that the prosecution will bring bad publicity on to your business.

7   Will a prosecution lead to trouble with others in your workforce? Examples:
   (*a*) Are any trade unions concerned on your side? Sometimes, workers' organisations apply pressure to prosecute—perhaps because continuing pilfering or 'shrinkage' causes ill will among the workforce; perhaps because property has been stolen from members. Sometimes the pressure is in the opposite direction. It is totally proper to bear this in mind.
   (*b*) Is it in the best interests of your business to prosecute—to

discourage thefts by others or because you have a specific policy that all those caught thieving are handed over to the law?

(c) Will the prosecution add to the temptation for other employees by (for instance) revealing a shrewd mode of dishonesty which they have probably not thought of?

(d) Will a prosecution lead to bad publicity because it will show how poorly the person concerned was paid in comparison to his responsibilities; the extent of the temptation open to him; or the inadequate system which you have operated for the protection of your property?

8   Are there special mitigating circumstances in the case of the individual concerned which would encourage you not to prosecute?

(a) Is the theft a minor one and the employee a person whom you wish to keep on your books, in spite of his slip from grace?

(b) Is the employee a person who has given long service; a man from a decent background; a family man with heavy responsibilities; a normally decent person who acted in an uncharacteristic way under particular stress—of ill-health or debt?

(c) Is the employee willing to resign—or will you wish to dismiss him—and do you feel that the loss of his job is sufficient punishment, both from his point of view and from that of others who will hear of your decision?

9   What are the views of the police as to the prosecution? How far are they prepared to help? Do they consider that the prosecution is likely to succeed? And what is their estimate of the length of the trial?

10   What are the costs likely to be involved? Assuming that the prosecution is brought properly, your legal expenses should be recoverable from the Crown, even if the prosecution fails. But consult your solicitor to find out what risk there may be to your pocket.

11   How much time would have to be devoted by how many (and which) of your staff, if the appropriate evidence is to be placed before the court? If the accused pleads guilty, both the costs and the time

will be minimal; but a plea of not guilty will inevitably involve time —and possibly anxiety.

12   Finally: If the offender is convicted, is he likely to receive such a leniency that other potential offenders will actually be encouraged? If the case is likely to be heard by your local bench, how do they generally treat pilferers, petty thieves or other villains of the category concerned?

*   *   *

Having checked the list, if you are still in doubt then consult your solicitor. If you prosecute privately you will in any event need his help. So get it before you make your decision, if you are in any doubt as to what the decision should be.

Chapter 109

The Rehabilitation of Offenders

The Rehabilitation of Offenders Act is now in full force. Among *exceptions* to the general benevolent rules are those which deal with sections of the society regarded as being especially vulnerable—the old and the young, the sick and the handicapped. Doctors, nurses, pharmacists, teachers and youth workers rank alongside policemen and Judges, solicitors and Counsel, probation and prison officers. They retain their bad names for life. But most others may now wipe clean the criminal slate.

The new Act raises important questions for the employer, particularly when he is asked to provide references not merely for his own staff but also for customers or clients. So consider: What can and should you reveal about a disreputable past when you give them a reference? How far can you expect an applicant for a job to go back in his past if he has served time, when considering appointing him to a post of trust? And are you free to ignore a person's past improprieties, when giving him a reference which will affect not only his future, but also that of others—including especially those who are intending to employ him?

*   *   *

Anyone who applied for a job with you could have been required to reveal his criminal past. If you did not see fit to enquire, then that was your misfortune and the applicant's good luck. Assuming that the applicant told no lies, you were (and are) not entitled to dismiss him merely because you discover some unpleasant truth about his past.

The new Act goes much further. It allows everyone who has ever been convicted of a criminal offence and has been given a sentence not exceeding *two and a half years* in prison, to become a so-called 'rehabilitated person' at the end of a specified period. The 'rehabilitation period' will generally restart, if the person is again convicted of anything other than a minor offence during that period. Once the period has passed, the conviction is 'spent'. He has what amounts to a clean licence to show prospective employers.

In general, 'a person who has become a rehabilitated person . . . in respect of a conviction, shall be treated for all purposes in law as a person who has not committed or been charged with or prosecuted for or convicted of or sentenced for the offence or offences which were the subject of that conviction'. Evidence of the conviction will not be admissible in any Civil Court. The Act does not appear to apply, though, to criminal prosecutions or to proceedings involving the care or custody of children.

Next: 'Any person who, in the course of his official duties, has or at any time has had custody of or access to any official record or the information contained therein, shall be guilty of an offence if—knowing or having reasonable cause to suspect that any specified information he has obtained in the course of those duties is specified information—he discloses it, otherwise than in the course of those duties, to another person'.

So there is a maximum fine of £200 for anyone who makes improper disclosure from his records—and that includes doctors or nurses giving away secrets. When you or your colleagues or subordinates give references, be careful not to reveal any conviction which is 'spent'.

Again: 'Any person who obtains any specified information from any official record by means of any fraud, dishonesty or bribe' may be fined up to £400 and/or imprisoned for up to six months. Those behind-the-scenes, private investigations of other people's files have become legally perilous operations.

How long, then, is the 'rehabilitation period' which must pass before a person's conviction is 'spent'? That depends upon the length of the sentence; for example:

> Absolute discharge—six months.
> Fine or community service order—five years.
> Imprisonment for six months or less—seven years.
> Imprisonment for between six months and 2½ years—ten years.

The rehabilitation period for people under 17 is halved, except in the case of an absolute discharge. And where a sentence may only be imposed on the young person, the periods of rehabilitation are fixed. On the other hand, where the person has been sentenced to more than 30 months in prison—or to life or to preventative detention or their equivalents for young offenders—the period can never be suspended.

Note: what matters is the period imposed by the Court, and not the actual time served. So even if a sentence is suspended, the above periods apply. Where a man is imprisoned while serving in the armed forces, the rehabilitation periods are the same as in civilian life. And where a serviceman is discharged with ignominy or disgrace, the period is ten years.

Here, then, are the main consequences, in the law of employment:

1   It is normally unlawful to refuse to employ or to dismiss an employee on the ground that he or she has a criminal record, once that record is 'spent'.
2   You may give a reference about the rehabilitated person, without mentioning any spent conviction.
3   If the spent conviction comes to light, the employee must not be prejudiced for having failed to disclose it.

Over a million people are said to have stale convictions for indictable offences. In general, they now no longer live under the fear of the threat of their past being brought to light. And yet another opportunity for blackmail has been removed. But (as I said) certain professional people will have no such legal luck. And it will be small consolation for them to know that their long-term misery is shared by men of the law who have strayed from the required paths of righteousness.

Finally: note that when a person has become rehabilitated, this applies for all purposes—including the making of insurance contracts. In general, insurers are entitled to avoid liability if there has been any 'material non-disclosure'. The assured is bound to reveal any facts which would be likely to affect the mind of the prudent insurer, when considering whether or not to grant protection and if so, then at what premium.

Today, though, you are not usually bound to reveal the criminal past of people engaged in your business. Indeed, to do so may itself constitute an offence against the law.

Part ten

Courts and Cases

Chapter 110

To Sue or Not to Sue?

THE AVERAGE businessman tends to regard the courts as places of last resort. To an extent, he is right. Civil litigation is a luxury and criminal prosecutions (as we saw in Chapter 108) should only be brought after careful thought and consideration. But if you know your courts and how best to use them, you can save a great deal of time and worry. And they are designed to bring justice not only to criminals and their kind, but also to business and professional men . . . to the world of commerce. . . .

So we now consider the question: To sue or not to sue?

*   *   *

Leaving matters of arbitration on one side, the alternative to justice meted out by an impartial judge is war. In the old days, the tribal chief or king used to sit on his throne (or under the leafy tree in his courtyard) and do justice to his loyal subjects. As the tribe grew, so the royal powers had to be delegated. Judges were appointed. The squire was created a 'justice', empowered to keep the king's peace, by acting as a mediator between his subjects, or by imposing discipline upon them. Princes of power, temporal and spiritual, acquired the power to judge, each in his own sphere.

'Hear ye, hear ye, hear ye . . . all those who have business before Her Majesty's Justices of Oyer and Terminer of the City of London, draw nigh and give your attendance. God save the Queen!' The court usher's cry rings down through the centuries. No longer claiming to represent divine infallibility on earth, the Crown is still the symbol of justice. And Her Majesty's judges and justices and the members of all juries do their best to fail as rarely as possible.

Naturally, the courts cost money. If you appoint an arbitrator, you would expect him to be paid for his time and trouble. The courts are provided as part of the facilities of every civilised State. But the litigant must pay the lawyer. If he manages to win his case, then he should get an indemnity from the other side.

Normally, 'costs go with the event'. The loser in a civil suit is ordered to pay the costs of the winner. All those costs regarded by the law as essential for the doing of justice must normally be paid by the party whose intransigence, unreasonableness or error has resulted in those costs being incurred. Still, there is usually a balance of legal costs, properly incurred but not regarded as essential, which have to be paid by the winner out of his own pocket. These costs sometimes dig deep into the winnings.

Nor can the litigant expect to be paid for his own time. The loser will usually have to pay the expenses of witnesses, lay and professional. There is no recompense, though, for the litigant's loss of his own time—still less for the worry and aggravation involved in the legal proceedings.

Naturally, if the potential winnings are sufficiently high, it is well worth investing your own time and money in legal process. So when deciding whether or not to sue, the first question is: Is there sufficient cash involved? If not, then write off the debt or the row and put it down to experience . . . deduct the losses from your taxed income or profits . . . and keep away from the law. Battles over principles are all very well—but in business and professional life, it is seldom worth fighting over trifles.* The most principled of litigants tend to settle, when they see the costs mounting up and the time bearing down on their already heavy days.

Next, time must be considered. A sensible settlement today is usually better than a potential victory, the day after tomorrow— or the year after next. Maybe yours is a claim so clear and unanswerable that you could get 'summary judgment'. Where the defendant cannot raise a 'triable' or 'arguable' issue, then you may be given swift, cheap judgment in the High Court. For a smaller sum, a default summons in the County Court may do the trick.

On the other hand, has the other man a good defence to your claim? If he were to argue that the goods you supplied were delivered defective or late or that the services rendered were inadequate or unworkmanlike, might he be believed? The greater the opposition, the less you should be inclined to do battle.

Then consider the documentation involved. How intricate are the issues, of fact or of law? The greater the stakes and the more involved the problems, the more time the lawyers will have to spend and the

* Indeed, it is said that a good businessman will sell the shirt off his back to become a millionaire.

longer the case is likely to last if it reaches trial. In addition, the weightier the matter, the more experienced (and expensive) the lawyer whom you will want to instruct.

So before you launch litigation, by all means ask your solicitors to attempt to estimate the likely costs involved. They will doubtless hedge vigorously and explain how impossible it is to give any precise assessment. They will be right. On the other hand, they will at least be able to tell you the sort of sums involved, if you take the case through its various stages.

Maybe it is worth while to hazard a certain sum at the start, to see whether proceedings bring results. You will have sent out the usual letters of demand. Your solicitor will have tried a 'letter before action', threatening proceedings if monies due are not paid. Those two steps usually bring results. If they fail, though, and a writ or summons is issued, the debtor generally pays up. Only a tiny minority of cases ever reach trial.

Even if the start of the proceedings does not spell the end of the opposition, you should get some sort of compromise settlement, before the day of trial arrives. But this cannot be guaranteed. Once you start a case, you should be prepared if necessary to fight it or else to throw in a certain figure as costs, in return for withdrawing the action. Alternatively, you could probably 'let it go to sleep' (as lawyers put it), hoping that the other party will not seek to 'wake it up', or to have it 'dismissed for lack of prosecution' merely for the sake of costs which he himself has incurred to date.

Unfortunately, though, there are other worries to be put into the balance. Do you know where to find the debtor? Will you have to throw good money after bad, in setting up a search for him? If you obtain your judgment, is it likely to be satisfied? Suing a man of straw or a shell company is a profitless pastime.

So before you waste powder and shot in court proceedings, look at the issues; tot up the likely or potential legal costs; examine the defences and the defendants—and then decide on your legal action in a cool, commercial way, and with due regard to the advice you receive from your experts.

Chapter 111

Representing Yourself

MOST BUSINESSES are blessed with limited liability. They operate through companies. A company is a brilliant invention of the law, which has no existence apart from those who run it. It is defined as a 'person', by certain statutes. But its personality is distinctly inhuman.

Still, a company may sue and be sued—and it may also be convicted of criminal offences. It may be fined, banned or otherwise punished. It may not, of course, be imprisoned. For that, you need flesh, blood and bones.

The same applies to appearing in court. There is nothing whatsoever to prevent a company from employing its own lawyer, to act as company secretary, accounts administrator, property supervisor or any other sort of general factotum. If he is a qualified solicitor, holding a current practising certificate, then he may appear in court and represent the company. True, he is limited to those courts at which solicitors may appear—they have no right of audience in the High Court, for instance, but County Courts, Magistrates' Courts, tribunals and certain Crown Courts are open to them.

What of any other company employee? He has no right of audience. In practice, companies do sometimes obtain a cheaper representation through putting their staff into a court in the guise of witnesses. This is particularly common when it comes to debt collecting. But in general, corporations must appear through solicitor or counsel.

Individuals (including professional men and women), on the other hand, may fight their way up to the House of Lords, if they wish, entirely in person. Take, for instance, the recent case of a Mr Robin Samuel Buckland, shopkeeper, who conducted a successful action in person against a chartered surveyor, against whom he alleged professional negligence.

In general, 'costs go with the event'. If you win your case, you are entitled to your costs. There will often be a balance left over which a client must pay to his own solicitor, even though the case is won. The only costs which will be allowed against the other side are normally those which are regarded as absolutely essential for the doing of justice. But apart from the 'solicitor and client' costs, the winner is usually entitled to force the loser to pay up.

'I won my case,' said Mr Buckland, in effect. 'I had to study my law books in an attempt to "do it myself". I have had to draft Particulars of Claim, to prepare the case for trial, to consider the law and so on. I estimate that I had to spend a vast amount of my time—which is also my money. I have been awarded costs, but nothing for my time. This is wrong.'

'Sorry,' said the Court of Appeal. Lord Justice Danckwerts put it like this:

'Although solicitors who act in person for themselves and claim to be remunerated for necessary professional services may recover these costs, a layman not skilled in the law may recover only out-of-pocket expenses. . . . A layman cannot charge for his time. . . .' So Mr Buckland got nothing for his 'time and labour expended'.

Sir Gordon Willmer: 'When a solicitor successfully conducts his own case, there has been an exercise of professional skill and he is treated differently from any other litigant in person. The court is not concerned with the exercise of other skills. Other professional people who become involved in litigation might recover something in so far as they are qualified witnesses and are called as such. But nobody except a solicitor is entitled to make charges in respect of the exercise of professional legal skill, which is what Mr. Buckland seeks to do in this case.'

The learned judge expressed 'much sympathy for Mr Buckland'. But he could find 'no ground either in principle or in authority for allowing him anything by way of remuneration for the exercise of professional skill which he had not got'.

That's the essence of it, then. No professional skill exercised? Then you get no costs from the other side. You may recover your out-of-pocket expenses . . . your disbursements . . . what you have to lay out in order to win your judgment. But you provide your time and labour, at your own expense, win or lose.

This, of course, is a mighty argument for obtaining legal representation. An even better one? That the lawyer is likely to do a far better job for you. You are dealing with parking summonses and the like? Then by all means represent yourself. But if (for instance) you are likely to lose your licence because you are coming up for your third conviction for an endorsable offence, within the magic period of three years, then it is the height of folly to attempt to handle the court without the assistance of the best lawyer whom you can afford to instruct.

You have a lawyer for your business? He is no good? Then find another. He is a splendid fellow? Then do not keep a dog and do your own barking. Even if you are allowed to appear and you win your case, you may still find yourself out of pocket on costs . . . as the unfortunate Mr Buckland discovered.

Chapter 112

When You Need Your Lawyer—a Checklist

To KNOW when your lawyer's services are vital may be worth a fortune to you or your business. Here is a check list of occasions when the wise business or professional man will not attempt to go it alone.

1   Drafting and vetting standard terms of service. *The Contracts of Employment Act, 1972* (as amended), requires written particulars of all main terms to be supplied within 13 weeks of the start of the employment or any variation within four weeks of the change. At least once in a business lifetime it is worth getting the terms drafted by experts. If you are offered a document containing your own proposed terms of service and you do not fully understand it, then take it to your lawyer.

2   Restraint clauses—new or old, yours or those of your employees —need professional drafting and interpretation. In the absence of a reasonable (and hence binding) restraint clause, an employee may compete against the company immediately he leaves its service. Definition of 'reasonableness' depends upon all the circumstances of the case—and upon knowledge of all recent decided cases. Do not attempt to draft restraints upon your own employees—you are likely to fail, disastrously. Conversely, if there is no restraint clause in your own contract of service, you may leave and compete as you see fit;

but if you find a restraint clause, it may not be binding on you. Obtain and follow your solicitor's advice.

3 Standard documents require legal drafting. In particular, as the Supply of Goods (Implied Terms) Act has now made exclusion clauses in contracts for 'consumer sales' void—and similar clauses in business contracts voidable if they are 'unfair and unreasonable'—conditions of trading should be either drafted or re-drafted by lawyers.

4 Disputes over complicated contracts need expert sorting out. To find out, for instance, whether you can cancel, bring all the documents (order forms, 'acceptances', acknowledgements, correspondence and the like) to your lawyers. They may find loopholes for you—or advise you whether there are any available to your suppliers or customers.

5 Court actions can seldom be fought without legal help. An individual may represent himself; a company must (except in comparatively rare and unimportant cases) have solicitor or Counsel. If you are sued, ask your solicitors the following questions:

(*a*) What are the plaintiff's prospects of success?

(*b*) When is the case likely to come on for trial?

(*c*) Can you give any estimate of the legal costs likely to be involved—if not in the entire proceedings, then at least within the foreseeable future?

(*d*) Do you advise attempting a settlement—and if so, then should we wait for the approach to come from the other side; should it be made between solicitors; or should we wave the olive branch personally?

(*e*) What additional documents, statements or information do you require from us?

6 If you wish to sue, then ask your solicitor the questions posed in (*a*) to (*e*) above (in reverse, where necessary), plus the following:

(*a*) If we obtain judgment, what are our prospects of getting it enforced?

(*b*) Have we—or could we obtain—information about the liquidity or means of the defendant? It is useless to sue a man or a company 'of straw', however successfully.

(c) Would the defendant (if an individual) be likely to obtain legal aid? If so, then he may not be worth suing because even if you win, it is most unlikely that he would be ordered to pay any substantial part of your costs;

(d) Should we place a limit on the costs which we are prepared to incur, without re-assessing the situation? After all, very few cases reach trial; a writ or a summons usually brings the desired result; but litigation is a gamble and it is often wise to assess and limit that gamble in advance.

7   If you are prosecuted for anything other than a parking summons (which you might as well deal with on your own), then you need your lawyer—as soon as possible and preferably before you have made any incriminating statements. In civil and in criminal cases alike, clients habitually go to lawyers when their cases are already ruined—through incautious oral statements or careless correspondence. Do not ruin your own case beyond repair—particularly when that ruin could cost you a fine, your driving licence—or prison.

Typical prosecution cases which may require swift legal help include the following:

Trade Descriptions Act.

Factories Act.

Offices, Shops and Railway Premises Act.

Serious driving offences—including
those involving allegations of drink or danger—plus problems under the 'totting up' rules (three convictions within three years equals probable disqualification).

Also (and more serious) theft; taking or driving away a motor vehicle or other conveyance; handling (or receiving) stolen property.

8   Before prosecuting a suspected thief, if in doubt then take advice. While a civil action may be withdrawn on payment of the costs of the other side, the prosecutor may only discontinue a prosecution with the leave of the Court.

9   Do not draft your own will. There are too many snags. Samples: A witness cannot get a legacy; if both parents are dead, the executors may automatically become guardians of the children; and there are complicated formalities, the absence of any one of which can make

the will invalid. Anyway: You are unlikely to achieve your wishes if you draft your will yourself.

10 The acquisition or sale of premises needs an expert in conveyancing. Traps include: problems of title; plans for compulsory purchase for development or road widening; complicated clauses in leases—particularly concerned with repairs; and technical terms which the layman cannot hope to understand.

11 When dealing with tenancies or tenants, let solicitors vet or prepare and serve (as the case may be) all necessary notices—including notices to quit; notices required for increases of rent following a break or rent revision clauses; counter-notices or applications to the Court in connection with business tenancies (under *The Landlord and Tenant Act, 1954*).

12 When approaching liquidation or bankruptcy (personal or corporate, your own or other peoples) there are too many intricacies for the business or professional man to cope with on his own.

13 Where an accident causes personal injuries either to you or to another person for whom you are responsible, a solicitor's help is vital. While special damage (items like loss of earnings or cost of repairing a vehicle) are easily assessed, 'general damage' (compensation for pain and suffering, loss of expectation of life and loss of future earnings, for instance) is extremely difficult; based upon decisions of courts in similar cases; and leaves the layman totally out of his legal depth.

In any of these 13 cases, you need the help of your lawyer. If in doubt in any other case, the sooner you consult your lawyer, the less his services are likely to cost you in the long run.

Chapter 113

Problems of Legal Aid

ONE OF the greatest joys of winning your case is collecting the costs from the loser. 'Costs go with the event', says the law. He who emerges triumphant from court is entitled to have at least the bulk of his costs paid by the other side. But what happens if the loser has Legal Aid.

Conversely, what are your chances (as a business concern or as a private individual) of having your litigation financed as part of the wonders of the Welfare State? If you need solicitor and counsel, it is best to be rich or poor. But the middle-grade executive or professional man is out of luck.

So let us look at legal aid from every commercial angle.

*   *   *

If one of your operatives is injured and wishes to sue you, the chances are that he will get legal aid. This will not necessarily be free. His income will be assessed; various items of expenditure will be deducted; and if the balance is sufficiently high, he will have to make a contribution towards his costs. Still, the chances are that his legal battle will cost him far less than it would if he had to finance it on his own.

Perhaps the greatest advantage of legal aid comes to the loser. The chances are that he will have to contribute exactly the same towards the cost of the winner as he does to the Legal Aid Fund for his certificate. If his contribution was nil, then the winner will probably have to bear all his own costs, even if he emerged from court, unruffled and triumphant in every respect.

No winner can be sure of getting all his costs. Generally, these will be 'taxed' (or assessed, by an official of the court) and the loser will have to pay those which are regarded as essential for the doing of justice ('party and party' costs, so called). There is usually a balance ('solicitor and client costs') which the winner will have to pay in any event. Litigation is always a luxury, to be avoided where possible.

Still, it is possible in most cases to rescue a great deal from the wreckage if you can only convince the court of the justice of your cause. But when you fight a legally assisted person, whatever happens you are almost always bound to lose. If you cave in at the start and pay up, the chances are that you will not only save time, worry and aggravation but that you will have to pay out less than if you had taken the case to court and fought it to a conclusion. In other words, if you are advised by your solicitors that if you win against a legally assisted person your own costs will exceed the amount of his claim, the sooner you come to a sensible compromise, the better. This is a form of blackmail, if you like. But it is legitimate and it works.

'What about my litigation, then?' you say. 'If I want my doctor on the National Health, I can have him. Can I force the State to pay for my lawyer as well?'

The chances are that—as a reader of this book—your income will exceed the prescribed limit for Legal Aid. If you operate through a company, then even if it is on the rocks . . . about to go up the spout . . . operating at a loss . . . legal aid will certainly not be available to that company. If you are an individual and your income exceeds the limit, the fact that you cannot afford to litigate without legal aid does not mean that the State will help you by paying one single penny towards your costs—or by saving you from the grim necessity of finding the costs of the other party, if you lose.

The departmental manager of a substantial factory recently settled a High Court case. He dropped his claim and even agreed to pay his own costs. His counsel pointed out to the judge that if the hearing were to last, as expected, for the best part of a week, to lose would have meant complete financial ruin. The stakes were too high. He had to throw in his hand and lose every penny that he had spent on the litigation.

'I sometimes feel,' said the judge, 'that our courts are like the restaurant in the Ritz. In theory, they are open to all. . . .'

American lawyers avoid this problem by agreeing to work on a contingency basis. If he loses, the client may pay nothing. If he wins, as much as 50 per cent of the proceeds may go to the lawyers. This system is forbidden to counsel and solicitors in Britain. There are many who feel that while both the rich and the poor are better off without it, at least it would enable the industrial and commercial executive, professional man, and even the better paid modern operative or engineer to fight cases which he ought to win but which today he does not even dare to fight. It is a brave man who risks ruin, even when his cause is just.

Chapter 114

Laws on Arbitrations

KING SOLOMON used to sit under a palm tree, dispensing justice. In the main, his loyal subjects willingly submitted their disputes for his wise decision. The modern equivalent of this procedure is arbitration. Its success or failure depends almost entirely upon how much of the wisdom and experience of Solomon has passed to the arbitrator.

Every commercial community (alas) has its disputes. It is essential to understand how these may best be settled. And you need that understanding not merely before trouble breaks out but preferably before a contract is even made.

So consider the vices and virtues of arbitration, as opposed to the efforts of courts of law. When can you be forced to arbitrate—and when is it to your advantage? If you do not like the arbitrator's decision, what can be done? When will a court set aside an arbitration award?

*　　*　　*

There can seldom be arbitration without the consent of the parties. That consent may have been given when they agreed on their terms of business. It may come later. But whereas you can drag an opponent unwillingly to the courts of the land, you cannot lay him (or your case) at the feet of an arbitrator, without his consent.

It follows that the form of arbitration is also a matter for agreement. Just as the variety of disputes and disputants is almost endless, so arbitrators may be individual businessmen, Presidents of Chambers of Commerce, former Official Referees or other court officials, or the Chief Rabbi's court (known as the 'Beth Din'—or 'House of Judgment'). Just as you may choose the persons with whom you do business, so you may pick your arbitrator.

Most arbitrations are held because the original agreement contained a clause under which the businessmen agreed to settle their disputes through arbitration. Most such clauses provide that either party may give notice, requiring arbitration; that an arbitrator shall be chosen by consent; and that if the parties cannot agree upon an appropriate arbitrator, then he shall be chosen by person holding a particular office—maybe the President of the Royal Institute of

British Architects or the President for the time being of the local Chamber of Commerce.

On the other hand, there is nothing whatsoever to prevent people from saying: 'We cannot agree. Let us submit our dispute to an independent engineer, surveyor, or suitably qualified person whom we both trust.'

Once a case gets before an arbitrator, he has the power to settle it and both parties are bound by his decision. The rules are laid down by various Arbitration Acts—but the procedure is generally informal. In most cases, the parties will set out their contentions in 'points of claim' and 'points of defence'; the arbitrator will give directions as to the trial; documents will be disclosed—and, with good fortune and a first-class arbitrator, the result may be obtained quicker and cheaper than if the parties had gone through the courts.

In practice, though, arbitrations have a number of snags. First, the party who is being kept out of his money and who could get 'summary judgment' in the High Court will have his patience sorely tried. In that case, arbitration takes much longer to produce results than do the courts of law.

Next, whereas judges at every level are skilled in deciding disputes—that is, in hearing and sifting evidence and coming to a just conclusion—most arbitrators have little or no judicial experience. Unless they happen to be retired judges, or perhaps practising lawyers, they will lack judicial experience and training. However great their knowledge of the particular trade or industry, their acquaintance with the law will probably be minimal.

Again, rights of appeal from courts of law are far greater than from arbitrators—which is a double pity when you consider the judicial inexperience of many of those who arbitrate. In general, the courts will only upset an arbitrator's decision if it is made in bad faith, contrary to the rules of natural justice or in disregard of the law of the land.

There have been cases where arbitrators have heard one side while the other was out of the room or where the documents themselves show some clear error. But however many dissatisfied litigants there undoubtedly may be (and are) in courts of law, most lawyers consider that dissatisfaction is far more common with arbitrations.

Still, arbitrations do have their advantages. For instance, there may, be no formal hearing. An arbitration is, in any event, generally held in private—and one or both parties may welcome a total absence of publicity. Only if the arbitrator's award is appealed is the press likely to be involved. Again, although the parties may be represented by solicitor or counsel before an arbitrator, the costs are generally lower than they would be in a legal proceeding of equivalent complexity and length. But it would be interesting to know (although impossible to find out) whether there is truth in the general belief that a far higher percentage of arbitrations in fact reach hearing, than commercial cases in which writs or summonses are issued.

Finally, consider one of the most recent arbitration cases, in which Mr Justice Willis dismissed a motion in which builders sought to set aside an arbitrator's decision that they make payments to a Mr Pywell.

'Only within a very limited sphere,' said the Judge, 'will the courts interfere with arbitration awards. An error in law or in fact on the faith of an award means that there can be found in the award—or in a document actually incorporated thereto—some legal or factual proposition which was the basis of the award and which could be said to be erroneous.' In other words, only where the arbitrator is in obvious and patent error will the courts interfere. Whether or not that is a happy thought depends entirely upon your view of the decision of the arbitrator.

So before you decide to incorporate an arbitration clause in your commercial contract—or to appoint an arbitrator to sort out your dispute—consider the pros and cons with care. There are many of each.

Chapter 115

When You Owe the World a Living

IF WE lived in China, no doubt the present time would be dubbed: 'The Era of the Great Debt'. As each New Year arrives, the prospect of anyone emerging into it in universal credit is remote. Both for business, professional and personal reasons, the debtor needs to know some basic law. So here are some thoughts on staving off your creditors.

If you owe money, then (assuming that the time for payment has arrived) your creditor is entitled to sue. Unless you have some special credit arrangement, the moment that a debt falls due, he may use the law as a stick to beat your money out of you. And—in spite of an almost universal belief to the contrary—there is some point to the Sword of Justice, which may somehow be wielded to swift effect.

Where the defendant can raise no 'triable issue' . . . where there is not even an arguable answer to the claim . . . then a plaintiff can get 'summary judgment'—he can short-circuit the usual, lengthy legal procedures and obtain his judgment in a matter of weeks and at a fairly low cost.

So if you are sued, look for a 'triable issue'. Maybe the goods delivered turned out to be defective or the contractors' workmanship was shoddy. Do you suspect errors in accounting? The old gambit, 'I ordered the goods for my company not for myself', is treated with merited suspicion. The company in question is, no doubt, teetering on the brink of liquidation. But if that is the best you can do then at least put it on paper as soon as you can.

In fact, the time to prepare your issues is before they arise. If you have no correspondence to corroborate your alleged complaints, then your purported defence will probably be regarded as a sham and you will be refused 'leave to defend'. If you do have genuine grounds for refusing to pay any account which is at present on your 'Damn'd Bills' clip, the sooner you write off to the alleged creditor, setting out those complaints in clear and unequivocal terms, the better.

This procedure is, at the worst, likely to deter or at least to postpone the issue of the writ. With luck, your creditor will have as sound a realisation as yourself that litigation (at least for the non-legally-aided) is a luxury, to be avoided wherever possible. He will know that while an order is normally made that the loser pay the winner's costs, there may well be some part of the winner's legal expenses that he will still have to meet out of his own pocket. Then there's the time and energy expended, the loss of goodwill, the general aggravation and the risk (however remote) of failure.

However much the creditor may despise litigation, it is worse for the debtor. So if you do receive a 'letter before action' from a solicitor, you should either put your own man of law into action—or else see whether you cannot come to some reasonable arrangement for payment by instalments.

This sort of gambit is particularly apt for your bank manager.

As we saw in Chapter 2 a bank loan is like any other. And an overdraft is a form of loan. In the absence of some special agreement to the contrary, it is repayable on demand. So if the Bank of England squeezes those honoured with your custom and they react by requiring you to liquidate your debt to them, the odds are that they are within their rights. If you refuse to comply, then they may be able to dispose of the securities you have lodged with them, to repay themselves from the proceeds and to hand over any balance.

If you would like to keep your shares or other securities, then off you go to the manager's office. The stars foretell that the most fashionable future position in such circumstances will be prostrate. But if you can manage to convince the man that you are only waiting to be paid what you are owed, you may find him a good deal more patient than the law could require.

Many of us (especially those who are self-employed—or whose incomes depend upon receipts of family companies) could pay off all our debts with ease, if only others would do the same courtesy to us. If your creditors become nasty, you will have to pass the misery along the line to those who owe you a living. Demand your money. If it is not received, let your solicitor send a 'letter before action'. If this fails and you are advised to issue a writ, go ahead—remembering that you may get summary judgment. Console yourself, too, with the thought that most people pay up when they get a solicitor's letter and that those who do not will seldom allow a case to get to trial. Even where a writ is issued, the odds are heavily against eventual legal battle.

My advice, then, in a hard-up future? Treat thy debtor as thyself. If your creditors are cruel to you, the least you can do is to return the compliment—to those in your debt. When solvency is at stake, the forthcoming years are unlikely to be known as 'The Era of the Gentlemen'.

Chapter 116

Legal Aspects of Billing*

THE LARGER and more modern the aircraft, the greater the tragedy when the crash occurs. The finer the computer, the greater the hazard if

---

* See also Chapter 86, for the Rights of the Unpaid.

it hiccups—or is fed the wrong material—and the wrong bills emerge.

So consider: If you send out the wrong account, can you later correct it? If you undercharge, are you bound by your mistakes? If you overcharge and your client or customer has a heart attack as a result, can you be held liable in law?

* * *

A bill is born of a contract. When the contract contemplates that payment is due, the debtor is bound to pay.

The bill merely takes account of existing circumstances. An error in that account in no way affects the obligations of the parties, one towards the other—at least for the first few years.

If you charge too much, your customer is still only bound to pay the proper contractual price. If the customer overpays, then he is entitled to the return of any balance overpaid.

Conversely, if you undercharge, you are entitled to demand the difference between the sum on your account and the amount which should have been billed.

The creditor is not bound by the mistakes that he makes in accounts which are 'post-contractual documents'. They do not contain the deal between the parties. The bargain remains the same and either may still enforce his rights.

The situation is, of course, entirely different where the supplier agrees to provide goods or services at a mistakenly low cost. Suppose, for instance that you receive a firm quotation for repairs to your premises. The contractor has under-quoted. This is his misfortune. The law will not let him say: 'I made a mistake—so I must charge more.'

Equally, you may accept a quotation and then find someone else prepared to do the job (or, for that matter, to provide the goods) at a much lower cost. You are bound by your error.

There are some possible legal loopholes. For instance, if goods are advertised or shown in a shop window, marked with a price, and you write (or say) that you will have them, you are making the offer. The supplier is merely (in law) issuing an 'invitation to treat'—he is inviting you to offer to pay the sum which he has indicated that he will accept. He is not bound by his indication (see Chapter 62).

Anyway, the bill has nothing to do with the bargain. It comes afterwards. Mistakes will cause ill-will—but they have no legally binding effect.

What if an overcharge causes ill health?

The law is very unlikely to provide any balm for the customer's wounds. The damage is 'too remote', from the wrongful act or omission. I know of no case in which an overcharge—even a deliberate one made by a public utility to jolt the customer into action—has led to successful legal proceedings. Not every wrong leads to a legal remedy.

As for undercharging, the creditor runs one risk only—that time may run out on him. The law says that all good things—and all bad ones—must come to an end. It applies a 'period of limitation' even on claims for debts when there is and can be no valid answer to the original claim, and even where the account is both accurate and entirely justified.

A claim for a debt becomes 'statute barred' when six years have passed from the date when the debt was originally incurred or (in appropriate cases) the date when the debtor last gave a written acknowledgement of his debt. If someone owes you money and asks for time to pay and you grant his request, then 'time begins to run' all over again, from the date of his request. But if he simply sits tight and says nothing, you must start your proceedings within six years from the date when the money originally fell due for payment.

Conversely, if you do not receive an account for a while, do not rejoice too soon. Only when six years have passed can you relax and regard the transaction as closed.

Chapter 117

The 'Harassment' of Debtors

A DEBT collecting firm attempted to obtain money from a housewife, in payment for goods. It sent a letter threatening that a van marked 'debt collection company' would arrive at her home. Charged and convicted of an offence under *The Administration of Justice Act, 1970*, the proprietor made legal history—and emphasised that traders who are owed money are going to find it even harder to collect in the future than they have done in the past.

So before you put a list of debtors in your window or threaten to humiliate your debtors in some other way, consider the recent rules.

Section 40 of the Act says this: 'A person commits an offence if, with the object of coercing another person to pay money claimed from the other as a debt due under a contract, he—

'(a) harasses the other with demands for payment which, in respect of their frequency or the manner or occasion of making any such demand, or of any threat or publicity by which any demand is accompanied, are calculated to subject him or members of his family or household to alarm, distress or humiliation.'

The object of telling a customer that a van will arrive at her home marked 'debt collection company' is obviously to subject her and her household to 'distress or humiliation'. To put the name and address of the debtor in the window would produce the same result. Either way, the odds are that the trader commits an offence.

Equally, it is unlawful 'falsely to represent, in relation to the money claimed, that criminal proceedings lie for failure to pay it.' By all means threaten to put the matter in the hands of your solicitors or of a debt collecting agency. But do not say that you will call in the police when you know perfectly well that no prosecution lies for failure to comply with your contract.

Further, it is unlawful to represent that you are 'authorised in some official capacity to claim or enforce payment'. So do not tell the debtor that you are a court official or the like. Also, if you send out a document which you have falsely represented to have some official character, you will commit an offence.

If a trader 'concerts with others' in the taking of such action under (a) above, then he may be guilty of an offence 'notwithstanding that his own course of conduct does not by itself amount to harassment'. If you plan harassment with some debt collecting agency, you may find yourself in the dock, even though you have taken no specific action on your own behalf.

Penalties? For the first offence, a fine of up to £100; on the second or subsequent conviction, a fine of not more than £400. You cannot be imprisoned for your pains, but it may cost you a great deal more to break the law than it would to write off the debt.

The Section does provide one defence: The above rules do not apply 'to anything done by a person which is reasonable (and otherwise permissible in law) for the purpose—

(a) of securing the discharge of an obligation due, or believed by him to be due, to himself or to persons for whom he acts, or

protecting himself or them from future loss; or
(*b*) of the enforcement of any liability by legal process.'

Lawyers may still harass debtors by serving writs or summonses—and the wise course now is quite clearly to let your lawyers get on with the job for you. On the other hand, if you are owed money—or honestly believe that a particular person is in your debt—then you you may take such steps as are 'reasonable and otherwise permissible in law' in order to get payment. What is 'reasonable', as always, will depend on all the circumstances of the case.

Chapter 118

Time

IF A train or a plane arrives late, its occupants may be aggravated, but the effects of the delay will not be fatal. In law, though, delay may spell death.

When suing for damages for personal injuries, for instance, the claim must normally be brought within three years of the accident. But 'time' may run from the date when the patient first could or should have known of the existence of the ailment or of its cause. Claims against the estate of the deceased person must generally be brought within 12 months from the grant of probate or, in the case of an intestacy, of letters of administration, of the start of the winding up of his affairs. Actions for debt must (as we saw in the previous Chapter) be brought within six years of the date when the debt was incurred or the date when it was last acknowledged to be due, in writing. Most other actions for breach of contract have a six year limit.

If you are to be sued for professional negligence, the time limit is also six years (unless, of course, you caused personal injuries, in which case the three-year limit applies). Negligence is a 'tort'—a civil wrong—as is nuisance, defamation or assault. Six years with no writ or summons means that the potential action disappears.

There are other and much shorter limits imposed by individual statutes. The most important for the business or professional man? Those laid down by *The Landlord And Tenant Act, 1954*—which protects business and professional tenants whose leases or tenancies are coming to an end (see Chapter 8).

Suppose that you are tenant of your shop or office. Unless and until your landlords serve a notice on you, in the prescribed form, stating whether or not he is prepared to grant a new tenancy, you may remain—on the old terms.

Once you have received a notice, though, you must take appropriate action. You must serve a counter-notice, saying whether or not you are prepared to give up possession of the property. You must give your notice within two months—and you must do so in writing.

Now suppose that you give your notice and the haggling procedure begins. Your landlords ask for a rent that you regard as too high. You offer terms which are unacceptably low. Still, there is no doubt that you are entitled to a new tenancy. Your landlord cannot show (for instance) that he needs the place for the purposes of his own business or home, or that he intends to redevelop the premises.

Unfortunately for you, the haggling goes on too long. You are suddenly faced with Section 29 (3) of the Act: 'No application . . .' to the court for a new tenancy 'shall be entertained unless it is made not less than two nor more than four months after the giving of the landlord's notice . . .'. The four-month period has passed. You are out of luck. No court, however mighty, can restore your rights. You are at your landlord's mercy.

If you decide to handle your own legal affairs, you do so at your own risk—if you make a mistake . . . if you forget to take action within the appropriate time . . . then you have only yourself to blame. In that case, you will have to bear any loss on your own shoulders.

If, on the other hand, you have seen fit to put your problems into the hands of solicitors, it is up to them to watch out for the time limits. Whether you are seeking a new tenancy of your old office or shop—or whether the local planning authority is challenging your use of the premises—it is highly dangerous to go it alone.

"IF I HAD ONLY KNOWN . . . !"

Part eleven

Appendices

Appendix 1

The Trade Descriptions Act, 1968

ARRANGEMENT OF SECTIONS

Prohibition of false trade descriptions

* Note: As a result of the *Criminal Justice Act, 1972*, a person who suffers as a result of a breach of the Trade Descriptions Act may be awarded up to £400 by the Court that convicts the offender.

Prohibition of false trade descriptions

1.—(1) Any person who, in the course of a trade or business,—
    (*a*) applies a false trade description to any goods; or
    (*b*) supplies or offers to supply any goods to which a false trade
        description is applied;
shall, subject to the provisions of this Act, be guilty of an offence.

(2) Section 2 to 6 of this Act shall have effect for the purposes of this
section and for the interpretation of expressions used in this section, where-
ever they occur in this Act.

2.—(1) A trade description is an indication, direct or indirect, and by
whatever means given, of any of the following matters with respect to any
goods or parts of goods, that is to say—
    (*a*) quantity, size or gauge;
    (*b*) method of manufacture, production, processing or reconditioning;
    (*c*) composition;
    (*d*) fitness for purpose, strength, performance, behaviour or accuracy;
    (*e*) any physical characteristics not included in the preceding para-
        graphs;
    (*f*) testing by any person and results thereof;
    (*g*) approval by any person or conformity with a type approved by any
        person;
    (*h*) place or date of manufacture, production, processing or recon-
        ditioning;
    (*i*) person by whom manufactured, produced, processed or recon-
        ditioned;
    (*j*) other history, including previous ownership or use.

(2) The matters specified in subsection (1) of this section shall be taken—
    (*a*) in relation to any animal, to include sex, breed or cross, fertility
        and soundness;
    (*b*) in relation to any semen, to include the identity and characteristics
        of the animal from which it was taken and measure of dilution.

(3) In this section 'quantity' includes length, width, height, area,
volume, capacity, weight and number.

(4) Notwithstanding anything in the preceding provisions of this section,
the following shall be deemed not to be trade descriptions, that is to say,
any description or mark applied in pursuance of—
    (*a*) the Seeds Act 1920;
    (*b*) section 2 of the Agricultural Produce (Grading and Marking) Act
        1928 (as amended by the Agricultural Produce (Grading and
        Marking) Amendment Act 1931) or any corresponding enactment
        of the Parliament of Northern Ireland;
    (*c*) the Plant Varieties and Seeds Act 1964;
    (*d*) the Agriculture and Horticulture Act 1964;
    (*e*) the Seeds Act (Northern Ireland) 1965;
    (*f*) the Horticulture Act (Northern Ireland) 1966;
any description applied in pursuance of the Fertilisers and Feeding Stuffs
Act 1926 to an article included in the first column of Schedule 1 to that

Act, and any mark prescribed by a system of classification compiled under section 5 of the Agriculture Act 1967.

(5) Notwithstanding anything in the preceding provisions of this section, where provision is made under the Food and Drugs Act 1955, the Food and Drugs (Scotland) Act 1956 or the Food and Drugs Act (Northern Ireland) 1958 prohibiting the application of a description except to goods in the case of which the requirements specified in that provision are complied with, that description, when applied to such goods, shall be deemed not to be a trade description.

3.—(1) A false trade description is a trade description which is false to a material degree.

(2) A trade description which, though not false, is misleading, that is to say, likely to be taken for such an indication of any of the matters specified in section 2 of this Act as would by false to a material degree, shall be deemed to be false trade description.

(3) Anything which, though not a trade description, is likely to be taken for an indication of any of those matters and, as such an indication, would be false to a material degree, shall be deemed to be false trade description.

(4) A false indication, or anything likely to be taken as an indication which would be false, that any goods comply with a standard specified or recognised by any person or implied by the approval of any person shall be deemed to be a false trade description, if there is no such person or no standard so specified, recognised or implied.

4.—(1) A person applies a trade description to goods if he—

(*a*) affixes or annexes it to or in any manner marks it on or incorporates it with—

    (i) the goods themselves, or

    (ii) anything in, on or with which the goods are supplied; or

(*b*) places the goods in, on or with anything which the trade description has been affixed or annexed to, marked on or incorporated with, or places any such thing with the goods; or

(*c*) uses the trade description in any manner likely to be taken as referring to the goods.

(2) An oral statement may amount to the use of a trade description.

(3) Where goods are supplied in pursuance of a request in which a trade description is used and the circumstances are such as to make it reasonable to infer that the goods are supplied as goods corresponding to that trade description, the person supplying the goods shall be deemed to have applied that trade description to the goods.

5.—(1) The following provisions of this section shall have effect where in an advertisement a trade description is used in relation to any class of goods.

(2) The trade description shall be taken as referring to all goods of the class, whether or not in existence at the time the advertisement is published

(*a*) for the purpose of determining whether an offence has been committed under paragraph (*a*) of section 1(1) of this Act; and

(*b*) where goods of the class are supplied or offered to be supplied by a person publishing or displaying the advertisement, also for the purpose of determining whether an offence has been committed under paragraph (*b*) of the said section 1(1).

(3) In determining for the purposes of this section whether any goods are of a class to which a trade description used in an advertisement relates regard shall be had not only to the form and content of the advertisement but also to the time, place, manner and frequency of its publication and all other matters making it likely or unlikely that a person to whom the goods are supplied would think of the goods as belonging to the class in relation to which the trade description is used in the advertisement.

6. A person exposing goods for supply or having goods in his possession for supply shall be deemed to offer to supply them.

Power to define terms and to require display, etc. of information

7. Where it appears to the Board of Trade—
 (*a*) that it would be in the interest of persons to whom any goods are supplied; or
 (*b*) that it would be in the interest of persons by whom any goods are exported and would not be contrary to the interest of persons to whom such goods are supplied in the United Kingdom;

that any expressions used in relation to the goods should be understood as having definite meanings, the Board may by order assign such meanings either—
 (i) to those expressions when used in the course of a trade or business as, or as part of, a trade description applied to the goods; or
 (ii) to those expressions when so used in such circumstances as may be specified in the order;

and where such a meaning is so assigned to an expression it shall be deemed for the purposes of this Act to have that meaning when used as mentioned in paragraph (i) or, as the case may be, paragraph (ii) of this section.

8.—(1) Where it appears to the Board of Trade necessary or expedient in the interest of persons to whom any goods are supplied that the goods should be marked with or accompanied by any information (whether or not amounting to or including a trade description) or instruction relating to the goods, the Board may, subject to the provisions of this Act, by order impose requirements for securing that the goods are so marked or accompanied, and regulate or prohibit the supply of goods with respect to which the requirements are not complied with; and the requirements may extend to the form and manner in which the information or instruction is to be given.

(2) Where an order under this section is in force with respect to goods of any description, any person who, in the course of any trade or business, supplies or offers to supply goods of that description in contravention of the order shall, subject to the provisions of this Act, be guilty of an offence.

(3) An order under this section may make different provision for different circumstances and may, in the case of goods supplied in circumstances where the information or instruction required by the order would not be conveyed until after delivery, require the whole or part thereof to be also displayed near the goods.

9.—(1) Where it appears to the Board of Trade necessary or expedient in the interest of persons to whom any goods are to be supplied that any description of advertisements of the goods should contain or refer to any information (whether or not amounting to or including a trade description) relating to the goods the Board may, subject to the provisions of this Act, by order impose requirements as to the inclusion of that information, or of an indication of the means by which it may be obtained, in such description of advertisements of the goods as may be specified in the order.

(2) An order under this section may specify the forms and manner in which any such information or indication is to be included in advertisements of any description and may make different provision for different circumstances.

(3) Where an advertisement of any goods to be supplied in the course of any trade or business fails to comply with any requirement imposed under this section, any person who publishes the advertisement shall, subject to the provisions of this Act, be guilty of an offence.

10.—(1) A requirement imposed by an order under section 8 or section 9 of this Act in relation to any goods shall not be confined to goods manufactured or produced in any one country or any one of a number of countries or to goods manufactured or produced outside any one or more countries, unless—

> (*a*) it is imposed with respect to a description of goods in the case of which the Board of Trade are satisfied that the interest of persons in the United Kingdom to whom goods of that description are supplied will be sufficiently protected if the requirement is so confined; and
>
> (*b*) the Board of Trade are satisfied that the order is compatible with the international obligations of the United Kingdom.

(2) Where any requirements with respect to any goods are for the time being imposed by such an order and the Board of Trade are satisfied, on the representation of persons appearing to the Board to have a substantial interest in the matter, that greater hardship would be caused to such persons if the requirements continued to apply than is justified by the interest of persons to whom such goods are supplied, the power of the Board to relax or discontinue the requirements by a further order may be exercised without the consultation and notice required by section 38(3) of this Act.

Misstatements other than false trade descriptions

11.—(1) If any person offering to supply goods of any description gives, by whatever means, any false indication to the effect that the price at which the goods are offered is equal to or less than—

> (*a*) a recommended price; or
>
> (*b*) the price at which the goods or goods of the same description were previously offered by him;

or is less than such a price by a specified amount, he shall, subject to the provisions of this Act, be guilty of an offence.

(2) If any person offering to supply any goods gives, by whatever means, any indication likely to be taken as an indication that the goods are being

offered at a price less than that at which they are in fact being offered he shall, subject to the provisions of this Act, be guilty of an offence.

(3) For the purposes of this section—

(*a*) an indication that goods were previously offered at a higher price or at a particular price—

(i) shall be treated as an indication that they were so offered by the person giving the indication, unless it is expressly stated that they were so offered by others and it is not expressed or implied hat they were, or might have been, so offered also by that person; and

(ii) shall be treated, unless the contrary is expressed, as an indication that they were so offered within the preceding six months for a continuous period of not less than twenty-eight days;

(*b*) an indication as to a recommended price—

(i) shall be treated, unless the contrary is expressed, as an indication that it is a price recommended by the manufacturer or producer; and

(ii) shall be treated, unless the contrary is expressed, as an indication that it is a price recommended generally for supply by retail in the area where the goods are offered;

(*c*) anything likely to be taken as an indication as to a recommended price or as to the price at which goods were previously offered shall be treated as such an indication; and

(*d*) a person advertising goods as available for supply shall be taken as offering to supply them.

12.—(1) If any person, in the course of any trade or business, gives, by whatever means, any false indication, direct or indirect, that any goods or services supplied by him or any methods adopted by him are or are of a kind supplied to or approved by Her Majesty or any member of the Royal Family, he shall, subject to the provisions of this Act, be guilty of an offence.

(2) If any person, in the course of any trade or business, uses, without the authority of Her Majesty, any device or emblem signifying the Queen's Award to Industry or anything so nearly resembling such a device or emblem as to be likely to deceive, he shall, subject to the provisions of this Act, be guilty of an offence.

13. If any person, in the course of any trade or business, gives, by whatever means, any false indication, direct or indirect, that any goods or services supplied by him are of a kind supplied to any person he shall, subject to the provisions of this Act, be guilty of an offence.

14.—(1) It shall be an offence for any person in the course of any trade or business—

(*a*) to make a statement which he knows to be false; or

(*b*) recklessly to make a statement which is false;

as to any of the following matters, that is to say,—

(i) the provision in the course of any trade or business of any services, accommodation or facilties;

    (ii) the nature of any services, accommodation or facilities provided in the course of any trade or business;

    (iii) the time at which, manner in which or persons by whom any services, accommodation or facilities are so provided;

    (iv) the examination, approval or evaluation by any person of any services, accommodation or facilities so provided; or

    (v) the location or amenities of any accommodation so provided.

(2) For the purposes of this section—

    (*a*) anything (whether or not a statement as to any of the matters specified in the preceding subsection) likely to be taken for such a statement as to any of those matters as would be false shall be deemed to be a false statement as to that matter; and

    (*b*) a statement made regardless of whether it is true or false shall be deemed to be made recklessly, whether or not the person making it had reasons for believing that it might be false.

(3) In relation to any services consisting of or including the application of any treatment or process or the carrying out of any repair, the matters specified in subsection (1) of this section shall be taken to include the effect of the treatment, process or repair.

(4) In this section 'false' means false to a material degree and 'services' does not include anything done under a contract of service.

15. Where it appears to the Board of Trade that it would be in the interest of persons for whom any services, accommodation or facilities are provided in the course of any trade or business that any expressions used with respect thereto should be understood as having definite meanings, the Board may by order assign such meanings to those expressions when used as, or as part of, such statements as are mentioned in section 14 of this Act with respect to those services, accommodation or facilities; and where such a meaning is so assigned to an expression it shall be deemed for the purposes of this Act to have that meaning when so used.

Prohibition of importation of certain goods

16. Where a false trade description is applied to any goods outside the United Kingdom and the false indication, or one of the false indications, given, or likely to be taken as given, thereby is an indication of the place of manufacture, production, processing or reconditioning of the goods or any part thereof, the goods shall not be imported into the United Kingdom.

17. In the Trade Marks Act 1938 the following shall be inserted after section 64:—

    '64A.—(1) The person who is registered as the proprietor or registered user of a trade mark in respect of any goods may give notice in writing to the Commissioners of Customs and Excise (in this section referred to as the Commissioners)—

    (*a*) that he is the proprietor or registered user of that trade mark, and

    (*b*) that such goods bearing the trade mark are expected to arrive in the United Kingdom at a time and place and by a consignment specified in the notice, and (*c*) that the use within the United Kingdom of the trade mark in relation to the goods would infringe the proprietor's exclusive right to that use, and

(*d*) that he requests the Commissioners to treat the goods as prohibited goods.

(2) Where a notice has been given under this section in respect of any goods bearing a trade mark and has not been withdrawn and the requirements of any regulations made under this section are complied with, then, subject to the following provisions of this section, the importation into the United Kingdom of the goods shall, if the condition of paragraph (*c*) of the preceding subsection is satisfied, be deemed to be prohibited unless the importation is for the private and domestic use of the person importing the goods.

(3) The Commissioners may make regulations prescribing the form in which notices are to be given under this section, and requiring a person giving such a notice, either at the time of giving the notice or at the time when the goods in question are imported, or at both those times, to furnish the Commissioners with such evidence, and to comply with such other conditions (if any), as may be specified in the regulations, and any such regulations may include such incidental and supplementary provisions as the Commissioners consider expedient for the purposes of this section.

(4) Without prejudice to the generality of the preceding subsection, regulations made under that subsection may include provision for requiring a person who has given a notice under subsection (1) of this section, or a notice purporting to be a notice under that subsection,—

(*a*) to pay such fees in respect of the notice as may be prescribed by the regulations;

(*b*) to give to the Commissioners such security as may be so prescribed, in respect of any liability or expense which they may incur in consequence of the detention of any goods to which the notice relates, or in consequence of anything done in relation to goods so detained;

(*c*) whether any such security is given or not, to keep the Commissioners indemnified against any such liability or expense as is mentioned in the preceding paragraph.

(5) For the purposes of section 11 of the Customs and Excise Act 1952 (which relates to the disposal of duties) any fees paid in pursuance of regulations made under this section shall be treated as money collected on account of customs.

(6) Regulations under subsection (3) of this section shall be made by statutory instrument, which shall be subject to annulment in pursuance of a resolution of either House of Parliament.'

Provisions as to offences

18. A person guilty of an offence under this Act for which no other penalty is specified shall be liable—

(*a*) on summary conviction, to a fine not exceeding four hundred pounds; and

(*b*) on conviction on indictment, to a fine or imprisonment for a term not exceeding two years or both.

19.—(1) No prosecution for an offence under this Act shall be commenced after the expiration of three years from the commission of the offence or one year from its discovery by the prosecutor, whichever is the earlier.

(2) Notwithstanding anything in section 104 of the Magistrates' Courts Act 1952, a magistrates' court may try an information for an offence under this Act if the information was laid at any time within twelve months from the commission of the offence.

(3) Notwithstanding anything in section 23 of the Summary Jurisdiction (Scotland) Act 1954 (limitation of time for proceedings in statutory offences) summary proceedings in Scotland for an offence under this section may be commenced at any time within twelve months from the time when the offence was committed, and subsection (2) of the said section 23 shall apply for the purposes of this subsection as it applies for the purposes of that section.

(4) Subsections (2) and (3) of this section do not apply where—

(*a*) the offence was committed by the making of an oral statement; or

(*b*) the offence was one of supplying goods to which a false trade description is applied, and the trade description was applied by an oral statement; or

(*c*) the offence was one where a false trade description is deemed to have been applied to goods by virtue of section 4(3) of this Act and the goods were supplied in pursuance of an oral request.

20.—(1) Where an offence under this Act which has been committed by a body corporate is proved to have been committed with the consent and connivance of, or to be attributable to any neglect on the part of, any director, manager, secretary or other similar officer of the body corporate, or any person who was purporting to act in any such capacity, he as well as the body corporate shall be guilty of that offence and shall be liable to be proceeded against and punished accordingly.

(2) In this section 'director', in relation to any body corporate established by or under any enactment for the purpose of carrying on under national ownership any industry or part of an industry or undertaking, being a body corporate whose affairs are managed by the members thereof, means a member of that body corporate.

21.—(1) Any person who, in the United Kingdom, assists in or induces the commission in any other country of an act in respect of goods which, if the act were committed in the United Kingdom, would be an offence under section 1 of this Act shall be guilty of an offence, except as provided by subsection (2) of this section, but only if either—

(*a*) the false trade description concerned is an indication (or anything likely to be taken as an indication) that the goods or any part thereof were manufactured, produced, processed or reconditioned in the United Kingdom; or (*b*) the false trade description concerned—

    (i) consists of or comprises an expression (or anything likely to be taken as an expression) to which a meaning is assigned by an order made by virtue of section 7(*b*) of this Act, and

    (ii) where that meaning is so assigned only in circumstances specified in the order, the trade description is used in those circumstances.

(2) A person shall not be guilty of an offence under sub-section (1) of this section if, by virtue of section 32 of this Act, the act, though committed in the United Kingdom, would not be an offence under section 1 of this Act had the goods been intended for despatch to the other country.

(3) Any person who, in the United Kingdom, assists in or induces the commission outside the United Kingdom of an act which, if committed in the United Kingdom, would be an offence under section 12 of this Act shall be guilty of an offence.

22.—(1) Where any act or omission constitutes both an offence under this Act and an offence under any provision contained in or having effect by virtue of Part IV of the Weights and Measures Act 1963 or Part IV of the Weights and Measures Act (Northern Ireland) 1967—

    (*a*) proceedings for the offence shall not be instituted under this Act, except by virtue of section 23 thereof, without the service of such a notice as is required by sub-section (2) of section 51 of the said Act of 1963 or, as the case may be, subsection (2) of section 33 of the said Act of 1967, nor after the expiration of the period mentioned in paragraph (*c*) of that subsection; and

    (*b*) subsections (2), (3) and (5) to (7) of section 26 of the said Act of 1963 or, as the case may be, of section 20 of the said Act of 1967, shall, with the necessary modifications, apply as if the offence under this Act were an offence under Part IV of that Act or any instrument made thereunder.

(2) Where any act or omission constitutes both an offence under this Act and an offence under the food and drugs laws, evidence on behalf of the prosecution concerning any sample procured for analysis shall not be admissible in proceedings for the offence under this Act unless the relevant provisions of those laws have been complied with.

In this subsection 'the food and drugs laws' means the Food and Drugs Act 1955, the Food and Drugs (Scotland) Act 1956, the Food and Drugs Act (Northern Ireland) 1958 and any instrument made thereunder and 'the relevant provisions' means—

    (*a*) in relation to the said Act of 1955, sections 93 and 97 and Part I of Schedule 7;

    (*b*) in relation to the said Act of 1956, sections 30 and 33; and

    (*c*) in relation to the said Act of 1958, sections 35 and 38;

or any provision replacing any of the said provisions by virtue of section 123 of the said Act of 1955, section 56 of the said Act of 1956, or section 68 of the said Act of 1958.

(3) The Board of Trade may by order provide that in proceedings for an offence under this Act in relation to such goods as may be specified in the

order (other than proceedings for an offence falling within the preceding provisions of this section) evidence on behalf of the prosecution concerning any sample procured for analysis shall not be admissible unless the sample has been dealt with in such manner as may be specified in the order.

23. Where the commission by any person of an offence under this Act is due to the act or default of some other person that other person shall be guilty of the offence, and a person may be charged with and convicted of the offence by virtue of this section whether or not proceedings are taken against the first-mentioned person.

Defences

24.—(1) In any proceedings for an offence under this Act it shall, subject to subsection (2) of this section, be a defence for the person charged to prove—

(*a*) that the commission of the offence was due to a mistake or to reliance on information supplied to him or to the act or default of another person, an accident or some other cause beyond his control; and

(*b*) that he took all reasonable precautions and exercised all due diligence to avoid the commission of such an offence by himself or any person under his control.

(2) If in any case the defence provided by the last foregoing subsection involves the allegation that the commission of the offence was due to the act or default of another person or to reliance on information supplied by another person, the person charged shall not, without leave of the court, be entitled to rely on that defence unless, within a period ending seven clear days before the hearing, he has served on the prosecutor a notice in writing giving such information identifying or assisting in the identification of that other person as was then in his possession.

(3) In any proceedings for an offence under this Act of supplying or offering to supply goods to which a false trade description is applied it shall be a defence for the person charged to prove that he did not know, and could not with reasonable diligence have ascertained, that the goods did not conform to the description or that the description had been applied to the goods.

25. In proceedings for an offence under this Act committed by the publication of an advertisement it shall be a defence for the person charged to prove that he is a person whose business it is to publish or arrange for the publication of advertisements and that he received the advertisement for publication in the ordinary course of business and did not know and had no reason to suspect that its publication would amount to an offence under this Act.

Enforcement

26.—(1) It shall be the duty of every local weights and measures authority to enforce within their area the provisions of this Act and of any order made under this Act; and section 37 of the Weights and Measures Act 1963 (power of local authorities to combine) shall apply with respect to the functions of such authorities under this Act as it applies with respect to their functions under that Act.

(2) Every local weights and measures authority shall, whenever the Board of Trade so direct, make to the Board a report on the exercise of their functions under this Act in such form and containing such particulars as the Board may direct.

(3) Where a complaint is made to the Board of Trade that all or any of the functions conferred by this Act on a local weights and measures authority are not being properly discharged in any area, or the Board are of opinion that an investigation should be made as to whether those functions are being properly discharged in any area, the Board may cause a local inquiry to be held, and—

> (a) in relation to such an inquiry in England or Wales, subsections (2) to (5) of section 290 of the Local Government Act 1933 (evidence and costs at local inquiries), but subsection (4) (costs of department) only in a case where the Board so direct, shall apply as if the inquiry were held in pursuance of subsection (1) of that section;

> (b) in relation to such an inquiry held in Scotland, sub-sections (2) to (9) of section 355 of the Local Government (Scotland) Act 1947 (provisions as to local inquiries) shall apply as if the inquiry were held in pursuance of subsection (1) of that section.

(4) The person appointed to hold an inquiry under the preceding subsection shall report the results thereof in writing to the Board of Trade, who shall publish the report together with such observations, if any, as they think fit to make thereon.

(5) Nothing in this section shall be taken as authorising a local weights and measures authority in Scotland to institute proceedings for an offence.

27. A local weights and measures authority shall have power to make, or to authorise any of their officers to make on their behalf, such purchases of goods, and to authorise any of their officers to secure the provision of such services, accommodation or facilities, as may appear expedient for the purpose of determining whether or not the provisions of this Act and any order made thereunder are being complied with.

28.—(1) A duly authorised officer of a local weights and measures authority or of a Government department may, at all resonable hours and on production, if required, of his credentials, exercise the following powers, that is to say,—

> (a) he may, for the purpose of ascertaining whether any offence under this Act has been committed, inspect any goods and enter any premises other than premises used only as a dwelling;

> (b) if he has reasonable cause to suspect that an offence under this Act has been committed, he may, for the purpose of ascertaining whether it has been committed, require any person carrying on a trade or business or employed in connection with a trade or business to produce any books or documents relating to the trade or business and may take copies of, or of any entry in, any such book or document;

> (c) if he has reasonable cause to believe that an offence under this Act

has been committed, he may seize and detain any goods for the purpose of ascertaining, by testing or otherwise, whether the offence has been committed;

(*d*) he may seize and detain any goods or documents which he has reason to believe may be required as evidence in proceedings for an offence under this Act;

(*e*) he may, for the purpose of exercising his powers under this subsection to seize goods, but only if and to the extent that it is reasonably necessary in order to secure that the provisions of this Act and of any order made thereunder are duly observed, require any person having authority to do so to break open any container or open any vending machine and, if that person does not comply with the requirement, he may do so himself.

(2) An officer seizing any goods or documents in the exercise of his powers under this section shall inform the person from whom they are seized and, in the case of goods seized from a vending machine, the person whose name and address are stated on the machine as being the proprietor's or, if no name and address are so stated, the occupier of the premises on which the machine stands or to which it is affixed.

(3) If a justice of the peace, on sworn information in writing—

(*a*) is satisfied that there is reasonable ground to believe either—

(i) that any goods, books or documents which a duly authorised officer has power under this section to inspect are on any premises and that their inspection is likely to disclose evidence of the commission of an offence under this Act; or

(ii) that any offence under this Act has been, is being or is about to be committed on any premises; and

(*b*) is also satisfied either—

(i) that admission to the premises has been or is likely to be refused and that notice of intention to apply for a warrant under this subsection has been given to the occupier; or

(ii) that an application for admission, or the giving of such a notice, would defeat the object of the entry or that the premises are unoccupied or that the occupier is temporarily absent and it might defeat the object of the entry to await his return.

the justice may by warrant under his hand, which shall continue in force for a period of one month, authorise an officer of a local weights and measures authority or of a Government department to enter the premises, if need be by force.

In the application of this subsection to Scotland, 'justice of the peace' shall be construed as including a sheriff and a magistrate.

(4) An officer entering any premises by virtue of this section may take with him such other persons and such equipment as may appear to him necessary; and on leaving any premises which he has entered by virtue of a warrant under the preceding subsection he shall, if the premises are unoccupied or the occupier is temporarily absent, leave them as effectively secured against trespassers as he found them.

(5) If any person discloses to any person—

(*a*) any information with respect to any manufacturing process or trade secret obtained by him in premises which he has entered by virtue of this section; or

(*b*) any information obtained by him in pursuance of this Act;

he shall be guilty of an offence unless the disclosure was made in or for the purpose of the performance by him or any other person of functions under this Act.

(6) If any person who is not a duly authorised officer of a local weights and measures authority or of a Government department purports to act as such under this section he shall be guilty of an offence.

(7) Nothing in this section shall be taken to compel the production by a solicitor of a document containing a privileged communication made by or to him in that capacity or to authorise the taking of possession of any such document which is in his possession.

29.—(1) Any person who—

(*a*) wilfully obstructs an officer of a local weights and measures authority or of a Government department acting in pursuance of this Act; or

(*b*) wilfully fails to comply with any requirement properly made to him by such an officer under section 28 of this Act; or

(*c*) without reasonable cause fails to give such an officer so acting any other assistance or information which he may reasonably require of him for the purpose of the performance of his functions under this Act,

shall be guilty of an offence and liable, on summary conviction, to a fine not exceeding fifty pounds.

(2) If any person, in giving any such information as is mentioned in the preceding subsection, makes any statement which he knows to be false, he shall be guilty of an offence.

(3) Nothing in this section shall be construed as requiring a person to answer any question or give any information if to do so might incriminate him.

30.—(1) Where any goods seized or purchased by an officer in pursuance of this Act are submitted to a test, then—

(*a*) if the goods were seized, the officer shall inform the person mentioned in section 28(2) of this Act of the result of the test;

(*b*) if the goods were purchased and the test leads to the institution of proceedings for an offence under this Act, the officer shall inform the person from whom the goods were purchased, or, in the case of goods sold through a vending machine, the person mentioned in section 28(2) of this Act, of the result of the test;

and shall, where as a result of the test proceedings for an offence under this Act are instituted against any person, allow him to have the goods tested on his behalf if it is reasonably practicable to do so.

(2) No proceedings for an offence under this Act, other than an offence under section 28(5) or 29, shall be instituted by a local weights and measures authority unless they have given to the Board of Trade notice of the intended proceedings and either a period of twenty-eight days has

elapsed since the giving of the notice or the Board of Trade have before the end of that period issued a certificate under this section.

(3) A notice under subsection (2) of this section must be accompanied by a summary of the facts on which the charges are to be founded.

(4) A certificate of the Board of Trade that a notice under subsection (2) of this section was given on a date specified in the certificate and was accompanied by the summary required under subsection (3) of this section shall be conclusive evidence that the notice was given on that date and was accompanied by such a summary; and any document purporting to be such a certificate and to be signed on behalf of the Board shall be deemed such a certificate, unless the contrary is shown.

31.—(1) The Board of Trade may by regulations provide that certificates issued by such persons as may be specified by the regulations in relation to such matters as may be so specified shall, subject to the provisions of this section, be received in evidence of those matters in any proceedings under this Act.

(2) Such a certificate shall not be received in evidence—

    (*a*) unless the party against whom it is to be given in evidence has been served with a copy thereof not less than seven days before the hearing; or

    (*b*) if that party has, not less than three days before the hearing, served on the other party a notice requiring the attendance of the person issuing the certificate.

(3) In any proceedings under this Act in Scotland, a certificate received in evidence by virtue of this section, or where the attendance of a person issuing a certificate is required under subsection (2)(*b*) of this section, the evidence of that person, shall be sufficient evidence of the matters stated in the certificate.

(4) For the purposes of this section any document purporting to be such a certificate as is mentioned in this section shall be deemed to be such a certificate unless the contrary is shown.

(5) Regulations under this section shall be made by statutory instrument which shall be subject to annulment in pursuance of a resolution of either House of Parliament.

Miscellaneous and supplemental

32. In relation to goods which are intended—

    (*a*) for despatch to a destination outside the United Kingdom and any designated country within the meaning of section 21(5)(*b*) of the Weights and Measures Act 1963 or section 15(5)(*b*) of the Weights and Measures Act (Northern Ireland) 1967; or

    (*b*) for use as stores within the meaning of the Customs and Excise Act 1952 in a ship or aircraft on a voyage or flight to an eventual destination outside the United Kingdom; or

    (*c*) for use by Her Majesty's forces or by a visiting force within the meaning of any of the provisions of Part I of the Visiting Forces Act 1952; or

    (*d*) for industrial or constructional use within the meaning of the

Weights and Measures Act 1963 or the Weights and Measures
Act (Northern Ireland) 1967;

section 1 of this Act shall apply as if there were omitted from the matters
included in section 2(1) of this Act those specified in paragraph (*a*) thereof;
and, if the Board of Trade by order specify any other of those matters for
the purposes of this section with respect to any description of goods, the
said section 1 shall apply, in relation to goods of that description which are
intended for despatch to a destination outside the United Kingdom and
such country (if any) as may be specified in the order, as if the matters so
specified were also omitted from those included in the said section 2(1).

33.—(1) Where, in the exercise of his powers under section 28 of this
Act, an officer of a local weights and measures authority or of a Government department seizes and detains any goods and their owner suffers loss
by reason thereof or by reason that the goods, during the detention, are lost
or damaged or deteriorate, then, unless the owner is convicted of an offence
under this Act committed in relation to the goods, the authority or department shall be liable to compensate him for the loss so suffered.

(2) Any disputed question as to the right to or the amount of any compensation payable under this section shall be determined by arbitration
and, in Scotland, by a single arbiter appointed, failing agreement between
the parties, by the sheriff.

34. The fact that a trade description is a trade mark, or part of a trade
mark, within the meaning of the Trade Marks Act 1938 does not prevent it
from being a false trade description when applied to any goods, except
where the following conditions are satisfied, that is to say—

(*a*) that it could have been lawfully applied to the goods if this Act had
not been passed; and

(*b*) that on the day this Act is passed the trade mark either is registered
under the Trade Marks Act 1938 or is in use to indicate a connection in the course of trade between such goods and the
proprietor of the trade mark; and

(*c*) that the trade mark as applied is used to indicate such a connection between the goods and the proprietor of the trade mark
or a person registered under section 28 of the Trade Marks Act
1938 as a registered user of the trade mark; and

(*d*) that the person who is the proprietor of the trade mark is the same
person as, or a successor in title of, the proprietor on the day this
Act is passed.

35. A contract for the supply of any goods shall not be void or unenforceable by reason only of a contravention of any provision of this Act.

36.—(1) For the purposes of this Act goods shall be deemed to have been
manufactured or produced in the country in which they last underwent a
treatment or process resulting in a substantial change.

(2) The Board of Trade may by order specify—

(*a*) in relation to any description of goods, what treatment or process
is to be regarded for the purposes of this section as resulting or not
or not resulting in a substantial change;

(*b*) in relation to any description of goods different parts of which were manufactured or produced in different countries, or of goods assembled in a country different from that in which their parts were manufactured or produced, in which of those countries the goods are to be regarded for the purposes of this Act as having been manufactured or produced.

37.—(1) In this section 'market research experiment' means any activities conducted for the purpose of ascertaining the opinion of persons (in this section referred to as 'participants') of—

(*a*) any goods; or

(*b*) anything in, on or with which the goods are supplied; or

(*c*) the appearance or any other characteristic of the goods or of any such thing; or

(*d*) the name or description under which the goods are supplied.

(2) This section applies to any market research experiment with respect to which the following conditions are saitsfied, that is to say,—

(*a*) that any participant to whom any goods are supplied in the course of the experiment is informed, at or before the time at which they are supplied to him, that they are supplied for such a purpose as is mentioned in subsection (1) of this section, and

(*b*) that no consideration in money or money's worth is given by a participant for the goods or any goods supplied to him for comparison.

(3) Neither section 1 nor section 8 of this Act shall apply in relation to goods supplied or offered to be supplied, whether to a participant or any other person, in the course of a market research experiment to which this section applies.

38.—(1) Any power to make an order under the preceding provisions of this Act shall be exercisable by statutory instrument, which shall be subject to annulment in pursuance of a resolution of either House of Parliament, and includes power to vary or revoke such an order by a subsequent order.

(2) Any order under the preceding provisions of this Act which relates to any agricultural, horticultural or fishery produce, whether processed or not, food, feeding stuffs or ingredients of food or feeding stuffs, fertilisers or any goods used as pesticides or for similar purposes shall be made by the Board of Trade acting jointly with the following Ministers, that is to say, if the order extends to England and Wales, the Minister of Agriculture, Fisheries and Food, and if it extends to Scotland or Northern Ireland, the Secretary of State concerned.

(3) The following provisions shall apply to the making of an order under section 7, 8, 9, 15 or 36 of this Act, except in the case mentioned in section 10(2) thereof, that is to say—

(*a*) before making the order the Board of Trade shall consult with such organisations as appear to them to be representative of interests substantially affected by it and shall publish, in such manner as the Board think appropriate, notice of their intention to make the order and of the place where copies of the proposed order may be obtained; and

(*b*) the order shall not be made until the expiration of a period of twenty-eight days from the publication of the notice and may then be made with such modifications (if any) as the Board of Trade think appropriate having regard to any representations received by them.

39.—(1) The following provisions shall have effect, in addition to sections 2 to 6 of this Act, for the interpretation in this Act of expressions used therein, that is to say,—

'advertisement' includes a catalogue, a circular and a price list;

'goods' includes ships and aircraft, things attached to land and growing crops;

'premises' includes any place and any stall, vehicle, ship or aircraft; and

'ship' includes any boat and any other description of vessel used in navigation.

(2) For the purposes of this Act, a trade description or statement published in any newspaper, book or periodical or in any film or sound or television broadcast shall not be deemed to be a trade description applied or statement made in the course of a trade or business unless it is or forms part of an advertisement.

40.—(1) This Act shall apply to Northern Ireland subject to the following modifications, that is to say—

(a) section 19(2) shall apply as if for the references to section 104 of the Magistrates' Courts Act 1952 and the trial and laying of an information there were substituted respectively references to section 34 of the Magistrates' Courts Act (Northern Ireland) 1964 and the hearing and determination and making of a complaint;

(b) section 26 and subsections (2) to (4) of section 30 shall not apply but it shall be the duty of the Ministry of Commerce for Northern Ireland to enforce the provisions of this Act and of any order made under it (other than the provisions of section 42 of this Act);

(c) sections 27 to 29 and 33 shall apply as if for references to a local weights and measures authority and any officer of such an authority there were substituted respectively references to the said Ministry and any of its officers.

(2) In paragraph (13) of section 4(1) of the Government of Ireland Act 1920 (which excludes, among other things, merchandise marks from the matters with respect to which the Parliament of Northern Ireland has power to make laws) the words 'merchandise marks' shall be omitted and shall be deemed never to have been included; but the following provisions of this section shall (in addition to any other limitation) apply with respect to the powers of that Parliament to make laws for purposes similar to those of this Act.

(3) The Parliament of Northern Ireland shall not have power to make provision requiring any information as to the country of manufacture or production of any goods to be marked on or to accompany the goods or to be included in advertisements except—

(a) in the case of any agricultural, horticultural or fishery produce, whether processed or not, which for the purposes of this Act is deemed to have been produced or manufactured in Northern Ireland; or

(b) if the provision is made for the purpose of preventing or controlling the introduction into Northern Ireland, or the spreading within Northern Ireland, of diseases or pests affecting animals or plants.

(4) If the Parliament of Northern Ireland enacts any law for purposes similar to those of section 7 or section 15 of this Act, any provision of or made in pursuance of that law which would be inconsistent with any provision made (whether before or after the first-mentioned provision) under either of those sections shall be void so far as it would be so inconsistent.

(5) The Board of Trade shall for each financial year pay into the Exchequer of Northern Ireland such sum as the Board and the Ministry of Commerce for Northern Ireland may agree to be appropriate as representing the expenses incurred by that Ministry in enforcing so much of this Act as relates to matters with respect to which the Parliament of Northern Ireland does not have power to make laws.

(6) Nothing in this Act shall authorise any department of the Government of Northern Ireland to incur any expenses attributable to the provisions of this Act until provision has been made by the Parliament of Northern Ireland for those expenses to be defrayed out of moneys provided by that Parliament.

(7) This Act, so far as it relates to matters with respect to which the Parliament of Northern Ireland has power to make laws, shall be deemed for the purposes of section 6 of the Government of Ireland Act 1920 to have been passed before the day appointed for the purposes of that section.

41.—(1) The enactments mentioned in Schedule 1 to this Act shall have effect subject to the amendments specified in that Schedule.

(2) The enactments mentioned in Schedule 2 to this Act are hereby repealed to the extent specified in the third column of that Schedule.

42.—(1) Until the end of the period of three years beginning with the commencement of this Act the repeals made by this Act shall not affect—

(a) any Order in Council made under section 2 of the Merchandise Marks Act 1926, or the prohibition on the importation of any goods required by such an Order to bear an indication of origin at the time of importation, or

(b) the powers conferred by section 9 of that Act on local authorities and their officers with respect to goods to which such an Order applies;

and a person who contravenes the provisions of such an Order shall, subject to the provisions of this Act, be guilty of an offence and liable on summary conviction to a fine not exceeding five pounds, and in the case of a second or subsequent conviction to a fine not exceeding twenty pounds.

(2) Nothing in this Act shall be taken to affect the meaning of the expression 'indication of origin' in any such Order in Council.

(3) Her Majesty may by Order in Council vary or revoke any Order in Council made under the said section 2.

(4) Where any requirements with respect to any goods are for the time being imposed by an Order in Council made under the said section 2 and the Board of Trade are satisfied, on the representation of persons appearing to the Board to have a substantial interest in the matter, that the continued application of any of those requirements has caused or is likely to cause injury or hardship to such persons, or any of them, the Board may by statutory instrument direct that the Order, or any particular provisions of the Order, shall cease to apply to those goods or shall apply to such goods subject only to such modifications and conditions as the Board think fit; and where such a direction is in force the Order shall have effect subject to the direction.

(5) Any direction under this section which relates to goods of any description mentioned in subsection (2) of section 38 of this Act shall be given by the Board of Trade acting jointly as mentioned in that subsection.

(6) A direction under this section, if not given for a shorter period or withdrawn earlier, shall cease to be in force at whichever of the following dates is the earlier, that is to say, twelve months after the date on which it was given or the date on which an Order in Council under this section varying the Order with respect to which the direction was given comes into force.

(7) The Board of Trade shall publish any direction given under this section in such manner as they think appropriate.

(8) A draft of any Order in Council to be made under this section shall be laid before Parliament.

(9) The duty of local weights and measures authorities under section 26 of this Act to enforce the provisions of this Act shall not extend to the provisions of this section.

43.—(1) This Act may be cited as the Trade Descriptions Act 1968.

(2) This Act shall come into force on the expiration of the period of six months beginning with the day on which it is passed.

SCHEDULES

SCHEDULE 1

CONSEQUENTIAL AMENDMENTS

1. In section 1 of the Anglo-Portuguese Commercial Treaty Act 1914 for the words 'the Merchandise Marks Act 1887' there shall be substituted the words 'the Trade Descriptions Act 1968'.

2. In section 1(1) of the Anglo-Portuguese Commercial Treaty Act 1916 for the words 'the Merchandise Marks Act 1887' there shall be substituted the words 'the Trade Descriptions Act 1968'.

3. In section 4(2) of the Agricultural Produce (Grading and Marking) Act 1928, after the words 'indication of origin' there shall be inserted the words 'or an order under section 8 of the Trade Descriptions Act 1968 is in force imposing requirements for securing that such eggs are marked with or accompanied by such an indication'.

4—(1) In section 47(1) of the Road Traffic Act 1962 for the words from 'and the use' to the end of the subsection there shall be substituted the words 'and any markings so designated shall be deemed for the purposes of the Trade Descriptions Act 1968 to be a trade description, whether or not the markings fall within the definition of that expression in section 2 of that Act'.

(2) In subsection (2) of that section for the words from 'offence' to '1887' there shall be substituted the words 'offence under the Trade Descriptions Act 1968'.

SCHEDULE 2

REPEALS

Chapter	Short Title	Extent of Repeal
50 & 51 Vict. c. 28.	The Merchandise Marks Act 1887.	The whole Act.
54 Vict. c. 15.	The Merchandise Marks Act 1891.	The whole Act.
57 & 58 Vict. c. 19.	The Merchandise Marks (Prosecutions) Act 1894.	The whole Act.
3 Edw. 7. c. 31.	The Board of Agriculture and Fisheries Act 1903.	Section 1(8).
9 Edw. 7. c. 21.	The Irish Handloom Weavers Act 1909.	The whole Act.
1 & 2 Geo. 5. c. 31.	The Merchandise Marks Act 1911.	The whole Act.
10 & 11 Geo. 5. c. 67.	The Government of Ireland Act 1920.	In section 4, in paragraph (13), the words 'merchandise marks'.
16 & 17 Geo. 5. c. 53.	The Merchandise Marks Act 1926.	The whole Act.
1 & 2 Geo. 6. c. 29.	The Patents &c. (International Coventions) Act 1938.	Section 10, and in section 12, subsection (6).
1 & 2 Eliz. 2. c. 48.	The Merchandise Marks Act 1953.	The whole Act.
10 & 11 Eliz. 2. c. 59.	The Road Traffic Act 1962.	Section 47(3).
1964 c. 14.	The Plant Varieties and Seeds Act 1964.	Section 31(2).
1964 c. 28.	The Agriculture and Horticulture Act 1964.	Section 22(2).
1965 c. 22 (N.I.)	The Seeds Act (Northern Ireland) 1965.	Section 15(2).

The Trade Descriptions Act, 1972

1.—(1) Where a name or mark which—

(*a*) is a United Kingdom name or mark; or

(*b*) is likely to be taken for a United Kingdom name or mark (whether or not such a United Kingdom name or mark actually exists);

is applied to goods manufactured or produced outside the United Kingdom, subsection (2) of this section shall apply except as otherwise provided by or under this section.

(2) If any person, in the course of a trade or business, supplies or offers to supply the goods, then, unless—

(*a*) the name or mark is accompanied by a conspicuous indication of the country in which the goods were manufactured or produced; or

(*b*) the name or mark is neither visible in the state in which the goods are supplied or offered nor likely to become visible on such inspection as may reasonably be expected to be made of the goods by a person to whom they are to be supplied;

the person supplying or offering to supply the goods shall, subject to the provisions of this Act, be guilty of an offence.

(3) Subsection (2) of this section does not apply to second-hand goods.

(4) Subsection (2) of this section does not apply to goods used or to be used as containers or labels for other goods supplied or offered to be supplied in the course of a trade or business.

(5) If the Secretary of State is satisfied, after considering such representations (if any) as may be made to him by persons appearing to him to have a substantial interest in the matter, that the interests of persons in the United Kingdom to whom goods of any description may be supplied or to whom goods may be supplied under any designation would not be materially

impaired by his doing so and that it is desirable for him to do so, he may by statutory instrument give directions for excluding or relaxing the provisions of subsection (2) of this section in relation to goods of that description or in relation to that designation, either generally or in such circumstances or subject to such conditions as may be specified in the direction; and any such direction may be given for a limited time or indefinitely and may be withdrawn or varied by a further direction under this subsection.

(6) In this Act—

" container or label " includes anything in, on or with which goods are supplied or offered to be supplied;

" name " includes any abbreviation of a name;

" United Kingdom name or mark " means any of the following, that is to say—

> (*a*) the name of any person carrying on a trade or business in the United Kingdom;

> (*b*) the name of any part of, or area, place, or geographical feature in, the United Kingdom ;

> (*c*) a trade mark of which a person carrying on a trade or business in the United Kingdom is the proprietor or registered user; and

> (*d*) a certification trade mark of which a person in the United Kingdom is the proprietor; and

" trade mark " and " certification trade mark " have the same meanings as in the Trade Marks Act 1938.

2.—(1) Without prejudice to section 24 of the Trade Descriptions Act 1968 as applied by section 3 of this Act, where a person is charged with an offence under this Act it shall be a defence for him to prove—

(*a*) that the name or mark had not been applied by him and that he did not know, and could not, with reasonable diligence, have ascertained that the goods were manufactured or produced outside the United Kingdom; or

(*b*) that he did not know, and had no reason to believe, that the name or mark was, or was likely to be taken for, a United Kingdom name or mark.

(2) The definition of "United Kingdom name or mark" in section 1(6) of this Act shall apply for the purposes of this section with the omission of paragraph (*b*).

3. Section 4(1) of the Trade Descriptions Act 1968 shall apply, with the necessary modifications and with the omission of paragraph (*c*), for determining for the purposes of this Act whether a name or mark (whether a trade description or not) is applied to any goods; and this Act shall be construed, and that Act shall have effect, as if this Act were included among the provisions of that Act.

4.—(1) This Act may be cited as the Trade Descriptions Act 1972 and this Act and the Trade Descriptions Act 1968 may be cited together as the Trade Descriptions Acts 1968 and 1972.

(2) This Act, except section 1(5), shall not come into force until the expiration of the period of six months beginning with the date on which it is passed.

(3) This Act extends to Northern Ireland.

The Contracts of Employment Act, 1972

Minimum period of notice

1.—(1) The notice required to be given by an employer to terminate the contract of employment of a person who has been continuously employed for thirteen weeks or more—

    (a) shall be not less than one week's notice if his period of continuous employment is less than two years,

    (b) shall be not less than two weeks' notice if his period of continuous employment is two years or more but less than five years,

    (c) shall be not less than four weeks' notice if his period of continuous employment is five years or more but less than ten years,

    (d) shall be not less than six weeks' notice if his period of continuous employment is ten years or more but less than fifteen years, and

    (e) shall be not less than eight weeks' notice if his period of continuous employment is fifteen years or more.

(2) The notice required to be given by an employee who has been continuously employed for thirteen weeks or more to terminate his contract of employment shall be not less than one week.

(3) Any provision for shorter notice in any contract of employment with a person who has been continuously employed for thirteen weeks or more shall have effect subject to the foregoing subsections, but this section shall not be taken to prevent either party from waiving his right to notice on any occasion, or from accepting a payment in lieu of notice.

(4) Any contract of employment of a person who has been continuously employed for thirteen weeks or more which is a contract for a term certain of four weeks or less shall have effect as if it were for an indefinite period and, accordingly, subsections (1) and (2) of this section shall apply to the contract.

*This Act has been extensively amended by *The Employment Protection Act, 1975*

(5) Schedule 1 to this Act shall apply for the purposes of this and the next following section for ascertaining the length of an employee's period of employment and whether that period of employment has been continuous.

(6) It is hereby declared that this section does not affect any right of either party to treat the contract as terminable without notice by reason of such conduct by the other party as would have enabled him so to treat it before the passing of this Act.

2.—(1) If an employer gives notice to terminate the contract of employment of a person who has been continuously employed for thirteen weeks or more, the provisions of Schedule 2 to this Act shall have effect as respects the liability of the employer for the period of notice required by section 1(1) of this Act.

(2) If an employee who has been continuously employed for thirteen weeks or more gives notice to terminate his contract of employment, the provisions of Schedule 2 to this Act shall have effect as respects the liability of the employer for the period of notice required by section 1(2) of this Act.

(3) This section shall not apply in relation to a notice given by the employer or the employee if the notice to be given by the employer to terminate the contract must be at least one week more than the notice required by section 1(1) of this Act.

(4) So far as a contract purports to exclude or limit the obligations imposed on an employer by this section it shall be void.

3. If an employer fails to give the notice required by section 1 of this Act, the rights conferred by section 2 of this Act (with Schedule 2 to this Act) shall be taken into account in assessing his liability for breach of the contract.

Written particulars of terms of employment

4.—(1) Not later than thirteen weeks after the beginning of an employee's period of employment with an employer, the employer shall give to the employee a written statement identifying the parties, specifying the date when the employment began, and giving the following particulars of the terms of employment as at a specified date not more than one week before the statement is given, that is—

(a) the scale or rate of remuneration, or the method of calculating remuneration,

(b) the intervals at which remuneration is paid (that is,

whether weekly or monthly or by some other period),

(c) any terms and conditions relating to hours of work (including any terms and conditions relating to normal working hours),

(d) any terms and conditions relating to—

(i) entitlement to holidays, including public holidays, and holiday pay (the particulars given being sufficient to enable the employee's entitlement, including any entitlement to accrued holiday pay on the termination of employment, to be precisely calculated),

(ii) incapacity for work due to sickness or injury, including any provisions for sick pay,

(iii) pensions and pension schemes, and

(e) the length of notice which the employee is obliged to give and entitled to receive to determine his contract of employment:

Provided that paragraph (d)(iii) of this subsection shall not apply to the employees of any body or authority if the employees' pension rights depend on the terms of a pension scheme established under any provision contained in or having effect under an Act of Parliament and the body or authority are required by any such provision to give to new employees information concerning their pension rights, or concerning the determination of questions affecting their pension rights.

(2) Every statement given to an employee under subsection (1) of this section shall include a note—

(a) indicating the nature of the employee's rights under section 5 of the Industrial Relations Act 1971 (which relates to the rights of workers in respect of trade union membership and activities) including, where an agency shop agreement or an approved closed shop agreement is in force which applies to him, the effect of that agreement on those rights, and

(b) specifying by description or otherwise a person to whom the employee can apply for the purpose of seeking redress of any grievance relating to his employment, and the manner in which any such application should be made, and

(c) either explaining the steps consequent upon any such application or referring to a document which is reasonably accessible to the employee and which explains those steps, and any reference in subsection (5) of this section, in subsections (1) or (3) of section 5 of this Act or in subsections (1) to (6) of section 8 of this Act to that which is, or is to be, included, given or referred to in a statement under subsection (1) of this section shall be construed as including a reference to a note under this subsection, and any reference to that which is, or is to be, included, given or referred to in a statement under section 5(1) of this Act shall be construed accordingly.

(3) If there are no particulars to be entered under any of the heads of paragraph (*d*) or under any of the other provisions of subsection (1) of this section, that fact shall be stated.

(4) If the contract is for a fixed term, the statement given under subsection (1) of this section shall state the date when the contract expires.

(5) A statement given under subsection (1) of this section may, for all or any of the particulars to be given by the statement, refer the employee to some document which the employee has reasonable opportunities of reading in the course of his employment or which is made reasonably accessible to him in some other way.

(6) If not more than six months after the termination of an employee's period of employment, a further period of employment is begun with the same employer, and the terms of employment are the same, no statement need be given under subsection (1) of this section in respect of the second period of employment, but without prejudice to the operation of subsection (1) of the next following section if there is a change in the terms of employment.

(7) No account shall be taken under this section of employment during any period when the hours of employment are normally less than twenty-one hours weekly, and this section shall apply to an employee who at any time comes or ceases to come within the exception in this subsection as if a period of employment terminated or began at that time.

5.—(1) If after the date to which a statement given under section 4(1) of this Act relates there is a change in the terms of employment to be included, or referred to, in that statement, the employer shall, not more than one month after the change, inform the employee of the nature of the change by a written statement and, if he does not leave a copy of the statement with the employee, shall preserve the statement and ensure that the employee has reasonable opportunities of reading it in the course of his employment, or that it is made reasonably accessible to him in some other way.

(2) A statement given under subsection (1) of this section may, for all or any of the particulars to be given by the statement, refer the employee to some document which the employee has reasonable opportunities of reading in the course of his employment, or which is made reasonably accessible to him in some other way.

(3) If the employer in referring in the statement given under section 4(1) of this Act, or under subsection (1) of this section, to any such document indicates to the employee that future changes in the terms the particulars of which are given in the document will be entered up in the document (or recorded by some other means for the information of persons referring to the document), the employer need not under subsection (1) of this section inform the employee of any such change which is duly entered up or recorded not more than one month after the change is made.

(4) Where, after an employer has given to an employee a written statement in accordance with section 4(1) of this Act—

> (*a*) the name of the employer (whether an individual or a body corporate or partnership) is changed, without any change in the identity of the employer, or

> (*b*) the identity of the employer is changed, in such circumstances that, in accordance with paragraph 9 or paragraph 10 of Schedule 1 to this Act, the continuity of the employee's period of employment is not broken,

and (in either case) the change does not involve any change in the terms (other than the names of the parties) included or referred to in the statement, then, the person who, immediately after the change, is the employer shall not be required to give to the employee a statement in accordance with section 4(1) of this Act, but the change shall be treated as a change falling within subsection (1) of this section.

6. Sections 4 and 5 of this Act shall not apply to an employee if and so long as the following conditions are fulfilled in relation to him, that is to say—

(a) the employee's contract of employment is a contract which has been reduced to writing in one or more documents and which contains express terms affording

the particulars to be given under each of the paragraphs in subsection (1) of section 4 of this Act, and under each head of paragraph (d) of that subsection;

(b) there has been given to the employee a copy of the contract (with any variations made from time to time), or he has reasonable opportunities of reading such a copy in the course of his employment, or such a copy is made reasonably accessible to him in some other way; and

(c) such a note as is mentioned in section 4(2) of this Act has been given to the employee or he has reasonable opportunities of reading such a note in the course of his employment or such a note is made reasonably accessible to him in some other way:

Provided that if at any time after the beginning of an employee's period of employment these conditions cease to be fulfilled in relation to him, the employer shall give the employee a written statement under section 4(1) of this Act not more than one month after that time.

7.—(1) The Secretary of State shall have power by order to provide that section 4 of this Act shall have effect as if such further particulars as may be specified in the order were included in the particulars to be included in a statement under that section.

(2) An order under subsection (1) of this section may contain such transitional and other supplemental and incidental provisions, including provisions amending subsection (1) of the said section 4, as appear to the Secretary of State to be expedient, and may be varied or revoked by a further order so made.

(3) Any such order shall be made by statutory instrument subject to annulment in pursuance of a resolution of either House of Parliament.

8.—(1) Where an employer is required by section 4(1) or section 5(1) of this Act to give an employee a written statement, and the employer does not give such a statement to the employee within the time limited by those sections, the employee may require a reference to be made to an industrial tribunal to determine what particulars ought to have been included or referred to in a statement given so as to comply with the requirements of the said section 4 or the said section 5, as the case may be.

(2) Where a statement purporting to be a statement under section 4(1) or section 5(1) of this Act is given by an employer to an employee, and a question arises as to the particulars which ought to have been included or referred to in the statement so as to comply with the requirements of the said section 4 or the said section 5, as the case may be, either the employer or the employee may require that question to be referred to an industrial tribunal.

(3) Where a statement under section 4(1) or section 5(1) of this Act given by an employer to an employee contains such an indication as is mentioned in section 5(3) of this Act, and

> (a) any particulars purporting to be particulars of a change to which that indication relates are entered up or recorded in accordance with that indication, and

> (b) a question arises as to the particulars which ought to have been so entered up or recorded,

either the employer or the employee may require that question to be referred to an industrial tribunal.

(4) Where, on a reference under subsection (1) of this section a tribunal determines particulars as being those which ought to have been included or referred to in a statement, the employer shall be deemed to have given to the employee a statement in which those particulars were included, or referred to, as specified in the decision of the tribunal.

(5) On determining a reference under subsection (2) of this section, a tribunal may either confirm the particulars as included or referred to in the statement given by the employer, or may amend those particulars, or may substitute other particulars for them, as the tribunal may determine to be appropriate ; and the statement shall be deemed to have been given by the employer to the employee in accordance with the decision of the tribunal.

(6) On determining a reference under subsection (3) of this section, a tribunal may either confirm the particulars to which the reference relates, or may amend those particulars or may substitute other particulars for them, as the tribunal may determine to be appropriate ; and particulars of the change to which the reference relates shall be deemed to have been entered up or recorded in accordance with the decision of the tribunal.

(7) Any matter required to be referred to an industrial tribunal in pursuance of this section shall be referred to, and determined by, an industrial tribunal in accordance with regulations made under Schedule 6 to the Industrial Relations Act 1971.

(8) An industrial tribunal shall not entertain a reference under this section in a case where the employment to which the reference relates has ceased unless an application requiring the reference to be made was, in accordance with the regulations referred to in subsection (7) of this section, made before the end of the period of three months beginning with the date on which the employment ceased.

(9) In this section "industrial tribunal" means a tribunal established under section 12 of the Industrial Training Act 1964.

Excluded categories of employees

9.—(1) The foregoing sections of this Act shall not apply to any registered dock worker as defined by any scheme in force under the Dock Workers (Regulation of Employment) Act 1946 except when engaged in work which is not dock work as defined by the scheme.

(2) The foregoing sections of this Act shall not apply to—

(a) a person employed as master of or a seaman on a seagoing British ship having a gross registered tonnage of 80 tons or more, including a person ordinarily employed as a seaman who is employed in or about such a ship in port by the owner or charterer of the ship to do work of a kind ordinarily done by a seaman on such a ship while it is in port, or

(b) a person working under an indenture of apprenticeship recorded in accordance with the requirements of section 108 of the Merchant Shipping Act 1894 (apprenticeship to the sea service), or

(c) a person employed as a skipper of or a seaman on a fishing boat for the time being required to be registered under section 373 of the said Act.

(3) Sections 4 and 5 of this Act shall not apply where the employee is the father, mother, husband, wife, son or daughter of the employer.

(4) Sections 4 and 5 of this Act shall apply to an employee who at any time comes or ceases to come within the exceptions provided for by or under this section as if a period of employment terminated or began at that time.

(5) The Secretary of State shall have power by order—

   (*a*) to provide that all or any of the foregoing sections of this Act shall not apply to persons or to employment of such classes or descriptions as may be prescribed by the order, and

   (*b*) to vary or revoke any of the provisions of subsections (1), (2) and (3) of this section.

(6) An order under the subsection (5) of this section may contain such transitional and other supplemental and incidental provisions as appear to the Secretary of State to be expedient, and may be varied or revoked by a further order so made.

(7) Any order under this section shall be made by statutory instrument, but no such order shall be made unless a draft of the order has been laid before Parliament and approved by a resolution of each House.

Supplemental

10.—(1) The Secretary of State shall have power by order to provide that this Act shall have effect—

   (*a*) as if for the reference to twenty-one hours in section 4(7), or

   (*b*) as if for each of the references to twenty-one hours in paragraphs 3 and 4 of Schedule 1 and paragraph 3(3) of Schedule 2,

there were substituted a reference to such other number of hours less than twenty-one as may be specified in the order.

(2) Orders under the foregoing subsection may specify different numbers of hours for the purposes of paragraphs (*a*) and (*b*), and an order under paragraph (*b*) shall affect the operation of Schedule 1 to this Act as respects periods before the order takes effect for the purposes of sections 1 and 2 of this Act, as well as respects later periods.

(3) An order under this section may contain such transitional and other supplemental and incidental provisions as appear to the Secretary of State to be expedient, and may be varied or revoked by a further order so made.

(4) An order under this section shall be made by statutory instrument, but no such order shall be made unless a draft of the order has been laid before Parliament and approved by a resolution of each House.

11.—(1) In this Act—

"agency shop agreement" has the meaning assigned to it by section 11(1) of the Industrial Relations Act 1971;

"approved closed shop agreement" has the meaning assigned to it by section 17(1) of that Act;

"employee" means an individual who has entered into or works under (or, where the employment has ceased, worked under) a contract with an employer, whether the contract be for manual labour, clerical work or otherwise, be expressed or implied, oral or in writing, and whether it be a contract of service or of apprenticeship; and cognate expressions shall be construed accordingly.

(2) Sections 1 and 2 of this Act shall apply in relation to a contract all or any of the terms of which are terms which take effect by virtue of any provision contained in or having effect under an Act of Parliament, whether public or local, as they apply in relation to any other contract; and the reference in this subsection to an Act of Parliament includes, subject to any express provision to the contrary, an Act passed after this Act.

12.—(1) Sections 1 to 5 of this Act shall not apply in relation to employment during any period when the employee is engaged in work wholly or mainly outside Great Britain unless the employee ordinarily works in Great Britain and the work outside Great Britain is for the same employer.

(2) Subject to the foregoing subsection, this Act shall apply whatever the law governing the contract between the employer and the employee.

13.—(1) The enactments specified in Schedule 3 to this Act are hereby repealed to the extent specified in the third column of that Schedule.

(2) Sections 1 and 2 of this Act shall apply in relation to any contract made before the commencement of this Act.

(3) Any notice, statement, particulars, information, copy or note given, date specified, order, application, determination, reference, indication, record or entry made or other thing done under any enactment repealed by this Act shall, if in force at the commencement of this Act, continue in force, and have effect as if given, specified, made or done under the corresponding provision of this Act.

(4) Where any period of time specified in an enactment repealed by this Act is current at the commencement of this Act, this Act shall have effect as if the corresponding provision thereof had been in force when that period began to run.

(5) Notwithstanding anything in Schedule 1 to this Act, any week which counted as a period of employment for the purposes of the Contracts of Employment Act 1963 shall count as a period of employment for the purposes of this Act, and any week which did not break the continuity of a period of employment for the purposes of the Contracts of Employment Act 1963 shall not break the continuity of a period of employment for the purposes of this Act.

(6) Any enactment or other document referring to an enactment repealed by this Act shall be construed as referring to the corresponding provision of this Act.

(7) Nothing in the foregoing provisions of this section shall be taken as prejudicing the operation of section 38 of the Interpretation Act 1889 (which relates to the effect of repeals).

14.—(1) This Act may be cited as the Contracts of Employment Act 1972.

(2) This Act shall not form part of the law of Northern Ireland.

SCHEDULES

SCHEDULE 1

COMPUTATION OF PERIOD OF EMPLOYMENT

Preliminary

1.—(1) The employee's period of employment shall be computed in weeks in accordance with this Schedule, and the periods of two, five, ten and fifteen years mentioned in section 1 of this Act shall be taken as 104, 260, 520 and 780 weeks respectively.

(2) For the purpose of computing an employee's period of employment (but not for any other purpose), the provisions of this Schedule apply to periods during which the employee is engaged in work wholly or mainly outside Great Britain, and periods during which the employee is excluded by or under section 9 of this Act, as they apply to other periods.

General provisions as to continuity of period of employment

2. Except so far as otherwise provided by the following provisions of this Schedule, any week which does not count under paragraphs 3 to 6 of this Schedule breaks the continuity of the period of employment.

Normal working weeks

3. Any week in which the employee is employed for twenty-one hours or more shall count in computing a period of employment.

Employment governed by contract

4. Any week during the whole or part of which the employee's relations with the employer are governed by a contract of employment which normally involves employment for twenty-one hours or more weekly shall count in computing a period of employment.

Periods in which there is no contract of employment

5.—(1) If in any week the employee is, for the whole or part of the week—

   (*a*) incapable of work in consequence of sickness or injury, or
   (*b*) absent from work on account of a temporary cessation of work, or
   (*c*) absent from work in circumstances such that, by arrangement or custom, he is regarded as continuing in the employment of his employer for all or any purposes,

that week shall, notwithstanding that it does not fall under paragraph 3 or paragraph 4 of this Schedule, count as a period of employment.

(2) Not more than twenty-six weeks shall count under paragraph (*a*) of the foregoing sub-paragraph between any two periods falling under paragraphs 3 and 4 of this Schedule.

(3) Paragraph (*b*) of sub-paragraph (1) of this paragraph shall not apply to a temporary cessation of work on account of a strike in which the employee takes part.

Industrial disputes

6.—(1) A week shall not count under paragraph 3, paragraph 4 or paragraph 5 of this Schedule if in that week, or any part of that week, the employee takes part in a strike.

(2) The continuity of an employee's period of employment is not broken by a week which does not count under this Schedule, and which begins after this Act comes into force, if in that week, or any part of that week, the employee takes part in a strike.

(3) Sub-paragraph (2) applies whether or not the week would, apart from sub-paragraph (1), have counted under this Schedule.

7. The continuity of the period of employment is not broken by

a week which begins after this Act comes into force and which does not count under this Schedule, if in that week, or any part of that week, the employee is absent from work because of a lock-out by the employer.

Re-instatement after service with the armed forces, etc.

8.—(1) If a person who is entitled to apply to his former employer under Part II of the National Service Act 1948 (re-instatement in civil employment) enters the employment of that employer not later than the end of the six months period mentioned in section 35(2)(*b*) of that Act, his previous period of employment with that employer (or if there was more than one such period, the last of those periods) and the period of employment beginning in the said period of six months shall be treated as continuous.

(2) The reference in this paragraph to Part II of the National Service Act 1948 includes a reference to that Part of that Act as amended, applied or extended by any other Act passed before or after this Act.

Change of employer

9.—(1) Subject to this paragraph and paragraph 10 of this Schedule, the foregoing provisions of this Schedule relate only to employment by the one employer.

(2) If a trade or business or an undertaking (whether or not it be an undertaking established by or under an Act of Parliament) is transferred from one person to another, the period of employment of an employee in the trade or business or undertaking at the time of the transfer shall count as a period of employment with the transferee, and the transfer shall not break the continuity of the period of employment.

(3) If by or under an Act of Parliament, whether public or local and whether passed before or after this Act, a contract of employment between any body corporate and an employee is modified and some other body corporate is substituted as the employer, the employee's period of employment at the time when the modification takes effect shall count as a period of employment with the second mentioned body corporate, and the change of employer shall not break the continuity of the period of employment.

(4) If on the death of an employer the employee is taken into the employment of the personal representatives or trustees of the deceased, the employee's period of employment at the time of the death shall count as a period of employment with the employer's personal representatives or trustees, and the death shall not break the continuity of the period of employment.

(5) If there is a change in the partners, personal representatives or trustees who employ any person, the employee's period of

employment at the time of the change shall count as a period of employment with the partners, personal representatives or trustees after the change, and the change shall not break the continuity of the period of employment.

10.—(1) If an employee of a company is taken into the employment of another company which, at the time when he is taken into its employment is an associated company of the first-mentioned company, his period of employment at that time shall count as a period of employment with the associated company and the change of employer shall not break the continuity of the period of employment.

(2) In this paragraph company and associated company have the meanings assigned to them by section 48 of the Redundancy Payments Act, 1965.

Interpretation

11.—(1) In this Schedule, unless the context otherwise requires,—

" lock-out " means the closing of a place of employment, or the suspension of work, or the refusal by an employer to continue to employ any number of persons employed by him in consequence of a dispute, done with a view to compelling those persons, or to aid another employer in compelling persons employed by him, to accept terms or conditions of or affecting employment ;

" strike " means the cessation of work by a body of persons employed acting in combination, or a concerted refusal or a refusal under a common understanding of any number of persons employed to continue to work for an employer in consequence of a dispute, done as a means of compelling their employer or any person or body of persons employed, or to aid other employees in compelling their employer or any person or body of persons employed, to accept or not to accept terms or conditions of or affecting employment ;

" week " means a week ending with Saturday.

(2) For the purposes of this Schedule the hours of employment of an employee who is required by the terms of his employment to live on the premises where he works shall be the hours during which he is on duty or during which his services may be required.

SCHEDULE 2

RIGHTS OF EMPLOYEE IN PERIOD OF NOTICE

Preliminary

1.—(1) For the purposes of this Schedule the cases where there are
normal working hours include cases where the employee is entitled
to overtime pay when employed for more than a fixed number of
hours in a week or other period, and, subject to the following sub-
paragraph, in those cases that fixed number of hours (in this paragraph referred to as " the number of hours without overtime ") shall
be the normal working hours.

(2) If in such a case—

> (*a*) the contract of employment fixes the number, or the
> minimum number, of hours of employment in the said
> week or other period (whether or not it also provides for
> the reduction of that number or minimum number of hours
> in certain circumstances), and

> (*b*) that number or minimum number of hours exceeds the
> number of hours without overtime,

that number or minimum number of hours (and not the number of
hours without overtime) shall be the normal working hours.

(3) In this Schedule the " period of notice " means the period of
notice required by section 1(1) or, as the case may be, section 1(2)
of this Act.

Employments for which there are normal working hours

2.—(1) This paragraph shall apply if there are normal working
hours for the employee when employed under the contract of
employment in force in the period of notice, and if during any part
of those normal working hours—

> (*a*) the employee is ready and willing to work but no work is
> provided for him by his employer, or

> (*b*) the employee is incapable of work because of sickness or
> injury, or

> (*c*) the employee is absent from work in accordance with the
> terms of his employment relating to holidays.

(2) If the employee's remuneration for employment in normal
working hours, whether by the hour or week or other period, does
not vary with the amount of work done in the period, the employer
shall be liable to pay the employee for the normal working hours
as much as the amount which would have been payable if the
employee had been employed throughout the part of the normal
working hours covered by paragraphs (*a*), (*b*) and (*c*) of sub-paragraph (1) of this paragraph.

(3) If sub-paragraph (2) does not apply, the employer shall be liable for the part of the normal working hours covered by paragraphs (*a*), (*b*) and (*c*) of sub-paragraph (1) of this paragraph to pay to the employee a sum not less than remuneration for that part of the normal working hours calculated at the average hourly rate of remuneration payable to him by the employer in respect of the period of four weeks ending with the last complete week before the notice was given.

(4) In arriving at the said average hourly rate of remuneration only the hours when the employee was working, and only the remuneration payable for, or apportionable to, those hours of work, shall be brought in ; and if for any of the said four weeks no such remuneration was payable by the employer to the employee, account shall be taken of remuneration in earlier weeks so as to bring the number of weeks of which account is taken up to four.

(5) Where, in arriving at the said average hourly rate of remuneration, account has to be taken of remuneration payable for, or apportionable to, work done in hours other than normal working hours, and the amount of that remuneration was greater than it would have been if the work had been done in normal working hours, account shall be taken of that remuneration as if—

   (*a*) the work had been done in normal working hours, and

   (*b*) the amount of that remuneration had been reduced accordingly.

(6) For the purposes of the application of sub-paragraph (5) of this paragraph to a case falling within paragraph 1(2) of this Schedule, sub-paragraph (5) shall be construed as if, for the words " had been done in normal working hours ", in each place where those words occur, there were substituted the words " had been done in normal working hours falling within the number of hours without overtime (as defined by paragraph 1 of this Schedule) ".

(7) Any payments made to the employee by his employer in respect of the relevant part of the period of notice, whether by way of sick pay, holiday pay or otherwise, shall go towards meeting the employer's liability under this paragraph.

(8) Where the notice was given by the employee, the employer's liability under this paragraph shall not arise unless and until the employee leaves the service of the employer in pursuance of the notice.

(9) References in this paragraph to remuneration varying with the amount of work done include references to remuneration which may include any commission or similar payment which varies in amount.

Employments for which there are no normal working hours

3.—(1) This paragraph shall apply if there are no normal working hours for the employee when employed under the contract of employment in force in the period of notice.

(2) For each week of the period of notice the employer shall be liable to pay the employee a sum not less than his average weekly rate of remuneration in the period of twelve weeks ending with the last complete week before the notice was given.

(3) In arriving at the said average weekly rate of remuneration no account shall be taken of a week in which the employee worked for the employer for less than twenty-one hours; and where, as a result, the period for which the average is to be taken would be less than eight weeks, account shall be taken of remuneration in earlier weeks so as to bring the number of weeks averaged up to eight.

(4) Subject to the next following sub-paragraph, the employer's obligation under this paragraph shall be conditional on the employee being ready and willing to do work of a reasonable nature and amount to earn remuneration at the rate mentioned in sub-paragraph (2).

(5) Sub-paragraph (4) shall not affect the liability of the employer—

    (*a*) in respect of any period during which the employee is incapable of work because of sickness or injury, or

    (*b*) in respect of any period during which the employee is absent from work in accordance with the terms of his employment relating to holidays,

and any payment made to an employee by his employer in respect of such a period, whether by way of sick pay, holiday pay or otherwise, shall be taken into account for the purposes of this paragraph as if it were remuneration paid by the employer in respect of that period.

(6) Where the notice was given by the employee, the employer's liability under this paragraph shall not arise unless and until the employee leaves the service of the employer in pursuance of the notice.

Sickness or industrial injury benefit

4.—(1) The following provisions of this paragraph shall have effect where the arrangements in force relating to the employment are such that—

    (*a*) payments by way of sick pay are made by the employer to employees to whom the arrangements apply, in cases where any such employees are incapable of work because of sickness or injury, and

    (*b*) in calculating any payment so made to any such employee an amount representing, or treated as representing, sickness benefit or industrial injury benefit is taken into account, whether by way of deduction or by way of calculating the payment as a supplement to that amount.

(2) If during any part of the period of notice the employee is incapable of work because of sickness or injury, and—

    (*a*) one or more payments, either by way of sick pay or as amounts required to be paid by virtue of this Schedule, are made to him by the employer in respect of that part of the period of notice, and

(*b*) in calculating any such payment such an amount as is referred to in sub-paragraph (1)(*b*) of this paragraph is taken into account as therein mentioned,

then for the purposes of this Schedule the amount so taken into account shall be treated as having been paid by the employer to the employee by way of sick pay in respect of that part of that period, and shall go towards meeting the liability of the employer under paragraph 2 or paragraph 3 of this Schedule accordingly.

Absence on leave granted at request of employee

5. The employer shall not be liable under the foregoing provisions of this Schedule to make any payment in respect of a period during which the employee is absent from work with the leave of the employer granted at the request of the employee.

Notice given before a strike

6. No payment shall be due under this Schedule in consequence of a notice to terminate a contract given by an employee if, after the notice is given and on or before the termination of the contract, the employee takes part in a strike of employees of the employer.

In this paragraph " strike " has the same meaning as in Schedule 1 to this Act.

Termination of employment during period of notice

7.—(1) If, during the period of notice, the employer breaks the contract of employment, payments received under this Schedule in respect of the part of the period after the breach shall go towards mitigating the damages recoverable by the employee for loss of earnings in that part of the period of notice.

(2) If, during the period of notice, the employee breaks the contract and the employer rightfully treats the breach as terminating the contract, no payment shall be due to the employee under this Schedule in respect of the part of the period of notice falling after the termination of the contract.

Supplemental

8. In arriving at an average hourly rate or average weekly rate of remuneration under this Schedule—

(*a*) account shall be taken of work for a former employer within the period for which the average is to be taken if by virtue of paragraph 9 of Schedule 1 to this Act a period of employment with the former employer counted as part of the employee's continuous period of employment with the later employer, and

(b) " week " means, for an employee whose remuneration is
calculated weekly by a week ending with a day other than
Saturday, a week ending with that other day, and, for
other employees, means a week ending with Saturday.

9. Where under this Schedule account is to be taken of remuneration or other payments for a period which does not coincide with
the periods for which the remuneration or other payments are
calculated, the remuneration or other payments shall be apportioned
in such manner as may be just.

SCHEDULE 3

REPEALS

Chapter	Short Title	Extent of Repeal
1963 c. 49.	The Contracts of Employ- ment Act 1963.	The whole Act.
1965 c. 62.	The Redundancy Pay- ments Act 1965.	Sections 37 to 39. Section 48(7). In section 59(2), paragraphs (a) and (b) of the proviso.
1971 c. 72.	The Industrial Relations Act 1971.	Sections 19 to 21. Schedule 2.

Appendix 4

The Sale of Goods Act, 1893

PART I

FORMATION OF THE CONTRACT

Contract of Sale

1.—(1) A contract of sale of goods is a contract whereby the seller
transfers or agrees to transfer the property in goods to the buyer for a
money consideration, called the price. There may be a contract of sale
between one part owner and another.

(2) A contract of sale may be absolute or conditional.

(3) Where under a contract of sale the property in the goods is transferred from the seller to the buyer the contract is called a sale; but where
the transfer of the property in the goods is to take place at a future time or
subject to some condition thereafter to be fulfilled the contract is called an
agreement to sell.

(4) An agreement to sell becomes a sale when the time elapses or the conditions are fulfilled subject to which the property in the goods is to be transferred.

2. Capacity to buy and sell is regulated by the general law concerning capacity to contract, and to transfer and acquire property:

Provided that where necessaries are sold and delivered to an infant, minor, or to a person who by reason of mental incapacity or drunkenness is incompetent to contract, he must pay a reasonable price therefor.

Necessaries in this section mean goods suitable to the condition in life of such infant or minor or other person, and to his actual requirements at the time of the sale and delivery.

Formalities of the Contract

3. Subject to the provisions of this Act and of any statute in that behalf, a contract of sale may be made in writing (either with or without seal), or by word of mouth, or partly in writing and partly by word of mouth, or may be implied from the conduct of the parties.

Provided that nothing in this section shall affect the law relating to corporation.

Provided that nothing in this section shall affect the law relating to corporations.

4.—(1) A contract for the sale of any goods of the value of ten pounds or upwards shall not be enforceable by action unless the buyer shall accept part of the goods so sold, and actually receive the same, or give something in earnest to bind the contract, or in part payment, or unless some note or memorandum in writing of the contract be made and signed by the party to be charged or his agent in that behalf.

(2) The provisions of this section apply to every such contract, notwithstanding that the goods may be intended to be delivered at some future time, or may not at the time of such contract be actually made, procured, or provided, or fit or ready for delivery, or some act may be requisite for the making or completing thereof, or rendering the same fit for delivery.

(3) There is an acceptance of goods within the meaning of this section when the buyer does any act in relation to the goods which recognizes a pre-existing contract of sale whether there be an acceptance in performance of the contract or not.

(4) The provisions of this section do not apply to Scotland.

Subject Matter of Contract

5.—(1) The goods which form the subject of a contract of sale may be either existing goods, owned or possessed by the seller, or goods to be manufactured or acquired by the seller after the making of the contract of sale, in this Act called 'future goods'.

(2) There may be a contract for the sale of goods, the acquisition of which by the seller depends upon a contingency which may or may not happen.

(3) Where by a contract of sale the seller purports to effect a present sale of future goods, the contract operates as an agreement to sell the goods.

6. Where there is a contract for the sale of specific goods, and the goods without the knowledge of the seller have perished at the time when the contract is made, the contract is void.

7. Where there is an agreement to sell specific goods, and subsequently the goods, without any fault on the part of the seller or buyer, perish before the risk passes to the buyer, the agreement is thereby avoided.

The Price

8.—(1) The price in a contract of sale may be fixed by the contract, or may be left to be fixed in manner thereby agreed, or may be determined by the course of dealing between the parties.

(2) Where the price is not determined in accordance with the foregoing provisions the buyer must pay a reasonable price. What is a reasonable price is a question of fact dependent on the circumstances of each particular case.

9.—(1) Where there is an agreement to sell goods on the terms that the price is to be fixed by the valuation of a third party, and such third party cannot or does not make such valuation, the agreement is avoided; provided that if the goods or any part thereof have been delivered to and appropriated by the buyer he must pay a reasonable price therefor.

(2) Where such third party is prevented from making the valuation by the fault of the seller or buyer, the party not in fault may maintain an action for damages against the party in fault.

Conditions and Warranties

10.—(1) Unless a different intention appears from the terms of the contract stipulations as to time of payment are not deemed to be of the essence of a contract of sale. Whether any other stipulation as to time is of the essence of the contract or not depends on the terms of the contract.

(2) In a contract of sale 'month' means prima facie calendar month.

11.—(1) In England or Ireland—

(a) Where a contract of sale is subject to any condition to be fulfilled by the seller, the buyer may waive the condition, or may elect to treat the breach of such condition as a breach of warranty, and not as a ground for treating the contract as repudiated:

(b) Whether a stipulation in a contract of sale is a condition, the breach of which may give rise to a right to treat the contract as repudiated, or a warranty, the breach of which may give rise to a claim for damages but not to a right to reject the goods and treat the contract as repudiated, depends in each case on the construction of the contract. A stipulation may be a condition, though called a warranty in the contract:

(c) Where a contract of sale is not severable, and the buyer has accepted the goods, or part thereof, or where the contract is for specific goods, the property in which has passed to the buyer, the breach of any condition to be fulfilled by the seller can only be treated as a breach of warranty, and not as a ground for rejecting the goods and treating the contract as repudiated, unless there be a term of the contract, express or implied, to that effect.

(2) In Scotland, failure by the seller to perform any material part of a contract of sale is a breach of contract, which entitles the buyer either within a reasonable time after delivery to reject the goods and treat the contract as repudiated, or to retain the goods and treat the failure to perform such material part as a breach which may give rise to a claim for compensation or damages.

(3) Nothing in this section shall affect the case of any condition or warranty, fulfilment of which is excused by law by reason of impossibility or otherwise.

12. In a contract of sale, unless the circumstances of the contract are such as to show a different intention, there is—

(1) An implied condition on the part of the seller that in the case of a sale he has a right to sell the goods, and that in the case of an agreement to sell he will have a right to sell the goods at the time when the property is to pass:

(2) An implied warranty that the buyer shall have and enjoy quiet possession of the goods:

(3) An implied warranty that the goods shall be free from any charge or encumbrance in favour of any third party, not declared or known to the buyer before or at the time when the contract is made.

13. Where there is a contract for the sale of goods by description, there is an implied condition that the goods shall correspond with the description; and if the sale be by sample, as well as by description, it is not sufficient that the bulk of the goods corresponds with the sample if the goods do not also correspond with the description..

14. Subject to the provisions of this Act and of any statute in that behalf, there is no implied warranty or condition as to the quality or fitness for any particular purpose of goods supplied under a contract of sale, except as follows:

(1) Where the buyer, expressly or by implication, makes known to the seller the particular purpose for which the goods are required, so as to show that the buyer relies on the seller's skill or judgment, and the goods are of a description which it is in the course of the seller's business to supply (whether he be the manufacturer or not), there is an implied condition that the goods shall be reasonably fit for such purpose, provided that in the case of a contract for the sale of a specified article under its patent or other trade name, there is no implied condition as to its fitness for any particular purpose:

(2) Where goods are bought by description from a seller who deals in goods of that description (whether he be the manufacturer or not), there is an implied condition that the goods shall be of merchantable quality; provided that if the buyer has examined the goods, there shall be no implied condition as regards defects which such examination ought to have revealed:

(3) An implied warranty or condition as to quality or fitness for a particular purpose may be annexed by the usage of trade:

(4) An express warranty or condition does not negative a warranty or condition implied by this Act unless inconsistent therewith.

Sale by Sample

15.—(1) A contract of sale is a contract for sale by sample where there is a term in the contract, express or implied, to that effect.

(2) In the case of a contract for sale by sample:

(*a*) There is an implied condition that the bulk shall correspond with the sample in quality:

(*b*) There is an implied condition that the buyer shall have a reasonable opportunity of comparing the bulk with the sample:

(*c*) There is an implied condition that the goods shall be free from any defect, rendering them unmerchantable, which would not be apparent on reasonable examination of the sample.

PART II

EFFECTS OF THE CONTRACT

Transfer of Property as between Seller and Buyer

16. Where there is a contract for the sale of unascertained goods no property in the goods is transferred to the buyer unless and until the goods are ascertained.

17.—(1) Where there is a contract for the sale of specific or ascertained goods the property in them is transferred to the buyer at such time as the parties to the contract intend it to be transferred.

(2) For the purpose of ascertaining the intention of the parties regard shall be had to the terms of the contract, the conduct of the parties, and the circumstances of the case.

18. Unless a different intention appears, the following are rules for ascertaining the intention of the parties as to the time at which the property in the goods is to pass to the buyer.

Rule 1.—Where there is an unconditional contract for the sale of specific goods, in a deliverable state, the property in the goods passes to the buyer when the contract is made, and it is immaterial whether the time of payment or the time of delivery, or both, be postponed.

Rule 2.—Where there is a contract for the sale of specific goods and the seller is bound to do something to the goods, for the purpose of putting them into a deliverable state, the property does not pass until such thing be done, and the buyer has notice thereof.

Rule 3.—Where there is a contract for the sale of specific goods in a deliverable state, but the seller is bound to weigh, measure, test, or do some other act or thing with reference to the goods for the purpose of ascertaining the price, the property does not pass until such act or thing be done, and the buyer has notice thereof.

Rule 4.—When goods are delivered to the buyer on approval or 'on sale or return' or other similar terms the property therein passes to the buyer:—

(*a*) When he signifies his approval or acceptance to the seller or does any other act adopting the transaction:

(*b*) If he does not signify his approval or acceptance to the seller but retains the goods without giving notice of rejection, then, if a time has been fixed for the return of the goods, on the expiration of such time, and, if no time has been fixed, on the expiration of a reasonable time. What is a reasonable time is a question of fact.

Rule 5.—(1) Where there is a contract for the sale of unascertained or future goods by description, and goods of that description and in a deliverable state are unconditionally appropriated to the contract, either by the seller with the assent of the buyer, or by the buyer with the assent of the seller, the property in the goods thereupon passes to the buyer. Such assent may be express or implied, and may be given either before or after the appropriation is made.

(2) Where, in pursuance of the contract, the seller delivers the goods to the buyer or to a carrier or other bailee or custodier (whether named by the buyer or not) for the purpose of transmission to the buyer, and does not reserve the right of disposal, he is deemed to have unconditionally appropriated the goods to the contract.

19.—(1) Where there is a contract for the sale of specific goods or where goods are subsequently appropriated to the contract, the seller may, by the terms of the contract or appropriation, reserve the right of disposal of the goods until certain conditions are fulfilled. In such case, notwithstanding the delivery of the goods to the buyer, or to a carrier or other bailee or custodier for the purpose of transmission to the buyer, the property in the goods does not pass to the buyer until the conditions imposed by the seller are fulfilled.

(2) Where goods are shipped, and by the bill of lading the goods are deliverable to the order of the seller or his agent, the seller is prima facie demmed to reserve the right of disposal.

(3) Where the seller of goods draws on the buyer for the price, and transmits the bill of exchange and bill of lading to the buyer together to secure acceptance or payment of the bill of exchange, the buyer is bound to return the bill of lading if he does not honour the bill of exchange, and if he wrongfully retains the bill of lading the property in the goods does not pass to him.

20. Unless otherwise agreed, the goods remain at the seller's risk until the property therein is transferred to the buyer, but when the property therein is transferred to the buyer, the goods are at the buyer's risk whether delivery has been made or not.

Provided that where delivery has been delayed through the fault of either buyer or seller the goods are at the risk of the party in fault as regards any loss which might not have occurred but for such fault.

Provided also that nothing in this section shall affect the duties or liabilities of either seller or buyer as a bailee or custodier of the goods of the other party.

Transfer of Title

21.—(1) Subject to the provisions of this Act, where goods are sold by a person who is not the owner thereof, and who does not sell them under the authority or with the consent of the owner, the buyer acquires no better title to the goods than the seller had, unless the owner of the goods is by his conduct precluded from denying the seller's authority to sell.

(2) Provided also that nothing in this Act shall affect:

    (*a*) The provisions of the Factors Acts, or any enactment enabling the apparent owner of goods to dispose of them as if he were the true owner thereof;

    (*b*) The validity of any contract of sale under any special common law or statutory power of sale or under the order of a court of competent jurisdiction.

22.—(1) Where goods are sold in market overt, according to the usage of the market, the buyer acquires a good title to the goods, provided he buys them in good faith and without notice of any defect or want of title on the part of the seller.

(2) Nothing in this section shall affect the law relating to the sale of horses.

(3) The provisions of this section do not apply to Scotland.

23. When the seller of goods has a voidable title thereto, but his title has not been avoided at the time of the sale, the buyer acquires a good title to the goods, provided he buys them in good faith and without notice of the seller's defect of title.

24.—(1) Where goods have been stolen and the offender is prosecuted to conviction, the property in the goods so stolen revests in the person who was the owner of the goods, or his personal representative, notwithstanding any intermediate dealing with them, whether by sale in market overt or otherwise.

(2) Notwithstanding any enactment to the contrary, where goods have been obtained by fraud or other wrongful means not amounting to larceny, the property in such goods shall not revest in the person who was the owner of the goods, or his personal representative, by reason only of the conviction of the offender.

(3) The provisions of this section do not apply to Scotland.

25.—(1) Where a person having sold goods continues or is in possession of the goods, or of the documents of title to the goods, the delivery or transfer by that person, or by a mercantile agent acting for him, of the goods or documents of title under any sale, pledge, or other disposition thereof, to any person receiving the same in good faith and without notice of the previous sale, shall have the same effect as if the person making the delivery or transfer were expressly authorized by the owner of the goods to make the same.

(2) Where a person having bought or agreed to buy goods obtains, with the consent of the seller, possession of the goods or the documents of title to the goods, the delivery or transfer by that person, or by a mercantile agent acting for him, of the goods or documents of title, under any sale, pledge, or other disposition thereof, to any person receiving the same in good faith and without notice of any lien or other right of the original seller in respect of the goods, shall have the same effect as if the person making the delivery or transfer were a mercantile agent in possession of the goods or documents of title with the consent of the owner.

(3) In this section the term 'mercantile agent' has the same meaning as in the Factors Acts.

26.—(1) A writ of *fieri facias* or other writ of execution against goods shall bind the property in the goods of the execution debtor as from the time when the writ is delivered to the sheriff to be executed; and, for the better manifestation of such time, it shall be the duty of the sheriff, without fee, upon the receipt of any such writ to endorse upon the back thereof the hour, day, month, and year when he received the same.

Provided that no such writ shall prejudice the title to such goods acquired by any person in good faith and for valuable consideration, unless such person had at the time when he acquired his title notice that such writ or any other writ by virtue of which the goods of the execution debtor might be seized or attached had been delivered to and remained unexecuted in the hands of the sheriff.

(2) In this section the term 'sheriff' includes any officer charged with the enforcement of a writ of execution.

(3) The provisions of this section do not apply to Scotland.

PART III

PERFORMANCE OF THE CONTRACT

27. It is the duty of the seller to deliver the goods, and of the buyer to accept and pay for them, in accordance with the terms of the contract of sale.

28. Unless otherwise agreed, delivery of the goods and payment of the price are concurrent conditions, that is to say, the seller must be ready and willing to give possession of the goods to the buyer in exchange for the price and the buyer must be ready and willing to pay the price in exchange for possession of the goods.

29.—(1) Whether it is for the buyer to take possession of the goods or for the seller to send them to the buyer is a question depending in each case on the contract, express or implied, between the parties. Apart from any such contract, express or implied, the place of delivery is the seller's place of business, if he have one, and if not, his residence: Provided that, if the contract be for the sale of specific goods, which to the knowledge of the parties when the contract is made are in some other place, then that place is the place of delivery.

(2) Where under the contract of sale the seller is bound to send the goods to the buyer, but no time for sending them is fixed, the seller is bound to send them within a reasonable time.

(3) Where the goods at the time of sale are in the possession of a third person, there is no delivery by seller to buyer unless and until such third person acknowledges to the buyer that he holds the goods on his behalf; provided that nothing in this section shall affect the operation of the issue or transfer of any document of title to goods.

(4) Demand or tender of delivery may be treated as ineffectual unless made at a reasonable hour. What is a reasonable hour is a question of fact.

(5) Unless otherwise agreed, the expenses of and incidental to putting the goods into a deliverable state must be borne by the seller.

30.—(1) Where the seller delivers to the buyer a quantity of goods less than he contracted to sell, the buyer may reject them, but if the buyer accepts the goods so delivered he must pay for them at the contract rate.

(2) Where the seller delivers to the buyer a quantity of goods larger than he contracted to sell, the buyer may accept the goods included in the contract and reject the rest, or he may reject the whole. If the buyer accepts the whole of the goods so delivered he must pay for them at the contract rate.

(3) Where the seller delivers to the buyer the goods he contracted to sell mixed with goods of a different description not included in the contract, the buyer may accept the goods which are in accordance with the contract and reject the rest, or he may reject the whole.

(4) The provisions of this section are subject to any usage of trade, special agreement, or course of dealing between the parties.

31.—(1) Unless otherwise agreed, the buyer of goods is not bound to accept delivery thereof by instalments.

(2) Where there is a contract for the sale of goods to be delivered by stated instalments, which are to be separately paid for, and the seller makes defective deliveries in respect of one or more instalments, or the buyer neglects or refuses to take delivery of or pay for one or more instalments, it is a question in each case depending on the terms of the contract and the circumstances of the case, whether the breach of contract is a repudiation of the whole contract or whether it is a severable breach giving rise to a claim for compensation but not to a right to treat the whole contract as repudiated.

32.—(1) Where, in pursuance of a contract of sale, the seller is authorised or required to send the goods to the buyer, delivery of the goods to a carrier, whether named by the buyer or not, for the purpose of transmission to the buyer is prima facie deemed to be a delivery of the goods to the buyer.

(2) Unless otherwise authorised by the buyer, the seller must make such contract with the carrier on behalf of the buyer as may be reasonable having regard to the nature of the goods and the other circumstances of the case. If the seller omit so to do, and the goods are lost or damaged in course of transit, the buyer may decline to treat the delivery to the carrier as a delivery to himself, or may hold the seller responsible in damages.

(3) Unless otherwise agreed, where goods are sent by the seller to the buyer by a route involving sea transit, under circumstances in which it is usual to insure, the seller must give such notice to the buyer as may enable him to insure them during their sea transit, and, if the seller fails to do so, the goods shall be deemed to be at his risk during such sea transit.

33. Where the seller of goods agrees to deliver them at his own risk at a place other than that where they are when sold, the buyer must, nevertheless, unless otherwise agreed, take any risk of deterioration in the goods necessarily incident to the course of transit.

34.—(1) Where goods are delivered to the buyer, which he has not previously examined, he is not deemed to have accepted them unless and until he has had a reasonable opportunity of examining them for the purpose of ascertaining whether they are in conformity with the contract.

(2) Unless otherwise agreed, when the seller tenders delivery of goods to the buyer, he is bound on request, to afford the buyer a reasonable opportunity of examining the goods for the purpose of ascertaining whether they are in conformity with the contract.

35. The buyer is deemed to have accepted the goods when he intimates to the seller that he has accepted them, or when the goods have been delivered to him, and he does any act in relation to them which is inconsistent with the ownership of the seller, or when after the lapse of a reasonable time, he retains the goods without intimating to the seller that he has rejected them.

36. Unless otherwise agreed, where goods are delivered to the buyer, and he refuses to accept them having the right so to do, he is not bound to return them to the seller but it is sufficient if he intimates to the seller that he refuses to accept them.

37. When the seller is ready and willing to deliver the goods, and requests the buyer to take delivery, and the buyer does not within a reasonable time after such request take delivery of the goods, he is liable to the seller for any loss occasioned by his neglect or refusal to take delivery, and also for a reasonable charge for the care and custody of the goods: Provided that nothing in this section shall affect the rights of the seller where the neglect or refusal of the buyer to take delivery amounts to a repudiation of the contract.

PART IV

RIGHTS OF UNPAID SELLER AGAINST THE GOODS

38.—(1) The seller of goods is deemed to be an 'unpaid seller' within the meaning of this Act—

    (*a*) When the whole of the price has not been paid or tendered;

    (*b*) When a bill of exchange or other negotiable instrument has been received as conditional payment, and the condition on which it was received has not been fulfilled by reason of the dishonour of the instrument or otherwise.

(2) In this Part of this Act the term 'seller' includes any person who is in the position of a seller, as, for instance, an agent of the seller to whom the bill of lading has been indorsed, or a consignor or agent who has himself paid, or is directly responsible for, the price.

39.—(1) Subject to the provisions of this Act, and of any statute in that behalf, notwithstanding that the property in the goods may have passed to the buyer, the unpaid seller of goods, as such, has by implication of law:

    (*a*) A lien on the goods or right to retain them for the price while he is in possession of them;

    (*b*) In case of the insolvency of the buyer, a right of stopping the goods *in transitu* after he has parted with the possession of them;

    (*c*) A right of re-sale as limited by this Act.

(2) Where the property in goods has not passed to the buyer, the unpaid

seller has, in addition to his other remedies, a right of withholding delivery similar to and co-extensive with his rights of lien and stoppage *in transitu* where the property has passed to the buyer.

40. In Scotland a seller of goods may attach the same while in his own hands or possession by arrestment or poinding; and such arrestment or poinding shall have the same operation and effect in a competition or otherwise as an arrestment or poinding by a third party.

Unpaid Seller's Lien

41.—(1) Subject to the provisions of this Act, the unpaid seller of goods who is in possession of them is entitled to retain possession of them until payment or tender of the price in the following cases, namely:

(a) Where the goods have been sold without any stipulation as to credit;

(b) Where the goods have been sold on credit, but the term of credit has expired;

(c) Where the buyer becomes insolvent.

(2) The seller may exercise his right of lien notwithstanding that he is in possession of the goods as agent or bailee or custodier for the buyer.

42. Where an unpaid seller has made part delivery of the goods, he may exercise his right of lien or retention on the remainder, unless such part delivery has been made under such circumstances as to show an agreement to waive the lien or right of retention.

43.—(1) The unpaid seller of goods loses his lien or right of retention thereon:

(a) When he delivers the goods to a carrier or other bailee or custodier for the purpose of transmission to the buyer without reserving the right of disposal of the goods;

(b) When the buyer or his agent lawfully obtains possession of the goods;

(c) By waiver thereof.

(2) The unpaid seller of goods, having a lien or right of retention thereon, does not lose his lien or right of retention by reason only that he has obtained judgment or decree for the price of the goods.

Stoppage 'in Transitu'

44. Subject to the provisions of this Act, when the buyer of goods becomes insolvent, the unpaid seller who has parted with the possession of the goods has the right of stopping them *in transitu*, that is to say, he may resume possession of the goods as long as they are in course of transit, and may retain them until payment or tender of the price.

45.—(1) Goods are deemed to be in course of transit from the time when they are delivered to a carrier by land or water, or other bailee or custodier for the purpose of transmission to the buyer, until the buyer, or his agent in that behalf, takes delivery of them from such carrier or other bailee or custodier.

(2) If the buyer or his agent in that behalf obtains delivery of the goods before their arrival at the appointed destination, the transit is at an end.

(3) If, after the arrival of the goods at the appointed destination, the

carrier or other bailee or custodier acknowledges to the buyer, or his agent, that he holds the goods on his behalf and continues in possession of them as bailee or custodier for the buyer, or his agent, the transit is at an end, and it is immaterial that a further destination for the goods may have been indicated by the buyer.

(4) If the goods are rejected by the buyer, and the carrier or other bailee or custodier continues in possession of them, the transit is not deemed to be at an end, even if the seller has refused to receive them back.

(5) When goods are delivered to a ship chartered by the buyer it is a question depending on the circumstances of the particular case, whether they are in the possession of the master as a carrier, or as agent to the buyer.

(6) Where the carrier or other bailee or custodier wrongfully refuses to deliver the goods to the buyer, or his agent in that behalf, the transit is deemed to be at an end.

(7) Where part delivery of the goods has been made to the buyer, or his agent in that behalf, the remainder of the goods may be stopped *in transitu*, unless such part delivery has been made under such circumstances as to show an agreement to give up possession of the whole of the goods.

46.—(1) The unpaid seller may exercise his right of stoppage *in transitu* either by taking actual possession of the goods, or by giving notice of his claim to the carrier or other bailee or custodier in whose possession the goods are. Such notice may be given either to the person in actual possession of the goods or to his principal. In the latter case the notice, to be effectual, must be given at such time and under such circumstances that the principal, by the exercise of reasonable diligence, may communicate it to his servant or agent in time to prevent a delivery to the buyer.

(2) When notice stoppage *in transitu* is given by the seller to the carrier, or other bailee or custodier in possession of the goods, he must re-deliver the goods to, or according to the directions of, the seller. The expenses of such re-delivery must be borne by the seller.

Re-sale by Buyer or Seller

47. Subject to the provisions of this Act, the unpaid seller's right of lien or retention or stoppage *in transitu* is not affected by any sale, or other disposition of the goods which the buyer may have made, unless the seller has assented thereto.

Provided that where a document of title to goods has been lawfully transferred to any person as buyer or owner of the goods, and that person transfers the document to a person who takes the document in good faith and for valuable consideration, then, if such last-mentioned transfer was by way of sale the unpaid seller's right of lien or retention or stoopage *in transitu* is defeated, and if such last-mentioned transfer was made by way of pledge or other disposition for value, the unpaid seller's right of lien or retention or stoppage *in transitu* can only be exercised subject to the rights of the transferee.

48.—(1) Subject to the provisions of this section, a contract of sale is not rescinded by the mere exercise by an unpaid seller of his right of lien or retention or stoppage *in transitu*.

(2) Where an unpaid seller who has exercised his right of lien or retention or stoppage *in transitu* re-sells the goods, the buyer acquires a good title thereto as against the original buyer.

(3) Where the goods are of a perishable nature, or where the unpaid seller gives notice to the buyer of his intention to re-sell, and the buyer does not within a reasonable time pay or tender the price, the unpaid seller may re-sell the goods and recover from the original buyer damages for any loss occasioned by his breach of contract.

(4) Where the seller expressly reserves the right of re-sale in case the buyer should make default, and on the buyer making default, re-sells the goods, the original contract of sale is thereby rescinded, but without prejudice to any claim the seller may have for damages.

PART V
ACTIONS FOR BREACH OF THE CONTRACT
Remedies of the Seller

49.—(1) Where, under a contract of sale, the property in the goods has passed to the buyer, and the buyer wrongfully neglects or refuses to pay for the goods according to the terms of the contract, the seller may maintain an action against him for the price of the goods.

(2) Where, under a contract of sale, the price is payable on a day certain irrespective of delivery, and the buyer wrongfully neglects or refuses to pay such price, the seller may maintain an action for the price, although the property in the goods has not passed, and the goods have not been appropriated to the contract.

(3) Nothing in this section shall prejudice the right of the seller in Scotland to recover interest on the price from the date of tender of the goods, or from the date on which the price was payable, as the case may be.

50.—(1) Where the buyer wrongfully neglects or refuses to accept and pay for the goods, the seller may maintain an action against him for damages for non-acceptance.

(2) The measure of damages is the estimated loss directly and naturally resulting, in the ordinary course of events, from the buyer's breach of contract.

(3) Where there is an available market for the goods in question the measure of damages is prima facie to be ascertained by the difference between the contract price and the market or current price at the time or times when the goods ought to have been accepted or, if no time was fixed for acceptance, then at the time of the refusal to accept.

Remedies of the Buyer

51.—(1) Where the seller wrongfully neglects or refuses to deliver the goods to the buyer, the buyer may maintain an action against the seller for damages for non-delivery.

(2) The measure of damages is the estimated loss directly and naturally

resulting, in the ordinary course of events, from the seller's breach of contract.

(3) Where there is an available market for the goods in question the measure of damages is prima facie to be ascertained by the difference between the contract price and the market or current price of the goods at the time or times when they ought to have been delivered, or, if no time was fixed, then at the time of the refusal to deliver.

52. In any action for breach of contract to deliver specific or ascertained goods the Court may, if it thinks fit, on the application of the Plaintiff, by its judgment or decree direct that the contract shall be performed specifically, without giving the Defendant the option of retaining the goods on payment of damages. The judgment or decree may be unconditional, or upon such terms and conditions as to damages, payment of the price, and otherwise, as to the Court may seem just, and the application by the Plaintiff may be made at any time before judgment or decree.

The provisions of this section shall be deemed to be supplementary to, and not in derogation of, the right of specific implement in Scotland.

53.—(1) Where there is a breach of warranty by the seller, or where the buyer elects, or is compelled, to treat any breach of a condition on the part of the seller as a breach of warranty, the buyer is not by reason only of such breach of warranty entitled to reject the goods; but he may

    (*a*) set up against the seller the breach of warranty in diminution or extinction of the price; or

    (*b*) maintain an action against the seller for damages for the breach of warranty.

(2) The measure of damages for breach of warranty is the estimated loss directly and naturally resulting, in the ordinary course of events, from the breach of warranty.

(3) In the case of breach of warranty of quality such loss is prima facie the difference between the value of the goods at the time of delivery to the buyer and the value they would have had if they had answered to the warranty.

(4) The fact that the buyer has set up the breach of warranty in diminution or extinction of the price does not prevent him from maintaining an action for the same breach of warranty if he has suffered further damage.

(5) Nothing in this section shall prejudice or affect the buyer's right of rejection in Scotland as declared by this Act.

54. Nothing in this Act shall affect the right of the buyer or the seller to recover interest or special damages in any case where by law interest or special damages may be recoverable, or to recover money paid where the consideration for the payment of it has failed.

PART VI

SUPPLEMENTARY

55. Where any right, duty, or liability would arise under a contract of sale by implication of law, it may be negatived or varied by express agreement or by the course of dealing between the parties, or by usage, if the usage be such as to bind both parties to the contract.

56. Where, by this Act, any reference is made to a reasonable time the question what is a reasonable time is a question of fact.

57. Where any right, duty, or liability is declared by this Act, it may, unless otherwise by this Act provided, be enforced by action.

58. In the case of a sale by auction:

(1) Where goods are put up for sale by auction in lots, each lot is prima facie deemed to be the subject of a separate contract of sale:

(2) A sale by auction is complete when the auctioneer announces its completion by the fall of the hammer, or in other customary manner. Until such announcement is made any bidder may retract his bid:

(3) Where a sale by auction is not notified to the subject to a right to bid on behalf of the seller, it shall not be lawful for the seller to bid himself or to employ any person to bid at such sale, or for the auctioneer knowingly to take any bid from the seller or any such person: Any sale contravening this rule may be treated as fraudulent by the buyer:

(4) A sale by auction may be notified to be subject to a reserve or upset price, and a right to bid may also be reserved expressly by or on behalf of the seller.

Where a right to bid is expressly reserved, but not otherwise, the seller, or any one person on his behalf, may bid at the auction.

59. In Scotland where a buyer has elected to accept goods which he might have rejected, and to treat a breach of contract as only giving rise to a claim for damages, he may, in an action by the seller for the price, be required, in the discretion of the Court before which the action depends, to consign or pay into court the price of the goods, or part thereof, or to give other reasonable security for the due payment thereof.

60. The enactments mentioned in the schedule to this Act are hereby repealed as from the commencement of this Act to the extent in that schedule mentioned.

Provided that such repeal shall not affect anything done or suffered, or any right, title, or interest acquired or accrued before the commencement of this Act, or any legal proceeding or remedy in respect of any such thing, right, title or interest.

61.—(1) The rules in bankruptcy relating to contracts of sale shall continue to apply thereto, notwithstanding anything in this Act contained.

(2) The rules of the common law, including the law merchant, save in so far as they are inconsistent with the express provisions of this Act, and in particular the rules relating to the law of principal and agent and the effect of fraud, misrepresentation, duress or coercion, mistake, or other invalidating cause, shall continue to apply to contracts for the sale of goods.

(3) Nothing in this Act or in any repeal effected thereby shall affect the enactments relating to bills of sale, or any enactment relating to the sale of goods which is not expressly repealed by this Act.

(4) The provisions of this Act relating to contracts of sale do not apply to

any transaction in the form of a contract of sale which is intended to operate by way of mortgage, pledge, charge, or other security.

(5) Nothing in this Act shall prejudice or affect the landlord's right of hypothec or sequestration for rent in Scotland.

62.—(1) In this Act, unless the context or subject matter otherwise requires:

'Action' includes counter-claim and set off, and in Scotland condescendence and claim and compensation:

'Bailee' in Scotland includes custodier:

'Buyer' means a person who buys or agrees to buy goods:

'Contract of sale' includes an agreement to sell as well as a sale:

'Defendant' includes in Scotland defender, respondent, and claimant in a multiplepoinding:

'Delivery' means voluntary transfer of possession from one person to another:

'Document of title to goods' has the same meaning as it has in Factors Acts:

'Factors Acts' mean the Factors Act, 1889, the Factors (Scotland) Act, 1890, and any enactment amending or substituted for the same:

'Fault' means wrongful act or default:

'Future goods' means goods to be manufactured or acquired by the seller after the making of the contract of sale:

'Goods' include all chattels personal other than things in action and money, and in Scotland all corporeal moveables except money. The term includes emblements, industrial growing crops, and things attached to or forming part of the land which are agreed to be severed before sale or under the contract of sale:

'Lien' in Scotland includes right of retention:

'Plaintiff' includes pursuer, complainer, claimant in a multiplepoinding and defendant or defender counter-claiming:

'Property' means the general property in goods, and not merely a special property:

'Quality of goods' includes their state or condition.

'Sale' includes a bargain and sale as well as a sale and delivery:

'Seller' means a person who sells or agrees to sell goods:

'Specific goods' means goods identified and agreed upon at the time a contract of sale is made:

'Warranty' as regards England and Ireland means an agreement with reference to goods which are the subject of a contract of sale, but collateral to the main purpose of such contract, the breach of which gives rise to a claim for damages, but not to a right to reject the goods and treat the contract as repudiated.

As regards Scotland a breach of warranty shall be deemed to be a failure to perform a material part of the contract.

(2) A thing is deemed to be done 'in good faith' within the meaning of this Act when it is in fact done honestly, whether it be done negligently or not.

(3) A person is deemed to be insolvent within the meaning of this Act who either has ceased to pay his debts in the ordinary course of business, or

cannot pay his debts as they become due, whether he has committed an act of bankruptcy or not, and whether he has become a notour bankrupt or not.

(4) Goods are in a 'deliverable state' within the meaning of this Act when they are in such a state that the buyer would under the contract be bound to take delivery of them.

63. This Act shall come into operation on the first day of January one thousand eight hundred and ninety-four.

64. This Act may be cited as the Sale of Goods Act, 1893.

The Supply of Goods (Implied Terms) Act, 1973

BE IT ENACTED by the Queen's most Excellent Majesty, by and with the advice and consent of the Lords Spiritual and Temporal, and Commons, in this present Parliament assembled, and by the authority of the same, as follows:—

Sale of Goods

1. For section 12 of the principal Act (implied conditions as to title, and implied warranties as to quiet possession and freedom from encumbrances) there shall be substituted the following section:—

Implied undertakings as to title, etc.

" Implied under-takings as to title, etc.

12.—(1) In every contract of sale, other than one to which subsection (2) of this section applies, there is—

    (*a*) an implied condition on the part of the seller that in the case of a sale, he has a right to sell the goods, and in the case of an agreement to sell, he will have a right to sell the goods at the time when the property is to pass ; and

    (*b*) an implied warranty that the goods are free, and will remain free until the time when the property is to pass, from any charge or encumbrance not disclosed or known to the buyer before the contract is made and that the buyer will enjoy quiet possession of the goods except so far as it may be disturbed by the owner or other person entitled to the benefit of any charge or encumbrance so disclosed or known.

(2) In a contract of sale, in the case of which there appears from the contract or is to be inferred from the circumstances of the contract an intention that the seller should transfer only such title as he or a third person may have, there is—

    (*a*) an implied warranty that all charges or encumbrances known to the seller and not known to the buyer have been disclosed to the buyer before the contract is made ; and

    (*b*) an implied warranty that neither—

        (i) the seller ; nor

(ii) in a case where the parties to the contract intend that the seller should transfer only such title as a third person may have, that person ; nor

(iii) anyone claiming through or under the seller or that third person otherwise than under a charge or encumbrance disclosed or known to the buyer before the contract is made ;

will disturb the buyer's quiet possession of the goods."

Sale by description.

2. Section 13 of the principal Act (sale by description) shall be renumbered as subsection (1) of that section, and at the end there shall be inserted the following subsection : —

" (2) A sale of goods shall not be prevented from being a sale by description by reason only that, being exposed for sale or hire, they are selected by the buyer."

Implied undertakings as to quality or fitness.

3. For section 14 of the principal Act (implied undertakings as to quality or fitness) there shall be substituted the following section : —

" Implied under-takings as to quality or fitness.

14.—(1) Except as provided by this section, and section 15 of this Act and subject to the provisions of any other enactment, there is no implied condition or warranty as to the quality or fitness for any particular purpose of goods supplied under a contract of sale.

(2) Where the seller sells goods in the course of a business, there is an implied condition that the goods supplied under the contract are of merchantable quality, except that there is no such condition—

(*a*) as regards defects specifically drawn to the buyer's attention before the contract is made ; or

(*b*) if the buyer examines the goods before the contract is made, as regards defects which that examination ought to reveal.

(3) Where the seller sells goods in the course of a business and the buyer, expressly or by implication, makes known to the seller any particular purpose for which the goods are being bought, there is an implied condition that the goods supplied under the contract are reasonably fit for that purpose, whether or not that is a purpose for which such goods

are commonly supplied, except where the circumstances show that the buyer does not rely, or that it is unreasonable for him to rely, on the seller's skill or judgment.

(4) An implied condition or warranty as to quality or fitness for a particular purpose may be annexed to a contract of sale by usage.

(5) The foregoing provisions of this section apply to a sale by a person who in the course of a business is acting as agent for another as they apply to a sale by a principal in the course of a business, except where that other is not selling in the course of a business and either the buyer knows that fact or reasonable steps are taken to bring it to the notice of the buyer before the contract is made.

(6) In the application of subsection (3) above to an agreement for the sale of goods under which the purchase price or part of it is payable by instalments any reference to the seller shall include a reference to the person by whom any antecedent negotiations are conducted; and section 58(3) and (5) of the Hire-Purchase Act 1965, section 54(3) and (5) of the Hire-Purchase (Scotland) Act 1965 and section 65(3) and (5) of the Hire-Purchase Act (Northern Ireland) 1966 (meaning of antecedent negotiations and related expressions) shall apply in relation to this subsection as they apply in relation to each of those Acts, but as if a reference to any such agreement were included in the references in subsection (3) of each of those sections to the agreements there mentioned."

1965 c. 66.
1965 c. 67.

1966 c. 42, (N.I.).

4. For section 55 of the principal Act (exclusion of implied terms and conditions) there shall be substituted the following section:—

Exclusion of implied terms and conditions.

"Exclusion of implied terms and conditions.

55.—(1) Where any right, duty or liability would arise under a contract of sale of goods by implication of law, it may be negatived or varied by express agreement, or by the course of dealing between the parties, or by usage if the usage is such as to bind both parties to the contract, but the foregoing provision shall have effect subject to the following provisions of this section.

(2) An express condition or warranty does not negative a condition or warranty implied by this Act unless inconsistent therewith.

(3) In the case of a contract of sale of goods, any term of that or any other contract exempting from

all or any of the provisions of section 12 of this Act shall be void.

(4) In the case of a contract of sale of goods, any term of that or any other contract exempting from all or any of the provisions of section 13, 14 or 15 of this Act shall be void in the case of a consumer sale and shall, in any other case, not be enforceable to the extent that it is shown that it would not be fair or reasonable to allow reliance on the term.

(5) In determining for the purposes of subsection (4) above whether or not reliance on any such term would be fair or reasonable regard shall be had to all the circumstances of the case and in particular to the following matters—

> (*a*) the strength of the bargaining positions of the seller and buyer relative to each other, taking into account, among other things, the availability of suitable alternative products and sources of supply;
>
> (*b*) whether the buyer received an inducement to agree to the term or in accepting it had an opportunity of buying the goods or suitable alternatives without it from any source of supply;
>
> (*c*) whether the buyer knew or ought reasonably to have known of the existence and extent of the term (having regard, among other things, to any custom of the trade and any previous course of dealing between the parties);
>
> (*d*) where the term exempts from all or any of the provisions of section 13, 14 or 15 of this Act if some condition is not complied with, whether it was reasonable at the time of the contract to expect that compliance with that condition would be practicable;
>
> (*e*) whether the goods were manufactured, processed, or adapted to the special order of the buyer.

(6) Subsection (5) above shall not prevent the court from holding, in accordance with any rule of law, that a term which purports to exclude or restrict any of the provisions of section 13, 14 or 15 of this Act is not a term of the contract.

(7) In this section "consumer sale" means a sale of goods (other than a sale by auction or by competitive tender) by a seller in the course of a business where the goods—

(*a*) are of a type ordinarily bought for private use or consumption ; and

(*b*) are sold to a person who does not buy or hold himself out as buying them in the course of a business.

(8) The onus of proving that a sale falls to be treated for the purposes of this section as not being a consumer sale shall lie on the party so contending.

(9) Any reference in this section to a term exempting from all or any of the provisions of any section of this Act is a reference to a term which purports to exclude or restrict, or has the effect of excluding or restricting, the operation of all or any of the provisions of that section, or the exercise of a right conferred by any provision of that section, or any liability of the seller for breach of a condition of warranty implied by any provision of that section.

(10) It is hereby declared that any reference in this section to a term of a contract includes a reference to a term which although not contained in a contract is incorporated in the contract by another term of the contract.

(11) This section is subject to section 61(6) of this Act."

5.—(1) After section 55 of the principal Act there shall be inserted the following section :— Conflict of laws.

"Conflict of laws. 55A. Where the proper law of a contract for the sale of goods would, apart from a term that it should be the law of some other country or a term to the like effect, be the law of any part of the United Kingdom, or where any such contract contains a term which purports to substitute, or has the effect of substituting, provisions of the law of some other country for all or any of the provisions of sections 12 to 15 and 55 of this Act, those sections shall, notwithstanding that term but subject to section 61(6) of this Act, apply to the contract."

(2) In section 1(4) of the Uniform Laws on International Sales Act 1967 (which provides that no provision of the law of any part of the United Kingdom shall be regarded as a mandatory provision for the purposes of the Uniform Law on the International Sale of Goods so as to override the choice of the parties) for the words from " no provision " to the end of the subsection there shall be substituted the words " no provision of the law of any part of the United Kingdom, except sections 12 to 15, 55 and 55A of the Sale of Goods Act 1893, shall be 1967 c. 45.

56 & 57 Vict. c. 71.

regarded as a mandatory provision within the meaning of that
Article."

International
sales.

6. In section 61 of the principal Act (savings) there shall be
inserted after subsection (5) thereof the following subsection—

" (6) Nothing in section 55 or 55A of this Act shall
prevent the parties to a contract for the international sale
of goods from negativing or varying any right, duty or
liability which would otherwise arise by implication of law
under sections 12 to 15 of this Act."

Interpretation.

7.—(1) In section 62(1) of the principal Act (definitions) at
the appropriate points in alphabetical order there shall be
inserted the following definitions:

" business " includes a profession and the activities of any
government department (including a department of the
Government of Northern Ireland), local authority or
statutory undertaker ;

" contract for the international sale of goods " means a
contract of sale of goods made by parties whose places
of business (or, if they have none, habitual residences)
are in the territories of different States (the Channel
Islands and the Isle of Man being treated for this purpose as different States from the United Kingdom) and
in the case of which one of the following conditions is
satisfied, that is to say—

(*a*) the contract involves the sale of goods which
are at the time of the conclusion of the contract in
the course of carriage or will be carried from the
territory of one State to the territory of another ;
or

(*b*) the acts constituting the offer and acceptance
have been effected in the territories of different
States ; or

(*c*) delivery of the goods is to be made in the
territory of a State other than that within whose
territory the acts constituting the offer and the
acceptance have been effected."

(2) After section 62(1) of the principal Act there shall be
inserted the following subsection : —

" (1A) Goods of any kind are of merchantable quality
within the meaning of this Act if they are as fit for the
purpose or purposes for which goods of that kind are
commonly bought as it is reasonable to expect having
regard to any description applied to them, the price (if

relevant) and all the other relevant circumstances ; and any reference in this Act to unmerchantable goods shall be construed accordingly."

Hire-purchase agreements

8.—(1) In every hire-purchase agreement, other than one to which subsection (2) below applies, there is— *Implied terms as to title.*

- (*a*) an implied condition on the part of the owner that he will have a right to sell the goods at the time when the property is to pass ; and
- (*b*) an implied warranty that the goods are free, and will remain free until the time when the property is to pass, from any charge or encumbrance not disclosed or known to the hirer before the agreement is made and that the hirer will enjoy quiet possession of the goods except so far as it may be disturbed by any person entitled to the benefit of any charge or encumbrance so disclosed or known.

(2) In a hire-purchase agreement, in the case of which there appears from the agreement or is to be inferred from the circumstances of the agreement an intention that the owner should transfer only such title as he or a third person may have, there is—

- (*a*) an implied warranty that all charges or encumbrances known to the owner and not known to the hirer have been disclosed to the hirer before the agreement is made ; and
- (*b*) an implied warranty that neither—
  - (i) the owner ; nor
  - (ii) in a case where the parties to the agreement intend that any title which may be transferred shall be only such title as a third person may have, that person ; nor
  - (iii) anyone claiming through or under the owner or that third person otherwise than under a charge or encumbrance disclosed or known to the hirer before the agreement is made ;

  will disturb the hirer's quiet possession of the goods.

9.—(1) Where under a hire purchase agreement goods are let by description, there is an implied condition that the goods will correspond with the description ; and if under the agreement the goods are let by reference to a sample as well as a description, it is not sufficient that the bulk of the goods corresponds with the sample if the goods do not also correspond with the description. *Letting by description.*

(2) Goods shall not be prevented from being let by description by reason only that, being exposed for sale or hire, they are selected by the hirer.

Implied undertakings as to quality or fitness.

10.—(1) Except as provided by this section and section 11 below and subject to the provisions of any other enactment, including any enactment of the Parliament of Northern Ireland, there is no implied condition or warranty as to the quality or fitness for any particular purpose of goods let under a hire-purchase agreement.

(2) Where the owner lets goods under a hire purchase agreement in the course of a business, there is an implied condition that the goods are of merchantable quality, except that there is no such condition—

    (a) as regards defects specifically drawn to the hirer's attention before the agreement is made ; or

    (b) if the hirer examines the goods before the agreement is made, as regards defects which that examination ought to reveal.

(3) Where the owner lets goods under a hire purchase agreement in the course of a business and the hirer, expressly or by implication, makes known to the owner or the person by whom any antecedent negotiations are conducted, any particular purpose for which the goods are being hired, there is an implied condition that the goods supplied under the agreement are reasonably fit for that purpose, whether or not that is a purpose for which such goods are commonly supplied, except where the circumstances show that the hirer does not rely, or that it is unreasonable for him to rely, on the skill or judgment of the owner or that person.

(4) An implied condition or warranty as to quality or fitness for a particular purpose may be annexed to a hire-purchase agreement by usage.

(5) The foregoing provisions of this section apply to a hire-purchase agreement made by a person who in the course of a business is acting as agent for the owner as they apply to an agreement made by the owner in the course of a business, except where the owner is not letting in the course of a business and either the hirer knows that fact or reasonable steps are taken to bring it to the notice of the hirer before the agreement is made.

1965 c. 66.
1965 c. 67.
1966 c. 42
(N.I.).

(6) Section 58(3) and (5) of the Hire-Purchase Act 1965, section 54(3) and (5) of the Hire-Purchase (Scotland) Act 1965 and section 65(3) and (5) of the Hire-Purchase Act (Northern Ireland) 1966 (meaning of antecedent negotiations and related

expressions) shall apply in relation to subsection (3) above as they apply in relation to each of those Acts.

11. Where under a hire-purchase agreement goods are let Samples. by reference to a sample, there is an implied condition—

(a) that the bulk will correspond with the sample in quality ; and

(b) that the hirer will have a reasonable opportunity of comparing the bulk with the sample ; and

(c) that the goods will be free from any defect, rendering them unmerchantable, which would not be apparent on reasonable examination of the sample.

12.—(1) An express condition or warranty does not negative Exclusion of a condition or warranty implied by this Act unless inconsistent implied therewith. terms and conditions.

(2) A term of a hire purchase agreement or any other agreement exempting from all or any of the provisions of section 8 above shall be void.

(3) A term of a hire purchase agreement or any other agreement exempting from all or any of the provisions of section 9, 10 or 11 above shall be void in the case of a consumer agreement and shall, in any other case, not be enforceable to the extent that it is shown that it would not be fair or reasonable to allow reliance on the term.

(4) In determining for the purpose of subsection (3) above whether or not reliance on any such term would be fair or reasonable regard shall be had to all the circumstances of the case and in particular to the following matters—

(a) the strength of the bargaining positions of the owner and hirer relative to each other, taking into account, among other things, the availability of suitable alternative products and sources of supply ;

(b) whether the hirer received an inducement to agree to the term or in accepting it had an opportunity of acquiring the goods or suitable alternatives without it from any source of supply ;

(c) whether the hirer knew or ought reasonably to have known of the existence and extent of the term (having regard, among other things, to any custom of the trade and any previous course of dealing between the parties) ;

(d) where the term exempts from all or any of the provisions of section 9, 10 or 11 above if some condition is not complied with, whether it was reasonable at the time of the agreement to expect that compliance with that condition would be practicable ;

(e) whether the goods were manufactured, processed or adapted to the special order of the hirer.

(5) Subsection (4) above shall not prevent the court from holding, in accordance with any rule of law, that a term which purports to exclude or restrict any of the provisions of section 9, 10 or 11 above is not a term of the hire-purchase agreement.

(6) In this section " consumer agreement " means a hire-purchase agreement where the owner makes the agreement in the course of a business and the goods to which the agreement relates—

(a) are of a type ordinarily supplied for private use or consumption ; and

(b) are hired to a person who does not hire or hold himself out as hiring them in the course of a business.

(7) The onus of proving that a hire-purchase agreement falls to be treated for the purposes of this section as not being a consumer agreement shall lie on the party so contending.

(8) Any reference in this section to a term exempting from all or any of the provisions of any section of this Act is a reference to a term which purports to exclude or restrict, or has the effect of excluding or restricting, the operation of all or any of the provisions of that section, or the exercise of a right conferred by any provision of that section, or any liability of the owner for breach of a condition or warranty implied by any provision of that section.

(9) It is hereby declared that any reference in this section to a term of an agreement includes a reference to a term which although not contained in an agreement is incorporated in the agreement by another term of the agreement.

Conflict of laws.

13. Where the proper law of a hire purchase agreement would, apart from a term that it should be the law of some other country or a term to the like effect, be the law of any part of the United Kingdom, or where any such agreement contains a term which purports to substitute, or has the effect of substituting, provisions of the law of some other country for all or any of the provisions of sections 8 to 12 above, those sections shall, notwithstanding that term, apply to the agreement.

Special provisions as to conditional sale agreements.

14.—(1) Section 11(1)(c) of the principal Act (whereby in certain circumstances a breach of a condition in a contract of sale is treated only as a breach of warranty) shall not apply to conditional sale agreements which are agreements for consumer sales.

(2) In England and Wales and Northern Ireland a breach of a condition (whether express or implied) to be fulfilled by the seller under any such agreement shall be treated as a breach of warranty, and not as grounds for rejecting the goods and treating the agreement as repudiated, if (but only if) it would have fallen to be so treated had the condition been contained or implied in a corresponding hire-purchase agreement as a condition to be fulfilled by the owner.

15.—(1) In sections 8 to 14 above and this section—

    " conditional sale agreement ", " hire-purchase agreement ", " hirer " and " owner " have the same meanings respectively as in the Hire-Purchase Act 1965 or, as the case may be, the Hire-Purchase (Scotland) Act 1965 ;

    " business " includes a profession and the activities of any government department (including a department of the Government of Northern Ireland), local authority or statutory undertaker ;

    " consumer sale " has the same meaning as in section 55 of the principal Act, as amended by section 4 above ; and

    " condition " and " warranty ", in relation to Scotland, mean stipulation, and any stipulation referred to in sections 8(1)(*a*), 9, 10 and 11 above shall be deemed to be material to the agreement.

Supplementary.
1965 c. 66.
1965 c. 67.

(2) In the application of subsection (1) above to Northern Ireland—

    (*a*) " hirer " has the same meaning as in section 65(1) of the Hire Purchase Act (Northern Ireland) 1966 ; and

    (*b*) subject to paragraph (*a*) above, for the reference to the Hire-Purchase Act 1965 there shall be substituted a reference to the Hire-Purchase Act (Northern Ireland) 1966.

1966 c. 42 (N.I.).
1965 c. 66.
1966 c. 42 (N.I.).

(3) Goods of any kind are of merchantable quality within the meaning of section 10(2) above if they are as fit for the purpose or purposes for which goods of that kind are commonly bought as it is reasonable to expect having regard to any description applied to them, the price (if relevant) and all the other relevant circumstances ; and in section 11 above " unmerchantable " shall be construed accordingly.

(4) In section 14(2) above " corresponding hire-purchase agreement " means, in relation to a conditional sale agreement, a hire-purchase agreement relating to the same goods as the conditional sale agreement and made between the same parties and at the same time and in the same circumstances and, as nearly as may be, in the same terms as the conditional sale agreement.

(5) Nothing in sections 8 to 13 above shall prejudice the operation of any other enactment including any enactment of the Parliament of Northern Ireland or any rule of law whereby any condition or warranty, other than one relating to quality or fitness, is to be implied in any hire-purchase agreement.

Trading Stamps

Terms to be implied on redemption of trading stamps for goods.

1964 c. 71.

"Warranties to be implied on redemption of trading stamps for goods.

16.—(1) For section 4 of the Trading Stamps Act 1964 (warranties to be implied on redemption of trading stamps for goods) there shall be substituted the following section:—

4.—(1) In every redemption of trading stamps for goods, notwithstanding any terms to the contrary on which the redemption is made, there is—

(*a*) an implied warranty on the part of the promoter of the trading stamp scheme that he has a right to give the goods in exchange;

(*b*) an implied warranty that the goods are free from any charge or encumbrance not disclosed or known to the person obtaining the goods before, or at the time of, redemption and that that person will enjoy quiet possession of the goods except so far as it may be disturbed by the owner or other person entitled to the benefit of any charge or encumbrance so disclosed or known;

(*c*) an implied warranty that the goods are of merchantable quality, except that there is no such warranty—

(i) as regards defects specifically drawn to the attention of the person obtaining the goods before or at the time of redemption; or

(ii) if that person examines the goods before or at the time of redemption, as regards defects which that examination ought to reveal.

(2) Goods of any kind are of merchantable quality within the meaning of this section if they are as fit for the purpose or purposes for which goods of that kind are commonly bought as it is reasonable to expect having regard to any description

applied to them and all the other relevant circumstances.

(3) In the application of this section to Scotland for any reference to a warranty there shall be substituted a reference to a stipulation."

(2) The section so substituted, without subsection (3) thereof, shall be substituted for section 4 of the Trading Stamps Act 1965 c. 6 (Northern Ireland) 1965 (warranties to be implied on redemption (N.I.). of trading stamps for goods).

Miscellaneous

17.—(1) It is hereby declared that this Act extends to Northern Northern Ireland. Ireland.

(2) For the purposes of section 6 of the Government of Ireland 1920 c. 67. Act 1920 this Act shall, so far as it relates to matters within the powers of the Parliament of Northern Ireland, be deemed to be an Act passed before the appointed day within the meaning of that section.

18.—(1) This Act may be cited as the Supply of Goods Short title, (Implied Terms) Act 1973. citation, interpretation,

(2) In this Act " the principal Act " means the Sale of Goods commence-Act 1893. ment, repeal and saving.

(3) This Act shall come into operation at the expiration of a 56 & 57 Vict. period of one month beginning with the date on which it is c. 71. passed.

(4) Sections 17 to 20 and 29(3)(*c*) of each of the following Acts, that is to say, the Hire-Purchase Act 1965, the Hire-Purchase 1965 c. 66. (Scotland) Act 1965 and the Hire Purchase Act (Northern Ire- 1965 c. 67. land) 1966 (provisions as to conditions, warranties and stipula- 1966 c. 42 tions in hire-purchase agreements) shall cease to have effect. (N.I.).

(5) This Act does not apply to contracts of sale or hire-purchase agreements made before its commencement.

The Health and Safety at Work etc. Act, 1974 (extracts)

1974 CHAPTER 37

An Act to make further provision for securing the health, safety and welfare of persons at work, for protecting others against risks to health or safety in connection with the activities of persons at work, for controlling the keeping and use and preventing the unlawful acquisition, possession and use of dangerous substances, and for controlling certain emissions into the atmosphere; to make further provision with respect to the employment medical advisory service; to amend the law relating to building regulations, and the Building (Scotland) Act 1959; and for connected purposes.   [31st July 1974]

B E IT ENACTED by the Queen's most Excellent Majesty, by and with the advice and consent of the Lords Spiritual and Temporal, and Commons, in this present Parliament assembled, and by the authority of the same, as follows:—

PART I

HEALTH, SAFETY AND WELFARE IN CONNECTION WITH WORK, AND CONTROL OF DANGEROUS SUBSTANCES AND CERTAIN EMISSIONS INTO THE ATMOSPHERE

Preliminary

1.—(1) The provisions of this Part shall have effect with a view to—

(a) securing the health, safety and welfare of persons at work ;

(b) protecting persons other than persons at work against risks to health or safety arising out of or in connection with the activities of persons at work ;

(*c*) controlling the keeping and use of explosive or highly flammable or otherwise dangerous substances, and generally preventing the unlawful acquisition, possession and use of such substances ; and

(*d*) controlling the emission into the atmosphere of noxious or offensive substances from premises of any class prescribed for the purposes of this paragraph.

(2) The provisions of this Part relating to the making of health and safety regulations and agricultural health and safety regulations and the preparation and approval of codes of practice shall in particular have effect with a view to enabling the enactments specified in the third column of Schedule 1 and the regulations, orders and other instruments in force under those enactments to be progressively replaced by a system of regulations and approved codes of practice operating in combination with the other provisions of this Part and designed to maintain or improve the standards of health, safety and welfare established by or under those enactments.

(3) For the purposes of this Part risks arising out of or in connection with the activities of persons at work shall be treated as including risks attributable to the manner of conducting an undertaking, the plant or substances used for the purposes of an undertaking and the condition of premises so used or any part of them.

(4) References in this Part to the general purposes of this Part are references to the purposes mentioned in subsection (1) above.

General duties

2.—(1) It shall be the duty of every employer to ensure, so far as is reasonably practicable, the health, safety and welfare at work of all his employees.

(2) Without prejudice to the generality of an employer's duty under the preceding subsection, the matters to which that duty extends include in particular—

(*a*) the provision and maintenance of plant and systems of work that are, so far as is reasonably practicable, safe and without risks to health ;

(*b*) arrangements for ensuring, so far as is reasonably practicable, safety and absence of risks to health in connection with the use, handling, storage and transport of articles and substances ;

(*c*) the provision of such information, instruction, training and supervision as is necessary to ensure, so far as is reasonably practicable, the health and safety at work of his employees ;

(d) so far as is reasonably practicable as regards any place of work under the employer's control, the maintenance of it in a condition that is safe and without risks to health and the provision and maintenance of means of access to and egress from it that are safe and without such risks ;

(e) the provision and maintenance of a working environment for his employees that is, so far as is reasonably practicable, safe, without risks to health, and adequate as regards facilities and arrangements for their welfare at work.

(3) Except in such cases as may be prescribed, it shall be the duty of every employer to prepare and as often as may be appropriate revise a written statement of his general policy with respect to the health and safety at work of his employees and the organisation and arrangements for the time being in force for carrying out that policy, and to bring the statement and any revision of it to the notice of all of his employees.

(4) Regulations made by the Secretary of State may provide for the appointment in prescribed cases by recognised trade unions (within the meaning of the regulations) of safety representatives from amongst the employees, and those representatives shall represent the employees in consultations with the employers under subsection (6) below and shall have such other functions as may be prescribed.

(5) Regulations made by the Secretary of State may provide for the election in prescribed cases by employees of safety representatives from amongst the employees, and those representatives shall represent the employees in consultations with the employers under subsection (6) below and may have such other functions as may be prescribed.

(6) It shall be the duty of every employer to consult any such representatives with a view to the making and maintenance of arrangements which will enable him and his employees to co-operate effectively in promoting and developing measures to ensure the health and safety at work of the employees, and in checking the effectiveness of such measures.

(7) In such cases as may be prescribed it shall be the duty of every employer, if requested to do so by the safety representatives mentioned in subsections (4) and (5) above, to establish, in accordance with regulations made by the Secretary of State, a safety committee having the function of keeping under review the measures taken to ensure the health and safety at work of his employees and such other functions as may be prescribed.

3.—(1) It shall be the duty of every employer to conduct his undertaking in such a way as to ensure, so far as is reasonably practicable, that persons not in his employment who may be affected thereby are not thereby exposed to risks to their health or safety.

(2) It shall be the duty of every self-employed person to conduct his undertaking in such a way as to ensure, so far as is reasonably practicable, that he and other persons (not being his employees) who may be affected thereby are not thereby exposed to risks to their health or safety.

(3) In such cases as may be prescribed, it shall be the duty of every employer and every self-employed person, in the prescribed circumstances and in the prescribed manner, to give to persons (not being his employees) who may be affected by the way in which he conducts his undertaking the prescribed information about such aspects of the way in which he conducts his undertaking as might affect their health or safety.

4.—(1) This section has effect for imposing on persons duties in relation to those who—

    (*a*) are not their employees ; but

    (*b*) use non-domestic premises made available to them as a place of work or as a place where they may use plant or substances provided for their use there,

and applies to premises so made available and other non-domestic premises used in connection with them.

(2) It shall be the duty of each person who has, to any extent, control of premises to which this section applies or of the means of access thereto or egress therefrom or of any plant or substance in such premises to take such measures as it is reasonable for a person in his position to take to ensure, so far as is reasonably practicable, that the premises, all means of access thereto or egress therefrom available for use by persons using the premises, and any plant or substance in the premises or, as the case may be, provided for use there, is or are safe and without risks to health.

(3) Where a person has, by virtue of any contract or tenancy, an obligation of any extent in relation to—

    (*a*) the maintenance or repair of any premises to which this section applies or any means of access thereto or egress therefrom ; or

    (*b*) the safety of or the absence of risks to health arising from plant or substances in any such premises ;

that person shall be treated, for the purposes of subsection (2) above, as being a person who has control of the matters to which his obligation extends.

(4) Any reference in this section to a person having control of any premises or matter is a reference to a person having control of the premises or matter in connection with the carrying on by him of a trade, business or other undertaking (whether for profit or not).

5.—(1) It shall be the duty of the person having control of any premises of a class prescribed for the purposes of section 1(1)(*d*) to use the best practicable means for preventing the emission into the atmosphere from the premises of noxious or offensive substances and for rendering harmless and inoffensive such substances as may be so emitted.

(2) The reference in subsection (1) above to the means to be used for the purposes there mentioned includes a reference to the manner in which the plant provided for those purposes is used and to the supervision of any operation involving the emission of the substances to which that subsection applies.

(3) Any substance or a substance of any description prescribed for the purposes of subsection (1) above as noxious or offensive shall be a noxious or, as the case may be, an offensive substance for those purposes whether or not it would be so apart from this subsection.

(4) Any reference in this section to a person having control of any premises is a reference to a person having control of the premises in connection with the carrying on by him of a trade, business or other undertaking (whether for profit or not) and any duty imposed on any such person by this section shall extend only to matters within his control.

6.—(1) It shall be the duty of any person who designs, manufactures, imports or supplies any article for use at work—

(*a*) to ensure, so far as is reasonably practicable, that the article is so designed and constructed as to be safe and without risks to health when properly used ;

(*b*) to carry out or arrange for the carrying out of such testing and examination as may be necessary for the performance of the duty imposed on him by the preceding paragraph ;

(*c*) to take such steps as are necessary to secure that there will be available in connection with the use of the article at work adequate information about the use for which it is designed and has been tested, and about any conditions necessary to ensure that, when put to that use, it will be safe and without risks to health.

(2) It shall be the duty of any person who undertakes the design or manufacture of any article for use at work to carry out

or arrange for the carrying out of any necessary research with a view to the discovery and, so far as is reasonably practicable, the elimination or minimisation of any risks to health or safety to which the design or article may give rise.

(3) It shall be the duty of any person who erects or installs any article for use at work in any premises where that article is to be used by persons at work to ensure, so far as is reasonably practicable, that nothing about the way in which it is erected or installed makes it unsafe or a risk to health when properly used.

(4) It shall be the duty of any person who manufactures, imports or supplies any substance for use at work—

- (*a*) to ensure, so far as is reasonably practicable, that the substance is safe and without risks to health when properly used ;

- (*b*) to carry out or arrange for the carrying out of such testing and examination as may be necessary for the performance of the duty imposed on him by the preceding paragraph ;

- (*c*) to take such steps as are necessary to secure that there will be available in connection with the use of the substance at work adequate information about the results of any relevant tests which have been carried out on or in connection with the substance and about any conditions necessary to ensure that it will be safe and without risks to health when properly used.

(5) It shall be the duty of any person who undertakes the manufacture of any substance for use at work to carry out or arrange for the carrying out of any necessary research with a view to the discovery and, so far as is reasonably practicable, the elimination or minimisation of any risks to health or safety to which the substance may give rise.

(6) Nothing in the preceding provisions of this section shall be taken to require a person to repeat any testing, examination or research which has been carried out otherwise than by him or at his instance, in so far as it is reasonable for him to rely on the results thereof for the purposes of those provisions.

(7) Any duty imposed on any person by any of the preceding provisions of this section shall extend only to things done in the course of a trade, business or other undertaking carried on by him (whether for profit or not) and to matters within his control.

(8) Where a person designs, manufactures, imports or supplies an article for or to another on the basis of a written undertaking by that other to take specified steps sufficient to ensure, so far as is reasonably practicable, that the article will be safe and

without risks to health when properly used, the undertaking shall have the effect of relieving the first-mentioned person from the duty imposed by subsection (1)(*a*) above to such extent as is reasonable having regard to the terms of the undertaking.

(9) Where a person (" the ostensible supplier ") supplies any article for use at work or substance for use at work to another (" the customer ") under a hire-purchase agreement, conditional sale agreement or credit-sale agreement, and the ostensible supplier—

(*a*) carries on the business of financing the acquisition of goods by others by means of such agreements ; and

(*b*) in the course of that business acquired his interest in the article or substance supplied to the customer as a means of financing its acquisition by the customer from a third person (" the effective supplier "),

the effective supplier and not the ostensible supplier shall be treated for the purposes of this section as supplying the article or substance to the customer, and any duty imposed by the preceding provisions of this section on suppliers shall accordingly fall on the effective supplier and not on the ostensible supplier.

(10) For the purposes of this section an article or substance is not to be regarded as properly used where it is used without regard to any relevant information or advice relating to its use which has been made available by a person by whom it was designed, manufactured, imported or supplied.

7. It shall be the duty of every employee while at work—

(*a*) to take reasonable care for the health and safety of himself and of other persons who may be affected by his acts or omissions at work ; and

(*b*) as regards any duty or requirement imposed on his employer or any other person by or under any of the relevant statutory provisions, to co-operate with him so far as is necessary to enable that duty or requirement to be performed or complied with.

8. No person shall intentionally or recklessly interfere with or misuse anything provided in the interests of health, safety or welfare in pursuance of any of the relevant statutory provisions.

9. No employer shall levy or permit to be levied on any employee of his any charge in respect of anything done or provided in pursuance of any specific requirement of the relevant statutory provisions.

The Health and Safety Commission and the Health and Safety Executive

10.—(1) There shall be two bodies corporate to be called the Health and Safety Commission and the Health and Safety Executive which shall be constituted in accordance with the following provisions of this section.

(2) The Health and Safety Commission (hereafter in this Act referred to as " the Commission ") shall consist of a chairman appointed by the Secretary of State and not less than six nor more than nine other members appointed by the Secretary of State in accordance with subsection (3) below.

(3) Before appointing the members of the Commission (other than the chairman) the Secretary of State shall—

(a) as to three of them, consult such organisations representing employers as he considers appropriate ;

(b) as to three others, consult such organisations representing employees as he considers appropriate ; and

(c) as to any other members he may appoint, consult such organisations representing local authorities and such other organisations, including professional bodies, the activities of whose members are concerned with matters relating to any of the general purposes of this Part, as he considers appropriate.

(4) The Secretary of State may appoint one of the members to be deputy chairman of the Commission.

(5) The Health and Safety Executive (hereafter in this Act referred to as " the Executive ") shall consist of three persons of whom one shall be appointed by the Commission with the approval of the Secretary of State to be the director of the Executive and the others shall be appointed by the Commission with the like approval after consultation with the said director.

(6) The provisions of Schedule 2 shall have effect with respect to the Commission and the Executive.

(7) The functions of the Commission and of the Executive, and of their officers and servants, shall be performed on behalf of the Crown.

11.—(1) In addition to the other functions conferred on the Commission by virtue of this Act, but subject to subsection (3) below, it shall be the general duty of the Commission to do such things and make such arrangements as it considers appropriate for the general purposes of this Part except as regards matters relating exclusively to agricultural operations.

(2) It shall be the duty of the Commission, except as aforesaid—

(*a*) to assist and encourage persons concerned with matters relevant to any of the general purposes of this Part to further those purposes ;

(*b*) to make such arrangements as it considers appropriate for the carrying out of research, the publication of the results of research and the provision of training and information in connection with those purposes, and to encourage research and the provision of training and information in that connection by others ;

(*c*) to make such arrangements as it considers appropriate for securing that government departments, employers, employees, organisations representing employers and employees respectively, and other persons concerned with matters relevant to any of those purposes are provided with an information and advisory service and are kept informed of, and adequately advised on, such matters ;

(*d*) to submit from time to time to the authority having power to make regulations under any of the relevant statutory provisions such proposals as the Commission considers appropriate for the making of regulations under that power.

(3) It shall be the duty of the Commission—

(*a*) to submit to the Secretary of State from time to time particulars of what it proposes to do for the purpose of performing its functions ; and

(*b*) subject to the following paragraph, to ensure that its activities are in accordance with proposals approved by the Secretary of State; and

(*c*) to give effect to any directions given to it by the Secretary of State.

(4) In addition to any other functions conferred on the Executive by virtue of this Part, it shall be the duty of the Executive—

(*a*) to exercise on behalf of the Commission such of the Commission's functions as the Commission directs it to exercise ; and

(*b*) to give effect to any directions given to it by the Commission otherwise than in pursuance of paragraph (*a*) above ;

but, except for the purpose of giving effect to directions given to the Commission by the Secretary of State, the Commission shall not give to the Executive any directions as to the enforcement of any of the relevant statutory provisions in a particular case.

(5) Without prejudice to subsection (2) above, it shall be the duty of the Executive, if so requested by a Minister of the Crown—

    (a) to provide him with information about the activities of the Executive in connection with any matter with which he is concerned ; and

    (b) to provide him with advice on any matter with which he is concerned on which relevant expert advice is obtainable from any of the officers or servants of the Executive but which is not relevant to any of the general purposes of this Part.

(6) The Commission and the Executive shall, subject to any directions given to it in pursuance of this Part, have power to do anything (except borrow money) which is calculated to facilitate, or is conducive or incidental to, the performance of any function of the Commission or, as the case may be, the Executive (including a function conferred on it by virtue of this subsection).

17.—(1) A failure on the part of any person to observe any provision of an approved code of practice shall not of itself render him liable to any civil or criminal proceedings ; but where in any criminal proceedings a party is alleged to have committed an offence by reason of a contravention of any requirement or prohibition imposed by or under any such provision as is mentioned in section 16(1) being a provision for which there was an approved code of practice at the time of the alleged contravention, the following subsection shall have effect with respect to that code in relation to those proceedings.

(2) Any provision of the code of practice which appears to the court to be relevant to the requirement or prohibition alleged to have been contravened shall be admissible in evidence in the proceedings ; and if it is proved that there was at any material time a failure to observe any provision of the code which appears to the court to be relevant to any matter which it is necessary for the prosecution to prove in order to establish a contravention of that requirement or prohibition, that matter shall be taken as proved unless the court is satisfied that the requirement or prohibition was in respect of that matter complied with otherwise than by way of observance of that provision of the code.

(3) In any criminal proceedings—

    (a) a document purporting to be a notice issued by the Commission under section 16 shall be taken to be such a notice unless the contrary is proved ; and

(*b*) a code of practice which appears to the court to be
the subject of such a notice shall be taken to be the
subject of that notice unless the contrary is proved.

Enforcement

18.—(1) It shall be the duty of the Executive to make
adequate arrangements for the enforcement of the relevant statutory provisions except to the extent that some other authority
or class of authorities is by any of those provisions or by
regulations under subsection (2) below made responsible for
their enforcement.

(2) The Secretary of State may by regulations—

(*a*) make local authorities responsible for the enforcement
of the relevant statutory provisions to such extent as
may be prescribed ;

(*b*) make provision for enabling responsibility for enforcing
any of the relevant statutory provisions to be, to such
extent as may be determined under the regulations—

(i) transferred from the Executive to local authorities or from local authorities to the Executive ;
or

(ii) assigned to the Executive or to local authorities
for the purpose of removing any uncertainty as to
what are by virtue of this subsection their respective
responsibilities for the enforcement of those
provisions ;

and any regulations made in pursuance of paragraph (*b*) above
shall include provision for securing that any transfer or assignment effected under the regulations is brought to the notice of
persons affected by it.

(3) Any provision made by regulations under the preceding
subsection shall have effect subject to any provision made by
health and safety regulations or agricultural health and safety
regulations in pursuance of section 15(3)(*c*).

(4) It shall be the duty of every local authority—

(*a*) to make adequate arrangements for the enforcement
within their area of the relevant statutory provisions
to the extent that they are by any of those provisions
or by regulations under subsection (2) above made
responsible for their enforcement ; and

(*b*) to perform the duty imposed on them by the preceding
paragraph and any other functions conferred on them
by any of the relevant statutory provisions in accordance with such guidance as the Commission may give
them.

(5) Where any authority other than the appropriate Agriculture Minister, the Executive or a local authority is by any of the relevant statutory provisions or by regulations under subsection (2) above made responsible for the enforcement of any of those provisions to any extent, it shall be the duty of that authority—

(*a*) to make adequate arrangements for the enforcement of those provisions to that extent ; and

(*b*) to perform the duty imposed on the authority by the preceding paragraph and any other functions conferred on the authority by any of the relevant statutory provisions in accordance with such guidance as the Commission may give to the authority.

(6) Nothing in the provisions of this Act or of any regulations made thereunder charging any person in Scotland with the enforcement of any of the relevant statutory provisions shall be construed as authorising that person to institute proceedings for any offence.

(7) In this Part—

(*a*) " enforcing authority " means the Executive or any other authority which is by any of the relevant statutory provisions or by regulations under subsection (2) above made responsible for the enforcement of any of those provisions to any extent ; and

(*b*) any reference to an enforcing authority's field of responsibility is a reference to the field over which that authority's responsibility for the enforcement of those provisions extends for the time being ;

but where by virtue of paragraph (*a*) of section 13(1) the performance of any function of the Commission or the Executive is delegated to a government department or person, references to the Commission or the Executive (or to an enforcing authority where that authority is the Executive) in any provision of this Part which relates to that function shall, so far as may be necessary to give effect to any agreement under that paragraph, be construed as references to that department or person ; and accordingly any reference to the field of responsibility of an enforcing authority shall be construed as a reference to the field over which that department or person for the time being performs such a function.

36.—(1) Where the commission by any person of an offence under any of the relevant statutory provisions is due to the act or default of some other person, that other person shall be guilty of the offence, and a person may be charged with and convicted of the offence by virtue of this subsection whether or not proceedings are taken against the first-mentioned person.

(2) Where there would be or have been the commission of an offence under section 33 by the Crown but for the circumstance that that section does not bind the Crown, and that fact is due to the act or default of a person other than the Crown, that person shall be guilty of the offence which, but for that circumstance, the Crown would be committing or would have committed, and may be charged with and convicted of that offence accordingly.

(3) The preceding provisions of this section are subject to any provision made by virtue of section 15(6).

37.—(1) Where an offence under any of the relevant statutory provisions committed by a body corporate is proved to have been committed with the consent or connivance of, or to have been attributable to any neglect on the part of, any director, manager, secretary or other similar officer of the body corporate or a person who was purporting to act in any such capacity, he as well as the body corporate shall be guilty of that offence and shall be liable to be proceeded against and punished accordingly.

(2) Where the affairs of a body corporate are managed by its members, the preceding subsection shall apply in relation to the acts and defaults of a member in connection with his functions of management as if he were a director of the body corporate.

40. In any proceedings for an offence under any of the relevant statutory provisions consisting of a failure to comply with a duty or requirement to do something so far as is practicable or so far as is reasonably practicable, or to use the best practicable means to do something, it shall be for the accused to prove (as the case may be) that it was not practicable or not reasonably practicable to do more than was in fact done to satisfy the duty or requirement, or that there was no better practicable means than was in fact used to satisfy the duty or requirement.

The Employment Protection Act, 1975 (extracts)

Disclosure of information

17.—(1) For the purposes of all the stages of such collective bargaining between an employer and representatives of an independent trade union as is referred to in subsection (2) below, it shall be the duty of the employer, subject to section 18 below, to disclose to those representatives on request all such information relating to his undertaking as is in his possession, or that of any associated employer, and is both— *(General duty of employers to disclose information.)*

    (a) information without which the trade union representatives would be to a material extent impeded in carrying on with him such collective bargaining, and

    (b) information which it would be in accordance with good industrial relations practice that he should disclose to them for the purposes of collective bargaining.

(2) The collective bargaining for the purposes of which an employer must disclose information under subsection (1) above is collective bargaining about matters, and in relation to descriptions of workers,—

    (a) in respect of which the trade union is recognised by that employer ; or

    (b) falling within the scope of an operative recommendation for recognition (within the meaning of section 15 above) relating to the union,

and in this section and sections 19 to 21 below " representative ", in relation to a trade union, means an official or other person authorised by the trade union to carry on such collective bargaining.

(3) Where a request for information is made by trade union representatives under this section, the request shall, if the employer so requests, be in writing or be confirmed in writing.

(4) In determining, for the purposes of subsection (1)(b) above, what would be in accordance with good industrial relations practice, regard shall be had to the relevant provisions of any Code of Practice issued by the Service under section 6 above, but not so as to exclude any other evidence of what that practice is.

(5) Where an employer is required by virtue of this section to disclose any information to trade union representatives, the disclosure of it shall, if they so request, be in writing or be confirmed in writing.

Restrictions on general duty under s. 17.

18.—(1) No employer shall, by virtue of section 17 above, be required to disclose—

(a) any information the disclosure of which would be against the interests of national security, or

(b) any information which he could not disclose without contravening a prohibition imposed by or under an enactment, or

(c) any information which has been communicated to the employer in confidence, or which the employer has otherwise obtained in consequence of the confidence reposed in him by another person, or

(d) any information relating specifically to an individual, unless he has consented to its being disclosed, or

(e) any information the disclosure of which would cause substantial injury to the employer's undertaking for reasons other than its effect on collective bargaining, or

(f) any information obtained by the employer for the purpose of bringing, prosecuting or defending any legal proceedings ;

and in formulating the provisions of any Code of Practice relating to the disclosure of information, the Service shall have regard to the provisions of this subsection.

(2) In the performance of his duty under section 17 above an employer shall not be required—

(a) to produce, or allow inspection of, any document (other than a document prepared for the purpose of conveying or confirming the information) or to make a copy of or extracts from any document, or

(b) to compile or assemble any information where the compilation or assembly would involve an amount of work or expenditure out of reasonable proportion to the value of the information in the conduct of collective bargaining.

Guarantee payments

Right to guarantee payment.

22.—(1) Where an employee throughout a day during any part of which he would normally be required to work in accordance with his contract of employment is not provided with work by his employer by reason of—

(a) a diminution in the requirements of the employer's business for work of the kind which the employee is employed to do, or

(b) any other occurrence affecting the normal working of the employer's business in relation to work of the kind which the employee is employed to do,

he shall, subject to the following provisions of this Act, be entitled to be paid by his employer a payment, referred to in this Act as a guarantee payment, in respect of that day and hereafter in this section and sections 23 to 26 below—

(i) such a day is referred to as a " workless day ", and

(ii) " workless period " has a corresponding meaning.

(2) In this section and sections 23 to 27 below " day " means the period of 24 hours from midnight to midnight, and where a period of employment begun on any day extends over midnight into the following day, or would normally so extend, then—

(a) if the employment before midnight is, or would normally be, of longer duration than that after midnight, that period of employment shall be treated as falling wholly on the first day ; and

(b) in any other case, that period of employment shall be treated as falling wholly on the second day.

(3) An employee shall not be entitled to a guarantee payment under subsection (1) above in respect of a workless day unless he has been continuously employed for a period of four weeks ending with the last complete week before that day.

23.—(1) An employee shall not be entitled to a guarantee payment in respect of a workless day if the failure to provide him with work occurs in consequence of a trade dispute involving any employee of his employer or of an associated employer. *General exclusions from right under s. 22.*

(2) An employee shall not be entitled to a guarantee payment in respect of a workless day if—

(a) his employer has offered to provide alternative work for that day which is suitable in all the circumstances, whether or not work which the employee is under his contract employed to perform, and the employee has unreasonably refused that offer ; or

(b) he does not comply with reasonable requirements imposed by his employer with a view to ensuring that his services are available.

25.—(1) The amount of guarantee payment payable to an employee in respect of any day shall not exceed £6. *Limits on amount of and entitlement to guarantee payment.*

(2) An employee shall not be entitled to guarantee payments in respect of more than the specified number of days in any one of the relevant periods, that is to say, the periods of three months commencing on 1st February, 1st May, 1st August and 1st November in each year.

(3) The specified number of days for the purposes of subsection (2) above shall be, subject to subsection (4) below,—

(a) the number of days, not exceeding five, on which the employee normally works in a week under the contract of employment in force on the day in respect of which the guarantee payment is claimed ; or

(b) where that number of days varies from week to week or over a longer period, the average number of such days, not exceeding five, calculated by dividing by 12 the total number of such days during the period of 12 weeks ending with the last complete week before the day in respect of which the guarantee payment is claimed, and rounding up the resulting figure to the next whole number ; or

(c) in a case falling within paragraph (b) above but where the employee has not been employed for a sufficient period to enable the calculation to be made under that paragraph, a number which fairly represents the number of the employee's normal working days in a week, not exceeding five, having regard to such of the following considerations as are appropriate in the circumstances, that is to say,—

(i) the average number of normal working days in a week which the employee could expect in accordance with the terms of his contract ;

(ii) the average number of such days of other employees engaged in relevant comparable employment with the same employer.

(4) If in any case an employee's contract has been varied, or a new contract has been entered into, in connection with a period of short-time working, subsection (3) above shall have effect as if for the references to the day in respect of which the guarantee payment is claimed there were substituted references to the last day on which the original contract was in force.

(5) The Secretary of State may vary any of the limits referred to in this section, and may in particular vary the relevant periods referred to in subsection (2) above, after a review under section 86 below, by order made in accordance with that section.

Rights of employee in connection with pregnancy and confinement.

35.—(1) An employee who is absent from work wholly or partly because of pregnancy or confinement shall, subject to the following provisions of this Act, be entitled—

(a) in accordance with sections 36 to 38 below, to be paid by her employer a sum to be known as maternity pay ; and

(b) in accordance with sections 48 to 50 below and Schedule

(2) An employee shall be entitled to the rights referred to in subsection (1) above whether or not a contract of employment subsists during the period of her absence but, subject to subsection (3) below, she shall not be so entitled unless—

(a) she continues to be employed by her employer (whether or not she is at work) until immediately before the beginning of the 11th week before the expected week of confinement ;

(b) she has at the beginning of that 11th week been continuously employed for a period of not less than two years ; and

(c) she informs her employer (in writing if he so requests) at least three weeks before her absence begins or, if that is not reasonably practicable, as soon as reasonably practicable,—

(i) that she will be (or is) absent from work wholly or partly because of pregnancy or confinement, and

(ii) in the case of the right to return, that she intends to return to work with her employer.

(3) An employee who has been dismissed by her employer for a reason falling within section 34(1)(a) or (b) above and has not been re-engaged in accordance with that section, shall be entitled to the rights referred to in subsection (1) above notwithstanding that she has thereby ceased to be employed before the beginning of the 11th week before the expected week of confinement if, but for that dismissal, she would at the beginning of that 11th week have been continuously employed for a period of not less than two years, but she shall not be entitled to the right to return unless she informs her employer (in writing if he so requests), before or as soon as reasonably practicable after the dismissal takes effect, that she intends to return to work with him.

(4) An employee shall not be entitled to either of the rights referred to in subsection (1) above unless, if requested to do so by her employer, she produces for his inspection a certificate from a registered medical practitioner or a certified midwife stating the expected week of her confinement.

(5) The Secretary of State may by order vary the periods of two years referred to in subsections (2) and (3) above, or those periods as varied from time to time under this section, but no such order shall be made unless a draft of the order has been laid before Parliament and approved by resolution of each House of Parliament.

36.—(1) Maternity pay shall be paid in respect of a period not Maternity pay. exceeding, or periods not exceeding in the aggregate, six weeks during which the employee is absent from work wholly or partly because of pregnancy or confinement (hereafter in this section and sections 37 and 38 below referred to as the payment period or payment periods).

(2) An employee shall not be entitled to maternity pay for any absence before the beginning of the 11th week before the expected week of confinement, and her payment period or payment periods shall be the first six weeks of absence starting on or

falling after the beginning of that 11th week.

(3) The Secretary of State may by order vary the periods of six weeks referred to in subsections (1) and (2) above, or those periods as varied from time to time under this section, but no such order shall be made unless a draft of the order has been laid before Parliament and approved by resolution of each House of Parliament.

(4) Where an employee gives her employer the information required by section 35(2)(c) above or produces any certificate requested under section 35(4) above after the beginning of the payment period or the first of the payment periods, she shall not be entitled to maternity pay for any part of that period until she gives him that information or certificate, but on giving him the information or as the case may be producing the certificate, she shall be entitled to be paid in respect of that part of the period or periods which fell before the giving of the information or the production of the certificate.

Calculation of maternity pay.

1975 c. 14.

37.—(1) The amount of maternity pay to which an employee is entitled as respects any week shall be 9/10ths of a week's pay reduced by the amount of maternity allowance payable for that week under Part I of Schedule 4 to the Social Security Act 1975, whether or not the employee in question is entitled to the whole or any part of that allowance.

(2) Maternity pay shall accrue due to an employee from day to day and in calculating the amount of maternity pay payable for any day—

(a) there shall be disregarded Sunday or such other day in each week as may be prescribed in relation to that employee under section 22(10) of the Social Security Act 1975 for the purpose of calculating the daily rate of maternity allowance under that Act ; and

(b) the amount payable for any other day shall be taken as 1/6th of the amount of the maternity pay for the week in which the day falls.

(3) Subject to subsection (4) below, a right to maternity pay shall not affect any right of an employee in relation to remuneration under any contract of employment (hereafter in this section referred to as " contractual remuneration ").

(4) Any contractual remuneration paid to an employee in respect of a day within a payment period shall go towards discharging any liability of the employer to pay maternity pay in respect of that day, and conversely any maternity pay paid in respect of a day shall go towards discharging any liability of the employer to pay contractual remuneration in respect of that day.

(5) For the purposes of Part II of Schedule 4 to this Act as it applies for the calculation of a week's pay for the purposes of this section, the calculation date is the last day on which the

employee worked under the contract of employment in force immediately before the beginning of her absence.

48.—(1) The right to return to work of an employee who has been absent from work wholly or partly because of pregnancy or confinement is, subject to the following provisions of this Act, a right to return to work with her original employer, or, where appropriate, his successor, at any time before the end of the period of 29 weeks beginning with the week in which the date of confinement falls, in the job in which she was employed under the original contract of employment and on terms and conditions not less favourable than those which would have been applicable to her if she had not been so absent.

(2) In subsection (1) above—

> (a) " job ", in relation to an employee, means the nature of the work which she is employed to do in accordance with her contract and the capacity and place in which she is so employed ; and

> (b) " terms and conditions not less favourable than those which would have been applicable to her if she had not been so absent " means, as regards seniority, pension rights and other similar rights, that the period or periods of employment prior to the employee's absence shall be regarded as continuous with her employment following that absence.

(3) In sections 35 and 49 to 51 of, and Schedule 3 to, this Act, except where the context otherwise requires, " to return to work " means to return to work in accordance with subsection (1) above, and cognate expressions shall be construed accordingly.

(4) If an employee is entitled to return to work in accordance with subsection (1) above, but it is not practicable by reason of redundancy for the employer to permit her so to return to work, she shall be entitled, where there is a suitable available vacancy, to be offered alternative employment wi'h her employer (or his successor), or an associated employer, under a new contract of employment complying with subsection (5) below.

(5) The new contract of employment must be such that—

> (a) the work to be done under the contract is of a kind which is both suitable in relation to the employee and appropriate for her to do in the circumstances : and

> (b) the provisions of the new contract as to the capacity and place in which she is to be employed and as to the other terms and conditions of her employment are not substantially less favourable to her than if she had returned to work in accordance with subsection (1) above.

(6) The remedies of an employee for infringement of either of the rights mentioned in this section are those conferred by or by virtue of the provisions of sections 49 and 50 below and Schedule 3 to this Act.

Exercise of right to return. **49.**—(1) An employee shall exercise her right to return to work by notifying the employer (who may be her original employer or a successor of that employer) at least one week before the day on which she proposes to return of her proposal to return on that day (hereafter in this section and section 50 below and Schedule 3 to this Act referred to as the " notified day of return ").

(2) An employer may postpone an employee's return to work until a date not more than four weeks after the notified day of return if he notifies her before that day that for specified reasons he is postponing her return until that date, and accordingly she will be entitled to return to work with him on that date.

(3) Subject to subsection (4) below, an employee may—

(a) postpone her return to work until a date not exceeding four weeks from the notified day of return, notwithstanding that that date falls after the end of the period of 29 weeks mentioned in section 48(1) above ; and

(b) where no day of return has been notified to the employer, extend the time during which she may exercise her right to return in accordance with subsection (1) above, so that she returns to work not later than four weeks from the expiration of the said period of 29 weeks ;

if before the notified day of return or, as the case may be, the expiration of the period of 29 weeks she gives the employer a certificate from a registered medical practitioner stating that by reason of disease or bodily or mental disablement she will be incapable of work on the notified day of return or the expiration of that period, as the case may be.

(4) Where an employee has once exercised a right of postponement or extension under subsection (3)(a) or (b) above, she shall not again be entitled to exercise a right of postponement or extension under that subsection in connection with the same return to work.

(5) If an employee has notified a day of return but there is an interruption of work (whether due to industrial action or some other reason) which renders it unreasonable to expect the employee to return to work on the notified day of return, she may instead return to work when work resumes after the interruption or as soon as reasonably practicable thereafter.

(6) If no day of return has been notified and there is an interruption of work (whether due to industrial action or some other reason) which renders it unreasonable to expect the employee to return to work before the expiration of the period of 29 weeks referred to in section 48(1) above, or which appears likely to have that effect, and in consequence the employee does not notify a day of return, the employee may exercise her right to return in accordance with subsection (1) above so that she returns to work at any time before the end of the period of 14 days from the end of the interruption notwithstanding that she returns to work outside the said period of 29 weeks.

(7) Where the employee has either—

(a) exercised the right under subsection (3)(b) above to extend the period during which she may exercise her right to return ; or

(b) refrained from notifying the day of return in the circumstances described in subsection (6) above,

the other of those subsections shall apply as if for the reference to the expiration of the period of 29 weeks there were substituted a reference to the expiration of the further period of four weeks or, as the case may be, of the period of 14 days from the end of the interruption of work.

(8) Where—

(a) an employee's return is postponed under subsection (2) or (3)(a) above, or

(b) the employee returns to work on a day later than the notified day of return in the circumstances described in subsection (5) above,

then, subject to subsection (4) above, references in those sub-sections and in section 50 below and Schedule 3 to this Act to the notified day of return shall be construed as references to the day to which the return is postponed or, as the case may be, that later day.

50.—(1) Where an employee is entitled to return to work and has exercised her right to return in accordance with section 49 above but is not permitted to return to work, then, she shall be treated for the purposes of— _{Failure to permit to return treated as dismissal.}

(a) the provisions of this Act and the 1974 Act relating to unfair dismissal ; and

(b) the Redundancy Payments Act 1965 ;   1965 c. 62.

as if she had been employed until the notified day of return, and, if she would not otherwise be so treated, as having been continuously employed until that day, and as if she had been dismissed with effect from that day for the reason for which she was not permitted to return.

(2) The provisions of Schedule 3 to this Act shall have effect for the purpose of supplementing the foregoing provisions of this Act relating to an employee's right to return to work.

Dismissal of replacement.

51. Where an employer—

(*a*) on engaging an employee informs the employee in writing that his employment will be terminated on the return to work of another employee who is, or will be, absent wholly or partly because of pregnancy or confinement ; and

(*b*) dismisses the first-mentioned employee in order to make it possible to give work to the other employee ;

then, for the purposes of paragraph 6(1)(*b*) of Schedule 1 to the 1974 Act (employer to show substantial reason for dismissal), but without prejudice to the application of paragraph 6(8) of that Schedule (whether dismissal fair or unfair to depend on whether employer acted reasonably), the dismissal shall be regarded as having been for a substantial reason of a kind such as to justify the dismissal of an employee holding the position which that employee held.

Time off work

Time off for carrying out trade union duties.

57.—(1) An employer shall permit an employee of his who is an official of an independent trade union recognised by him to take time off, subject to and in accordance with subsection (2) below, during the employee's working hours for the purpose of enabling him—

(*a*) to carry out those duties of his as such an official which are concerned with industrial relations between his employer and any associated employer, and their employees ; or

(*b*) to undergo training in aspects of industrial relations which is—

(i) relevant to the carrying out of those duties ; and

(ii) approved by the Trades Union Congress or by the independent trade union of which he is an official.

(2) The amount of time off which an employee is to be permitted to take under this section and the purposes for which, the occasions on which and any conditions subject to which time off may be so taken are those that are reasonable in all the circumstances having regard to any relevant provisions of a Code of Practice issued by the Service under section 6 above.

(3) In the Code of Practice referred to in section 6(2)(*b*)(i) above the Service shall in particular provide practical guidance on the circumstances in which a trade union official is to be permitted to take time off under this section in respect of duties connected with industrial action.

(4) An employer who permits an employee to take time off under this section for any purpose shall, subject to the following provisions of this section, pay him for the time taken off for that purpose in accordance with the permission—

    (*a*) where the employee's remuneration for the work he would ordinarily have been doing during that time does not vary with the amount of work done, as if he had worked at that work for the whole of that time ;

    (*b*) where the employee's remuneration for that work varies with the amount of work done, an amount calculated by reference to the average hourly earnings for that work.

(5) The average hourly earnings referred to in subsection (4)(*b*) above shall be the average hourly earnings of the employee concerned or, if no fair estimate can be made of those earnings, the average hourly earnings for work of that description of persons in comparable employment with the same employer or, if there are no such persons, a figure of average hourly earnings which is reasonable in the circumstances.

(6) Subject to subsection (7) below, a right to be paid any amount under subsection (4) above shall not affect any right of an employee in relation to remuneration under his contract of employment (hereafter in this section referred to as " contractual remuneration ").

(7) Any contractual remuneration paid to an employee in respect of a period of time off to which subsection (1) above applies shall go towards discharging any liability of the employer under subsection (4) above in respect of that period, and conversely any payment of any amount under subsection (4) above in respect of a period shall go towards discharging any liability of the employer to pay contractual remuneration in respect of that period.

(8) An employee who is an official of an independent trade union recognised by his employer may present a complaint to an industrial tribunal that his employer has failed to permit him to take time off as required by this section or to pay him the whole or part of any amount so required to be paid.

58.—(1) An employer shall permit an employee of his who *Time off for* is a member of an appropriate trade union to take time off, *trade union* subject to and in accordance with subsection (3) below, during *activities.* the employee's working hours for the purpose of taking part in any trade union activity to which this section applies.

(2) In this section "appropriate trade union", in relation to an employee of any description, means an independent trade union which is recognised by his employer in respect of that description of employee, and the trade union activities to which this section applies are—

(a) any activities of an appropriate trade union of which the employee is a member ; and

(b) any activities, whether or not falling within paragraph (a) above, in relation to which the employee is acting as a representative of such a union,

excluding activities which themselves consist of industrial action whether or not in contemplation or furtherance of a trade dispute.

(3) The amount of time off which an employee is to be permitted to take under this section and the purposes for which, the occasions on which and any conditions subject to which time off may be so taken are those that are reasonable in all the circumstances having regard to any relevant provisions of a Code of Practice issued by the Service under section 6 above.

(4) In the Code of Practice referred to in section 6(2)(b)(ii) above the Service shall in particular provide practical guidance on the following matters, that is to say, the question whether, and the circumstances in which a trade union member is to be permitted to take time off under this section for trade union activities connected with industrial action.

(5) An employee who is a member of an independent trade union recognised by his employer may present a complaint to an industrial tribunal that his employer has failed to permit him to take time off as required by this section.

Time off for public duties.   **59.**—(1) An employer shall permit an employee of his who is—

(a) a justice of the peace ;

(b) a member of a local authority ;

(c) a member of any statutory tribunal ;

(d) a member of, in England and Wales, a Regional Health Authority or Area Health Authority or, in Scotland, a Health Board;

(e) a member of, in England and Wales, the managing or governing body of an educational establishment maintained by a local education authority, or, in Scotland, a school or college council or the governing body of a central institution or a college of education ; or

(f) a member of, in England and Wales, a water authority or, in Scotland, river purification board, to take time off, subject to and in accordance with subsection (4) below, during the employee's working hours for the purposes of performing any of the duties of his office or, as the case may be, his duties as such a member.

(2) In subsection (1) above—

(a) " local authority " in relation to England and Wales includes the Common Council of the City of London but otherwise has the same meaning as in the Local Government Act 1972, and in relation to Scotland has the same meaning as in the Local Government (Scotland) Act 1973 ;

(b) " Regional Health Authority " and " Area Health Authority " have the same meaning as in the National Health Service Reorganisation Act 1973, and " Health Board " has the same meaning as in the National Health Service (Scotland) Act 1972 ;

(c) " local education authority " means the authority designated by section 192(1) of the Local Government Act 1972, " school or college council " means a body

61.—(1) An employee who is given notice of dismissal by reason of redundancy shall, subject to the following provisions of this section, be entitled before the expiration of his notice to be allowed by his employer reasonable time off during the employee's working hours in order to look for new employment or make arrangements for training for future employment.

Time off to look for work or make arrangements for training.

(2) An employee shall not be entitled to time off under this section unless, on whichever is the later of the following dates, that is to say,—

(a) the date on which the notice is due to expire ; or

(b) the date on which it would expire were it the notice required to be given by section 1(1) of the Contracts of Employment Act 1972 (minimum period of notice),

he will have been or, as the case may be, would have been continuously employed for a period of two years or more.

(3) An employee who is allowed time off during his working hours under subsection (1) above shall, subject to the following provisions of this section, be entitled to be paid remuneration by his employer for the period of absence at the appropriate hourly rate.

(4) The appropriate hourly rate in relation to an employee shall be the amount of one week's pay divided by—

(a) the number of normal working hours in a week for that employee when employed under the contract of employment in force on the day when notice was given ; or

(b) where the number of such normal working hours differs from week to week or over a longer period, the average number of such hours calculated by dividing by 12 the total number of the employee's normal working hours during the period of 12 weeks ending with the last complete week before the day on which notice was given.

(5) For the purposes of Part II of Schedule 4 to this Act as it applies for the calculation of a week's pay for the purposes of this section, the calculation date is the day on which the employer's notice was given.

(6) In this section, " week " in relation to an employee whose remuneration is calculated weekly by a week ending with a day other than Saturday, means a week ending with that other day, and in relation to any other employee means a week ending with Saturday.

(7) If an employer unreasonably refuses to allow an employee time off from work under this section, the employee shall, subject to subsection (11) below, be entitled to be paid an amount equal to the remuneration to which he would have been entitled under subsection (3) above if he had been allowed the time off.

Written statement of reasons for dismissal

Written statement of reasons for dismissal.

70.—(1) An employee shall be entitled—

(a) if he is given by his employer notice of termination of his contract of employment ;

(b) if his contract of employment is terminated by his employer without notice ; or

(c) if, where he is employed under a contract for a fixed term, that term expires without being renewed under the same contract,

to be provided by his employer, on request, within 14 days of that request, with a written statement giving particulars of the reasons for his dismissal.

(2) An employee shall not be entitled to a written statement under subsection (1) above unless on the effective date of termination he has been, or will have been, continuously employed for a period of 26 weeks ending with the last complete week before that date.

(3) A written statement provided under this section shall be admissible in evidence in any proceedings.

(4) A complaint may be presented to an industrial tribunal by an employee against his employer on the ground that the employer unreasonably refused to provide a written statement under subsection (1) above or that the particulars of reasons

given in purported compliance with that subsection are inadequate or untrue, and if the tribunal finds the complaint well-founded—

    (*a*) it may make a declaration as to what it finds the employer's reasons were for dismissing the employee; and

    (*b*) it shall make an award that the employer pay to the employee a sum equal to the amount of two weeks' pay.

(5) An industrial tribunal shall not entertain a complaint under this section relating to the reasons for a dismissal unless it is presented to the tribunal at such a time that the tribunal would, in accordance with paragraph 21(4) or (4A) of Schedule 1 to the 1974 Act, entertain a complaint of unfair dismissal in respect of that dismissal presented at the same time.

(6) For the purposes of Part II of Schedule 4 to this Act as it applies for the calculation of a week's pay for the purposes of this section, the calculation date where the dismissal was with notice is the date on which the employer's notice was given and in any other case is the effective date of termination.

Remedies for unfair dismissal

71.—(1) Where on a complaint under paragraph 17 of Schedule 1 to the 1974 Act (unfair dismissal) an industrial tribunal finds that the grounds of the complaint are well-founded, it shall explain to the complainant what orders for reinstatement or re-engagement may be made under this section and in what circumstances they may be made, and shall ask him whether he wishes the tribunal to make such an order, and if he does express such a wish the tribunal may make an order under this section.

Order for reinstatement or re-engagement.

(2) An order under this section may be an order for reinstatement (in accordance with subsections (3) and (4) below) or an order for re-engagement (in accordance with subsection (5) below), as the tribunal may decide, and in the latter case may be on such terms as the tribunal may decide.

(3) An order for reinstatement is an order that the employer shall treat the complainant in all respects as if he had not been dismissed, and on making such an order the tribunal shall specify—

    (*a*) any amount payable by the employer in respect of any benefit which the complainant might reasonably be expected to have had but for the dismissal, including arrears of pay, for the period between the date of termination of employment and the date of reinstatement;

(b) **any rights and privileges,** including seniority and pension rights, which must be restored to the employee; and

(c) the date by which the order must be complied with.

(4) Without prejudice to the generality of subsection (3) above, if the complainant would have benefited from an improvement in his terms and conditions of employment had he not been dismissed, an order for reinstatement shall require him to be treated as if he had benefited from that improvement from the date on which he would have done so but for being dismissed.

(5) An order for re-engagement is an order that the complainant be engaged by the employer, or by a successor of the employer or by an associated employer, in employment comparable to that from which he was dismissed or other suitable employment, and on making such an order the tribunal shall specify the terms on which re-engagement is to take place including—

(a) the identity of the employer;

(b) the nature of the employment;

(c) the remuneration for the employment;

(d) any amount payable by the employer in respect of any benefit which the complainant might reasonably be expected to have had but for the dismissal, including arrears of pay, for the period between the date of termination of employment and the date of re-engagement;

(e) any rights and privileges, including seniority and pension rights, which must be restored to the employee; and

(f) the date by which the order must be complied with.

(6) In exercising its discretion under this section the tribunal shall first consider whether to make an order for reinstatement and in so doing shall take into account the following considerations, that is to say—

(a) whether the complainant wishes to be reinstated;

(b) whether it is practicable for the employer to comply with an order for reinstatement;

(c) where the complainant caused or contributed to some extent to the dismissal, whether it would be just to order his reinstatement.

(7) If the tribunal decides not to make an order for reinstatement it shall then consider whether to make an order for re-engagement and if so on what terms; and in so doing the

tribunal shall take into account the following considerations, that is to say—

(a) any wish expressed by the complainant as to the nature of the order to be made;

(b) whether it is practicable for the employer or, as the case may be, a successor or associated employer to comply with an order for re-engagement;

(c) where the complainant caused or contributed to some extent to the dismissal, whether it would be just to order his re-engagement and if so on what terms;

and except in a case where the tribunal takes into account contributory fault under paragraph (c) above it shall, if it orders re-engagement, do so on terms which are, so far as is reasonably practicable, as favourable as an order for reinstatement.

(8) Where in any case an employer has engaged a permanent replacement for a dismissed employee the tribunal shall not take that fact into account in determining, for the purposes of subsection (6)(b) or (7)(b) above whether it is practicable to comply with an order for reinstatement or re-engagement unless the employer shows—

(a) that it was not practicable for him to arrange for the dismissed employee's work to be done without engaging a permanent replacement; or

(b) that he engaged the replacement after the lapse of a reasonable period, without having heard from the dismissed employee that he wished to be reinstated or re-engaged, and that when the employer engaged the replacement it was no longer reasonable for him to arrange for the dismissed employee's work to be done except by a permanent replacement.

(9) In calculating for the purpose of subsection (3)(a) or (5)(d) above any amount payable by the employer the tribunal shall take into account, so as to reduce the employer's liability, any sums received by the complainant in respect of the period between the date of termination of employment and the date of reinstatement or re-engagement by way of—

(a) wages in lieu of notice or ex gratia payments paid by the employer;

(b) remuneration paid in respect of employment with another employer;

and such other benefits as the tribunal thinks appropriate in the circumstances.

72.—(1) If an order under section 71 above is made and the complainant is reinstated or, as the case may be, re-engaged but the terms of the order are not fully complied with, then, subject to paragraph 20 of Schedule 1 to the 1974 Act (limit on compensation), an industrial tribunal shall make an award of compensation, to be paid by the employer to the employee, of such amount as the tribunal thinks fit having regard to the loss sustained by the complainant in consequence of the failure to comply fully with the terms of the order.

Enforcement
of s. 71
order and
compensation.

(2) Subject to subsection (1) above, if an order under section 71 above is made but the complainant is not reinstated or, as the case may be, re-engaged in accordance with the order—

> (a) the tribunal shall make an award of compensation for unfair dismissal, calculated in accordance with sections 73 to 76 below, to be paid by the employer to the employee ; and

> (b) unless the employer satisfies the tribunal that it was not practicable to comply with the order, the tribunal shall make an additional award of compensation to be paid by the employer to the employee of an amount—

>> (i) where the dismissal is of a description referred to in subsection (3) below, not less than 26 or more than 52 weeks' pay, or

>> (ii) in any other case, not less than 13 or more than 26 weeks' pay.

(3) The descriptions of dismissal in respect of which an employer may incur a higher additional award in accordance with subsection (2)(b)(i) above are the following, that is to say,—

> (a) a dismissal which is unfair by virtue of paragraph 6(4) or (5) of Schedule 1 to the 1974 Act (dismissal for membership or non-membership of a trade union, or for taking part in the activities of an independent trade union) ;

> (b) a dismissal which is an unlawful act of discrimination by virtue of section 3(1) of the Race Relations Act 1968 ;

> (c) a dismissal which is an act of discrimination (within the meaning of the Sex Discrimination Act 1975) which is unlawful by virtue of that Act.

1968 c. 71.

1975 c. 65.

(4) Where in any case an employer has engaged a permanent replacement for a dismissed employee the tribunal shall not take that fact into account in determining, for the purposes of subsection (2)(b) above whether it was practicable to comply with the order for reinstatement or re-engagement unless the employer

shows that it was not practicable for him to arrange for the dismissed employee's work to be done without engaging a permanent replacement.

(5) If on a complaint under paragraph 17 of Schedule 1 to the 1974 Act the tribunal finds that the grounds of the complaint are well-founded, and no order is made under section 71 above the tribunal shall make an award of compensation for unfair dismissal, calculated in accordance with sections 73 to 76 below, to be paid by the employer to the employee.

(6) Where in any case the tribunal makes an award of compensation for unfair dismissal, calculated in accordance with sections 73 to 76 below, and the tribunal finds that the complainant has unreasonably prevented an order under section 71 above from being complied with, it shall, without prejudice to the generality of section 76(4) below, take that conduct into account as a failure on the part of the complainant to mitigate his loss.

(7) For the purposes of Part II of Schedule 4 as it applies for the calculation of a week's pay for the purpose of subsection (2)(*b*) above, the calculation date where the dismissal was with notice is the date on which the notice was given and in any other case the effective date of termination.

(8) Notwithstanding anything in the said Part II, the amount of a week's pay for the purpose of calculating an additional award under subsection (2)(*b*) above shall not exceed £80.

73. Where a tribunal makes an award of compensation for unfair dismissal under section 72(2)(*a*) or (5) above, the award shall consist of a basic award (calculated in accordance with sections 74 and 75 below) and a compensatory award (calculated in accordance with section 76 below). *Compensation for unfair dismissal.*

74.—(1) The amount of the basic award shall be the amount calculated in accordance with subsections (3) to (7) and sections 75(1) to (6) below, subject to the following provisions of this Act, namely— *Calculation of basic award.*

(*a*) subsection (2) below (which provides for an award of two weeks' pay in certain cases) ;

(*b*) section 75(7) below (which provides for the amount of the award to be reduced where the employee contributed to the dismissal) ;

(*c*) section 75(8) below (which provides for the amount of the award to be reduced where the employee received a payment in respect of redundancy) ; and (*d*) section 77 below (which prohibits double compensation where compensation in respect of the same matter is also awarded under the Sex Discrimination Act 1975).

1975 c. 65.

(2) In the following cases the amount of the basic award shall be two weeks' pay:—

(*a*) where the tribunal finds that the reason or principal reason for the dismissal of the employee was that he was redundant and the employee—

(i) by virtue of section 2(5) or (6) of the Redundancy Payments Act 1965 (unreasonable refusal or relinquishment of suitable alternative employment) is not, or if he were otherwise entitled would not be, entitled to a redundancy payment ; or

1965 c. 62.

(ii) by virtue of the operation of section 3(3) of that Act (renewal of employment or re-engagement) is not treated as dismissed for the purposes of Part I of that Act ;

(*b*) where the amount calculated in accordance with sub-sections (3) to (7) and section 75(1) to (7) below is less than the amount of two weeks' pay.

(3) The amount of the basic award shall be calculated by reference to the period, ending with the effective date of termination, during which the employee has been continuously employed, by starting at the end of that period and reckoning backwards the numbers of years of employment falling within that period, and allowing—

(*a*) one and a half weeks' pay for each such year of employment which consists wholly of weeks in which the employee was not below the age of 41 ;

(*b*) one week's pay for each such year of employment which consists wholly of weeks in which the employee was below the age of 41 and was not below the age of 22 ; and

(*c*) half a week's pay for each such year of employment which consists wholly of weeks in which the employee was below the age of 22 and was not below the age of 18.

(4) In ascertaining for the purpose of subsection (3) above the period for which an employee has been continuously employed, where the effective date of termination falls to be determined in accordance with paragraph 5(6) of Schedule 1 to the 1974 Act, a period falling within such an interval as is referred to in paragraph 30(1A) of that Schedule (period of continuous employment) shall count as a period of employment notwithstanding that it does not count under Schedule 1 to the Contracts of Employment Act 1972 (computation of period of employment).

1972 c. 53.

(5) Where in reckoning the number of years of employment in accordance with subsection (3) above 20 years of employment have been reckoned no account shall be taken of any year of employment earlier than those 20 years.

(6) Where in the case of an employee the effective date of termination is after the specified anniversary the amount of the basic award calculated in accordance with subsections (3) to (5) above shall be reduced by the appropriate fraction.

(7) In subsection (6) above " the specified anniversary " in relation to a man means the 64th anniversary of the day of his birth, and in relation to a woman means the 59th anniversary of the day of her birth, and " the appropriate fraction " means the fraction of which—

> (a) the numerator is the number of whole months reckoned from the specified anniversary in the period beginning with that anniversary and ending with the effective date of termination ; and
>
> (b) the denominator is 12.

75.—(1) For the purposes of Part II of Schedule 4 to this Act as it applies for the calculation of a week's pay for the purposes of section 74 above, the calculation date is, subject to subsection (3) below, the date on which notice would have been given by the employer had the conditions referred to in subsection (2) below been fulfilled (whether those conditions were in fact fulfilled or not). Provisions supplementary to s. 74.

(2) Those conditions are that the contract was terminable by notice and was terminated by the employer giving such notice as is required to terminate that contract by section 1(1) of the Contracts of Employment Act 1972 (minimum period of notice), and that the notice expired on the effective date of termination. 1972 c. 53.

(3) Where by virtue of paragraph 5(6) of Schedule 1 to the 1974 Act a date is to be treated as the effective date of termination for the purposes of section 74(3) above which is later than the effective date of termination as defined by paragraph 5(5) of that Schedule, then, for the purposes of Part II of Schedule 4 to this Act as it applies for the calculation of a week's pay for the purpose of section 74 above, the calculation date is the effective date of termination as defined by the said paragraph 5(5).

(4) Notwithstanding anything in the said Part II, the amount of a week's pay for the purpose of calculating a basic award shall not exceed £80.

(5) The Secretary of State may, after a review under section 86 below, vary the limit referred to in subsection (4) above by order made in accordance with that section.

(6) Without prejudice to the generality of the power to make transitional provision in an order under subsection (5) above, such an order may provide that it shall apply in the case of a dismissal in relation to which the effective date of termination for the purposes of this subsection (as defined by paragraph 5(6) of Schedule 1 to the 1974 Act) falls after the order comes into operation, notwithstanding that the effective date of termination for the purposes of other provisions of this Act or the 1974 Act (as defined by paragraph 5(5) of Schedule 1 to the 1974 Act) falls before the order comes into operation.

(7) Where the tribunal finds that the dismissal was to any extent caused or contributed to by any action of the complainant it shall, except in a case where the dismissal was by reason of redundancy, reduce the amount of the basic award by such proportion as it considers just and equitable having regard to that finding.

(8) The amount of the basic award shall be reduced or, as the case may be, be further reduced, by the amount of any redundancy payment awarded by the tribunal under the Redundancy Payments Act 1965 in respect of the same dismissal or of any payment made by the employer to the employee on the ground that the dismissal was by reason of redundancy, whether in pursuance of the said Act of 1965 or otherwise.

1965 c. 62.

Itemised pay statement

Right to itemised pay statement.

81. Every employee shall have the right to be given by his employer at or before the time at which any payment of wages or salary is made to him an itemised pay statement, in writing, containing the following particulars, that is to say,—

    (a) the gross amount of the wages or salary ;

    (b) the amounts of any variable and, subject to section 82 below, any fixed deductions from that gross amount and the purposes for which they are made ;

    (c) the net amount of wages or salary payable ; and

    (d) where different parts of the net amount are paid in different ways, the amount and method of payment of each part-payment.

Duty of employer to consult trade union representatives on redundancy.

99.—(1) An employer proposing to dismiss as redundant an employee of a description in respect of which an independent trade union is recognised by him shall consult representatives of that trade union about the dismissal in accordance with the following provisions of this section.

(2) In this section and sections 100 and 101 below, " trade union representative " in relation to a trade union means an official or other person authorised to carry on collective

bargaining with the employer in question by that trade union.

(3) The consultation required by this section shall begin at the earliest opportunity, and shall in any event begin—

    (a) where the employer is proposing to dismiss as redundant 100 or more employees at one establishment within a period of 90 days or less, at least 90 days before the first of those dismissals takes effect; or

    (b) where the employer is proposing to dismiss as redundant 10 or more employees at one establishment within a period of 30 days or less, at least 60 days before the first of those dismissals takes effect.

(4) In determining for the purpose of subsection (3) above whether an employer is proposing to dismiss as redundant 100 or more, or, as the case may be, 10 or more, employees within the periods mentioned in that subsection, no account shall be taken of employees whom he proposes to dismiss as redundant in respect of whose proposed dismissals consultation has already begun.

(5) For the purposes of the consultation required by this section the employer shall disclose in writing to trade union representatives—

    (a) the reasons for his proposals;

    (b) the numbers and descriptions of employees whom it is proposed to dismiss as redundant;

    (c) the total number of employees of any such description employed by the employer at the establishment in question;

    (d) the proposed method of selecting the employees who may be dismissed; and

    (e) the proposed method of carrying out the dismissals, with due regard to any agreed procedure, including the period over which the dismissals are to take effect.

(6) The information which is to be given to trade union representatives under this section shall be delivered to them, or sent by post to an address notified by them to the employer, or sent by post to the union at the address of its head or main office.

(7) In the course of the consultation required by this section the employer shall—

    (a) consider any representations made by the trade union representatives; and

    (b) reply to those representations and, if he rejects any of those representations, state his reasons.

(8) If in any case there are special circumstances which render it not reasonably practicable for the employer to comply with

any of the requirements of subsections (3), (5) or (7) above, the employer shall take all such steps towards compliance with that requirement as are reasonably practicable in those circumstances.

(9) This section shall not be construed as conferring any rights on a trade union or an employee except as provided by sections 101 to 103 below.

Duty of employer to notify Secretary of State of certain redundancies.

100.—(1) An employer proposing to dismiss as redundant—

    (*a*) 100 or more employees at one establishment within a period of 90 days or less ; or

    (*b*) 10 or more employees at one establishment within a period of 30 days or less,

shall notify the Secretary of State, in writing, of his proposal—

    (i) in a case falling within paragraph (*a*) above, at least 90 days before the first of those dismissals takes effect ; and

    (ii) in a case falling within paragraph (*b*) above, at least 60 days before the first of those dismissals takes effect,

and where the notice relates to employees of any description in respect of which an independent trade union is recognised by him, he shall give a copy of the notice to representatives of that union.

(2) In determining for the purpose of subsection (1) above whether an employer is proposing to dismiss as redundant 100 or more, or, as the case may be, 10 or more, employees within the periods mentioned in that subsection, no account shall be taken of employees whom he proposes to dismiss as redundant in respect of whose proposed dismissals notice has already been given to the Secretary of State.

(3) A notice under this section shall—

    (*a*) be given to the Secretary of State by delivery to him or by sending it by post to him, at such address as the Secretary of State may direct in relation to the establishment where the employees proposed to be dismissed are employed ;

    (*b*) in a case where consultation with trade union representatives is required by section 90 above, identify the trade union concerned and state the date when consultation began ; and

    (*c*) be in such form and contain such particulars, in addition to those required by paragraph (*b*) above, as the Secretary of State may direct.

(4) The copy of the notice under this section which is to be given to trade union representatives shall be delivered to them, or sent by post to an address notified by them to the employer,

or sent by post to the union at the address of its head or main office.

(5) At any time after receiving a notice under this section from an employer the Secretary of State may by written notice require the employer to give him such further information as may be specified in the requirement.

(6) If in any case there are special circumstances rendering it not reasonably practicable for the employer to comply with any of the requirements of subsections (1) to (5) above, he shall take all such steps towards compliance with that requirement as are reasonably practicable in those circumstances.

101.—(1) An appropriate trade union may present a complaint to an industrial tribunal on the ground that an employer has dismissed as redundant or is proposing to dismiss as redundant one or more employees and has not complied with any of the requirements of section 99 above.

Complaint by trade union and protective award.

(2) If on a complaint under this section a question arises as to the matters referred to in section 99(8) above, it shall be for the employer to show—

    (*a*) that there were special circumstances which rendered it not reasonably practicable for him to comply with any requirement of section 99 above ; and

    (*b*) that he took all such steps towards compliance with that requirement as were reasonably practicable in those circumstances.

(3) Where the tribunal finds a complaint under subsection (1) above well-founded it shall make a declaration to that effect and may also make a protective award in accordance with subsection (4) below.

(4) A protective award is an award that in respect of such descriptions of employees as may be specified in the award, being employees who have been dismissed, or whom it is proposed to dismiss, as redundant, and in respect of whose dismissal or proposed dismissal the employer has failed to comply with any requirement of section 99 above, the employer shall pay remuneration for a protected period.

(5) The protected period under an award under subsection (4) above shall be a period beginning with the date on which the first of the dismissals to which the complaint relates takes effect, or the date of the award, whichever is the earlier, of such length as the tribunal shall determine to be just and equitable in all the circumstances having regard to the seriousness of the employer's default in complying with any requirement of section 99 above, not exceeding—

    (*a*) in a case falling within section 99(3)(*a*) above, 90 days ;

    (*b*) in a case falling within section 99(3)(*b*) above, 60 days ;
      or

(c) in any other case, 28 days.

(6) An industrial tribunal shall not consider a complaint under subsection (1) above in respect of an employer's default in relation to a dismissal or proposed dismissal unless it is presented to the tribunal before the proposed dismissal takes effect or before the end of the period of three months beginning with the date on which the dismissal takes effect or within such further period as the tribunal considers reasonable in a case where it is satisfied that it was not reasonably practicable for the complaint to be presented within the period of three months.

(7) " Appropriate trade union ", in relation to an employee of any description, means an independent trade union recognised by his employer in respect of that description of employee.

Entitlement under protective award.   **102.**—(1) Where an industrial tribunal has made a protective award under section 101 above, every employee of a description to which the award relates shall be entitled, subject to the following provisions of this section, to be paid remuneration by his employer for the protected period specified in the award.

(2) The rate of remuneration payable under a protective award shall be a week's pay for each week of the protected period, and if remuneration falls to be calculated for a period less than one week the amount of a week's pay shall be reduced proportionately.

(3) Any payment made to an employee by an employer under his contract of employment, or by way of damages for breach of that contract, in respect of a period falling within a protected period, shall go towards discharging the employer's liability to pay remuneration under the protective award in respect of that first mentioned period, and conversely any payment of remuneration under a protective award in respect of any period shall go towards discharging any liability of the employer under, or in respect of breach of, the contract of employment in respect of that period.

(4) In respect of a period during which he is employed by the employer an employee shall not be entitled to remuneration under a protective award unless he would be entitled to be paid by the employer in respect of that period, either by virtue of his contract of employment or by virtue of Schedule 2 to the Contracts of Employment Act 1972 (rights of employee in period of notice), if that period fell within the period of notice required to be given by section 1(1) of that Act.

(5) Where the employee is employed by the employer during the protected period and—

(a) he is fairly dismissed by his employer for a reason other than redundancy ; or

(b) he unreasonably terminates the contract of employment,

then, subject to the following provisions of this section, he shall not be entitled to remuneration under the protective award in respect of any period during which but for that dismissal or termination he would have been employed.

(6) If an employer makes an employee an offer (whether in writing or not and whether before or after the ending of his employment under the previous contract) to renew his contract of employment, or to re-engage him under a new contract, so that the renewal or re-engagement would take effect before or during the protected period and either—

    (*a*) the provisions of the contract as renewed, or of the new contract, as to the capacity and place in which he would be employed, and as to the other terms and conditions of his employment, would not differ from the corresponding provisions of the previous contract ; or

    (*b*) the first mentioned provisions would differ from those corresponding provisions, but the offer constitutes an offer of suitable employment in relation to the employee ;

the provisions of subsections (7) to (11) below shall effect.

(7) If, in a case to which subsection (6) above applies, the employee unreasonably refuses that offer, then, he shall not be entitled to any remuneration under a protective award in respect of any period during which but for that refusal he would have been employed.

(8) If an employee's contract of employment is renewed, or he is re-engaged under a new contract of employment, in pursuance of such an offer as is referred to in subsection (6)(*b*) above, there shall be a trial period in relation to the contract as renewed, or the new contract (whether or not there has been a previous trial period under this section).

(9) The trial period shall begin with the ending of the employee's employment under the previous contract and end with the expiration of the period of four weeks beginning with the date on which the employee starts work under the contract as renewed, or the new contract, or such longer period as may be agreed in accordance with subsection (10) below for the purpose of retraining the employee for employment under that contract.

(10) Any such agreement shall—

    (*a*) be made between the employer and the employee or his representative before the employee starts work under the contract as renewed or, as the case may be, the new contract ;

    (*b*) be in writing ;

    (*c*) specify the date of the end of the trial period ; and

    (*d*) specify the terms and conditions of employment which will apply in the employee's case after the end of that period.

(11) If during the trial period—

> (a) the employee, for whatever reason, terminates the contract, or gives notice to terminate it and the contract is thereafter, in consequence, terminated ; or

> (b) the employer, for a reason connected with or arising out of the change to the renewed, or new, employment, terminates the contract, or gives notice to terminate it and the contract is thereafter, in consequence, terminated,

then, the employee shall remain entitled under the protective award unless, in a case falling within paragraph (a) above, he acted unreasonably in terminating or giving notice to terminate the contract.

PART II

1972 c. 53.

CONTRACTS OF EMPLOYMENT ACT 1972

1. In sections 1(1) to (3) and 2 (minimum period of notice) for the words " thirteen weeks ", wherever they occur, substitute the words " four weeks ".

2. In section 1(1) for paragraphs (b) to (e) substitute the following paragraphs—

> " (b) shall be not less than one week's notice for each year of continuous employment if his period of continuous employment is two years or more but less than twelve years ; and

> (c) shall be not less than twelve weeks' notice if his period of continuous employment is twelve years or more.".

3. In section 1(4) (contract for a term certain to be treated in certain cases as a contract for an indefinite period) for the words " thirteen weeks " substitute the words " twelve weeks ".

4. In section 4(1) (written statement of terms of employment),—

> (a) after the words " the date when the employment began ", insert the words " stating whether any employment with a previous employer counts as part of the employee's continuous period of employment with him, and if so specifying the date on which the continuous period of employment began " ; and

> (b) after paragraph (e) insert " and

>> (f) the title of the job which the employee is employed to do: ".

5. In section 4(2) (written particulars to contain note about grievance procedure)—

> (a) at the beginning insert the words " Subject to subsection (2A) of this section " ; and

> (b) for paragraphs (b) and (c) substitute the following paragraphs : —

>> " (a) specifying any disciplinary rules applicable to the employee, or referring to a document which is reasonably accessible to the employee and which specifies such rules ;

(*b*) specifying, by description or otherwise—

    (i) a person to whom the employee can apply if he is dissatisfied with any disciplinary decision relating to him ; and

    (ii) a person to whom the employee can apply for the purpose of seeking redress of any grievance relating to his employment,

    and the manner in which any such applications should be made ; and

(*c*) where there are further steps consequent upon any such application, explaining those steps or referring to a document which is reasonably accessible to the employee and which explains them,".

6. After section 4(2) insert the following subsection—

" (2A) The provisions of paragraphs (*b*) to (*d*) of subsection (2) of this section shall not apply to rules, disciplinary decisions, grievances or procedures relating to health or safety at work.".

7. In section 4(7) (part-time employment)—

(*a*) at the beginning insert the words " Subject to the following provisions of this section," ; and

(*b*) for the words " twenty-one hours " substitute the words " sixteen hours ".

8. After section 4(7) insert the following subsections—

" (8) If the employee's relations with his employer cease to be governed by a contract which normally involves work for sixteen hours or more weekly and become governed by a contract which normally involves employment for eight hours or more, but less than sixteen hours, weekly, the employee shall nevertheless for a period of twenty-six weeks computed in accordance with the next following subsection be treated for the purposes of the foregoing subsection as if his contract normally involved employment for sixteen hours or more weekly.

(9) In computing the said period of twenty-six weeks no account shall be taken of any week—

(*a*) during which the employee is in fact employed for sixteen hours or more ;

(*b*) during which the employee takes part in a strike (as defined in paragraph 11 of Schedule 1 to this Act), or is absent from work because of a lock-out (as so defined) by his employer ; or

(*c*) during which there is no contract of employment but which, by virtue of paragraph 5(1) of Schedule 1 to this Act, counts in computing a period of continuous employment.

(10) An employee whose relations with his employer are governed by a contract of employment which normally involves employment for eight hours or more, but less than sixteen hours,

SCH. 16

weekly shall nevertheless, if he has been continuously employed for a period of five years or more (computed in accordance with Schedule 1 to this Act) be treated for the purposes of subsection (7) of this section as if his contract normally involved employment for sixteen hours or more weekly.".

9. In section 5(4) (written statement of change in terms of employment), after the word " but " insert the words " subject to subsection (5) of this section ", and after that subsection insert the following subsection—

" (5) A written statement under this section which informs an employee of such a change in his terms of employment as is referred to in subsection (4)(*b*) of this section shall specify the date on which the employee's continuous period of employment began.".

10. In section 9 (excluded categories of employees)—

(*a*) after subsection (2) insert the following subsection: —

" (2A) Section 1 of this Act shall not apply to a person employed under a contract made in contemplation of the performance of a specific task which is not expected to last for more than twelve weeks, unless the employee has been continuously employed for a period of more than twelve weeks (computed in accordance with Schedule 1 to this Act)." ; and

(*b*) in subsection (3) for the words from " father " to " daughter " substitute the words " husband or wife ".

11. For section 10 (power to vary number of weekly hours of employment necessary to qualify for rights) substitute the following section: —

'* Power to vary number of weekly hours of employment necessary to qualify for rights.*

10.—(1) The Secretary of State shall have power by order to provide that this Act shall have effect as if—

(*a*) for each of the references to sixteen hours in section 4(7) to (10) of this Act and in paragraphs 3, 4, 4A, 4B and 4C of Schedule 1 to this Act there were substituted a reference to such other number of hours less than sixteen as may be specified in the order ; and

(*b*) as if for each of the references to eight hours in section 4(7), (8) and (10) of this Act and in paragraphs 4B and 4C of the said Schedule there were substituted a reference to such other number of hours less than eight as may be specified in the order.

(2) An order under the foregoing subsection shall affect the operation of Schedule 1 to this Act as respects periods before the order takes effect as well as respects later periods.

(3) An order under this section may contain such transitional and other supplemental and incidental provisions as appear to the Secretary of State to be expedient, and may be varied or revoked by a further order so made.

(4) An order under this section shall be made by statutory instrument, but no such order shall be made unless a draft of the order has been laid before Parliament and approved by resolution of each House.".

12. For paragraph 1(1) of Schedule 1 (computation of period of employment) substitute the following sub-paragraph—

" (1) Where an employee's period of employment is, for the purposes of any enactment (including any enactment contained in this Act), to be computed in accordance with this Schedule, it shall be computed in weeks, and in any such enactment which refers to a period of employment expressed in years, a year means 52 weeks (whether continuous or discontinuous) which count in computing a period of employment.".

13. In paragraph 3 and 4 of Schedule 1 for the words " twenty-one hours" wherever they occur substitute the words " sixteen hours ".

14. After paragraph 4 of Schedule 1 insert the following paragraphs—

" 4A.—(1) If the employee's relations with his employer cease to be governed by a contract which normally involves work for sixteen hours or more weekly and become governed by a contract which normally involves employment for eight hours or more, but less than sixteen hours, weekly, and but for that change the later weeks would count in computing a period of employment, or would not break the continuity of a period of employment, then those later weeks shall count in computing a period of employment or, as the case may be, shall not break the continuity of a period of employment, notwithstanding that change.

(2) Not more than twenty-six weeks shall count under this paragraph between any two periods falling under paragraph 4 of this Schedule, and in computing the said figure of twenty-six weeks no account shall be taken of any week which counts in computing a period of employment, or does not break the continuity of a period of employment, otherwise than by virtue of this paragraph.

4B.—(1) An employee whose relations with his employer are governed, or have been from time to time governed, by a contract of employment which normally involves employment for eight hours or more, but less than sixteen hours, weekly shall nevertheless, if he satisfies the condition referred to in the next following sub-paragraph, be treated for the purposes of this Schedule (apart from this paragraph) as if his contract normally involved employment for sixteen hours or more weekly, and had at all times at which there was a contract during the period of employment of five years or more referred to in the next following sub-paragraph normally involved employment for sixteen hours or more weekly.

(2) The foregoing sub-paragraph shall apply if the employee, on the date by reference to which the length of any period

SCH. 16

of employment falls to be ascertained in accordance with the provisions of this Schedule, has been continuously employed, within the meaning of the next following sub-paragraph, for a period of five years or more.

(3) In computing, for the purposes of the foregoing sub-paragraph, an employee's period of employment the provisions of this Schedule (apart from this paragraph) shall apply but as if, in paragraphs 3 and 4, for the words "sixteen hours" wherever they occur, there were substituted the words "eight hours".

4C.—(1) If an employee has, at any time during the relevant period of employment, been continuously employed for a period which qualifies him for any right which requires a qualifying period of continuous employment computed in accordance with this Schedule, then, he shall be regarded for the purposes of qualifying for that right as continuing to satisfy that requirement until the condition referred to in sub-paragraph (3) of this paragraph occurs.

(2) In this paragraph the relevant period of employment means the period of employment ending on the date by reference to which the length of any period of employment falls to be ascertained which would be continuous (in accordance with the provisions of this Schedule) if at all relevant times the employee's relations with the employer had been governed by a contract of employment which normally involved employment for sixteen hours or more weekly.

(3) The condition which defeats the operation of sub-paragraph (1) of this paragraph is that in a week subsequent to the time at which the employee qualified as referred to in that sub-paragraph—

(a) his relations with his employer are governed by a contract of employment which normally involves employment for less than eight hours weekly ; and

(b) he is employed in that week for less than sixteen hours.

(4) If, in a case in which an employee is entitled to any right by virtue of sub-paragraph (1) of this paragraph, it is necessary for the purpose of ascertaining the amount of his entitlement to determine for what period he has been continuously employed, he shall be regarded for that purpose as having been continuously employed throughout the relevant period.".

15. In paragraph 5(1) of Schedule 1 after paragraph (c) insert the following paragraph : —

" or

(d) absent from work wholly or partly because of pregnancy or confinement,"

and for the words " or paragraph 4 " substitute the words " , 4 or 4A."

16. In paragraph 5(2) of Schedule 1, after the words " paragraph (a) " insert the words " or, subject to paragraph 5A below, paragraph

(*d*) ", and for the words " two periods falling under paragraphs 3 and 4 " substitute the words " periods falling under paragraph 3, 4 or 4A ".

17. After paragraph 5 of Schedule 1, insert the following paragraph : —

" 5A. If an employee returns to work in accordance with section 49 of the Employment Protection Act 1975 after a period of absence from work wholly or partly occasioned by pregnancy or confinement, every week during that period shall count in computing a period of employment, notwithstanding that it does not fall under paragraph 3, 4 or 4A of this Schedule.".

18. In paragraph 6(1) of Schedule 1, for the words " paragraph 4 or paragraph 5 ", substitute the words " 4, 4A, 5, or 5A ".

19. For paragraph 10 of Schedule 1, substitute the following paragraph : —

" 10.—(1) If an employee of an employer is taken into the employment of another employer who, at the time when the employee enters his employment is an associated employer of the first mentioned employer, the employee's period of employment at that time shall count as a period of employment with the second mentioned employer and the change of employer shall not break the continuity of the period of employment.

(2) For the purposes of this paragraph, any two employers are to be treated as associated if one is a company of which the other (directly or indirectly) has control, or if both are companies of which a third person (directly or indirectly) has control ; and the expression " associated employer " shall be construed accordingly.".

Appendix 8

The Sex Discrimination Act, 1975 (extracts)

An Act to render unlawful certain kinds of sex discrimination and discrimination on the ground of marriage, and establish a Commission with the function of working towards the elimination of such discrimination and promoting equality of opportunity between men and women generally; and for related purposes.

[12th November 1975]

BE IT ENACTED by the Queen's most Excellent Majesty, by and with the advice and consent of the Lords Spiritual and Temporal, and Commons, in this present Parliament assembled, and by the authority of the same, as follows:—

PART I

DISCRIMINATION TO WHICH ACT APPLIES

1.—(1) A person discriminates against a woman in any circumstances relevant for the purposes of any provision of this Act if—

(a) on the ground of her sex he treats her less favourably than he treats or would treat a man, or

(b) he applies to her a requirement on condition which he applies or would apply equally to a man but—

(i) which is such that the proportion of women who can comply with it is considerably smaller than the proportion of men who can comply with it, and

(ii) which he cannot show to be justifiable irrespective of the sex of the person to whom it is applied, and

(iii) which is to her detriment because she cannot comply with it.

(2) If a person treats or would treat a man differently according to the man's marital status, his treatment of a woman is for the purposes of subsection (1)(a) to be compared to his treatment of a man having the like marital status.

2.—(1) Section 1, and the provisions of Parts II and III relating to sex discrimination against women, are to be read as applying equally to the treatment of men, and for that purpose shall have effect with such modifications as are requisite.

(2) In the application of subsection (1) no account shall be taken of special treatment afforded to women in connection with pregnancy or childbirth.

3.—(1) A person discriminates against a married person of either sex in any circumstances relevant for the purposes of any provision of Part II if—

(a) on the ground of his or her marital status he treats that person less favourably than he treats or would treat an unmarried person of the same sex, or

(b) he applies to that person a requirement or condition which he applies or would apply equally to an unmarried person but—

(i) which is such that the proportion of married persons who can comply with it is considerably smaller than the proportion of unmarried persons of the same sex who can comply with it, and

(ii) which he cannot show to be justifiable irrespective of the marital status of the person to whom it is applied, and

(iii) which is to that person's detriment because he cannot comply with it.

(2) For the purposes of subsection (1), a provision of Part II framed with reference to discrimination against women shall be treated as applying equally to the treatment of men, and for that purpose shall have effect with such modifications as are requisite.

4.—(1) A person ("the discriminator") discriminates against another person ("the person victimised") in any circumstances relevant for the purposes of any provision of this Act if he treats the person victimised less favourably than in those circumstances he treats or would treat other persons, and does so by reason that the person victimised has—

(a) brought proceedings against the discriminator or any other person under this Act or the Equal Pay Act 1970, or

(*b*) given evidence or information in connection with proceedings brought by any person against the discriminator or any other person under this Act or the Equal
Pay Act 1970 or

(*c*) otherwise done anything under or by reference to this
Act or the Equal Pay Act 1970 in relation to the
discriminator or any other person, or

(*d*) alleged that the discriminator or any other person has
committed an act which (whether or not the allegation
so states) would amount to a contravention of this Act
or give rise to a claim under the Equal Pay Act 1970,

or by reason that the discriminator knows the person victimised
intends to do any of those things, or suspects the person
victimised has done, or intends to do, any of them.

(2) Subsection (1) does not apply to treatment of a person by
reason of any allegation made by him if the allegation was false
and not made in good faith.

(3) For the purposes of subsection (1), a provision of Part II
or III framed with reference to discrimination against women
shall be treated as applying equally to the treatment of men
and for that purpose shall have effect with such modifications
as are requisite.

5.—(1) In this Act —

(*a*) references to discrimination refer to any discrimination
falling within sections 1 to 4 ; and

(*b*) references to sex discrimination refer to any discrimination falling within section 1 or 2,

and related expressions shall be construed accordingly.

(2) In this Act—

" woman " includes a female of any age, and

" man " includes a male of any age.

(3) A comparison of the cases of persons of different sex or
marital status under section 1(1) or 3(1) must be such that the
relevant circumstances in the one case are the same, or not
materially different, in the other.

PART II

DISCRIMINATION IN THE EMPLOYMENT FIELD

Discrimination by employers

6.—(1) It is unlawful for a person, in relation to employment by him at an establishment in Great Britain, to discriminate
against a woman—

(*a*) in the arrangements he makes for the purpose of determining who should be offered that employment, or

(*b*) in the terms on which he offers her that employment, or

(*c*) by refusing or deliberately omitting to offer her that employment.

(2) It is unlawful for a person, in the case of a woman employed by him at an establishment in Great Britain, to discriminate against her—

(*a*) in the way he affords her access to opportunities for promotion, transfer or training, or to any other benefits, facilities or services, or by refusing or deliberately omitting to afford her access to them, or

(*b*) by dismissing her, or subjecting her to any other detriment.

(3) Except in relation to discrimination falling within section 4, subsections (1) and (2) do not apply to employment—

(*a*) for the purposes of a private household, or

(*b*) where the number of persons employed by the employer, added to the number employed by any associated employers of his, does not exceed five (disregarding any persons employed for the purposes of a private household).

(4) Subsections (1)(*b*) and (2) do not apply to provision in relation to death or retirement.

(5) Subject to section 8(3), subsection (1)(*b*) does not apply to any provision for the payment of money which, if the woman in question were given the employment, would be included (directly or by reference to a collective agreement or otherwise) in the contract under which she was employed.

(6) Subsection (2) does not apply to benefits consisting of the payment of money when the provision of those benefits is regulated by the woman's contract of employment.

(7) Subsection (2) does not apply to benefits, facilities or services of any description if the employer is concerned with the provision (for payment or not) of benefits, facilities or services of that description to the public, or to a section of the public comprising the woman in question, unless—

(*a*) that provision differs in a material respect from the provision of the benefits, facilities or services by the employer to his employees, or

(*b*) the provision of the benefits, facilities or services to the woman in question is regulated by her contract of employment, or

(*c*) the benefits, facilities or services relate to training.

7.—(1) In relation to sex discrimination—

(a) section 6(1)(a) or (c) does not apply to any employment where being a man is a genuine occupational qualification for the job, and

(b) section 6(2)(a) does not apply to opportunities for promotion or transfer to, or training for, such employment.

(2) Being a man is a genuine occupational qualification for a job only where—

(a) the essential nature of the job calls for a man for reasons of physiology (excluding physical strength or stamina) or, in dramatic performances or other entertainment, for reasons of authenticity, so that the essential nature of the job would be materially different if carried out by a woman ; or

(b) the job needs to be held by a man to preserve decency or privacy because—

(i) it is likely to involve physical contact with men in circumstances where they might reasonably object to its being carried out by a woman, or

(ii) the holder of the job is likely to do his work in circumstances where men might reasonably object to the presence of a woman because they are in a state of undress or are using sanitary facilities ; or

(c) the nature or location of the establishment makes it impracticable for the holder of the job to live elsewhere than in premises provided by the employer, and—

(i) the only such premises which are available for persons holding that kind of job are lived in, or normally lived in, by men and are not equipped with separate sleeping accommodation for women and sanitary facilities which could be used by women in privacy from men, and

(ii) it is not reasonable to expect the employer either to equip those premises with such accommodation and facilities or to provide other premises for women ; or

(d) the nature of the establishment, or of the part of it within which the work is done, requires the job to be held by a man because—

(i) it is, or is part of, a hospital, prison or other establishment for persons requiring special care, supervision or attention, and

(ii) those persons are all men (disregarding any woman whose presence is exceptional), and

(iii) it is reasonable, having regard to the essential character of the establishment or that part, that the job should not be held by a woman ; or

(e) the holder of the job provides individuals with personal services promoting their welfare or education, or similar personal services, and those services can most effectively be provided by a man, or

(f) the job needs to be held by a man because of restrictions imposed by the laws regulating the employment of women, or

(g) the job needs to be held by a man because it is likely to involve the performance of duties outside the United Kingdom in a country whose laws or customs are such that the duties could not, or could not effectively, be performed by a woman, or

(h) the job is one of two to be held by a married couple.

(3) Subsection (2) applies where some only of the duties of the job fall within paragraphs (a) to (g) as well as where all of them do.

(4) Paragraph (a), (b), (c), (d), (e), (f) or (g) of subsection (2) does not apply in relation to the filling of a vacancy at a time when the employer already has male employees—

(a) who are capable of carrying out the duties falling within that paragraph, and

(b) whom it would be reasonable to employ on those duties, and

(c) whose numbers are sufficient to meet the employer's likely requirements in respect of those duties without undue inconvenience.

8.—(1) In section 1 of the Equal Pay Act 1970, the following are substituted for subsections (1) to (3)—

" (1) If the terms of a contract under which a woman is employed at an establishment in Great Britain do not include (directly or by reference to a collective agreement or otherwise) an equality clause they shall be deemed to include one.

(2) An equality clause is a provision which relates to terms (whether concerned with pay or not) of a contract under which a woman is employed (the " woman's contract "), and has the effect that—

(a) where the woman is employed on like work with a man in the same employment—

(i) if (apart from the equality clause) any term of the woman's contract is or becomes less favourable to the woman than a term of a similar kind in the contract under which that man is employed, that term of the woman's contract shall be treated as so modified as not to be less favourable, and

(ii) if (apart from the equality clause) at any time the woman's contract does not include a term corresponding to a term benefiting that man included in the contract under which he is employed, the woman's contract shall be treated as including such a term ;

(b) where the woman is employed on work rated as equivalent with that of a man in the same employment—

(i) if (apart from the equality clause) any term of the woman's contract determined by the rating of the work is or becomes less favourable to the woman than a term of a similar kind in the contract under which that man is employed, that term of the woman's contract shall be treated as so modified as not to be less favourable, and

(ii) if (apart from the equality clause) at any time the woman's contract does not include a term corresponding to a term benefiting that man included in the contract under which he is employed and determined by the rating of the work, the woman's contract shall be treated as including such a term.

(3) An equality clause shall not operate in relation to a variation between the woman's contract and the man's contract if the employer proves that the variation is genuinely due to a material difference (other than the difference of sex) between her case and his."

(2) Section 1(1) of the Equal Pay Act 1970 (as set out in subsection (1) above) does not apply in determining for the purposes of section 6(1)(b) of this Act the terms on which employment is offered.

(3) Where a person offers a woman employment on certain terms, and if she accepted the offer then, by virtue of an equality clause, any of those terms would fall to be modified, or any additional term would fall to be included, the offer shall be taken to contravene section 6(1)(b).

(4) Where a person offers a woman employment on certain terms, and subsection (3) would apply but for the fact that, on her acceptance of the offer, section 1(3) of the Equal Pay Act 1970 (as set out in subsection (1) above) would prevent the equality clause from operating, the offer shall be taken not to contravene section 6(1)(b).

(5) An act does not contravene section 6(2) if—

(a) it contravenes a term modified or included by virtue of an equality clause, or

(b) it would contravene such a term but for the fact that the equality clause is prevented from operating by section 1(3) of the Equal Pay Act 1970.

(6) The Equal Pay Act 1970 is further amended as specified in Part I of Schedule 1, and accordingly has effect as set out in Part II of Schedule 1.

9.—(1) This section applies to any work for a person (" the principal ") which is available for doing by individuals (" contract workers ") who are employed not by, the principal himself but by another person, who supplies them under a contract made with the principal.

(2) It is unlawful for the principal, in relation to work to which this section applies, to discriminate against a woman who is a contract worker—

(a) in the terms on which he allows her to do that work, or

(b) by not allowing her to do it or continue to do it, or

(c) in the way he affords her access to any benefits, facilities or services or by refusing or deliberately omitting to afford her access to them, or

(d) by subjecting her to any other detriment.

(3) The principal does not contravene subsection (2)(b) by doing any act in relation to a woman at a time when if the work were to be done by a person taken into his employment being a man would be a genuine occupational qualification for the job.

(4) Subsection (2)(c) does not apply to benefits, facilities or services of any description if the principal is concerned with the provision (for payment or not) of benefits, facilities or services of that description to the public, or to a section of the public to which the woman belongs, unless that provision differs in a material respect from the provision of the benefits, facilities or services by the principal to his contract workers.

10.—(1) For the purposes of this Part and section 1 of the Equal Pay Act 1970 (" the relevant purposes "), employment is to be regarded as being at an establishment in Great Britain unless the employee does his work wholly or mainly outside Great Britain.

(2) Subsection (1) does not apply to—

(a) employment on board a ship registered at a port of registry in Great Britain, or (*b*) employment on aircraft or hovercraft registered in the United Kingdom and operated by a person who has his principal place of business, or is ordinarily resident, in Great Britain ;

but for the relevant purposes such employment is to be regarded as being at an establishment in Great Britain unless the employee does his work wholly outside Great Britain.

(3) In the case of employment on board a ship registered at a port of registry in Great Britain (except where the employee does his work wholly outside Great Britain, and outside any area added under subsection (5)) the ship shall for the relevant purposes be deemed to be the establishment.

(4) Where work is not done at an establishment it shall be treated for the relevant purposes as done at the establishment from which it is done or (where it is not done from any establishment) at the establishment with which it has the closest connection.

(5) In relation to employment concerned with exploration of the sea bed or subsoil or the exploitation of their natural resources, Her Majesty may by Order in Council provide that subsections (1) and (2) shall each have effect as if the last reference to Great Britain included any area for the time being designated under section 1(7) of the Continental Shelf Act 1964, except an area or part of an area in which the law of Northern Ireland applies.

(6) An Order in Council under subsection (5) may provide that, in relation to employment to which the Order applies, this Part and section 1 of the Equal Pay Act 1970 are to have effect with such modifications as are specified in the Order.

(7) An Order in Council under subsection (5) shall be of no effect unless a draft of the Order was laid before and approved by each House of Parliament.

Discrimination by other bodies

11.—(1) It is unlawful for a firm consisting of six or more partners, in relation to a position as partner in the firm, to discriminate against a woman—

(*a*) in the arrangements they make for the purpose of determining who should be offered that position, or

(*b*) in the terms on which they offer her that position, or

(*c*) by refusing or deliberately omitting to offer her that position, or

(*d*) in a case where the woman already holds that position—

    (i) in the way they afford her access to any benefits, facilities or services, or by refusing or deliberately omitting to afford her access to them, or

(ii) by expelling her from that position, or subjecting her to any other detriment.

(2) Subsection (1) shall apply in relation to persons proposing to form themselves into a partnership as it applies in relation to a firm.

(3) Subsection (1)(*a*) and (*c*) do not apply to a position as partner where, if it were employment, being a man would be a genuine occupational qualification for the job.

(4) Subsection (1)(*b*) and (*d*) do not apply to provision made in relation to death or retirement.

(5) In the case of a limited partnership references in subsection (1) to a partner shall be construed as references to a general partner as defined in section 3 of the Limited Partnerships Act 1907.

12.—(1) This section applies to an organisation of workers, an organisation of employers, or any other organisation whose members carry on a particular profession or trade for the purposes of which the organisation exists.

(2) It is unlawful for an organisation to which this section applies, in the case of a woman who is not a member of the organisation, to discriminate against her—

(*a*) in the terms on which it is prepared to admit her to membership, or

(*b*) by refusing, or deliberately omitting to accept, her application for membership.

(3) It is unlawful for an organisation to which this section applies, in the case of a woman who is a member of the organisation, to discriminate against her—

(*a*) in the way it affords her access to any benefits, facilities or services, or by refusing or deliberately omitting to afford her access to them, or

(*b*) by depriving her of membership, or varying the terms on which she is a member, or

(*c*) by subjecting her to any other detriment.

(4) This section does not apply to provision made in relation to the death or retirement from work of a member.

The Registration of Business Names Act, 1916

1. Subject to the provisions of this Act:

(*a*) Every firm having a place of business in the United Kingdom and carrying on business under a business name which does not consist of the true surnames of all partners who are individuals and the corporate names of all partners who are corporations without any addition other than the true Christian names of individual partners or initials of such Christian names;

(*b*) Every individual having a place of business in the United Kingdom and carrying on business under a business name which does not consist of his true surname without any addition other than his true Christian names or the initials thereof:

(*c*) Every individual or firm having a place of business in the United Kingdom, who, or a member of which, has either before or after the passing of this Act changed his name, except in the case of a woman in consequence of marriage;

shall be registered in the manner directed by this Act:

Provided that:

(i) where the addition merely indicates that the business is carried on in succession to a former owner of the business, that addition shall not of itself render registration necessary; and

(ii) where two or more individual partners have the same surname, the addition of an *s* at the end of that surname shall not of itself render registration necessary: and

(iii) where the business is carried on by a trustee in bankruptcy or a receiver or manager appointed by any court, registration shall not be necessary; and

(iv) a purchase or acquisition of property by two or more persons as joint tenants or tenants in common is not of itself to be deemed carrying on a business whether or not the owners share any profits arising from the sale thereof.

2. Where a firm, individual, or corporation having a place of business within the United Kingdom carries on the business wholly or mainly as nominee or trustee of or for another person, or other persons, or another corporation, or acts as general agent for any foreign firm, the first-mentioned firm, individual, or corporation shall be registered in manner provided by this Act, and, in addition to the other particulars required to be furnished and registered, there shall be furnished and registered the particulars mentioned in the schedule to this Act:

Provided that where the business is carried on by a trustee in bankruptcy or a receiver or manager appointed by any court, registration under this section shall not be necessary.

3.—(1) Every firm or person required under this Act to be registered shall furnish by sending by post or delivering to the registrar at the register office in that part of the United Kingdom in which the principal place of business of the firm or person is situated a statement in writing in the prescribed form containing the following particulars:

(*a*) The business name;

(*b*) The general nature of the business;

(*c*) The principal place of the business;

(*d*) Where the registration to be effected is that of a firm, the present Christian name and surname, any former Christian name or surname, the nationality, and if that nationality is not the nationality of origin, the nationality of origin, the usual residence, and the other business occupation (if any) of each of the individuals who are partners, and the corporate name and registered or principal office of every corporation which is a partner;

(*e*) Where the registration to be effected is that of an individual, the present Christian name and surname, any former Christian name or surname, the nationality, and if that nationality is not the nationality of origin, the nationality of origin, the usual residence, and the other business occupation (if any) of such individual;

(*f*) Where the registration to be effected is that of a corporation, its corporate name and registered or principal office;

(*g*) If the business is commenced after the passing of this Act, the date of the commencement of the business.

(2) Where a business is carried on under two or more business names, each of those business names must be stated.

4. The statement required for the purpose of registration must in the case of an individual be signed by him, and in the case of a corporation by a director or secretary thereof, and in the case of a firm either by all the individuals who are partners, and by a director or the secretary of all corporations which are partners or by some individual who is a partner, or a director or the secretary of some corporation which is a partner, and in either of the last two cases must be verified by a statutory declaration made by the signatory: Provided that no such statutory declaration stating that any person other than the declarant is a partner, or omitting to state that any person other than as aforesaid is a partner, shall be evidence for or against any such other person in respect of his liability or non-liability as a partner, and that the High Court or a judge thereof may on application of any person alleged or claiming to be a partner direct the rectification of the register and decide any question arising under this section.

5. The particulars required to be furnished under this Act shall be furnished within fourteen days after the firm of person commences business or the business in respect of which registration is required, as the case may be; Provided that if such firm or person has carried on such business before the passing of this Act or commences such business within two months thereafter, the statement of particulars shall be furnished after the expiration of two months and before the expiration of three months from the passing of this Act, and that if at the expiration of the said two months the conditions affecting the firm or persons have ceased to be such as to require registration under this Act, the firm or person need not be registered so long as such conditions continue.

This section shall apply, in the case where registration is required in consequence of a change of name, as if for references to the date of the commencement of the business there were substituted references to the date of such change.

6. Wherever a change is made or occurs in any of the particulars registered in respect of any firm or person such firm or person shall, within fourteen days after such change, or such longer period as the Board of Trade may, on application being made in any particular case, whether before or after the expiration of such fourteen days, allow, furnish by sending by post or delivery to the registrar in that part of the United Kingdom in which the aforesaid particulars are registered a statement in writing in the prescribed form specifying the nature and date of the change signed, and where necessary verified, in like manner as the statement required on registration.

7. If any firm or person by this Act required to furnish a statement of particulars or of any change in particulars shall without reasonable excuse make default in so doing in the manner and within the time specified by this Act, every partner in the firm or the person so in default shall be liable on summary conviction to a fine not exceeding five pounds for every day during which the default continues, and the court shall order a statement of the required particulars or change in the particulars to be furnished to the registrar within such time as may be specified in the order.

8.—(1) Where any firm or person by this Act required to furnish a statement of particulars or of any change in particulars shall have made default in so doing, then the rights of that defaulter under or arising out of any contract made or entered into by or on behalf of such defaulter in relation to the business in respect to the carrying on of which particulars were required to be furnished at any time while he is in default shall not be enforceable by action or other legal proceeding either in the business name or otherwise:

Provided always as follows:

    (*a*) The defaulter may apply to the Court for relief against the disability imposed by this section, and the Court, on being satisfied that the default was accidental, or due to inadvertence, or some other sufficient cause, or that on other grounds it is just and equitable to grant relief, may grant such relief either generally, or as respects any particular contracts, on condition of the costs of the application being paid by the defaulter, unless the Court otherwise orders, and on such other conditions (if any) as the Court may impose, but such relief shall not be granted except on such service and such publication of notice of the application as the Court may order, nor shall relief be given in respect of any contract if any party to the contract proves to the satisfaction of the Court that, if this Act has been complied with, he would not have entered into the contract;

(*b*) Nothing herein contained shall prejudice the rights of any other parties as against the defaulter in respect of such contract as aforesaid;

(*c*) If any action or proceeding shall be commenced by any other party against the defaulter to enforce the rights of such party in respect of such contract, nothing herein contained shall preclude the defaulter from enforcing in that action or proceeding, by way of counter-claim set off or otherwise, such rights as he may have against that party in respect of such contract.

(2) In this section the expression 'court' means the 'High Court' or a judge thereof:

Provided that, without prejudice to the power of the High Court or a judge thereof to grant such relief as aforesaid, if any proceeding to enforce any contract is commenced by a defaulter in a county court, the county court may, as respects that contract, grant such relief as aforesaid.

9. If any statement required to be furnished under this Act contains any matter which is false in any material particular to the knowledge of any person signing it, that person shall, on summary conviction, be liable to imprisonment with or without hard labour for a term not exceeding three months, or to a fine not exceeding twenty-pounds, or to both such imprisonment and fine.

10.—(1) The Board of Trade may require any person to furnish to the Board such particulars as appear necessary to the Board for the purpose of ascertaining whether or not he or the firm of which he is partner should be registered under this Act, or an alteration made in the registered particulars, and may also in the case of a corporation require the secretary or any other officer of a corporation performing the duties of secretary to furnish such particulars, and if any persons when so required fails to supply such particulars as it is in his power to give, or furnishes particulars which are false in any material particular, he shall on summary conviction be liable to imprisonment with or without hard labour for a term not exceeding three months or to a fine not exceeding twenty pounds or to both such imprisonment and fine.

(2) If from any information so furnished it appears to the Board of Trade that any firm or person ought to be registered under this Act, or an alteration ought to be made in the registered particulars, the Board may require the firm or person to furnish to the registrar the required particulars

within such times as may be allowed by the Board, but, where any default under this Act has been discovered from the information acquired under this section, no proceedings under this Act shall be taken against any person in respect of such default prior to the expiration of the time within which the firm or person is required by the Board under this section to furnish particulars to the registrar.

11. On receiving any statement or statutory declaration made in pursuance of this Act the registrar shall cause the same to be filed, and he shall send by post or deliver a certificate of the registration thereof to the firm or person registering and the certificate or a certified copy thereof shall be kept exhibited in a conspicuous position at the principal place of business of the firm or individual, and if not kept so exhibited, every partner in the firm or the person, as the case may be, shall be liable on summary conviction to a fine not exceeding twenty pounds.

12. At each of the register offices herein-after referred to the registrar shall keep an index of all the firms and persons registered at that office under this Act.

13.—(1) If any firm or individual registered under this Act ceases to carry on business, it shall be the duty of the persons who were partners in the firm at the time when it ceased to carry on business or of the individual or if he is dead his personal representative, within three months after the business has ceased to be carried on, to send by post or deliver to the registrar notice in the prescribed form that the firm or individual has ceased to carry on business, and if any person whose duty it is to give such notice fails to do so within such time as aforesaid, he shall be liable on summary conviction to a fine not exceeding twenty pounds.

(2) On receipt of such a notice as aforesaid the registrar may remove the firm or individual from the register.

(3) Where the registrar has reasonable cause to believe that any firm or individual registered under this Act is not carrying on business he may send to the firm or individual by registered post a notice that, unless an answer is received to such notice within one month from the date thereof, the firm or individual may be removed from the register.

(4) If the registrar either receives an answer from the firm or individual to the effect that the firm or individual is not carrying on business or does not within one month after sending the notice receive an answer, he may remove the firm or individual from the register.

14.—(1) Where any business name under which the business of a firm or individual is carried on contains the word 'British' or any other word which, in the opinion of the registrar, is calculated to lead to the belief that the business is under British ownership or control, and the registrar is satisfied that the nationality of the persons by whom the business is wholly or mainly owned or controlled is at any time such that the name is misleading, the registrar shall refuse to registrer such business name or, as the case may be, remove such business name from the register, but any person aggrieved by a decision of the registrar under this provision may appeal to the Board of Trade, whose decision shall be final.

(2) The registration of a business name under this Act shall not be con-

strued as authorising the use of that name if apart from such registration the use thereof could be prohibited.

15. There shall be offices in London, Edinburgh, and Dublin for the registration of firms and persons whose principal places of business are respectively situated in England and Wales, Scotland, and Ireland, and the registrar of companies in each of those cities or such other person as the Board of Trade may determine shall be the registrar for the purposes of this Act.

16. At any time after the expiration of six months from the passing of this Act or of such longer period, not being more than nine months from the passing of this Act, as the Board of Trade may by order direct, any person may inspect the documents filed by the registrar on payment of such fees as may be prescribed not exceeding one shilling for each inspection; and any person may require a certificate of the registration of any firm or person, or a copy of or extract from any registered statement to be certified by the registrar or assistant registrar, and there shall be paid for such certificate of registration, certified copy, or extract such fees as may be prescribed not exceeding two shillings for the certificate of registration, and not exceeding sixpence for each folio of seventy-two words, or in Scotland for each sheet of two hundred words, of the entry, copy, or extract.

A certificate of registration, or a copy of or extract from any statement registered under this Act, if duly certified to be a true copy or extract under the hand of the registrar or one of the assistant registrars (whom it shall not be necessary to prove to be the registrar or assistant registrar) shall, in all legal proceedings, civil or criminal, be received in evidence.

17.—(1) The Board of Trade may make rules (but as to fees with the concurrence of the Treasury) concerning any of the following matters:

(*a*) The fees to be paid to the registrar under this Act, so that they do not exceed the sum of five shillings for the registration of any one statement;

(*b*) The forms to be used under this Act;

(*c*) The duties to be performed by any registrar under this Act;

(*d*) The performance by assistant registrars and other officers of acts by this Act required to be done by the registrar;

(*e*) Generally the conduct and regulation of registration under this Act, and any matters incidental thereto.

(2) All fees payable in pursuance of any such rules shall be applied as the Treasury may direct.

18.—(1) After the expiration of three months from the passing of this Act every individual and firm required by this Act to be registered shall, in all trade catalogues, trade circulars, showcards, and business letters, on or in which the business name appears and which are issued or sent by the individual or firm to any person in any part of His Majesty's dominions, have mentioned in legible characters:

(*a*) in the case of an individual, his present Christian name or the initials thereof and present surname, any former Christian name or surname, his nationality if not British, and if his nationality is not his nationality of origin his nationality of origin; and (*b*) in the case of a firm, the present Christian names, or the initials thereof and present surnames, any former Christian names and surnames, and the nationality if not British, and if the nationality is not the nationality of origin the nationality of origin of all the partners in the firm or, in the case of a corporation being a partner, the corporate name.

(2) If default is made in compliance with this section the individual or, as the case may be, every member of the firm shall be liable on summary conviction for each offence to a fine not exceeding five pounds:

Provided that no proceedings shall in England or Ireland be instituted under this section except by or with the consent of the Board of Trade.

19. Where a corporation is guilty of an offence under this Act every director, secretary, and officer of the corporation who is knowingly a party to the default shall be guilty of a like offence and liable to a like penalty.

20. Anything required or authorised by this Act to be done by the Board of Trade may be done by the President or a Secretary or Assistant Secretary of the Board, or any other person authorized in that behalf by the President of the Board.

21. There shall be paid out of moneys to be provided by Parliament such remuneration in respect of the duties performed under this Act as the Treasury may assign.

22. In the construction of this Act the following words and expressions shall have the meanings in this section assigned to them, unless there be something in the subject or context repugnant to such construction:

'Firm' shall mean an unincorporate body of two or more individuals, or one or more individuals and one or more corporations, or two or more corporations, who have entered into partnership with one another with a view to carrying on business for profit, but shall not include any unincorporated company which was in existence on the second day of November eighteen hundred and sixty-two:

'Business' shall include profession:

'Individual' shall mean a natural person and shall not include a corporation:

'Christian name' shall include any forename:

'Initials' shall include any recognised abbreviation of a Christian name:

In the case of a peer or person usually known by a British title different from his surname, the title by which he is known shall be substituted in this Act for his surname:

References in this Act to a former Christian name or surname shall not, in the case of natural-born British subjects, include a former Christian name or surname where that name or surname has been changed or disused before the person bearing the name had attained the age of eighteen years, and, in the case of a married woman, shall not include the name or surname by which she was known previous to the marriage:

References in this Act to a change of name shall not include, in the case of natural-born British subjects, a change of name which has taken place before the person whose name has been changed has attained the age of eighteen years; or, in the case of a peer or a person usually known by a British title different from his surname, the adoption of or succession to the title:

'Business name' shall mean the name or style under which any business is carried on, wehther in partnership or otherwise:

'Foreign firm' shall mean any firm, individual, or corporation whose principal place of business is situate outside His Majesty's dominions.

'Showcards' shall mean cards containing or exhibiting articles dealt with, or samples or representations thereof:

'Prescribed' shall mean prescribed by rules made in pursuance of this Act.

23.—(1) In the application of this Act to Scotland:

'Court of Session' shall be substituted for 'High Court';

'Sheriff court' shall be substituted for 'county court';

'Trustee on a sequestrated estate' shall be substituted for 'trustee in bankruptcy';

'Receiver or manager appointed by any Court' shall include 'judicial factor'; and

'Joint tenants' and 'tenants in common' shall mean *pro indiviso* proprietors.

24. In the application of this Act to Ireland the expression 'trustee in bankruptcy' shall be construed as including an assignee in bankruptcy and a trustee of the estate of an arranging debtor.

25. This Act may be cited as the Registration of Business Names Act, 1916.

SCHEDULE

Description of Firm, &c.	The additional Particulars
Where the firm, individual, or corporation required to be registered carries on business as nominee or trustee.	The present Christian name and surname, any former name, nationality, and, if that nationality is not the nationality of origin, the nationality of origin, and usual residence, or, as the case may be, the corporate name, of every person or corporation on whose behalf the business is carried on: Provided that if the business is carried on under any trust and any of the beneficiaries are a class of children or other persons, a description of the class shall be sufficient.

SCHEDULE (*cont.*)

Description of Firm, &c.	The additional Particulars
Where the firm, individual, or corporation required to be registered carries on business as general agent for any foreign firm.	The business name and address of the firm or person as agent for whom the business is carried on: Provided that if the business is carried on as agent for three or more foreign firms it shall be sufficient to state the fact that the business is so carried on, specifying the countries in which such foreign firms carry on business.

The Partnership Act, 1890

Nature of Partnership

1.—(1) Partnership is the relation which subsists between persons carrying on a business in common with a view of profit.

(2) But the relation between members of any company or association which is—

(a) Registered as a company under the Companies Act, 1862, or any other Act of Parliament for the time being in force and relating to the registration of joint stock companies; or

(b) Formed or incorporated by or in pursuance of any other Act of Parliament or letters patent, or Royal Charter; or

(c) A company engaged in working mines within and subject to the jurisdiction of the Stannaries:

is not a partnership within the meaning of this Act.

2. In determining whether a partnership does or does not exist, regard shall be had to the following rules:

(1) Joint tenancy, tenancy in common, joint property, common property or part ownership does not of itself create a partnership as to anything so held or owned, whether the tenants or owners do or do not share any profits made by the use thereof.

(2) The sharing of gross returns does not of itself create a partnership, whether the persons sharing such returns have or have not a joint or

common right or interest in any property from which or from the use of which the returns are derived.

(3) The receipt by a person of a share of the profits of a business is prima facie evidence that he is a partner in the business, but the receipt of such a share, or of a payment contingent on or varying with the profits of a business, does not of itself make him a partner in the business; and in particular:

(*a*) The receipt by a person of a debt or other liquidated amount by instalments, or otherwise out of the accruing profits of a business does not of itself make him a partner in the business or business or liable as such:

(*b*) A contract for the remuneration of a servant or agent of a person engaged in a business by a share of the profits of the business does not of itself make the servant or agent a partner in the business or liable as such:

(*c*) A person being the widow or child of a deceased partner, and receiving by way of annuity a portion of the profits made in the business in which the deceased person was a partner, is not by reason only of such receipt a partner in the business or liable as such:

(*d*) The advance of money by way of loan to a person engaged or about to engage in any business on a contract with that person that the lender shall receive a rate of interest varying with the profits, or shall receive a share of the profits arising from carrying on the business, does not of itself make the lender a partner with the person or persons carrying on the business or liable as such. Provided that the contract is in writing, and signed by or on behalf of all the parties thereto:

(*e*) A person receiving by way of annuity or otherwise a portion of the profits of a business in consideration of the sale by him of the goodwill of the business is not by reason only of such receipt a partner in the business or liable as such.

3. In the event of any person to whom money has been advanced by way of loan upon such a contract as is mentioned in the last foregoing section, or of any buyer of a goodwill in consideration of a share of the profits of the business, being adjudged a bankrupt, entering into an arrangement to pay his creditors less than twenty shillings in the pound, or dying in insolvent circumstances, the lender of the loan shall not be entitled to recover anything in respect of his loan, and the seller of the goodwill shall not be entitled to recover anything in respect of the share of profits contracted for, until the claims of the other creditors of the borrower or buyer for valuable consideration in money or money's worth have been satisfied.

4.—(1) Persons who have entered into partnership with one another are for the purposes of this Act called collectively a firm, and the name under which their business is carried on is called the firm-name.

(2) In Scotland a firm is a legal person distinct from the partners of whom it is composed, but an individual partner may be charged on a decree or diligence directed against the firm, and on payment of the debts is entitled to relief *pro rata* from the firm and its other members.

Relations of Partners to Persons Dealing with Them

5. Every partner is an agent of the firm and his other partners for the purpose of the business of the partnership; and the acts of every partner who does any act for carrying on in the usual way business of the kind carried on by the firm of which he is a member bind the firm and his partness, unless the partner so acting has in fact no authority to act for the firm in the particular matter, and the person with whom he is dealing either knows that he has no authority, or does not know or believe him to be a partner.

6. An act or instrument relating to the business of the firm and done or executed in the firm-name, or in any other manner showing an intention to bind the firm, by any person thereto authorized, whether a partner or not, is binding on the firm and all the partners.

Provided that this section shall not affect any general rule of law relating to the execution of deeds or negotiable instruments.

7. Where one partner pledges the credit of the firm for a purpose apparently not connected with the firm's ordinary course of business, the firm is not bound, unless he is in fact specially authorized by the other partners; but this section does not affect any personal liability incurred by an individual partner.

8. If it has been agreed between the partners that any restriction shall be placed on the power of any one or more of them to bind the firm, no act done in contravention of the agreement is binding on the firm, with respect to persons having notice of the agreement.

9. Every partner in a firm is liable jointly with the other partners, and in Scotland severally also, for all debts and obligations of the firm incurred while he is a partner; and after his death his estate is also severally liable in a due course of administration for such debts and obligations, so far as they remain unsatisfied, but subject in England or Ireland to the prior payment of his separate debts.

10. Where, by any wrongful act or omission of any partner acting in the ordinary course of the business of the firm, or with the authority of his co-partners, loss or injury is caused to any person not being a partner in the firm, or any penalty is incurred, the firm is liable therefor to the same extent as the partner so acting or omitting to act.

11. In the following cases; namely—
   (a) Where one partner acting within the scope of his apparent authority receives the money or property of a third person and misapplies it; and
   (b) Where a firm in the course of its business receives money or property of a third person, and the money or property so received is misapplied by one or more of the partners while it is in the custody of the firm;

the firm is liable to make good the loss.

12. Every partner is liable jointly with his co-partners and also severally for everything for which the firm while he is a partner therein becomes liable under either of the two last preceding sections.

13. If a partner, being a trustee, improperly employs trust-property in the business or on the account of the partnership, no other partner is liable for the trust-property to the persons beneficially interested therein.

Provided as follows:—

(1) This section shall not affect any liability incurred by any partner by reason of his having notice of a breach of trust; and

(2) Nothing in this section shall prevent trust money from being followed and recovered from the firm if still in its possession or under its control.

14.—(1) Every one who by words spoken or written or by conduct represents himself, or who knowingly suffers himself to be represented, as a partner in a particular firm, is liable as a partner to any one who has on the faith of any such representation given credit to the firm, whether the representation has or has not been made or communicated to the person so giving credit by or with the knowledge of the apparent partner making the representation or suffering it to be made.

(2) Provided that where after a partner's death the partnership business is continued in the old firm-name, the continued use of that name or of the deceased partner's name as part thereof shall not of itself make his executors' or administrators' estate or effects liable for any partnership debts contracted after his death.

15. An admission or representation made by any partner concerning the partnership affairs and in the ordinary course of its business, is evidence against the firm.

16. Notice to any partner who habitually acts in the partnership business of any matter relating to partnership affairs operates as notice to the firm, except in the case of a fraud on the firm committed by or with the consent of that partner.

17.—(1) A person who is admitted as a partner into an existing firm does not thereby become liable to the creditors of the firm for anything done before he became a partner.

(2) A partner who retires from a firm does not thereby cease to be liable for partnership debts or obligations incurred before his retirement.

(3) A retiring partner may be discharged from any existing liabilities, by an agreement to that effect between himself and the members of the firm as newly constituted and the creditors, and this agreement may be either express or inferred as a fact from the course of dealing between the creditors and the firm as newly constituted.

18. A continuing guaranty or cautionary obligation given either to a firm or to a third person in respect of the transactions of a firm is, in the absence of agreement to the contrary, revoked as to future transactions by any constitution of the firm to which, or of the firm in respect of the transactions of which, the guaranty or obligation was given.

Relations of Partners to One Another

19. The mutual rights and duties of partners, whether ascertained by agreement or defined by this Act, may be varied by the consent of all the partners, and such consent may be either express or inferred from a course of dealing.

20.—(1) All property and rights and interests in property originally brought into the partnership stock or acquired, whether by purchase or otherwise, on account of the firm or for the purposes and in the course of the partnership business, are called in this Act partnership property and must be held and applied by the partners exclusively for the purposes of the partnership and in accordance with the partnership agreement.

(2) Provided that the legal estate or interest in any land, or in Scotland the title to and interest in any heritable estate, which belongs to the partnership shall devolve according to the nature and tenure thereof, and the general rules of law thereto applicable, but in trust, so far as necessary, for the persons beneficially interested in the land under this section.

(3) Where co-owners of an estate or interest in any land, or in Scotland of any heritable estate, not being itself partnership property, are partners as to profits made by the use of that land or estate, and purchase other land or estate out of the profits to be used in like manner the land or estate so purchased belongs to them, in the absence of an agreement to the contrary, not as partners but as co-owners for the same respective estates and interests as are held by them in the land or estate first mentioned at the date of the purchase.

21. Unless the contrary intention appears, property bought with money belonging to the firm is deemed to have been bought on account of the firm.

22. Where land or any heritable interest therein has become partnership property, it shall, unless the contrary intention appears, be treated as between the partners (including the representatives of a deceased partner), and also as between the heirs of a deceased partner and his executors or administrators, as personal or moveable and not real or heritable estate.

23.—(1) After the commencement of this Act a writ of execution shall not issue against any partnership property except on a judgement against the firm.

(2) The High Court, or a judge thereof, or the Chancery Court of the county palatine of Lancaster, or a county court, may, on the application by summons of any judgment creditor of a partner, make an order charging that partner's interest in the partnership property and profits with payment of the amount of the judgment debt and interest thereon, and may by the same or a subsequent order appoint a receiver of that partner's share of profits (whether already declared or accruing), and of any other money which may be coming to him in respect of the partnership, and direct all accounts and inquiries, and give all other orders and directions which might have been directed or given if the charge had been made in favour of the judgment creditor by the partner, or which the circumstances of the case may require.

(3) The other partner or partners shall be at liberty at any time to redeem the interest charged, or in case of a sale being directed, to purchase the same.

(4) This section shall apply in the case of a cost-book company as if the company were a partnership within the meaning of this Act.

(5) This section shall not apply to Scotland.

24. The interests of partners in the partnership property and their rights and duties in relation to the partnership shall be determined, subject to any agreement express or implied between the partners, by the following rules:

(1) All the partners are entitled to share equally in the capital and profits of the business, and must contribute equally towards the losses whether of capital or otherwise sustained by the firm.

(2) The firm must indemnify every partner in respect of payments made and personal liabilities incurred by him:

(*a*) In the ordinary and proper conduct of the business of the firm; or,

(*b*) In or about anything necessarily done for the preservation of the business or property of the firm.

(3) A partner making, for the purpose of the partnership, any actual payment or advance beyond the amount of capital which he has agreed to subscribe, is entitled to interest at the rate of five per cent per annum from the date of the payment or advance.

(4) A partner is not entitled, before the ascertainment of profits, to interest on the capital subscribed by him.

(5) Every partner may take part in the management of the partnership business.

(6) No partner shall be entitled to remuneration for acting in the partnership business.

(7) No person may be introduced as a partner without the consent of all existing partners.

(8) Any difference arising as to ordinary matters connected with the partnership business may be decided by a majority of the partners, but no change may be made in the nature of the partnership business without the consent of all existing partners.

(9) The partnership books are to be kept at the place of business of the partnership (or the principal place, if there is more than one), and every partner may, when he thinks fit, have access to and inspect and copy any of them.

25. No majority of the partners can expel any partner unless a power to do so has been conferred by express agreement between the partners.

26.—(1) Where no fixed term has been agreed upon for the duration of the partnership, any partner may determine the partnership at any time on giving notice of his intention so to do to all the other partners.

(2) Where the partnership has originally been constituted by deed, a notice in writing, signed by the partner giving it, shall be sufficient for this purpose.

27.—(1) Where a partnership entered into for a fixed term is continued after the term has expired, and without any express new agreement, the rights and duties of the partners remain the same as they were at the expiration of the term, so far as is consistent with the incidents of a partnership at will.

(2) A continuance of the business by the partners or such of them as habitually acted therein during the term, without any settlement or liquidation of the partnership affairs, is presumed to be a continuance of the partnership.

28. Partners are bound to render true accounts and full information of all things affecting the partnership to any partner or his legal representatives.

29.—(1) Every partner must account to the firm for any benefit derived by him without the consent of the other partners from any transaction concerning the partnership, or from any use by him of the partnership property name or business connexion.

(2) This section applies also to transactions undertaken after a partnership has been dissolved by the death of a partner, and before the affairs thereof have been completely wound up, either by any surviving partner or by the representatives of the deceased partner.

30. If a partner, without the consent of the other partners, carries on any business of the same nature as and competing with that of the firm, he must account for and pay over to the firm all profits made by him in that business.

31.—(1) An assignment by any partner of his share in the partnership, either absolute or by way of mortgage or redeemable charge, does not, as against the other partners, entitle the assignee, during the continuance of the partnership, to interfere in the management or administration of the partnership business or affairs, or to require any accounts of the partnership transactions, or to inspect the partnership books, but entitles the assignee only to receive the share of profits to which the assigning partner would otherwise be entitled, and the assignee must accept the account of profits agreed to by the partners.

(2) In case of a dissolution of the partnership, whether as respects all the partners or as respects the assigning partner, the assignee is entitled to receive the share of the partnership assets to which the assigning partner is entitled as between himself and the other partners, and, for the purpose of ascertaining that share, to an account as from the date of the dissolution.

Dissolution of Partnership, and its Consequences

32. Subject to any agreement between the partners a partnership is dissolved:

(*a*) If entered into for a fixed term, by the expiration of that term:

(*b*) If entered into for a single adventure or undertaking, by the termination of that adventure or undertaking:

(*c*) If entered into for an undefined time, by any partner giving notice to the other or others of his intention to dissolve the partnership.

In the last-mentioned case the partnership is dissolved as from the date mentioned in the notice as the date of dissolution, or, if no date is so mentioned, as from the date of the communication of the notice.

33.—(1) Subject to any agreement between the partners, every partnership is dissolved as regards all the partners by the death or bankruptcy of any partner.

(2) A partnership may, at the option of the other partners, be dissolved if any partner suffers his share of the partnership property to be charged under this Act for his separate debt.

34. A partnership is in every case dissolved by the happening of any event which makes it unlawful for the business of the firm to be carried on or for the members of the firm to carry it on in partnership.

35. On application by a partner the Court may decree a dissolution of the partnership in any of the following cases:

(*a*) When a partner is found lunatic by inquisition, or in Scotland by cognition, or is shown to the satisfaction of the Court to be of permanently unsound mind, in either of which cases the application may be made as well on behalf of that partner by his committee or next friend or person having title to intervene as by any other partner:

(*b*) When a partner, other than the partner suing, becomes in any other way permanently incapable of performing his part of the partnership contract:

(*c*) When a partner, other than the partner suing, has been guilty of such conduct as, in the opinion of the Court, regard being had to the nature of the business, is calculated to prejudicially affect the carrying on of the business:

(*d*) When a partner, other than the partner suing, wilfully or persistently commits a breach of the partnership agreement, or otherwise so conducts himself in matters relating to the partnership business that it is not reasonably practicable for the other partner or partners to carry on the business in partnership with him:

(*e*) When the business of the partnership can only be carried on at a loss:

(*f*) Whenever in any case circumstances have arisen which, in the opinion of the Court, render it just and equitable that the partnership be dissolved.

36.—(1) Where a person deals with a firm after a change in its constitution he is entitled to treat all apparent members of the old firm as still being members of the firm until he has notice of the change.

(2) An advertisement in the London Gazette as to a firm whose principal place of business is in England or Wales, in the Edinburgh Gazette as to a firm whose principal place of business is in Scotland, and in the Dublin Gazette as to a firm whose principal place of business is in Ireland, shall be notice as to persons who had not dealings with the firm before the date of the dissolution or change so advertised.

(3) The estate of a partner who dies, or who becomes bankrupt, or of a partner who, not having been known to the person dealing with the firm to be a partner, retires from the firm, is not liable for partnership debts, contracted after the date of the death, bankruptcy, or retirement respectively.

37. On the dissolution of a partnership or retirement of a partner any partner may publicly notify the same, and may require the other partner or partners to concur for that purpose in all necessary or proper acts, if any, which cannot be done without his or their concurrence.

38. After the dissolution of a partnership the authority of each partner to bind the firm, and the other rights and obligations of the partners, continue notwithstanding the dissolution so far as may be necessary to wind up the affairs of the partnership, and to complete transactions begun but unfinished at the time of the dissolution, but not otherwise.

Provided that the firm is in no case bound by the acts of a partner who has become bankrupt; but this proviso does not affect the liability of any person who has after the bankruptcy represented himself or knowingly suffered himself to be represented as a partner of the bankrupt.

39. On the dissolution of a partnership every partner is entitled, as against the other partners in the firm, and all persons claiming through them in respect of their interests as partners, to have the property of the partnership applied in payment of the debts and liabilities of the firm, and to have the surplus assets after such payment applied in payment of what may be due to the partners respectively after deducting what may be due from them as partners to the firm; and for that purpose any partner or his representatives may on the termination of the partnership apply to the Court to wind up the business and affairs of the firm.

40. Where one partner has paid a premium to another on entering into a partnership for a fixed term, and the partnership is dissolved before the expiration of that term otherwise than by the death of a partner, the Court may order the repayment of the premium, or of such part thereof as it thinks just, having regard to the terms of the partnership contract and to the the length of time during which the partnership has continued; unless

(a) the dissolution is, in the judgment of the Court, wholly or chiefly due to the misconduct of the partner who paid the premium, or

(b) the partnership has been dissolved by an agreement containing no provision for a return of any part of the premium.

41. Where a partnership contract is rescinded on the ground of the fraud or misrepresentation of one of the parties thereto, the party entitled to rescind is, without prejudice to any other right, entitled:

(a) to a lien on, or right of retention of, the surplus of the partnership assets, after satisfying the partnership liabilities, for any sum of money paid by him for the purchase of a share in the partnership and for any capital contributed by him, and is

(b) to stand in the place of the creditors of the firm for any payments made by him in respect of the partnership liabilities, and

(c) to be indemnified by the person guilty of the fraud or making the representation against all the debts and liabilities of the firm.

42.—(1) Where any member of a firm has died or otherwise ceased to be a partner, and the surviving or continuing partners carry on the business of the firm with its capital or assets without any final settlement of accounts as between the firm and the outgoing partner or his estate, then, in the absence of any agreement to the contrary, the outgoing partner or his estate is entitled at the option of himself or his representatives to such share of the profits made since the dissolution as the Court may find to be attributable to the use of his share of the partnership assets, or to interest at the rate of five per cent per annum on the amount of his share of the partnership assets.

(2) Provided that where by the partnership contract an option is given to surviving or continuing partners to purchase the interest of a deceased or outgoing partner, and that option is duly exercised, the estate of the deceased partner, or the outgoing partner or his estate, as the case may be,

is not entitled to any further or other share of profits; but if any partner assuming to act in exercise of the option does not in all material respects comply with the terms thereof, he is liable to account under the foregoing provisions of this section.

43. Subject to any agreement between the partners, the amount due from surviving or continuing partners to an outgoing partner or the representatives of a deceased partner in respect of the outgoing or deceased partner's share is a debt accruing at the date of the dissolution or death.

44. In settling accounts between the partners after a dissolution of partnership, the following rules shall, subject to any agreement, be observed:

(*a*) Losses, including losses and deficiences of capital, shall be paid first out of profits, next out of capital, and lastly, if necessary, by the partners individually in the proportion in which they were entitled to share profits:

(*b*) The assets of the firm including the sums, if any, contributed by the partners to make up losses or deficiencies of capital, shall be applied in the following manner and order:

1. In paying the debts and liabilities of the firm to persons who are not partners therein:
2. In paying to each partner rateably what is due from the firm to him for advances as distinguished from capital:
3. In paying to each partner rateably what is due from the firm to him in respect of capital:
4. The ultimate residue, if any, shall be divided among the partners in the proportion in which the profits are divisible.

Supplemental

45. In this Act, unless the contrary intention appears:

The expression 'court' includes every Court and judge having jurisdiction in the case:

The expression 'business' includes every trade, occupation, or profession.

46. The rules of equity and of common law applicable to partnership shall continue in force except so far as they are inconsistent with the express provisions of this Act.

47.—(1) In the application of this Act to Scotland the bankruptcy of a firm or of an individual shall mean sequestration under the Bankruptcy (Scotland) Acts, and also in the case of an individual the issue against him of a decree of *cessio bonorum.*

(2) Nothing in this Act shall alter the rules of the law of Scotland relating to the bankruptcy of a firm or of the individual partners thereof.

48.—The Acts mentioned in the schedule to this Act are hereby repealed to the extent mentioned in the third column of that schedule.

49. This Act shall come into operation on the first day of January one thousand eight hundred and ninety-one.

50. This Act may be cited as the Partnership Act, 1890.

Sample Memorandum and Articles of Association

No. 123456

No. 123456

The Companies Act, 1948

COMPANY LIMITED BY SHARES

MEMORANDUM

AND

ARTICLES OF ASSOCIATION

OF

SWISH LIMITED

(*A Private Company adopting Part II of Table A with modifications*)

Incorporated the 18th day of December, 1967

MEMORANDUM OF ASSOCIATION

1. The name of the Company is 'SWISH LIMITED'.
2. The registered office of the Company will be situate in England.
3. The objects for which the Company is established are:
   (A) To carry on the business of a self-service launderette or launderettes either on the system known as the Bendix System, or on any other system, the business of manufacturers, repairers, hirers, servicers and dealers in washing machines or parts or components thereof, the business of launderers, cleaners, dry cleaners, dyers, carpet and upholstery cleaners and dyers, and the business of repairing or renovating, altering, waterproofing, mending or invisibly mending all articles or goods left with or sent to the Company for laundering, cleaning, dry cleaning or dyeing.
   (B) To carry on any other trade or business whatsoever which can, in the opinion of the Board of Directors, be advantageously carried on by the Company in connexion with or as ancillary to any of the above businesses or the general business of the Company.
   (C) To purchase, taken on lease or in exchange, hire or otherwise acquire and hold for any estate or interest any lands, buildings, easements, rights, privileges, concessions, patents, patent rights, licences, secret processes, machinery, plant, stock-in-trade, and any real or personal property of any kind necessary or convenient for the purposes of or in connexion with the Company's business or any branch or department thereof.
   (D) To erect, construct, lay down, enlarge, alter and maintain any roads, railways, tramways, sidings, bridges, reservoirs, shops, stores, factories, buildings, works, plant and machinery necessary or convenient for the Company's business, and to contribute to or subsidise the erection, construction and maintenance of any of the above.
   (E) To borrow or raise or secure the payment of money for the purposes of or in connexion with the Company's business, and for the purposes of or in connexion with the borrowing or raising of money by the Company to become a member of any building society.
   (F) To mortgage and charge the undertaking and all or any of the real and personal property and assets, present or future, and all or any of the uncalled capital for the time being of the Company, and to issue at par or at a premium or discount, and for such consideration and with and subject to such rights, powers, privileges and conditions as may be thought fit, debentures or debenture stock, either permanent or redeemable or repayable, and collaterally or further to secure any securities of the Company by a trust deed or other assurance.
   (G) To issue and deposit any securities which the Company has power to issue by way of mortgage to secure any sum less than the nominal amount of such securities, and also by way of security for the performance of any contracts or obligations of the Company

or of its customers or other persons or corporations having dealings with the Company, or in whose businesses or undertakings the Company is interested, whether directly or indirectly.

(H) To receive money on deposit or loan upon such terms as the Company may approve, and to guarantee the obligations and contracts of customers and others.

(I) To make advances to customers and others with or without security, and upon such terms as the Company may approve, and generally to act as bankers for customers and others.

(J) To grant pensions, allowances, gratuities and bonuses to officers, ex-officers, employees or ex-employees of the Company or its predecessors in business or the dependants or connexions of such persons, to establish and maintain or concur in establishing and maintaining trusts, funds or schemes (whether contributory or non-contributory) with a view to providing pensions or other benefits for any such persons as aforesaid, their dependants or connexions, and to support or subscribe to any charitable funds or institutions, the support of which may, in the opinion of the Directors, be calculated directly or indirectly to benefit the Company or its employees, and to institute and maintain any club or other establishment or profit-sharing scheme calculated to advance the interests of the Company or its officers or employees.

(K) To draw, make, accept, endorse, negotiate, discount and execute promissory notes, bills of exchange and other negotiable instruments.

(L) To invest and deal with the moneys of the Company not immediately required for the purposes of its business in or upon such investments or securities and in such manner as may from time to time be determined.

(M) To pay for any property or rights acquired by the Company, either in cash or fully or partly paid-up shares, with or without preferred or deferred or special rights or restrictions in respect of dividend, repayment of capital, voting or otherwise, or by any securities which the Company has power to issue, or partly in one mode and partly in another, and generally on such terms as the Company may determine.

(N) To accept payment for any property or rights sold or otherwise disposed of or dealt with by the Company, either in cash, by instalments or otherwise, or in fully or partly paid-up shares of any company or corporation, with or without deferred or preferred or special rights or restrictions in respect of dividend, repayment of capital, voting or otherwise, or in debentures or mortgage debentures or debenture stock, mortgages or other securities of any company or corporation, or partly in one mode and partly in another, and generally on such terms as the Company may determine, and to hold, dispose of or otherwise deal with any shares, stock or securities so acquired.

(o) To enter into any partnership or joint-purse arrangement or arrangement for sharing profits, union of interests or co-operation with any company, firm or person carrying on or proposing to carry on any business within the objects of this Company, and to acquire and hold, sell, deal with or dispose of shares, stock or securities of any such company, and to guarantee the contracts or liabilities of, or the payment of the dividends, interest or capital of any shares, stock or securities of and to subsidize or otherwise assist any such company.

(p) To establish or promote or concur in establishing or promoting any other company whose objects shall include the acquisition and taking over of all or any of the assets and liabilities of this Company or the promotion of which shall be in any manner calculated to advance directly or indirectly the objects or interests of this Company, and to acquire and hold or dispose of shares, stock or securities of and guarantee the payment of the dividends, interest or capital of any shares, stock or securities issued by or any other obligations of any such company.

(q) To purchase or otherwise acquire and undertake all or any part of the business, property, assets, liabilities and transactions of any person, firm or company carrying on any business which this Company is authorized to carry on.

(r) To sell, improve, manage, develop, turn to account, exchange, let on rent, royalty, share of profits or otherwise, grant licences, easements and other rights in or over, and in any other manner deal with or dispose of the undertaking and all or any of the property and assets for the time being of the Company for such consideration as the Company may think fit.

(s) To amalgamate with any other company whose objects are or include objects similar to those of this Company, whether by sale or purchase (for fully or partly paid-up shares or otherwise) of the undertaking, subject to the liabilities of this or any such other company as aforesaid, with or without winding up, or by sale or purchase (for fully or partly paid-up shares or otherwise) of all or a controlling interest in the shares or stock of this or any such other company as aforesaid, or by partnership, or any arrangement of the nature of partnership, or in any other manner.

(t) To distribute among the members in specie any property of the Company, or any proceeds of sale or disposal of any property of the Company, but so that no distribution amounting to a reduction of capital be made except with the sanction (if any) for the time being required by law.

(u) To do all or any of the above things in any part of the world, and either as principals, agents, trustees, contractors or otherwise, and either alone or in conjunction with others, and either by or through agents, trustees, sub-contractos or otherwise.

(v) To do all such other things as are incidental or conducive to the above objects or any of them.

4. The liability of the members is limited.

5. The share capital of the Company is £100, divided into 400 shares of 25p each. The shares in the original or any increased capital may be divided into several classes, and there may be attached thereto respectively any preferential, deferred or other special rights, privileges, conditions or restrictions as to dividend, capital, voting or otherwise.

WE, the several persons whose names and addresses are subscribed, are desirous of being formed into a Company in pursuance of this Memorandum of Association, and we respectively agree to take the number of shares in the capital of the Company set opposite our respective names.

NAMES, ADDRESSES AND DESCRIPTIONS OF SUBSCRIBERS	Number of Shares taken by each Subscriber
Polly Porthole, *1 Suds Rd., London, N.W.1,* *Travel Agent.*	One
Desmond Drain, *2 Overflow Drive,* *Birmingham,* *Company Director*	One

Dated this 24th day of October, 1967.
Witness to the above Signatures:
    Bertram Bibb,
      1 Lawyer Court,
        Temple, EC4,
          Barrister's Clerk

The Companies Act, 1948

COMPANY LIMITED BY SHARES

Articles of Association

OF

SWISH LIMITED

PRELIMINARY

1. Subject as hereinafter provided, the regulations contained or incorporated in Part II of Table A in the First Schedule to the Companies Act, 1948 (hereinafter referred to as 'Table A, Part II'), shall apply to the Company.

2. Regulations 3, 5, 24, 53, 60, 71, 75, 79, 88, 89, 90, 91, 92, 93, 96, 97 and 136 of Part I of Table A in the said Schedule (hereinafter referred to as 'Table A, Part I') shall not apply to the Company, but the Articles hereinafter contained, and the remaining regulations of Table A, Part I, and regulations 2 to 6 of Table A, Part II, subject to the modifications hereinafter expressed, shall constitute the regulations of the Company.

SHARES

3. The shares shall be at the disposal of the Directors, who may allot or otherwise dispose of them, subject to regulation 2 of Table A, Part II, and to the provisions of the next following Article, to such persons at such times and generally on such terms and conditions as they think proper, and provided that no shares shall be issued at a discount, except as provided by section 57 of the Act.

4. Unless otherwise determined by the Company in General Meeting any original shares for the time being unissued and any new shares from time to time to be created shall, before they are issued, be offered to the members in proportion, as nearly as may be, to the number of shares held by them. Such offer shall be made by notice specifying the number of shares offered, and limiting a time within which the offer, if not accepted, will be deemed to be declined, and after the expiration of such time, or on the receipt of an intimation from the person to whom the offer is made that he declines to accept the shares offered, the Directors may, subject to these Articles, dispose of the same in such manner as they think most

beneficial to the Company. The Directors may, in like manner, dispose of any such new or original shares as aforesaid, which, by reason of the proportion borne by them to the number of persons entitled to such offer as aforesaid or by reason of any other difficulty in apportioning the same, cannot in the opinion of the Directors be conveniently offered in manner hereinbefore provided.

5. Subject to the provisions of section 58 of the Act, any Preference Shares may with the sanction of a Special Resolution be issued upon the terms that they are or at the option of the Company are liable to be redeemed.

LIEN

6. In regulation 11 of Table A, Part I, the words '(not being a fully paid share)' and the words '(other than fully paid shares') shall be omitted.

TRANSFER OF SHARES

7. (A) Subject as in these Articles provided, any share may be transferred to any member of the Company, and any share may be transferred by a member to his or her father or mother, or to any lineal descendant of his or her father or mother, or to his or her wife or husband, and any share of a deceased member may be transferred to the widow or widower or any other such relative as aforesaid of such deceased member or may be transferred to or placed in the names of his or her executors or trustees; and in any such circumstances (but subject as aforesaid) regulation 3 of Table A, Part II, shall not apply save to ensure that the number of members shall not exceed the prescribed limit or to prevent a transfer of shares on which the Company has a lien.

(B) A share shall not be transferred otherwise than as provided in paragraph (A) of this Article unless it first be offered to the members at a fair value to be fixed by the Company's Auditors. Any member desiring to sell a share (hereinafter referred to as a 'retiring member') shall give notice thereof in writing to the Company (hereinafter referred to as a 'sale notice') constituting the Company his agent for the purpose of such sale. No sale notice shall be withdrawn without the Directors' sanction. The Directors shall offer any share comprised in a sale notice to the existing members, and if within twenty-eight days after the sale notice has been given a purchasing member is found, such purchasing member shall be bound to complete the purchase within seven days. Notice of the finding of the purchasing member shall be given to the retiring member, who shall be bound on payment of the fair value to transfer the share to the purchasing member. If the retiring member fails to complete the transfer, the Directors may authorize some person to transfer the share to the purchasing member and may receive the purchase money and register the purchasing member as holder of the share, issuing him a certificate therefor. The retiring member shall deliver up his certificate and shall thereupon be paid the purchase money. If within twenty-eight days after the sale notice has been given the Directors shall not find a purchasing member for the share and shall give notice accordingly, or if through no default of the retiring member the purchase is not duly completed, the retiring member may at any time within six months after the sale notice was given, but subject to regulation 3 of Table A, Part II, sell such share to any person and at any price.

(c) No share shall be issued or transferred to any infant, bankrupt or person of unsound mind.

TRANSMISSION OF SHARES

8. The proviso to regulation 32 of Table A, Part I, shall be omitted.

PROCEEDINGS AT GENERAL MEETINGS

9. The words "or not carried by a particular majority" shall be inserted after the words "or lost" in regulation 58 of Table A, Part I.

DIRECTORS

10. Unless and until otherwise determined by the Company in General Meeting, the number of the Directors shall not be less than two nor more than ten. The following shall be the first Directors of the Company, that is to say—*Polly Porthole and Desmond Drain.*

11. The word 'Directors' shall be substituted for the words 'Company in General Meeting' in regulation 76 of Table A, Part I.

12. The words 'in General Meeting' shall be inserted after the words 'unless the Company' in regulation 78 of Table A, Part I.

BORROWING POWERS

13. The Directors may exercise all the powers of the Company to borrow money, and to mortgage or charge its undertaking, property and uncalled capital, or any part thereof, and to issue debentures, debenture stock and other securities whether outright or as security for any debt, liability or obligation of the Company or of any third party.

POWERS AND DUTIES OF DIRECTORS

14. A Director may vote in respect of any contract or arrangement in which he is interested and be counted in the quorum present at any meeting at which any such contract or arrangement is proposed or considered, and if he shall so vote his vote shall be counted. This article shall have effect in substitution for paragraphs (2) and (4) of regulation 84 of Table A, Part I, which paragraphs shall not apply to the Company.

15. The office of a Director shall be vacated—

    (1) If by notice in writing to the Company he resigns the office of Director.

    (2) If he ceases to be a Director by virtue of section 182 of the Act.

    (3) If he becomes bankrupt or enters into any arrangement with his creditors.

    (4) If he is prohibited from being a Director by an order made under any of the provisions of section 188 of the Act.

    (5) If he becomes of unsound mind.

(6) If he is removed from office by a resolution duly passed under section 184 of the Act.

16. Any person may be appointed or elected as a Director, whatever may be his age, and no Director shall be required to vacate his office by reason of his attaining or having attained the age of seventy years or any other age.

ROTATION OF DIRECTORS

17. The words 'and may also determine in what rotation the increased or reduced number is to go out of office' shall be omitted in regulation 94 of Table A, Part I.

18. The last sentence shall be omitted in regulation 95 of Table A, Part I.

19. In addition and without prejudice to the provisions of section 184 of the Act, the Company may by Extraordinary Resolution remove any Director before the expiration of his period of office, and may by Ordinary Resolution appoint another Director in his stead.

PROCEEDINGS OF DIRECTORS

20. The third sentence shall be omitted in regulation 98 of Table A, Part I.

21. The words 'and in the case of an equality of votes, the Chairman shall have a second or casting vote' shall be omitted in regulation 104 of Table A, Part I.

22. A Director may from time to time by notice in writing to the Company appoint any person approved by his co-Directors to act as an alternate Director at any meeting of the Board from which he is himself absent, and may in like manner remove any person so appointed from office. An alternate Director so appointed may also be removed from his office by notice in writing to the Company given by the co-Directors of the Director by whom he was appointed. An alternate Director appointed under this Article shall not be required to hold any qualification or be entitled to any remuneration from the Company, but he shall be entitled, while holding office as such, to receive notice of meetings of Directors and to attend and vote thereat in place of and in the absence of the Director appointing him.

ACCOUNTS

23. In regulation 127 of Table A, Part I, the words 'and shall only have effect subject and without prejudice to the provisions of section 158 (1) (c) of the Act' shall be inserted immediately after the words 'joint holders of any shares or debentures' at the end of that regulation.

WINDING UP

24. In regulation 135 of Table A, Part I, the words 'with the like sanction' shall be inserted immediately before the words 'determine how such division', and the word 'members' shall be substituted for the word 'contributories'.

INDEMNITY

25. Every Director or other officer of the Company shall be entitled to be indemnified out of the assets of the Company against all losses or liabilities which he may sustain or incur in or about the execution of the duties of his office or otherwise in relation thereto, including any liability incurred by him in defending any proceedings, whether civil or criminal, in which judgment is given in his favour or in which he is acquitted or in connexion with any application under section 448 of the Act in which relief is granted to him by the court, and no Director or other officer shall be liable for any loss, damage or misfortune which may happen to or be incurred by the Company in the execution of the duties of his office or in relation thereto. But this Article shall only have effect in so far as its provisions are not avoided by section 205 of the Act.

NAMES, ADDRESSES AND DESCRIPTIONS OF SUBSCRIBERS

> *Polly Porthole,*
> > *1 Suds Rd., London, NW1,*
> > > *Travel Agent*
> *Desmond Drain,*
> > *2 Overflow Drive,*
> > > *Birmingham.*
> > > > *Company Director,*

Dated this 24th day of October, 1967.
Witness to the above Signatures—
> *Bertram Bibb,*
> > *1 Lawyer's Court,*
> > > *Temple, EC4,*
> > > > *Barrister's Clerk.*

Appendix 12

Table A of *The Companies Act, 1948*

TABLE A

PART I

REGULATIONS FOR THE MANAGEMENT OF A COMPANY LIMITED BY SHARES NOT BEING A PRIVATE COMPANY

INTERPRETATION

1. In these regulations:

'the Act' means the Companies Act, 1948.

'the seal' means the common seal of the company.

'secretary' means any person appointed to perform the duties of the secretary of the company.

'the United Kingdom' means Great Britain and Northern Ireland.

Expressions referring to writing shall, unless the contrary intention appears, be construed as including references to printing, lithography, photography, and other modes of representing or reproducing words in a visible form.

Unless the context otherwise requires, words or expressions contained in these regulations shall bear the same meaning as in the Act or any statutory modification thereof in force at the date at which these regulations become binding on the company.

SHARE CAPITAL AND VARIATION OF RIGHTS

2. Without prejudice to any special rights previously conferred on the holders of any existing shares or class of shares, any share in the company may be issued with such preferred, deferred or other special rights or such restrictions, whether in regard to dividend, voting, return of capital or otherwise as the company may from time to time by ordinary resolution determine.

3. Subject to the provisions of section 58 of the Act, any preference shares may, with the sanction of an ordinary resolution, be issued on the

533

terms that they are, or at the option of the company are liable, to be redeemed on such terms and in such manner as the comapny before the issue of the shares may by special resolution determine.

4. If at any time the share capital is divided into different classes of shares, the rights attached to any class (unless otherwise provided by the terms of issue of the shares of that class) may, whether or not the company is being wound up, be varied with the consent in writing of the holders of three-fourths of the issued shares of that class, or with the sanction of an extraordinary resolution passed at a separate general meeting of the holders of the shares of the class. To every such separate general meeting the provisions of these regulations relating to general meetings shall apply, but so that the necessary quorum shall be two persons at least holding or representing by proxy one-third of the issued shares of the class and that any holder of the class present in person or by proxy may demand a poll.

5. The rights conferred upon the holders of the shares of any class issued with preferred or other rights shall not, unless otherwise expressly provided by the terms of issue of the shares of that class, be deemed to be varied by the creation or issue of further shares ranking *pari passu* therewith.

6. The Company may exercise the powers of paying commissions conferred by section 53 of the Act, provided that the rate per cent or the amount of the commission paid or agreed to be paid shall be disclosed in the manner required by the said section and the rate of the commission shall not exceed the rate of 10 per cent of the price at which the shares in respect whereof the same is paid are issued or an amount equal to 10 per cent of such price (as the case may be). Such commission may be satisfied by the payment of cash or the allotment of fully or partly paid shares or partly in one way and partly in the other. The company may also on any issue of shares pay such brokerage as may be lawful.

7. Except as required by law, no person shall be recognized by the company as holding any share upon any trust, and the company shall not be bound by or be compelled in any way to recognize (even when having notice thereof) any equitable, contingent, future or partial interest in any share or any interest in any fractional part of a share or (except only as by these Regulations or by law otherwise provided) any other rights in respect of any share except an absolute right to the entirety thereof in the registered holder.

8. Every person whose name is entered as a member in the register of members shall be entitled without payment to receive within two months after allotment or lodgement of transfer (or within such other period as the conditions of issue shall provide) one certificate for all his shares or several certificates each for one or more of his shares upon payment of 2s 6d for every certificate after the first or such less sum as the directors shall from time to time determine. Every certificate shall be under the seal and shall specify the shares to which it relates and the amount paid up thereon. Provided that in respect of a share or shares held jointly by several persons the company shall not be bound to issue more than one certificate, and delivery of a certificate for a share to one

of several joint holders shall be sufficient delivery to all such holders.

9. If a share certificate be defaced, lost or destroyed, it may be renewed on payment of a fee of 2s 6d or such less sum and on such terms (if any) as to evidence and indemnity and the payment of out-of-pocket expenses of the company of investigating evidence as the directors think fit.

10. The company shall not give, whether directly or indirectly, and whether by means of a loan, guarantee, the provision of security or otherwise, any financial assistance for the purpose of or in connexion with a purchase or subscription made or to be made by any person of or for any shares in the company or in its holding company, nor shall the company make a loan for any purpose whatsoever on the security of its shares or those of its holding company, but nothing in this regulation shall prohibit transactions mentioned in the proviso to section 54 (1) of the Act.

LIEN

11. The company shall have a first and paramount lien on every share (not being a fully paid share) for all moneys (whether presently payable or not) called or payable at a fixed time in respect of that share, and the company shall also have a first and paramount lien on all shares (other than fully paid shares) standing registered in the name of a single person for all moneys presently payable by him or his estate to the company; but the directors may at any time declare any share to be wholly or in part exempt from the provisions of this regulation. The company's lien, if any, on a share shall extend to all dividends payable thereon.

12. The company may sell, in such manner as the directors think fit, any shares on which the company has a lien, but no sale shall be made unless a sum in respect of which the lien exists is presently payable, nor until the expiration of fourteen days after a notice in writing, stating and demanding payment of such part of the amount in respect of which the lien exists as is presently payable, has been given to the registered holder for the time being of the share, or the person entitled thereto by reason of his death or bankruptcy.

13. To give effect to any such sale the directors may authorize some person to transfer the shares sold to the purchaser thereof. The purchaser shall be registered as the holder of the shares comprised in any such transfer, and he shall not be bound to see to the application of the purchase money, nor shall his title to the shares be affected by any irregularity or invalidity in the proceedings in reference to the sale.

14. The proceeds of the sale shall be received by the company and applied in payment of such part of the amount in respect of which the lien exists as is presently payable, and the residue, if any, shall (subject to a like lien for sums not presently payable as existed upon the shares before the sale) be paid to the person entitled to the shares at the date of the sale.

CALLS ON SHARES

15. The directors may from time to time make calls upon the members in respect of any moneys unpaid on their shares (whether on account of the

nominal value of the shares or by way of premium) and not by the conditions of allotment thereof made payable at fixed times, provided that no call shall exceed one-fourth of the nominal value of the share or be payable at less than one month from the date fixed for the payment of the last preceding call, and each member shall (subject to receiving at least fourteen days' notice specifying the time or times and place of payment) pay to the company at the time or times and place so specified the amount called on his shares. A call may be revoked or postponed as the directors may determine.

16. A call shall be deemed to have been made at the time when the resolution of the directors authorizing the call was passed and may be required to be paid by instalments.

17. The joint holders of a share shall be jointly and severally liable to pay all calls in respect thereof.

18. If a sum called in respect of a share is not paid before or on the day appointed for payment thereof, the person from whom the sum is due shall pay interest on the sum from the day appointed for payment thereof to the time of actual payment at such rate not exceeding 5 per cent per annum as the directors may determine, but the directors shall be at liberty to waive payment of such interest wholly or in part.

19. Any sum which by the terms of issue of a share becomes payable on allotment or at any fixed date, whether on account of the nominal value of the share or by way of premium, shall for the purposes of these regulations be deemed to be a call duly made and payable on the date on which by the terms of issue the same becomes payable, and in case of non-payment all the relevant provisions of these regulations as to payment of interest and expenses, forfeiture or otherwise shall apply as if such sum had become payable by virtue of a call duly made and notified.

20. The directors may, on the issue of shares, differentiate between the holders as to the amount of calls to be paid and the times of payment.

21. The directors may, if they think fit, receive from any member willing to advance the same, all or any part of the moneys uncalled and unpaid upon any shares held by him, and upon all or any of the moneys so advanced may (until the same would, but for such advance become payable) pay interest at such rate not exceeding (unless the company in general meeting shall otherwise direct) 5 per cent per annum, as may be agreed upon between the directors and the member paying such sum in advance.

TRANSFER OF SHARES

22. The instrument of transfer of any share shall be executed by or on behalf of the transferer and transferee, and, except as provided by sub-paragraph (4) of paragraph 2 of the Seventh Schedule to the Act, the transferer shall be deemed to remain a holder of the share until the name of the transferee is entered in the register of members in respect thereof.

23. Subject to such of the restrictions of these regulations as may be applicable, any member may transfer all or any of his shares by instrument in writing in any usual or common form or any other form which the directors may approve.

24. The directors may decline to register the transfer of a share (not being a fully paid share) to a person of whom they shall not approve, and they may also decline to register the transfer of a share on which the company has a lien.

25. The directors may also decline to recognize any instrument of transfer unless:

(a) a fee of 2s. 6d. or such lesser sums as the directors may from time to time require is paid to the company in respect thereof;

(b) the instrument of transfer is accompanied by the certificate of the shares to which it relates, and such other evidence as the directors may reasonably require to show the right of the transfer or to make the transfer; and

(c) the instrument of transfer is in respect of only one class of share.

26. If the directors refuse to register a transfer they shall within two months after the date on which the transfer was lodged with the company send to the transferee notice of the refusal.

27. The registration of transfers may be suspended at such times and for such periods as the directors may from time to time determine, provided always that such registration shall not be suspended for more than thirty days in any year.

28. The company shall be entitled to charge a fee not exceeding 2s. 6d. on the registration of every probate, letters of administration, certificate of death or marriage, power of attorney, notice in lieu of distringas, or other instrument.

TRANSMISSION OF SHARES

29. In case of the death of a member the survivor or survivors where the deceased was a joint holder, and the legal personal representatives of the deceased where he was a sole holder, shall be the only persons recognized by the company as having any title to his interest in the shares; but nothing herein contained shall release the estate of a deceased joint holder from any liability in respect of any share which had been jointly held by him with other persons.

30. Any person becoming entitled to a share in consequence of the death or bankruptcy of a member may, upon such evidence being produced as may from time to time properly be required by the directors and subject as hereinafter provided, elect either to be registered himself as holder of the share or to have some person nominated by him registered as the transferee thereof, but the directors shall, in either case, have the same right to decline or suspend registration as they would have had in the case of a transfer of the share by that member before his death or bankruptcy, as the case may be.

31. If the person so becoming entitled shall elect to be registered himself, he shall deliver or send to the company a notice in writing signed by him, stating that he so elects. If he shall elect to have another person registered he shall testify his election by executing to that person a transfer of the share. All the limitations, restrictions and provisions of these regulations relating to the right to transfer and the registration of transfers of shares

shall be applicable to any such notice or transfer as aforesaid as if the death or bankruptcy of the member had not occurred and the notice or transfer were a transfer signed by that member.

32. A person becoming entitled to a share by reason of the death or bankruptcy of the holder shall be entitled to the same dividends and other advantages to which he would be entitled if he were the registered holder of the share, except that he shall not, before being registered as a member in respect of the share, be entitled in respect of it to exercise any right conferred by membership in relation to meetings of the company:

Provided always that the directors may at any time give notice requiring any such person to elect either to be registered himself or to transfer the share, and if the notice is not complied with within ninety days the directors may thereafter withhold payment of all dividends, bonuses or other moneys payable in respect of the share until the requirements of the notice have been complied with.

FORFEITURE OF SHARES

33. If a member fails to pay any call or instalment of a call on the day appointed for payment thereof, the directors may, at any time thereafter during such time as any part of the call or instalment remains unpaid, serve a notice on him requiring payment of so much of the call or instalment as is unpaid, together with any interest which may have accrued.

34. The notice shall name a further day (not earlier than the expiration of fourteen days from the date of service of the notice) on or before which the payment required by the notice is to be made, and shall state that in the event of non-payment at or before the time appointed the shares in respect of which the call was made will be liable to be forfeited.

35. If the requirements of any such notice as aforesaid are not complied with, any share in respect of which the notice has been given may at any time thereafter, before the payment required by the notice has been made, be forfeited by a resolution of the directors to that effect.

36. A forfeited share may be sold or otherwise disposed of on such terms and in such manner as the directors think fit, and at any time before a sale or disposition the forfeiture may be cancelled on such terms as the directors think fit.

37. A person whose shares have been forfeited shall cease to be a member in respect of the forfeited shares, but shall, notwithstanding, remain liable to pay to the company all moneys which, at the date of forfeiture, were payable by him to the company in respect of the shares, but his liability shall cease if and when the company shall have received payment in full of all such moneys in respect of the shares.

38. A statutory declaration in writing that the declarant is a director or the secretary of the company, and that a share in the company has been duly forfeited on a date stated in the declaration, shall be conclusive evidence of the facts therein stated as against all persons claiming to be entitled to the share. The company may receive the consideration, if any, given for the share on any sale or disposition thereof and may execute a transfer of the share in favour of the person to whom the share is sold

or disposed of and he shall thereupon be registered as the holder of the share, and shall not be bound to see to the application of the purchase money, if any, nor shall his title to the share be affected by any irregularity or invalidity in the proceedings in reference to the forfeiture, sale or disposal of the share.

39. The provisions of these regulations as to forfeiture shall apply in the case of non-payment of any sum which, by the terms of issue of a share, becomes payable at a fixed time, whether on account of the nominal value of the share, or by way of premium, as if the same had been payable by virtue of a call duly made and notified.

CONVERSION OF SHARES INTO STOCK

40. The company may by ordinary resolution convert any paid-up shares into stock, and reconvert any stock into paid-up shares of any demonination.

41. The holders of stock may transfer the same, or any part thereof, in the same manner, and subject to the same regulations, as and subject to which the shares from which the stock arose might previously to conversion have been transferred, or as near thereto as circumstances admit; and the directors may from time to time fix the minimum amount of stock transferable, but so that such minimum shall not exceed the nominal amount of the shares from which the stock arose.

42. The holders of stock shall, according to the amount of stock held by them, have the same rights, privileges and advantages as regards dividends, voting at meetings of the company and other matters as if they held the shares from which the stock arose, but no such privilege or advantage (except participation in the dividends and profits of the company and in the assets on winding up) shall be conferred by an amount of stock which would not, if existing in shares, have conferred that privilege or advantage.

43. Such of the regulations of the company as are applicable to paid-up shares shall apply to stock, and the words 'share' and 'shareholder' therein shall include 'stock' and 'stockholder'.

ALTERATION OF CAPITAL

44. The company may from time to time by ordinary resolution increase the share capital by such sum, to be divided into shares of such amount, as the resolution shall prescribe.

45. The company may by ordinary resolution:
  (a) consolidate and divide all or any of its share capital into shares of larger amount than its existing shares;
  (b) sub-divide its existing shares, or any of them, into shares of smaller amount than is fixed by the Memorandum of Association subject, nevertheless, to the provisions of section 61 (1) (d) of the Act;
  (c) cancel any shares which, at the date of the passing of the resolution, have not been taken or agreed to be taken by any person.

46. The company may by special resolution reduce its share capital

redemption reserve fund or any share premium account in any manner and with, and subject to, any incident authorized, and consent required, by law.

GENERAL MEETINGS

47. The company shall in each year hold a general meeting as its annual general meeting in addition to any other meetings in that year, and shall specify the meeting as such in the notices calling it; and not more than fifteen months shall elapse between the date of one annual general meeting of the company and that of the next. Provided that so long as the company holds its first annual general meeting within eighteen months of its incorporation, it need not hold it in the year of its incorporation or in the following year. The annual general meeting shall be held at such time and place as the directors shall appoint.

48. All general meetings other than annual general meetings shall be called extraordinary general meetings.

49. The directors may, whenever they think fit, convene an extraordinary general meeting, and extraordinary general meetings shall also be convened on such requisition, or, in default, may be convened by such requisitionists, as provided by section 132 of the Act. If at any time there are not within the United Kingdom sufficient directors capable of acting to form a quorum, any director or any two members of the company may convene an extraordinary general meeting in the same manner as nearly as possible as that in which meetings may be convened by the directors.

NOTICE OF GENERAL MEETINGS

50. An annual general meeting and a meeting called for the passing of a special resolution shall be called by twenty-one days' notice in writing at the least, and a meeting of the company other than an annual general meeting or a meeting for the passing of a special Resolution shall be called by fourteen days' notice in writing at the least. The notice shall be exclusive of the day on which it is served or deemed to be served and of the day for which it is given, and shall specify the place, the day and the hour of meeting and, in case of special business, the general nature of that business, and shall be given, in manner hereinafter mentioned or in such other manner, if any, as may be prescribed by the company in general meeting, to such persons as are, under the regulations of the company, entitled to receive such notices from the company:

Provided that a meeting of the company shall, notwithstanding that it is called by shorter notice than that specified in this regulation be deemed to have been duly called if it is so agreed:

(*a*) in the case of a meeting called as the annual general meeting, by all the members entitled to attend and vote thereat; and

(*b*) in the case of any other meeting, by a majority in number of the members hainag a right to attend and vote at the meeting, being a majority together holding not less than 95 per cent in nominal value of the shares giving that right.

51. The accidental omission to give notice of a meeting to, or the

non-receipt of notice of a meeting by, any person entitled to receive notice shall not invalidate the proceedings at that meeting.

PROCEEDINGS AT GENERAL MEETINGS

52. All business shall be deemed special that is transacted at an extra-ordinary general meeting, and also all that is transacted at an annual general meeting, with the exception of declaring a dividend, the consideration of the accounts, balance sheets, and the reports of the directors and auditors, the election of directors in the place of those retiring and the appointment of, and the fixing of the remuneration of, the auditors.

53. No business shall be transacted at any general meeting unless a quorum of members is present at the time when the meeting proceeds to business; save as herein otherwise provided, three members present in person shall be a quorum.

54. If within half an hour from the time appointed for the meeting a quorum is not present, the meeting, if convened upon the requisition of members, shall be dissolved; in any other case it shall stand adjourned to the same day in the next week, at the same time and place or to such other day and at such other time and place as the directors may determine, and if at the adjourned meeting a quorum is not present within half an hour from the time appointed for the meeting, the members present shall be a quorum.

55. The chairman, if any, of the board of directors shall preside as chairman at every general meeting of the company, or if there is no such chairman or if he shall not be present within fifteen minutes after the time appointed for the holding of the meeting or is unwilling to act the directors present shall elect one of their number to be chairman of the meeting.

56. If at any meeting no director is willing to act as chairman or if no director is present within fifteen minutes after the time appointed for holding the meeting, the members present shall choose one of their number to be chairman of the meeting.

57. The chairman may, with the consent of any meeting at which a quorum is present (and shall if so directed by the meeting), adjourn the meeting from time to time and from place to place, but no business shall be transacted at any adjourned meeting other than the business left unfinished at the meeting from which the adjournment took place. When a meeting is adjourned for thirty days or more notice of the adjourned meeting shall be given as in the case of an original meeting. Save as aforesaid it shall not be necessary to give any notice of an adjournment or of the business to be transacted at an adjourned meeting.

58. At any general meeting a resolution put to the vote of the meeting shall be decided on a show of hands unless a poll is (before or on the declaration of the result of the show of hands) demanded:

(*a*) by the chairman; or

(*b*) by at least three members present in person or by proxy; or

(*c*) by any member or members present in person or by proxy and representing not less than one-tenth of the total voting rights of all the members having the right to vote at the meeting; or (*d*) by a member or members holding shares in the company conferring a right to vote at the meeting being shares on which an aggregate sum has been paid up equal to not less than one-tenth of the total sum paid up on the shares conferring that right.

Unless a poll be so demanded a declaration by the chairman that a resolution has on a show of hands been carried or carried unanimously, or by a particular majority, or lost and an entry to that effect in the book containing the minutes of the proceedings of the company shall be conclusive evidence of the fact without proof of the number or proportion of the votes recorded in favour of or against such resolution.

The demand for a poll may be withdrawn.

59. Except as provided in regulation 61, if a poll is demanded it shall be taken in such manner as the chairman directs, and the result of the poll shall be deemed to be the resolution of the meeting at which the poll was demanded.

60. In the case of an equality of votes, whether on a show of hands or on a poll, the chairman of the meeting at which the show of hands takes place or at which the poll is demanded, shall be entitled to a second or casting vote.

61. A poll demanded on the election of a chairman or on a question of adjournment shall be taken forthwith. A poll demanded on any other question shall be taken at such time as the chaiman of the meeting directs, and any business other than that upon which a poll has been demanded may be proceeded with pending the taking of the poll.

VOTES OF MEMBERS

62. Subject to any rights or restrictions for the time being attached to any class or classes of shares, on a show of hands every member present in person shall have one vote, and on a poll every member shall have one vote for each share of which he is the holder.

63. In the case of joint holders the vote of the senior who tenders a vote, whether in person or by proxy, shall be accepted to the exclusion of the votes of the other joint holders; and for this purpose seniority shall be determined by the order in which the names stand in the register of members.

64. A member of unsound mind, or in respect of whom an order has been made by any court having jurisdiction in lunacy, may vote, whether on a show of hands or on a poll, by his committee, receiver, curator bonis, or other person in the nature of a committee, receiver or curator bonis appointed by that Court, and any such committee, receiver, curator bonis or other person may, on a poll, vote by proxy.

65. No member shall be entitled to vote at any general meeting unless all calls or other sums presently payable by him in respect of shares in the company have been paid.

66. No objection shall be raised to the qualification of any voter except at the meeting or adjourned meeting at which the vote objected to is given or tendered, and every vote not disallowed at such meeting shall be valid for all purposes. Any such objection made in due time shall be referred

to the chairman of the meeting, whose decision shall be final and conclusive.

67. On a poll votes may be given either personally or by proxy.

68. The instrument appointing a proxy shall be in writing under the hand of the appointer or of his attorney duly authorized in writing or, if the appointer is a corporation, either under seal, or under the hand of an officer or attorney duly authorized. A proxy need not be a member of the company.

69. The instrument appointing a proxy and the power of attorney or other authority, if any, under which it is signed or a notarially certified copy of that power or authority shall be deposited at the registered office of the company or at such other place within the United Kingdom as is specified for that purpose in the notice convening the meeting, not less than 48 hours before the time for holding the meeting or adjourned meeting, at which the person named in the instrument proposes to vote, or, in the case of a poll, not less than 24 hours before the time appointed for the taking of the poll, and in default the instrument of proxy shall not be treated as valid.

70. An instrument appointing a proxy shall be in the following form, or a form as near thereto as circumstances admit:

‘   LIMITED.

I/We   , of   in the county of   , being a member/members of the above-named company, hereby appoint   of or failing him   of   , as my/our proxy to vote for me/us on my/our behalf at the [annual or extra-ordinary as the case may be] general meeting of the company to be held on the   day of   19 , and at any adjournment thereof.

Signed this   day of   19 .’

71. Where it is desired to afford members an opportunity of voting for or against a resolution the instrument appointing a proxy shall be in the following form or a form as near thereto as circumstances admit:

‘   LIMITED.

I/We   , of   in the county of   , being a member/members of the above-named company, hereby appoint   of or failing him   of   , as my/our proxy to vote for me/us on my/our behalf at the [annual or extra-ordinary, as the case may be] general meeting of the company to be held on the   day of   19 , and at any adjournment thereof.

Signed this   day of   19 .

This form is to be used in favour of/against the resolution.

Unless otherwise instructed, the proxy will vote as he thinks fit.’

72. The instrument appointing a proxy shall be deemed to confer authority to demand or join in demanding a poll.

73. A vote given in accordance with the terms of an instrument of proxy shall be valid notwithstanding the previous death or insanity of the principal or revocation of the proxy or of the authority under which the proxy was executed, or the transfer of the share in respect of which the proxy is given, provided that no intimation in writing of such death, insanity, revocation or transfer as aforesaid shall have been received by the company at the office before the commencement of the meeting or adjourned meeting at which the proxy is used.

CORPORATIONS ACTING BY REPRESENTATIVES AT MEETINGS

74. Any corporation which is a member of the company may by resolution of its directors or other governing body authorize such person as it thinks fit to act as its representative at any meeting of the company or of any class of members of the company, and the person so authorized shall be entitled to exercise the same powers on behalf of the corporation which he represents as that corporation could exercise if it were an individual member of the company.

DIRECTORS

75. The number of the directors and the names of the first directors shall be determined in writing by the subscribers of the Memorandum of Association or a majority of them.

76. The remuneration of the directors shall from time to time be determined by the company in general meeting. Such remuneration shall be deemed to accrue from day to day. The directors may also be paid all travelling, hotel and other expenses properly incurred by them in attending and returning from meetings of the directors or any committee of the directors or general meetings of the company or in connexion with the business of the company.

77. The shareholding qualification for directors may be fixed by the company in general meeting, and unless and until so fixed no qualification shall be required.

78. A director of the company may be or become a director or other officer, of, or otherwise interested in, any company promoted by the company or in which the company may be interested as shareholder or otherwise, and no such director shall be accountable to the company for any remuneration or other benefits received by him as a director or officer of, or from his interest in, such other company unless the company otherwise direct.

BORROWING POWERS

79. The directors may exercise all the powers of the company to borrow money, and to mortgage or charge its undertaking, property and uncalled capital, or any part thereof, and to issue debentures, debenture stock, and other securities whether outright or as security for any debt, liability or obligation of the company or of any third party:

Provided that the amount for the time being remaining undischarged of moneys borrowed or secured by the directors as aforesaid (apart from temporary loans obtained from the company's bankers in the ordinary course of business) shall not at any time, without the previous sanction of the company in general meeting, exceed the nominal amount of the share capital of the company for the time being issued, but nevertheless, no lender or other person dealing with the company shall be concerned to see or inquire whether this limit is observed. No debt incurred or security given in excess of such limit shall be invalid or ineffectual except in the case of express notice to the lender or the recipient of the security at the time when the debt was incurred or security given that the limit hereby imposed had been or was thereby exceeded.

POWERS AND DUTIES OF DIRECTORS

80. The business of the company shall be managed by the directors, who may pay all expenses incurred in promoting and registering the company, and may exercise all such powers of the company as are not, by the Act or by these regulations, required to be exercised by the company in general meeting, subject, nevertheless, to any of these regulations to the provisions of the Act, and to such regulations, being not inconsistent with the aforesaid regulations or provisions, as may be prescribed by the company in general meeting; but no regulation made by the company in general meeting shall invalidate any prior act of the directors which would have been valid if that regulation had not been made.

81. The directors may from time to time and at any time by power of attorney appoint any company, firm or person or body of persons, whether nominated directly or indirectly by the directors, to be the attorney or attorneys of the company for such purposes and with such powers, authorities and discretions (not exceeding those vested in or exercisable by the directors under these regulations) and for such period and subject to such conditions as they may think fit, and any such powers of attorney may contain such provisisions for the protection and convenience of persons dealing with any such attorney as the directors may think fit and may also authorize any such attorney to delegate all or any of the powers, authorities and discretions vested in him.

82. The company may exercise the powers conferred by section 35 of the Act with regard to having an official seal for use abroad, and such powers shall be vested in the directors.

83. The company may exercise the powers conferred upon the company by sections 199 to 123 (both inclusive) of the Act with regard to the keeping of a dominion register, and the directors may (subject to the provisions of those sections) make and vary such regulations as they may think fit respecting the keeping of any such register.

84.—(1) A director who is in any way, whether directly or indirectly, interested in a contract or proposed contract with the company shall declare the nature of his interest at a meeting of the directors in accordance with section 199 of the Act.

(2) A director shall not vote in respect of any contract or arrangement in which he is interested, and if he shall do so his vote shall not be counted, nor shall he be counted in the quorum present at the meeting, but neither of these prohibitions shall apply to:

(*a*) any arrangement for giving any director any security or indemnity in respect of money lent by him to or obligations undertaken by him for the benefit of the company; or

(*b*) to any arrangement for the giving by the company of any security to a third party in respect of a debt or obligation of the company for which the director himself has assumed responsibility in whole or in part under a guarantee or indemnity or by the deposit of a security; or

(*c*) any contract by a director to subscribe for or underwrite shares or debentures of the company; or

(*d*) any contract or arrangement with any other company in which he is interested only as an officer of the company or as holder of shares or other securities;

and these prohibitions may at any time be suspended or relaxed to any extent, and either generally or in respect of any particular contract, arrangement or transaction, by the company in general meeting.

(3) A director may hold any other office or place of profit under the company (other than the office of auditor) in conjunction with his office of director for such period and on such terms (as to remuneration and otherwise) as the directors may determine and no director or intending director shall be disqualified by his office from contracting with the company either with regard to his tenure of any such office or place of profit or as vendor, purchaser or otherwise, nor shall any such contract, or any contract or arrangement entered into by or on behalf of the company in which any director is in any way interested, be liable to be avoided, nor shall any director so contracting or being so interested be liable to account to the comapny for any profit realized by any such contract or arrangement by reason of such director holding that office or of the fiduciary relation thereby established.

(4) A director, notwithstanding his interest, may be counted in the quorum present at any meeting whereat he or any other director is appointed to hold any such office or place of profit under the company or whereat the terms of any such appointment are arranged, and he may vote on any such appointment or arrangement other than his own appointment or the arrangement of the terms thereof.

(5) Any director may act by himself or his firm in a professional capacity for the company, and he or his firm shall be entitled to remuneration for professional services as if he were not a director; provided that nothing herein contained shall authorize a director or his firm to act as auditor to the company.

85. All cheques, promissory notes, drafts, bills of exchange and other negotiable instruments, and all receipts for moneys paid to the company, shall be signed, drawn, accepted, endorsed, or otherwise executed, as the case may be, in such manner as the directors shall from time to time by resolution determine.

86. The directors shall cause minutes to be made in books provided for the purpose:

(*a*) of all appointments of officers made by the directors;

(*b*) of the names of the directors present at each meeting of the directors and of any committee of the directors;

(*c*) of all resolutions and proceedings at all meetings of the company, and of the directors, and of committees of directors;

and every director present at any meeting of directors or committee of directors shall sign his name in a book to be kept for that purpose.

87. The directors on behalf of the company may pay a gratuity or pension or allowance on retirement to any director who has held any other salaried office or place of profit with the company or to his widow or dependents and may make contributions to any fund and pay premiums for the purchase or provision of any such gratuity, pension or allowance.

DISQUALIFICATION OF DIRECTORS

88. The office of director shall be vacated, if the director:

(*a*) ceases to be a director by virtue of section 182 or 185 of the Act; or

(*b*) becomes bankrupt or makes any arrangement or composition with his creditors generally; or

(*c*) becomes prohibited from being a director by reason of any order made under section 188 of the Act; or

(*d*) becomes of unsound mind; or

(*e*) resigns his office by notice in writing to the company; or

(*f*) shall for more than six months have been absent without permission of the directors from meetings of the directors held during that period.

ROTATION OF DIRECTORS

89. At the first annual general meeting of the company all the directors shall retire from office, and at the annual general meeting in every subsequent year one-third of the directors for the time being, or, if their number is not three or a multiple of three, then the number nearest one-third, shall retire from office.

90. The directors to retire in every year shall be those who have been longest in office since their last election, but as between persons who became directors on the same day those to retire shall (unless they otherwise agree among themselves) be determined by lot.

91. A retiring director shall be eligible for re-election.

92. The company at the meeting at which a director retires in manner aforesaid may fill the vacated office by electing a person thereto, and in default the retiring director shall if offering himself for re-election be deemed to have been re-elected, unless at such meeting it is expressly resolved not to fill such vacated office or unless a resolution for the re-election of such director shall have been put to the meeting and lost.

93. No person other than a director retiring at the meeting shall unless recommended by the directors be eligible for election to the office of director at any general meeting unless not less than three nor more than twenty-one days before the date appointed for the meeting there shall have been left at the registered office of the company notice in writing

signed by a member duly qualified to attend and vote at the meeting for which such notice is given of his intention to propose such person for election, and also notice in writing signed by that person of his willingness to be elected.

94. The company may from time to time by ordinary resolution increase or reduce the number of directors, and may also determine in what rotation the increased or reduced number is to go out of office.

95. The directors shall have power at any time, and from time to time, to appoint any person to be director, either to fill a casual vacancy or as an addition to the existing directors, but so that the total number of directors shall not at any time exceed the number fixed in accordance with these regulations. Any director so appointed shall hold office only until the next following annual general meeting, and shall then be eligible for re-election but shall not be taken into account in determining the directors who are to retire by rotation at such meeting.

96. The company may by ordinary resolution, of which special notice has been given in accordance with section 142 of the Act, remove any director before the expiration of his period of office notwithstanding anything in these regulations or in any agreement between the company and such director. Such removal shall be without prejudice to any claim such director may have for damages for breach of any contract of service between him and the company.

97. The company may by ordinary resolution appoint another person in place of a director removed from office under the immediately preceding regulation, and without prejudice to the powers of the directors under regulation 95 the company in general meeting may appoint any person to be a director either to fill a casual vacancy or as an additional director. A person appointed in place of a director so removed or to fill such a vacancy shall be subject to retirement at the same time as if he had become a director on the day on which the director in whose place he is appointed was last elected a director.

PROCEEDINGS OF DIRECTORS

98. The directors may meet together for the dispatch of business, adjourn, and otherwise regulate their meetings, as they think fit. Questions arising at any meeting shall be decided by a majority of votes. In case of an equality of votes the chairman shall have a second or casting vote. A director may, and the secretary on the requisition of a director shall, at any time summon a meeting of the directors. It shall not be necessary to give notice of a meeting of directors to any director for the time being absent from the United Kingdom.

99. The quorum necessary for the transaction of the business of the directors may be fixed by the directors, and unless so fixed shall be two.

100. The continuing directors may act notwithstanding any vacancy in their body, but, if and so long as their number is reduced below the number fixed by or pursuant to the regulations of the company as the necessary quorum of directors, the continuing directors or director may act for the purpose of increasing the number of directors to that number,

or of summoning a general meeting of the company, but for no other purpose.

101. The directors may elect a chairman of their meetings and determine the period for which he is to hold office; but if no such chairman is elected, or if at any meeting the chairman is not present within five minutes after the time appointed for holding the same, the directors present may choose one of their number to be chairman of the meeting.

102. The directors may delegate any of their powers to committees consisting of such member or members of their body as they think fit; any committee so formed shall in the exercise of the powers so delegated conform to any regulations that may be imposed on it by the directors.

103. A committee may elect a chairman of its meetings; if no such chairman is elected, or if at any meeting the chairman is not present within five minutes after the time appointed for holding the same, the members present may choose one of their number to be chairman of the meeting.

104. A committee may meet and adjourn as it thinks proper. Questions arising at any meeting shall be determined by a majority of votes of the members present, and in the case of an equality of votes the chairman shall have a second or casting vote.

105. All acts done by any meeting of the directors or of a committee of directors, or by any person acting as a director shall, notwithstanding that it be afterwards discovered that there was some defect in the appointment of any such director or person acting as aforesaid, or that they or any of them were disqualified, be as valid as if every such person had been duly appointed and was qualified to be a director.

106. A resolution in writing, signed by all the directors for the time being entitled to receive notice of a meeting of the directors, shall be as valid and effectual as if it had been passed at a meeting of the directors duly convened and held.

MANAGING DIRECTOR

107. The directors may from time to time appoint one or more of their body to the office of managing director for such period and on such terms as they think fit, and, subject to the terms of any agreement entered into in any particular case, may revoke such appointment. A director so appointed shall not, whilst holding that office, be subject to retirement by rotation or be taken into account in determining the rotation of retirement of directors, but his appointment shall be automatically determined if he cease from any cause to be a director.

108. A managing director shall receive such remuneration (whether by way of salary, commission or participation in profits, or partly in one way and partly in another) as the directors may determine.

109. The directors may entrust to and confer upon a managing director any of the powers exercisable by them upon such terms and conditions and with such restrictions as they may think fit, and either collaterally with or to the exclusion of their own powers and may from time to time revoke, withdraw, alter or vary all or any of such powers.

SECRETARY

110. The secretary shall be appointed by the directors for such term, at such remuneration and upon such conditions as they may think fit; and any secretary so appointed may be removed by them.

111. No person shall be appointed or hold office as secretary who is:
   (a) the sole director of the company; or
   (b) a corporation the sole director of which is the sole director of the company; or
   (c) the sole director of a corporation which is the sole director of the company.

112. A provision of the Act or these regulations requiring or authorising a thing to be done by or to a director and the secretary shall not be satisfied by its being done by or to the same person acting both as director and as, or in place of, the secretary.

THE SEAL

113. The directors shall provide for the safe custody of the seal, which shall only be used by the authority of the directors or of a committee of the directors authorized by the directors in that behalf, and every instrument to which the seal shall be affixed shall be signed by a director and shall be counter-signed by the secretary or by a second director or by some other person appointed by the directors for the purpose.

DIVIDENDS AND RESERVE

114. The company in general meeting may declare dividends, but no dividend shall exceed the amount recommended by the directors.

115. The directors may from time to time pay to the members such interim dividends as appear to the directors to be justified by the profits of the company.

116. No dividend shall be paid otherwise than out of profits.

117. The directors may, before recommending any dividend, set aside out of profits of the company such sums as they think proper as a reserve or reserves which shall, at the discretion of the directors, be applicable for any purpose to which the profits of the company may be properly applied, and pending such application may, at the like discretion, either be employed in the business of the company or be invested in such investments (other than shares of the company) as the directors may from time to time think fit. The directors may also without placing the same to reserve carry forward any profits which they may think prudent not to divide.

118. Subject to the rights of persons, if any, entitled to shares with special rights as to dividend, all dividends shall be declared and paid according to the amounts paid or credited as paid on the shares in respect whereof the dividend is paid, but no amount paid or credited as paid on a share in advance of calls shall be treated for the purpose of this regulation as paid on the share. All dividends shall be apportioned and paid proportionately to the amounts paid or credited as paid on the shares during any portion or portions of the period in respect of which the dividend is paid; but if any share is issued on terms providing that it shall rank for

dividend as from a particular date such share shall rank for dividend accordingly.

119. The directors may deduct from any dividend payable to any member all sums of money (if any) presently payable by him to the company on account of calls or otherwise in relation to the shares of the company.

120. Any general meeting declaring a dividend or bonus may direct payment of such dividend or bonus wholly or partly by the distribution of specific assets and in particular of paid up shares, debentures or debenture stock of any other company or in any one or more of such ways, and the directors shall give effect to such resolution and where any difficulty arises in regard to such distribution, the directors may settle the same as they think expedient, and in particular may issue fractional certificates and fix the value for distribution of such specific assets or any part thereof and may determine that cash payments shall be made to any members upon the footing of the value so fixed in order to adjust the rights of all parties, and may vest any such specific assets in trustees as may seem expedient to the directors.

121. Any dividend, interest or other moneys payable in cash in respect of shares may be paid by cheque or warrant sent through the post directed to the registered address of the holder or, in the case of joint holders, to the registered address of that one of the joint holders who is first named on the register of members or to such person and to such address as the holder or joint holders may in writing direct. Every such cheque or warrant shall be made payable to the order of the person to whom it is sent. Any one, two or more joint holders may give effectual receipts for any dividends, bonuses or other moneys payable in respect of the shares held by them as joint holders.

122. No dividend shall bear interest against the company.

ACCOUNTS

123. The directors shall cause proper books of account to be kept with respect to:

    (*a*) all sums of moneys received and expended by the company and the matters in respect of which the receipt and expenditure takes place;

    (*b*) all sales and purchases of goods by the company; and

    (*c*) the assets and liabilities of the company.

Proper books shall not be deemed to be kept if there are not kept such books of account as are necessary to give a true and fair view of the state of the company's affairs and to explain its transactions.

124. The books of account shall be kept at the registered office of the company, or, subject to section 147 (3) of the Act, at such other place or places as the directors think fit, and shall always be open to the inspection of the directors.

125. The directors shall from time to time determine whether and to what extent and at what times and places and under what conditions or regulations the accounts and books of the company or any of them shall be open to the inspection of members not being directors, and no member

(not being a director) shall have any right of inspecting any account or book or document of the company except as conferred by statute or authorized by the directors or by the company in general meeting.

126. The directors shall from time to time, in accordance with sections 148, 150 and 157 of the Act, cause to be prepared and to be laid before the company in general meeting such profit and loss accounts, balance sheets, group accounts (if any) and reports as are referred to in those sections.

127. A copy of every balance sheet (including every document required by law to be annexed thereto) which is to be laid before the company in general meeting, together with a copy of the auditors' report shall not less than twenty-one days before the date of the meeting be sent to every member of, and every holder of debentures of the company and to every person registered under regulation 31. Provided that this regulation shall not require a copy of those documents to be sent to any person of whose address the company is not aware or to more than one of the joint holders of any shares or debentures.

CAPITALIZATION OF PROFITS

128. The company in general meeting may upon the recommendation of the directors resolve that it is desirable to capitalize any part of the amount for the time being standing to the credit of any of the companys' reserve accounts or to the credit of the profit and loss account or otherwise available for distribution, and accordingly that such sum be set free for distribution amongst the members who would have been entitled thereto if distributed by way of dividend and in the same proportions on condition that the same be not paid in cash but be applied either in or towards paying up any amounts for the time being unpaid on any shares held by such members respectively or paying up in full unissued shares or debentures of the company to be allotted and distributed credited as fully paid up to and amongst such members in the proportion aforesaid, or partly in the one way and partly in the other, and the directors shall give effect to such resolution:

Provided that a share premium account and a capital redemption reserve fund may, for the purposes of this regulation, only be applied in the paying up of unissued shares to be issued to members of the company as fully paid bonus shares.

129. Whenever such a resolution as aforesaid shall have been passed the directors shall make all appropriations and applications of the undivided profits resolved to be capitalized thereby, and all allotments and issues of fully-paid shares or debentures, if any, and generally shall do all acts and things required to give effect thereto, with full power to the directors to make such provision by the issue of fractional certificates or by payment in cash or otherwise as they think fit for the case of shares or debentures becoming distributable in factions, and also to authorize any person to enter on behalf of all the members entitled thereto into an agreement with the company providing for the allotment to them respectively, credited as fully paid up, of any further shares or debentures to which they may be entitled upon such capitalization, or (as the case may require) for the

payment up by the company on their behalf, by the application thereto of their respective proportions of the profits resolved to be capitalized, of the amounts or any part of the amounts remaining unpaid on their existing shares and any agreement made under such authority shall be effective and binding on all such members.

AUDIT

130. Auditors shall be appointed and their duties regulated in accordance with sections 159 to 162 of the Act.

NOTICES

131. A notice may be given by the company to any member either personally or by sending it by post to him or to his registered address, or (if he has no registered address within the United Kingdom) to the address, if any, within the United Kingdom supplied by him to the company for the giving of notice to him. Where a notice is sent by post, service of the notice shall be deemed to be effected by properly addressing, prepaying, and posting a letter containing the notice, and to have been effected in the case of a notice of a meeting at the expiration of 24 hours after the letter containing the same is posted, and in any other case at the time at which the letter would be delivered in the ordinary course of post.

132. A notice may be given by the company to the joint holders of a share by giving the notice to the joint holder first named in the register of members in respect of the share.

133. A notice may be given by the company to the persons entitled to a share in consequence of the death or bankruptcy of a member by sending it through the post in a prepaid letter addressed to them by name, or by the title of representatives of the deceased, or trustee of the bankrupt, or by any like description, at the address, if any, within the United Kingdom supplied for the purpose by the persons claiming to be so entitled, or (until such an address has been so supplied) by giving the notice in any manner in which the same might have been given if the death or bankruptcy had not occurred.

134. Notice of every general meeting shall be given in any manner hereinbefore authorized to:

  (a) every member except those members who (having no registered address within the United Kingdom) have not supplied to the company an address within the United Kingdom for the giving of notices to them;

  (b) every person upon whom the ownership of a share devolves by reason of his being a legal personal representative or a trustee in bankruptcy of a member where the member but for his death or bankruptcy would be entitled to receive notice of the meeting; and

  (c) the auditor for the time being of the company.

No other person shall be entitled to receive notices of general meetings.

WINDING UP

135. If the company shall be wound up the liquidator may, with the sanction of an extraordinary resolution of the company and any other sanction required by the Act, divide amongst the members in specie or kind the whole or any part of the assets of the company (whether they shall consist of property of the same kind or not) and may, for such purpose set such value as he deems fair upon any property to be divided as aforesaid and may determine how such division shall be carried out as between the members or different classes of members. The liquidator may, with the like sanction, vest the whole or any part of such assets in trustees upon such trusts for the benefit of the contributories as the liquidator, with the like sanction, shall think fit, but so that no member shall be compelled to accept any shares or other securities whereon there is any liability.

INDEMNITY

136. Every director, managing director, agent, auditor, secretary and other officer for the time being of the company shall be indemnified out of the assets of the company against any liability incurred by him in defending any proceedings, whether civil or criminal, in which judgment is given in his favour or in which he is acquitted or in connexion with any application under section 448 of the Act in which relief is granted to him by the Court.

PART II

REGULATIONS FOR THE MANAGEMENT OF A PRIVATE COMPANY LIMITED BY SHARES

1. The regulations contained in Part I of Table A (with the exception of regulations 24 and 53) shall apply.

2. The company is a private company and accordingly:
   (*a*) the right to transfer shares is restricted in manner hereinafter prescribed;
   (*b*) the number of members of the company (exclusive of persons who are in the employment of the company and of persons who having been formerly in the employment of the company were while in such employment and have continued after the determination of such employment to be members of the company) is limited to fifty. Provided that where two or more persons hold one or more shares in the company jointly they shall for the purpose of this regulation be treated as a single member;
   (*c*) any invitation to the public to subscribe for any shares or debentures of the company is prohibited;
   (*d*) the company shall not have power to issue share warrants to bearer.

3. The directors may, in their absolute discretion and without assigning any reason therefor, decline to register any transfer of any share, whether or not it is a fully paid share.

4. No business shall be transacted at any general meeting unless a

quorum of members is present at the time when the meeting proceeds to business; save as herein otherwise provided two members present in person or by proxy shall be a quorum.

5. Subject to the provisions of the Act, a resolution in writing signed by all the members for the time being entitled to receive notice of and to attend and vote at general meetings (or being corporations by their duly authorized representatives) shall be as valid and effective as if the same had been passed at a general meeting of the company duly convened and held.

6. The directors may at any time require any person whose name is entered in the register of members of the company to furnish them with any information, supported (if the directors so require) by a statutory declaration, which they may consider necessary for the purpose of determining whether or not the company is an exempt private company within the meaning of subsection (4) of section 129 of the Act.

Index

Absenteeism, 140-2
Absolute offences, 90
Accident
  damages for, 298-301
  divisible liability for, 301-2
  employee, to, 310-4
Accountant
  importance of engaging, 58
  tax advice by, 79
Accounts
  duty to keep, 22
  error in, 251
  inspection of, 21
Administration of Justice Act, 1920,
  262
Administration of Justice Act, 1970,
  368
Advertisements
  deposits, for, 110
Advertising, restraints on, 63-64
Advice
  gratuitous, negligence in, 292-3
  solicitor, by, liability for, 318
Advisory, Conciliation etc. Service,
  183
Agency shop agreements, 169
Agent
  authority of, 247-8
  corruption of, 333
  employee as, 247-9
  fiduciary relationship of, 85
  meaning, 247
Agreement. *See* Contract
Alsatian dog, dangerous, 307-8
Appropriation of property, 325
Arbitration
  consent of parties, 362
  procedure, 363-4
Architect
  drawings, rights in, 13
  misrepresentation by, 85
Articles of association, 000
Artist, copyright vesting in, 13, 14
Artistic work, copyright in, 12
Assault, examples of, 313
Assignment of leases, 22
Atmospheric pollution, 226-31
Attachment of earnings
  debts for which available, 127

earnings attachable, 128
employer's expenses, 128-9
orders, 127-8
rate of deduction, 128
Attachment of Earnings Act, 1971,
  127
Audience in court, 48, 354-6

Bank
  cheque. *See* Cheque
  facilities granted by, 7
  loan
    evidence as to, 8
    period of, 8
    repayable on demand, 7, 366
    securities, realising, 8
    suing on, 8
  reference by, 150
Bankruptcy obtaining credit, 35
Bankruptcy
  director, of, 108
  employer, of, 194
  fraudulent preference in, 36
  preferred debts, 35-36
  priority of debts, 35
  receiving order, 35
Barrister. *See* Counsel
Bicycle, taking, 324
Bill, mistake in, 251, 367-8
Bills of Exchange Act 1882, 271
Biological male case, 78
Blackmail, 324
Boardroom battles, 96-98
Bomb scares, 220
Bonfire nuisance, 296
Bonus schemes, 138-9
Breach of confidence, 307
Bribery, 332-5
British Medical Journal, libel, 75
British Syphon Co. v. *Homewood,* 131
Building Society, control of, 108-9
Burglary, 323
Business
  accounts, keeping, 22
  buying a, 40-43
  closing. *See* Closing business
  expenses, tax position, 17-20
  insurance cover, 24
  short lived, 359

557